Programming with JAVA

Mahesh P. Bhave

Former Vice Principal and HOD
Department of Computer Technology
Veermata Jijabai Technological Institute, Mumbai

Sunil A. Patekar

Dean, Research & Development
Vidyalankar Institute of Technology, Mumbai

Copyright © 2009 by Dorling Kindersley (India) Pvt. Ltd

This book is sold subject to the condition that it shall not, by way of trade or otherwise, be lent, resold, hired out, or otherwise circulated without the publisher's prior written consent in any form of binding or cover other than that in which it is published and without a similar condition including this condition being imposed on the subsequent purchaser and without limiting the rights under copyright reserved above, no part of this publication may be reproduced, stored in or introduced into a retrieval system, or transmitted in any form or by any means (electronic, mechanical, photocopying, recording or otherwise), without the prior written permission of both the copyright owner and the above-mentioned publisher of this book.

Although the author and publisher have made every effort to ensure that the information in this book was correct at the time of editing and printing, the author and publisher do not assume and hereby disclaim any liability to any party for any loss or damage arising out of the use of this book caused by errors or omissions, whether such errors or omissions result from negligence, accident or any other cause. Further, names, pictures, images, characters, businesses, places, events and incidents are either the products of the author's imagination or used in a fictitious manner. Any resemblance to actual persons, living or dead or actual events is purely coincidental and do not intend to hurt sentiments of any individual, community, sect or religion.

In case of binding mistake, misprints or missing pages etc., the publisher's entire liability and your exclusive remedy is replacement of this book within reasonable time of purchase by similar edition/reprint of the book.

ISBN 978-81-317-2080-6

First Impression, 2009
Twelfth Impression, 2022
Thirteenth Impression, 2024

Published by Pearson India Education Services Pvt. Ltd, CIN: U72200TN2005PTC057128

Head Office: 1st Floor, Berger Tower, Plot No. C-001A/2, Sector 16B, Noida – 201 301,Uttar Pradesh, India.

Registered Office: Featherlite, 'The Address' 5th Floor, Survey No 203/10B, 200 Ft MMRD Road, Zamin Pallavaram, Chennai - 600044
Website: in.pearson.com; Email:companysecretary.india@pearson.com

Digitally printed in India by Trinity Academy for Corporate Training Ltd, New Delhi in the year of 2024.

Dedicated to our beloved teachers
Dr S. K. Kulkarni
Dr S. D. Varwandkar
The Late Dr A. D. Mokashi

Preface

We are glad to present our fourth textbook to readers. This is a textbook of a programming language called Java. In early days, Java was considered to be some sort of a tool for Internet programming. Now, it is slowly getting the status of a full-fledged programming language. In the early days of C language, we felt the need for a disciplined language. However, we could not convince our colleagues about it. Java language is now appreciated by everyone because it is highly disciplined and forces type checking. It does not allow `goto` command, and there is no arbitrary pointer arithmetic. Hence, in our opinion, it can become the first programming language to be introduced to students.

We have tried to structure the chapters in such a way that this book can be used as a standard textbook in a class room. By reading this book, chapter by chapter, students can develop more complex programs, step by step. At no time, facilities which are discussed at a later stage are used in the chapter. There are only a few exceptions to this rule. The chapter on graphics uses Frames. We feel that a topic like graphics increases the interest in a subject which is otherwise dry. This book has been written with the intention that it can also be used as a self-study guide.

Normally, Java is taught after C++ in most of the universities. Hence, a comparison of the two languages is inevitable in this book. Those who are good at C++ will be able to study Java using this book in a very short time. In spite of the above fact, we have written the initial chapters with a lot of care. Those who do not know any programming language will also find this book simple and useful.

We have taken some liberty with the standard English. We have used terms like "commented out" and "subclassing". We believe they are more expressive and hence, convey the meaning of the sentence more empathetically.

Professor K. M. Kulkarni has been our inspiration for all these years. His area of interest is Computer-Assisted Instruction. Many programs in this book are templates for effectively teaching various subjects (not necessarily computer programming). The complete multimedia experience and programs like Projectile, drawing from files, and many other programs are a tribute to Professor Kulkarni.

This book is accompanied by a 'Teachers Supplement' which will be available to teachers. It contains solutions to selected exercises and a section called "Java Practical", useful in selecting the problems for laboratory work.

The programs in this book are developed with a program called `BPsimple`. It is an integrated development environment (IDE) designed by us on the lines of Turbo C++ version 3.0. Authors are also planning to develop a separate Web site to discuss problems and solutions for benefit of those who are using this textbook. The outputs in the text display a line "press any key to continue". It originates from `BPsimple`. If you use any other IDE or command line, you will not see this line.

At the end of the book, we have provided an extensive Glossary and the RuleBook. Appendixes include 10 mini projects. These projects are useful if the language is taught at a higher level.

We have provided the best possible material needed to study core Java. However, the study of Java cannot be complete if one does not study "Java Tutorial". It is available as free download. Please visit http://java.sun.com/docs/books/tutorial for the same. The Data Tables of methods and constructors for various classes used in the book have been taken from the API specification downloaded from <http://java.sun.com/jvase/6/docs/api/>. Teachers and post-graduate students should also have a close look at "Java Languages Specifications" available on the Web site of Sun Microsystem.

Acknowledgements

A lot of people have helped us during the writing of this text. It will not be possible to remember and enlist every name but we hope that all those whose names have not appeared in this list will forgive us.

We are thankful to all our reviewers whose suggestions have helped us to improve the quality of the text. We are also thankful to the editorial team of Pearson, specially, Thomas Mathew Rajesh, Sachin Saxena and Shadan Perween for their constant support.

We thank Deepak Malshe from Tata Consultancy Services, who helped us in the early days of writing this text. Special thanks to Rajanikant Patkar. We are thankful to Dr Medha Dixit, Principal, K. J. Somaiya Engineering College, for giving Professor Bhave the opportunity to class test the book. We are also thankful to Professor Deepak Sharma, Head, Computer Department, and Professor Uday Joshi of Somaiya Engineering College for their cooperation.

We eagerly await suggestions from our readers and can be contacted at bhavemp@gmail.com

Mahesh P. Bhave
Sunil A. Patekar

Contents

Chapter 10: Strings 145

Chapter 11: Simple Input/Output 171

Chapter 16: Inheritance Revisited 342

Chapter 17: Files 357

Chapter 24: Multimedia Experience 564

Chapter 25: Moving From C++ to Java 589

Chapter 26: Collection of Programs 610

List of Programs

List of Boxes

List of Figures

List of Tables

INTRODUCTION

CHAPTER 1

Welcome to the world of Java programming. In this book, we will start from the most basic concepts and try to reach a reasonably higher level. We hope you will enjoy the tour of Java language with us. We do not assume knowledge of any particular programming language. However, it is expected that many of our readers have a prior introduction to the object-oriented language C++. You will find the comparison of C++ and Java useful. Let us start our study in a more formal manner.

1.1 A Brief History of Java

Java was developed at Sun Microsystems in 1991, by a team comprising James Gosling, Patrick Naughton, Chris Warth, Ed Frank, and Mike Sheridan as its members. The language was initially called Oak. It was later termed as Java. Java was launched on 23 May, 1995. The Java software was released as a development kit. The first two versions were named JDK 1.0 and JDK 1.1. In 1998, while releasing the next version, Sun Microsystems changed the nomenclature from Java Development Kit (JDK) to Software Development Kit (SDK). Also, it added "2" to the name. The released version of Java was called Java 2 SDK 1.2.

With every version, Java became stronger and stronger. At the time of writing of the book, Java had come up with its version 6, known as JDK 6. Java has already released the beta of its next version. In our text, we will be describing version 6.

The following table illustrates the various versions released till date:

Version	Release date	Major additions
JDK 1.0	January 1996	Initial release
JDK 1.1	February 1997	Inner classes, JavaBeans, JDBC, RMI
J2SE 1.2	December 1998	Swing and Collections Framework
J2SE 1.3	May 2000	HotSpot JVM, RMI, JavaSound
J2SE 1.4	February 2002	Regular expressions, Java Web Start
J2SE 5.0	September 2004	Generics, autoboxing, enumeration
Java SE 6	December 2006	Database manager and many new facilities
Java SE 7	To be released	—

1.2 Why Is Java Popular for the Internet?

The main reason why Java is popular on the Internet is that Java offers applets. Applets are tiny programs which run inside the browser. Before the introduction of applets, the web pages were mostly static. After the use of this application, they have become dynamic, making browsing richer. When we will study chapter on applets (Chapter 20), you will get the proof of this statement.

Applets are very safe. They cannot write to the local hard disk. Hence, there is no threat of viruses while surfing the Internet. This has made applets (and thereby Java) highly popular on the Internet.

However, this is only one aspect. Because applets are Java programs, they inherit strengths of Java. They also support graphical user interface (GUI). Hence, surfing the Internet can be quite enjoying when web pages use applets. Please note that applets are only one aspect of Java.

Java is a complete programming language. We can write applications in different walks of life. As we move along the text, we will be discussing them thoroughly.

1.3 Features of Java

The features of Java, which make Java a powerful, popular language, can be stated briefly as

- Simple
- Secure
- Portable
- Object oriented
- Robust
- Multi-threaded
- Architecture neutral
- Interpreted
- Distributed

Let us discuss these features one by one.

1.3.1 Simple

As compared to C++, Java is simpler because of many reasons. The most important thing is the absence of pointers. Many unnecessary features of C++, like overloading of operators, are removed from Java.

1.3.2 Secure

Java language becomes secure because of the following properties/components:

- No pointers
- Bytecode verifier
- Class loader
- Security manager

1.3.3 Portable

The Java code is highly portable. Write Once Run Anywhere (WORA) is the basic Java slogan. Every platform will always have its own Java runtime machine. What you need is the Java bytecode. You are free to write the Java source code on any platform and compile to bytecode there. The bytecode so generated is platform independent. It will run on any platform.

1.3.4 Object oriented

Java is object oriented. During the last many years, every new language introduced is object oriented. We will be discussing the advantages of "object-oriented" programming language in Chapter 2.

1.3.5 Robust

Java is a robust language. It does not crash the computer, even when it encounters minor mistakes in a program. It has the ability to withstand the threats. This is considered as a great advantage for a programming language.

1.3.6 Multi-threaded

With the introduction of high-speed microprocessors a few years ago, users wanted to perform many tasks at a time. This is possible on a single-chip processor only by the use of multi-threading. Multi-threading means ability of a program to run multiple (more than one) pieces of program code simultaneously. This is possible by time slicing in a single processor system. Every thread is assigned a small time slice to run. It creates a feeling that all the tasks are running simultaneously in time.

1.3.7 Interpreted

Java is an interpreted language. When we write a program, it is compiled into a class file. The interpreter executes this class file. However, the interpreters 30 years ago were interpreting the statement in textual form. It was a very slow process. Java interprets bytecode; hence, it is considerably fast. Actually, Java gets all the advantages of interpretation, without suffering from major disadvantages.

1.3.8 Architecture neutral

The Java programming language is dependent neither on any particular microprocessor family, nor on any particular architecture. Any standard computer or even a microcomputer can run Java programs. The mobile phones also have software based on Java.

1.3.9 Distributed

Java has many in-built faculties which make it easy to use language in distributed systems.

1.4 How Java Programs Run

Earlier we had said that Java is an interpreted language. Some of us may be familiar with languages C and C++, which are not interpreted languages. Let us try to understand the difference.

While developing a program in non-interpreted languages (like C/C++), the following steps occur. A program is written in higher level language (HLL). It is called the source code, typically a `.c` or `.cpp` file.

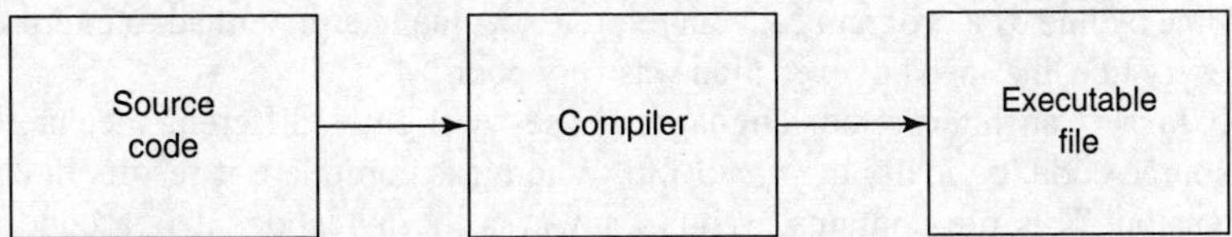

Figure 1.1 **Compilation in Other Languages**

Next, this program is compiled completely, resulting in an executable file, as shown in Figure 1.1. It typically has an `.exe` extension. This file contains a machine language program (sometimes called machine code). This file can be executed on machine (computer) with the help of an operating system.

To understand how Java programs run, we must understand two new terms. These are *bytecode* and *virtual machine* (VM).

- *Bytecode*: This code is actually platform independent. We can consider it as a machine code for a hypothetical computer. When you compile an `anyName.java` file successfully, you get this code. It is in the form of `anyName.class` file.
- *Virtual machine*: The name virtual suggests that this is not an actual machine. It is just a program which simulates a machine on which Java programs are supposed to run. Actually, you can suppose that VM is a hardware which runs programs in bytecode (as its own machine language).

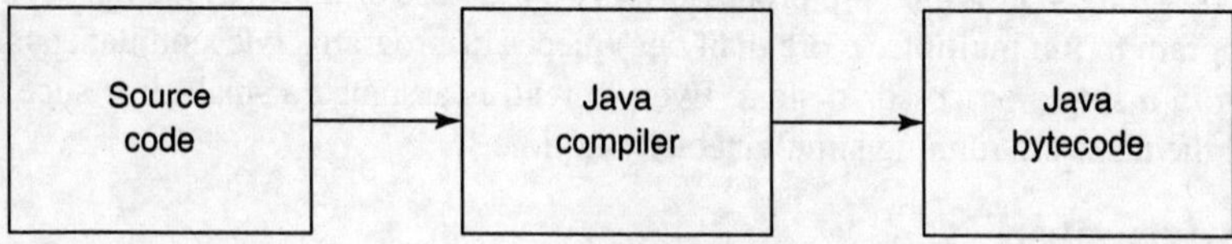

Figure 1.2 Compilation in Java

Now we can understand how Java programs are executed. First, a program is written in Java. It is called the source code. The file has `.java` extension. Next, this program is compiled by a Java compiler. It produces a bytecode. The file extension is `.class`. This process is shown in Figure 1.2.

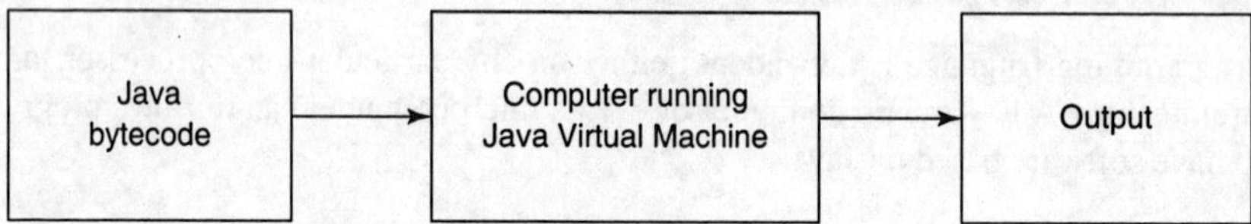

Figure 1.3 Running a Java Program

The computer does not directly execute this bytecode. Instead, a program known as Java Virtual Machine (JVM) runs on a computer. We pass this bytecode as an input to this program. This program interprets and executes this bytecode. This fact is explained in Figure 1.3.

1.5 Advantages and Disadvantages of an Interpreted Language

In the early days of computing, the compilation of interpreted languages was quite different. The source code was executed line by line by a program called interpreter. As the interpreter had to interpret (understand) and then execute every line, the speed of execution was very poor.

Although Java is an interpreted language, it uses a slightly different mechanism. A program is written as a source code, typically a `.java` file. When it is compiled, it results in another file that has `.class` extension. This file contains a code known as the bytecode. It is a code for a hypothetical machine. This file is executed by another program called interpreter. Since the interpreter interprets the bytecode (and not the text lines), the speed of execution is much higher as compared to the old interpreted languages.

Still today, Java programs run at lesser speed as compared to other language programs which are completely compiled.

Third-party softwares have already started appearing which compile and produce executable code from bytecode. Because of this and other developments that will occur in future, Java programs are expected to run as fast as any other language programs.

However, the major advantage of Java being an interpreted language is that it is machine (hardware platform) independent. If there is any computer in the world of any specific type (make/hardware) and if a JVM exists for that machine, then the Java bytecode runs on that machine in exactly the same way as being run on any other machine. In today's world of the Internet, where heterogeneous collection of hardware and software platforms exists, this machine independence is considered as a great advantage.

1.6 Java Applets and Applications

We can use Java for writing two types of programs, namely applets and applications. Applets are executed in (Java-enabled) browsers. Applet is like a small Java program. It can be dynamically downloaded from the Internet.

Applications are programs similar to the ones that we find in any other languages. Since they do not need a browser, they are sometimes referred to as stand-alone applications.

The only difference between these two is that applet cannot write to local disk whereas an application can.

1.7 Advantages of Java Technology

Out of the available technologies, Java promises many advantages, which are described in a famous book *Java Tutorial* under the heading "How Will Java Technology Change My Life?" They are reproduced here for the readers benefit.

How Will Java Technology Change My Life?

- *Get started quickly*: Although the Java programming language is a powerful object-oriented language, it's easy to learn, especially for programmers already familiar with C or C++.
- *Write less code*: Comparisons of program metrics (class counts, method counts, and so on) suggest that a program written in the Java programming language can be four times smaller than the same program in C++.
- *Write better code*: The Java programming language encourages good coding practices, and its garbage collection helps you avoid memory leaks. Its object orientation, its Java Beans component architecture, and its wide-ranging, easily extendible API let you reuse other people's tested code and introduce fewer bugs.
- *Develop programs faster*: Your development time may be as much as twice as fast versus writing the same program in C++. Why? You write fewer lines of code and it is a simpler programming language than C++.
- *Avoid platform dependencies with 100% Pure Java*: You can keep your program portable by following the purity tips mentioned throughout this tutorial and avoiding the use of libraries written in other languages.
- *Write once, run anywhere*: Because 100% Pure Java programs are compiled into machine-independent bytecodes, they run consistently on any Java platform.
- *Distribute software more easily*: You can upgrade applets easily from a central server. Applets take advantage of the feature of allowing new classes to be loaded "on the fly," without recompiling the entire program.

1.8 Java Platform

The Java platform consists of the following.

- A language for writing programs
- A set of APIs
- Class libraries
- Other programs used in developing, compiling, and error-checking
- A VM which loads and executes the class files

The Java language is the one which we are going to study in detail in this book. Language consists of syntax (rules) and semantics. Syntax means rules of grammar. Semantics means the description of what will happen when statements (instructions) that follow syntax rules are executed.

API as defined by Java is "the specification of how a programmer writing an application accesses the behaviour and state of classes and objects". This is rather a terse definition. While writing Java programs we need many classes which are designed and developed by Java language creators. Programs simply would not run without them. The library of such classes is nothing but API.

To develop Java programs, we need a compiler, and other programs and tools. They are also part and parcel of the Java platform.

A program named JVM is needed to execute the Java programs. This is the most important component of the platform.

1.9 Java Development Kit

The JDK is a development environment for building applications, applets, and components using the Java programming language. In more technical terms, the current version is called Java™ Platform, Standard Edition 6 JDK. For simplicity, let us refer it as JDK 6. It is possible that you have heard the term SDK. You might wonder what is the difference between JDK and SDK. Actually, they mean the same thing. During the development of Java, different terms were more popular at different times.

The JDK 6 includes tools useful for developing and testing programs written in Java. They help us running them on the Java platform. These tools are designed to be used from the command line. They do not provide a GUI. The only exception is the "applet viewer". Let us describe the contents of JDK 6 in detail.

1. *Development tools*: Tools and utilities that will help one to develop, execute, debug, and document programs written in the Java programming language are provided in the "bin" sub-directory. These tools are the foundation of the JDK 6. The basic tools are described in the following table.

Tool	Description
`javac`	The compiler for the Java programming language
`java`	The launcher for Java applications. In this release, a single launcher is used for both development and deployment
`javadoc`	API documentation generator
`appletviewer`	Run and debug applets without a web browser
`jar`	Manage Java Archive (JAR) files
`jdb`	The Java Debugger

`javah`	C header and stub generator. Used to write native methods
`javap`	Class file disassembler
`extcheck`	Utility to detect JAR conflicts

2. *Runtime environment*: An implementation of the Java 2 runtime environment for use by the SDK. The runtime environment includes a JVM, class libraries, and other files that support the execution of programs written in the Java programming language. These are present in the "jre" sub-directory.
3. *Additional libraries*: Additional class libraries and support files required by the development tools are present in the "lib" sub-directory.
4. *Demo applets and applications*: Examples, with source code, (of programming for the Java platform) are present in the "demo" sub-directory. These include examples that use Swing and other Java Foundation Classes, and the Java Platform Debugger Architecture.
5. *JDK documentation*: The documentation is available online. It contains API specifications, feature description, developer guides, reference pages for SDK tools and utilities, demos, and links to related information. We can download this documentation and install on our machine.

1.10 How to Run Simple Java Programs

Java is a machine-independent language. Java programs can be run on any system. However, Windows operating system is quite popular. Hence, let us assume that we are working on any Pentium class machine with Windows XP as the operating system.

A good number of integrated development environments (IDEs) are available for writing and running Java programs. They provide lot of useful features to the users. However, most of them are complex. First-time users *many a times* become uncomfortable using them. Hence, experts feel that beginners should run Java from basic technique, that is, from "command prompt". Only at the later stage, they should start using an IDE.

In this section, we will describe how to run our Java programs from command prompt.

1.10.1 How to organize our computer for command prompt operation

Before we start using Java, we have to organize our computer (directory structure) for it. We must first install Java in our computer. We can use any available hard drive (C: or D: drive) for this purpose. We have to install it in a directory. Shakespeare said, "What is in the name". But it will be a good idea to name this directory "JDK 6". In my computer, I have this directory in the C: drive. (When you install the kit using default directory, it is normally loaded in "program files" directory. Since this name contains a blank character, some experts feel that it should be avoided.) For keeping programs, we should have a separate directory. In my computer, I have a directory named Jprog for this purpose.

Also, we should have one plain text editor in our Java directory. Normally we have a program Notepad in our machine. We should copy it in the Java directory.

1.10.2 How to run a simple program in command prompt environment

The *first step* in running any program is to write (code) it. To write a program, we have to use a text editor. If we are using Windows, we may select Notepad. We are free to use any available "Text Editor". Using any of these text editors, we must create a file. This file should have the extension `.java`. Let us say we have created a file `first.java` in Jprog directory.

The *second step* is to compile this file. We must execute the command `javac` as follows:

```
C:\Jprog> javac  first.java
```

If there are any errors in our program, they will be displayed on the screen. We have to note them and correct our file accordingly. If the compilation is successful, a file `first.class` will be created. Once compilation is successful, we should be ready for the next step.

In the *third step*, we can run our program by executing the command `java` as

```
C:\Jprog> java   first
```

Please note that while compiling we have to give full file name (including extension `.java`). While running we have to use only the class name (without the extension `.class`).

The tips for working from command prompt environment are given in Box 1.1.

1.10.3 How to run programs in integrated development environments

Earlier we had seen that to develop a program first, we have to edit the code using an editor. Next, we have to run the compiler. If there are any errors, we have to edit the code again. Then, we have to run "JVM". To facilitate the handling of all these tasks, special programs are written. Since they provide us an environment which integrates various activities, they are called IDEs.

Like other programming languages, there are many programs (IDEs) available from different vendors. The most common are

- Jbuilder from Borland
- Sun ONE studio
- Eclipse (available from www.eclipse.org)

BOX 1.1 Tips For Working In Command Prompt Environment

Please note that for convenience we have to keep all our programs in a particular directory. It is a nice idea to give it name "**Jprog**".

In Windows there is an environment variable "PATH". We can set it by using the set command. When we issue any command (like `javac`), Windows searches it in the path. If our `javac` program is in the directory (folder) specified by the path, then we can simply invoke it (even without a fully qualified path name).

Once you enter the DOS command prompt, you should change the (working) directory to Jprog and start working.

In our computer, we have created a batch file named `cmdjdk6.bat` as

```
set PATH=%path%;C:\JDK6\bin;C:\Jprog
set classpath=.;C:\Jprog;
cd C:\Jprog
command
```

When we run this batch file, it sets the PATH for us, and also sets classpath and takes us to our normal working folder. After completing our work, we should type exit to come out of command mode.

- JCreator
- BlueJ (available from www.bluej.org)

To run programs in these environments, you have to become familiar with them. After that, they offer you facilities to edit, compile, and run programs. Their text editors are normally user-friendly. They take you to appropriate locations where the compiler has indicated errors.

Keywords

Applet, `appletviewer`, application, bytecode, integrated development environment (IDE), the Internet, interpreter, `javac`, `java` command, Java Virtual Machine (JVM), Jbuilder, Sun Microsystems, virus

RuleBook

Bytecode The type of code generated by a Java compiler

Review Questions

1. Explain "write once and run anywhere" nature of Java.
2. Write a short note on Java Virtual Machine.
3. Why is Java popular on the Internet?
4. Describe the various features of Java.
5. List at least three development tools from JDK.
6. What are the advantages that IDE provides to a programmer?

OBJECT ORIENTATION AN INTRODUCTION

Java is an object-oriented programming (OOP) language. In this chapter, we will make ourselves familiar with concepts of OOP. As we study Java, these concepts will be covered in depth gradually.

2.1 Programming Languages Before Object Orientation Became Popular

Before the concept of object orientation (OO) was introduced, the general purpose programming languages were procedure oriented. Emphasis was on functions to introduce modularity. Data was organized in terms of a unit called "record". Records were supported by both COBOL and Pascal. They are renamed as structures in C.

However, programmers were not satisfied with what they had. Programs tended to be problem specific, and changing them was difficult. The techniques at that time were not at all suitable for large programs. Simulation programs were difficult to develop. It may be noted that the programmers at that time (and even today) were highly paid. There was a need to make use of their programming efforts in cost-effective manner.

It led to the new paradigm of OO and OOP.

Consider an example of "time". "Time" is part and parcel of all our activities. We will miss a local train even if we are late by a minute. If we wanted to handle time in a program, we used to define a structure like

```
Struct time0 {int hour;
              int minute;
              int second;

              };
```

And later on declare variables of type `time0`. Figure 2.1 illustrates a simple view of structure time.

If a programmer used this structure in one program, it was not helpful or convenient in writing another program. The time variable could be modified inadvertently and produce errors, which are very difficult to trace. The functions written to manipulate time were scattered in the program and not bound to structure time.

Let us now see a typical class declaration in object-oriented language like Java. (Do not worry about the details. We will be discussing them at appropriate place.)

```
class Time0
{ private int hour, minute, second;
public void set_time(int h ,int m ,int s);
```

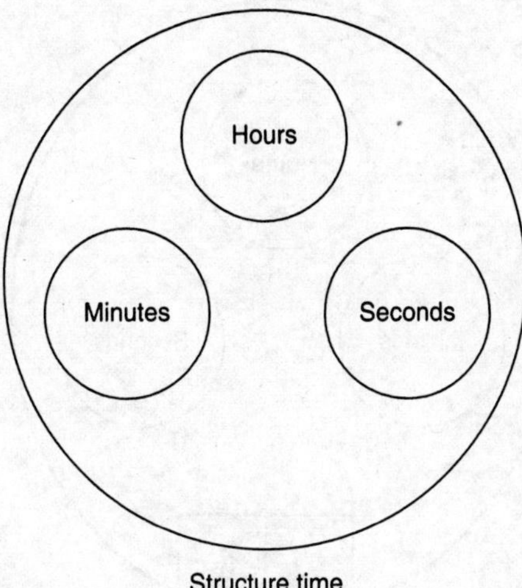

Figure 2.1 Simple View of Structure Time

```
public void show_time(int h ,int m ,int s);
} ;
Time0 t1;
```

Here we are defining a variable time t1, where t1 is an object. In the object, data hour, minute, and second and the functions `set_time()` and `show_time()` are tightly coupled. Once this class is fully tested, it can be easily reused in any new application.

You are not allowed to modify date in an arbitrary manner. You have to use function `set_time()`. Similarly, you can see (print) time only with the help of a function `show_time()`.

This is depicted in Figure 2.2. A dark, thick circle is indicative of the encapsulation. The only way to reach the data is through methods.

Now let us describe the features of object-oriented languages in detail.

2.2 Features of Object-Oriented Language

2.2.1 Encapsulation

In the earlier example, we are putting three variables and two functions in a bundle. There is an invisible shell around "time". In other words, we are encapsulating the data. It is more secure. We cannot modify data without using functions specifically designed for that object. This adds much safety to the code. Let us take an every day example.

Every schoolboy sports a water bottle in Mumbai these days. Every office goer carries, it too. Here water is like data. It is encapsulated in a bottle. It is safe from contamination. To use this data (water), we must unscrew the lid. It means we have to use standard method only. Compare this with the water in a pond or an open well. There is no fixed method to use it. Also, it may not be safe or may be contaminated.

2.2.2 Data hiding

As discussed earlier, we cannot tamper, i.e. modify, hour, minute, and second. Actually, they are hidden from our program (main and other functions). We are not allowed to see (use or copy) these values. If

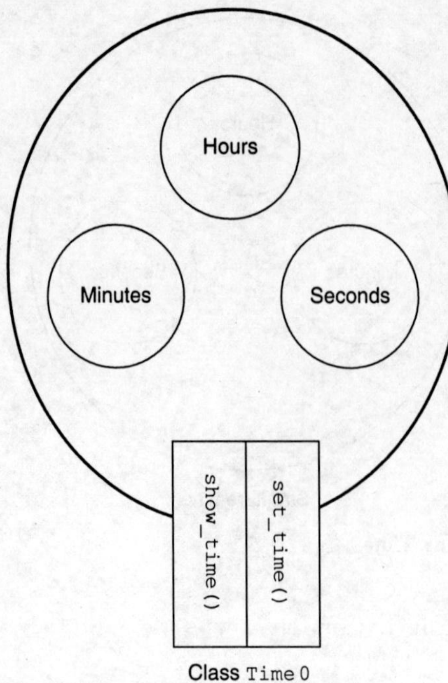

Figure 2.2 Detailed View of Class `Time0`

we say second = 30, compiler will say variable not known. This is the principle of data hiding. Data is available only through pre-defined manner [methods `set_time()` and `show_time()`], otherwise it is invisible.

2.2.3 Inheritance

If a particular application needs more functions to operate on class `Time0`, we can inherit the properties of this class in a new class. Here we define a new class, say `Time1` based on class `Time0`. All the definitions of class `Time0` are available to class `Time1`. In other words, the work done earlier is intact. We can add few new functions, such as `display_analog()`, as required in an application. It is a great saving in development time.

2.2.4 Polymorphism

We can design new classes based on a single class. Suppose that we have defined a general class component. Now we may develop new classes like `Textwindow`, `Button`, and `Scrollbar`. These classes have many things in common with class component. They have few properties which are different from class component. They will have many functions with same name like paint, which paints (displays) the component on the screen. They all share a similar interface. A component may be a label or a button, but method `paint()` will draw them properly on the screen. The same method acts differently (appropriately) in case of different sub-classes. This is the principle of polymorphism.

2.2.5 Message passing

The concept of object is very powerful and general. Object may not be simple structures. They can represent any real life entity like a running train or a plane. Now it is quite logical that these want to communicate with each other. This is done in terms of messages. Message is the information sent by one object to the other. Message passing (also receiving) environment is supported by the operating system. How simple or complex the messages and message passing can be depends on the operating system.

If Object technology has many new features, you are bound to ask what benefit we get out of these. There are many benefits of these new features. Let us discuss them one by one.

2.3 The Benefits of OOP

2.3.1 Software reusability

Nowadays, we develop software using objects. Objects are nothing but data abstractions. Hence, they have some existence even outside the program. When we write a new program requiring similar data, all these objects can be used directly. It means we have 50% of the job done in the first minute of software development. In other words, the time required will be less (as compared to a case when these objects are not available).

2.3.2 Code sharing

We can look at code sharing from two angles. When a large project is being handled, many groups work on it simultaneously. A code developed by one group has to be used by another group. Consider a second situation. A company has started a new project. It is quite similar to previous one developed by the company. The code developed in previous project must come handy now. If the code is in terms of objects, half of the job is done. Objects once developed and tested are usable straightaway. Hence, developing and testing objects enhance the code sharing process.

2.3.3 Rapid prototyping

To develop a software project requires lot of time and energy. After the project ends, if the client says that he wanted it in a different way, there will be a great loss. Hence, a small model is required to be developed first. This process is called prototyping. When client approves the prototype, the project starts in full swing. OO helps in rapid prototyping. While basic design is done, important classes can be designed with minimum number of methods.

Only at the later stage, all the remaining methods can be developed.

2.3.4 Information hiding

Information hiding is the most important advantage of OOP. It adds lot of safety to the software. Consider a case that we are developing one part of a program, inadvertently (and of course unintentionally) we modify some data in some other part. It leads to bugs, which are very difficult to detect. Debugging takes up lot of project time. When we use Object technology, lot of information can be easily hidden from the programmers. The compiler does not allow us to modify this data inadvertently. It saves considerable amount of debugging time.

Keywords

Class, code sharing, data hiding, encapsulation, information hiding, inheritance, message, message passing, object, object orientation, object-oriented languages, object-oriented programming, polymorphism, rapid prototyping, software reusability

Review Questions

1. Describe features of object-oriented language.
2. Discuss the benefits of OOP.
3. Explain the principal advantages of OOP.
4. What is a Class? How does it accomplish data hiding?
5. List any five object-oriented languages other than Java.

CHAPTER 3

JAVA LANGUAGE BASICS

It is said that the best way to learn swimming is to jump into the water right away. Similarly, the best way to learn a programming language is to start coding straight away. Let us start our study of Java programming in an informal way. Let us write a simple Java program and run it.

3.1 Introduction

In our first Java program, we will find the area of a circle with radius 5.

Problem: Write a program to find area of a circle with radius 5.

Solution: See Program 3.1.

PROGRAM 3.1 Area of a Circle

```
//     first.java
class first
 {
public static void main( String args[] )
   {
     int r  ;
     r = 5 ;
     System.out.println(3.14 * r * r);
   }
 }
```

If you run the program, you will get the following output.

Output

```
78.5
```

The output was as expected. Though the program was very simple still it had many components (parts). Let us describe its every part (Table 3.1).

Table 3.1 Program Parts Illustrated

Program code	Explanation
`//     first.java`	This is a comment
`class first`	The name of the class is `first`. This program must be in a file `first.java`
`{`	Left brace: start of class
`public static void main`	The execution of program starts with method `main ()`
`( String args[] )`	
`{`	Left brace: start of main method
`int r ;`	Declaration of variable `r`
`r = 5 ;`	Initialization of `r`
`System.out.println (3.14 * r * r);`	Program statement. Prints the value
`}`	Right brace: end of method main
`}`	Right brace: end of class `first`

3.2 Java Program Structure

A useful Java program will consist of many parts. It will have many features. It will not be easy to absorb every thing at one go. Therefore, we should first think of very simple programs, then simple programs, and so on. We should study Java step by step. Now in light of this program, let us study structure of a **very simple** Java program.

Structure of a **very simple** Java program can be summarized as follows:

1. A program say `first` is written in a file named `first.java`.
2. The file contains a class `first`, as a rule.
3. The class contains method `main`. It has to be declared with parameters: `String args[]`, as shown in Table 3.1.
4. The method main contains declarations and program statements.
5. Java applications begin execution at method `main()`.

As a matter of the rule, name of the class which contains method `main()` and the name of the file (without extension) must be identical.

Please note that this is description of a very simple program. As we start studying more and more features, we will refine this definition.

3.3 Basic Building Blocks

Any Java program (or a program in any other language for that matter) consists of few building blocks like comments, declarations, statements, and methods. These blocks are formed by some small atomic quantities known as tokens. Here we will not go into the grammar in depth. Still we will discuss step by step how programs, that is declarations and statements, are written. We will talk about grammar in a later chapter.

3.3.1 Comments

Comments are that part of the program, which are supposed to give more information (or explanation) to the reader. They increase the readability of the program. The compiler does not convert it into code. (We may say compiler ignores it.) Therefore, presence of comments has no relevance to program (execution) speed. In Java, comments are enclosed in pair of /* and */. Such comments can be of one or more lines. It may be noted that, such comment can appear anywhere, where a white space can appear in a program.

In addition Java uses double slash (//) for single-line comments. Any text from // to the end of that line is treated as comment.

In this text, you will see every program starts with the program name as a comment. It is not merely a style. It is a discipline which helps in long run.

3.3.2 Character set

When we write a program, we actually write characters. The console input and output also uses characters. Character set stands for the collection of characters used by any programming language. Java supports Unicode character set. Unicode characters need 16 bits (instead of 8 for ASCII) to store a character. It will be heartening to know that in Unicode there is representation for scripts (languages), like Japanese, Chinese, and many Indian ones, like Devnagri and Tamil.

Earlier languages used ASCII character set. Java also supports it as Unicode encompasses the ASCII character set.

A Java program can generate all of these characters. If we talk of writing Java program, that is source code, then there are some restrictions. We cannot use each and every character in writing a program. Table 3.2 illustrates the characters used in writing a program.

All Unicode characters can be written to file. However, if we are writing them to screen, some of them may not be shown properly.

Let us write a small program to verify this fact.

Table 3.2 Characters for Writing Java Programs

Group	Details
Letters—English alphabets	a to z and A to Z
Letters—non-English alphabets	All characters that are considered to be a letter by the Unicode 2.0 standard.
Digits	0, 1, 2, 3, 4, 5, 6, 7, 8, 9
Special characters I	dollar mark ($) and underscore (_) character
Special characters II	! @ # % ^ & * - = + \ < > / ?
Special characters III	{ } [ ] ( ) ; ,
Separator	blank, tab, new line

Problem: Write a program to print all ASCII characters on the screen.

Solution: We know that first 31 characters are used for special purpose. Hence, we will show characters with value 32 to 255. To restrict limited say 16 characters in one line, we will use 2 for loops (see Program 3.2).

PROGRAM 3.2 ASCII Characters

```
//    char1.java
class  char1
{   public static void main(String args[])
  {   char x= 65 ;
      int i,j,key ;
        for(j=2;j<16;j++)
         {   System.out.print(j*16 + " : ");
             for(i=0;i<16;i++)
              { key = j*16 + i;
                System.out.print( (char) key + " ");
              }
             System.out.println();
         }
  }
}
```

If you run the program, you will get the following output.

Output

```
32  :   ! " # $ % & ' ( ) * + , - . /
48  : 0 1 2 3 4 5 6 7 8 9 : ; < = > ?
64  : @ A B C D E F G H I J K L M N O
80  : P Q R S T U V W X Y Z [ \ ] ^ _
96  : ` a b c d e f g h i j k l m n o
112 : p q r s t u v w x y z { | } ~ ⌂
128 : ? ? ? ? ? ? ? ? ? ? ? ? ? ? ? ?
144 : ? ? ? ? ? ? ? ? ? ? ? ? ? ? ? ?
160 : á í ó ú ñ Ñ ª º ¿ ⌐ ¬ ½ ¼ ¡ « »
176 : ░ ▒ ▓ │ ┤ ╡ ╢ ╖ ╕ ╣ ║ ╗ ╝ ╜ ╛ ┐
192 : └ ┴ ┬ ├ ─ ┼ ╞ ╟ ╚ ╔ ╩ ╦ ╠ ═ ╬ ╧
208 : ╨ ╤ ╥ ╙ ╘ ╒ ╓ ╫ ╪ ┘ ┌ █ ▄ ▌ ▐ ▀
224 : α ß Γ π Σ σ µ τ Φ Θ Ω δ ∞ φ ε ∩
240 : ≡ ± ≥ ≤ ⌠ ⌡ ÷ ≈ ° · · √ n 2 ■ a
```

Please note that some characters are not shown properly on the screen. Hence, the computer (Windows OS) is showing question mark (?) in their place.

3.3.3 Constants

The most basic things in a program are the variables and the values they take. We have seen a statement:

```
r = 5 ;
```

Here, *r* is a variable and it takes value "5".

We will call this value appearing in a program as constant. (In strict computer jargon, it is called literal).

Constants can be divided into following three categories:

1. Integer constants
2. Real constants
3. Character constants

Integer constants

Integers can be expressed in three possible notations, that is octal, decimal, and hexadecimal.

In daily use, we use integer constants in decimal form. These constants are either positive or negative. Plus sign is optional.

Following are examples of valid integer constants in decimal notation:

23

−55

+2367

If we have to state an integer constant in octal notation (format), we must precede it with zero. This is the way we tell the computer that we mean octal representation. Please note that digits 8 and 9 are not valid in octal notation.

Following are examples of valid integer constants in octal notation:

023

055

02367

Hexadecimal number system consist of digits 0 to 9 and alphabets "a" to "f". These constants are preceded by `0x`

Following are examples of valid integer constants in hexadecimal notation:

```
0x23
0x5B
0Xff23
```

Please note that alphabets "a" to "f" and "x" can be in either small or capital.

Let us study these constants in a simple program.

Problem: Write a program to study octal, decimal, and hexadecimal notation for integers.

Solution: See Program 3.3.

PROGRAM 3.3 The Octal Notation

```
//     const1.java
class  const1
{  public static void main(String args[])
      {    int i,j,k ;
           i = 23 ;    // decimal notation
           j = 023 ;   // octal notation
           k = 0X23 ; // hexadecimal notation
           System.out.println("--->const1.java starts<---");
           System.out.println("Decimal      notation    23 -> " + i );
           System.out.println("Octal        notation   023 -> " + j );
           System.out.println("Hexadecimal notation 0x23 -> " + k );
      }
}
```

If you run this program, you will get the following output.

Output

```
--->const1.java starts<---
Decimal     notation   23 -> 23
Octal       notation  023 -> 19
Hexadecimal notation 0x23 -> 35
```

Real constants

Real or floating-point constants are written in either fixed point or scientific notation. Following are examples of valid real constants in fixed point notation.

2.3

−5.54

236.7

Notice the presence of decimal point. Also note, optional sign. Following are examples of valid real constants in scientific notation:

0.2e3

−5E5

2E67

Following conventions are used with scientific notation:

1. For both mantissa and exponent, sign is optional.
2. Use of capital "E" is allowed in place of small "e".

When we write numerical constants, they may belong to different types like `float`, `double`, `integer`, or `long`. There may be some confusion in the mind of compiler. If we write 2 it can very well represent an `integer` or `long` or `float` value. Hence, Java allows us to specify the data type of a constant using a suffix. If we use suffixes f, F, l, L, d, D they tell the compiler the necessary data type of the constant. Type `float` is specified by f or F. Type `long` is specified by l or L. Similarly, type `double` is specified by d or D.

Can you figure out why type `integer` is not given a suffix? The answer is simple; the type `integer` is the default numeric type. Any constant if not specified is treated as `integer`.

Character constants

Enclosing a single character in single quotes forms simple character constants:

Example: 'A', 'B', ')'

There are many characters in ASCII character set which are used for special purpose (for example, carriage return, form feed). Some of them cannot be typed with a keyboard. Naturally, they cannot be placed within single quotes. Therefore, alternate notation (format) has been developed. It uses a backslash character. It is also referred as escape codes.

Table 3.3 illustrates commonly used special characters.

It is interesting to note that to denote a single backslash character we use two such characters. Please note that unlike C++, Java does not define escape codes for vertical tab and the bell characters. See escape codes in action at the end of chapter example.

If we have to specify Unicode character, we have to write its hexadecimal value preceded by character u. For example,

```
'\u0100'
```

Please note that you cannot use uppercase U. Also, there must be four (no more no less) hexadecimal digits. Hence, constants like

```
'\U0100' or \u100
```

are invalid.

String constants

A collection of characters is known as `string`. Putting characters in the pair of double quotes forms a `string` constant.

Table 3.3 Escape Characters

Character	Represented by
Backspace	`'\b'`
Form feed	`'\f'`
New line	`'\n'`
Carriage return	`'\r'`
Horizontal tab	`'\t'`
Single quote	`'\''`
Double quote	`'\"'`
Backslash	`'\\'`

Following are examples of valid `string` constants:

```
"Hello"
"World"
"good morning" *
```

Java has an in-built class `String` to deal with character `strings`. We will deal with it later in a separate chapter.

3.4 Variables

We have seen constants. To store their values we need what is called variables. As name suggests, computer allows us to vary (change, manipulate) the values stored in a variable. In earlier programs, we have used variable names like *area1*. Grammatically variable name is an identifier. Hence, rule for forming variables are same as those for forming identifiers.

Rules for forming variable names can be stated as follows:

1. Variable names are formed with the help of letters and digits.
2. Alphabets can be in upper or lower case.
3. Only letters are allowed as starting character. Underscore character (_) and Dollar symbol ($) are treated as letter as far as variables are concerned.
4. The first character cannot be a digit.
5. There is no restriction on number of characters in a variable.
6. As white space characters (such as space and tab) are used to separate tokens, they cannot be part of a variable.

Following are valid variable names:

marks

Marks

K3G

Kabhi_Kushi_Kabhi_Gum

$JamesBond

Following are invalid variable names:

mark's

4you

m.x

These rules are general. Java treats few non-letter characters for use in variable names. We will discuss this again in Chapter 9 on "Wrapper Classes".

Every language reserve few words for its own use. They are termed as keywords or reserved words. We can group keywords of Java in three separate groups. Some keywords are in use as of today. Some are reserved for future use. Some of them actually represent values. It goes without saying that we cannot use keywords as variables (or user-defined name for any other entity like method).

Table 3.4 illustrates the keywords from Java which are currently in use.

Table 3.4 Keywords in Java

abstract	assert	boolean	break	byte
case	catch	char	class	continue
default	do	double	else	enum
extends	final	finally	float	for
if	implements	import	instanceof	int
interface	long	native	new	package
private	protected	public	return	short
static	strictfp	super	switch	synchronized
this	throw	throws	transient	try
void	volatile	while		

Table 3.5 illustrates the keywords from Java which are reserved for future use.

Table 3.5 Keywords Reserved for Future Use

const	goto

Table 3.6 Keywords which are Value Defined

false	null	true

Table 3.6 illustrates the keywords from Java which are value defined.

3.5 Data Types

We have said that variables store values. They basically represent **data**. In computer, data may be numeric or non-numeric. Therefore, various data types have been defined. The basic classification of data types can be numeric and non-numeric. These can be sub-classified further. Let us study these data types one by one.

3.5.1 Numeric data types

Numeric data types are for storing numbers. Not all of our school and college days number types are supported by Java. It basically supports only integers and real numbers. (As a programmer, we have to write code ourselves for numbers like rational numbers.)

Integer data type has a peculiarity that it has an exact representation in a computer. In different programs, we may be using large or small values. To store small numbers, we need fewer bytes and to store big number we need many bytes. Earlier computers had very little memory. Hence, different sub-data types for storing integers were defined. They are `byte`, `short`, `int`, and `long`. Java supports all these types. The memory required to store them varies from 1–4 bytes.

In C++ there is a qualifier named unsigned. There is no such qualifier in Java. Hence, all `integer` types can handle positive as well as negative numbers in Java.

To store real numbers, Java uses floating-point method. That is the reason for type name `float`. The beauty of `float` type is that in a given space (number of bits) it can store a very large as well as small numbers. (This is not possible in fixed point notation.)

To store real numbers, Java defines two sub-types, namely `float` and `double`. They require 4 and 8 bytes, respectively. They are capable of handling fairly large as well as fairly small values. Table 3.7 illustrates the length in bytes and range of numeric data types.

Type `float` and `double` are capable of storing very small values. The smallest values they can store are **`1.4E-45`** and **`4.9E-324`**, respectively.

3.5.2 Non-numeric data types

We will now discuss non-numeric data types one by one.

Character

Variables of type `char` store characters. Java supports 16 bits Unicode characters. If you have studied ASCII character set, for simplicity you can assume that Java supports ASCII character set.

Boolean

Variable of type `boolean` store `true` or `false` values.

Void

Void means nothing. We cannot have a variable of type `void`. When a function (called method in Java) does not return anything, we say it returns a value of type `void`. Data type `void` is used only with reference to functions.

Reference

Programming languages like C and C++ have a type called `pointer`. It stores the address of the

Table 3.7 Length and Range of Numeric Data Types

Type	Length in bytes	Range
byte	1	−128 to +127
short	2	−32,768 to 32,767
intent	4	−2,147,473,648 to 2,147,483,647
long	8	−9,223,372,036,854,775,808 to 9,223,372,036,854,775,807
float	4	−3.4E38 to +3.4 E38
double	8	−1.7E308 to +1.7E308

variable it references. A similar data type in Java is termed as `reference`. However, Java does not allow any numeric processing on this type. `Arrays, strings`, and `classes` are handled by type `reference`.

At this stage just assume that it is some mechanism to represent complex (or in general multi valued) data type. We will discuss this in more details when we discuss objects and methods.

3.5.3 Declarations of variables

Variables are declared with the help of its data type.

A declaration

```
int j ;
```

tells the compiler that *j* is a variable of type `int (integer)`. If you have more than one variable of type `int`, they are separated by comma, for example

```
int j, k, m ;
```

Please note that we must assign initial values (using assignment operator) to these variables before using them in a program. Otherwise, compiler will fail to compile the program. This helps in avoiding many unintended errors. Note that C++ does not behave like this. It assigns arbitrary values to the variable. In this respect, Java scores over C++.

Java allows us to initialize a variable at the time of declaration as shown hereafter.

```
int marks = 100;
```

This statement declares a variable `marks` of type `integer` and assigns value 100 to it.

3.6 Operators

Operator performs operations on operands. Operands may be one, two, or three. Operands are either variables or constants. The operators, which take single operand, are called unary operators. Those taking two are known as binary operators and one having three operands is called ternary operator.

Most of the operators are binary operators, few are unary while there is only one ternary operator (for example "?:" operator).

For further study, we can group operators depending on functionality.

- Arithmetic operators
- Relational (or Conditional) operators
- Shift and Logical operators
- Assignment operators
- Other operators

Let us discuss all of them one by one.

3.6.1 Arithmetic operators

From our school days, we are familiar with following arithmetic operators:

addition (+)
subtraction (-)
multiplication (*)
division (/) and
modulo (%).

All these operators are binary operators and work on all integer and floating-point types. Please note that in Java, you can use modulo operator (`%`) with floating-point operands. (This is not a case with C++.) Following unary operators also work on integers and floating-point numbers:

Unary plus +

Unary minus –

Pre-increment or post-increment ++

Pre-decrement or post-decrement --

Please note that last two operators work only with variables (not constants). Consider a case where we use say for example `mark++` (post-increment) in an expression. First current value of mark is used in evaluating that expression and then variable mark is incremented by one.

Consider a case where we use say for example `++mark` (pre-increment) in an expression. First variable mark is incremented by one and then the new value of mark is used in evaluating that expression.

Operation with decrement is similar in nature. Here value of the variable is decremented by one.

Advice

Mixing too many pre- and post-increment/decrement operators in a single expression is quite confusing. It must be avoided. Language has given this facility as convenience. We should not make our life miserable with it.

Problem: Write a program to demonstrate use of modulo operator.

Solution: See Program 3.4.

PROGRAM 3.4 Modulo Operator

```
//      modulo1.java
class  modulo1
{  public static void main(String args[])
       {   int amount = 320;
           int rupees,paise;
           System.out.println("--->modulo1.java starts<---");
           rupees = amount / 100 ;
           paise = amount % 100 ;
           System.out.println("rupees = " + rupees);
           System.out.println("paise = " + paise);
       }
}
```

If you run the program, you will get the following output.

Output

```
--->modulo1.java starts<---
rupees = 3
paise = 20
```

Table 3.8 **Relational Operators**

Operator	Description
<	Less than
<=	Less than or equal to
>	Greater than
>=	Greater than or equal to
==	Equal to
!=	Not equal to

Table 3.8 illustrates the various relational operators available in Java.

Here we have seen a simple application of modulo operator. It involved integers as operands. The "modulo division" may be applied to floating-point values in Java. This is not permitted in C/C++. However, we have not come across any decent use of this facility.

3.6.2 Relational operators

When we use relational operator in an expression it returns Boolean value, that is true or false. Please note that in C++, such expressions actually return number 1 for true and number 0 for false. Hence, a code

```
int k ;
      k = 5>4 ;
```

is valid in C++, but not in Java. Java will flag compilation error saying "Can't convert `boolean` to `int`". See Program 3.8 `relop1.java` in the end of chapter programs.

3.6.3 Logical operators

To work with variables and constants of type `Boolean`, we have logical operators. They are also termed as Boolean operators. Some texts call them conditional operators. Table 3.9 illustrates these operators.

Table 3.9 **Logical Operators**

Operator	Description
`&&`	Logical AND short-circuit evaluation
`&`	Logical `AND` operator
`||`	Logical `OR` short-circuit evaluation
`|`	Logical `OR` operator
`!`	Logical negation `(NOT)`
`^`	Exclusive `OR`

Let us study a simple program.

Problem: Write a program to demonstrate evaluation of Boolean expression.

Solution: Let us take the question closest to the heart of first-year students. Whether they will enter second year or not? Consider that there are two semesters whose results are stored as Boolean. Rules of University A are lenient. If a student passes any one semester, he is allowed to go to next year. Rules of University B are stringent. Student must pass both the semesters (see Program 3.5).

PROGRAM 3.5 Evaluating Boolean Expression

```
//      logical1.java
class  logical1
{  public static void main(String args[])
      {   boolean semI  = true ;
          boolean semII = false ;
          boolean resultA, resultB ;
          System.out.println("<---logical1--->");
          resultA = semI || semII ;
          resultB = semI && semII ;
          System.out.println("resultA ->" +resultA);
          System.out.println("resultB ->" +resultB);
      }
}
```

If you run the program, you will get the following output.

Output

```
<---logical1--->
resultA ->true
resultB ->false
```

It goes without saying that these logical/Boolean operators need Boolean operands. Any attempt to use it with operands of type `integer` (as allowed in C/C++) will result in error.
For example, in Program 3.5, `resultA` and `semI` are Boolean variables. A statement like

```
resultA = semI || 3 ;
```

results in compilation error.

Short-circuit evaluation

Consider an expression

```
op1 || op2 ;
```

Here first `op1` is evaluated. If it is true, the value of expression is true. Naturally, there is no need to evaluate `op2`. Hence, `op2` is not evaluated.

If `op2` was a method, it will not be invoked.

If we are executing

```
op1 | op2
```

`op2` will always be evaluated.

Table 3.10 Bit-Wise Operators

Operator	Description
~	Bit-wise (1's) complement
&	Bit-wise AND
^	Bit-wise XOR
|	Bit-wise OR

In case of doubt do not use short-circuit operation.
(Please note that | stands for vertical bar character. It is seen on keyboard as "¦".)

3.6.4 Bit-wise operators

Twenty-five years ago when programming language C was introduced, there was lot of noise regarding bit manipulation. Bit-wise operators were in limelight. However, over the years the enthusiasm has subsided. In the past 5 years, we hardly remember any program written by us using bit manipulation. However, it is still required in specific fields like communication engineering.
Table 3.10 illustrates the bit-wise operators.
The following points may be noted regarding use of bit-wise operators:

1. The operands must be of integral (`char, byte, short, int,` or `long`) type. It means `float` and `double` are not allowed as operands.
2. If one of the operand is of type `long`, result is of type `long`.
3. If none of the operand is `long`, result is of type `int`.

Let us see a simple program using bit-wise operators.

Problem: Write a program to demonstrate bit-wise operators.

Solution: In this program we have one example of AND and OR operator each (see Program 3.6).

PROGRAM 3.6 Bit Manipulation

```
//     bit1.java
class  bit1
{  public static void main(String args[])
       {   int i=5;
           long a=2,b ;
           short c=4,d=3 ;
           System.out.println("<---bit1--->");
            b = i | a ;  // 101 | 010
            d = (short)( d & c ); // 011 &  100
           System.out.println(" ->" + b );
           System.out.println(" ->" + d );
       }
}
```

If you run the program, you will get the following output.

Output

```
<---bit1--->
->7
->0
```

Are the results as expected? You may note that `d & c` produce a result of type `integer`. Hence, typecasting to `short` is required. Effective use of bit-wise operators can be seen in Chapter 24 on "Multimedia Experience".

3.6.5 Shift operators

A shift operator also performs bit manipulation by shifting the bits left or right. The bits of the first operand are shifted number of places as specified by the second operand. Java has three operators for this purpose. Table 3.11 summarizes these operators.

Table 3.11 Shift Operators

Operator	Use	Operation
>>	`op1 >> op2`	Shift bits of `op1` right by distance `op2`
<<	`op1 << op2`	Shift bits of `op1` left by distance `op2`
>>>	`op1 >>> op2`	Shift bits of `op1` right by distance `op2` (unsigned)

It goes without saying that these operators work with only operands, which are integral in nature (sorry no floating-point operands).

When we shift right with >> the sign bit (left most) is copied in the left most position. With >>> sign is ignored. Zero is entered in MSB position.

Let us study a problem with shift operators.

Problem: Write a program to study shift operators.

Solution: See Program 3.7.

PROGRAM 3.7 Shift Operator

```
//      shift1.java
class  shift1
{  public static void main(String args[])
      {   int i,j;
          byte k = 4 ;
          i =  6 << 2 ;
          j = 23 >> 2;
          k = (byte)  (k >> 1)   ;
          System.out.println("--->shift1.java starts<---");
          System.out.println("1)  " + i );
          System.out.println("2)  " + j );
          System.out.println("3)  " + k );
      }
}
```

If you run this program, you will get the following output.

Output

```
--->shift1.java starts<---
1) 24
2) 5
3) 2
```

Note the following:

"<<" is left shift operator. Shifting a binary number by 2 bits left is equal to multiplying by `4 (=2*2)`. Hence, `6 * 4 = 24` is the output.
">>" is right shift operator. Shifting a binary number by 2 bits right is equal to dividing (integer mode) by `4 (= 2 raised to 2)`. Hence, `23/4 = 5` is the output.

Here 4 is divided by 2. Hence, the answer. The point to note is `k>>1` is evaluated as an integer. Hence, before substituting in `k` we have to typecast it to byte.

3.6.6 Assignment operators

We have seen equal sign as basic assignment operator. It assigns value on right-hand side to variable on left-hand side. For example, `marks = 95.`

Many times we need expressions as `marks = marks + 3;` (grace marks). To handle such situations, Java provides shortcut operators. For example, += is a shortcut operator. If you write `marks=+3` it means a shortcut for longer expression `marks = marks+3`. There are many such shortcut operators. They are listed in Table 3.12

Table 3.12 Shortcut Assignment Operators

Operator	Description
=	Simple assignment
*=	Assign product
/=	Assign quotient
%=	Assign remainder (modulus)
+=	Assign sum
-=	Assign difference
&=	Assign bit-wise AND
^=	Assign bit-wise XOR
|=	Assign bit-wise OR
<<=	Assign left shift
>>=	Assign right shift

Table 3.13 Special Operators

Operator	Description
`?:`	For conditional evaluation
`()`	Used in Function call
`[]`	Used for Array subscript
`.`	Used as reference to member
`new`	Used for creating an object or an array
`(type)`	Used in typecasting the operand
`instanceof`	Used for checking an object for belonging to a class

3.6.7 Other (special) operators

Table 3.13 lists other special operators.
Please note that these are not operators in strict mathematical sense. It is the requirement of grammar that forces Java to call them as operators. Let us not worry about it. We will study these operators later at appropriate time.

Those who know C++ will notice the absence of comma operator. In our opinion, this is a good thing because there are not many uses of this operator. Inadvertent use of this operator produces many bugs in C++ programs. Many times we may use a two-dimensional matrix element as A[j,k]. (This is an error as we must be using A[j][k].) C++ accepts this assuming that we are consciously using comma operator. It produces unexpected results. This does not happen in Java as error is caught at compile time only.

3.7 Expressions

We are faced with all sorts of calculations from our school days. Calculations primarily involve numeric expressions. In Java, we will see numeric as well as non-numeric expressions. Expressions are combinations of operators and operands; operands are literals (constants), variables or keywords, or symbols that evaluate a value of some type (for example true). Let us start with arithmetic expressions.

3.7.1 Arithmetic expressions

Simple arithmetic expressions can be classified as unary expressions or binary expressions.

3.7.2 Arithmetic expressions with single operand

When we apply unary + or − operator to a constant or variable we get unary expression. If we have expression `-Marks`, it is evaluated as `-1 *` Marks. Similarly, expression `+Y` is evaluated as `+1 * Y`.

3.7.3 Arithmetic expressions with two operands

These expressions involve two operands and a binary operand. If one fruit costs 3 rupees, five fruits costs

3 * 5 equal to 15 rupees.

Here 3 and 5 are operands and * (for multiplication) is the operator.

3.7.4 General arithmetic expressions

General expressions involve many operands and operators. Their evaluation follows standard rules known to us from our school days.

1. When brackets are present, expressions within brackets are evaluated first.
2. Operators with highest precedence are operated before those of lower precedence.
3. With all operators of same precedence, expression is evaluated from left to right.

All the operators and their precedence are shown in Appendix C.

Associativity

Strictly speaking, when more than one operator with same precedence appears in an expression, we have to look for the associativity of the operators. Most of the operators have left to right associativity. The important exceptions are assignment operator and all of shorthand assignment operators. They operate from right to left.

3.7.5 Logical expressions

Expressions involving logical operators are called logical expressions. Alternate name is Boolean expressions. These evaluations follow the Boolean algebra. They result in only true or false answer.

Rules for evaluating such expressions (precedence and left to right) are similar to that of arithmetic expressions.

3.7.6 Assignment expressions

Assignment expressions are evaluated as follows. First right-hand side sub-expression is evaluated. Then this result is assigned to variable of left-hand side. It must be noted that at left-hand side we must have something, which can store the value.

`j = 5+5;` is fine, but `3 = 5` is not acceptable. If you write such an expression compiler will generate error message as L-value required.

Java is a strongly typed language. Hence, it does not allow you to assign value of one type to variable of other type in arbitrary manner. Consider following declarations:

```
long n = 2 ;
int j = 5 ;
j = n ;
```

Here `n` is a `long` integer. Its value is assigned to a variable of type `int`. We know that `long` can store values larger than capacity of type `int`. Hence, there is a possibility of error. Hence, Java does not compile this code. It gives error. On the contrary if we write

```
n = j;
```

Java allows this. Reason is very simple. Capacity of `long` is much more than `int`, therefore, `long` can accept any `int` value without error. This is called "widening" principle.

Table 3.14 illustrates the assignment compatibility of numeric types

Table 3.14 Assignment Compatibility

Type on left-hand side	Type on right-hand side
short	byte
int	short, byte
long	int, short, byte
float	int, short, byte
double	float, int, short, byte

Right from Fortran days, programmers are interested in knowing whether integer values can be put to real variables and vice versa. Let us first talk of substituting integer values in real variables. Type `float` handles values much greater than the largest value of type `integer`. Hence, it can accept integer values. Similarly, `double` can take `long`.

On the other side, conversion from `float` to `int` is not permitted directly. A `float` may contain a fraction, which is not acceptable in `integers`. Hence, specific conversion is required. From our knowledge of school mathematics, we know that there are two well-known ways for conversion. They are truncation and rounding. Java supports method `round()` for rounding. There is no first-hand support for truncation. Java supports methods `ceil()` and `floor()` for this purpose.

Table 3.15 describes the methods `ceil`, `floor`, and `round`.
Figure 3.1 will illustrate their action graphically.
Please note that in this diagram a represents a whole number, which can be either positive or negative. If we want to truncate a real value we can use methods `ceil` and floor (details are left to you as an exercise). Alternately, we can use brute force and use typecasting to truncate a floating-point value. See Program 3.10 `trunc1.java` in the end of chapter programs.

3.7.7 Type `char` in assignment

In C language, type `integer` and type `char` are treated as equal and exchangeable. A highly typed Java does not make such assumption. Also, size in bytes of these types also differs. Still Java considers type

Table 3.15 Methods for Converting Real to Integer

Return type	Method	Description
Static double	ceil (double x)	Returns the smallest (closest to negative infinity) `double` value that is, not less than the argument and is equal to a mathematical integer
Static double	floor (double x)	Returns the largest (closest to positive infinity) `double` value that is, not greater than the argument and is equal to a mathematical integer
Static long	round (double x)	Returns the closest `long` to the argument
Static int	round (float x)	Returns the closest `int` to the argument

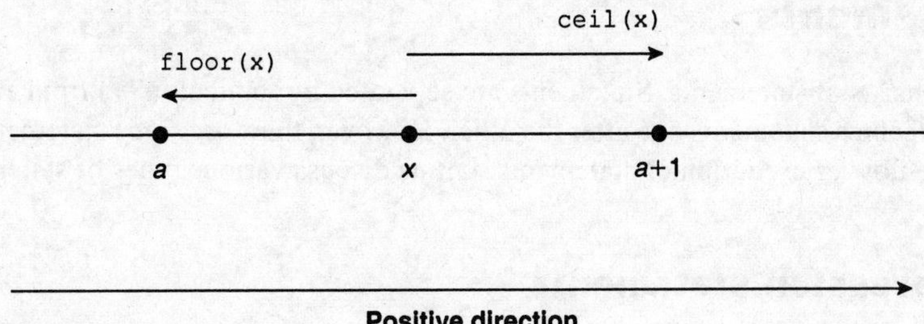

Figure 3.1 **`ceil` and `floor`**

`char` as something like an (16 bits) `integer`. We are allowed to use operators like (++) with variables of type `char`. As far as assignment is concerned, type `char` can appear on right side of `int` or `float` or `double` assignment expression. However, we cannot assign any non-character variable even of type `byte` to character variable.

3.8 Typecasting

All these were natural and logical conversions. What about brute force? What if we want to convert anyway? What if we do not want to care about ensuing error? Well solution in that case is straightforward. We must use a technique called "typecasting".

If we specify a type inside brackets ahead of any expression, then value of that expression is converted to value of type specified in a bracket. For example,

```
(int) 3.5 ;
```

This type of conversion will not alert us even if there is loss of information. Hence, such typecasting must be used with caution.

3.9 Keyword `Final`

The variables are for holding different values at different times. If we want to keep a value constant, we may declare a variable as final. Such a variable has to be initialized only once. For example,

```
final int j;
   .
   .
   j = 30 ; // first initialization
```

If we try to modify its values at later stage, we will get compilation error.

It is possible to initialize such a variable at the time of declaration only.

For example,

```
final int j= 30 ;
```

See Program 3.12 on `final1` at the end of chapter programs.

Please note that use of keyword final is equivalent to const declaration of C++. However, `const` is a reserved word for future use in Java.

3.10 Statements

Program code consists of statements. Statements are separated by semicolon (`;`) from each other. In general, computer executes statements one after the other. However, there are some statements, which changes or controls the flow of execution of statements. Let us discuss various types of statements briefly.

3.10.1 Expression statements

Any valid expression can be considered as expression statement. In general, expressions return a value. Hence, if it is not stored anywhere, action of such statement will not have any effect on the program. For example,

```
i+j;
```

The computer will add two values. But the result is not stored anywhere. Hence, such statements will be redundant. Hence, Java does not allow such expressions as statement. Note that in C++, such statements are valid.

Java allows only two types of expressions as statements. They are

Assignment expression and

Auto-increment/decrement expression.

This is fine as both these expression leave some effect after their evaluation.

Assignment expression statements

See the following statement. It consists of assignment expression.

```
i = j+5;
```

This is a valid statement in Java.

Here right-hand side is evaluated and then the value is stored in variable appearing on the left-hand side. It means there is action associated with it.

This is the most fundamental statement in any programming language.

Auto-increment/decrement expression statements

Another effective expression statement consists of auto-increment/decrement expressions. For example,

```
i++;
--j;
```

Such expressions are evaluated and its effect is stored in the computer.

Method call

A call to a method is technically an expression. It returns a value after executing the body (which may imply action). Grammatically a method call is a valid statement.

Object creation expression

When we write an expression with new operator, it creates an object.

That is,

```
Point origin = new Point (0,0);
```

This is a valid statement in Java. We will discuss this type of expression in detail in chapter on objects.

3.10.2 Declaration statement

We need variables to be declared explicitly. Such statements can be considered as declaration statements. For example,

```
int myMarks =99; // out of 100!
```

3.10.3 Flow control statements

We can group these statements in following manner:
The first group consists of decision-making statements.

Examples are `if-else` and `switch-case` statements.

Second group consist of looping statements.

Examples are `while, do-while`, and `for` statements.

The third group consists of branching statements.

Examples are `break, continue, label`, and `return` statements.

The last group consists of exception handling statements.

Examples are `try-catch-finally` and `throw` statements.

These statements are discussed separately at a later stage.

3.10.4 Empty statement

When we do not write any statement, it effectively becomes null or empty statement. Consider two consecutive semicolons with some blanks in between.

```
;   ;
```

These semicolons are containing a blank statement. Such blank statements are allowed in Java. (They are allowed in C/C++ too.) Here no action is involved. We do not know the logic in allowing such statements in a program.

These are source of errors when coupled with loops. The investor lost most of the interest on a fixed deposit when the programmer (of the bank) wrote the following code:

```
int_rate = 0.08;
balance = 1000;
for ( j=0;j<10;j++ );
balance = balance + balance * int_rate;
```

3.10.5 Labelled statement

Strictly speaking, this is not a separate type of statement. Java allows us to attach a label to a statement. Most of the times, it will have no significance. Only when we use labelled `break` or `continue` statements, the label will have some importance. We are discussing such statements in a later chapter.

3.11 Description of Very Simple Java Program

Officially, there is no distinction as simple or difficult Java program. Java is a very vast language. We cannot study it in one go. We have to study it step by step. Naturally, the programs in initial chapter must be very simple. They must be using only few of the large number of language facilities (or concepts). We are, therefore, describing (not defining) very simple Java program.

Very simple Java programs are as follows:

- Programs less than 50 lines
- Program must be in a single file
- No user-defined classes or interfaces

Special suggestion: Though it is not necessary, we should follow the practice of keeping every program in separate directory.

3.12 End of Chapter Programs

3.12.1 Relational expression

Problem: Write a program to demonstrate relational expression.

Solution: See Program 3.8.

PROGRAM 3.8 Relational Expression Returns Boolean

```
//      relop1.java
class relop1
{ public static void main(String args[])
    { int k ;
      boolean flag ;
     System.out.println("--->relop1.java<---");
//     k = 5>4 ;
       flag = 5>4 ;
       System.out.println(" value of flag is : " + flag);
    }
}
```

If you run the program, you will get the following output.

Output

```
--->relop1.java<---
value of flag is : true
```

Notice the commented statement. If present, it would have resulted in following compilation error:

```
relop1.java:6: Incompatible type for =. Can't convert
boolean to int.
   k = 5>4 ;
     ^
1 error
press any key to continue
```

3.12.2 Study of special characters

Problem: Write a program to study special characters.

Solution: See Program 3.9.

PROGRAM 3.9 Special Characters

```
//       char3n.java
class  char3n
{public static void main(String args[])
  {  char x[]={'\b','\f','\n', '\r',
              '\t'}  ;
     int i ;
     System.out.println("program char3n.java starts");
     System.out.println("1. Writing back space --->"
                                   + x[0] + "<---") ;
     System.out.println("2. Writing form feed  --->"
                                   + x[1] + "<---" );
     System.out.println("3. Writing new line   --->"
                                   + x[2] + "<---" );
     System.out.println("4. Writing return     --->"
                                   + x[3] + "<---" );
     System.out.println("5. Writing tab        --->"
                                   + x[4] + "<---" );
     System.out.println("--->the end<---");
  }
}
```

If you run the program, you will get the following output.

Output

```
program char3n.java starts
1. Writing back space ---<---
2. Writing form feed  --->†<---
3. Writing new line   --->
<---
<---riting return     --->
5. Writing tab        --->     <---
--->the end<---
```

It is very surprising that characters `4. W` are missing from the output. Can you interpret the result?

3.12.3 Truncating a real number

Problem: Write a program to study truncation of a real number.

Solution: See Program 3.10.

PROGRAM 3.10 Truncating a Real Number

```
//       trunc1.java
class  trunc1
{  public static void main(String args[])
       {   double  a = 5.1;
           double  b = -3.99 ;
           long i=0,j=0;
           System.out.println("--->trunc1<---");
           i = (long) a;
           j = (long) b;
           System.out.println("truncating a -> " +i);
           System.out.println("truncating b -> " +j);
       }
}
```

If you run this program, you will get the following output.

Output

```
--->trunc1<---
truncating a -> 5
truncating b -> -3
```

In this example we have used a brute force, that is typecast.

3.12.4 A straight line

In school geometry, we learn equation of a straight line as

$$y = m^*x + c$$

where m is the slope and c is the intercept on y-axis (Figure 3.2).
Let us write a program to compute them.

Problem: Write a program to find the slope and intercept on y-axis of a straight line. Assume that two points on the given straight line are specified.

Solution: Assume that two points are specified with coordinates as `x1, y1` and `x2, y2` (see Figure 3.2). By substituting these coordinates in the standard equation and rearranging the terms, we get following formulae:

```
m = (y2 - y1) / (x2 - x1)
c = y1 - m * x1
```

See Program 3.11.

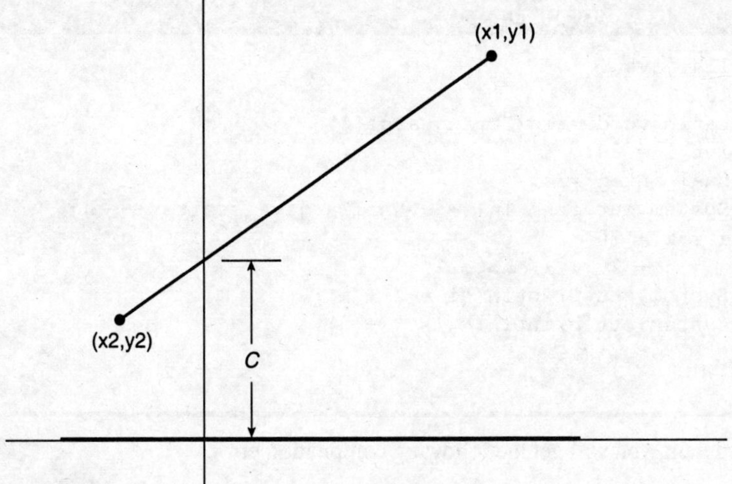

Figure 3.2 Straight Line Slope and Intercept

PROGRAM 3.11 Straight Line Slope and Intercept

```
//      PROGRAM 3.12  Straight Line slope and intercept
//      line1.java
class line1
{ public static void main(String args[])
   { double x1, y1, x2, y2 ;
     double m , c ;
     System.out.println("<---line1.java--->");
     x1= -1; y1 = 1;
     x2=11; y2 =13;
     m= (y2 - y1) / (x2 - x1);
     c = y1- m*x1;
     System.out.println(" slope= " + m);
     System.out.println(" intercept = " + c);
   }
}
```

If you run the program, you will get the following output.

Output

```
<---line1.java--->
slope= 1.0
intercept = 2.0
```

3.12.5 Keyword `final`

Problem: Write a program to study keyword final.

Solution: See Program 3.12.

PROGRAM 3.12 Keyword Final

```
//      final1a.java
class  final1a
{  public static void main(String args[])
       {    int i = 20;
            final int j =30;
            System.out.println("--->final1a.java starts<---");
            i = i + 30 ;
            j = j + 20 ; // note 1
            System.out.println("i = " + i);
            System.out.println("j = " + j);
        }
}
```

If you run the program, you will get the following compilation error.

Output

```
Compiling \JDK6\bin\javac final1a.java
final1a.java:10: cannot assign a value to final variable j
            j = j + 20 ; // note 1
            ^
1 error
press any key to continue
```

Let us remove that line by commenting it out and run the program. In that case, you will get the following output.

Output

```
--->final1.java starts<---
i = 50
j = 30
```

Keywords

AND operator, Arithmetic Operators, Assignment operators, Bit-wise operators, Boolean operators, character set, comment, conditional operators, constant-character, constant-integer, constant-real, Constants, constant-string, Data types, Empty statement, Expression, final, keywords, literal, method `main()`, modulo operator, Operators, OR operator, post-decrement, post-increment, Pre-decrement, Pre-increment, reference, relational operators, shift operators, Statements, string-constant, Typecasting, Unicode character, variable

RuleBook

escape codes	In Java, there are no escape codes defined for vertical tab and the bell character.
final	A final variable cannot change from its initialized value.

unsigned	`integer` types are always signed in Java. There is no unsigned qualifier in Java.
modulo division	Modulo divisor operator can be used with floating point values in Java. This is not allowed in C/C++.
Relational expressions	Relational expressions return Boolean value. Note C++ returns `integer`.
Assignment	You can assign a character variable to integer but not vice versa.
Expression statement	Only certain types of expressions are allowed in expression statement. They are assignment, inc/dec and method call.
Variable name	A variable name can contain as well as start with character `$`.
Variable initialization	Java flags compilation error if we try to use ordinary variables without initialization.
`const`	In Java, `const` is a reserved word, reserved for future use.
Unicode character	Unicode character can be expressed as \u followed by four hexadecimal digits. Note character u is in lowercase. There must be exactly four digits. No more no less.
Bit-wise operator	Bit-wise operators accept only integral operands (`char, byte, short, int,` and `long`). `float` and `double` are not allowed.
Comma operator	Java does not support the comma operator (of C++).
`main()`	Java applications begin execution at method `main()`.
Comments	Comments increase the readability of the program.
Comments	Comments have no relevance to program (execution) speed.
Keywords reserved for future use	`const goto`
Keywords which are values defined	`false null true`

Keywords currently in use	`abstract`	`assert`	`boolean`
	`break`	`byte`	`case`
	`catch`	`char`	`class`
	`continue`	`default`	`do`
	`double`	`else`	`enum`
	`extends`	`final`	`finally`
	`float`	`for`	`if`
	`implements`	`import`	`instanceof`

`int`	`interface`	`long`
`native`	`new`	`package`
`private`	`protected`	`public`
`return`	`short`	`static`
`strictfp`	`super`	`switch`
`synchronized`	`this`	`throw`
`throws`	`transient`	`try`
`void`	`volatile`	`while`

`long` — The number of bytes used by Java primitive `long` is 8.

Expressions — *Expressions* are combinations of variables, keywords or symbols that evaluate to a value of some type.

Character constant — Character constant (literal) is formed by enclosing a single character in pair of single quotes.

`String` constant — `String` constant (literal) is formed by enclosing a zero or more characters in pair of double quotes.

Source file public class — If a source file includes a public class, the class name must match the unextended filename. In other words, there cannot be two public classes in a single source file.

Program file name — A simple Java application source file must have extension ".java" The name of the file and the name of the public class must be identical (case sensitive).

Boolean variable — In Java, Boolean variable **does not** take the value 1 or 0, it takes true or false values only.

Boolean type — The Boolean type cannot be converted from or to any other data type.

C++ Corner

Relational expressions return Boolean value. Note C++ returns `int`.

You can assign a character variable to integer but not vice versa. In C++, you are allowed to do so.

"`j+k`"; which is valid statement in C++, is invalid in Java

`$` is not allowed as part or start of a variable name in C++. It is allowed in Java.

C++ does not flag compilation error, when un-initialized variables are used. This is sure to create unexpected errors. In this case, Java is a better language than C++.

There is no direct equivalent of "`enum`" in Java. However, its effect can be obtained by defining an interface. Interface is discussed later in chapter on inheritance.

At present Java does not support keyword `const`. If we want C++ like action of const on a variable, we have to make use of keyword final.

Java does not support the comma operator of C++. Inadvertent use of this operator produces many bugs in C++ programs.

Review Questions

1. Describe the structure of a simple Java program.
2. Describe the various methods of writing comments in Java.
3. At what place can a Java comment appear?
4. What is the advantage of Unicode character set?
5. Describe the method to tell the compiler that whether the literal constant is binary, octal, or hexadecimal.
6. We normally use decimal notation. Why then octal and hexadecimal notations are supported?
7. State the rules for forming a variable name.
8. Explain the rules for assigning the values of expression to a variable.
9. What do you understand by the term widening?
10. How can we truncate a number with the help of methods, like `round`, `ceil`, and `floor`?
11. What is the significance of keyword final used with a variable?
12. Why word float is used to represent real numbers?
13. Why bit-wise operators accept type `char` as operands?

Exercises

1. Find the average of five given numbers (integers).
2. Find whether given number N is divisible by 23.
3. Find the perimeter and area of circle with given radius.
4. Find the distance between two points (20,20) and (40,50).
5. Find the roots of a given quadratic equation.
6. Convert given temperature in Fahrenheit to Centigrade.
7. Estimate the time needed for a stone to fall from height of 3,000 meters. Assume g = 9.8 meter/sec2.
8. State whether following program will compile. If yes, describe the output. If no, give reasons.

```
*************************************
//      default1.java
class  default1
{ public static void main(String args[])
    {   int i ;
        float f ;
        boolean b ;
        System.out.println("<---default1.java starts--->");
        System.out.println(" int i = " + i );
        System.out.println(" float f = " + f );
        System.out.println(" boolean b = " + b );
    }
}
*************************************
```

9. State whether following program will compile. If yes, describe the output. If no, give reasons.

```
************************************
//      logical2.java
class  logical2
{  public static void main(String args[])
      {   boolean semI  = true ;
          boolean semII = false ;
          boolean resultA, resultB ;
          System.out.println("<---logical2--->");
          resultA = semI || 3 ;
          resultB = 5 & 6;
          System.out.println("resultA ->" +resultA);
          System.out.println("resultB ->" +resultB);
      }
}
************************************
```

10. State whether following program will compile. If yes, describe the output. If no, give reasons.

```
************************************
//      bit2.java
class  bit2
{ public static void main(String args[])
      {  float j ;
         System.out.println("<---bit2--->");
         j = 3.2f & 4.2;
         System.out.println("j ->" + j );
      }
}
************************************
```

11. State whether following program will compile. If yes, describe the output. If no, give reasons and suggest minimum changes in the code.

```
************************************
//      tcheck1.java
class  tcheck1
{ public static void main(String args[])
      {  char ch = 'A' ;
         int i = ch ;
         System.out.println("<---tcheck1.java--->");
         System.out.println(ch + "   " + i );
         i  = 66 ;
         ch =  i ;
         System.out.println(ch + "   " + i );
      }
}
************************************
```

12. State whether following program will compile. If yes, describe the output. If no, give reasons and suggest minimum changes in the code.

```
************************************
//      tcheck2.java
class  tcheck2
```

```
{ public static void main(String args[])
   { char ch = 'A' ;
     int i ;
     short j = 32000;
     byte k = 5;
     float a = ch;
     System.out.println("<---tcheck2.java--->");
     i  = 66 + ch*4 ;
     System.out.println("66 +ch  " + i );
     System.out.println("float a = " + a );
   }
}
*************************************
```

CONTROL STRUCTURES

In Chapter 3, we saw a few simple statements. In a program, these statements are executed one after the other. However, these statements are not sufficient to effectively solve the problems. To solve these problems, flow control statements are used. When we use them, statement to be executed need not be the very next statement. This gives tremendous power to the code.

Java supports many flow control statements. We can group these statements in the following manner.

1. The first group consists of decision-making statements. Examples are `If-else` and `switch-case` statements.
2. The second group consists of looping statements. Examples are `while`, `do-while`, and `for` statements.
3. The third group consists of branching statements Examples are `break`, `continue`, `label`, and `return` statements.
4. The last group consists of exception handling statements. Examples are `Try-catch-finally` and `throw` statements.

Let us start our study with a simple `if` statement.

4.1 Simple `If` Statement

Right from our first exam, we are faced with pass or fail dilemma. If we get minimum marks, then we pass. If we have enough money, we may go to the theatre. The action depends on a condition. This is characterized in `if` statement. Its general syntax is as follows:

```
if ( condition ) statement;
```

It can be described as follows:

- It starts with keyword `if`.
- It is followed by a condition, which is a Boolean expression.
- This condition has to be put in round brackets.
- A statement follows it.
- As usual, semicolon marks the end of statement.
- A block, meaning a group of statements enclosed in curly brackets, is considered as a (single) statement from grammar point of view.

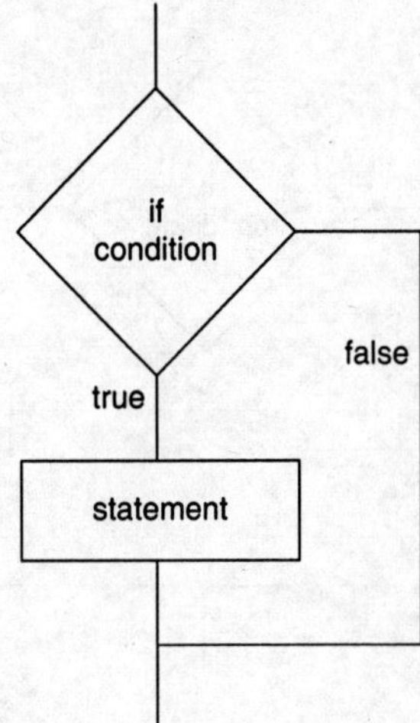

Figure 4.1 `If Statement`

Figure 4.1 describes the `if statement` pictorially.

When a computer executes this statement, it first evaluates the condition. If it evaluates to true, computer executes the statement. If the condition fails, no action is taken.

4.2 `If-Else` Statement

Right from our first exam, we are faced with pass or fail dilemma. If we get more than specified marks, we pass otherwise we fail. There are two different actions, depending on a Boolean condition. This is characterized in `if-else` statement. Its general syntax is as follows:

```
if  ( condition )  statement1 ;
     else  statement2 ;
```

It can be described as follows:

- It starts with keyword `if`.
- It is followed by a condition, which is a Boolean expression.
- This condition has to be put in round brackets.
- It is followed by a statement 1.
- As usual, semicolon marks the end of this statement.
- Next comes keyword `else`.
- It is followed by a statement 2.
- Finally, semicolon marks the end of this statement.
- A block, meaning a group of statements enclosed in curly brackets, is considered as a (single) statement.

Figure 4.2 pictorially illustrates this description.

When a computer executes this statement, it first evaluates the condition. If it evaluates to true, the computer executes statement1. If the condition fails, it executes statement2.

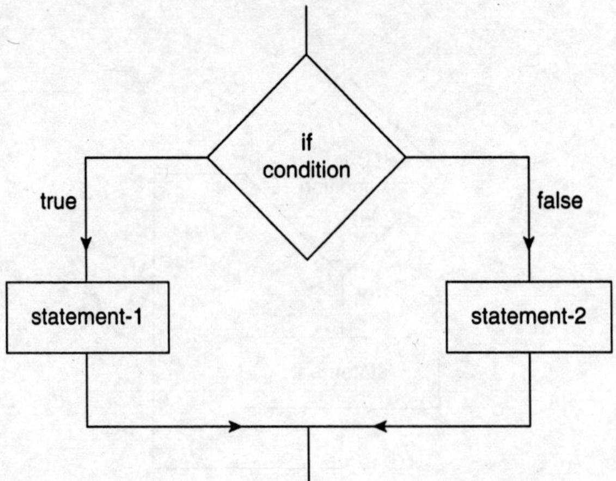

Figure 4.2 If-Else Statement

Now let us study a simple program.

Problem: Write a program to read marks out of 100 and declare result. The rules are as follows:

60 or more marks	first class
50 to 59 marks	second class
40 to 49 marks	pass class
less than 40 marks	fail

Solution: See Program 4.1.

PROGRAM 4.1 If Statement I

```
//      ifthen1.java
class ifthen1
  { public static void main(String args[])
      {   int  marks = 55 ;
          if (marks >=50 )
                if (marks >= 60)
                           System.out.println("First class");
                     else  System.out.println("Second class");

              else
                  if (marks >= 40)
                           System.out.println("Pass class");
                    else  System.out.println("Fails");
      }
}
```

If you run this program, you will get the following output.

Output

```
Second class
```

4.3 Switch-Case Statement

Many times, specific actions take place for specific conditions (cases). Coding becomes complicated on using `if-else` statement. To help the programmers, language supports this new construct, that is, `switch-case` statement. There are some variations in this statement. Hence, let us study it step by step.

In the simplest form, the statement appears as follows.

```
switch (  n )
   { case 1 : statement_1;
     case 2 : statement_2;
     case 3 : statement_4;
     case 4 : statement_4;
   }
```

Figure 4.3 illustrates the logic of this statement.

When control enters the switch construct, it tries to match `n` with values in case clause. If any value matches, then corresponding statement is executed. Thereafter, all the statements (without caring for matching case) are executed. It goes without saying that if there is no match, no statement is executed.

It is understood that `n` stands for any variable or expression of type `byte`, `short`, `int`, or `char`. It cannot be of type `long`.

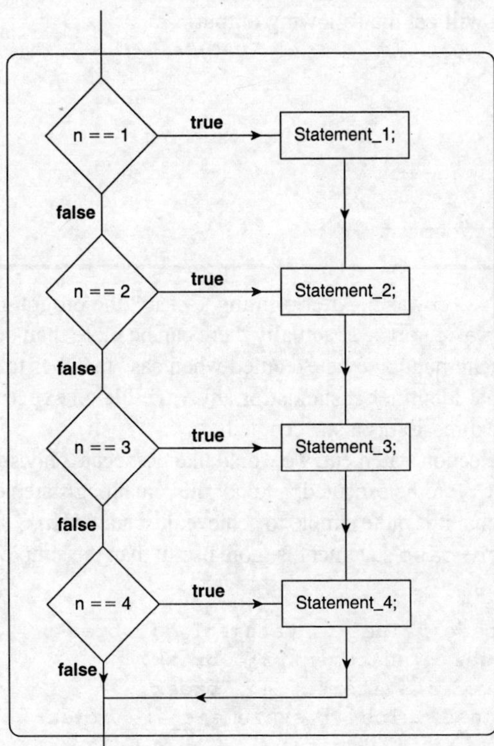

Figure 4.3 `Switch-Case` **Simple Form**

Let us try this with a program.

Problem: Write a program to demonstrate the general form of `switch-case` statement.

Solution: See Program 4.2.

PROGRAM 4.2 Switch-Case Statement Simple Form

```
//     switch5.java
class switch5
{ public static void main(String args[])
  { int n = 2;
    System.out.println("<---switch5.java--->");
    switch (n)
      { case 1  : System.out.println("I am 1");
        case 2  : System.out.println("I am 2");
        case 3  : System.out.println("I am 3");
        case 4  : System.out.println("I am 4");
      }
    System.out.println("Out of switch case statement");
  }
};
```

If you run this program, you will get the following output.

Output

```
<---switch5.java--->
I am 2
I am 3
I am 4
Out of switch case statement
```

Please note that in Program 4.2, `n` was 2. After printing `I am 2` the program printed few more lines.

Though we have said `statement_2`, actually there can be more than one statement. The nomenclature is only to indicate that this statement is to be executed when case matches to 2.

Another point to note that identifier `n` stands for any **variable or expression**, which represents integral value. It means a character expression is also accepted.

In a rational use of any selection statement, we would like to execute only specific statements. If case is 2, we would like only `statement_2` to be executed, and not the remaining statements thereafter. By this time, you must have guessed correctly that it is quite simple to achieve; just add "*break*" statement after every statement.

The new form of `switch-case` statement is more useful than the simple form. It will appear as follows:

```
switch ( int_value )
              { case value1 : statement_1;  break;
        case value2 : statement_2;  break;
        case value3 : statement_4;  break;
               case value4 : statement_4;  break;
              }
```

Figure 4.4 illustrates the logic of this statement.

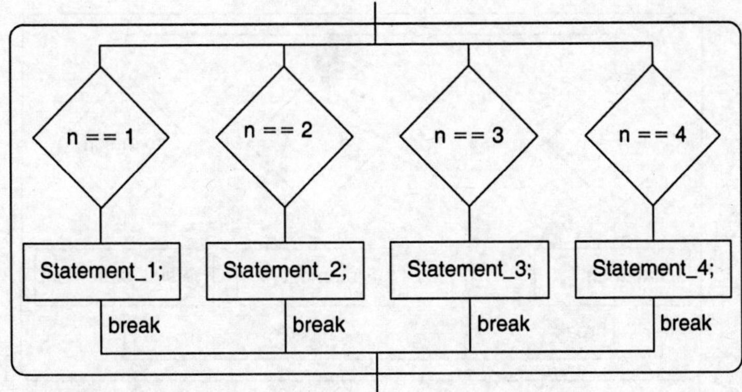

Figure 4.4 `Switch-Case` **Useful Form**

Let us study a simple program using "`switch`" statement (see Program 4.3 in action).

Problem: Write a program to simulate calculator. Assume operands as two given integers. Operation should be performed as specified.

Solution: In this program, we will use simple arithmetic operations like addition subtraction, multiplication, and division. For the sake of simplicity, the action character will be specified in a program (instead of being accepted from the keyboard; see Program 4.3).

PROGRAM 4.3 Calculator Simulation

```
//     switch8.java
class switch8
{ public static void main(String args[])
  {   int i=3,j=7,k=0 ;
      System.out.println("---switch8.java---");
      // specifying input
      char ch ='*' ;
      switch(ch)
          {   case '+' : k = i+j ;break;
              case '-' : k = i-j ;break;
              case '*' : k = i*j ;break;
              case '/' : k = i/j ;break;
          };
       System.out.println("k=" + k);
      //   else    System.out.println("Invalid date");
  }
}
```

If you run this program, you will get the following output.

Output

```
---switch8.java---
k= 21
```

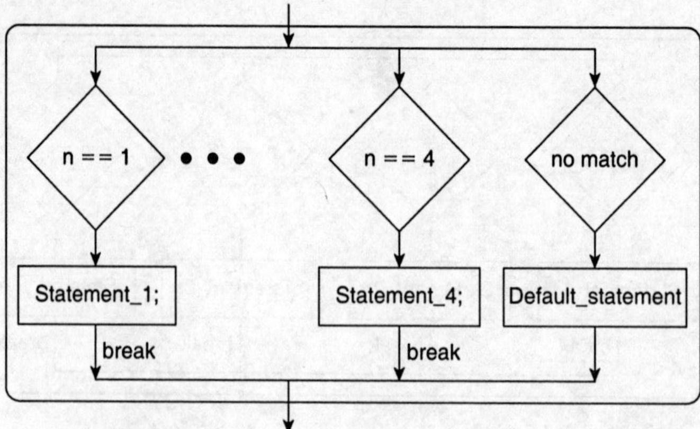

Figure 4.5 Switch-Case **Most Practical Form**

We can add a default clause (case) to this statement. When the value of switch expression does not match with any of the case values, statements in default clause are executed.

You may wonder what is the necessity of "default clause". In a properly designed program, all cases must be considered. If something is missing by error, there should be some indication of it. A small error message in default clause will be helpful in debugging.

Alternately, if some assignment or action pertains to all remaining cases, we can use default clause. Hence, most practical form of a `switch-case` statement is one having both break and default clause.

```
switch (  int_value )

  { case value1 : statement_1;  break;
          case value2 : statement_2;  break;
          case value3 : statement_4;  break;
     case value4 : statement_4;  break;
            default      : default_satement;  // note no break required here.
  }
```

Figure 4.5 illustrates the most practical form of `switch-case` statement.

Problem: Write a program to decide whether a given date is valid date for a non-leap year. Read only date and month. Use `switch` statement for maximum days of a month. Use default clause for valid value of the month.

Solution: In English calendar, number of days is defined for every month. We will use case values 1 to 12 for months January to December. Checking a valid date means checking two things. First, value of month is between 1 and 12, and second, date is within 1 and max-value for that month (see Program 4.4).

PROGRAM 4.4 Switch with Default

```
//      switch6.java
class switch6
{ public static void main(String args[])
```

```
  {   boolean result = true ; // boolean answer;
      int maxdays= 0 ;
      System.out.println("<---switch6.java--->");
      // specifying input
      int date  = 3 ;
      int month = 14 ; // invalid month

              { switch(month)
                { case 1 : maxdays = 31;break;
                  case 2 : maxdays = 28;break;
                  case 3 : maxdays = 31;break;
                  case 4 : maxdays = 30;break;
                  case 5 : maxdays = 31;break;
                  case 6 : maxdays = 30;break;
                  case 7 : maxdays = 31;break;
                  case 8 : maxdays = 31;break;
                  case 9 : maxdays = 30;break;
                  case 10 : maxdays = 31; break;
                  case 11 : maxdays = 30; break;
                  case 12 : maxdays = 31; break;
                 default :  result = false  ;
                };
               if (date > maxdays) result = false ;
              };
      if ( result )  System.out.println("Valid date");
           else   System.out.println("Invalid date");
  }
}
```

If you run this program, you will get the following output.

Output

```
<---switch6.java--->
Invalid date
```

Let us try one more program.

If the action taken is identical, for certain cases, we can use the absence of break with convenience. We have to write the action only once. Let us see with the concrete example.

Problem: Rewrite Program 4.4 on valid date with different style.

Solution: See Program 4.5.

PROGRAM 4.5 Switch Statement Different Style

```
//     switch4.java
class switch4
{ public static void main(String args[])
  {   boolean result = true ; // boolean answer;
      int maxdays= 0 ;
```

```
    System.out.println("---switch4.java---");
    // specifying input
    int date  = 31 ;
    int month = 8 ;

    if ( (month < 1) || (month > 12) || (date<1) )
            result = false;
       else
        {     switch(month)
             {  case 2  : maxdays = 28;break;

                case 1  : ;
                case 3  : ;
                case 5  : ;
                case 7  : ;
                case 8  : ;
                case 10 : ;
                case 12 : maxdays = 31; break;

                case 4  : ;
                case 6  : ;
                case 9  : ;
                case 11 : maxdays = 30; break;
             };
            if (date > maxdays) result = false ;
        };
    if ( result )  System.out.println("Valid date");
        else   System.out.println("Invalid date");
  }
}
```

If you run this program, you will get the following output.

Output

```
---switch4.java---
Valid date
```

In Program 4.5, we have used data value for month as 8. When `switch` statement is executed, control comes up to case 8. There is no executable statement against 8. Hence, control passes to case 10 and subsequently to case 12. It executes assignment max-days = 31 and breaks. It means that when the value of the month is anything like 1, 3, and 5 there is only one action that is max-days = 31.

Advance Note

In addition to basic types, the switch variable can be of a wrapper class like `character`, `byte`, `short`, and `integer`. It can be also of any enumerated type. Wrapper classes and enumerated types are discussed later in the book.

Keywords

`case`, default, `if statement`, `if-else statement`, `switch`, `switch-case statement`

RuleBook

`switch` default	Default clause is optional in Java
`switch` expression	`Switch` expression can be of basic type `byte`, `short`, `int` or `character`. It can be also be Wrapper class type like `Character`, `Byte`, `Short`, or `Integer`. It can be also of any enumerated type

Review Questions

1. If there are many `if` clauses before the first `else`, to which `if` clause the `else` belongs?
2. Is presence of `switch-case statement` a must in a programming language?
3. Can any `case statement` be replaced by an `if statement`?
4. Can `case statement` substitute for an `if statement`?

Exercises

1. Given the temperature, print whether water will be in solid, liquid, or vapour form.
2. Find roots of a given quadratic equation.
3. Find if integer is odd or even.
4. Find the largest of three integers.
5. Find the largest of four given real numbers.
6. Find if a given point lies in a given circle or not.
7. State whether the following program will compile. If yes, describe the output. If no, give reasons and suggest minimum changes in the code.

```
**************************************

//      switch2.java
class switch2
{ public static void main(String args[])
  {   boolean result = true ; // boolean answer;
      int maxdays= 0 ;
      System.out.println("---switch2.java---");
      // specifying input
      int date  = 31 ;
      int month = 4 ;

      if ( (month < 1) || (month > 12) || (date<1) )
```

```
            result = false;
        else
         {  switch(month)
            {   case 1 : maxdays = 31;break;
                case 2 : maxdays = 28;break;
                case 3 : maxdays = 31;break;
                case 4 : maxdays = 30;break;
                case 5 : maxdays = 31;break;
                case 6 : maxdays = 30;break;
                case 7 : maxdays = 31;break;
                case 8 : maxdays = 31;break;
                case 9 : maxdays = 30;break;
                case 10 : maxdays = 31; break;;
                case 11 : maxdays = 30; break;
                case 12 : maxdays = 31; break;
            };
          if (date > maxdays) result = false ;
         };
    if ( result )  System.out.println("Valid date");
        else     System.out.println("Invalid date");
  }
}
*************************************
```

In this program, input was specified in the program itself. Consider that this program is modified to read the date and the month from keyboard. Will the program give correct result in that case?

LOOPS

The real strength of computers and computer programs is in looping. A computer can execute thousands of instructions in no time. If we have to code each and every instruction, we will need days to write a single program. The few instructions we write are repeated hundreds of time faithfully by the computer. For this purpose, we need loops.

In Java, just like C or C++, there are three structures for looping around a given code. They are

- `for` loop
- `while` loop
- `do-while` loop

Statements `break` and `continue` are used mainly in these structures. Therefore, we will be discussing these statements too. Let us start with the `for` loop statement.

5.1 `for` Loop

`for` loop is the most useful statement (facility) in any programming language. A typical statement looks like

```
for(i=0; i<10; i++)
    statement_1;
```

Syntax of `for` loop can be described as follows:

1. The statement starts with the key word `for`.
2. Then come three expressions in round bracket.
3. A statement follows it.
4. In the above example, we will call variable *i* as control variable (cv).
5. First expression initializes cv.
6. Next expression is a condition involving cv.
7. The third expression decides how much cv is incremented (or decremented).

Here `statement_1` is executed repeatedly. The action of the `for` statement can be explained as follows:

1. First control variable *i* in this statement is initialized, that is *i* is set to zero.
2. Next `statement_1 is executed.`
3. Thereafter control variable is incremented, that is *i*++.

4. Now the condition is tested ($i < 10$).
5. If the condition is true, statements from step 2 are repeated.
6. Otherwise, the loop terminates and the program goes to the next statement.

Let us study this action with the help of a simple program.

Problem: Write a program to find the factorial of a given integer.

Solution: As we are studying `for` *loop*, we will also show intermediate results in this program. These intermediate results are also factorials themselves (see Program 5.1).

PROGRAM 5.1 Factorial I

```
//    factor2.java
class factor2
{ public static void main(String args[])
   { int factorial, n, product;
     int number = 10 ; // given number
     if (number== 1)
            factorial = 1 ;
        else
        { System.out.println("<---factor2.java--->");
          product=1;
          for( n=2; n <= number; n++)
               {  product=product*n ;
System.out.printf("%4d%10d\n",n,product);
               }
          factorial=product;
          System.out.println("");
          System.out.println("The final answer is : "
                                        + factorial);
        }
   }
}
```

If you run the program, you will get the following output.

Output

```
<---factor2.java--->
  2         2
  3         6
  4        24
  5       120
  6       720
  7      5040
  8     40320
  9    362880
 10   3628800

The final answer is : 3628800
```

Java allows us to declare the control variable of `for` loop in `for` statement itself; for example,

```
for ( int n =0; n<4;n++)
{
};
```

In this example, control variable is *n*. It is declared in the `for` statement itself. This variable is available inside the `for` loop. However, when the `for` loop terminates, this variable becomes invisible (technically out of scope). If you try to use it outside `for` loop, it will result in compilation error. See Program 5.11 to verify this fact. Please see Box 5.1 for many other issues with `for` loop.

So far, our control variable was only an integer. It can be a character as well. It is quite possible to have a `for` loop such as

```
for(ch='A';ch<='Z';ch++)
```

See this code in action in Program 5.13.

BOX 5.1 for loop

The syntax of `for` loop does not talk of control variable. The control variable is a legacy of Fortran. Java follows the rules of C/C++. A `for` loop heading contains only `expression1`, `expression2`, and `expression3`. The only difference is expression2 if exits must be of type Boolean. C programmers have wasted (in our opinion) 100s of hours finding how `for` loop can work as `while` loop and so on. In a disciplined language like Java, programmers should not waste their energy in such an exercise.

`for` loop should be used only when some code is to be repeated specific number of times, depending on values of an integral control variable. In any other case `while` loop is the most appropriate.

Problem: Write a program to demonstrate how an amount grows year by year with compound interest. Assume the initial amount as Rs. 100,000. Assume the rate of interest as 8%.

Solution: We can compute the interest as

```
interest = principle * rate
```

Note that for this formula, rate of interest is per unit, that is percent rate divided by 100. In this problem rate of interest is 8%. Hence, rate will be 8 divided by 100, that is 0.08. See Program 5.2.

PROGRAM 5.2 Compound Interest

```
//      for2.java
class for2
{ public static void main(String args[])
    { double amount = 100000.0;
      double rate= 0.08; // rate per unit
      int i ;
      for(i=1;i<=10;i++)
        { amount = amount * (1+ rate) ;
          System.out.printf("%4d %10.4f \n",i, amount);
        }
    }
}
```

If you run this program, you will get the following output.

Output

```
  1    108000.0000
  2    116640.0000
  3    125971.2000
  4    136048.8960
  5    146932.8077
  6    158687.4323
  7    171382.4269
  8    185093.0210
  9    199900.4627
 10    215892.4997
```

The output is fine. We are using `printf()` statement instead of `print()` statement. Please see Program 5.10 to know how life without this facility was.

It is possible to have a `for` loop within a `for` loop. You will see its use in programs on matrices.

5.2 `while` Loop

Sometimes we need to loop around till a particular condition is true. A `while` statement is very suitable for the purpose. The general form of the `while` statement is as follows:

```
while ( condition )
   statement_1 ;
```

The `statement_1` is repeated `while` the condition remains true. When the condition becomes false, looping stops. Program control moves ahead. If you want to execute more than one statement, you have to put them in a pair of curly brackets.

Consider a problem in which we want to know the number of years after which the amount grows three times the original. Here, we have to repeat adding interest. We should continue looping while the amount is less than three times its original value. Let us write a program and study it.

Problem: Write a program to find after how many years an amount in fixed deposit becomes three times. Assume the rate of interest as 8%.

Solution: See Program 5.3.

PROGRAM 5.3 Fixed Deposit

```
//     while2.java
class while2
{ public static void main(String args[])
   { double amount = 100000.0;
     double limit = 3 * amount ;
     double rate= 0.08; // rate per unit
     int y = 0 ;
     System.out.println("<---while2.java--->");
     while ( amount < limit)
       {  y = y+1;
```

```
            amount = amount * (1+ rate) ;
            System.out.printf("%4d %10.2f\n", y,amount);//Note 1
         }
       System.out.println("\nAfter "+ y + " years amount becomes three times");
    }
}
```

If you run this program, you will get the following output.

Output

```
<---while2.java--->
  1     108000.00
  2     116640.00
  3     125971.20
  4     136048.90
  5     146932.81
  6     158687.43
  7     171382.43
  8     185093.02
  9     199900.46
 10     215892.50
 11     233163.90
 12     251817.01
 13     271962.37
 14     293719.36
 15     317216.91

After 15 years amount becomes three times
```

Consider the line marked Note 1. You will think that this line is not required. Strictly speaking, yes! But a good programming practice recommends that such lines be present, at least when the program is under development. Consider that you have made a small mistake in the earlier line. Now the program will go in endless loop and you will be just waiting for the output without any clue. When this statement is present and you see the amount reducing instead of increasing, you can break the program. You also have some clue regarding the error.

Let us write another program.

Problem: Write a program to find the sine of a given angle in degrees by series expansion.

Solution: We know that the formula for sin(*x*) is

$$\sin(x) = \frac{x}{1!} - \frac{x^3}{3!} + \frac{x^5}{5!} - \frac{x^7}{7!}$$

where! stands for factorial. See Program 5.4.

PROGRAM 5.4 Computing Sine by Expansion

```
//      while1.java
//      to cal Sin(X) value by using series method.

import java.io.*;
class while1
{  static int read_int() throws IOException
```

```
    { int k;
      InputStreamReader reader
          =new InputStreamReader(System.in);
      BufferedReader input =new
BufferedReader(reader);
      String temp=input.readLine();
      k=Integer.parseInt(temp);
      return k;
    }
 public static void main(String arg[]) throws
IOException
    { int deg,i;
      double sum,term,rad;
      System.out.println("--->while1.java starts<---");
      System.out.print("Enter angle in degrees 0..90 : ");
      deg = read_int();
      rad=deg * 3.14159 /180;
      System.out.println("Value of angle in degrees= " + deg);
      System.out.println("Value of angle in radians= " +rad);
      i=1;
      sum=term=rad;
      while(Math.abs(term) > 0.0001)
      {   i=i+2;
          term=-1 *term *rad *rad / i/(i-1);
          sum=sum+term;
          System.out.println("Intermediate value = " + sum);
      }
     System.out.println(
          "\nValue of Sin(" + deg + ") is = " +   sum);
    }
 }
```

If you run the program, you will see the following output.

Output

```
--->while1.java starts<---
Enter angle in degrees 0..90 : 45
Value of angle in degrees= 45
Value of angle in radians= 0.7853975
Intermediate value = 0.7046521924199955
Intermediate value = 0.7071425764724745
Intermediate value = 0.707106000484554

Value of Sin(45) is = 0.707106000484554
```

In Program 5.4, we have accepted the input from the keyboard. We have defined a method `readint()` for this purpose. Since something can go wrong while reading, we have to use the clause `throws IOException`. We will study the exceptions in detail in Chapter 19. Till that time treat it just as a syntax requirement.

If the loop has to terminate, there has to be at least one statement inside the loop body, which has an effect on the condition. Otherwise the loop will never end.

5.3 do-while Loop

The `do-while` construct is a slight variation of `while` construct. A typical structure looks like as follows:

```
do
    statement_1;
while ( condition ) ;
```

When the program enters this loop construct, `statements_1` is executed. Then the condition is evaluated. If the condition is true, then control passes to the start of the loop construct, that is keyword `do`.

Note that a semicolon after `statement_1` is mandatory. If you want to repeat more than one statement, put them in a pair of curly brackets.

The most important thing to note is that the body of the loop is executed at least once. In contrast, the `while` construct body may not be executed at all.

It is understood that if we want to execute more than one statement in the loop, we have to put them in a pair of curly brackets.

In older languages, like Algol and Pascal, a statement called `REPEAT UNTIL` was present. It was an exact opposite of the `while` statement. The `do-while` statement is similar to the `repeat until` statement. The only difference is that the `repeat until` statement terminates as the condition becomes true, whereas the `do-while` terminates when the condition becomes false. Probably developers of C language did not like the `repeat until` construct. Hence, they replaced it by this `do-while` construct which is somewhat similar to the `while` construct.

Let us study a simple program using the `do-while` statement.

Problem: Write a program to print all natural numbers and their squares such that the square is less than 101. Use `do-while` construct.

Solution: See Program 5.5.

PROGRAM 5.5 do-while Loop I

```
//      do1.java
class do1
{ public static void main ( String args[ ] )
  { System.out.println("<---do1.java--->") ;
    int i=1,j=i*i;
    do
     { System.out.printf("%4d %4d\n",i,j);
       i++;
       j= i*i ;
     }
    while(i*i<101);
  }
}
```

If you run the program, you will see the following output.

Output

```
<---do1.java--->
 1      1
 2      4
 3      9
```

```
 4     16
 5     25
 6     36
 7     49
 8     64
 9     81
10    100
```

Let us solve another problem based on a common riddle from school mathematics.

Problem: Ram pays Sham Rs. 10,000 every day. Sham pays Ram Re. 1 on the first day, Rs. 2 on the second, Rs. 4 on the third day, and so on. On which day the total amount received by Ram is greater than the total amount he has paid?

Solution: See Program 5.6.

PROGRAM 5.6 do-while Loop II

```
//     dowhile1.java
class dowhile1
{ public static void main(String args[])
   { int Ram_amt, Shyam_amt, RamTotal,ShyamTotal ;
     int i = 1;
     System.out.println("<---dowhile1.java--->");
     Ram_amt = 10000; Shyam_amt= 1;
     RamTotal = 0 ; ShyamTotal= 0 ;
     System.out.println(" Day RamTotal ShyamTotal" ) ;
     do
       {  RamTotal = RamTotal + Ram_amt;
          ShyamTotal = ShyamTotal + Shyam_amt;
          Shyam_amt = 2 * Shyam_amt ;
          System.out.printf(
              "%4d %9d %9d\n",i, RamTotal, ShyamTotal) ;
          i++ ;
       } while ( RamTotal > ShyamTotal );
     return;
   }
}
```

If you run the program, you will see the following output.

Output

```
<---dowhile1.java--->
Day   RamTotal     ShyamTotal
 1      10000           1
 2      20000           3
 3      30000           7
 4      40000          15
 5      50000          31
 6      60000          63
 7      70000         127
 8      80000         255
```

```
 9      90000          511
10     100000         1023
11     110000         2047
12     120000         4095
13     130000         8191
14     140000        16383
15     150000        32767
16     160000        65535
17     170000       131071
18     180000       262143
```

5.4 break and continue

After studying loops, we can study two additional statements `break` and `continue`. The `break` takes control out of the innermost loop. The `continue` statement takes control of the last line of the loop. Therefore, control goes to the beginning of the loop. In simple programs, you hardly need these statements.

5.4.1 break statement

It may be noted that the `break` statement can appear only in a loop. By loop, we mean body of `for`, `do`, or `while` statement. In addition, `break` can also appear in switch statement. When `break` statement is executed, control goes (just) out of the innermost loop.
Let us study a simple program.

Problem: Write a program to demonstrate the `break` statement. Assume that variable *m* reduces by 3 every time. Find out after how many loops the value of *m* becomes negative.

Solution: We will set a `for` loop. As we do not know the answer, we will set an arbitrary large value say 100 for looping. We will use `break` statement to jump out of the loop. See Program 5.7.

PROGRAM 5.7 Using break

```
//     break1.java
class break1
{  public static void main ( String args[ ] )
     { int m=7 ;
       int i;
       System.out.println("--->break1.java starts<---" ) ;
       for(i=1;i<100;i++)
        { m= m-3;
          System.out.println("m is " +m);
          if (m < 0) break;
        }
       System.out.println("No Of loops are " + i);
     }
}
```

If you run the program, you will see the following output.

Output

```
--->break1.java starts<---
m is 4
m is 1
m is -2
No Of loops are 3
```

The `for` loop is supposed to run 100 times. However, in the third looping, value of variable *m* becomes negative. The statement `break` is executed and looping terminates.

5.4.2 continue statement

It may be noted that `continue` statement can appear only in a loop. By loop, we mean body of `for`, `do`, or `while` statement. When `continue` statement is executed, control goes to the end of the innermost loop.

Let us study a simple program.

Problem: Write a program to illustrate `continue`.

Solution: We will take a case of marks of four students. We will set a `for` loop. In this program, we want to list all the students who have passed. If marks are less than 40, use `continue`. It will bypass the listing of that particular student. See Program 5.8.

PROGRAM 5.8 Using continue

```
//     continue1.java
class continue1
{   public static void main ( String args[ ] )
    { int marks[] ={ 55 , 35, 88 , 10 } ;
      System.out.println("--->continue1.java<-- -") ;
      int i;
      for(i=0;i<4;i++)
        {   System.out.println("first line in loop " + i +"  , marks
                                                    =" + marks[i] );

            if (marks[i] <40) continue ;
            System.out.println("---last line in loop " + i );
        }
    }
}
```

If you run the program, you will see the following output.

Output

```
--->continue1.java<---
first line in loop 0 , marks =55
---last line in loop 0
first line in loop 1 , marks =35
first line in loop 2 , marks =88
---last line in loop 2
first line in loop 3 , marks =10
```

If we study the output, the string `---last line` does not appear in loop no. 1 and 3. In these loops, value of marks[i] is less than 40. Therefore, statement `continue` gets executed.

It may be noted that Java supports labelled `break` and `continue` statements. These are discussed in later chapters.

5.5 Comparison of all the Three Constructs

So far, we have seen all the three loop statements. You may wonder when to prefer one to the other. All these constructs have been used for quite some time in computer programming. Hence, the advice of the experts is readily available.

The `for` construct is very straightforward. It is to be used when we have to repeat things for fixed number of times. There exists a flexibility that value of control variable need not increment by one only. Whenever we see problem statement like for first 100 natural numbers or compound interest for 10 years, `for` loop becomes the natural choice. The control variable is an essentially important part of `for` statement. (Please note that as per grammar rules, control variable is not mandatory.)

If we are processing array elements and going to look at every element one by one, `for` loop is most natural. Our advice is that under all these circumstances use `for` loop.

Many times, we do not know how many times to loop; for example, in how many years an amount grows two-folds? Well, we do not know whether the answer is six, seven, or eight. In such cases we have to loop around till a particular condition is satisfied. In this case, `while` or `do-while` comes handy.

Someone will point out that `for` loop with `break` statement can solve the problem. Well, our aim is not just to solve a problem, but solve it elegantly and comfortably too.

In our opinion `break` and `continue` statements are provided as the last resort. Only when we cannot write a code without them, we should use these constructs, not otherwise.

`do-while` and `while` loops are more or less identical. The `while` loop is executed zero or more times. Do loop is executed one or more times. Hence, `while` loop becomes more general than the other one. Hence, experts advise us to use `while` loop as far as possible. Only in cases where you are 100% sure that loop executes at least once, you may use `do-while` loop.

5.6 End of Chapter Programs

5.6.1 Fibonacci numbers

Problem: Write a program to find first 15 Fibonacci numbers.

Solution: We know that

```
            fib(1) = 0 ;
            fib(2) = 1 ;
and         fib (n) = fib(n-1) + fib (n -2) ;
```

Hence, any new value is the sum of the two previous values. See Program 5.9.

PROGRAM 5.9 First 15 Fibonacci Numbers

```
//      fibb1.java
class fibb1
{ public static void main(String args[])
   { int first, second, value ;
     int i ;
```

```
        System.out.println("<---fibb1.java--->");
        first = 0; second = 1;
        System.out.println("1\t" + first) ;
        System.out.println("2\t" + second) ;
        for(i=3; i<=15; i++)
          { value = first+ second;
            first = second;
            second = value;
            System.out.println(i+ "\t" + value) ;
          }
        return;
    }
}
```

If you run this program, you will get the following output.

Output

```
<---fibb1.java--->
 1      0
 2      1
 3      1
 4      2
 5      3
 6      5
 7      8
 8     13
 9     21
10     34
11     55
12     89
13    144
14    233
15    377
```

5.6.2 Compound interest

So far we have written programs with `printf` statement. This was introduced only in version 5. Life before this statement was miserable. Formatting required complex statements. This program is retained only to show how newer and newer versions of Java are making programming an enjoyable experience.

Problem: Write a program to find how your amount grows with interest.

Solution: Let us assume that we have a deposit of Rs. 100,000. Let us assume that compound interest rate is 8%. Let us assume a period of 10 years. At the end of every year, we have to add interest to the capital. So we have to set a `for` loop for 10 years. Within the loop, we have to compute and add interest. See Program 5.10.

PROGRAM 5.10 Compound Interest

```
//      for3.java
import java.text.* ;
class  for3
```

```
{ public static void main(String args[])
   { double amount = 100000.0;
     double rate= 0.08; // rate per unit
     DecimalFormat twodigits = new DecimalFormat("###.00");
     String result =new String("");
     int i ;
     for(i=1;i<=10;i++)
      {   amount = amount * (1+ rate) ;
          result = twodigits.format(amount) ;
          System.out.println(i +"\t"+ result ) ;
      }
   }
}
```

If you run this program, you will get the following output.

Output

```
 1       108000.00
 2       116640.00
 3       125971.20
 4       136048.90
 5       146932.81
 6       158687.43
 7       171382.43
 8       185093.02
 9       199900.46
10       215892.50
```

Note the lines marked in bold in the aforementioned program. They help in getting a decent output. We will discuss formatting at a later stage.

5.6.3 for loop control variable

Problem: Write a program to demonstrate that control variable declared inside the `for` clause is not available outside the loop.

Solution: See Program 5.11.

PROGRAM 5.11 Declaring cv Inside the `for` Statement

```
//     cv2.java
class cv2
{ public static void main(String args[])
    {    long factorial, product;
         System.out.println("<---cv2.java--->");
         product=1;
         for(int n=2;n<=10;n++)
             {  product = product * n ;
                System.out.println(n + " : " + product);
```

```
        }
        factorial=product;
        System.out.println("\n factorial of " + n);
        System.out.println("The factorial is : " + factorial);
    }
}
```

If you run the program, you will see the following error message.

Output

```
Compiling \java\bin\javac cv2.java
cv2.java:12: Undefined variable: n
System.out.println("\n factorial of " + n);
^
1 error
press any key to continue
```

Please note the line marked in bold. The compiler refuses to accept "n". Just two lines above, it accepts "n". The reason behind this is that at that place it is inside the scope of the `for` loop.

It goes without saying that if you remove the line in bold, program compiles as well as runs.

5.6.4 Java is great!

Earlier, we had said that Java allows a blank expression as a Boolean expression. Let us test this premise in a simple program.

Problem: Write a program to find factorials of five.

Solution: We will use a blank expression as `expression2`. See Program 5.12.

PROGRAM 5.12 Factorial

```
//      for7.java
class for7
{ public static void main(String args[])
    { int n, product, k=3;
      int number = 5 ;
      System.out.println("<---for7.java--->");

      product=1;
      for( n=2; ; n++ ) //Note 1
          { product= n * product ;
            System.out.println(product);
          // if ( n>=5 ) break;
          }
      System.out.println("The answer is " + product);
    }
}
```

If you run this program, you will get the following compilation error.

Output

```
for7.java:14: unreachable statement
System.out.println("The answer is " + product);
^
1 error
```

Note that Java has allowed a blank expression as a Boolean expression. However, it has also understood that this loop will never terminate. Hence, control will never reach the `println()` statement.

Also, note the commented statement. If you bring it back in the program, the program will not only compile but will also give you a factorial of five.

5.6.5 cv can be a character

Problem: Write a program to demonstrate that `for` loop control variable can be a character.

Solution: See Program 5.13.

PROGRAM 5.13 cv Can Be a Character

```
//      for5.java
class for5
{ public static void main(String args[])
    { char ch;
      System.out.println("<---for5.java--->");
      for(ch='A';ch<='Z';ch++)
        { System.out.print(ch +" ");
        }
    }
}
```

If you run this program, you will get the following output.

Output

```
<---for5.java--->
A B C D E F G H I J K L M N O P Q R S T U V W X Y Z
```

Keywords

`break`, compound interest, `continue`, control variable, `do-while` , factorial, Fibonacci numbers, `for` loop, `while`

RuleBook

labelled `break;` labelled `continue`	Labelled `break` and labelled `continue` statements are allowed in Java.

`cv for`	The control variable declared in `for` loop is visible only within the scope of the loop. But in C/C++, it is visible even after the loop is exited.
`break`	A `break` statement can be used only within loop or switch case statements.
`do-while`	`do-while` loop construct will always be executed at least once.
`for` loop	The second expression in for statement must be a Boolean expression. As a special case, it can be a blank expression which is considered as having a value true.

C++ Corner

`break` and `continue` in C++ cannot have labels.

Review Questions

1. What is the significance of *break* and *continue* statements?
2. Is `do-while` statement really essential (considering the presence of `while` statement)?
3. Can for statement be used as a `while` statement? If so, is it advisable to do it?
4. When the program goes into infinite loop, how can we (to certain extent) ensure that the program will not go in infinite loop?

Exercises

1. Find the cosine of a given angle using the series expansion formula.
2. Find GCD of two numbers.
3. Find LCM of given two integers.
4. Find the largest integer value *n*, such that its factorial can be correctly stored in variable of type `long`.
5. Find first 50 prime numbers.
6. If a deposit attracts compound interest, find its maturity value for a given period with given rate of interest.
7. Write a program to print fixed deposit table. Assume the period as 1 to 5 years. Assume compound interest rates as 5%, 6%, 6.5%, 7%, and 7.5%. Assume the deposit amount as Rs. 1,000.
8. Find the sum of first 50 natural numbers.
9. Find all the divisors (prime as well as non prime) of a given integer.
10. Given a positive integer between 1 and 9,999, find the number of digits needed to express it.
11. Find the sum of sequence $1 - 1/2 + 1/3 - 1/4 + 1/5$.
12. Find the sum of sequence $2/9 - 5/13 + 8/17$.
13. Find the sum of sequence $1 + 1/1! + 1/2! + 1/3!$.
14. Reverse the digits of a given integer.

15. Find the sum of all digits of an integer.
16. Generate Pascal's triangle.
17. State whether the following program will compile. If yes, describe the output. If no, give reasons.

```
********************************************

//      for9.java
class for9
{ public static void main(String args[])
    { int number, product, k=3;
      System.out.println("--->for9.java<---");
      product=1;
      for(number=2; k++; number++ )
        {   product=product*number ;
            System.out.println(product);
        }
    }
}

********************************************
```

FUNCTIONS

Every programming language supports functions in two categories: (1) user-defined functions, and (2) language-supplied functions (also known as library functions). To begin with, let us start with user-defined functions.

6.1 Functions in Java

In most object-oriented languages, either functions belong to a class or they do not belong to any particular class (free or global). In Java, every function must be a part of some class. There is no concept of free or global function.

Functions are small pieces of code doing a particular task. Functions are called **methods** in Java. Hence, the name of the topic should have been "methods in Java".

So far, we have not introduced objects. Hence, you may not appreciate the significance of keyword `static` at this stage. For the time being, let us assume that it is just a syntax requirement.

Let us study a simple method `convert` which converts amount in rupees and paise into paise.

Problem: Write a function `convert()` to convert rupees and paise into paise.

Solution: See Program 6.1.

PROGRAM 6.1 Conversion to Paise

```
//     method2.java
class method2
{
  public static void main(String args[])
    { int rupees=3;
      int paise =25;
      int total;
      total = convert(rupees,paise);
      System.out.println("Total paise = " + total);
    }
  public static int convert(int x, int y)
    { int temp;
      temp = x*100 + y;
      return temp;
    }
}
```

The following output is obtained on running Program 6.1.

Output

```
Total paise = 325
```

6.1.1 Syntax of methods

A method has a header line and a body.

The header line consists of

- optional access specifier
- return type
- method name
- optional parameter list

The body consists of a block. Block means zero or more statement within curly brackets. If the return type is anything other than `void`, the last statement must be `return` statement.

Please note that access specifier (like public or private) is optional. Also, methods may not have any parameters.

6.2 Recursive Functions

Like most programming languages, functions can call themselves. This technique is called recursion. There are both advantages and disadvantages of this technique. Let us first see a common example.

Problem: Write a function factorial using recursive technique.

Solution: See Program 6.2.

PROGRAM 6.2 Introducing Recursion

```
//      factor5.java
//      demonstrates recursion
class factor5
{  static int factorial ( int number)
     { System.out.println("parameter value = " + number);
       if (number<=1) return 1 ;
          else
             return number*factorial(number -1);
     };
   public static void main(String args[])
     { int number = 8 ;
       int result;
       // it is assumed that number is >= 2 result = factorial( number );
       System.out.println("--------------------");
       System.out.println("number=" + number);
       System.out.println("The factorial is : " + result);
     }
}
```

The following output is obtained on running Program 6.2.

Output

```
parameter value = 8
parameter value = 7
parameter value = 6
parameter value = 5
parameter value = 4
parameter value = 3
parameter value = 2
parameter value = 1
---------------------
number=8
The factorial is : 40320
```

Advantages of recursion: If you see the aforementioned code, there is only one critical line.

```
number*factorial(number -1);
```

It does the task of finding the factorial. It means that the code written is small and crisp (in most of the cases). Many data structures are recursive in nature. Their handling becomes easy using recursion. The tree structure is the most common example. There are two interesting programs ahead in the text which emphasize the advantage of recursion. One is listing all the files in a directory. Another builds and displays a binary search tree.

Disadvantages of recursion: If a code is not written carefully, there is a chance that program goes in a loop. Recursive methods normally require more memory and possibly more time too.

When to use recursion: As a rule of thumb, recursion should be used if we are dealing with algorithms which are recursive in nature or data structures which are recursive in definition (e.g. tree).

When not to use recursion: Recursion should not be used when we can code without it without any difficulty. Hence, factorial is not a good case for recursion.

6.3 Parameter Passing

Right from our school days, we know that most of the functions have parameters. Consider method sin(x). Here x is the parameter. The method calculates the value of sine of x. In this sense, parameter x is an input to the method.

The basic method of passing parameters in Java is pass-by-value. It means that if the method modifies the parameter, its effect will not remain after the method is over. It may be noted that in other languages like Pascal and C/C++, parameters can be passed in two different ways (pass-by-value and pass-by-reference).

Passing of parameters can be divided into two sections: (1) passing parameters of simple or primitive type (like `int` and `char`), and (2) passing parameters aggregate of type (like objects or arrays).

6.3.1 Simple data types as parameters

Ordinary parameters are passed-by-value. This implies that when a method modifies it; the modified value will exist till the method is running. As soon as the method ends (returns), value of the parameter will be as earlier. In other words, copy of the parameter is passed. Hence, the original parameter value remains intact.

Let us try a simple program.

Problem: Write a program to show that the method `clear()` fails to clear an integer parameter.

Solution: See Program 6.3.

PROGRAM 6.3 Passing Parameters

```
//     para1.java
class para1
{ public static void main(String args[])
    { int marks = 95 ;
      System.out.println("--->para1.java<---");
      System.out.println(" before clear marks = " + marks);
      clear(marks);
      System.out.println(" after clear marks = " + marks);
    }
   public static void clear(int n)
    { n = 0;
    }
}
```

The following output is obtained on running Program 6.3.

Output

```
--->para1.java<---
before clear marks = 95
after clear marks = 95
```

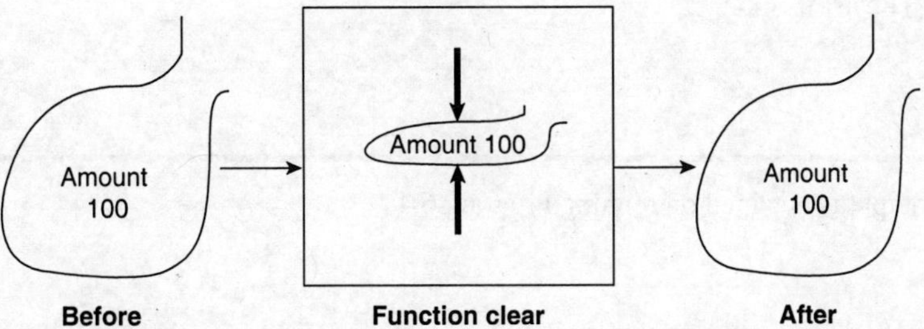

Figure 6.1 Pass-by-Value

The principle of Program 6.3 can be shown in Figure 6.1.

Can you imagine what will happen if someone writes a method `swap` for swapping two integers? Program 6.3 tells us that such a method would simply fail. If we want to swap two integers, say *m* and *n* (or any simple variables for that matter), we should write the standard three line code in place of function `swap`. The code is as follows:

```
temp = m;
m=n ;
n= temp;
```

6.3.2 Objects as parameters

So far we have seen simple data types as parameters. In Java, we can also pass objects as parameters. As mentioned earlier, there is only one way to pass parameters, that is pass-by-value. This is true. But in Java, objects are created with the help of object reference (something like a pointer in C/C++). Hence, when we pass objects as parameter, they effectively get passed by reference. Hence, changes made by a method are seen even after the method is over.

Java creates arrays and strings with the help operator `new`. Java treats them as objects. Therefore, passing arrays or strings also behaves in the same manner.

Let us write a small program and test how an array behaves when passed as a parameter.

Problem: Write a program to demonstrate the fact that when an array is passed as a parameter, it is passed by reference.

Solution: See Program 6.4.

PROGRAM 6.4 Array as Parameter

```
//      ref1.java
class ref1
{  public static void main(String args[])
    { int A[]= { 20, 30, 40, 50, 60 };
      int i, n = 5 ;
      System.out.println("before clear A[3] = " +A[3]);
      clear(A,n);
      System.out.println("after clear A[3] = " +A[3]);
    }
   public static void clear(int X[],int n)
    { int i;
      for(i=0;i<n;i++)
        X[i] =0;
    }
}
```

The following output is obtained on running Program 6.4.

Output

```
before clear A[3] = 50
after clear A[3] = 0
```

The principle of passing parameters by reference is shown in Figure 6.2.

6.4 Method swap

Swapping is a very common process in programming. It is needed in many applications. Sorting is a common example. Swapping means exchanging. Let us see what happens if we try to write method `swap` for swapping objects.

Earlier we had mentioned that ordinary variables cannot be swapped. But the previous example has shown that the contents of an object can change. It means that swapping of objects is possible. Let us try it in a program.

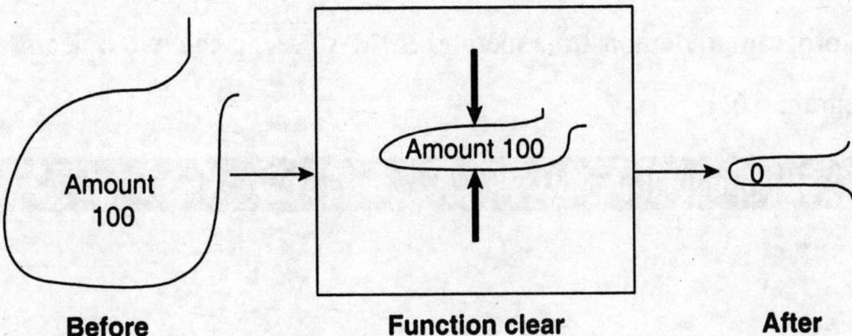

Figure 6.2 Pass-by-Reference

Problem: Write a program to demonstrate the method swap to exchange two objects.

Solution: See Program 6.5.

PROGRAM 6.5 Swapping Objects I

```
//      swap1.java
class marks
{       int a;
}
class swap1
{ public static void main(String args[])
     {    marks ramesh,suresh;
          ramesh=new marks();
          suresh=new marks();
          ramesh.a=90;
          suresh.a=80;
          swap(ramesh,suresh);
          System.out.println("--->swap1.java starts<---");
          System.out.println("Ramesh " + ramesh.a );
          System.out.println("Suresh " + suresh.a );
     }
  static void swap(marks X,marks Y)
  {    marks temp=new marks();
       temp=X;
       X=Y;
       Y=temp;
  }
}
```

The following output is obtained on running Program 6.5.

Output

```
--->swap1.java starts<---
Ramesh 90
Suresh 80
```

We observe that the desired result "swapping of objects" is not obtained on running Program 6.5. To obtain the desired result, let us study Program 6.6.

Problem: Write a program to demonstrate method `SWAP` to `swap` the two objects.

Solution: See Program 6.6.

PROGRAM 6.6 Swapping Objects II

```
//      swap2.java
class marks
{         int a;
}
class swap2
{    public static void main(String args[])
        { marks ramesh,suresh;
         ramesh=new marks();
         suresh=new marks();
         ramesh.a=90;
         suresh.a=80;
         SWAP(ramesh,suresh);
         System.out.println("--->swap2.java starts<---");
         System.out.println("Ramesh " + ramesh.a );
         System.out.println("Suresh " + suresh.a );
        }
     static void SWAP(marks X,marks Y)
      {  marks temp=new marks();
         temp.a=X.a;
         X.a=Y.a;
         Y.a=temp.a;
      }
}
```

The following output is obtained on running Program 6.6.

Output

```
--->swap2.java starts<---
Ramesh 80
Suresh 90
```

Now, the desired result is obtained. Please note that when we swap objects in a method we should swap all the fields of the objects individually. (Concept of fields will be clear when we discuss objects in Chapter 7.)

Let us summarize the process of swapping.

a. If we want to swap two ordinary variables, do it just as it is done in any programming language, for example

   temp = a;
   $a = b$;
   b = temp;

   Simple code, no parameters no methods! If you want to swap p and q at some other place, write a similar (not same) code at that place.

b. If we want to swap two objects, write and use method swap. That method should swap all fields individually as shown in Program 6.6.

6.5 In-built Methods or Library Methods

Java has defined many packages and classes for the use of the programmer. They contain highly useful methods. Since all of us are familiar with number crunching and mathematics, let us have a look at methods found in class Math. Table 6.1 summarizes the important methods from class Math.

Table 6.1 Methods Summary: Class Math

static double	**abs**(double a)	Returns the absolute value of a double value
static float	**abs**(float a)	Returns the absolute value of a float value
Static int	**abs**(int a)	Returns the absolute value of an int value
static long	**abs**(long a)	Returns the absolute value of a long value
static double	**acos**(double a)	Returns the arc cosine of an angle, in the range of 0.0 through *pi*
static double	**asin**(double a)	Returns the arc sine of an angle, in the range of −*pi*/2 through *pi*/2
static double	**atan**(double a)	Returns the arc tangent of an angle, in the range of −*pi*/2 through *pi*/2
static double	**atan2**(double y, double x)	Converts rectangular coordinates (*x*, *y*) to polar (*r*, *theta*)
static double	**cbrt**(double a)	Returns the cube root of a double value
static double	**ceil**(double a)	Returns the smallest (closest to negative infinity) double value that is greater than or equal to the argument and is equal to a mathematical integer
static double	**cos**(double a)	Returns the trigonometric cosine of an angle
static double	**cosh**(double x)	Returns the hyperbolic cosine of a double value
static double	**exp**(double a)	Returns Euler's number *e* raised to the power of a double value
static double	**expm1**(double x)	Returns $e^x - 1$
static double	**floor**(double a)	Returns the largest (closest to positive infinity) double value that is less than or equal to the argument and is equal to a mathematical integer
static double	**hypot**(double x, double y)	Returns sqrt($x^2 + y^2$) without intermediate overflow or underflow

(*Continued*)

Table 6.1 *(Continued)*

static double	**IEEEremainder** (double f1, double f2)	Computes the remainder operation on two arguments as prescribed by the IEEE 754 standard
static double	**log**(double a)	Returns the natural logarithm (base *e*) of a double value
static double	**log10**(double a)	Returns the base 10 logarithm of a double value
static double	**log1p**(double x)	Returns the natural logarithm of the sum of the argument and 1
static double	**max**(double a, double b)	Returns the greater of two double values
static float	**max**(float a, float b)	Returns the greater of two float values
Static int	**max**(int a, int b)	Returns the greater of two int values
static long	**max**(long a, long b)	Returns the greater of two long values
static double	**min**(double a, double b)	Returns the smaller of two double values
static float	**min**(float a, float b)	Returns the smaller of two float values
Static int	**min**(int a, int b)	Returns the smaller of two int values
static long	**min**(long a, long b)	Returns the smaller of two long values
static double	**pow**(double a, double b)	Returns the value of the first argument raised to the power of the second argument
static double	**random**()	Returns a double value with a positive sign, greater than or equal to 0.0 and less than 1.0.
static double	**rint**(double a)	Returns the double value that is closest in value to the argument and is equal to a mathematical integer
static long	**round**(double a)	Returns the closest long to the argument
Static int	**round**(float a)	Returns the closest int to the argument
static double	**signum**(double d)	Returns the signum function of the argument; zero if the argument is zero, 1.0 if the argument is greater than zero, and −1.0 if the argument is less than zero

(Continued)

Table 6.1 *(Continued)*

static float	**signum**(float f)	Returns the `signum` function of the argument; zero if the argument is zero, 1.0f if the argument is greater than zero, and −1.0f if the argument is less than zero
static double	**sin**(double a)	Returns the trigonometric sine of an angle
static double	**sinh**(double x)	Returns the hyperbolic sine of a `double` value
static double	**sqrt**(double a)	Returns the correctly rounded positive square root of a `double` value
static double	**tan**(double a)	Returns the trigonometric tangent of an angle
static double	**tanh**(double x)	Returns the hyperbolic tangent of a `double` value
static double	**toDegrees**(double angrad)	Converts an angle measured in radians into an approximately equivalent angle measured in degrees
static double	**toRadians**(double angdeg)	Converts an angle measured in degrees into an approximately equivalent angle measured in radians
static double	**ulp**(double d)	Returns the size of an `ulp` of the argument
static float	**ulp**(float f)	Returns the size of an `ulp` of the argument

Please note that Table 6.1 contains many transcendental functions. The functions which are not algebraic are called transcendental functions. These functions include exponential and trigonometric functions.

We will see a few methods in action in Section 6.6. Java provides many useful classes. These classes provide programmers with useful methods. These methods will be discussed as and when needed.

6.6 End of Chapter Programs

6.6.1 Method `pow()`

A story from a village goes as follows. A poor old man celebrated his hundredth birthday. All the villagers were thrilled with the idea that someone from their village could be so lucky. They contributed generously and presented a purse of Rs. 1000 to him. The old man said, "If I had got this gift at my birth, I would have been 'Karodpati' by now".

Let us test whether what the old man thought is accurate or not with the help of a program.

Problem: Write a program to demonstrate the power of method `pow()` from class `Math`.

Solution: Assume that the villager in the aforementioned story deposited the money in a bank at 10% compound interest.

Normally, we use R for rate specified as percent. Then r is used as rate per unit and is calculated as R/100.

If one invests Re. 1 at rate r per unit, after N years he gets back $(1 + r)$ raised to N.

Hence, method `pow` is handy in calculations.

See Program 6.7.

PROGRAM 6.7 Use of Method pow()

```
//    pow1.java
class pow1
{
   public static void main(String args[])
     {     double deposit= 1000.00 ;
           double R = 10.0 ;
           double r = R /100.0 ;
           double amount=0;
           System.out.println("<---pow1.java--->");
           amount = deposit * Math.pow( (1.0+r) , 100);
           System.out.println("The amount is : " + (long)amount);
     }
}
```

The following output is obtained on running Program 6.7.

Output

```
<---pow1.java--->
The amount is : 13780612
```

6.6.2 Method Math.atan2( )

The method `atan()` helps us getting arctan in the range −pi/2 to +pi/2. If we consider a problem of rectangular to polar coordinates, we want angle in all possible (four) coordinates. Hence, Java supplies an additional method `atan2()`. Let us check it in action.

Problem: Write a program to find an angle theta for a point with given *x* and *y* coordinates.

Solution: For simplicity, let us take a condition $x = y$. If the point is in the first quadrant, the angle should be pi/4. If the point is in the third quadrant, the angle should be 3*pi/4. Figure 6.3 illustrates the use of method `atan()` to find angle theta.

See Program 6.8.

PROGRAM 6.8 Method atan2()

```
//     pt1.java
class pt1
{
   public static void main(String args[])
     {     double x1 = 1.0, y1=1.0 ;
           double x3 = -1.0,y3=-1.0 ;
           double theta1,theta3 ;
           double pi_by_4= Math.PI / 4.0;
           System.out.println("<---pt1.java--->");
           System.out.println("pi_by_4 is : " + pi_by_4);
           theta1 = Math.atan2( x1 , y1);
```

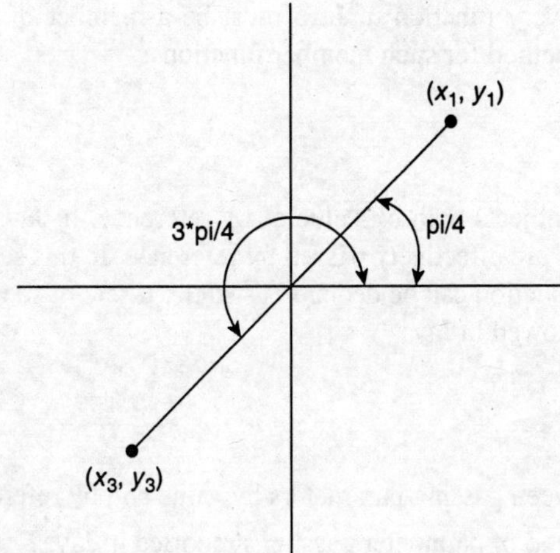

Figure 6.3 **Method** atan2()

```
        System.out.println("Theta1 is : " + theta1);
        theta3 = Math.atan2( x3 , y3);
        System.out.println("Theta3 is : " + theta3);
    }
}
```

If you run the program, you will get following output.

Output

```
<---pt1.java--->
pi_by_4 is : 0.7853981633974483
Theta1 is : 0.7853981633974483
Theta3 is : -2.356194490192345
```

Actually, method `atan2` is developed (written) very carefully. It takes care of many special cases regarding the parameter values. Readers are requested to see the relevant documentation.

Keywords

array as parameter, `atan()`, `atan2()`, class `Math`, objects as parameters, pass-by-reference, pass-by-value, `pow()`, recursion, `swap`

RuleBook

parameter passing	Basic parameter passing in Java is call-by-value. All simple types are passed by call-by-value. However all aggregate types effectively get passed by "call-by-reference".
static for local variables.	Keyword `static` not allowed for local variables of any method.

`void`	In Java if a method does not return any value, then it must be declared as `void`.
functions	Every function in Java must be a member of some class. Java uses the term method for such member functions.

C++ Corner

In C++, it is possible to pass objects both by value or by reference. In Java basic data types are passed by value and aggregate data types are effectively passed by reference. In this sense, C++ is richer than Java. In C++, a local variable of a function can be declared as static. It retains the value after the execution of that function is over. This is not allowed in Java.

Review Questions

1. What is the difference between passing parameters by value and by reference?
2. Which is the standard method of parameter passing supported in Java?
3. If you pass an object or an array to a method, what is the effective method of parameter passing?
4. Why method `swap` is not available for simple (in-built) data types?
5. What are the advantages and disadvantages of recursion?
6. What are transcendental functions?

Exercises

1. Write a program to find first 20 prime numbers.
2. Study any one random number generation algorithm and develop a function to return a pseudo-random number between 0 and *n*.
3. Write a function to find the largest number from a given integer array.
4. Develop a method to count the number of vowels in a given array of characters.
5. Assume that a 4 bit binary number is stored in an array of characters. Write a program to print its value in decimal format.
6. Develop a recursive method to find GCD of two integers.
7. Develop a recursive method to compute the *n*th Fibonacci number. Is this technique suitable for this problem?

ARRAYS

An array is by far the most powerful data structure in a programming language. This is the reason why it is in-built in all the HLLs, old as well as modern. We may not find any useful program without using an array.

7.1 Arrays in Java

An array is nothing but a sequential collection of items. We are allowed to refer to any item with the help of an index.

An item can be any of the following:

- Any simple data type like `int`, `char`, and so on.
- A `string`
- An object of a given class
- An array itself

The great strength of an array is that any particular element can be accessed with the help of the index. Just like C/C++, Java uses zero-based indexing. It means that index of the first element is always zero. It is not possible to define an array of elements, indexed say 1 to 10 or −5 to +5.

Let us assume we have a class of 20 students. They have recently obtained test marks. Every student has scored marks, which is of type `int`. To store all 20 marks, we need an array capable of storing 20 integers. If an array `Marks[ ]` is used for this purpose, `Marks[0]`, `Marks[1]`, . . ., `Marks[19]` are the twenty elements (variables); each of type `int` is used to store the data.

Short Questions and Answers

Q. What is an array?

A. An array is sequential collection of similar items.

Q. What is the great strength of an array?

A. Any particular element can be accessed directly with the help of the index.

For simplicity, at this stage, let us assume that arrays consist of elements belonging to simple data types. An array has a dimension (size). If an array has dimension 10, it means it can store 10 items. Each element of an array is referred with an array name and index. We may specify its dimension implicitly or explicitly. Once specified, the dimension cannot be changed later in a program.

7.2 Creating an Array

The first step in creating an array is to declare it. Arrays can be declared as follows:

```
int [] marks ;
```

Here, the variable `marks` is declared as an array of integer.

Alternatively, we can also declare the array as

```
int marks[] ;
```

This also means the same.

After declaring, we have to create an array with operator `new`.

```
marks = new int [3];
```

The above statement creates the array. This statement also allocates memory to it.

Here, the array is created with dimension three. Please note that while declaring, we have not specified the dimension. At this stage all the elements are initialized to zero.

Just like the declaration of other variables, we can couple declaration and initialization. See the following statement:

```
int marks[] = { 3,4,5 };
```

Here, we are declaring an array with the name `Marks`. We are initializing array elements as 3, 4, and 5. We have not specified the array dimension ourselves. As we have initialized with 3 values, array dimension is fixed as three. We may call it as implicit specification.

Those using C/C++ should note that declaration syntax `int a[5]` is not allowed in Java.

Let us try a program with arrays.

Problem: Write a program to find the average of given array elements.

Solution: Finding an average is simplest of all tasks. First, we have to add all the elements and then divide the sum by the number of elements (see Program 7.1).

PROGRAM 7.1 Finding Average

```
//   array21.java
class array21
{ public static void main(String args[])
    { float total=0, avg ;
      int i ;
      int Marks[];
      Marks = new int[5] ;
      System.out.println("---array21.java---");
      Marks[0] = 36;
      Marks[1] = 46;
      Marks[2] = 56;
      Marks[3] = 66;
      Marks[4] = 76;

      for(i=0;i<5;i++)
          total = total + Marks[i];
      avg = (float) ( total / 5.0) ;
      System.out.println("Average Marks are " + avg);
    }
}
```

If you run this program, you will get the following output.

Output

```
---array21.java---
Average Marks are 56.0
```

Note that (total/5.0) returns a double value. Hence, it has to be typecast to float.

7.3 Array Index Checking

Java checks array index during runtime. If a program tries to use index out of bound, a runtime error occurs. You can see this in action in Program 7.6 (`array3.java`). This is a very good feature for a programming language. Non-checking can introduce hard-to-diagnose bugs. A Java programmer is protected from such trouble.

Discussion

Does Java check index at the compile time? The answer is "no". The possible reason is that arrays are used with constant index very few times. Only in such cases the checking of compile time is possible. Most of the time array index is in the form of expression. Value of this expression is not known at the time of compilation. Hence, index checking in such cases is not possible. See program `array5a.java` in Section 7.6.

The size of the array is specified by the programmers. But for some reason, we may want to know the size of an array. Java has attached a property `length` to arrays. If we say

```
array_name.length
```

it will represent the length of the array named `array_name`. For example, in the previous example, if we say

```
Marks.length
```

it will represent the value 5. Please note that length is not a method. Hence, no brackets are used with it.

7.4 Multi-Dimensional Arrays

Arrays in Java can have more than one dimension. Such arrays are termed as multi-dimensional arrays. Let us first study two-dimensional arrays. We are all familiar with N × N matrices. These can be stored using array with two dimensions. Let us start our study with a simple program for printing a matrix.

Problem: Write a program to print a matrix.

Solution: See Program 7.2.

PROGRAM 7.2 Printing a Matrix

```
//      matrix1.java
//      matrix reading and printing
class matrix1
{ public static void main(String arg[])
    { int i,j;
      int matrix[][]={
                        {1,2,3},
```

```
                                {4,5,6},
                                {7,8,9}
                            };
        System.out.println("<---matrix1.java starts--->");
        for(i=0;i<=2;++i)
           { for(j=0;j<=2;++j)
                System.out.print("\t" + matrix[i][j]);
              System.out.println();
           }
    }
}
```

If you run the program, you will get the following output.

Output

```
<---matrix1.java starts--->
        1       2       3
        4       5       6
        7       8       9
```

Please note that we refer an element as `matrix [i][j]`. This syntax is same as that for C/C++. However, in mathematics, we write such an element as `matrix [i, j]`. In Java, we cannot write it in this form. We get compilation error.

7.4.1 Matrix addition

Matrix addition is a fairly simple task. The only condition is that both the matrices must be of the same size. Value of the resultant element is the sum of two corresponding elements.

Problem: Write a program to add two given matrices.

Solution: See Program 7.3.

PROGRAM 7.3 Matrix Addition

```
//    matrixadd.java
//addition of two matrices

class matrixadd
{
    public static void main(String arg[])
    {   int i,j;
        int matrix1[][]={  {1,2,3},
                           {4,5,6},
                           {7,8,9}
                        };
        int matrix2[][]={  {11,12,13},
                           {24,25,26},
                           {37,38,39}
                        };
        int matrix3[][]=new int[3][3];
        System.out.println("--->Program matrixadd.java starts<---");
```

```
//      calculating
        for(i=0;i<=2;++i)
          for(j=0;j<=2;++j)
            matrix3[i][j]=(matrix1[i][j] + matrix2[i][j]);
//      printing
        System.out.println("Matrix1");
        for(i=0;i<=2;++i)
          { for(j=0;j<=2;++j)
              System.out.print("\t" + matrix1[i][j]);
            System.out.println();
          }

        System.out.println("Matrix2");
        for(i=0;i<=2;++i)
          { for(j=0;j<=2;++j)
              System.out.print("\t" + matrix2[i][j]);
            System.out.println();
          }

        System.out.println("Matrix3");
        for(i=0;i<=2;++i)
          { for(j=0;j<=2;++j)
              System.out.print("\t" + matrix3[i][j]);
            System.out.println();
          }
    }
}
```

If you run the program, you will get the following output.

Output

```
--->Program matrixadd.java starts<---
Matrix1
            1       2       3
            4       5       6
            7       8       9
Matrix2
            11      12      13
            24      25      26
            37      38      39
Matrix3
            12      14      16
            28      30      32
            44      46      48
```

7.4.2 Matrix multiplication

We can multiply two matrices if the number of columns of the first is same as the number of rows of the second. The `(i, j)`th element of the product is computed by adding the product of elements of the `i`th row of the first matrix with corresponding elements of the `j`th column of the second matrix.

```
C [i, j] = sum of all A [i, k] * B [k, j]
```

Problem: Write a program to multiply two given matrices.

Solution: See Program 7.4.

PROGRAM 7.4 Matrix Multiplication

```
//      matrixmul1.java
//matrix multiplication
class matrixmul1
{ public static void main(String arg[])
    {   int i,j,k,sum;
        int matrix1[][]={    {1,0,0},
                             {0,1,0},
                             {0,0,1}
                        };
        int matrix2[][]={    { 1, 2, 3},
                             {14,15,16},
                             {27,28,29}
        };
        int matrix3[][]=new int [3][3];
        System.out.println("<---matrixmul1.java--->");
//      calculating
        for(i=0;i<=2;i++)
            for(j=0;j<=2;j++)
             {  sum=0;
                for(k=0;k<=2;k++)
                   sum+=matrix1[i][k] * matrix2[k][j];
                matrix3[i][j]=sum;
             }

        System.out.println("matrix1");
        for(i=0;i<=2;++i)
           {   for(j=0;j<=2;++j)
                   System.out.print("\t" + matrix1[i][j]);
               System.out.println();
           }
        System.out.println("matrix2");
        for(i=0;i<=2;++i)
           {   for(j=0;j<=2;++j)
                   System.out.print("\t" + matrix2[i][j]);
               System.out.println();
           }
        System.out.println("matrix3");
        for(i=0;i<=2;++i)
           {   for(j=0;j<=2;++j)
                   System.out.print("\t" + matrix3[i][j]);
               System.out.println();
           }
    }
}
```

If you run the program, you will get the following output.

Output

```
<---matrixmul1.java--->
matrix1
          1          0          0
          0          1          0
          0          0          1
matrix2
          1          2          3
          14         15         16
          27         28         29
matrix3
          1          2          3
          14         15         16
          27         28         29
```

7.5 Enhanced for Loop

From version 5, Java decided to give additional power to for loop. Many times, we work with a collection of objects. We are required to work with each and every item of the collection. As this situation is very common, new syntax covers it very elegantly. As arrays are the simplest collection, let us see it first.

Consider an array of marks defined as

```
int Marks[ ]
```

Now we can set a loop as

```
for ( int j : Marks )
  { body of the loop }
```

Here, body of the loop is executed for every value `j` which is present in an array. We can say that this is equivalent to a standard for loop like

```
for ( i=0;i<Marks.length;i++)
                { body of the loop }
```

where, integer `j` in the first example represents `Marks[i]` of the second example.

Earlier we had seen a program to find the average (`array21.java`). Let us rewrite it using enhanced for loop.

Problem: Write a program to find the average of a given array element using enhanced for loop.

Solution: See Program 7.5.

PROGRAM 7.5 Enhanced for Loop

```
//    array22.java
class array22
{ public static void main(String args[])
   {  float total=0, avg ;
      int i ;
      int Marks[];
```

```
        Marks = new int[5] ;
        System.out.println("<---array22.java--->");
        Marks[0] = 36;
        Marks[1] = 46;
        Marks[2] = 56;
        Marks[3] = 66;
        Marks[4] = 76;

        for(int j : Marks)
            total = total + j ;
        avg = (float)( total / 5.0) ;
        System.out.println("Average Marks are " + avg);
    }
}
```

If you run the program, you will get the following output.

Output

```
<---array22.java--->
Average Marks are 56.0
```

If you consider this as a trivial example, let us discuss a very complex collection like `HashSet`. Here, we have to move from element to element only with the help of Iterator. In such a collection, we can use enhanced for loop very easily. We will discuss this example in Chapter 23.

7.6 End of Chapter Programs

7.6.1 Array index out of bound

Problem: Write a program to show that Java checks array index.

Solution: See Program 7.6.

PROGRAM 7.6 Java Checks Array Index Automatically

```
//    array3.java
class array3
{ public static void main(String args[])
    {  float x=0,y=0 ;
       int i;
       int A[];
       A = new int[3] ;
       System.out.println("<---array3.java--->");
       A[0]=3;
       A[1]=4;
       A[2]=5;
       A[3]=6;

       for(i=0;i<4;i++)
```

```
        x=x+A[i];
      System.out.println("Average of A is" + x/4.0);
    }
}
```

If you run the program, you will get the following output.

Output

```
<---array3.java--->
Exception in thread "main"
java.lang.ArrayIndexOutOfBoundsException: 3
at array3.main(array3.java:12)
```

When an array index is out of bound, the program throws what is known as `ArrayIndexOutOfBoundsException`. We will study errors and exceptions in Chapter 19. At this stage, we will only say that exceptions are very useful in program development.

7.6.2 Binary search

Binary search is the fastest search technique. It requires data to be sorted. It finds the given number in much less efforts (log n) as compared to other searching techniques. The algorithm can be explained in brief as follows.

At any time, searching is confined to a range. To begin with, range is the entire array. First, we get the element at the middle of the range. We compare the search item with the value of this element.

If the value matches, we have successfully found the element.

If search element is smaller, new range is from start to middle.

If search element is larger, new range is middle to end.

When the search range reduces to one, we stop searching further. Let us try this algorithm.

Problem: Write a program to find a given number in a given array using binary search algorithm.

Solution: See Program 7.7.

PROGRAM 7.7 Binary Search

```
//                search1.java
class search1
{ public static void main(String args[])
  {  int i,l,r,n,k;
     int[] a = { 1,12,13,23,25,37,41,47,51,59};
     boolean found;
     n = 13; // number to find
     System.out.println("The input data is as follows");
     System.out.println("1,12,13,23,25,37,41,47,51,59");
     System.out.println("The number To be searched : " + n );
     found = false;
     l=0;r=9; // array index in java is 0 to 9
     do
      { k=(l+r)/2 ;
        if (a[k]==n)
```

```
                found=true;
            else { if (a[k]<n ) l=k+1;
                        else r=k-1;
                }
        } while ((!found)&&(l<=r));
          if (found)
                System.out.println ("The number is found");
          else
                System.out.println ("The number is NOT found");
        return ;
    }
}
```

If you run the program, you will get the following output.

Output

```
The input data is as follows
1,12,13,23,25,37,41,47,51,59
The number To be searched : 13
The number is found
```

7.6.3 Linear search

We have seen the fastest search just now. However, it requires that data must be sorted. What if the data is unsorted? Then we have to use a simple technique called linear search. It finds a given number simply by examining every array element one by one sequentially.

Problem: Write a program to find a given number in a given array using the linear search method.

Solution: See Program 7.8.

PROGRAM 7.8 Linear Search

```
//      search2.java
//      linear search
class search2
{ public static void main(String args[])
   {  int i,n;
      int[] a = {59,13,37,25,51,1,23,41,47,12};
      boolean found;
      n = 47; // number to find
      System.out.println ("<---search2.java--->");
      System.out.println("The input data is as follows");
      System.out.println("59,13,37,25,51,1,23,41,47,12");
      System.out.println("The number To be searched : " + n );
      found = false;
      for(i=0;i<10;i++)
        { System.out.println("checking " + i +" th number = "+ a[i]);
          if (a[i]==n)
            { found = true;
              break;
```

```
            }
        } ;
      if (found)
              System.out.println ("The number is found");
          else
              System.out.println ("The number is NOT found");
      return ;
   }
}
```

If you run the program, you will get the following output.

Output

```
<---search2.java--->
The input data is as follows
59,13,37,25,51,1,23,41,47,12
The number To be searched : 47
checking 0 th number = 59
checking 1 th number = 13
checking 2 th number = 37
checking 3 th number = 25
checking 4 th number = 51
checking 5 th number = 1
checking 6 th number = 23
checking 7 th number = 41
checking 8 th number = 47
The number is found
```

If you see the code carefully, you will notice the use of the `break` statement in the `for loop`. It is possible to replace this use of for with break by a `while loop`. Some experts will give more marks for such coding.

7.6.4 Checking for duplicate

In many applications, it is required that the data does not have any duplicate entries. Let us try a simple algorithm for checking duplicates.

Problem: Write a program to check for duplicate entries in a given array.

Solution: The simplest solution will have the following steps. First, consider the first entry (`a[0]`) as num. Then using a `for loop`, check it with all the remaining entries in an array. Now repeat this for all elements except the last one.

PROGRAM 7.9 Checking for Duplicates

```
//     dup1.java
//     checks for duplicate
//     linear search
class dup1
{  public static void main(String args[])
   {  int i,j,num;
```

```
      int[] a = {59,13,37,25,51,1,23,41,37,12};
      boolean found;
      System.out.println ("<---dup1.java--->");
      System.out.println("The input data is as follows");
      System.out.println("59,13,37,25,51,1,23,41,37,12");
      System.out.println("checking for duplicates" );
      found = false;
      for(i=0; i<10-1; i++)
      {  System.out.println("checking for " + a[i]);
         num = a[i];
         for(j=i+1;j<10;j++)
             if (num==a[j])
                { found = true;
                  System.out.println ("The duplicate number found");
                }
      } ;
      return ;
   }
}
```

If you run the program, you will get the following output.

Output

```
<---dup1.java--->
The input data is as follows
59,13,37,25,51,1,23,41,37,12
checking for duplicates
checking for 59
checking for 13
checking for 37
The duplicate number found
checking for 25
checking for 51
checking for 1
checking for 23
checking for 41
checking for 37
```

Well, checking is simple. Can you remove the duplicate entries?

Earlier we have said that referring an array element as matrix `[a, b]` produces compilation error. We know that it is safer and hence better to catch these errors at compilation time. In C/C++, such reference does not necessarily produce compilation error. The program gets compiled and also executed, albeit with surprising and of course incorrect results. At least in this respect we can say Java is better than C++. (C++ programmers will know that this happens because C++ supports the comma operator. Java does not support comma operator.)

Keywords

array, array index checking, `ArrayIndexOutOfBoundsException`, binary search, linear search, matrix addition, matrix multiplication, multi-dimensional arrays, two-dimensional arrays, zero-based indexing

RuleBook

array index checking	Java checks array index during runtime. If program tries to use index out of bound, a runtime error occurs.
array size	When an array size (dimension) is specified, it cannot be changed later in the program.
arrays methods	Arrays are passed to methods by call-by-reference.

C++ Corner

In C++ there is no in-built array index checking. It is the responsibility of a programmer. Index going out of bounds generates hard-to-detect errors in C++. In Java, memory to an array is allocated using operator new! In C++, you may allocate memory this way. Alternately, a simple declaration like `int a[5]` allocates memory to an array in C++.

Review Questions

1. Describe two methods to declare an array.
2. How do you get the size of an array?
3. Is index checking supported in Java?

Exercises

1. Write a function to find the largest number from a given integer array.
2. Write a function `binSearch()` to find a given number from a given sorted integer array.
3. Develop a method to count the number of vowels in a given array of characters.
4. Assume that a 4-bit binary number is stored in an array of characters. Write a program to print its value in Hexadecimal format.
5. An array of char of size 4 is supposed to contain a number in hexadecimal format. Write a method `validate()` which checks the validity of the stored number. Hint: anything other than 0,…, 9 and A,…, F is invalid.
6. Write a program to find the determinant of N × N matrix.
7. Write a program to subtract one N × N matrix from other.
8. An array contains marks obtained by students in a class test. Assume the number of students to be 60. The marks are between 0 and 100. Write a program to plot a Histogram. (As we have not studied graphics as yet, develop only in text mode. For convenience of programming, you may draw the bars in horizontal direction.)
9. Assume that different schemes offer compound interest at rate 3%, 4%, 6% and 7%. Prepare a table showing amount returned if an investor invests Rs. 1,000 for a period of 1, 2, 3, 4, and 5 years.
10. Write a program to remove duplicates from a given array.
11. Rewrite program search2.java such that we do not need `break` statement. Hint: Use `while`.

12. State whether the following program will compile. If yes, describe the output. If no, give reasons.

```
**********************************************

// array5b.java
class array5b
{ public static void main(String args[])
   {  int k=5;
      int a[] ;
      System.out.println("<---array5b--->");
      a=new int[5];
      k= a[3];
      System.out.println(k);
   }
}

**********************************************
```

CHAPTER 8

INTRODUCING CLASSES

So far, we have studied many basic features of Java. We know that Java is a highly object-oriented language. The study of this aspect of the language starts with the concept of class. Let us study classes step by step in this chapter.

8.1 Class Fundamentals

8.1.1 The general form of a class

Class can be considered as nothing but a user-defined type. It is a template for the object to be created. It holds some data. This data can be of different simple types we have studied earlier.

Let us take an example of time. It consists of hours, minutes, and seconds. To store these quantities, we need three different fields (variables). But together they constitute a single object.

A class in general has two types of members. They are as follows:

- Fields: These are variables associated with the class.
- Methods: These are the procedures which define the behaviour (executable code) of the object.

Let us draw a pictorial view of simple class `Time` (Figure 8.1).
This class consists of only three fields. We have not put any methods in it. We will see methods little later.

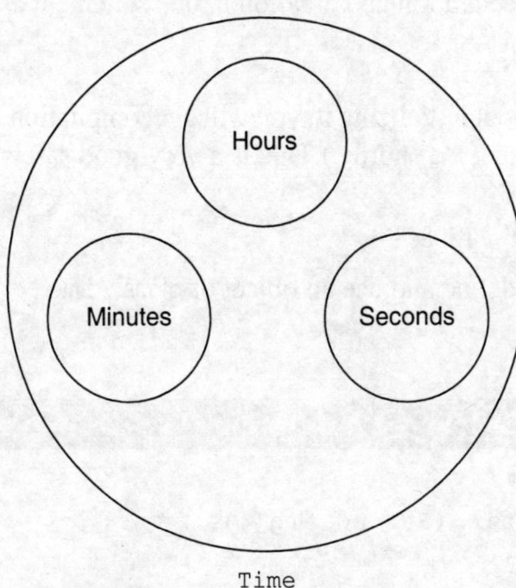

Figure 8.1 Pictorial View of Class **`Time`**

8.1.2 A simple class

We have just seen a pictorial view of class Time. If we have to use it in a program, we will have to define it. We can define a class Time as follows.

```
class Time
      {     int hour
            int minute;
            int second;
      };
```

Let us observe few details about class declaration.

1. It starts with keyword **class**.
2. Next comes class name. It is Time in this example.
3. Next comes "{" opening curly bracket.
4. It is followed by three data member declarations.
5. The declaration ends with "}" closing curly bracket and a semicolon.
6. The variables declared here are known as "instance variables".

The other type of variables is known as "class variables", we will discuss them little later.

8.2 Declaring and Creating Objects

An object is nothing but an instantiation of a class (variable of type class). Hence, an object declaration is like any other variable declaration.

```
Time t1;
```

However, it is just not sufficient to declare an object. You must create it as follows:

```
t1 = new Time();
```

Alternately, you can combine declaration and creation in one statement as follows:

```
Time t1 = new Time();
```

If you start using the object without initializing it, you will get compilation error. (An object is initialized at the time of creation; this will be discussed shortly.) This is a very good safety feature in Java. See Program 8.10 in Section 8.18 to this effect.
At this stage, let us study a simple program.

Problem: Write a program to define and use an object of class Time.

Solution: See Program 8.1.

PROGRAM 8.1 Class Time I

```
class time4
{ public static void main (String arg[])
   { int total ;
     Time t1= new Time() ;
     t1.hour = 5 ;
```

```
        t1.minute =30 ;
        t1.second = 0;
        total = t1.hour * 60 *60 + t1.minute*60 + t1.second ;
        System.out.println("<---time4.java--->");
        System.out.println("Total seconds " + total);
    }
}
class Time
{   int hour;
    int minute;
    int second ;
}
```

If you run the program, you will get the following output.

Output

```
<---time4.java--->
Total seconds 19800
```

8.3 Accessing Members

In Program 8.1, we have an object `t1` of class `Time`. This object has three fields. When we wanted to initialize "second", we wrote `t1.second`. Here we are using a dot operator. It associates field name with object name. The methods pertaining to objects are also referred using dot operator.

8.4 Access Control Parameters: Public and Private

Java allows us to declare variable as well as methods with access control parameters. They are typically public, protected, and private. These keywords are sometimes called as access specifiers. Out of these, we will discuss public and private here. We will discuss "protected" when we study inheritance.

If a variable in a class is declared as private, it is not accessible outside the class. A sample program is given at the end of chapter. **Please note** that a variable, which is private, can be accessed by methods of that same class.

If you drink tea at a small dhaba ("Cutting on Tapri" in Mumbai) and pay, you can see the cash box as shown in Figure 8.2. You can see the coins but not the wades of notes. This situation has been depicted in Figure 8.2.

As you are an outsider, you can see only coins (like public variables). You cannot see notes (like private variables). The tea stall vendor can see both, coins as well as notes (like any method of the same class).

In a good object design, practically all data members are to be declared private. Any inadvertent reference to them will be detected by the compiler. Compiler will not allow us to modify them arbitrarily.

You may ask me what the use of such data is? We have already said that these (private) variables can be accessed by the methods of the class. We are supposed to write methods to access private data.

Important

When we do not use any of the access specifier, like public or private, system treats it as default access. This access is sometimes termed as package access. We will discuss this access when we discuss packages in later

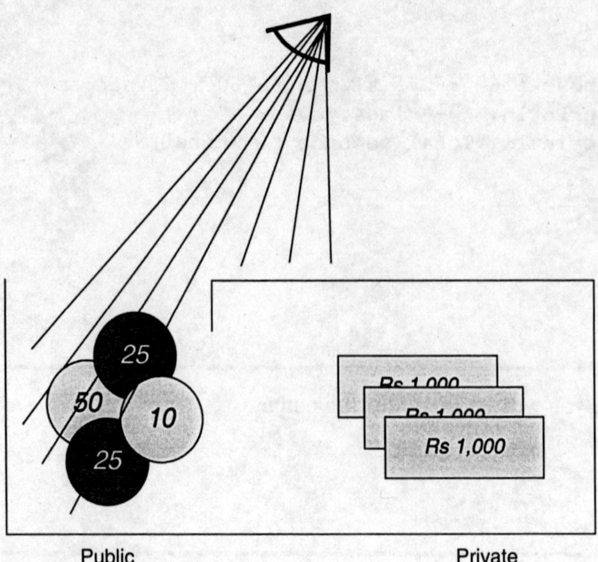

Figure 8.2 Public vs. Private

chapter. This access behaves as public access in "*Simple Java Programs*". As we found it convenient to use, in the text hereafter, we will use default access even when public access is intended.

8.5 Introducing Methods

A class in Java contains data in the form of variables. In addition, a class contains functions to work with these variables. These functions are termed as **methods** in Java.

Let us study a simple method to initialize the data elements.

Problem: Write a program to illustrate method `init()` to assign initial values to an object.

Solution: See Program 8.2.

PROGRAM 8.2 Introducing Methods

```
//   time6
class time6
{ public static void main (String argv[])
    { int result;
      Time t1= new Time() ;
      t1.hour = 7 ;
      t1.minute = 20 ;
      t1.second = 30 ;
      result = t1.total();
      System.out.println("<---Time6.java--->");
      System.out.println("Total seconds " + result);
    };
}
```

```
class Time
{  int hour;
   int minute;
   int second ;
   public int total()
    { return 3600 * hour + 60 * minute + second ;
    }
};
```

If you run the program, you will get the following output.

Output

```
<---Time6.java--->
Total seconds 26430
```

Here method `total()` is used to compute time in seconds.

8.6 Methods with Parameters

In earlier example, there were no parameters for method `total()`. You will agree that for methods to be very effective, they should, in general, have one or more parameters. All languages, old and new, support functions with parameters. Naturally, Java methods can also have parameters.

Here we show one example where one method `convert()` accepts parameters while another method `display()` does not have any parameters.

Problem: Write a program to illustrate methods with parameters.

Solution: Just opposite to total in previous program, we will have method convert, which will convert a given total number of seconds into equivalent hour, minutes, and seconds (see Program 8.3).

PROGRAM 8.3 Methods with Parameters

```
//       time7
class Time
{  int hour;
   int minute;
   int second ;
   void convert(int n)
   {  int temp = n ;
      second = n % 60;
      temp = temp / 60 ;
      minute = temp % 60;
      hour = temp /60 ;
   }
   void display()
   { System.out.println("**TIME**");
     System.out.println("Hours = " + hour);
     System.out.println("Minutes = " + minute);
     System.out.println("Seconds = " +second);
   } ;
};
```

```
class time7
{  public static void main (String argv[])
   { int total ;
     Time t1= new Time() ;
     t1.convert(7840);
     System.out.println("<---time7.java--->");
     t1.display();
   };
}
```

If you run the program, you will get the following output.

Output

```
<---time7.java--->
**TIME**
Hours = 2
Minutes = 10
Seconds = 40
```

8.7 Methods Returning a Value

Methods need not be of type void. They can return a value. In the previous example, we have seen an example where method `total()` returns integer. There is no restriction on variable type returned by a method. A method can return any primitive data type like `int` float. It can also return strings, arrays, vectors, or even object (reference). The return type of a method can also be `void`. It means, such a method does not return anything.

Short Questions and Answers

Q. Is return statement compulsory in Java?

A. If return type of a method is void, return statement is optional. For any other return type, it is compulsory.

8.8 Constructors

Earlier we made a statement that an object must not only be declared but also initialized. In earlier programs, we have done it in most haphazard way. In Java, the elegant way of initializing an object is use of constructor.

Constructor is a special **method**, which initializes an object. Constructor does not have any return type. Name of the class is name of the constructor method. Constructor can be declared (optionally) as public or protected. It cannot be declared as private.

Parameterized constructors: As with any method, constructors can also have parameters. Such constructors are termed as parameterized constructor.

Constructor overloading: Just like other methods, there can be more than one constructor in a class. Such constructors can be termed as overloaded constructors.

Let us study all these concepts in a simple program.

Problem: Write a program to illustrate constructor.

Solution: See Program 8.4.

PROGRAM 8.4 Introducing Constructor

```
//      const3
class Time
{  int hour;
   int minute;
   int second ;
   Time(int h,int m, int s)
    { hour = h ;
      minute = m ;
      second = s ;
    }
   Time()
    { second = 0;
      minute = 15;
      hour = 9;
    }
   void disp()
    { System.out.print("Time-->");
      System.out.print(hour+":");
      System.out.print(minute+":");
      System.out.println(second);
    }
};

class const3
{  public static void main (String argv[])
    { System.out.println("<---const3.java--->");
      Time t1 = new Time() ;
//    College opening time
      t1.disp();
//    time for morning walk!
      Time t2 = new Time(5,45,0);
      t2.disp();
    };
}
```

If you run the program, you will get the following output.

Output

```
<---const3.java--->
Time-->9:15:0
Time-->5:45:0
```

In Program 8.4, the first constructor initializes the time value to college opening time. The second constructor initializes to ideal time for morning walk.

8.9 System-Supplied Constructor

In a given class, when we do not write any constructor ourselves, the system supplies a constructor itself. We can term this constructor as "system-supplied constructor". It does not have any parameters. It initializes all numeric data members to zero. It initializes a Boolean member to false. Table 8.1 illustrates the values used for initializing different types of variables by the system supplied constructor.

Table 8.1 **Initialization by System-Supplied Constructor**

Type of variable	Values used for initialization
byte	0
Short	0
int	0
long	0
float	0
double	0
char	Character with value 0
boolean	false
String	null

Let us verify the fact with the help of a program.

Problem: Write a program to demonstrate that compiler provides a constructor when we do not define any constructor.

Solution: See Program 8.5.

PROGRAM 8.5 **System-Supplied Constructor I**

```
//       init1.vava
class init1
{ public static void main (String argv[])
   { test t1 = new test();
     System.out.println("<---init1.java--->");
     t1.show();
   }
}
class test
 { int a;
   double b;
   boolean c;
   char ch;
   String str;
   void show()
     { System.out.println("int a = " + a);
       System.out.println("double b = " +b);
       System.out.println("boolean c = " +c);
       System.out.println("character ch --->" + ch + "<---");
```

```
        System.out.println("integer value of ch is " + (int) ch);
        System.out.println("string str = --->" + str + "<---");
        //System.out.println("length of str =--->" +
        //        str.length() + "<---");
    }
}
```

If you run the program, you will get the following output.

Output

```
<---init1.java--->
int a = 0
double b = 0.0
boolean c = false
character ch ---> <---
integer value of ch is 0
string str = --->null<---
```

Note:

1. The last line is commented out in the program. In Program 8.5, value of `string` is null. It means un-initialized. Calling a method in this case causes an exception. We will discuss exceptions in a separate chapter later.
2. Character with value 0 is a non-printable character. That is why we get a blank in place of character `ch`.
3. The string `str` is not initialized. Therefore, it is printed as `null`.

If the class has one or more constructors defined, then system does not supply any constructor. Program 8.6 proves this fact.

Problem: Show that if a class has one or more constructor then system does not supply any constructor.

Solution: See Program 8.6.

PROGRAM 8.6 System-Supplied Constructor II

```
//      const4
class Time
{  int hour;
   int minute;
   int second ;
   Time(int h,int m, int s)
    { hour = h ;
      minute = m ;
      second = s ;
    }
   void disp()
    { System.out.print("Time-->");
      System.out.print(hour+":");
      System.out.print(minute+":");
```

```
        System.out.println(second);
    }
}
class const4
{  public static void main (String argv[])
    { System.out.println("<---const4.java--->");
        Time t1 = new Time() ;
        t1.disp();
    };
}
```

If you run the program, you will get the following error message.

Output

```
Compiling javac const4.java
const4.java:22: cannot find symbol
symbol : constructor Time()
location: class Time
Time t1 = new Time() ;
^
1 error
```

In this case, we must use the constructor that we have defined.

8.10 Default Constructor

We initialize objects using constructor. Most of the times, we specify the constructor we want to use. If we try to create an object without specifying any constructor, the Java environment has to find (or decide on) a constructor for us. Such a constructor can be termed as default constructor.
Let us examine three specific situations.

1. When we define a class without ***any*** constructor, the system (compiler) supplies what is called as system-supplied constructor. It initializes instance variables to zero values. It becomes the default constructor.
2. If we have defined one or more constructors, and one of them is without parameters, such a constructor becomes default constructor.
3. When we have defined one or more constructors, and **none** of them is without parameters, there is no default constructor. System also does not supply a default constructor in this case. Any code under these circumstances produces compilation error.

C++ programmers please note that basic concept of default constructor in C++ and Java is same. The only difference is that when the default constructor is supplied by the system, it does not initialize the variables in a C++ program.

8.11 Keyword `this`

Java provides a keyword `this` to refer to current object. Consider a definition of class `Amount`.

```
class Amount
   { int rupee ;
```

```
        int paisa ;
        Amount (int r1, int p1)
            { rupee = r1; paisa = p1 };
}
```

This is fine. But notice we have to use artificial identifiers `r1` and `p1`. If we wanted our program to look natural, the only alternative is to use parameter names rupee and paise. See the following definition:

```
class Amount
    { int rupee ;
      int paisa ;
      Amount (int rupee, int paisa)
          { rupee = rupee; paisa = paisa; } ;
}
```

It **is in our mind** that rupee on left-hand side is instance variable and that on right-hand side is the parameter. But the poor computer cannot resolve this ambiguity. Here keyword `this` comes handy. We can write the constructor as

```
Amount (int rupee, int paisa)
    { this.rupee = rupee; this.paisa = paisa; };
```

`this.rupee` refers to rupee for current object and `rupee` represents the parameter. You can see complete program `this2.java` in Program 8.13.

It will be interesting to modify and execute it, by removing `this` from it.

Instance variable hiding: Actually when you run such a program by removing `this`, you do not get the expected result. The reason is that as the parameter name say rupee is used, this hides the instance variable rupee. Any appearance of word rupee stands for the parameter. In this context, `this` is of great use to us.

In absence of such facility, we would have to use artificial identifiers like `rupee1` or `rup1` or worst `r1`.

8.12 Garbage Collection

In large applications, memory gets allocated to objects when created. After some time during program execution, these objects are no more needed. Hence, memory allocated to them can be brought back to OS. Earlier, languages put this responsibility on programmers. Java designers have done a nice thing by putting this responsibility on the system. This action of getting back the allocated memory by the system is known as garbage collection.

A word of caution: There is no defined time for garbage collection. System does it as and when it is free. Hence, you cannot program assuming it will take place at certain time.

For medium-sized programs or single-user environments, you need not worry about garbage collection.

8.13 The `finalize()` Method

Many objects acquire resources. When they are not needed any more, system takes back the memory allocated to them. But the resources remain still allocated to them. By resources, we mean opened files, printers etc. Other users of the system cannot use such resources. Hence, when an object is no more needed, we must see that it returns all resources to OS.

All objects in Java are derived from class `Object`. This class has defined a protected method `finalize()`. We should override this method for classes defined by us. When the garbage collector reclaims the memory allocated to a given object, it calls this method.

The only point to be noted is that after the object goes out of scope, garbage collector is called after some **unspecified** time. There is no guarantee that it will be called immediately.

We have discussed garbage collection again in a later chapter.

8.14 Overloading Methods and Constructors

It is possible to have different set of parameters for a method with a given name. For example, we can have function

```
void init( )
void init (long total_seconds);
void init(int h, int m, int s);
```

This is called method overloading. The list of parameters (having specific types) is called a signature of a method. Thus

```
void
int
int, int, int
```

are the three signatures of the overloading methods. Methods having same name and different signatures are allowed. We say that such methods are overloaded. It goes without saying that methods with same name and same signature will not be allowed. Reason being very simple. There is no way the computer can differentiate them. You may wonder what if they have different return types. For example, methods

```
int    init ( int h, int m, int s) and
void   init (int a, int b, int c ).
```

The rule is that such methods are not allowed in a given class. The reason for this is very simple. When you invoke any one in your program, the compiler cannot decide which method you want to invoke.

As constructors are basically methods, it goes without saying that constructors can also be overloaded. It gives us different ways to initialize an object.

8.15 Using Objects as Parameters

So far, we have seen parameters of ordinary or basic types. You may wonder whether we can pass objects as parameter to methods. The answer is yes, by all means.

But when methods work with objects, why use objects as parameter? Normally, a method is tied to one particular object. What if we want to compare two objects? In general, what if we want to deal with objects of two different types? In that case, we need object as a parameter.

Problem: Write a program to pass object as a parameter.

Solution: See Program 8.7.

PROGRAM 8.7 Object as Parameter

```
//      para2.java
class Date12
 { int dd ;
   int mm ;
   int yy ;
   Date12(int a, int b, int c)
```

```
      { dd=a; mm=b; yy=c;};
  }
 class para2
  { public static void show(Date12 dx)
      { System.out.println(dx.dd + ":" + dx.mm + ":" +
                                          dx.yy );
      }
    public static void next_date(Date12 dx)
    {    dx.dd ++ ;
    }
    public static void main (String argv[])
     {   Date12 d1 = new Date12(21,4,2005);
         System.out.println("---para1.java---");
         show(d1);
         next_date(d1);
         show(d1);
     };
  }
```

If you run the program, you will get the following output.

Output

```
---para2.java---
21:4:2005
22:4:2005
```

Please note that in this example we have simply increased the date. This will work in 90% of times. If the date is last day of month then both date and month should change. If it is the last day of the year, all three quantities should change. This task is left to our readers as exercise.

Have you found something surprising? The method could change the object, which is passed as parameter. So far, we have seen that parameters are passed by value. Hence, they are not supposed to change.

Why a different kind of result here? The reason is that Java passes the reference for all non-primitive types (strings, arrays, and objects). We know that reference is something like pointer in C. Hence, when we pass a reference as a parameter, behaviour is as if "pass by reference". We have discussed this aspect in detail at a later stage.

8.16 Keyword `Static`

Keyword static can be applied to variables as well as methods of a class. Let us first discuss use of static with variables.

8.16.1 Static variables

When we declare a variable as static there is single value (copy) of that variable for every object of that class. Consider a case of class Player defined for players from India. The class Player will have many variables for storing name, game, and other data regarding players. But they all belong to India. If we declare a field like country, it will have identical value for every player. Hence, there is no necessity to declare it separately for every player, that is every object. A single value for whole class is sufficient. Such variables are called **"class variables"**. It will be worth remembering that non-static variables are termed as "instance variable".

Let us see a concrete example.

Problem: Write a program to illustrate use of static inside a class.

Solution: See Program 8.8.

PROGRAM 8.8 Static Field (Class Variable)

```
//      static1.java
class static1
{  public static void main(String argv[])
   { PLAYER p1,p2,p3 ;
     p1 = new PLAYER("sachin","cricket");
     p2 = new PLAYER("leander","tennis");
     System.out.println("<---static1.java--->");
     p1.show();
     p2.show();
   }
}
class PLAYER
 {  String name;
    String game;
    static String nation ;
    void show()
     { System.out.println("showing details of a player") ;
       System.out.println("name " + name);
       System.out.println("game " + game);
       System.out.println("nation " + nation);
     }
    PLAYER(String s1, String g1)
     {  name = s1 ;
        game = g1 ;
        nation = "INDIA";
     }
 }
```

If you run the program, you will get the following output.

Output

```
<---static1.java--->
showing details of a player
name sachin
game cricket
nation INDIA
showing details of a player
name leander
game tennis
nation INDIA
```

Note:

1. Value of static variable nation is same for both the players, that is `INDIA`.
2. This variable is initialized in the constructor.

Now let us discuss keyword static with methods.

8.16.2 Static methods

When a method is declared as static, it belongs to a class. Hence, such a method is called a class method. You can invoke it with either a class name or object of that class. See Program 14.11 on complex numbers (`comp2.java`) in the chapter "Collection of Academic Programs". It has a static method which compares two complex numbers.

In class methods, you **cannot** make use of `this`, as these methods cannot be tied to any particular object. Please note that our everyday method `main()` is declared as static.

You may remember that in Chapter 6 on functions, we have studied lot of methods from class Math. Most of them were static.

Let us write a simple program to study class methods.

Problem: Write a program to study static methods.

Solution: See Program 8.9.

PROGRAM 8.9 A Class Method

```
//      static2.java
class static2
{  public static void main(String argv[])
   { Player p1,p2; ;
     System.out.println("--->static2.java<---");
     Player.disp();
   }
}
class Player
 {  String name;
    String game;
    static String nation ;
    void show()
     {    System.out.println("showing details of a player") ;
          System.out.println("name " + name);
          System.out.println("game " + game);
          System.out.println("nation " + nation);
     }
    Player(String s1, String g1)
     {  name = s1 ;
        game = g1 ;
        nation = "INDIA";
     }
   static  void disp()
     {   System.out.println("Static Method disp ") ;
         System.out.println(" Class Player has two main fields");
         System.out.println(" name and game ");
         //  System.out.println(name);
     }
 }
```

If you run the program, you will get the following output.

Output

```
--->static2.java<---
Static Method disp
Class Player has two main fields
name and game
```

The static methods cannot make any reference (in simple words **use**) to non-static variables of a class. It is very natural, as such variables are defined specifically for the object. As static method is not associated with any particular object, static methods cannot use them.

Notice the commenting of last line in a program. If you include it in the program, you will get following compilation error:

```
static2.java:30: Can't make a static reference to nonstatic variable name
in class Player.
            System.out.println(name);
                ^
```

At this time you would like to know, whether keyword static can be applied to local variables of any method (as permitted in C/C++)? The answer is NO. We cannot attach keyword static to ordinary local variables. See Program 8.14 in Section 8.18.

Short Questions and Answers

Q. What is an object?

A. In simple words, an object is an instantiation of a class.

Q. What is a class?

A. Prima-facie class is a user-defined type like structure. In addition to data members, it also contains definition of all the methods that operate on this type.

Q. What are the components of a class?

A. A class consists of two components, variables and methods. These components can be of type instance or class.

Q. What are instance variables?

A. Instance variables are variables of any type (in-built or user defined) used to store data.

Q. What are class variables?

A. Variables declared as static are class variables. Only one copy of such variables is maintained for all the objects of that class.

Q. What are methods?

A. Methods are functions associated with the class. They are able to access even private instance variables.

Q. What are class methods?

A. Methods declared as static are class methods. They can be invoked with the help of class name. They do not need any particular object for invocation.

Q. How to create a class definition?

A. We study the real-life object and its attributes are made as the data members of the class. A careful thinking is made of the functions required to access and process the data members. These functions are then made as the member methods of the class.

In the main program, we declare an object to this class and use methods to process the data.

Q. Do public and private declarations have effect on calling (invoking) of methods.

A. Yes. Just like private member variables, private methods cannot be called from outside the class. Does it imply that private methods are unusable? No. Any method of that same class can invoke this private method. It is well known that methods marked public are accessible from anywhere.

8.17 Description of Simple Java Program

At the beginning of the text, we have defined very simple Java programs. As we have studied classes and objects, now our programs will have more power. We are not writing very simple programs any more. We will be required to be more careful. This is the time to define simple Java programs. As the program contains many classes, we have to identify the class which has method `main()`. Program starts running with executing method `main()`. Let us coin a term "**program class**" for such a class.

Simple Java programs:

- Programs less than 100 lines
- Program must be in a single file
- User-defined classes or interfaces allowed
- No user-defined packages
- No inner classes

Special suggestions:

1. Every program in separate folder (directory)
2. Only one public class that is program class
3. Avoid static variables and methods
4. All user-defined classes either before or after program class.

Comments:

1. If you develop many programs in one folder, older programs start malfunctioning. It appears that your computer is infested by a virus. Worse, you may think of ghosts!
2. Language does not allow more than one public class in one file. There is no compulsion that program class must be declared public. But it is a good practice. When we develop applets, this discipline comes to our help.
3. Use interfaces for global constants. Use dummy classes for holding general methods. If we want general method `delay()`, use it as method of some user-defined class, say `MyTimer`. Reason for this guideline is very obvious. Once you start writing moderate size programs, you get lot of troubles with compilation errors. These types of errors occur because programmer tries to use his habits of global variables and methods from C++ programming to Java. At the middle stage, you should be a highly disciplined Java programmer.
4. Actually, location of the program class is a matter of choice. However, it should not be placed in the middle of other classes. The reader will have lot of trouble in understanding the program.

You may not appreciate the significance of these suggestions at this stage. But follow the guideline scrupulously. It will avoid many of the unnecessary hassles. It will make your programming experience, enjoyable.

8.18 End of Chapter Programs

8.18.1 Initializing an object is necessary

Problem: Write a program to show that initializing an object is necessary.

Solution: See Program 8.10.

PROGRAM 8.10 Initializing an Object is Necessary

```
//      time2,java
class time2
  { public static void main (String argv[])
    {  Time t1;
       System.out.println("<---time2.java--->");
//      t1 = new Time();
       System.out.println("hours are " +t1.hour);
    };
  }
class Time
  { int hour;
    int minute;
    int second ;
  };
```

If you try to compile, you will get the following error message.

Output

```
Compiling javac time2.java
time2.java:7: variable t1 might not have been initialized
System.out.println("hours are " +t1.hour);
^
1 error
press any key to continue
```

Do you think that there is any contradiction here? Earlier we have said that elements of the objects are initialized with zero value. The answer is that there is no contradiction here. Elements are initialized to zero values by a default constructor. The default constructor is invoked when we initialize the object. Add a statement which is commented out. Now the program will work well.

8.18.2 A non-static method can access private instance variables

Problem: Write a program to show that a non static method can access private instance variables. Use an example of complex number.

Solution: See Program 8.11.

PROGRAM 8.11 Introduction to Private

```
//    complex1.java
class Complex
     { private double x, y ;
       void show()
          { System.out.print(" Complex number: " );
            System.out.println(x +" +j "+ y);
          };
       void init()
          { x = 20;
            y = 30;
          };
     } ;
class complex1
{  public static void main(String arg[])
     {
       System.out.println("--->complex1.java starts<---");
       Complex a = new Complex();
       a.init();
       a.show();
     }
}
```

If you run the program, you will get the following output.

Output

```
--->complex1.java starts<---
Complex number: 20.0 +j 30.0
```

Please note that though we cannot modify x or y arbitrarily, we can see them easily with the help of method show().

8.18.3 Private variables are not accessible outside the class

Problem: Write a program to demonstrate that **private** variables are not accessible outside the class.

Solution: See Program 8.12.

PROGRAM 8.12 Private is Private

```
class time000
{  int hour;
   int minute;
   private int second ;
};

class time5A
{  public static void main (String argv[])
     { int total ;
       time000 t1= new time000() ;
       t1.hour = 5 ;
```

```
        t1.minute =30 ;
        t1.second = 0;
        total =t1.hour * 60 *60 + t1.minute*60 + t1.second ;
        System.out.println("---time5A.java---");
        System.out.println("Total seconds " + total);
    };
}
```

If you run the program, you will get the following error.

Error

```
time5A.java:13: Variable second in class time000 not accessible from class
time5A.
    t1.second = 0;
      ^
time5A.java:14: Variable second in class time000 not accessible from class
time5A.
    total =t1.hour * 60 *60 + t1.minute*60 + t1.second ;
                                                ^
2 errors
```

This is because of keyword `private` marked in bold. If you remove it, there will not be any problem.

8.18.4 Use of this keyword

Problem: Write a program to demonstrate use of keyword `this`.

Solution: See Program 8.13.

PROGRAM 8.13 Using this

```
//      this2.java
//  deliberate errors in prog
class AMOUNT
 { int rupee ;
   int paise ;
   AMOUNT (int rupee, int paise)
    { this.rupee = rupee; this.paise = paise; };
 }
class this2
 {  public static void main (String argv[])
      {  AMOUNT amt1 = new AMOUNT(30,0);
         System.out.println("Amount " );
         System.out.println("rupees = " + amt1.rupee + "
paise = " +amt1.paise);
      };
 }
```

If you run the program, you will get the following output.

Output

```
Amount
rupees = 30 paise = 0
```

The output is as expected. Replace the line marked in bold by removing keyword `this`, for example

```
rupee = rupee; paise = paise;
```

You will get unexpected (and of course unwanted) output.

And you will appreciate the power/necessity of `this`.

8.18.5 Keyword static not allowed for local variables

Problem: Write a program to show that keyword `static` not allowed for local variables.

Solution: See Program 8.14.

PROGRAM 8.14 Static with Local Variable

```
//      static3.java
class PLAYER
  { String name;
    String game;
  };
class static3
{  public static void main(String argv[])
    { PLAYER p1,p2,p3 ;
      /*static*/ int i ;
      p1 = new PLAYER();
      p1.name ="Anand" ;
      p1.game ="Chess" ;
      System.out.println("<---static3.java--->");
      System.out.println(p1.name + " plays " + p1.game );
    }
}
```

If you run the program, you will get the following output.

Output

```
<---static3.java--->
Anand plays Chess
```

So far so good. Everyone knows that Vishwanathan Anand is a world-class chess player. Notice the keyword `static`. It has been put inside a comment. Therefore, this program runs well.

If we include keyword `static` in the program, we will get following compilation errors. It shows that appearance of keyword `static` has put compiler in confused state.

Error

```
Compiling \java\bin\javac static3.java
static3.java:8: '}' expected.
     { PLAYER p1,p2,p3 ;
                       ^
static3.java:9: Statement expected.
          static int i ;
          ^
static3.java:10: Identifier expected.
          p1 = new PLAYER();
          ^
3 errors
```

8.18.6 Class Point

Let us define a class `Point`. It will have fields x and y representing the rectangular coordinates. We will have a constructor with two parameters. Earlier we have seen method `atan2` from class `Math`. We will use it in method `showPolar()` to represent the point in polar form.

Problem: Write a program to demonstrate a constructor with parameters.

Solution: See Program 8.15.

PROGRAM 8.15 Constructor with Parameters

```
//      pt2.java
class pt2
{
  public static void main(String args[])
    {   point p1 ;
        double pi_by_4= Math.PI / 4.0;
        System.out.println("<---pt2.java--->");
        p1 = new point(2,2);
        p1.show();
        System.out.println("pi_by_4 is : " + pi_by_4);
        p1.showPolar();
    }
}
class point
   {  double x,y ;
      point(double a, double b)
           { x=a;y=b;}
      public void show()
          { System.out.println("point is "+x+" , " +y);
          }
       public void showPolar()
          { double mag,angle;
            mag = Math.sqrt(x*x +y*y) ;
            angle = Math.atan2(x,y);
```

```
            System.out.println("Polar representation \n is "
                                  +mag + " /_ " + angle);
        }
    };
```

If you run this program, you will get the following output.

Output

```
<---pt2.java--->
point is 2.0 , 2.0
pi_by_4 is : 0.7853981633974483
Polar representation
Is 2.8284271247461903 /_ 0.7853981633974483
```

We tested this program with data 2.0. A normal program would have failed. But `atan2` is written so carefully that it does not produce runtime error.

Keywords

access control parameters, access specifiers, class, class method, class variables, constructor, constructor with parameters, default constructor, `finalize()`, garbage collection, instance variables, instantiation, method, method overloading, method with parameters, object declaring, overloading method, overloading constructor, pass by reference, private, protected, public, signature of a method, `static`, static methods, static variable, this

RuleBook

constructor	Constructors do not have a return type.
constructor	Name of the constructor is same as that of the class.
constructor	Constructors can be overloaded.
default constructor	If class definition does not contain a constructor, the compiler provides a default constructor which initializes all data members to null values.
overloading	Methods with a given name in a class can have different signatures. Such methods are said to be overloaded.
overloading	A method in a class cannot have two declarations with the same signature, even if return types are different.
static for local variables	Keyword `static` not allowed for local variables of any method.
static method	A static method cannot make a reference to non-static variables of a class.
static variable	A static variable indicates that there is only one copy of that variable.
`Main()`	`Main()` is a class method, not an object method.
constructor	A class constructor may have public or protected keyword before them, nothing else.
constructor	Constructor is a method used to initialize the instance variable of a class.
`finalize()`	Method `finalize()` is called before an unused object is recycled.

initialization of class variable	JVM automatically initializes every numeric instance of class variable.
return statement	If return type of a method is void, return statement is optional. For any other return type, it is compulsory.
static method	When a method is made static, it cannot use keywords `this` or `super`.

C++ Corner

C++ programmers please note that basic concept of default constructor in C++ and Java is same. The only difference is that when the default constructor is supplied by the system, it does not initialize the variables in a C++ program.

Local variables of methods could be static in C++. They retain their values after invocation of the method. This concept is not supported in Java. Keyword `static` cannot be applied to local variables.

Review Questions

1. What is a class? How does it accomplish data hiding? What is the need of a constructor?
2. What does the `static` keyword mean in front of a variable, a method, and a class?
3. Can all methods of a class be private?
4. What is the use of keyword `static` in case of a variable and in case of a method?
5. What are factory classes?
6. Write a short note on overloading of methods.
7. Write a short note on constructors.
8. Write a short note on access specifiers.

Exercises

Define suitable instance variables on your own and develop specified methods for following classes:

1. rational number—`display(), add()`
2. amount—`display(), add()`
3. point—`distance_from_origin()`
4. circle—`area(), perimeter()`
5. book—`show_name(), show_price()`

WRAPPER CLASSES

When we give gifts, we wrap them nicely in a box. The gift may be a doll or a toy car or something else. The box and the glossy paper around it make it attractive. We have worked with simple data types. Now Java wants to wrap them and make them more attractive (useful). For this, Java provides an interesting concept of wrapper classes.

9.1 Introduction

We have studied the basic data type `float`. It holds floating-point number. Now Java provides a class `Float`. As identifiers are case sensitive, `Float` and `float` are different. The new class **`Float`** is for storing floating-point values only. But it is a class, a wrapper class.

Similarly, a bare number of type `int` is wrapped nicely in a class `Integer`. We know that classes have methods. So this class has many methods that work with this class.

The class `Float` is an extension of an abstract class number. The other wrapper classes which are subclass of this number class are `Byte`, `Short`, `Integer`, `Long`, and `Double`.

Let us divide wrapper classes into groups:

Group I	`Byte`, `Short`, `Integer`, and `Long`
Group II	`Float` and `Double`
Group III	`Boolean` and `Char`

You may wonder what the necessity of such classes is. The one possible answer is that the language can give all of them uniform look and feel. At a later stage, you will find out that a given method working on class `Byte` works with similar meaning on `Long`. In a way you as a programmer have to remember less details. Another point is that as these numbers are stored as objects, they can take all the advantage of Object technology. They can be passed to methods as parameters.

Let us start our study with class `Byte`.

9.2 Class `Byte`

The first thing we should study about any class is its constructor. This class provides the following two constructors:

`Byte (byte b1)`

`Byte (string str1)` throws number format exception.

In the first constructor, we pass an existing `byte` variable (or constant) as the parameter. In the second one, we pass a `string` literal representing the `byte` value as the parameter. Naturally, the `string` may or may not represent a `byte`. Therefore, this constructor may throw an exception. We will discuss about exceptions at a later stage.

Let us write a program to study these constructors.

Problem: Write a program to demonstrate overloaded constructors for class `Byte`.

Solution: See Program 9.1.

PROGRAM 9.1 Class Byte

```
//      wp1.java
import java.io.* ;
class wp1
{ public static void main(String[] args)
     {
          System.out.println("<---wp1.java--->");
          byte b1 = 10 ;
          Byte b2 = new Byte( b1 );
          System.out.println("1 )  " + b2); // note1
          String st1 = b2.toString() ;
          System.out.println("2 )  " + st1);
          String st2 = new String("100");
          Byte b3 = new Byte(st2);
          System.out.println("3 )  " + b3);
     }
}
```

If you run this program, you will get the following output.

Output

```
<---wp1.java--->
1 ) 10
2 ) 10
3 ) 100
```

Note: Please note that `println` method could print the `Byte` without any difficulty.

At a later stage, we will study that the `println` method actually prints a `string` formed by a method tostring() in case of objects.

This program also illustrates constructing `Byte` object with

1. `byte value` and
2. `string`

Table 9.1 describes the various methods from class `Byte`. Other classes like `Short`, `Integer`, and `Long` have methods with same name and meaning.

Table 9.1 **Method Summary: Class Byte**

Byte	byteValue()	Returns the value of this Byte as a byte
Int	compareTo(Byte anotherByte)	Compares two Byte objects numerically
static Byte	decode(String nm)	Decodes a string into a Byte
double	doubleValue()	Returns the value of this Byte as a double
boolean	equals(Object obj)	Compares this object to the specified object
Float	floatValue()	Returns the value of this Byte as a float
Int	hashCode()	Returns a hash code for this Byte
int	intValue()	Returns the value of this Byte as an int
long	longValue()	Returns the value of this Byte as a long
Static byte	parseByte(String s)	Parses the string argument as a signed decimal byte
Static byte	parseByte(String s, int radix)	Parses the string argument as a signed byte in the radix specified by the second argument
short	shortValue()	Returns the value of this Byte as a short
String	toString()	Returns a string object representing this Byte's value
static String	toString(byte b)	Returns a new string object representing the specified byte
static Byte	valueOf(byte b)	Returns a Byte instance representing the specified byte value
static Byte	valueOf(String s)	Returns a Byte object holding the value given by the specified string
static Byte	valueOf(String s, int radix)	Returns a Byte object holding the value extracted from the specified string when parsed with the radix given by the second argument

Let us write a program to study some of the methods given in Table 9.1 in action.

Problem: Write a program to demonstrate method `byteValue()`.

Solution: In this case, we will take three wrapper classes `Byte`, `Integer`, and `Long`. Then we will apply method `byteValue()` to all these wrappers and print the value returned (see Program 9.2).

PROGRAM 9.2 Methods in Class `Byte` I

```
//       byte1.java
import java.io.* ;
class byte1
      { public static void main(String[] args) throws IOException
      { int k;
        Byte by1 = new Byte( (byte) 100 ); //Note 1
        Integer in1= new Integer( 101 );
        Long lg1 = new Long( 256*256+102);

        System.out.println("<---byte1.java--->");
        System.out.println( by1.byteValue() );
        System.out.println( in1.byteValue() );
        System.out.println( lg1.byteValue()) ;
     }
}
```

Note: When we use constant "100", it is treated as of type `integer`. Constructor for class `Byte` expects a value of type `byte`. Hence, we have to convert 100 by using typecast.

If you run this program, you will get the following output.

Output

```
<---byte1.java--->
100
101
102
```

Can you decipher the result? Why the `byteValue` of the `lg1` is 102? The variable of type `long` is 8 bytes long. When we say `byteValue`, it returns what is stored in the last byte. We have deliberately designed the value of `lg1` as 256 * 256 + 102. It ensures that last byte contains only 102. Try the program with `lg1` value as 257(= 256 + 1).

Let us see method `compareTo()` in action when parameter is of type `byte`.

Problem: Write a program to demonstrate use of method `compareTo( )` for class `Byte`.

Solution: See Program 9.3.

PROGRAM 9.3 Method `CompareTo( )`

```
//     wp3.java
import java.io.* ;
class wp3
      { public static void main(String[] args) throws IOException
          { int i,k;
            Byte BX = new Byte( "100" );
            Byte[] by = new Byte[3] ;
```

```
            by[0] = new Byte( "90" );
            by[1] = new Byte( "100" );
            by[2] = new Byte( "110" );

            System.out.println("<---wp3.java--->");

            for(i=0;i<3;i++)
              { System.out.print( "BX as compared to by[" +i+ "] is ");
                k= BX.compareTo( by[i] );
                if (k < 0) System.out.println("less");
                if (k ==0) System.out.println("equal");
                if (k > 0) System.out.println("more");
            }
        }
}
```

If we run the program, we will get the following output.

Output

```
<---wp3.java---> .
BX as compared to by[0] is more
BX as compared to by[1] is equal
BX as compared to by[2] is less
```

After discussing class `Byte` in detail, we need not discuss `Short`, `Integer`, and `Long` class. They will essentially behave in same way as that of class `Byte`. That is why Java defines wrapper classes. All these types are integer in nature. The classes `Float` and `Double` will also behave similarly. But there will be some differences. Hence, let us briefly discuss wrapper class `Float`.

9.3 Float

The wrapper class float will have the following three constructors:

- `Float(double value)`
- `Float(float value)`
- `Float(String s)`

Let us describe the third constructor first. If you pass a string which represents a `float` value, it will be converted as value of class `float`. The second constructor will take a `float` argument. That is also natural. The first constructor will accept a double argument. This is somewhat difficult to digest. A double value may not always get converted to `float` without loss of data. The apparent reason for this constructor is that when you want to supply a `float` value as literal, you may forget to put f at the end. You may say 2.5 and that will be a double value. It will lead to a compilation error. To avoid this unpleasantness, a constructor with double argument may have been provided.

The class `Float` supports two constants namely “MAX_VALUE” and “MIN_VALUE”. They tell us the value of largest positive number and the value of smallest positive number that can be stored in type `Float`. Let us find these values with the help of a program.

Problem: Write a program to illustrate wrapper class `Float`.

Solution: In this program, we will print the values of the constants discussed before. Additionally, we will show all the three constructors in action (see Program 9.4).

PROGRAM 9.4 Class `Float`

```
//      float1.java
import java.io.* ;
class float1
 { public static void main(String[] args)
     { Float f1 = new Float( 2.5);
       Float f2 = new Float( 2.6f);
       Float f3 = new Float( "2.7");
       System.out.println("<---float1.java--->");
       System.out.println(" f1 = " + f1);
       System.out.println(" f2 = " + f2);
       System.out.println(" f3 = " + f3);

       System.out.println( "Max value = " + Float.MAX_VALUE );
       System.out.println( "Min value = " + Float.MIN_VALUE );
     }
 }
```

If you run the program, you will get the following output.

Output

```
<---float1.java--->
f1 = 2.5
f2 = 2.6
f3 = 2.7
Max value = 3.4028235E38
Min value = 1.4E-45
```

At the end of the chapter, we have given a table summarizing important methods of class `Float`. Compare it with methods of class `Byte` and find out the similarities and differences between the two.

9.4 Boolean

Wrapper class `Boolean` stores a boolean value. It has very similar behaviour to other wrapper classes. There are two constructors available:

`Boolean ( boolean_value);` and
`Boolean ( boolean_string );`

Problem: Write a program to illustrate wrapper class `Boolean`.

Solution: See Program 9.5.

PROGRAM 9.5 Wrapper Class `Boolean`

```
//      BOOL1.java
class BOOL1
{ public static void main (String args [] )
      { Boolean flagA = new Boolean("true");
        Boolean flagB = new Boolean(false);
```

```
        System.out.println("--->BOOL1.java starts<---");
        System.out.println("1) " + flagA);
        System.out.println("2) " + flagB.toString()) ;
        System.out.println("3) " + String.valueOf(flagA) );

        if ( flagA.equals(flagB) )
                    System.out.println("4)" + " are equal");
            else    System.out.println("4)" + " not Equal");
    }
}
```

If you run the program, you will get the following output.

Output

```
--->BOOL1.java starts<---
1) true
2) false
3) true
4) not Equal
```

9.5 Character

Wrapper class `Character` stores a character value. It has very similar behaviour to other wrapper classes.

There is only one constructor available for this class.

For example, `Character( char ch);`

This constructor creates an object and initializes it to value specified by parameter `ch`.

The class contains a method **`charValue()`** which returns **`char`** value of the character contained in the object.

This class contains many static methods. It is interesting to note that most of these methods work on parameter which is simple **`char`** type variable (instead of object of type `Character`).

Table 9.2 illustrates methods defined in class `Character`.

Table 9.2 Methods from Class `Character`

`Char`	**`charValue()`**: Returns the value of this character object
`Int`	`compareTo(Character another Character)`: Compares two characters numerically
`int`	**`compareTo(Object o)`**: Compares this character to another object
`static int`	**`digit(char ch, int radix)`**: Returns the numeric value of the character `ch` in the specified radix
`boolean`	**`equals(Object obj)`**: Compares this object against the specified object
`static char`	**`forDigit(int digit, int radix)`**: Determines the character representation for a specific digit in the specified radix

(Continued)

Table 9.2 *(Continued)*

`static int`	**`getNumericValue(char ch)`**: Returns the Unicode numeric value of the character as a non-negative integer
`static int`	**`getType(char ch)`**: Returns a value indicating a character category
`int`	**`hashCode()`**: Returns a hash code for this character
`static boolean`	`isDefined(char ch)`: Determines if a character has a defined meaning in Unicode
`static boolean`	**`isDigit(char ch)`**: Determines if the specified character is a digit
`static boolean`	**`isIdentifierIgnorable(char ch)`**: Determines if the specified character should be regarded as an ignorable character in a Java identifier or a Unicode identifier
`static boolean`	**`isISOControl(char ch)`**: Determines if the specified character is an ISO control character
`static boolean`	**`isJavaIdentifierPart(char ch)`**: Determines if the specified character may be part of a Java identifier as other than the first character
`static boolean`	**`isJavaIdentifierStart(char ch)`**: Determines if the specified character is permissible as the first character in a Java identifier
`static boolean`	**`isLetter(char ch)`**: Determines if the specified character is a letter
`static boolean`	**`isLetterOrDigit(char ch)`**: Determines if the specified character is a letter or digit
`static boolean`	**`isLowerCase(char ch)`**: Determines if the specified character is a lowercase character
`static boolean`	**`isSpaceChar(char ch)`**: Determines if the specified character is a Unicode space character
`static boolean`	**`isTitleCase(char ch)`**: Determines if the specified character is a titlecase character
`static boolean`	**`isUnicodeIdentifierPart(char ch)`**: Determines if the specified character may be part of a Unicode identifier as other than the first character
`static boolean`	**`isUnicodeIdentifierStart(char ch)`**: Determines if the specified character is permissible as the first character in a Unicode identifier
`static boolean`	**`isUpperCase(char ch)`**: Determines if the specified character is an uppercase character
`static boolean`	**`isWhitespace(char ch)`**: Determines if the specified character is white space according to Java

(Continued)

Table 9.2 (*Continued*)

static char	**toLowerCase(char ch)** : The given character is mapped to its lowercase equivalent; if the character has no lowercase equivalent, the character itself is returned
String	**toString()** : Returns a String object representing this character's value
static char	**toTitleCase(char ch)** : Converts the character argument to titlecase
static char	**toUpperCase(char ch)** : Converts the character argument to uppercase
Following Methods have been deprecated.	
**static boolean	**isJavaLetter(char ch)** : Replaced by isJavaIdentifierStart (char)
**static boolean	**isJavaLetterOrDigit(char ch)** : Replaced by isJavaIdentif ierPart(char)
**static boolean	**isSpace(char ch)** : Replaced by isWhitespace(char)

It can be seen from Table 9.2 that it is possible to identify a type of a given character.

Problem: Write a program to study various methods from class Character to decide the type of a given character.

Solution: For all the characters, we can test whether they belong to any of the following type:

- White space
- Digit
- Letter
- Control character
- Java identifier start

It may be noted that some characters will belong to more than one type. We know that control characters like return and form feed interfere with the output. Hence, we have replaced all control characters by capital X (see Program 9.6).

PROGRAM 9.6 Testing Characters

```
//     char6.java
class char6
{ public static void main(String args[])
     { int i=0;
       char ch ;
       System.out.println("<---char6.java--->");

       for(i=0;i<256;i++)
            { ch = (char) i ;
               if ( Character.isISOControl(ch) ) ch = 'X';
               System.out.print(i + " ) " + ch + " : ");
```

```
            if (Character.isWhitespace(ch) )
                        System.out.print(" white ");
                else  System.out.print(" ..... ");
            if (Character.isDigit(ch) )
                        System.out.print( " digit ");
                else System.out.print( " ..... ");
        if ( Character.isLetter(ch) )
                        System.out.print( " Letter ");
                else System.out.print( " ...... ");
        if (Character.isJavaIdentifierStart(ch) )
                        System.out.print( " Start ");
                else System.out.print( " ..... ");
        if (Character.isJavaIdentifierPart(ch) )
                        System.out.print( " Part ");
                else System.out.print( " .... ");
        if ( Character.isISOControl(ch) )
                        System.out.print( " control ");
                else System.out.print( " ....... ");
            System.out.print( " Type = " + Character.getType(ch) );
            System.out.println();
          }
    }
}
```

When we run the program, we see only last few lines. Therefore, we have captured the output in a file. Since file is very long (256 lines), we have retained only selected lines.

Output

```
<---char6.java--->
0 ) X : ..... ..... Letter Start Part ....... Type = 1
1 ) X : ..... ..... Letter Start Part ....... Type = 1
31 ) X : ..... ..... Letter Start Part ....... Type = 1
32 )   : white ..... ...... ..... .... ....... Type = 12
33 ) ! : ..... ..... ...... ..... .... ....... Type = 24
34 ) " : ..... ..... ...... ..... .... ....... Type = 24
35 ) # : ..... ..... ...... ..... .... ....... Type = 24
36 ) $ : ..... ..... ...... Start Part ....... Type = 26
37 ) % : ..... ..... ...... ..... .... ....... Type = 24
38 ) & : ..... ..... ...... ..... .... ....... Type = 24
39 ) ' : ..... ..... ...... ..... .... ....... Type = 24
40 ) ( : ..... ..... ...... ..... .... ....... Type = 21
41 ) ) : ..... ..... ...... ..... .... ....... Type = 22
42 ) * : ..... ..... ...... ..... .... ....... Type = 24
43 ) + : ..... ..... ...... ..... .... ....... Type = 25
44 ) , : ..... ..... ...... ..... .... ....... Type = 24
45 ) - : ..... ..... ...... ..... .... ....... Type = 20
46 ) . : ..... ..... ...... ..... .... ....... Type = 24
47 ) / : ..... ..... ...... ..... .... ....... Type = 24
48 ) 0 : ..... digit ...... ..... Part ....... Type = 9
```

```
57 ) 9 : ..... digit ...... ..... Part ....... Type = 9
58 ) : : ..... ..... ...... ..... .... ....... Type = 24
59 ) ; : ..... ..... ...... ..... .... ....... Type = 24
60 ) < : ..... ..... ...... ..... .... ....... Type = 25
61 ) = : ..... ..... ...... ..... .... ....... Type = 25
62 ) > : ..... ..... ...... ..... .... ....... Type = 25
63 ) ? : ..... ..... ...... ..... .... ....... Type = 24
64 ) @ : ..... ..... ...... ..... .... ....... Type = 24
65 ) A : ..... ..... Letter Start Part ....... Type = 1
90 ) Z : ..... ..... Letter Start Part ....... Type = 1
91 ) [ : ..... ..... ...... ..... .... ....... Type = 21
92 ) \ : ..... ..... ...... ..... .... ....... Type = 24
93 ) ] : ..... ..... ...... ..... .... ....... Type = 22
94 ) ^ : ..... ..... ...... ..... .... ....... Type = 27
95 ) _ : ..... ..... ...... Start Part ....... Type = 23
96 ) ` : ..... ..... ...... ..... .... ....... Type = 27
97 ) a : ..... ..... Letter Start Part ....... Type = 2
122 ) z : ..... ..... Letter Start Part ....... Type = 2
123 ) { : ..... ..... ...... ..... .... ....... Type = 21
124 ) | : ..... ..... ...... ..... .... ....... Type = 25
125 ) } : ..... ..... ...... ..... .... ....... Type = 22
126 ) ~ : ..... ..... ...... ..... .... ....... Type = 25
127 ) X : ..... ..... Letter Start Part ....... Type = 1
128 ) X : ..... ..... Letter Start Part ....... Type = 1
129 ) X : ..... ..... Letter Start Part ....... Type = 1
159 ) X : ..... ..... Letter Start Part ....... Type = 1
160 )   : ..... ..... ...... ..... .... ....... Type = 12
161 ) ! : ..... ..... ...... ..... .... ....... Type = 24
162 ) ¢ : ..... ..... ...... Start Part ....... Type = 26
163 ) £ : ..... ..... ...... Start Part ....... Type = 26
164 ) □ : ..... ..... ...... Start Part ....... Type = 26
165 ) ¥ : ..... ..... ...... Start Part ....... Type = 26
166 ) ¦ : ..... ..... ...... ..... .... ....... Type = 28
167 ) § : ..... ..... ...... ..... .... ....... Type = 28
168 ) ¨ : ..... ..... ...... ..... .... ....... Type = 27
169 ) © : ..... ..... ...... ..... .... ....... Type = 28
170 ) ª : ..... ..... Letter Start Part ....... Type = 2
171 ) « : ..... ..... ...... ..... .... ....... Type = 29
172 ) ¬ : ..... ..... ...... ..... .... ....... Type = 25
173 ) – : ..... ..... ...... ..... .... ....... Type = 20
174 ) ® : ..... ..... ...... ..... .... ....... Type = 28
175 ) ¯ : ..... ..... ...... ..... .... ....... Type = 27
176 ) ° : ..... ..... ...... ..... .... ....... Type = 28
177 ) ± : ..... ..... ...... ..... .... ....... Type = 25
178 ) ² : ..... ..... ...... ..... .... ....... Type = 11
179 ) ³ : ..... ..... ...... ..... .... ....... Type = 11
180 ) ´ : ..... ..... ...... ..... .... ....... Type = 27
181 ) µ : ..... ..... Letter Start Part ....... Type = 2
182 ) ¶   ..... ..... ...... ..... .... ....... Type = 28
183 ) · : ..... ..... ...... ..... .... ....... Type = 24
184 ) ¸ : ..... ..... ...... ..... .... ....... Type = 27
```

```
185 ) ¹ : ..... ..... ...... ..... .... ....... Type = 11
186 ) º : ..... ..... Letter Start Part ....... Type = 2
187 ) » : ..... ..... ...... ..... .... ....... Type = 30
188 ) ¼ : ..... ..... ...... ..... .... ....... Type = 11
189 ) ½ : ..... ..... ...... ..... .... ....... Type = 11
190 ) ¾ : ..... ..... ...... ..... .... ....... Type = 11
191 ) ¿ : ..... ..... ...... ..... .... ....... Type = 24
192 ) À : ..... ..... Letter Start Part ....... Type = 1
214 ) Ö : ..... ..... Letter Start Part ....... Type = 1
215 ) × : ..... ..... ...... ..... .... ....... Type = 25
216 ) Ø : ..... ..... Letter Start Part ....... Type = 1
217 ) Ù : ..... ..... Letter Start Part ....... Type = 1
218 ) Ú : ..... ..... Letter Start Part ....... Type = 1
219 ) Û : ..... ..... Letter Start Part ....... Type = 1
220 ) Ü : ..... ..... Letter Start Part ....... Type = 1
221 ) Ý : ..... ..... Letter Start Part ....... Type = 1
222 ) Þ : ..... ..... Letter Start Part ....... Type = 1
223 ) ß : ..... ..... Letter Start Part ....... Type = 2
246 ) ö : ..... ..... Letter Start Part ....... Type = 2
247 ) ÷ : ..... ..... ...... ..... .... ....... Type = 25
248 ) ø : ..... ..... Letter Start Part ....... Type = 2
255 ) ÿ : ..... ..... Letter Start Part ....... Type = 2
```

We have not discussed type values in the text. Interested readers can study it on their own.

9.6 Autoboxing and Unboxing Principle

From version 5, Java introduced these new principles of autoboxing and unboxing for working with wrapper classes. Consider a case where we have a method say `half` which needs class `Integer` as parameter. As Java is a strict language, we cannot pass an `int` value as a parameter in place of wrapper class object `Integer`. Earlier versions resulted in compilation error. Now it will not. Now when you pass an `int`, it will be nicely wrapped (boxed) into an `Integer`. This is what autoboxing means.

Similarly, when we expect say `float` as a parameter, and we pass an object of type `Float`, the compiler will convert object `Float` into value `float` for you. This is called unboxing. Let us study these principles with a program.

Problem: Write a program to study principle of autoboxing and unboxing.

Solution: We will develop a method `half` with `Integer` as a parameter. We will pass an integer variable as a parameter and see the result. We will develop method triple with `float` as a parameter and pass object of class `Float` as a parameter (see Program 9.7).

PROGRAM 9.7 Autoboxing and Unboxing I

```
//     box2.java
import java.io.* ;
class box2
 { static void print_half(Integer I)
     { int temp = I.intValue();
```

```
            temp=temp/2;
            System.out.println(temp);
          }
      static void print_triple(float f )
          { float temp = f *3 ;
            System.out.println(temp);
          }
      public static void main(String[] args)
          { int i1 =100;
            Float Fl = new Float( 0.5);
            System.out.println("<---box2.java--->");
//               Example of Autoboxing
            print_half(i1);
//            Example of UnBoxing
            print_triple(Fl);
          }
}
```

If you run the program, you will get the following output.

Output

```
<---box2.java--->
50
1.5
```

Let us see another example. We will have both these actions in one expression.

Problem: Write a program to study principle of autoboxing and unboxing.

Solution: We will develop a program where both the principle will be in one expression.

PROGRAM 9.8 Autoboxing and Unboxing II

```
//    box3.java
class box3
      { public static void main(String[] args)
          { Integer K = new Integer( 7 );
            System.out.println("<---box3.java--->");

            K++ ;

            System.out.println( K.intValue() );
          }
}
```

If you run the program, you will get the following output.

Output

```
<---box3.java--->
8
```

Consider the expression K++. As K is a wrapper class it cannot have operation ++ associated with it. Therefore, Java first unboxes it to plain integer. Then this value is incremented. Now this value is again boxed. This is proved when we print the value of K next.

9.7 End of Chapter Programs

9.7.1 Java identifier start

Only specific characters can be the first characters of an identifier. Method `isJavaIdentifierStart()` helps us to decide whether a given character can fit this bill. Let us find few such characters with the help of a program.

Problem: Write a program to illustrate Java identifier start.

Solution: See Program 9.9.

PROGRAM 9.9 Java Identifier Start

```
//     char31.java
class char31
{ public static void main(String args[])
      { int count ;
        char ch ;
        char æçè = 'A' ;
        System.out.println("<---char31.java--->");

// start letter
              System.out.println("\n start letter");
        count = 0;
        for(ch=0;ch<255;ch++)
              if (Character.isJavaIdentifierStart(ch) )
                     { System.out.print( (int)ch + ") " + ch + ", " );
                       count++;
                       if ( ( count %8) == 0 )
                           System.out.println();
                     }
        System.out.println("\n total = "+ count);
      }
}
```

If you run the program, you will get the following output.

Output

```
<---char31.java--->

start letter
36) $, 65) A, 66) B, 67) C, 68) D, 69) E, 70) F, 71) G,
72) H, 73) I, 74) J, 75) K, 76) L, 77) M, 78) N, 79) O,
80) P, 81) Q, 82) R, 83) S, 84) T, 85) U, 86) V, 87) W,
```

```
 88) X,  89) Y,  90) Z, 95) _,   97) a,  98) b,  99) c, 100) d,
101) e, 102) f, 103) g, 104) h, 105) i, 106) j, 107) k, 108) l,
109) m, 110) n, 111) o, 112) p, 113) q, 114) r, 115) s, 116) t,
117) u, 118) v, 119) w, 120) x, 121) y, 122) z, 162) ó, 163) ú,
164) ñ, 165) Ñ, 170) ¬  181) ╡, 186) ║, 192) └, 193) ┴, 194) ┬,
195) ├, 196) ─, 197) ┼, 198) ╞, 199) ╟, 200) ╚, 201) ╔, 202) ╩,
203) ╦, 204) ╠, 205) ═, 206) ╬, 207) ╧, 208) ╨, 209) ╤, 210) ╥,
211) ╙, 212) ╘, 213) ╒, 214) ╓, 216) ╪, 217) ┘, 218) ┌, 219) █,
220) ▄, 221) ▌, 222) ▐, 223) ▀, 224) α, 225) ß, 226) Γ, 227) π,
228) Σ, 229) σ, 230) µ, 231) τ, 232) Φ, 233) Θ, 234) Ω, 235) δ,
236) ∞, 237) φ, 238) ε, 239) ∩, 240) ∩, 241) ±, 242) ≥,  243) ≤,
244) ⌠, 245) ⌡, 246) ÷, 248) °, 249) ∙, 250) ·, 251) √,  252) ⁿ,
253) ², 254) ■,
total = 122
```

Please note that the variable name **æçè** is permissible in Java. Out of first 255 characters, 122 can start a Java identifier. As Java supports Unicode, many more characters outside this range also qualify as Java identifier start. You can modify this program and test.

9.7.2 Method `valueOf()`

Now let us study method `valueOf()`. This method is present in many wrapper classes. It is capable of converting strings to a number. It is overridden to convert a number specified in any given radix. This method throws number format exception. Let us study it as offered by class `Integer`.

Problem: Write a program to demonstrate method `valueOf()` for class `Integer`.

Solution: See Program 9.10.

PROGRAM 9.10 Converting `Strings` to Number

```
//     wp4.java
import java.io.* ;
class wp4
    { public static void main(String[] args) throws IOException
        { int k;
            Integer i1= new Integer( 0 );
            Integer i2= new Integer( 0 );
            System.out.println("<---wp4.java--->");
            i1=Integer.valueOf("234",10);
            System.out.println( "234 base 10 " + i1.intValue() );
            i1=Integer.valueOf("234",8);
            System.out.println( "234 base 8 " + i1.intValue() );
            i1=Integer.valueOf("239",8);
            System.out.println( "239 base 8 " + i1.intValue() );
        }
    }
```

If we run the program, we will get the following output.

Output

```
<---wp4.java--->
234 base 10 234
234 base 8 156
Exception in thread "main" java.lang.NumberFormatException:
For input string: "239"
at java.lang.NumberFormatException.forInputString(Unknown Source)
at java.lang.Integer.parseInt(Unknown Source)
at java.lang.Integer.valueOf(Unknown Source)
at wp4.main(wp4.java:13)
```

Note: Error occurs because of digit 9 in 239. It is not a valid digit in base 8 system.

Table 9.3 illustrates useful methods from class `Float`.

Table 9.3 Summary of Methods from Class Float

`byte`	**`byteValue()`**: Returns the value of this `Float` as a `byte` (by casting to a `byte`)
`int`	**`compareTo(Float anotherFloat)`**: Compares two `Float`s numerically
`int`	**`compareTo(Object o)`**: Compares this `Float` to another object
`double`	`doubleValue()`: Returns the double value of this `Float` object
`boolean`	`equals(Object obj)`: Compares this object against some other object
`static int`	**`floatToIntBits(float value)`**: Returns the bit representation of a single-float value
`static int`	**`floatToRawIntBits(float value)`**: Returns the bit representation of a single-float value
`float`	**`floatValue()`**: Returns the `float` value of this `Float` object
`int`	**`hashCode()`**: Returns a hashcode for this `Float` object
`static float`	**`intBitsToFloat(int bits)`**: Returns the single-float corresponding to a given bit represention
`int`	**`intValue()`**: Returns the integer value of this `Float` (by casting to an `int`)
`boolean`	**`isInfinite()`**: Returns true if this `Float` value is infinitely large in magnitude
`static boolean`	**`isInfinite(float v)`**: Returns true if the specified number is infinitely large in magnitude
`boolean`	**`isNaN()`**: Returns true if this `Float` value is Not-a-Number (NaN)

(*Continued*)

Table 9.2 *(Continued)*

`static boolean`	**`isNaN(float v)`**: Returns true if the specified number is the special Not-a-Number (NaN) value
`long`	**`longValue()`**: Returns the long value of this `Float` (by casting to a `long`)
`static float`	**`parseFloat(String s)`**: Returns a new `float` initialized to the value represented by the specified string, as performed by the `valueOf` `method` of class `Double`
`short`	**`shortValue()`**: Returns the value of this `Float` as a short (by casting to a short)
`String`	**`toString()`**: Returns a string representation of this `Float` object
`static String`	**`toString(float f)`**: Returns a string representation for the specified `float` value
`static Float`	**`valueOf(String s)`**: Returns the floating-point value represented by the specified string

You can study methods from class `Double` and verify that those methods are nearly identical to these methods.

Some of the readers would still be unconvinced about the utility of wrapper classes. Java is a highly object-oriented language. At advanced level, we will study "generic programming" and collection framework. In these topics, we will be making full use of wrapper classes.

Keywords

autoboxing, `Boolean`, `Byte`, `Char`, `Character`, `Double`, `Float`, `Integer`, `isJavaIdentifierStart()`, `Long`, Number, `NumberFormatException`, radix, `Short`, unboxing, `valueOf`, wrapper class

RuleBook

`parseInt`	The method is used to convert string to an integer, assuming that the string represents an integer.

C++ Corner

The concept of wrapper classes is exclusive to Java. There is no equivalent concept in C/C++
C++ does not allow non-English letters as starting character for an identifier. Java allows many of them.

Review Questions

1. What are the advantages of wrapper classes?
2. Why static methods are provides in class `Character`?

3. Write a short note on wrapper classes.
4. Explain the terms autoboxing and unboxing.

Exercises

1. Find equivalent C++ methods for all the methods of class `Character`.
2. Write a program to list all the white space characters.
3. Write a program to find maximum and minimum values supported by type `double`.

STRINGS

Strings are inseparable part of computer programming. Hence, Java has provided an inbuilt class `String` to handle strings. In C/C++, strings are stored in array of characters terminated by null character. In Java, we need not worry about how it is implemented internally.

10.1 Introduction

Java has a class `String` defined in the package `java.lang.` We are given a rich set of methods to work with strings. Table 10.1 lists the important methods for our ready reference.

It may be noted that unlike C++, strings in Java are immutable. You can not modify any character from a string.

Normal operations with strings are

1. Declaring and constructing a string
2. Reading a string from a console
3. Writing a string to screen
4. Copying one string into other
5. Comparing two strings
6. Other operations

Let us study how these operations are handled in Java.

10.2 Declaring and Constructing a `String`

An object of class `String` is declared just like any other object declaration, for example

```
String s1;
```

Object cannot be used unless it is initialized (otherwise it will give error). To initialize objects, we have to use constructors. This class supports many constructors. Four important ways to construct a string are as follows:

A string can be initialized from another string (variable or literal).

```
String s1 = new String("Good Morning");
```

Another way is to use assignment operator.

```
String s2;
s2 = "Prof. Patekar";
```

The third way is by using a character array.

```
char [] box = {'B', 'h', 'a', 'v', 'e'};
String s3 = new String(box);
```

Finally, we can use a constructor without any parameters.

```
String s4 = new String( );
```

This creates an empty (null) string.

Let us study a program to see all these ways.

Problem: Write a program to study various constructors for class `String`.

Solution: See Program 10.1.

PROGRAM 10.1 Constructors for `String`

```
//   string12.java
class string12
{ public static void main(String args[])
     {   //..1
         String s1 = new String("Good Morning");
         //..2
         String s2;
         s2 = "Prof. " ;
         //..3
         char [] box = {'B','h','a','v','e'};
         String s3 = new String(box);
         //.. output
         System.out.println("--->string12.java<---");
         System.out.println(s1);
         System.out.print(s2);
         System.out.println(s3);
     }
}
```

If you run this program, you will get the following output.

Output

```
--->string12.java<---
Good Morning
Prof. Bhave
```

10.3 Reading a String

Reading a string from console is a bit cumbersome in Java. Reading anything is cumbersome for that matter. A program to read a string is present in Section 10.11. Let us postpone the discussion about reading for sometime. For the time being, we will use constructors or assignments in place of reading.

10.4 Writing a String

A simple statement

```
System.out.println(st1);
        OR
System.out.print(st1) ;
```

is capable of writing a string. Here the difference in print and println is that `println` adds a new-line character after printing the string.

10.5 Copying One String into Other

It is straightforward operation. Assignment operator = does the task.

For example, `st1 = st2;`

It is mentioned earlier that strings are immutable and cannot be modified. It is true. Hence, this case can be considered as an exception. We know that string is an object and variable names are actually object references. Hence, it is possible for a given reference to point to another string. Hence, we may conclude that a string can be replaced by another string.

10.6 Comparing Strings

Comparing strings can result in either `Boolean` or `integer` result. To compare two strings `st1` and `st2`, and to know whether they are equal or not, the following method may be used:

```
st1. equals st2);
```

The following can be used if we want it to ignore case of individual characters:

```
st1.equalsIgnoreCase (st2);
```

These methods give `Boolean` result which may be either true or false.

If we want applications like sorting strings, it is not sufficient to know about equality. We want to know if one string is less than, equal to, or greater than another string lexicographically. Here method `compareTo()` comes handy. An expression like

```
st1.compareTo (st2)
```

returns a negative, zero, or positive value.
Let us study this method with the help of a simple program (see Program 10.2)

PROGRAM 10.2 Comparing Strings III

```
//    string5.java
class string5
{    public static void main(String args[])
         {    int i,j,k;
              String st1 = "Bhave" ;
              String st2 = "Bhave" ;
              String st3 = "Chave";
```

```
            String st4 = "Ahave";
            System.out.println("<---string5 starts--->");
            i = st1.compareTo(st2);
            j = st1.compareTo(st3);
            k = st1.compareTo(st4);
            System.out.println("st1 is " + st1);
            System.out.println("st2 is " + st2);
            System.out.println("st3 is " + st3);
            System.out.println("st4 is " + st4);
            System.out.println("comparing st1 and st2, i is : " + i);
            System.out.println("comparing st1 and st3, j is : " + j);
            System.out.println("comparing st1 and st4, k is : " + k);
        }
}
```

If you run this program, you will get the following output.

Output

```
<---string5 starts--->
st1 is Bhave
st2 is Bhave
st3 is Chave
st4 is Ahave
comparing st1 and st2, i is : 0
comparing st1 and st3, j is : -1
comparing st1 and st4, k is : 1
```

Warning

Do not use comparator operators like ==, <, >= etc. on strings. They will not work. The reason is that they will give result based on the value of the reference (pointer) and not on the contents of the string. See Program 10.12 at the end of the chapter programs.

Table 10.1 illustrates various methods supported by the class `String`.

Table 10.1 Summary of Methods of Class String

Return type	Method	description
char	**charAt(int index)**	Returns the character at the specified index
int	**compareTo(Object o)**	Compares the given string to another object
int	**compareTo(String anotherString)**	Compares two strings lexicographically
int	**compareToIgnoreCase (String str)**	Compares two strings lexicographically, ignoring case considerations

(Continued)

Table 10.1 (*Continued*)

String	**concat(String str)**	Concatenates the specified string to the end of this string
static String	**copyValueOf(char[] data)**	Returns the string that is equivalent to the specified character array
static String	**copyValueOf(char[] data, int offset, int count)**	Returns the string that is equivalent to the specified character array
boolean	**endsWith(String suffix)**	Tests if the given string ends with the specified suffix
boolean	**equals(Object anObject)**	Compares the given string to a specified object
boolean	**equalsIgnoreCase (String anotherString)**	Compares the given string to another string, ignoring case considerations
byte[]	**getBytes()**	Converts the given string into bytes according to the platform's default character encoding and storing the result into a new byte array
byte[]	**getBytes(String enc)**	Converts the given string into bytes according to the specified character encoding and storing the result into a new byte array
void	**getChars(int srcBegin, int srcEnd, char[] dst, int dstBegin)**	Copies characters from the given string into the destination character array
int	**hashCode()**	Returns a hashcode for the given string
int	**indexOf(int ch)**	Returns the index within the given string at the first occurrence of the specified character
int	**indexOf(int ch, int fromIndex)**	Returns the index within the given string at the first occurrence of the specified character and starting the search at the specified index
int	**indexOf(String str)**	Returns the index within the given string at the first occurrence of the specified substring
int	**indexOf(String str, int fromIndex)**	Returns the index within this string of the first occurrence of the specified substring, starting at the specified index

(*Continued*)

Table 10.1 *(Continued)*

String	**intern()**	Returns a canonical representation for the string object
int	**lastIndexOf(int ch)**	Returns the index within the given string at the last occurrence of the specified character
int	**lastIndexOf(int ch, int fromIndex)**	Returns the index within the given string at the last occurrence of the specified character, starting backward search at the specified index
int	**lastIndexOf (String str)**	Returns the index within the string at the rightmost occurrence of the specified substring
int	**lastIndexOf(String str, int fromIndex)**	Returns the index within this string of the last occurrence of the specified substring
int	**length()**	Returns the length of the given string
String	**replace(char oldChar, char newChar)**	Returns a new string resulting from replacing all occurrences of **oldChar** in the given string with a **newChar**
boolean	**startsWith(String prefix)**	Tests if this string starts with the specified prefix
boolean	**startsWith(String prefix, int toffset)**	Tests if this string starts with the specified prefix beginning a specified index
String	**substring(int beginIndex)**	Returns a new string which is a substring of the given string
String	**substring(int beginIndex, int endIndex)**	Returns a new string which is a substring of this string
char[]	**toCharArray()**	Converts the given string to a new character array
String	**toLowerCase()**	Converts all of the characters in the given string to lower case using the rules of default locale which is returned by **Locale.getDefault**
String	**toString()**	This object (which is already a string) is itself returned
String	**toUpperCase()**	Converts all the characters in the given string to upper case using the rules of default locale which is returned by **Locale.getDefault**

(Continued)

Table 10.1 (*Continued*)

String	**toUpperCase (Locale locale)**	Converts all the characters in the given string to upper case using the rules of the given locale.
String	**trim()**	Removes white space from both ends of the given string
static String	**valueOf(boolean b)**	Returns the string representation of the Boolean argument
static String	**valueOf(char c)**	Returns the string representation of the char argument
static String	**valueOf(char[] data)**	Returns the string representation of the char array argument
static String	**valueOf(char[] data, int offset, int count)**	Returns the string representation of specific subarray of the char array argument
static String	**valueOf(double d)**	Returns the string representation of the double argument
static String	**valueOf(float f)**	Returns the string representation of the float argument
static String	**valueOf(int i)**	Returns the string representation of the int argument
static String	**valueOf(long l)**	Returns the string representation of the long argument
static String	**valueOf(Object obj)**	Returns the string representation of the object argument
	Less important	
String	**toLowerCase(Locale locale)**	Converts all of the characters in the given string to lower case using the rules of given Locale
boolean	**regionMatches(boolean ignoreCase, int toffset, String other, int ooffset, int len)**	Tests if the two string regions are equal
boolean	**regionMatches(int toffset, String other, int ooffset, int len)**	Tests if the two string regions are equal

If we want to know the size of the string, that is the number of characters in it, method `length()` can be used.

10.7 Other Operations on Strings

10.7.1 Testing for contents

Java allows various methods to peep into a given string. One of these methods is `charAt()`. It returns a character at the specified location. Many other languages treat string as an array. Hence, they do not need such a method. In Java, a string is an object of class `String`. Hence, such a method is essential.

If we are interested in finding a character or a substring, method `indexOf()` can be used. It returns the index of the character or a substring which is passed as a parameter. If such a thing is not found, it returns minus one.

Let us study it with a simple program.

Problem: Write a program to illustrate various methods used with `String` class.

Solution: See Program 10.3.

PROGRAM 10.3 Looking Inside a String

```
//    string8.java
class string8
{     public static void main(String args[])
          {   int i;
              char ch ;
              String st1 = "I love Java PROGRAMMING" ;
              String st3 ;
              String st4 ;
              System.out.println("<---string8 starts--->");
              ch = st1.charAt(2);
              System.out.println(
                  "character at index 2 is "+ch );
              i= st1.indexOf('o');
              System.out.println("char o is at index " + i);
              i= st1.indexOf("Java");
              System.out.println(
                  "substring Java is at index " + i);
          }
}
```

If you run this program, you will get the following output.

Output

```
<---string8 starts--->
character at index 2 is l
char o is at index 3
substring Java is at index 7
```

The output is as expected. So far we have not stated that these operations are case sensitive. Try modifying any case of any one character in Program 10.3 and check the result.

10.7.2 Changing the case

Java provides methods `toLowerCase()` and `toUppercase()` for changing case of all the characters in the string.

Problem: Write a program to illustrate methods `toLowerCase()` and `toUpperCase` ()used with **`String`** class.

Solution: See Program 10.4.

PROGRAM 10.4 Few More Methods

```
//    string6a.java
class string6a
{    public static void main(String args[])
         {    int i;
              char ch ;
              String st1 = "java" ;
              String st2 = "PROGRAMMING" ;
              String st3 ;
              String st4 ;
              System.out.println("<---string6a starts--->");
              st3 =st1.toUpperCase();
              st4 =st2.toLowerCase() ;
              System.out.println("st3 is " + st3);
              System.out.println("st4 is " + st4);
         }
}
```

If you run this program, you will get the following output.

Output

```
<---string6a starts--->
st3 is JAVA
st4 is programming
```

The output is self-explanatory.

10.7.3 Methods `valueOf()` and `toString()`

As for printing on paper or screen, we need string representation of any object. Java offers method `toString()` in class `Object`. (A detailed discussion of this class is present in later chapter.) This method is overridden in wrapper classes like `Integer` and `Double`. This method returns a string which represents the value of such classes. Just for uniformity, this method is defined in class `String` also. It returns the string itself.

For user-defined classes, user is supposed to write (rather overload) the aforementioned method for its class.

Just opposite to it, class `String` has a **static** method `valueOf()`. This method is overloaded for not only all basic simple types like `byte`, `int`, and `float`, but also for all corresponding wrapper classes like `Byte`, `Integer`, and `Float`. This method returns the string representation of the parameter. In a way, it is somewhat similar to method `toString()`. The name is quite misleading. The appropriate name could have been `StringValueOf()`. As this is a static method, it is called as `String.valueOf()`. Therefore, user automatically gets a feel of the fact.

Let us study a simple program to study these methods.

Problem: Write a program to illustrate various methods `toString()` and `valueOf()`.

Solution: See Program 10.5.

PROGRAM 10.5 valueOf and toString

```
//              string3b.java
import java.io.*;
class string3b
{     public static void main(String args[])
        throws IOException // note1
        {   String st1 , st2 , st3;
            System.out.println("--->string3b<---");
            // ...1
            Integer int1 = new Integer(17);
            st1 = int1.toString();
            System.out.println(st1);
            //...2
            float f1 = (float) 1.2;
            st2 = String.valueOf(f1);
            System.out.println(st2);
            //...3
            Double db1 = new Double(1.6);
            st3 = String.valueOf(db1);
            System.out.println(st3);
        }
}
```

If you run this program, you will get the following output.

Output

```
--->string3b<---
17
1.2
1.6
```

We have demonstrated following things in this program:

Example 1 illustrates the use of method `toString` with wrapper class `Integer`.

Example 2 illustrates the use of method `valueOf` with primitive class `Float`.

Example 3 illustrates use of method `valueOf` with wrapper class `Double`.

10.7.4 Concatenation of strings

In many applications, we have to join, that is concatenate, strings. Class `String` has a method `concat(String str)`. If we execute

```
str1.concat(str2) ;
```

it returns a new string which is constructed by appending `str2` to `str1`.

Java also supports "+" operation for adding strings.

```
str1+str2
```

The output received will represent a string which is a concatenation of `str1` and `str2`.

After this much study we are in a position to write a real-life application. We will sort strings.

10.8 Sorting Strings

Problem: Write a program to sort strings. Use keywords of Java as data.

Solution: We will use the standard bubble sort algorithm for this task (see Program 10.6).

PROGRAM 10.6 Sorting Strings

```
//   sortstr1.java
class sortstr1
{ static String box[]=
          {
          "case", "public", "int" , "continue", "while",
          "break", "void", "for", "double", "catch"",
          "super", "finally", "throws", "try", "private",
          "class", "if", "char", "this", "synchronized",
          "default", "protected", "long", "throw", "volatile",
          "switch", "const", "static", "return", "abstract",
          "else" , "boolean", "byte", "extends", "final",
          "implements", "import", "instanceof", "interface", "native",
          "package", "short", "strictfp", "transient", "new",
          "float", "do", "goto", "protected",
           } ;
      public static void main(String args[])
          {   String p;
              int i,j;
              sort(48);
              for (i=0;i<48;i++)
                  {   System.out.println( i + "]= " + box[i] );
                  }
          }
      static void sort(int n)
          {   int i, j;
              String k;
              for(i=0;i<n;i++)
              for(j=0;j<n-1;j++)
                  {   if  ( box[j].compareTo(box[j+1]) > 0 )
                          { // swap
                              k=box[j];
                              box[j]=box[j+1];
                              box[j+1]=k;
                          }
                  }
          };
};
```

If you run the program, you will get the following output.

Output

```
0]= abstract
1]= boolean
2]= break
3]= byte
4]= case
5]= catch
6]= char
7]= class
8]= const
9]= continue
10]= default
11]= do
12]= double
13]= else
14]= extends
15]= final
16]= finally
17]= float
18]= for
19]= goto
20]= if
21]= implements
22]= import
23]= instanceof
24]= int
25]= interface
26]= long
27]= native
28]= new
29]= package
30]= private
31]= protected
32]= public
33]= return
34]= short
35]= static
36]= strictfp
37]= super
38]= switch
39]= synchronized
40]= this
41]= throw
42]= throws
43]= transient
44]= try
45]= void
46]= volatile
47]= while
```

Please note that method swap is not used. Code for swapping is embedded directly inside the method sort. Comparing strings is done by using `compareTo()` method.

10.9 StringBuffer

String is a very useful class. But unfortunately, it is immutable. You cannot change a string. Consider a text-processing task. You have a sentence and you have to capitalize the first character and remove extra blanks. To do this, you have to use copy modify and replace for every task. Though memory is not a constraint these days, still this is unnecessary work. Can we modify a given string itself?

Yes, Java provided a new class `StringBuffer` for this. It is very similar to class `String`. But objects of this class are mutable.

At any point in time, it contains some particular sequence of characters, but the length and content can be changed through certain method calls.
There are following three different constructors available with class.

```
StringBuffer ()
StringBuffer (int size)
StringBuffer (String str1)
```

The first one creates a string buffer with default capacity of 16; second creates one with specified capacity; and the third creates an object by copying a given string.

Please note that every string buffer has a capacity. As long as the length of the character sequence contained in the string buffer does not exceed the capacity, it is not necessary to allocate a new internal buffer array. If the internal buffer overflows, it is automatically made larger.

The principal operations on a `StringBuffer` can be stated as follows:

- append
- insert
- reverse
- replace
- covert to string
- get substring
- convert to character array

Let us study them with some programs.

Problem: Write a program to illustrate insert operation on `StringBuffer`.

Solution: See Program 10.7.

PROGRAM 10.7 `StringBuffer` Insert Operation

```
//    strbuf3.java
class strbuf3
{ public static void main(String args[])
      {   System.out.println("<---strbuf3.java starts--->");
          StringBuffer st1 =
          new StringBuffer("1234567890123456789012345") ;
          System.out.println(" initial string");
          System.out.println(st1);
```

```
        System.out.println("after insertion");
        st1.insert(20,"At 20th col ");
        System.out.println(st1);
    }
}
```

If you run this program, you will get the following output.

Output

```
<---strbuf3.java starts--->
initial string
1234567890123456789012345
after insertion
12345678901234567890At 20th col 12345
```

Once when students were enrolled at NCST for a computer course, they were assigned login name as their own names. Reverse of the login name was used as the password. Reversing a string is an exercise in every computer programming text. But Java does not need any algorithm for it. `StringBuffer` provides a method `reverse()`, which reverses all the characters of the given `StringBuffer`.

In an advertisement endorsing an insurance company, a man stands on unsound platform saying "I DONT need Insurance". Unfortunately, the part of the platform falls off with the man. The caption on the broken platform reads "I need Insurance". For such a task, Java provides method `delete()`.

Let us study actions reverse and delete with a program.

Problem: Write a program to demonstrate operations **reverse** and **delete.**

Solution: See Program 10.8.

PROGRAM 10.8 More Operations on StringBuffer

```
//    strbuf4.java
class strbuf4
{ public static void main(String args[])
        {    System.out.println("<---strbuf4.java starts--->");
             StringBuffer st1 =
                 new StringBuffer("Bhave") ;
             System.out.print(" initial string is ->");
             System.out.println(st1);
             System.out.println("after reverse");
             st1.reverse();
             System.out.println(st1);
             StringBuffer st2 =
                 new StringBuffer("I DONT need Insurance") ;
             System.out.print(" initial string is ->");
             System.out.println(st2);
             System.out.println("after deleting");
             st2.delete(2,6);
             System.out.println(st2);
        }
}
```

If you run this program, you will get the following output.

Output

```
<---strbuf4.java starts--->
initial string is ->Bhave
after reverse
evahB
initial string is ->I DONT need Insurance
after deleting
I need Insurance
```

Please note that the syntax of delete. The parameters are start index and end index. One may mistake it for start index and number of characters.

Table 10.2 illustrates various methods from class `StringBuffer`.

Table 10.2 Method Summary: Class `StringBuffer`

`StringBuffer`	**append** `(boolean b)`	Appends the string representation of the Boolean argument to the sequence
`StringBuffer`	**append** `(char c)`	Appends the string representation of the `char` argument to the given sequence
`StringBuffer`	**append** `(char[] str)`	Appends the string representation of the `char` array argument to the given sequence
`StringBuffer`	**append** `(char[] str, int offset, int len)`	Appends the string representation of a subarray of the `char` array argument to the given sequence
`StringBuffer`	**append** `(CharSequence s)`	Appends the specified `Char Sequence` to the given sequence
`StringBuffer`	**append** `(CharSequence s, int start, int end)`	Appends a subsequence of the specified `CharSequence` to the given sequence
`StringBuffer`	**append** `(double d)`	Appends the string representation of the double argument to the given sequence
`StringBuffer`	**append** `(float f)`	Appends the string representation of the `float` argument to the given sequence
`StringBuffer`	**append** `(int i)`	Appends the string representation of the `int` argument to the given sequence
`StringBuffer`	**append** `(long lng)`	Appends the string representation of the `long` argument to the given sequence
`StringBuffer`	**append** (Object `obj`)	Appends the string representation of the `Object` argument

(Continued)

Table 10.2 (*Continued*)

StringBuffer	**append** (String str)	Appends the specified string to the given character sequence
StringBuffer	**append** (StringBuffer sb)	Appends the specified StringBuffer to the given sequence
StringBuffer	**appendCodePoint** (int codePoint)	Appends the string representation of the codePoint argument to the given sequence
int	**capacity** ()	Returns the current capacity
char	**charAt** (int index)	Returns the char value in the given sequence at the specified index
int	**codePointAt** (int index)	Returns the character (Unicode code point) at the specified index
int	**codePointBefore** (int index)	Returns the character (Unicode code point) before the specified index
int	**codePointCount** (int beginIndex, int endIndex)	Returns the number of Unicode code points in the specified text range of the given sequence
StringBuffer	**delete** (int start, int end)	Removes the characters in a substring of the given sequence
StringBuffer	**deleteCharAt** (int index)	Removes the char at the specified position in the given sequence
void	**ensureCapacity** (int minimumCapacity)	Ensures that the capacity is at least equal to the specified minimum
void	getChars (int srcBegin, int srcEnd, char[] dst, int dstBegin)	Characters are copied from the given sequence into the destination character array dst
int	**indexOf** (String str)	Returns the index within the given string of the first occurrence of the specified substring
int	**indexOf** (String str, int fromIndex)	Returns the index within the given string at the first occurrence of the specified substring, starting at the specified index
StringBuffer	**insert** (int offset, boolean b)	Inserts the string representation of the Boolean argument into the given sequence

(*Continued*)

Table 10.2 ***(Continued)***

StringBuffer	**insert** (int offset, char c)	Inserts the string representation of the char argument into the given sequence
StringBuffer	**insert** (int offset, char[] str)	Inserts the string representation of the char array argument into the given sequence
StringBuffer	**insert** (int index, char[] str, int offset, int len)	Inserts the string representation of a subarray of the str array argument into the given sequence
StringBuffer	**insert** (int dstOffset, CharSequence s)	Inserts the specified CharSequence into the given sequence
StringBuffer	**insert** (int dstOffset, CharSequence s, int start, int end)	Inserts a subsequence of the specified CharSequence into the given sequence
StringBuffer	**insert** (int offset, double d)	Inserts the string representation of the double argument into the given sequence
StringBuffer	**insert** (int offset, float f)	Inserts the string representation of the float argument into the given sequence
StringBuffer	**insert** (int offset, int i)	Inserts the string representation of the second int argument into the given sequence
StringBuffer	**insert** (int offset, long l)	Inserts the string representation of the long argument into the given sequence
StringBuffer	**insert** (int offset, Object obj)	Inserts the string representation of the object argument into the given character sequence
StringBuffer	**insert** (int offset, String str)	Inserts the string into the given character sequence
int	**lastIndexOf** (String str)	Returns the index within the given string of the rightmost occurrence of the specified substring
int	**lastIndexOf** (String str, int fromIndex)	Returns the index within the given string of the last occurrence of the specified substring
int	**length ()**	Returns the length (character count)

(Continued)

Table 10.2 (*Continued*)

int	**offsetByCodePoints** (int index, int codePointOffset)	Returns the index within the given sequence that is offset from the given index by codePointOffset code points
StringBuffer	**replace** (int start, int end, String str)	Replaces the characters in a substring of the given sequence with characters in the specified string
StringBuffer	**reverse** ()	Causes the given character sequence to be replaced by the reverse of the sequence
void	**setCharAt** (int index, char ch)	The character at the specified index is set to ch
void	**setLength** (int newLength)	Sets the length of the character sequence
CharSequence	**subSequence** (int start, int end)	Returns a new character sequence that is a subsequence of the given sequence
String	**substring** (int start)	Returns a new string that contains a subsequence of characters currently contained in the given character sequence
String	**substring** (int start, int end)	Returns a new string that contains a subsequence of characters currently contained in the given sequence
String	**toString ()**	Returns a string representing the data in the given sequence
void	**trimToSize ()**	Attempts to reduce storage used for the character sequence

Please note that just like class `String`, `method length()` also exists in `StringBuffer.`

10.9.1 How to modify strings using `StringBuffer`

`StringBuffer` can supply immutable strings. For any specific reason, we have to process and modify a given string; we may adopt the following procedure:

- Create (construct) a `StringBuffer` from the given string.
- Modify it.
- Use `toString()` method to convert it to a string.
- Replace the original string with this new string.

10.10 Class Vector

Array is the most powerful basic data structure in any programming language. It is a collection of similar items (objects or basic data elements). Its components can be accessed with the help of an integer known as index. However, it has some disadvantages also.

- Its size cannot grow or shrink
- Items cannot be inserted easily
- Items cannot be deleted easily

If you want to insert an item in between, all items after it are required to be moved. Same is the case for delete.

Now Java offers the class `Vector`, which implements a growable array of objects. It does not suffer from disadvantages of an array. Like an array, we can access its components using an integer index. The size of a vector can grow or shrink, as needed by the programmers. It is very easy to add or remove items after it has been created.

Another important difference between vector and array is that elements of the vector can only be objects. Ordinary data elements like `int`, `double`, and `char` cannot become elements of a vector.

A vector can be declared using following constructors:

- `Vector v1 = new Vector( ) ;`
- `Vector v2 = new Vector( 5 ) ;`

In the first case, a vector is generated with default capacity of 10 elements. In the second case, we are defining the capacity of the vector as 5.

It may be noted that this 10 or 5 is the initial (starting) capacity. It can grow or shrink as per our wish.

At this time, let us clarify the difference between the words **capacity** and **size.** The size of vector means the number of elements currently present in a Vector. The word capacity means the number of elements it can hold at this time with out going in for additional memory allocation.

When we define a vector, it will have capacity of 10 or as you have defined. But the size at that time will be zero.

Table 10.3 describes the useful basic operations (methods) on vector.

Table 10.3 Methods from Class `Vector`

Return type	Methods	Operation/Action
`void`	`add(int index, Object element)`	Adds an element at specified index
`void`	`addElement(Object obj)`	The object `obj` is added at the end of vector and capacity is automatically increased, if needed
`void`	`insertElementAt(Object obj, int index)`	Inserts object `obj` at a specified index
`int`	`capacity()`	Returns the current capacity of the given vector

(*Continued*)

Table 10.3 *(Continued)*

void	clear()	Clears all elements
void	copyInto(Object[] anArray)	Copies elements to an array
Object	elementAt(int index)	Returns the element at the specified index
Object	firstElement()	Returns the first element, that is item at index
Object	get(int index)	Returns the element at the specified position
void	insertElementAt(Object obj, int index)	Inserts the specified object as an element in the given vector at the specified index
boolean	isEmpty()	Checks if the vector is empty
Object	lastElement()	Returns the last element of the vector
void	removeElementAt(int index)	Deletes the element at the specified index
void	setSize(int newSize)	Sets the size of the given vector
int	size()	Returns the number of elements in the given vector
Object[]	toArray()	Returns an array containing all of the elements in the given vector in correct order
String	toString()	Returns the string representation of a given vector, containing the string representation of each element

Let us study a simple program.

Problem: Write a program to introduce class `Vector`.

Solution: First, we will declare a vector with capacity three. Then we will add three elements. This makes it full. Now, we will add few more elements (see Program 10.9).

PROGRAM 10.9 Class Vector

```
//    vec2.java
import java.util.*;
class vec2
{
        public static void main(String argv[])
        {       int i;
```

```
        int A[] = { 7, 4, 1, 9, 5};
        Vector vect1 = new Vector(3);
        System.out.println("<---Vec2.java starts--->");
        System.out.println("1) Size of Vector = " + vect1.size() );
        System.out.println("2) Capacity of Vector = " + vect1.capacity() );
        System.out.println("3) Now adding elements ");
        for(i=0;i<3;i++)
            {   vect1.addElement( new Integer(A[i]) ) ; }
        System.out.println("4)Printing vector ");
        for(i=0;i<3;i++)
                {   System.out.print( vect1.elementAt(i) + "\t") ;
                }
        System.out.println();
        System.out.println("5) adding More elements ");

        vect1.insertElementAt(new Integer(A[3]) , 0 );
        vect1.insertElementAt(new Integer(A[4]) , 2 );

        System.out.println("6) Vector at this time");
        for(i=0;i<5;i++)
            {   System.out.print( vect1.elementAt(i) + "\t") ;
            }
        System.out.println();
    }
}
```

On compiling, the following error message is received.

```
Compiling javac vec2.java
Note: vec2.java uses unchecked or unsafe operations.
Note: Recompile with -Xlint:unchecked for details.
press any key to continue
```

Program compiles successfully on compiling with option – Xlint.
If you run this program, you will get the following output.

Output

```
<---Vec2.java starts--->
1) Size of Vector = 0
2) Capacity of Vector = 3
3) Now adding elements
4)Printing vector
7     4     1
5) adding More elements
6) Vector at this time
9     7     5     4     1
```

Note:
Lines one and two in the output demonstrate the difference between size and capacity. On checking the source code around line five of output, it is observed that no special instruction is used to increase the capacity of the vector. Still we are able to insert an element in the vector which is otherwise full.

Earlier class Vector was so defined that it did not impose any condition that all the inserted elements had to be of same type. Though this was great thing, the responsibility of remembering what elements had been placed and where they had been placed was on the programmer. In the latest version, this class has been retrofitted in "Collection Framework". It expects that all the elements should be of some pre-declared class. In spite of this, we can use it in old style. It goes without saying that we have to compile using – Xlint option. We can check this by following program.

Problem: Write a program to demonstrate that all the elements of a vector need not be of same class.

Solution: In this example, we will add `integer`, `double`, and `object` of class `Point` (see Program 10.10).

PROGRAM 10.10 Vectors can have Different Elements

```
//    vec3.java
import java.util.*;
class Point
      {     int x,y ;
            Point(int a, int b)
            { x= a; y=b; }
            public void display()
            { System.out.println(" x="+ x +" y= "+y);}
      }
class vec3
{ public static void main(String argv[])
      {     int i;
            Vector vect1 = new Vector(5);
            System.out.println("<---Vec3.java starts--->");
            vect1.addElement( new Integer(5) ) ;
            vect1.addElement( new Double( 6.7)) ;
            vect1.addElement( new Point(3,4) ) ;
            System.out.println("Printing vector ");
            for(i=0;i<3;i++)
                  { System.out.print( vect1.elementAt(i) + "\t") ;
                  }
            System.out.println();
            System.out.println();
            System.out.println("Displaying Point");
//          vect1.elementAt(2).display(); //Note 1 compilation error
            ((Point)vect1.elementAt(2)).display();
      }
}
```

If you run this program, you will get the following output.

Output

```
<---Vec3.java starts--->
Printing vector
5     6.7     Point@f8b
Displaying Point
x=3 y= 4
```

Note 1: The following command is not allowed.

```
vect1.elementAt(2).display();
```

This results in compilation error because vector expects its elements as of class `Object`. Since it does not have method display, program fails to compile. However, when we typecast this object to Point, we are allowed to call display.

In this program, we have first element as `Integer`, second as `Double` and the third as `Point`.

10.11 End of Chapter Programs

10.11.1 Reading a string from console

We have not studied input/output as yet. Reading a string from a console is a bit cumbersome in Java. If a string variable `st1` is defined as the following:

```
String st1;
```

then it can be read with a statement

```
st1 = br.readLine();
```

You may feel that this is simple. `readLine` is an in-built method to read a line. Whatever we read is assigned to string. It goes without saying that br is a suitable input stream from Java language.

Try this in a program and you will get 100 compilation errors. The aforementioned statement works perfectly when many other helping lines are added. These are explained in Box 10.1.

BOX 10.1 In Reading a String

The standard input stream object is defined as is `System.in`. We have to create input stream reader object as

```
InputStreamReader(System.in)
```

But this is not efficient. Hence, we setup object `br` of class `BufferedReader` as

```
BufferedReader jin = new BufferedReader(new
                    InputStreamReader(System.in) ) ;
```

These classes are defined in `java.io package`.

Therefore, we have to add

```
import java.io.*;
```

This is not the end. There may be an error while reading. This possibility is handled by adding

```
throws IOException
```

to the class.

Problem: Write a program to read a string from console.

Solution: See Program 10.11.

PROGRAM 10.11 Reading a String

```
//    string21.java
import java.io.*;
class string21
{ public static void main(String args[])
          throws IOException // note1
          { BufferedReader br =new BufferedReader(new
                    InputStreamReader(System.in) ) ;
               String st1;
               System.out.println("<---string21--->");
               System.out.println("please type your name");
               st1 = br.readLine();
               System.out.println("Welcome " + st1);
          }
}
```

If you run this program, you will get the following output.

Output

```
<---string21--->
please type your name
raja
Welcome raja
```

Note 1: As explained earlier we have to specify `throws IOException`.

If you feel this is a bit cumbersome, you will find a better way in the next chapter based on improvements available in Java version 5.

10.11.2 Comparison operators == does not work on strings

Problem: Write a program to see the effect of comparison operator "==" on the string.

Solution: See Program 10.12.

PROGRAM 10.12 Comparison Operators on Strings

```
//    string7.java
import java.io.*;
class string7
{ public static void main(String args[])
     {    String st1 = "VJTI";
          String st2 = "VJTI";
          String st3 = new String (st1);
          System.out.println(st1+ " " + st2 +" " + st3);
          if( st1 == st2 ) System.out.println("1. true");
                   else    System.out.println("1. false");
//        if( st1 = st2 ) System.out.println("2. true");
//                 else    System.out.println("2. false");
          if( st1 == st3 ) System.out.println("3. true");
                   else    System.out.println("3. false");
```

```
        if( st1.equals (st2) ) System.out.println("4. true");
                else    System.out.println("4. false");
        if( st3.equals (st2) ) System.out.println("5. true");
                else    System.out.println("5. false");
    }
}
```

If you run this program, you will get the following output.

Output

```
VJTI VJTI VJTI
1. true
3. false
4. true
5. true
```

Can you interpret the results?

Please note that the following lines are commented out in Program 10.12.

```
// if( st1 = st2 )        System.out.println("2. true");
//          else          System.out.println("2. false");
```

If you include them, the program will not compile. It is a very common mistake to put "=" sign in place of "==" sign. In C++, this does not raise an alarm. It only gives unexpected results. In this context, Java is better than C++, as it does not allow the programmer to make such errors. In Java, condition needs to be a Boolean value, while `st1 = st2` returns a string.

Keywords

Capacity of the vector, `compareTo()`, empty string, `equals()`, `equalsIgnoreCase()`, immutable, null string, size of vector, string constructing, `StringBuffer`, string comparing, strings, `toLowerCase()`, `toString()`, `toUpperCase()`, `valueOf()`, `Vector`

RuleBook

Strings-null	Java provides class `String` for strings (objects). This implementation is different from C/C++, where strings are array of characters terminated by null character.
Strings-immutable	Strings in Java are immutable, meaning they cannot be changed. The methods which appear to modify a given string actually return a new (separate) string.
`StringBuffer` mutable	Objects of class `StringBuffer` are very much like strings. However, they are mutable(can be modified).
String operators	Strings can not be lexicographically compared using operators like ">" or "<=" etc.
`Vector`	Elements of the vector can only be objects. Simple data types like integers are not allowed as elements.

`StringBuffer`	When no specific buffer length is requested, `StringBuffer` allocates room for **16** additional characters.
`Vector size()`	The `size()` method determines the number of elements in `Vector` [NOT `sizeOf()`].
`trim()String`	String method `trim()` returns a new String object in which all white-space characters have been removed from the beginning and end of a string.

C++ Corner

Strings in Java are not null terminated, as in C++. Strings are objects of class `String`. This class is very rich in methods.

In C++ strings are not immutable, but in Java they are.

To provide mutable strings Java offers a separate class `StringBuffer`.

In Java, strings cannot be lexicographically compared using operators like ">" or "<=" etc.

Review Questions

1. Why comparison operators like > or == fail to compare strings?
2. Which method tells us the size of a given string?
3. What is the necessity of class `StringBuffer`?
4. Compare the tables of method for class `String` and `StringBuffer`, and find methods which are identical and which exist in particular class only.
5. What are the advantages of class `Vector`?
6. What is the difference between size and capacity of the vector?
7. Write a short note on `Vector` class.

Exercises

1. Write a method to check whether any white-space character is present in a string.
2. Write a program to count number of words in a given string.
3. Write a program to find whether a given string is palindrome or not.
4. Write a program to sort an array of strings in alphabetic order.
5. Write a program to remove duplicates from an unsorted array of strings.
6. Write a function test to check if new-line (`'\n'`) character is part of a string.
7. Write a program to check whether a given string represents an integer constant. If answer is yes, find its value.
8. Write a method to accept a vector as parameter and print its size and capacity.
9. Write a program in Java to check the input characters for upper case, lower case, number of digits, and other characters.

CHAPTER 11

SIMPLE INPUT/OUTPUT

Modern computers have many input/output (i/o) devices. Any modern programming language should provide methods to work with them. Java is no exception. However, at this stage, we will discuss only conventional devices like keyboard and monitor. We will discuss files in a separate chapter. These days most of the programs use GUI. Input/output techniques for these applications will be discussed later.

At this stage, we will concentrate only on console input/output.

11.1 Concepts of Streams, Stream Classes

From the days of C language, input/output is made stream based. The data is supposed to flow as a stream. Languages support methods to work with these streams.

When data flows from input device to computer (CPU to be more precise) it will be called input stream, while when computer sends data to output device it will be called output stream (see Figure 11.1).

Java has excellent organization of classes for handling these streams. There are two ways to classify the streams. The first way is based on the direction of flow, that is input stream and output stream.

Another way of classification is based on the nature of raw data. Basic data type in a computer is byte. Hence, basic streams handle bytes. However, most of the users are familiar only with characters. Hence, streams of another type are required which handle characters.

This makes four main types of streams which are as follows:

- Byte-oriented input stream
- Byte-oriented output stream
- Character-oriented input stream
- Character-oriented output stream

In the package `java.lang`, an important class named `System` is defined. It has objects (fields) `in` and `out` defined in it.

The object `in` belongs to class `InputStream`. Note that this object is declared as public, static, and final. Please note that we are not supposed to create this object ourselves. This object represents the "standard" input stream. This stream is already open and ready to supply input data. Typically, this stream corresponds to keyboard input or another input source specified by the host environment or user.

The object `out` belongs to class `PrintStream`. [Technically better description is that this object is of type/class `PrintStream`. It belongs to (or part of) class `System`]. This object is also declared as public, static, and final. It is the `standard` output stream. This stream is already open and ready to accept output data. Typically, this stream corresponds to display output or another output destination specified by the host environment or user.

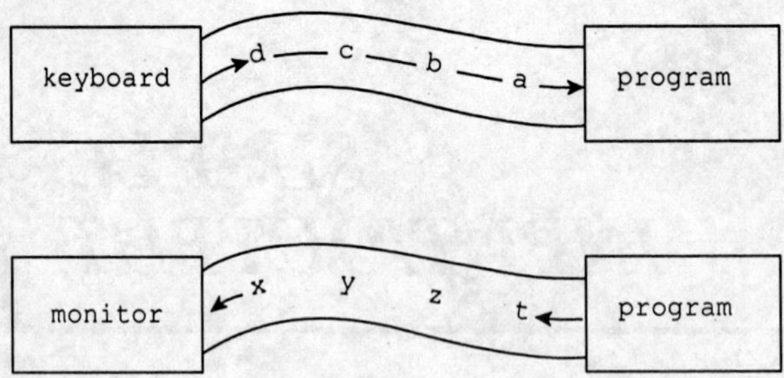

Figure 11.1 Input/Output Streams

11.2 Character Stream Classes

The most common output device for the past 50 years is the console (monitor). The most common output is of type text. Text is nothing but collections of characters. Similarly, the common input device is keyboard. Most of the keys represent characters. Therefore, when we start the study of input/output, we come across characters (and not bytes). Hence, in this chapter we will concentrate on character-based input/output streams. Java provides many classes for this purpose. Hierarchy of such classes is shown at the end of the chapter.

We will proceed first with output streams and then with input streams. We will introduce useful classes as and when required.

11.3 Writing to the Screen

So far we have used the method `System.out.println()`. We can straightaway write all standard primitive data type values as well as strings and objects with the help of this method. To use this method, we do not have to import any package. *The reason is class `System` belongs to package `java.lang`. Since this is the most important package, Java automatically imports it for us (programmers).* We can use any class from this package without importing it.

The class `System` has a field called `out`. This belongs to class `PrintStream`.

Let us start with a program to study it formally.

Problem: Write a program to illustrate the use of character-based output stream, for example `PrintStream`.

Solution: See Program 11.1.

PROGRAM 11.1 char1.java

```
// char1.java
import java.io.* ;
class money
  { int rupee;
  int paise ;
  public money(int a, int b)
     {  rupee =a;paise =b; };
  }
```

```
class char1
{ public static void main(String[] args) throws IOException
    { char k='A' ;
      int i = 100 ;
      double pi = 3.14;
      String st1= "GOD";
      money amt1 = new money(20,30);
      System.out.println("<---char1.java starts--->");
      System.out.println("1) character : " + k );
      System.out.println("2) integer   : " + i );
      System.out.println("3) double    : " + pi );
      System.out.println("4) string    : " + st1 );
      System.out.println("5) object    : " + amt1 );
    }
} ;
```

If you run the program, you will get the following output.

Output

```
<---char1.java starts--->
1) character : A
2) integer   : 100
3) double    : 3.14
4) string    : GOD
5) object    : money@3e25a5
```

Note that when we write object, a string supplied by `toString()` method of that object is written. Hence, we see a string `money@3e25a5`. If you want a decent output in its place, you have to write your own version of `toString()` for that object.

When we write one data element on one line, it is fine. But if we try to write two or more data items on one line, the result is confusing. All elements are written without any space in between. This calls for formatting the output.

11.4 Simple Formatting

So far, we have used a simple trick in `println` statement. We place either blanks or tab in between two values. Actually, we can do little better than that. Suppose we want that every value is written in a 10-column width. What we can do is as follows. First, get a `StringBuffer` with 10 blanks. (As strings are immutable, we have to use `StringBuffer`.) Now we prepare a string of value to be printed and insert it in this buffer. Actually method `insert()` does it automatically. It has the following form:

```
insert (position, variable) ;
```

It inserts the string value of a variable at a given position. In return, it gives us a string which is 10-character wide. Let us use this technique in a program.

Problem: Write a program to demonstrate simple formatting of output.

Solution: Consider a problem of square and cube. Write a program to print a table of square and cubes of first 10 natural numbers (see Program 11.2).

PROGRAM 11.2 Simple Formatting I

```
//    format1.java
//    Simple table
//    formatted output.
import java.io.* ;

class format1
{  public static void main(String[] args) throws IOException
   { int i , sq , cube ;
     System.out.println("<---format1.java starts--->");
     System.out.println("Unformatted output");

     for(i=1;i< =10;i++)
        { sq = i * i;
          cube = sq * i;
          System.out.println(i + " " + sq + " " + cube);
        }

     System.out.println("Formatted output");
     for(i=1;i<  =10;i++)
        { sq = i * i;
          cube = sq * i;
          StringBuffer st1 = new StringBuffer(" ") ;

          st1.insert(0,i);
          st1.insert(10,sq);
          st1.insert(20,cube);
          System.out.println(st1);
        }
   }
} ;
```

If you run the program, you will get the following output.

Output

```
<---format1.java starts--->
Unformatted output
1     1      1
2     4      8
3     9      27
4     16     64
5     25     125
6     36     216
7     49     343
8     64     512
9     81     729
10    100    1000
Formatted output
1     1      1
2     4      8
```

```
3    9     27
4    16    64
5    25    125
6    36    216
7    49    343
8    64    512
9    81    729
10   100   1000
```

If you have found this procedure a bit cumbersome, wait till you read the next section. In SDK 5, you are in for a pleasant surprise.

11.5 Formatting with `printf`

Now Java has introduced a new method `printf` which works more or less like one in language C. It is more convenient not only for those who know C language, but also for those who have no exposure to it. If you wish to print say two integers `i` and `j`, you can write

```
System.out.printf("format string", i, j);
```

Here format string will tell the computer in what format values of `i` and `j` should be printed. Please note the syntax of the statement. The format string is in a pair of quotes. Comma separates the `format string` and the variables to be printed. A format string may look like as follows:

```
% 1$ 0 20 0.1 f
```

The following diagram illustrates the details.

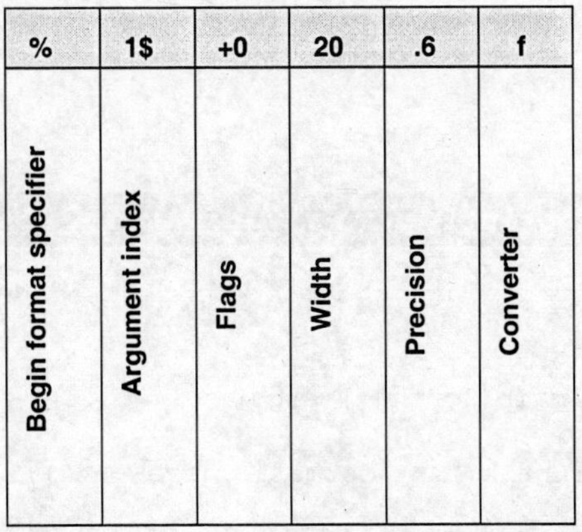

%	1$	+0	20	.6	f
Begin format specifier	Argument index	Flags	Width	Precision	Converter

Please note the following points with respect to the format specifier string.
The format string will have the following components in that order: format specifier, argument index, flags, width, precision, and converter (Table 11.1). Some of them are optional. Some of them are relevant under certain conditions.

Table 11.1 **Format Specifier**

Parameter	Nature	Example	Comments
Start symbol	Mandatory	Symbol %	–
Argument index	Optional	Integer$	Not much useful
Flags	Optional	Symbol + − 0	Any combination allowed
Width	Optional	Integer	Number of columns
Precision	Optional	Integer	Works with floating-point numbers as well as strings
Converter	Mandatory	Character d f s c	Any one

Flags: Result of individual flags is as follows:

+: prints plus sign for positive numbers

−: value printed left justified

0: prints leading zeros

Converters: The converters represent the following data types:

d: specifies decimal number

f: specifies floating-point number

s: specifies string

c: specifies character

With this much introduction, let us study it with a program.

Problem: Write a program to study method `printf`.

Solution: See Program 11.3.

PROGRAM 11.3 **Method `printf`**

```
//    format1a.java

class format 1a
{  public static void main(String[] args)
     {  int i,j ;
        System.out.println("<-- format1a.java--->");
        i= 234;
        j= 54;
        System.out.printf("i=%5d,j=%10d", i, j);
     }
}
```

If you run the program, you will get the following output.

Output

```
<-- format1a.java--->
i=  234,j=  54
xx12345xxx1234567890
```

The last row is added to verify the number of columns used.

Earlier we have seen program `format1.java`. Using `printf` statement, it can be rewritten in simple manner. See Program 11.16 in the end of chapter programs.

When it comes to printing floating-point numbers, we have to specify the precision as well. A specifier `10.3f` tells the computer to use minimum 10 columns with 3 digits for precision. "f" indicates a floating-point number. Let us see a simple program.

Problem: Write a program to find square root and cube root of first 10 natural numbers.

Solution: See Program 11.4.

PROGRAM 11.4 printf II

```
//    format3a.java
class format3a
{  public static void main(String[] args)
   {  int i;
      double j,k ;
      System.out.println("<---format3a.java--->");
      System.out.println("    Number squareroot cuberoot");

     for (i=1; i<11;i++)
       {  j= Math.sqrt(i);
          k= Math.pow(i,1.0/3.0);
          System.out.printf("%10d%10.3f%10.3f\n",i, j, k);
       }
   }
}
```

If you run the program, you will get the following output.

Output

```
<---format3a.java--->
Number     squareroot     cuberoot
   1       1.000          1.000
   2       1.414          1.260
   3       1.732          1.442
   4       2.000          1.587
   5       2.236          1.710
   6       2.449          1.817
   7       2.646          1.913
   8       2.828          2.000
   9       3.000          2.080
  10       3.162          2.154
```

Let us write one more program to test various properties of `printf` statement.

Problem: Write a program to study formatting with method `printf`.

Solution: See Program 11.5.

PROGRAM 11.5 printf III

```
//      format4.java
class format4
{ public static void main(String[] args)
   { int i=27 ;
     float   x = 5.67f ;
     double y = Math.PI ;
     System.out.println("<-- format4.java--->");
     System.out.printf("1) %d\n", i);
     System.out.printf("2) %10d\n", i);
     System.out.printf("3) %+010d\n", i);
     System.out.printf("4) %+10d\n", i);
     System.out.printf("5) %+-10d\n", i);
     System.out.printf("6) %10.5f\n", x);
     System.out.printf("7) %20.15e\n", y);
   }
}
```

If you run the program, you will get the following output.

Output

```
<-- format4.java--->
1) 27
2)         27
3) +000000027
4)        +27
5) +27
6)    5.67000
7) 3.141592653589793e+00
```

Note:

1. Plain decimal format nothing extra.
2. Width of 10 columns specified.
3. Sign appears as well as leading zeros.
4. No leading zeros.
5. Output left justified.
6. Width and precision in floating-point representation.
7. Scientific notation

Let us try one more program.

Problem: Write a program to study formatting of strings and character.

Solution: See Program 11.6.

PROGRAM 11.6 Formatting Strings and Character

```
//      format5.java

class format5
{ public static void main(String[] args)
    { String str1 = "This is a string" ;
      char x = 'X' ;
      System.out.println("<-- format5.java--->");
              System.out.printf("1) %s\n", str1);
              System.out.printf("2) %10s\n", str1);
              System.out.printf("3) %20.6s\n", str1);
              System.out.printf("4) %+10c\n", x);
    }
}
```

If you run the program, you will get the following output.

Output

```
<-- format5.java--->
1) This is a string
2) This is a string
3)              This i
4)          X
```

Note:

1. Simple formatting for string.
2. When specified width is insufficient, it is ignored.
3. Setting precision truncates string.
4. Even characters can be printed with width.

After studying output, let us go for input. Let us investigate how to read effectively.

11.6 Reading the Data

For reading character-oriented data, Java supplies us an abstract class `Reader`. For actual reading, we may use another non-abstract class derived from it known as `InputStreamReader`. You can see a simple example `read0.java` at the end of chapter.

However, for efficiency purpose Java recommends wrapping an `InputStreamReader` within a `BufferedReader`.

See the simple program which is mentioned hereafter.

Problem: Write a program to illustrate reading of characters from standard input, that is keyboard.

Solution: See Program 11.7.

PROGRAM 11.7 Reading a Character I

```
//      read1.java
import java.io.* ;
class read1
 { public static void main(String[] args) throws IOException
     { int i ,k;
       char ch ;
       BufferedReader Jin = new BufferedReader
       (new InputStreamReader (System.in) );
       System.out.println("program read1.java starts");
       System.out.print(" Input a characters and press enter: ");
       ch = (char) Jin.read();
       System.out.println("from Jin char read is->" + ch );
       System.out.println(" Character\'s integer value is " + (int) ch);
     }
 } ;
```

If you run the program, you will see the following output.

Output

```
program read1.java starts
  Input a characters and press enter: S
from Jin char read is->S
  Character's integer value is 83
```

The program is straight and simple. But please note that to input a character, we have to enter that character and press return key. The keyboard data goes into input stream only when we press the return key.

There is no simple way of getting to know (read) a key without pressing return. Those who know C/C++ will feel the absence of functions to read keys directly.

The first problem is questions like

```
Do you want to continue? (Y/N)
```

where it is expected that user only presses a key. If you want this action in Java, you have to type a key and press Return.

There is another misconception. When we say read, we expect to read what has been typed in response to this read instruction. However, when this method is executed there may be some characters already in the input stream (this happens in C/C++ also). The characters present in the stream are accepted. You may write a simple program and verify the fact.

In earlier example, we read a single character. It is possible to read an array of character. The syntax for this is

```
Jin.read(box,0,100);
```

The method returns number of characters that are actually read. It reads the characters in a character array named box (first parameter). It reads a maximum of 100 (third parameter) characters. The characters are placed in the array starting from 0th (second parameter) position.

So far, we have read only characters. What about strings? Yes, Java allows us to read strings too. Let us study it now.

11.7 Reading Strings

We have a method `readLine ( )` for this task (in class `BufferedReader`). It reads a line of text and returns it as a string. A line means any string (or sequence of characters) terminated by any one of the following:

line feed ('\n') character,

carriage return ('\r'), or

a carriage return followed immediately by a line feed

If the end of the stream has been reached, then it returns null.

Let us see this method in action.

Problem: Write a program to illustrate reading a string from standard input, that is keyboard.

Solution: See Program 11.8.

PROGRAM 11.8 Reading String I

```
//     io5.java
import java.io.* ;
class io5
  { public static void main(String[] args) throws IOException
      { char k='B',l='P';
        int i ;
        String st1;
        BufferedReader Jin = new BufferedReader
                  (new InputStreamReader (System.in) );
        System.out.println("Enter five lines");
        for(i=0;i<5;i++)
          { st1= Jin.readLine() ;
            System.out.println(i+ ") " + st1);
          }
      }
  }
```

If you run the program, you will see the following output.

Output

```
Enter five lines
good morning
0) good morning
Welcome to java programming
1) Welcome to java programming
Viru is man of the series
2) Viru is man of the series
Dravid is man of the match
3) Dravid is man of the match
India wins test series too!
4) India wins test series too!
```

11.8 Reading Data

Reading strings is fine, but one is more interested in reading data. It may be `integers`, `floats`, or `double`. We can read data first as a string, and then extracting individual element is possible.

Consider a case that a string contains a roll number and percentage marks of a student. It goes without saying that the first one is an integer and the second is a floating-point number. When we read this data, it will contain lot of white space characters in between the two data values.

Java provides us a class called `StringTokenizer` (see Box 11.1 for details). It helps in converting a line of data into what is called as tokens. Token is nothing but a string which does not contain any blanks. Once we have a token (string), we can convert it very easily into individual values.

BOX 11.1 StringTokenizer

Class StringTokenizer accepts a string while creating an object. Assume that the string is

" I love Java"

The class internally converts it to three tokens (strings) as

"I", "love", "Java"

It returns one token at a time when we invoke method `nextToken()`. We can test if tokens are still available with the help of method `hasMoreTokens()`.

Note that while converting string to tokens, all blanks, tabs, and other separating characters are ignored.

Problem: Write a program to illustrate reading data with the help of `StringTokenizer`.

Solution: See Program 11.9.

PROGRAM 11.9 Reading String II

```
//      reading2.java
//      format free input
import java.io.* ;
import java.util.* ;
class reading2
{  public static void main(String[] args) throws IOException
    {  int Rollnum ;
       double percent ;
       String st1,substr1="",substr2="";
       BufferedReader Jin = new BufferedReader
                (new InputStreamReader (System.in) );
       System.out.println("<---reading2.java--->");
       System.out.println("Give data roll no(int) and percentage(double)");
       st1= Jin.readLi ne();
    // System.out.println(st1);
       StringTokenizer st = new StringTokenizer(st1);
       if (st.hasMoreTokens() )
                substr1 = st.nextToken() ;
            else System.out.println("Error!!! no tokens to get");
       if (st.hasMoreTokens() )
       substr2 = st.nextToken() ;
       else System.out.println("Error!!! no tokens to get");
       System.out.println(" first substring : " + substr1);
```

```
        System.out.println("second substring : " + substr2);
        Rollnum = Integer.parseInt(substr1);
        percent = Double.parseDouble(substr2);
        System.out.println("    roll no = " +Rollnum);
        System.out.println("percentage = " +percent);
    }
  } ;
```

Run the program. While giving data, put any number of blanks and/or tabs in between. A sample output is shown hereafter.

Output

```
<---reading2.java--->
Give data roll no(int) and percentage(double)
22      97.3
 first   substring : 22
second  substring : 97.3
   roll no = 22
percentage = 97.3
```

You will agree that from Java version 5 onwards reading is fairly simple.

So far, we have used a few methods from the class `BufferedReader`. Table 11.2 describes all the methods from this class.

Table 11.2 Methods from Class `BufferedReader`

Return type	Method	Description
`Void`	`close()`	Close the stream.
`Void`	`mark(int readAheadLimit)`	Mark the present position in the stream.
`Boolean`	`markSupported()`	Tell whether this stream supports the `mark()` operation, which it does.
`int`	`read()`	Read a single character.
`int`	`read(char[] cbuf, int off, int len)`	Read characters into a portion of an array.
`String`	`readLine()`	Read a line of text.
`Boolean`	`ready()`	Tell whether this stream is ready to be read.
`void`	`reset()`	Reset the stream to the most recent mark.
`long`	`skip(long n)`	Skip characters.

11.9 Class Scanner

Just as printing is revolutionized in SDK 5 so is the reading. A class named `Scanner` is defined. Object of this class are useful in breaking down inputs (formatted as well as unformatted) into tokens. These tokens can be easily converted into individual data types. Let us study a program which achieves what is done in Program 11.9 in a much easier way.

Problem: Write a program to read an integer and a double using class `Scanner`.

Solution: See Program 11.10.

PROGRAM 11.10 Class Scanner I

```
//    scan1a.java
import java.io.* ;
import java.util.* ;
class scan1a
 { public static void main(String[] args) throws IOException
     { int    Rollnum, i ;
       double percent ;
       System.out.println("<-- scan1a.java--->");
       System.out.print(" Input Roll Number and Percentage");
       Scanner cin = new Scanner(System.in);
       Rollnum= cin.nextInt();
       percent = cin.nextDouble();
       System.out.println("   roll no = " +Rollnum);
       System.out.println("percentage = " +percent);
     }
 }
```

If you run the program, you will get the following output.

Output

```
<-- scan1a.java--->
Input Roll Number and Percentage 22 97.3
  roll no = 22
percentage = 97.3
```

Problem: Write another program to find to study class `Scanner`.

Solution: See Program 11.11.

PROGRAM 11.11 Class Scanner II

```
//    scanner2.java
//    copied from scanner1.java
import java.io.* ;
import java.util.* ;
class scanner2
```

```
{
    public static void main(String[] args) throws IOException
       { int i,j ;
         System.out.println("<-- scanner2.java--->");
         System.out.print(" Input two integers i and j : ");
         Scanner cin = new Scanner(System.in);
         i= cin.nextInt();
         j= cin.nextInt();
         System.out.println("Integers read are " + i +" "+ j);
       }
}
```

We have executed the program three times to get the following output.

Output

```
//First Run

<-- scanner2.java--->
 Input two integers i and j : 23 678
Integers read are 23 678

// Second run

<-- scanner2.java--->
 Input two integers i and j : 2345 67
Integers read are 2345 67
// third Run

<-- scanner2.java--->
 Input two integers i and j : 23 4.5
Exception in thread "main" java.util.InputMismatchException
      at java.util.Scanner.throwFor(Scanner.java:819)
      at java.util.Scanner.next(Scanner.java:1431)
      at java.util.Scanner.nextInt(Scanner.java:2040)
      at java.util.Scanner.nextInt(Scanner.java:2000)
      at scanner2.main(scanner2.java:13)
```

In the first run, we gave data in one line. In the second run, we typed first integer, then pressed return, and then gave the second integer. The program ran successfully. In the third run, we gave one integer and one floating-point number. The program failed because of `InputMismatchException`.

11.10 StreamTokenizer

Earlier we have studied class `StringTokenizer`. It was tokenizing a single string. The new class `StreamTokenizer` converts a stream of type reader into tokens.

Following facts can be noted about this class. See the following constructor:

```
StreamTokenizer (Reader r)
```

This creates a tokenizer that parses the given character stream.

1. The most important method is `nextToken()`. It extracts a token and returns an integer. It also initializes the field "ttype". The most important thing to note is that it does **not** return a string representing the token.
2. Fields nval and sval store the number or the string depending on the token read.
3. By using suitable methods, the C style or C++ style comments can be ignored.
4. Method `toString()` returns a string containing the token and the line number. However, its exact format is not guaranteed.

Let us study this class with the help of a program.

Problem: Write a program to introduce class `StreamTokenizer`.

Solution: See Program 11.12.

PROGRAM 11.12 Streamtokenizer

```
//   reading4.java
//   format free input
import java.io.* ;
import java.util.* ;
class reading4
 { public static void main(String[] args) throws IOException
     { int Rollnum ;
       double percent ;
       String st1,substr1="",substr2="";
       StreamTokenizer tok = new StreamTokenizer
                (new InputStreamReader (System.in) );
       tok.slashStarComments(true); // ignores C style comments
       System.out.println("<---reading4.java--->");
       System.out.println("Give few lines input");
       System.out.println("type CTRL-Z on fresh line to quit");
       while (tok.nextToken() != StreamTokenizer.TT_EOF) //NUMBER)
         { System.out.println("..."+ tok.toString());
           switch (tok.ttype)
           {
             case StreamTokenizer.TT_WORD :
                           System.out.println( tok.sval); break;
             case StreamTokenizer.TT_NUMBER :
                           System.out.println( tok.nval); break;
             default : System.out.println(
                           "Something went wrong");
           }
         }
     }
 }
```

If you run the program, you will get the following output.

Output

```
<---reading4.java--->
Give few lines input
type CTRL-Z on fresh line to quit
Good morning 23
...Token[Good], line 1
--->Good
...Token[morning], line 1
--->morning
...Token[n=23.0], line 1
--->23.0
// C++ style comment
/* C style comment */ ignored
...Token[ignored], line 3
--->ignored
```

Please note that C++ style comment is on line number 2. This has been ignored. However, the next line is properly taken as line number 3.

11.11 Hierarchies of Character-Based i/o Classes

In our programs, we mainly used `BufferedReader` and `InputStreamReader` classes. Package `java.io` provides all the needed APIs for input/output. For character streams, Java provides two abstract super-classes `Reader` and `Writer`. They provide support for reading and writing 16-bit characters. Package contains non-abstract subclasses derived from the above classes. Figures 11.2 and 11.3 show the hierarchy of these classes.

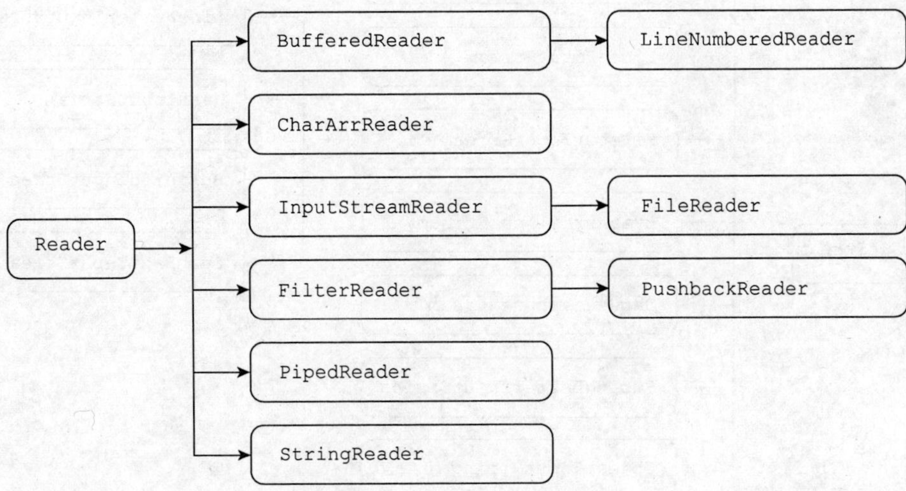

Figure 11.2 Character-Oriented Input Stream

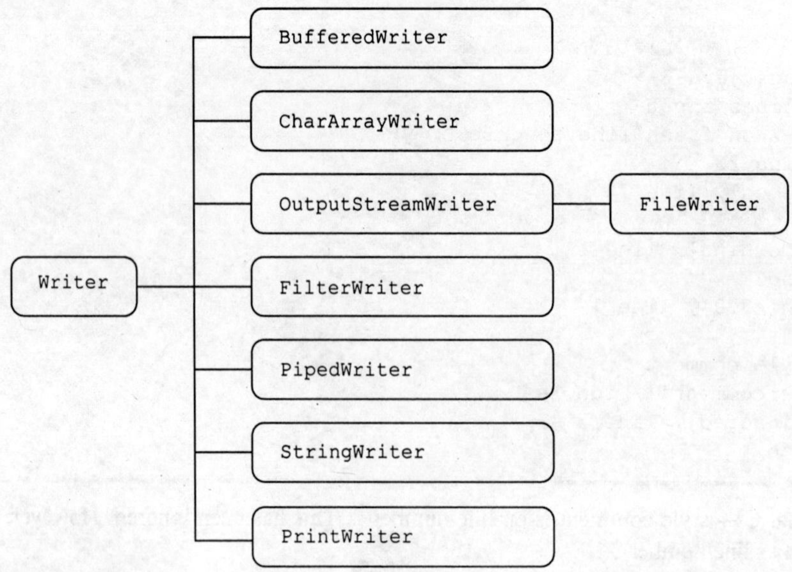

Figure 11.3 Output Stream

11.12 Hierarchies of Byte-Oriented i/o Classes

Though we use characters for input/output, most of the data in the computer is stored in 8-bit bytes. When we hear music or see a picture, the basic data is in terms of bytes. When we store data to files, again bytes are in action. Java has organized various classes nicely to handle byte streams. The most fundamental classes are `InputStream` and `OutputStream`. All other classes descend from them. Figures 11.4 and 11.5 show the hierarchy of these classes.

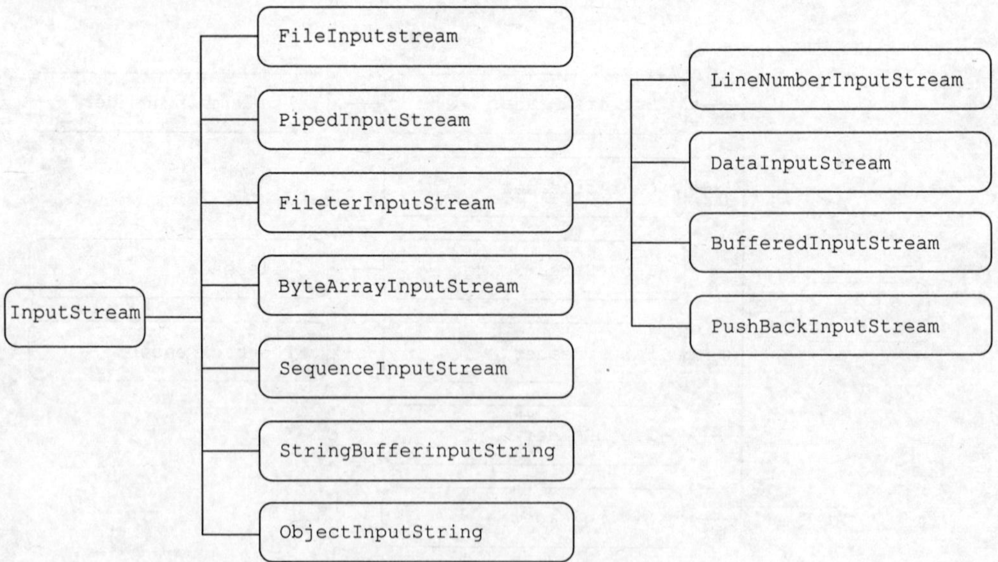

Figure 11.4 Byte-Oriented Input Stream

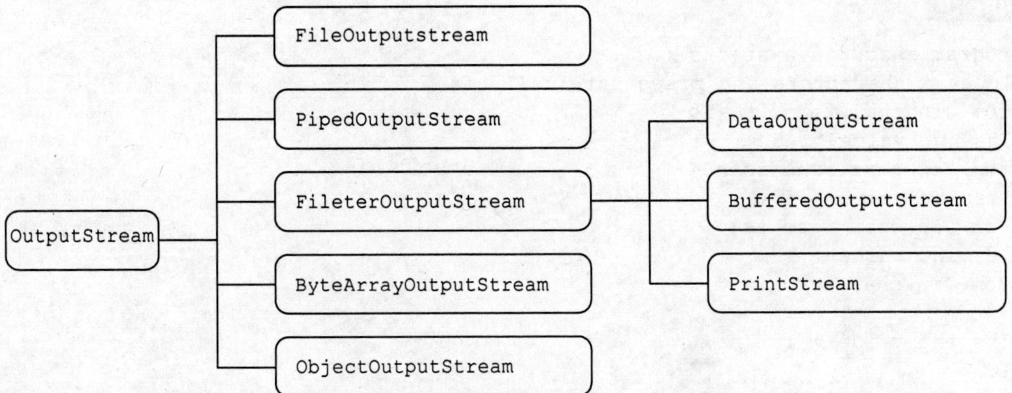

Figure 11.5 Byte-Oriented Output Stream

We will come across some of these classes later on in the chapter on files.

11.13 End of Chapter Programs

11.13.1 Using class `InputStreamReader`

Problem: Write a program to use basic class `InputStreamReader`.

Solution: See Program 11.13.

PROGRAM 11.13 Using `InputStreamReader`

```
//    read 0.java
//    copied from conio2c.java
import java.io.* ;
class read0
  { public static void main(String[] args) throws IOException
    { int i ;
      char ch ;
      InputStreamReader Jin =
                   new InputStreamReader(System.in) ;
      System.out.println("program read0.java starts");
      System.out.print(" Input a characters and press enter: ");
      for (i=0; i <7;i++)
        {  ch = (char) Jin.read();
           System.out.println("from Jin char read is->" + ch + "<-");
           System.out.println(" Its int value-> " + (int) ch);
        }
        Jin.close();
    }
  } ;
```

If you run the program, you will see the following output.

Output

```
program read0.java starts
 Input a characters and press enter: AB
from Jin char read is->A<-
 Its int value-> 65
from Jin char read is->B<-
 Its int value-> 66
<-om Jin char read is->
 Its int value-> 13
from Jin char read is->
<-
 Its int value-> 10
CDE
from Jin char read is->C<-
 Its int value-> 67
from Jin char read is->D<-
 Its int value-> 68
from Jin char read is->E<-
 Its int value-> 69
```

11.13.2 Reading integer

Problem: Write a program to develop method `getint()` which reads integer value from the keyboard.

Solution: Initially the value typed at the keyboard is read as a string. Then the string is converted into an integer (see Program 11.14).

PROGRAM 11.14 Developing `getint()`

```
//    coniol.java
//    copied from io8.java
import java.io.* ;
class coniol
  {
     public static void main(String[] args) throws IOException
       { int i ;
         System.out.println("program coniol.java starts");
         System.out.print(" Input an integer : ");
         i = getint();
         System.out.println("Integer read is " + i );
       }

     static int getint() throws IOException
       { String stl;
         BufferedReader Jin = new BufferedReader
                 (new InputStreamReader (System.in) );
         stl= Jin.readLine();
```

```
        Integer temp = new Integer (st1);
        return temp.intValue();
     } ;
  } ;
```

If you run the program, you will see the following output.

Output

```
program conio1.java starts
  Input an integer : 2004
Integer read is 2004
```

Please note that this program works correctly only when you type an integer value. Leading or trailing blanks are not allowed. They lead to errors. We can improve this program by using the method `trim()` from class `String`. We can write similar programs to read other primitive data types.

11.13.3 Reading into a character array

Problem: Write a program to use a character array to store characters read from the keyboard.

Solution: See Program 11.15.

PROGRAM 11.15 Reading a Character II

```
//    read2.java
//    copied from read1.java
import java.io.* ;
class read2
  {
    public static void main(String[] args) throws IOException
      {  int i ,k;
         char ch ;
         char box[] = new char[100];
         BufferedReader Jin = new BufferedReader
                     (new InputStreamReader (System.in) );
         System.out.println("program read2.java starts");
         System.out.print(" type few characters and press enter: ");
         k=Jin.read(box,0,100);
         System.out.println(" number of characters read :" +k);
         for(i=0;i <k;i++)
           System.out.println( i+ " ) character is " + box[i]);
      }
  } ;
```

If you run the program, you will see the following output.

Output

```
program read2.java starts
  type few characters and press enter: ABCD
  number of characters read :6
```

```
0 ) character is A
1 ) character is B
2 ) character is C
3 ) character is D
4 ) character is
5 ) character is
```

Why is the output showing six characters when only four characters have been typed? The reason is that the carriage return and line feed characters are also read. You can verify the fact by printing the numeric value of those characters.

11.13.4 Formatted output

We have solved the square–cube problem earlier. Let us apply formatting with method `printf()` to the same problem.

Problem: Write a program to find square and cube of first 10 natural numbers. The output should be well formatted.

Solution: The values of square and cube more digits than the basic number. Hence, different width will be in order. We will also use notation of '$' here (see Program 11.16).

PROGRAM 11.16 Formatted Output

```
//   format2.java
class format2
{  public static void main(String[] args)
     {  int i,j,k ;
        System.out.println("<-- format2.java--->");
        for (i=1; i <11;i++)-
          {  j= i*i;
             k= j*i;
             System.out.printf("%1$4d%2$6d%3$8d \n", i, j, k);
          }
     }
}
```

If you run the above program, you will get the following output.

Output

```
<-- format2.java--->
   1     1       1
   2     4       8
   3     9      27
   4    16      64
   5    25     125
   6    36     216
   7    49     343
   8    64     512
   9    81     729
  10   100    1000
```

Notice the width of four, six and, eight columns, respectively.

Table 11.3 illustrates constructors for class StringTokenizer.

Table 11.3 Constructor Summary: StringTokenizer

StringTokenizer(String str)	Constructs a string tokenizer for the specified string
StringTokenizer(String str, String delim)	Constructs a string tokenizer for the specified string
StringTokenizer(String str, String delim, boolean returnDelims)	Constructs a string tokenizer for the specified string

Table 11.4 illustrates methods from class StringTokenizer.

Table 11.4 Method Summary: StringTokenizer

int	**countTokens()**	Calculates the number of times that this tokenizer's nextToken method can be called before it generates an exception
Boolean	**hasMoreElements()**	Returns the same value as the hasMoreTokens method
Boolean	**hasMoreTokens()**	Tests if there are more tokens available from this tokenizer's string
Object	**nextElement()**	Returns the same value as the nextToken method, except that its declared return value is object rather than string
String	**nextToken()**	Returns the next token from this string tokenizer
String	**nextToken** (String delim)	Returns the next token in this string tokenizer's string

Table 11.5 illustrates constructors for class Scanner.

Table 11.5 Constructor Summary: Class Scanner

Scanner(File source)	Constructs a new Scanner that produces values scanned from the specified file
Scanner(File source, String charsetName)	Constructs a new Scanner that produces values scanned from the specified file

(Continued)

Table 11.5 *(Continued)*

Scanner(InputStream source)	Constructs a new Scanner that produces values scanned from the specified input stream
Scanner(InputStream source, String charsetName)	Constructs a new Scanner that produces values scanned from the specified input stream
Scanner(Readable source)	Constructs a new Scanner that produces values scanned from the specified source
.**Scanner**(ReadableByteChannel source)	Constructs a new Scanner that produces values scanned from the specified channel
Scanner(ReadableByteChannel source, String charsetName)	Constructs a new Scanner that produces values scanned from the specified channel
Scanner(String source)	Constructs a new Scanner that produces values scanned from the specified string

Table 11.6 illustrates methods from class Scanner.

Table 11.6 **Method Summary: Class Scanner**

void	close()	Closes this scanner
Pattern	delimiter()	Returns the Pattern this Scanner is currently using to match delimiters
String	findInLine(Pattern pattern)	Attempts to find the next occurrence of the specified pattern ignoring delimiters
String	findInLine(String pattern)	Attempts to find the next occurrence of a pattern constructed from the specified string, ignoring delimiters
String	findWithinHorizon (Pattern pattern, int horizon)	Attempts to find the next occurrence of the specified pattern
String	findWithinHorizon (String pattern, int horizon)	Attempts to find the next occurrence of a pattern constructed from the specified string, ignoring delimiters
boolean	hasNext()	Returns true if this scanner has another token in its input
boolean	hasNext(Pattern pattern)	Returns true if the next complete token matches the specified pattern

(Continued)

Table 11.6 *(Continued)*

boolean	hasNext(String pattern)	Returns true if the next token matches the pattern constructed from the specified string
boolean	hasNextBigDecimal()	Returns true if the next token in this scanner's input can be interpreted as a BigDecimal using the nextBigDecimal() method
boolean	hasNextBigInteger()	Returns true if the next token in this scanner's input can be interpreted as a BigInteger in the default radix using the nextBigInteger() method
boolean	hasNextBigInteger(int radix)	Returns true if the next token in this scanner's input can be interpreted as a BigInteger in the specified radix using the nextBigInteger() method
boolean	hasNextBoolean()	Returns true if the next token in this scanner's input can be interpreted as a boolean value using a case insensitive pattern created from the string true false
boolean	hasNextByte()	Returns true if the next token in this scanner's input can be interpreted as a byte value in the default radix using the nextByte() method
boolean	hasNextByte(int radix)	Returns true if the next token in this scanner's input can be interpreted as a byte value in the specified radix using the nextByte() method
boolean	hasNextDouble()	Returns true if the next token in this scanner's input can be interpreted as a double value using the nextDouble() method
boolean	hasNextFloat()	Returns true if the next token in this scanner's input can be interpreted as a float value using the nextFloat() method
boolean	hasNextInt()	Returns true if the next token in this scanner's input can be interpreted as an int value in the default radix using the nextInt() method
boolean	hasNextInt(int radix)	Returns true if the next token in this scanner's input can be interpreted as an int value in the specified radix using the nextInt() method
boolean	hasNextLine()	Returns true if there is another line in the input of this scanner

(Continued)

Table 11.6 *(Continued)*

boolean	hasNextLong()	Returns true if the next token in this scanner's input can be interpreted as a long value in the default radix using the nextLong() method
boolean	hasNextLong(int radix)	Returns true if the next token in this scanner's input can be interpreted as a long value in the specified radix using the nextLong() method
boolean	hasNextShort()	Returns true if the next token in this scanner's input can be interpreted as a short value in the default radix using the nextShort() method
boolean	hasNextShort(int radix)	Returns true if the next token in this scanner's input can be interpreted as a short value in the specified radix using the nextShort() method
IOException	ioException()	Returns the IOException last thrown by this Scanner's underlying Readable
Locale	locale()	Returns this scanner's locale
MatchResult	match()	Returns the match result of the last scanning operation performed by this scanner
String	next()	Finds and returns the next complete token from this scanner
String	next(Pattern pattern)	Returns the next token if it matches the specified pattern
String	next(String pattern)	Returns the next token if it matches the pattern constructed from the specified string
BigDecimal	nextBigDecimal()	Scans the next token of the input as a BigDecimal
BigInteger	nextBigInteger()	Scans the next token of the input as a BigInteger
BigInteger	nextBigInteger(int radix)	Scans the next token of the input as a BigInteger
boolean	nextBoolean()	Scans the next token of the input into a boolean value and returns that value
byte	nextByte()	Scans the next token of the input as a byte
byte	nextByte(int radix)	Scans the next token of the input as a byte
double	nextDouble()	Scans the next token of the input as a double

(Continued)

Table 11.6 *(Continued)*

float	nextFloat()	Scans the next token of the input as a float
int	nextInt()	Scans the next token of the input as an int
int	nextInt(int radix)	Scans the next token of the input as an int
String	nextLine()	Advances this scanner past the current line and returns the input that was skipped
long	nextLong()	Scans the next token of the input as a long
long	nextLong(int radix)	Scans the next token of the input as a long
short	nextShort()	Scans the next token of the input as a short
short	nextShort(int radix)	Scans the next token of the input as a short
int	radix()	Returns this scanner's default radix
void	remove()	The remove operation is not supported by this implementation of Iterator
Scanner	skip(Pattern pattern)	Skips input that matches the specified pattern, ignoring delimiters
Scanner	skip(String pattern)	Skips input that matches a pattern constructed from the specified string
String	toString()	Returns the string representation of this Scanner
Scanner	useDelimiter(Pattern pattern)	Sets this scanner's delimiting pattern to the specified pattern
Scanner	useDelimiter(String pattern)	Sets this scanner's delimiting pattern to a pattern constructed from the specified string
Scanner	useLocale(Locale locale)	Sets this scanner's locale to the specified locale
Scanner	useRadix(int radix)	Sets this scanner's default radix to the specified radix

RuleBook

import	Java by default imports package java.lang. We do not have to import it specifically.
in, out, err	In, out, and err are predefined stream variables.
Writer	Abstract class Writer is the super class of all classes used for writing characters.

`InputStream`	Abstract class `InputStream` is the super class of all classes used for reading bytes.
`Reader`	Abstract class `Reader` is the super class of all classes used for reading characters.
`in`	The object `in` belongs to class `InputStream`. It is standard input stream.
`out`	The object `out` belongs to class `printStream`. It is standard output stream.

C++ Corner

Redirection operators << and >> are not supported in Java. If someone likes these operators, for him i/o in C++ is more convenient.

Early versions of Java made reading and writing a bit tough. With the advent of version 1.5, i/o in Java has improved a lot. To some extent, it has become similar to i/o in "C".

Keywords

`BufferedReader`, format string, `hasMoreTokens()`, Hierarchies of character-based i/o classes, in, `InputMismatchException`, `InputStreamReader`, `nextToken()`, `Out`, `printf()`, `PrintStream`, `readLine()`, `readLine()`, `Scanner`, `StreamTokenizer`, `StringTokenizer`, System class

Review Questions

1. Object `System.out` belongs to which class?
2. Which are the simplest formatting techniques when we are using method `print()`?
3. Which classes are involved in reading from `System.in`?
4. What is the advantage of class `StringTokenizer` for reading data?
5. How does class scanner helps in reading data?
6. Describe various elements of format string in method `printf()`.

Exercises

1. Write a program to print a 3 × 3 matrix. Assume elements are of type `Double`.
2. Write a program to print salary records of a company.
3. Write an application that inputs a line of text, tokenizes the line with an object of class **StringTokenizer**, and outputs the tokens in reverse order.

4. In the following program, we want to print square and cubes of 10 natural numbers. Design suitable format string, so that the output will appear neat and correct. Do not modify any other sentence.

* *

```
//    format6.java
class format6
{  public static void main(String[] args)
     {  int i,j,k ;
        System.out.println("<---format6.java--->");
        System.out.println(" num square cube");
        for (i=1; i<11;i++)
          {j= i*i;
           k= j*i;
           System.out.printf("find suitable format string", k,j ,i );
          }
     }
}
```

* *

INHERITANCE

Let us imagine that a particular class is developed and used in some program. Now, another class is needed which is similar to this class but with more functionality (power). Does the time consumed in developing this class go waste? No, the Inheritance principle allows us to define a new class based on the previously designed class. We are required only to write a code related to additional functionality. The previously developed class is directly used. In technical jargon, the new class inherits the properties of old class.

12.1 Inheritance Basics

Consider a case where you want to develop class `Time12`. Assume that you have class `Time24`. Name `Time24` stands for twenty-four hours clock. The hours can take values between 0 and 23. In our routine life, we are accustomed to 12-hour clock. A class `Time12` need everything of `Time24` but should also have something more, that is specification AM or PM. This is an ideal situation for inheritance.

Here we say that class `Time12` inherits the properties of class `Time24`. Class `Time24` will be called the super-class while class `Time12` will be called the sub-class. (See Figure 12.1)
Consider the following declaration:

```
class Time12 extends Time24
{  String str;
}
```

Note the key word `extends`. It tells the compiler that sub-class `Time12` inherits properties of super-class `Time24`. Note that in C++ terminology, these classes are called derived classes and base classes.

Let us see a concrete example.

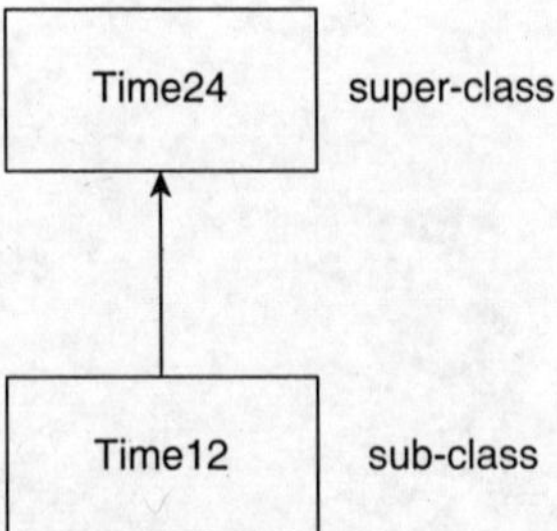

Figure 12.1 Simple Inheritance

Problem: Define class Time12 from class Time24.

Solution: See Program 12.1.

PROGRAM 12.1 Sub-Class extends Super-Class

```
//      inher1.java
class Time24
      { int numsec ; // (int n) ;
      } ;
class Time12 extends Time24
      { String st1;
      } ;
class inher1
{ public static void main (String argv[])
   { System.out.println("<---inher1.java--->");
     Time12 t1 = new Time12();
     t1.numsec =( 9*60+ 15)*60 ;// college opens in the morning
     if (t1.numsec >= 12*60*60) // 12 noon
              t1.st1 = "PM" ;
          else t1.st1 = "AM" ;

     System.out.println("Time in seconds " + t1.numsec);

     System.out.println("st1 is -->"+ t1.st1 +"<--");
   };
}
```

If you run this program, you will get the following output.

Output

```
<---inher1.java--->
Time in seconds 33300
St1 is -->AM<--
```

In the aforementioned example, class `Time12` is derived from class `Time24`. Variable `numsec` (for number of seconds) belongs to class `Time24`. It is not redefined in class `Time12`. Object t1 is of class `Time12`. Still we could initialize `t1.numsec`. It means that `numsec` is a member of class `Time12` now.

12.2 Member Access and Inheritance

As observed earlier, member access control is through keyword `public` and `private`. At this stage, we will be interested in knowing what happens to variables of super-class if keywords are declared specifically. The answer is simple and logical. The super-class variable declared `public` is available for use (accessible) in sub-class as observed in Program 12.1.

The nature of word private suggests that such a variable is not accessible in sub-class. This rule is tested in Program 12.11 in Section 12.10. Table 12.1 specifies these facts in tabular form.

Table 12.1 Access Control

Super-class access specifier	Effect in sub-class
`public`	accessible
`private`	not accessible

It is not mandatory to specify either `public` or `private`. When no particular access specifier is used, the access is considered as `default`. It is also termed as "package access".

At this moment, we are discussing small and simple programs (something like single-file programs of C++). So far, we have not used any user-defined packages. Under these circumstances, a member with default access specifier in super-class works as if declared `public`, as far as inheritance is concerned. Since it is more convenient to define variables without access specifier, we will use default access when we intend to use public access. See Program 12.12 in the end of chapter programs. At a later stage, we will study user-defined packages. We will study access `default` in detail at that time.

Inheritance is a mechanism that enables one class to inherit the behaviour and attributes of another class. However, we observe that the members marked `private` in super-class are not accessible in the sub-class. Hence, we cannot say that inheritance is a mechanism that enables one class to inherit **all the** behaviour and attributes of another class.

12.3 Keyword `super`

12.3.1 Use of `super` in sub-class constructor

Constructing a sub-class object

Any object needs a constructor for a disciplined initialization. The problem with sub-class is that it has to initialize not only its own (instance) variables but also the variables belonging to super-class.

While writing a sub-class constructor, we are supposed to initialize variables from super-class also. It means we have to call constructor for super-class. For this purpose, keyword `super` is used. If `Time12` is a sub-class having `Time24` as super-class and `Time24` has constructor `Time24(int h, int m, int s)`, then sub-class constructor must starts with a statement

```
super( int1,int2,int3);
```

where `int1, int2`, and `int3` are any integer expressions.

For example, the constructor for sub-class `Time12` will look like the following:

```
Time12(some_parameters)
    { super(h,m,s);// call to super-class constructor
               statement_1;
               statement_2;
          .
          .
    };
```

Here when a call to constructor of a sub-class is made, it first makes a call to constructor of super-class and then goes on initializing its own variables. We may say that "First statement of sub-class constructor should be call to `super()`".

Let us see this in a working program.

Problem: Show the use of keyword `super` in sub-class constructor.

Solution: See Program 12.2.

PROGRAM 12.2 Using super I

```
//      super1.java
class Time24
      { int hour,minute,second ;
        Time24(int h,int m, int s )
          { hour = h ;
            minute = m ;
            second = s ;
          }
      }
class Time12 extends Time24
      { String str;
        Time12(int h,int m, int s)
          { super(h,m,s);
            if (h>11) str = "PM" ;
                else str ="AM" ;
          }
      }
class super1
{  public static void main (String argv[])
   { System.out.println("<---super1.java--->");
     Time12 t1 = new Time12(9,15,0) ;
     System.out.println(t1.str) ;
   };
}
```

Please note that class `Time24` has a constructor `(int, int, int)`. The first statement of constructor of sub-class `Time12` is `super(h,m,s)`. It is used to initialize the variables of super-class.

If you run this program, you will get the following output.

Output

```
<---super1.java--->
AM
```

It is possible that the super-class may contain 2–3 constructors. In that case, sub-class constructor can call any of them. If super-class does not have any constructor, we have to call `super` without any parameters like `super()`.

In Program 12.2, you cannot simply say `super()`; compiler will complain that "No constructor matching `Time24 ()` found in class `Time24`".

One may think that if we have to call a super-class constructor, why not say `Time24(h,m,s)` at this position? Well syntax rules do not permit it.

We have seen a rule that "First statement of sub-class constructor should be call to `super()`". There are exceptions to this rule. When super-class has NO constructor or has a constructor without parameters (default constructor), we need not call `super()` in sub-class constructor. You can see this in Program 12.13 in end of chapter program.

12.3.2 Use of super in referencing a super-class variable

When a variable name, identical to that one in super class, is used in a sub-class, the variable from super-class gets hidden. Let us say that we define a variable hour in sub-class Time12 also. Now as far as object of the sub-class is concerned, it recognizes only one hour. The one which belongs to sub-class is recognised and the hour from super-class gets hidden. To refer to such a super-class variable, we have to use keyword super.

When we say

```
super.var_name
```

we are referring to a variable with name var_name present in super-class. Let us verify this in the following program.

Problem: Show that the keyword super used in sub-class refers to super-class variable.

Solution: See Program 12.3.

PROGRAM 12.3 Using super II

```
//      super3.java
class Time24
        { int hour,minute,second ;
          Time24(int h,int m, int s )
            { hour = h ;
              minute = m ;
              second = s ;
            }
        }
class Time12 extends Time24
        { int hour ;
          String str ;
          Time12(int h,int m, int s)
            { super(h,m,s);
              if (h>12) hour = h-12 ;
                  else hour = h ;
              if (h>11) str = "PM" ;
                  else str = "AM" ;
            }
          void show_super()
          { System.out.println(super.hour);
          }
        }
class super3
{   public static void main (String argv[])
    { System.out.println("<---super3.java--->");
      Time12 t1 = new Time12(17,15,0) ;
      System.out.println("time is :" ) ;
      System.out.print(t1.hour+":"+t1.minute);
      System.out.println(":"+ t1.second+" " +t1.str);
      t1.show_super();
    };
}
```

If you run this program, you will get the following output.

Output

```
<---super3.java--->
time is :
5:15:0 PM
17
```

Please note the word `super.hour` marked in bold. It refers to `hour` of super-class.

Also note that this has appeared in a method of a sub-class.

12.4 Use of `this` in Sub-Class Constructor

As mentioned earlier, the first statement in a sub-class constructor should be `super()`. This is true in principle. However, a minor variation can occur. The first statement can be `this(ABCD)` as well. Let us consider a case where class Guru is a super-class. Class `Shishya extends` class `Guru`.

Consider a case that we have a class `Shishya` with a valid constructor given as follows:

```
Shishya (String sy, String sx) // first constructor
        { super(sx);
          st2 = sy ;
        }
```

Now we want to have another constructor, say

```
Shishya (String sy)
```

You will immediately ask me what about `sx`, that is the value of the super-class variable. In light of previous example who is "Guru"?

In actual code for the constructor, we can call the previously defined constructor. This can be accomplished by a call using keyword `this`.

```
Shishya BOTTOM(String sy) // second constructor
   { this( sy , "GURU"); // note this
   }
```

In C++, there is a concept of default parameters. This example is somewhat similar to it.

Let us see this illustrated in the following program.

Problem: Write a program to demonstrate use of `this` in sub-class constructor.

Solution: See Program 12.4.

PROGRAM 12.4 Guru Shishya Example

```
//     guru1.java
class Guru
     {  String guruName ;
          Guru(String sx )
             { guruName = sx ; }
        } ;
class Shishya extends Guru
        {  String shishyaName;
```

```
            Shishya( String sy )
              { this(sy, "Drona") ;
              }
            Shishya(String sy, String sx)
              { super(sx);
                shishyaName = sy ;
              }
            void display()
            {  System.out.println(" Guru-->" + super.guruName) ;
               System.out.println("Shishya -->" + shishyaName ) ;
            }
        }
class guru1
{    public static void main (String argv[])
     { System.out.println("<---guru1.java--->");
       // example 1
       Shishya sh1 = new Shishya ("Narendra", "Rmakrishna") ;
       sh1.display();
       // example 2
       Shishya sh2 = new Shishya ("Arjun") ;
       sh2.display();
     };
}
```

If you run this program, you will see the following output.

Output

```
<---guru1.java--->
Guru-->Ramakrishna
Shishya -->Narendra
Guru-->Drona
Shishya -->Arjun
```

In this example, first we have a call to constructor with two parameters, Narendra (Famous Swami Vivekanand) and Ramakrishna (Parmahansa). This was a normal example.

In second example, we have a call to constructor for Shishya with only one parameter, Arjuna. Here a call to first constructor (as it has only one parameter) is made. In the code, there is keyword `this`. Here actually `this` means Shishya. It means `this` stands for call to second constructor (with two parameters).

Users of C++ are aware of facility of functions with default parameters. This facility is absent in Java. The aforementioned example is an **indirect** use of methods (functions) with default parameters.

12.5 Creating a Multi-Level Hierarchy

So far, we have seen one class extending the other. It is quite possible that the other class itself is a sub-class of another. Then this becomes the example of multi-level hierarchy.

Figure 12.2 illustrates this situation.

We can study this with a simple program. For simplicity, we will use an artificial example. Let us consider an example of an address book. It will typically contain entries like name, telephone number, and city. We will introduce one attribute at a time.

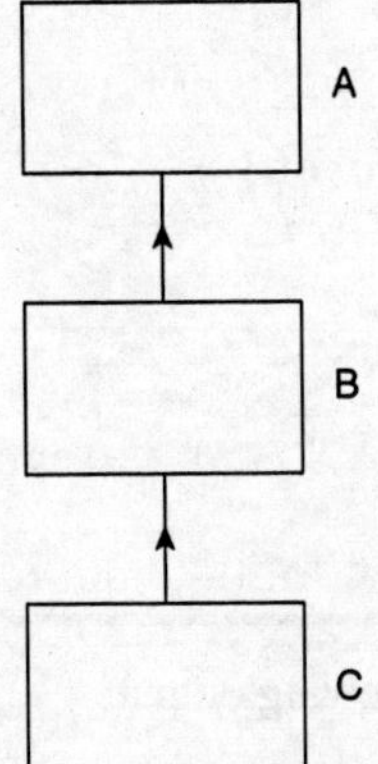

Figure 12.2 **Multi-Level Inheritance**

Problem: Write a program to demonstrate multi-level hierarchy.

Solution: Let us take the example of an address book (See Program 12.5).

PROGRAM 12.5 Multi-Level Hierarchy

```
//        multi1
class multi1
{   public static void main (String argv[])
    { int total ;
     System.out.println("<---multi1.java--->");
     System.out.println("");
     C me = new C("prof",24567890,"Mumbai");
     me.show();
    };
}

class A
    { public String name;
     A(String st1)
      { name = st1; }
     public void show()
      { System.out.println("name");
      }
    }
class B extends A
    {
     public long telephone ;
     B(String st1,long tn)
      { super(st1);
       telephone = tn ;
      }
     public void show()
      { System.out.println(super.name + " " + telephone);
      }
```

```
    }
class C extends B
    { public String city ;
      C(String st1, long n, String st3 )
        { super(st1, n);
          city = st3 ;
        }
      public void show()
       { System.out.println(name + " " + telephone+ " " + city);
       }
    }
```

If you run this program, you will get the following output.

Output

```
<---multi1.java--->
Prof 24567890 Mumbai
```

The aforementioned program works fine. It demonstrates multi-level inheritance. Please note that all the members were having public access. In an ideal situation data, members should be `private`. In that case, they will not be available to sub-classes. A simple program will fail to compile.

12.5.1 Keyword `protected`

Java offers the solution in terms of keyword `protected`. This access specifier works as `private` for outside world, but works as `public` for derived classes. Hence, it becomes extremely useful in multi-level inheritance.

Let us study it with the help of a program.

Problem: Write a program to demonstrate the use of access specifier `protected` in multi-level hierarchy.

Solution: Let us take a case of a telephone diary. Its entries may include name, telephone number, and a city. Let us create a simulated example from this. Let class A stores only name. Class B stores name and telephone number. The class C contains all the three entities. Class C `extends` class B, whereas class B `extends` class A. We will declare key fields as `protected`.

See Program 12.6.

PROGRAM 12.6 Keyword `protected`

```
//      multi4
class multi4
{ public static void main (String argv[])
  {
    System.out.println("<---multi4.java--->");
    System.out.println("");
    C me = new C("prof",24567890,"Mumbai");
    me.show();
    System.out.println( me.telephone);
  };
```

```
}
class A
  { protected String name;
    A(String st1)
     { name = st1; }
    public void show()
     { System.out.println("name");
     }
  }
class B extends A
  {
    protected long telephone ;
    B(String st1,long tn)
     { super(st1);
      telephone = tn ;
     }
    public void show()
     { System.out.println(super.name + " " + telephone);
     }
  }
class C extends B
    { public String city ;
      C(String st1, long n, String st3 )
        { super(st1, n);
          city = st3 ;
        }
    public void show()
     { System.out.println(name + " " + telephone+ " " + city);
    }
 }
```

If you run this program, you will get the following output.

Output

```
<---multi4.java--->
prof 24567890 Mumbai
24567890
```

You can see that the method shown from class C is capable of accessing protected variables in its super-classes.

The last program line

```
System.out.println( me.telephone);
```

is more critical. Here we are accessing a protected variable of class B in method `main()`. This method `main` is a part of class named `multi4`. This class is not a sub-class of class B.

This calls for a review of accessibility once again. Table 12.2 describes the rules for accessing variables of a given class, say X from some other class Y. We are assuming a single-file environment. It means that the classes X and Y are in the same file. (Technically speaking, they are in the same `package`. We will discuss the details of `package` in a later chapter.)

Table 12.2 Access Control in Single File Programs

Access specifier in a given class X	Accessibility in other class Y	
	When Y is Sub-class of X	When Y is not a sub-class of X
`public`	Accessible	Accessible
`protected`	Accessible	Accessible
`default`	Accessible	Accessible
`private`	Not accessible	Not accessible

Anyone who will scrutinize the table carefully will come up with a simple rule. If the access specifier is `private`, the variable is not accessible; in other access specifiers the variable is accessible.

We have used the term "variable" for simplicity. The correct word should be a member, as it will mean both variables (fields) and methods.

When we write a single-file program, all the classes it contains belong to same (unnamed) package. Since no specific name is given to this package, it is referred as "unnamed package", and hence, the above-mentioned rules are applied.

12.6 Method `overriding`

When same name appears for methods in both super- and sub-class, only method from sub-class is invoked. That is why it is said that the method of sub-class overrides the super-class method. However, super-class method is not lost, it is available. It has to be called with keyword `super` (only inside sub-class method).

Problem: Write a program to demonstrate method `overriding`.

Solution: See Program 12.7.

PROGRAM 12.7 Method `overriding` I

```
//      super5.java
class Time24
       { int hour,minute,second ;
         Time24(int h,int m, int s )
           { hour = h ;
             minute = m ;
             second = s ;
           }
         void show()
          {System.out.printf("***%3d%3d%3d",
               hour,minute,second);
           }
       }
class Time12 extends Time24
   { int hour ;
     String str ;
     Time12(int h,int m, int s)
       { super(h,m,s);
```

```
        if (h>12) hour = h-12 ;
              else hour = h ;
        if (h>11) str = "PM" ;
              else str = "AM" ;
      }
   void show()
      { System.out.printf("===%3d%3d%3d%3s\n",
                                hour,minute,second,str);
      }
   void show_super()
      { System.out.println("showing from super :");
        super.show();
      }
   }

class super5
{   public static void main (String argv[])
    { System.out.println("<---super5.java--->");
      Time12 t1 = new Time12(17,15,0) ;
      System.out.println("calling show of sub" ) ;
//      System.out.print(t1.hour+":"+t1.minute);
      t1.show();
      System.out.println("calling method show_super()");
      t1.show_super();
    };
}
```

If you run this program, you will get the following output.

Output

```
<---super5.java--->
calling show of sub
=== 5 15 0 PM
calling method show_super()
showing from super :
*** 17 15 0
```

Please note that we have used characters *** in show of super-class. Also note that we cannot call it as `t1.super.show()`. Language does not allow us to do it. We have to embed this call in some other method. Here we have chosen a name `show_super()` to draw attention to this fact.

12.7 Using final in Inheritance

Keyword `final` plays many roles in the process of inheritance. It can be used for a class or any method of a class. Let us study these situations one by one.

12.7.1 Using final with a class

It is possible to declare a normally behaving class as `final`. However, we cannot use it as a super-class. Any sub-classing is not allowed. There are two ways to look at this. When you think that the development of a class is complete and nobody should modify it by extending it, then you can use this keyword `final` with that class.

The other way is you feel that development is incomplete and no one use it (by extending) until you complete its development.

12.7.2 Using final with a method of a super-class

It is possible to declare a method in a class as `final`. That class behaves normally. We are allowed to sub-class it. However, we cannot override that method in a sub-class. Any such attempt generates compile time error. We can see this principle in action at the end of chapter program.

12.8 Introducing Interface

There are two ways of looking at interface facility. First one is simplistic. It considers it as a mask or interpretation of behaviour. The second one is complex. It looks at it as an effective tool for multiple inheritance. C++ supports multiple inheritance while Java does not. Hence, this technique is useful to affect two super-classes for one sub-class. However, only seasoned programmers need this facility. So we will discuss this concept at a later stage.

At this stage, let us study what interface offers us in simple terms.

12.8.1 Defining an interface

An interface can be defined as follows:

```
interface std // std = standard
{ void define();
  void show();
};
```

Please note the following points with respect to the interface definition:

- Interface definition starts with the keyword `interface`.
- Next is interface name.
- Then comes the definition within curly brackets.
- Interface may consist of variables (not seen in previous example). They are declared as `final`.
- There is no body to the methods defined.

12.8.2 Implementing interfaces

Once an interface is defined, one or more classes can implement it.

A typical class definition using an interface is shown as the following:

```
class  money implements std
    { int rupee;
      int paise;
      public void init(int a, int b)
         { rupee =a; paise = b; };
      public void show()
       {System.out.println("Rs "+ rupee + "="+paise);
       } ;
```

```
    public void define() { rupee =100; paise = 0; };
  };
```

Note the syntax:

```
class  class_name implements interface-name
       {
       }
```

Please note that methods `define` and `show` are fully defined here. In interface, they were simply declared.

As a rule, these methods must be declared `public`.

As a rule, any normal class must fully define all the methods declared in the interface. Let us see a working program.

Problem: Write a program to illustrate `interface`.

Solution: See Program 12.8.

PROGRAM 12.8 Interface I

```
//      impl33.java
interface std  // std = standard
   { void define();
     void show();
   };
class money implements std
       { int rupee;
         int paise;
         public void init(int a, int b)
           { rupee =a; paise = b; };
         public void show()
              { System.out.println("Rs "+ rupee + "="+paise);
              } ;
         public void define() { rupee =100; paise = 0; };
       };
class impl33
{   public static void main (String argv[])
    { //int total ;
      money amt1= new money() ;
      money amt2= new money();
      System.out.println("---impl33.java---");
      amt1.init(20,30);
      amt2.define();
      System.out.println("amt1 is ");
      amt1.show();
//      System.out.println(amt1.rupee + " " + amt1.paise);
      System.out.println("amt2 is ");
      amt2.show();
    };
}
```

If you run this program, you will get the following output.

Output

```
---impl33.java---
amt1 is
Rs 20=30
amt2 is
Rs 100=0
```

12.8.3 Variables in interfaces

All variables in the `interface` are declared as `final` and initialized. Therefore, they serve as enumerated constants.

Consider that we are working with money. We know that when we specify amount, paise cannot be more than 99 and less than 0. Naturally, our program needs two constants. We can define an `interface` for it as follows.

```
interface constP // constP = constants for paise
{ final int pmax =99;
    final int pmin = 0;
};
```

Let us see a complete program.

Problem: Write a program to show the use of `interface` in supplying constants to a class.

Solution: See Program 12.9.

PROGRAM 12.9 interface Supplies Constants

```
//      impl4.java
interface constP // constP = constants for paise
   { final int pmax =99;
     final int pmin = 0;
   };
class money implements constP
       { int rupee;
         int paise;
         money(int a, int b )
           { rupee =a; paise = b; };
         public void check()
           { if (paise > pmax)
                System.out.println("paise can not be more than "+ pmax);
             if(paise < pmin)
                System.out.println(" paise can not be less than " +pmin);
           };
       };
class impl4
{   public static void main (String argv[])
    { money amt1= new money(100,100) ;
      money amt2= new money(30,-20);
      System.out.println("---impl4.java---");
      System.out.println(amt1.rupee + " " + amt1.paise);
```

```
        amt1.check();
        System.out.println(amt2.rupee + " " + amt2.paise);
        amt2.check();
    };
}
```

If you run this program, you will get the following output.

Output

```
---impl4.java---
100 100
paise can not be more than 99
30 -20
Paise can not be less than 0
```

At this stage, we have seen two different useful interfaces for class `money`. If we want to redefine a class with both of them, Java permits us to do so. We can define our class, say `money1` as

```
class money1 implements std, constP
    {
    }
```

As a rule, a class can have more than one interface.

12.9 Abstract Methods and Classes

Sometimes, at the start of the project, we may want to define a class which is just some sort of a template or guideline for development of further classes. In that case, we need not define the class completely. Such a class is called `abstract` class. It goes without saying that such a class cannot be instantiated.

Consider a case that we have a class test. It has a number called num and method to show it. We want that implementation of show is left to the users of this class. We may want to define this class as

```
class test { int num;
             void show();
           }
```

This will not be acceptable to the compiler as there is no body to method `show`. A key word `abstract` comes in to a play.

We may write

```
class test
    { int num;
      abstract void show();
    }
```

Here we are declaring method `show()` as abstract method. This is fine as far as method `void` is concerned. Still the code will not compile. It will ask you to declare a class as `abstract`.

It will be acceptable if we declare it as follows:

```
abstract class test { int num;
                      abstract void show();
                    }
```

You may feel that there is redundancy in it. You are right. But this redundancy is deliberate. It increases the readability. When a programmer reads this code, he is not likely to miss that the class is `abstract`. He will also not miss the point that the method `show()` is abstract.

You can now extend this class yourselves. Only thing is that in the sub-class, you must define the method `show`. Let us study it with a program.

Problem: Write a program to study extending a class which is `abstract` class.

Solution: See Program 12.10.

PROGRAM 12.10 abstract class

```
//       abst3.java
abstract class test
    { int num;
      abstract void show();
    }
class newtest extends test
    {  void show()
        { System.out.println("num is " +num);
        }
    };
class abst3
{    public static void main (String argv[])
    {    newtest nt = new newtest();
         System.out.println("<---abst3.java--->");
         nt.show();
    }
}
```

If you run this program, you will get the following output.

Output

```
<---abst3.java--->
num is 0
```

Rules:

1. A method declared without the body is an abstract method. Such a method has to be declared as abstract.
2. A class containing an abstract method is an `abstract` class. Such a class must be explicitly declared as abstract.
3. An `abstract` class cannot be instantiated.
4. If a class `extends` an `abstract` class, it must define all the methods of the super-class, otherwise it has to be declared abstract.

12.10 Collection of Programs

12.10.1 private of super not accessible

Problem: Show that instance variable declared `private` in super-class is not accessible in sub-class.

Solution: See Program 12.11.

PROGRAM 12.11 private of super not Accessible

```
//       inher12.java
class Time24
    { private int numsec ; // (int n) ;
      Time24(int num )
      { numsec=num;}
    } ;
class Time12 extends Time24
    { String st1;
      Time12(int n)
        { super(n);
          if ( n >= 12*60*60) // 12 noon
                   st1 = "PM" ;
                   else st1 = "AM" ;
        }
    } ;
class inher12
{ public static void main (String argv[])
   { System.out.println("<---inher12.java--->");
     Time12 t1 = new Time12(3600);
     System.out.println("st1 is : " + t1.st1);
     System.out.println("variable numsec is :"+ t1.numsec);
   };
}
```

If you compile this program, you will get the following errors.

Compilation Error inher12.err

```
 Compiling javac inher12.java
inher12.java:22: numsec has private access in Time24
     System.out.println("variable numsec is :"+ t1.numsec);
                                                  ^

1 error
press any key to continue
```

If you comment out the last line you will get the following output.

Output

```
<---inher12.java--->
st1 is : AM
```

The key word `private` (marked in bold in source code) creates the problems.

12.10.2 This program proves that `default` acts as `public`

Problem: Write a program to show that `default` in `super` is accessible.

Solution: We have seen program `inher1` earlier. Let us use the same basic code. Let us remove either `public` or `private` to make access `default` (see Program 12.12).

PROGRAM 12.12 `default` of `super` is Accessible

```
//      inher13.java
class time0
        { int numsec ; // note absence of either
                        // public or private
        } ;
class clock extends time0
        { String st1;
         } ;
class inher13
{    public static void main (String argv[])
   { int total ;
     System.out.println("---inher13.java---");
     clock clk1 = new clock();
     clk1.numsec = ( 9*60+ 15)*60 ;; // college opens in the morning
     if (clk1.numsec >= 12*60*60) // 12 noon
               clk1.st1 = "PM" ;
          else clk1.st1 = "AM" ;
     System.out.println("Time in seconds " + clk1.numsec);
     System.out.println("st1 is -->"+ clk1.st1 +"<--");
   };
}
```

If you run this program, you will get the following output.

Output

```
---inher13.java---
Time in seconds 33300
st1 is -->AM<--
```

12.10.3 Is `super` always needed in sub-class constructor?

Problem: Show that the use of keyword `super` in sub-class constructor is not needed under certain conditions.

Solution: There are two distinct cases. When we have super-class which does not have any constructor, we need not use `super` in sub-class constructor. Alternately, if super-class has a constructor with no parameters (default constructor), call to `super` is not needed (see Program 12.13).

PROGRAM 12.13 super not Required

```
//      default1.java
//      No constructor in super class
class Super1
        { String st1=" ";
          int i;
          void init()
          { st1="I am super";}
        }
class Sub1 extends Super1
        { String st2 ;
          Sub1(String sy)
            {
              st2 = sy ;
            }
        }
class Super2
          { String st1;
            int i;
            Super2()
            { st1="I am super";}
          }
class Sub2 extends Super2
          { String st2 ;
            Sub2(String sy)
              {
                st2 = sy ;
              }
            void show()
            { System.out.println(st1);
              System.out.println(st2);
            }
          }
class default1
{    public static void main (String argv[])
     {
       System.out.println("<---default1.java--->");
       System.out.println(" No constructor case ");
       Sub1 s1 = new Sub1("Java") ;
       System.out.println("st1 is -->"+ s1.st2 ) ;
       System.out.println(" Default constructor case");
       Sub2 s2 = new Sub2("I am sub") ;
       s2.show();
   };
}
```

If you run this program, you will get the following output.

Output

```
<---default1.java--->
No constructor case
```

```
st1 is -->Java
Default constructor case
I am super
I am sub
```

Note the following points carefully.

First case: There is no constructor in super-class. Hence, we are not calling constructor of super-class explicitly. Still, object of sub-class comes into existence.

Second case: There is a constructor with no parameters. Here also no call to `super` is required.

12.10.4 A `final` class cannot be extended

Problem: Test whether a class declared as `final` can be sub-classed (extended).

Solution: See Program 12.14.

PROGRAM 12.14 Class Declared `final` I

```
//     final1.java
final class TOP
        { String st1 ;
          TOP() { st1="Guru" ; }
          void show()
            { System.out.println("+++ st1 is+++>"+ st1) ;}
         } ;
class BOTTOM extends TOP
         { String st2;
           BOTTOM() { st2 = "Shishya" ; }
           void show()
             { System.out.println("### st2 is###>"+ st2) ;}
           void attention()
             { super.show(); }
       }
class final1
{    public static void main (String argv[])
     { System.out.println("---final1---");
       BOTTOM b1 = new BOTTOM() ;
       b1.show();
       b1.attention();
     };
}
```

If you compile this program, you will get the following error.

Output

```
Compiling javac final1.java
final1.java:8: cannot inherit from final TOP
class BOTTOM extends TOP
                     ^
1 error
press any key to continue
```

Keywords

Abstract, `abstract` class, abstract method, access control, enumerated, constants, `extends`, `final`, implements, `interface`, method `overriding`, multiple, inheritance, `private`, `public`, `super`, `this`

RuleBook

method `interface`	Methods declared in interface must be declared `public` in class definition.
method `interface`	Any normal class (non-abstract) must fully define all the methods declared in the interface.
`interface`	A class can have more than one interface.
variables `interface`	Variables in interface must be declared as `final`.
`final` class	A class declared final cannot be sub-classed.
`final` method	A method declared as `final` cannot be overridden.
abstract method	A method declared without the body is an abstract method. Such a method has to be declared as abstract.
`abstract` class	A class containing an abstract method is an `abstract` class. Such a class must be explicitly declared as abstract.
`abstract` class	An `abstract` class cannot be instantiated.
`abstract` class extending	If a class `extends` an `abstract` class, it must define all the methods of the super-class. Other wise it has to be declared abstract.
sub-class constructor	Every constructor of a sub-class must have a call to super-class constructor as a first statement. Only exception is when Super-class has no constructor or has a default constructor (one without parameters).
multiple inheritances	Java allows multiple inheritances by means of interfaces.
Implements	A class can use an interface by using the `implements` clause.
Inheritance	Inheritance is a mechanism that enables one class to inherit, in general, the behaviour and attributes of another class. But we cannot say that it inherits all the behaviour and attributes.
override	A method is overridden when another method with the same signature is declared in a sub-class.
override	A `final` method cannot be overridden.
`interface`	An interface can extend any number of interfaces.

C++ Corner

1. There is no direct equivalent of `interface` in C++.
2. In early days, there was no `enum` keyword in Java. If one wants enumerated constants in Java, one has to define and use a suitable `interface`. Recently in version 5, a class `Enum` has been introduced. It can provide enumerated constants in a disciplined way.

Review Questions

1. What is the significance of keyword `super`?
2. What is the use of keyword `final` in inheritance?
3. What role does `interface` play in multiple inheritance?
4. How interface can be used to provide enumeration?
5. What is the meaning of abstract method?
6. What is the advantage of declaring a class `abstract`? What is the major difference between extending classes and extending interfaces?
7. Abstract identifier can be applied to classes as well as methods. Explain what this modifier indicates in each case.
8. What is the difference between `abstract` and `final` class.
9. Discuss the role of inheritance in object-oriented programming.
10. What do you understand by implementing interfaces? Explain with an example.
11. What is the difference between `abstract` class and an `interface`?
12. What does the `final` keyword mean in front of a variable, a method, and a class?
13. Write short notes on access specifiers `public, private`, and `protected`.
14. Write short notes on interfaces in Java.
15. Write short notes on Abstract classes in Java.

Exercises

1. State whether following program will compile. If yes, describe the output. If no, give reasons

```
*******************************************

//      final2.java
class TOP
      { String st1 ;
        TOP() { st1="Guru" ; }
        final void show()
          { System.out.println("+++ st1 is+++>"+ st1) ;}
      } ;
class BOTTOM extends TOP
      { String st2;
        BOTTOM() { st2 = "Shishya" ; }
        void show()
```

```
        { System.out.println("### st2 is###>"+ st2) ;}
      void attention()
        { super.show(); }
    }
class final2
{    public static void main (String argv[])
     { System.out.println("---final2---");
       BOTTOM b1 = new BOTTOM() ;
       b1.show();
       b1.attention();
     };
}
*******************************************
```

GRAPHICS

13.1 Introduction

So far, we have written many programs and seen their output on monitor screen. In all these outputs, monitor was displaying only text and not pictures. You may be surprised to know that 20 years before, 99% of the monitors could display only text. They could display images in very poor manner.

An image conveys any idea far more effectively than words. Therefore, we would like images to be shown on the screen. Even the text should be in various fonts and colours. This requires graphical capability. Modern monitors and operating systems have support for high-resolution graphics. In windows, the default screen itself is in high-resolution graphics.

Thus, today's computers can be used in computer-aided design (CAD), computer-aided manufacturing (CAM), image processing, and even computer-based training applications. The list will be incomplete if we do not mention the computer games.

In graphics mode, screen consists of pixels. Pixels are like fine points or dots, arranged in rows and columns and which can be illuminated. In monochrome monitors, pixel either glows (bright) or not (dark). If we are using colour monitors, pixels can glow with specified colour.

Study of graphics should actually start with points and line. However, to draw any thing we must have a canvas. And to hold it we need a frame. Hence, let us start our topic of graphics with class Frame.

13.2 Frame

A Frame is a top-level window with a title and a border. The size of the frame includes any area designated for the border. The Java supports a class `Frame` in advanced window toolkit (AWT) package. There are many methods to work with it. Let us jump straight away to an introductory program.

Problem: Write a program to introduce class `Frame`.

Solution: See Program 13.1.

PROGRAM 13.1 Using Frame

```
//      frame1.java
import java.awt.Frame;
import java.awt.Color;
class frame1 extends Frame
{ public static void main(String[] args)
    { frame1 f1= new frame1();
      f1.setSize(300,200);
```

```
    f1.setBackground(Color.yellow);
    f1.setVisible(true);
  }
}
```

If you run the program, you will get the following output.

Output

You may note the following:

The method `setSize(300, 200)` sets the output window to 300 × 200 pixels size.

The window has a title bar which has minimize, normal, and close **icons**.

The method `setBackground(Color.yellow)` sets the frame background yellow.

If you try to close this window by clicking the close icon (marked with X), it does not work. (If we add few more lines, we can close the window. However, our focus here is on graphics and not on frames. Interested readers should see Chapter 21 on AWT.) You will ask me how we close this window. The answer is that we should go back to running application and press Ctrl + C and then return. It terminates the application. This closes the frame.

There is a method `setTitle(String title_string)` which can be used to get a title to the frame.

If we want to draw in a frame, we must know the coordinate system of the frame. Luckily, it is similar to C/C++ `viewport`. Assume that the size of the frame is *w* by *h* (*w*, width and *h*, height). Now top left corner coordinates are (0, 0) and bottom right corner coordinates will be (*w*1, *h*1); the title bar height is approximately 20 pixels. Considering the borders, it will be safe to leave 25 pixels from the top while drawing.

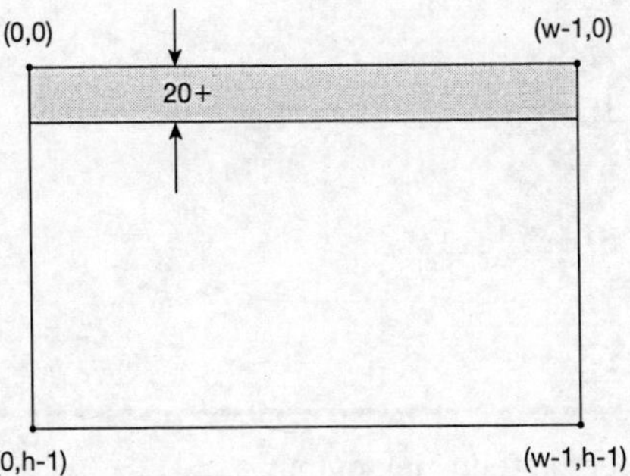

Figure 13.1 Frame Coordinates

13.3 Drawing a Line

After studying the frame, let us start drawing. The most fundamental or elementary instruction/method provided by Java is `drawLine()`. Its format is as shown hereafter:

```
public abstract void drawLine(int x1, int y1, int x2, int y2)
```

It draws a line between the points (x1, y1) and (x2, y2). It uses the current colour set for drawing.

13.4 Drawing a Rectangle

After drawing the lines you can draw any linear geometric figures like triangle and rectangle. In most of the drawings, we need to draw a rectangle. Java provides the following method:

```
drawRect (int x, int y, int width, int height)
```

It draws the outline of the specified rectangle. Please note that orientation of this rectangle is horizontal (/vertical). In strict geometrical terms, a rectangle is one with all angles of 90°. It does not assume any orientation. If you need to draw a rectangle with any other orientation, you have to draw all four lines.

Problem: Write a program to draw rectangles.

Solution: Here we will use both the alternatives. First, we will use `drawRect()`. Then we will use four straight lines to draw a rectangle (see Program 13.2).

PROGRAM 13.2 Rectangles

```
//    rect1.java
import java.awt.*;
class rect1 extends Frame
{  public void paint(Graphics g)
    {  g.setColor(Color.red);
       g.drawRect(50,50,100,50);
       g.setColor(Color.blue);
       g.drawLine(200,50,270,50);
       g.drawLine(270,50,270,100);
       g.drawLine(270,100,200,100);
       g.drawLine(200,100,200,50);
    };

   public static void main(String[] args)
    { rect1 f1= new rect1();
      f1.setSize(350,130);
      f1.setBackground(Color.yellow);
      f1.setVisible(true);
    }
}
```

If you run the program, you will get the following output.

Output

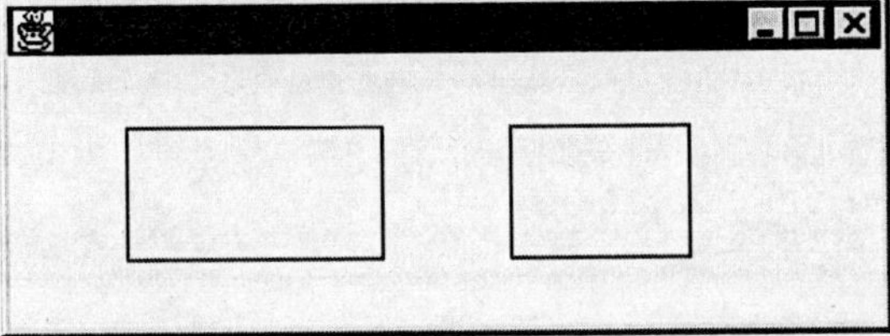

13.5 Drawing a Point

You will ask me if drawing a point is not more basic. I have no answer. But when I have to draw a point I draw a line with same values of *x* and *y* for both the end-points. A point is too tiny to see clearly on the screen. Hence, let us develop a method to draw a thick point.

This is our own method (see Program 13.3).

Problem: Write a program to develop and use method `drawPoint()`.

Solution: Such a method should have three parameters. The first two parameters are *x* and *y* coordinates where point is to be drawn and the third one is the thickness.

PROGRAM 13.3 Thick Points

```
//      thickp1.java
import java.awt.* ;
import java.applet.* ;
import java.util.* ;
//
class  VP extends Frame
   {  VP (int xdim, int ydim) //constructor
       { setSize(xdim,ydim);
         setBackground(Color.white);
         setVisible(true);
       }
   public void drawPoint(int x0 , int y0 , int thick )
   {  int k;
      Graphics g = getGraphics();
      g.setColor( Color.blue );
      for(k=0;k<thick; k++)
       { g.drawLine(x0,y0+k,x0+thick,y0+k) ;
       }
   }
   public void paint (Graphics g)
      {  int i,j,k ;
         int x0=50,y0 = 50 ;
         int x1,y1,x2,y2;
         int thickness ;
//         g.setColor( Color.green );
         for( i= 0; i<5 ;i++)
```

```
            for(j=0;j<4;j++)
                drawPoint( x0 +30*i , y0+30*j , 3);
        }
    }
 class thickp1
 {  public static void main(String[] args)
        { VP vp1= new VP( 220,180);
        };
 }
```

Output

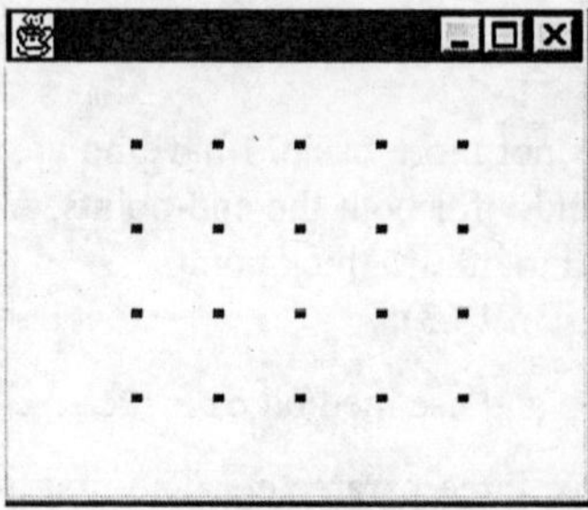

You will see points marked with thickness value three. It is possible to have any non-zero value for the thickness.

13.6 Drawing Circles

Java does not support method circle. Instead, it supports method `drawOval()`. The idea may be that this one method is just sufficient to draw both ovals and circles.

The syntax of the method is as shown hereafter:

```
drawOval (int x, int y, int width, int height)
```

This method draws the outline of an oval fitting a rectangle with coordinates of top left point as *x* and *y*. The `width` specifies the horizontal dimension while `height` stands for vertical dimension.

When we supply equal values for parameters width and height, we automatically get a circle.

Problem: Write a program to draw circles on the screen.

Solution: See Program 13.4.

PROGRAM 13.4 Circle I

```
 //      circle1.java
 import java.awt.* ;
 import java.applet.* ;
 class VP extends Frame
    { VP (int xdim, int ydim) //constructor
        { setSize(xdim,ydim);
          setBackground(Color.white);
          setVisible(true);
        }
```

```
public void delay(long n)
    { long t1,t2;
      t1 = System.currentTimeMillis();
      t1 = t1 + n;
      t2= System.currentTimeMillis();
      while ( t2 < t1 ) t2= System.currentTimeMillis();
    }

  public void paint (Graphics g)
     {  int k ;
        int x0=100, y0=100, r1=50;
        int x1 , y1 ;
        double mult = 3.1416 /180.0 ;
        g.setColor( Color.green );
        for(k=0; k< 6; k++)
          {  delay(1000);
             x1 = (int) Math.ceil( x0 + r1* Math.cos(60.0*mult*k) ) ;
             y1 = (int) Math.floor( y0 + r1* Math.sin(60.0*mult*k) ) ;
             g.drawOval(x1,y1,2*r1,2*r1);
          }
     }
 }
class circle1
{  public static void main(String[] args)
        { VP vp1= new VP( 300,300);
        };

}
```

If you run the program, you will get the following output.

Output

If you are drawing many circles, you may wish that there is a method

```
drawCircle( origin, radius)
```

It is very easy to develop such a method, using `drawOval()`. Details are left to you as exercise.

13.7 Introducing Colours

So far we have used the following two methods from the graphics package.

```
setColor(color);
setBackground(color);
```

These methods set the foreground and background colours for drawing. Let us study the colours in details now.

Class `color` is defined in package `java.awt`. Some colours are defined as static fields (constants). They are black, blue, cyan, grey, green, magenta, orange, pink, red, and yellow. We can use them directly to specify colours. Let us write a simple program to study these standard colours.

Problem: Write a program to introduce colours.

Solution: See Program 13.5.

PROGRAM 13.5 Colors I

```
//     col11.java
import java.awt.* ;
import java.applet.* ;

class Z { public int x0,y0,xdist,ydist ;
          public Z(int a, int b, int width, int hight )
           {    x0=a;  y0 = b;
             xdist=width; ydist= hight ; };
       }

class VIEWPORT extends Frame
   { Z z ;
     VIEWPORT (Color col, Z z1) //constructor
       { z = z1 ;
         setSize(z.xdist,z.ydist);
         setBackground(col);
         setVisible(true);
       }
    public void paint (Graphics g)
     { Color[] col = { Color.black , Color.blue , Color.cyan ,
                       Color.gray , Color.green , Color.magenta,
                       Color.orange , Color.pink , Color.red ,
                       Color.yellow } ;
       String[] name = { "black" , "blue" , "cyan" ,
                         "gray" , "green" , "magenta",
                         "orange" , "pink" , "red" ,
                         "yellow" } ;
       int i;
       for (i=0;i<10;i++)
        { g.setColor(col[i]);
          g.fillRect( 30,60+i*20, 100, 20);
          g.drawString(name[i], 30+100+30, 60+20 +i*20);
          delay(1000);
        }
     }
```

```
public  void delay(long n)
    { long t1,t2;
      t1 = System.currentTimeMillis();
      t1 = t1 + n;
      t2= System.currentTimeMillis();
      while ( t2 < t1 ) t2= System.currentTimeMillis();
    }
  }
public class col11
{
  public static void main(String[] args)
    {
      char x1 ;
      Z za = new Z(50,50,250,300);
      VIEWPORT win1= new VIEWPORT(Color.white, za);
    }
}
```

If you run the program, you will get the following output.

Output

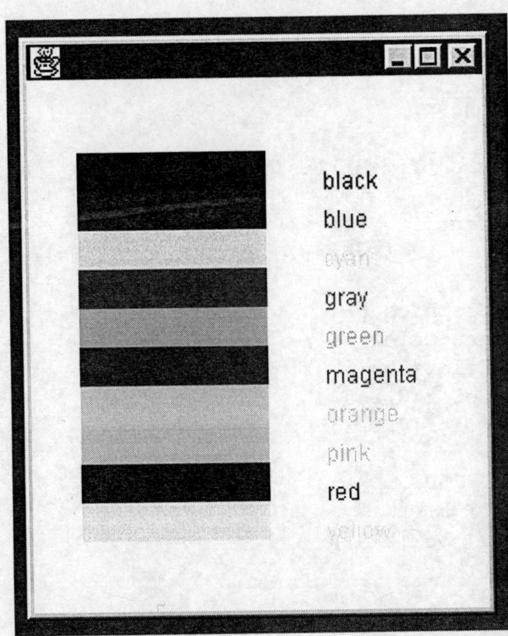

So far, we have seen predefined colours. Java helps us to achieve any colour on our own. Let us first understand its colour model. The computer graphics teaches us various colour models. Out of which RGB is simple to understand and use. Any colour is composed of three basic colours red, green, and blue. Java uses the sRGB model. Here, s stands for the transparence or alpha value. On 0 to 1 scale, 0 means totally transparent and 1 means opaque. Java stores colour values in a 32-bits integer word. Bits 0–7 is used for storing blue colour value. Bits 8–15 is used for storing green colour value. Bits 16–23 is used for storing red colour value. Bits 24–31 is used for storing alpha (transparency) value. To define a colour various constructors are defined. The simplest one is as follows. `Color (int r, int g, int b);` values of *r*, *g*, and *b* are in the range 0–255. The alpha value is by default 1.

If we say `color c1 = new color (255, 0, 0)`, then c1 will be pure red colour. The RGB model tells us that if values of *r*, *g*, and *b* are equal we get grey shades. $r = g = b = 0$ will represent black. $r = g = b = 255$ will represent white. The other constructors and methods can be seen at the end of chapter.

Let us try a program before proceeding.

Problem: Write a program to draw concentric filled circles with three alternate colours.

Solution: Earlier we have studied `drawOval` method to draw an outline of the oval. Method `fillOval` is similar except it fills the oval. We can use `fillOval` to draw a filled circle. When we draw circles, we have to remember that we should start from drawing largest circle. If we start from smallest circle, every new draw will overwrite the previous one (see Program 13.6).

PROGRAM 13.6 Colors II

```
//      circle3.java
import java.awt.* ;
import java.applet.* ;
class  VP extends Frame
{  VP (int xdim, int ydim) //constructor
        { setSize(xdim,ydim);
          setBackground(Color.white);
          setVisible(true);
        }
   public void delay(long n)
      { long t1,t2;
        t1 = System.currentTimeMillis();
        t1 = t1 + n;
        t2= System.currentTimeMillis();
        while ( t2 < t1 ) t2= System.currentTimeMillis();
      }
   public void paint (Graphics g)
      {  Color[] box= new Color[10];
         box[0] = new Color(255,0,0);
         box[1] = new Color(0,255,0);
         box[2] = new Color(0,0,255);
         int k ;
         int x0=250, y0=250, r = 50;
         for(k=0; k< 10; k++)
           { g.setColor( box[k%3]);
             delay(200);
             r = 200-20*k ;
             g.fillOval(x0-r,y0-r,2*r,2*r);
           }
      }
}
class circle3
{  public static void main(String[] args)
        { VP vp1= new VP( 500,500);
        };
}
```

If you run the program, you will get the following output.

Output

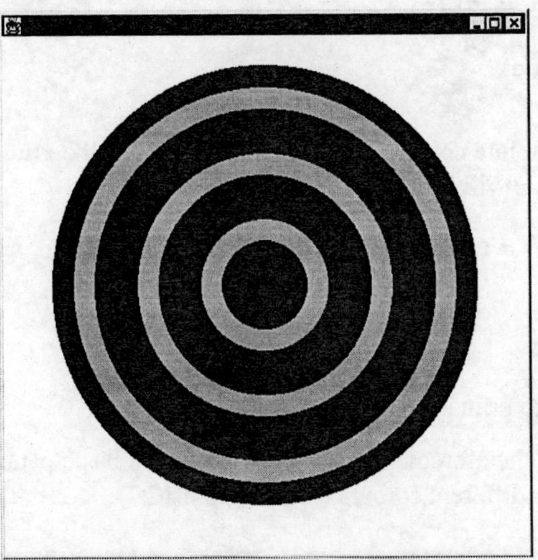

13.8 Designing a Fabric

Most of the clothes have a pattern. Theoretically, anything is possible. However, for convenience, repeating in horizontal and vertical directions is the easiest way of having a pattern. It means basic image (picture) should be a rectangle.

Hence, the simplest algorithm to draw a pattern is to draw an image in top left corner and repeat it horizontally and vertically. For this purpose, we have a method

```
copyArea (x,y,width,height,dx,dy);
```

This method copies an image from a rectangle with *x* and *y* as its top left corner. `width` and `height` represent the width and height of the image. Note that *dx* and *dy* represent the displacements. It means that the image is copied at a location whose top left corner is given by $(x + dx, y + dy)$.

However, this technique enters in trouble with threads. Hence, it has to be suitably modified. Instead of pasting what has been copied, we draw the image wherever we want.

Consider the canvas consists of a grid with blocks identified by its coordinates as shown in Figure 13.2.

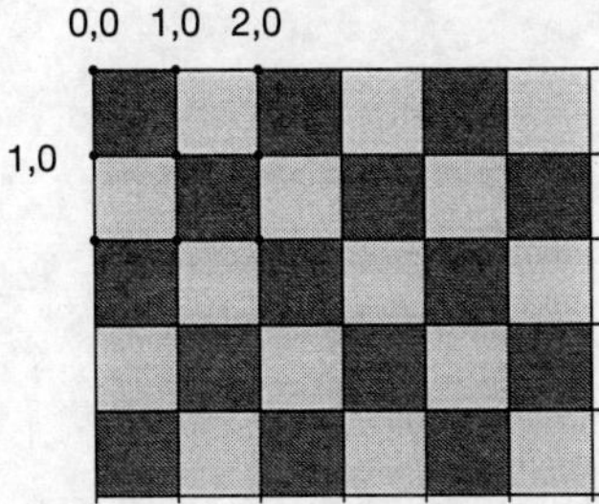

Figure 13.2 Grid

Let variables row and col represent the number of rows and number of columns.

Now simplest way to develop a pattern will be

```
for ( gx=0; gx <col ; gx++)
for ( gy=0; gy<row ; gy ++ )
{draw at gx, gy pane
}
```

Now if $x0$ and $y0$ are the absolute coordinates of top left corner of the grid then absolute values of x and y for the top left corner of a pane will be

```
X = x0 + gx * width ;
and
Y = y0 + gy * hight ;
```

With this derivation, let us try to create a design.

Problem: Write a program to print a design on a cloth.

Solution: We will be using the aforementioned algorithm. As a basic pattern, we will draw one rectangle and two filled rectangles with different colours (see Program 13.7).

PROGRAM 13.7 Cloth Design

```
//      cloth2.java
import java.awt.* ;

class VP extends Frame
{ VP (int xdim, int ydim) //constructor
      { setSize(xdim,ydim);
        setBackground(Color.white);
        setVisible(true);
      }
  public void delay(long n)
     { long t1,t2;
       t1 = System.currentTimeMillis();
       t1 = t1 + n;
       t2= System.currentTimeMillis();
       while ( t2 < t1 )  t2 = System.currentTimeMillis();
     }
  public void paint (Graphics g)
    { int i,j,k ;
      int x0=10,y0 = 40,x,y ;
      int hight = 100 , width = 100 ;
//    Drawing and Repeating the Pattern
      for(i=0;i<5;i++)
       for( j=0;j<4;j++)
        { delay(100);
          x= x0 + i * width ;
          y= y0 + j * hight;
          g.setColor( Color.green );
          g.drawRect(x,y,88,88);
          g.fillRect(x,y,70,70);
```

```
            g.setColor( Color.yellow );
            g.fillRect(x,y,40,40);
        }
    }
}
public class cloth2
{   public static void main(String[] args)
    { VP vp1= new VP( 550,450);
    };
}
```

If you run the program, you will get the following output.

Output

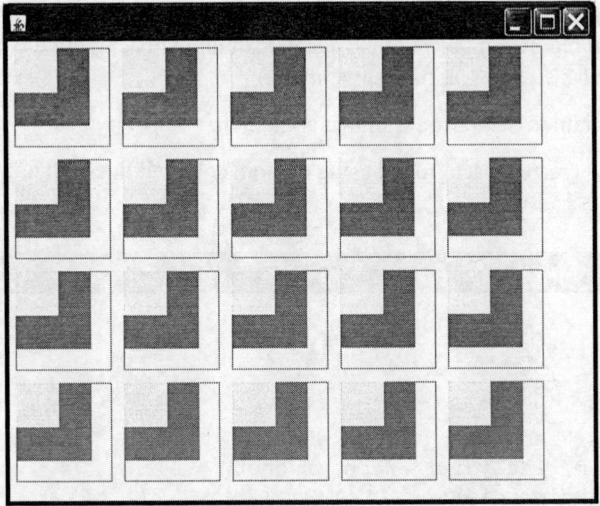

Can you modify the program to get the output as shown in figure 13.3?

Figure 13.3 Design for Trial

13.9 Simple Animation

Animation is the latest trend in digital art. Java has excellent capacity for animation. However, at this stage we have studied few graphics methods. Hence, we will discuss how to animate the screen with our limited repertoire.

A simple animation demo will have a background screen. It will have an object (picture/figure) which will move on this screen. So, the simplest algorithm will be repeating the following instructions:

draw a picture (figure) at new location

wait for short time

erase the picture.

However, there are many "ifs and buts" here. When you draw a figure, the background may be lost. Erasing a picture will not create the background properly. It may leave a shadow.

Here method `setXORMode(color)` comes handy. When this mode is set, picture is drawn in `XOR` mode. Hence, when you redraw an object at the same position the background is restored. (We know from Boolean algebra that (m1 `XOR` n1) `XOR` n1 results in m1.)

Problem: Write a program to demonstrate simple animation.

Solution: First, we will create a background using random coloured lines. Then we will set our picture as a filled circle (see Program 13.8).

PROGRAM 13.8 Simple Animation

```
import java.awt.* ;
import java.applet.* ;
import java.util.* ;
//      Animation
class  VP extends Frame
   {  VP (int xdim, int ydim) //constructor
        { setSize(xdim,ydim);
          setBackground(Color.white);
          setVisible(true);
        }

    public void delay(long n)
        { long t1,t2;
          t1 = System.currentTimeMillis();
          t1 = t1 + n;
          t2= System.currentTimeMillis();
          while ( t2 < t1 )  t2 = System.currentTimeMillis();
        }

      public void paint (Graphics g)
         {  int k ; int t1,t2;
            int x0=100, y0=100, r1=50;
            int x1=0 , y1=0 ;
            double mult = 3.1416 /180.0 ;
            g.setColor( Color.green );
            Random rand = new Random();
```

```
            for(k=0; k< 226; k++)
              {  t1= rand.nextInt( (int)(256*256*256) ) ;
                 Color c1 = new Color(t1);
                 g.setColor( c1 ) ;
                 g.drawLine( rand.nextInt(500),rand.nextInt(300),
                             rand.nextInt(500),rand.nextInt(300) );
              }
              g.setColor(Color.yellow);
              g.setXORMode(Color.red);
              for(k=0; k< 12; k++)
               { x1 = x0 +10*k ;
                 y1 = y0 ;
                 g.fillOval(x1,y1,2*r1,2*r1);
                 delay(300);
                 g.fillOval(x1,y1,2*r1,2*r1);
               }
               g.fillOval(x1,y1,2*r1,2*r1);
        }
  }
 class  copy2
 { public static void main(String[] args)
   { VP vp1= new VP( 520,320);
   };
 }
```

If you run the program, you will get the following output.

Output

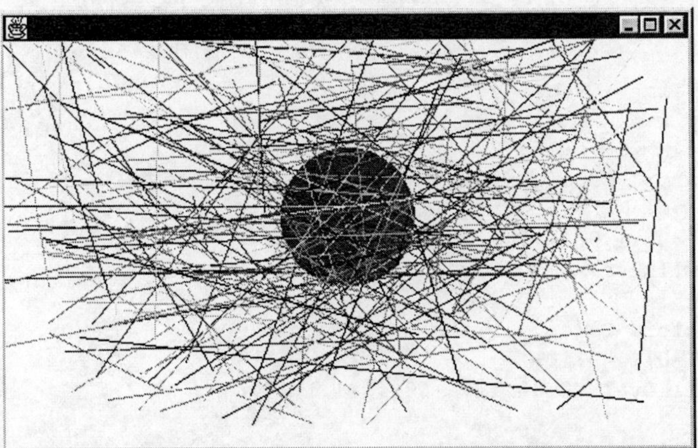

Warning

Please note that we have used method delay in method `paint()`. This is not a standard or approved procedure. We are using a graphical user interface (GUI) component `Frame`. The theory and practice of GUI does not recommend delay in method `paint()`. When we will study GUI and threads in detail, we will be able to improve these programs.

13.10 End of Chapter Programs

13.10.1 Thick point by other methods

Previously, we have created thick points with the help of lines. It is possible to create a thick point by other methods too. Let us try a simple program.

Problem: Write a program to draw thick points with alternative methods.

Solution: It is possible to get a thick point by filling either a rectangle or a circle (oval). See Program 13.9.

PROGRAM 13.9 Thick Point II

```
//     thickp2.java
import java.awt.* ;
import java.applet.* ;
import java.util.* ;
//
class  VP extends Frame
   {  VP (int xdim, int ydim) //constructor
        { setSize(xdim,ydim);
          setBackground(Color.blue);
          setVisible(true);
        }
  public void delay(long n)
      { long t1,t2;
        t1 = System.currentTimeMillis();
        t1 = t1 + n;
        t2= System.currentTimeMillis();
        while ( t2 < t1 )  t2= System.currentTimeMillis();
      }

  public void paint (Graphics g)
     {  int i,j,k ;
        int x0=40,y0 = 60 ;
        g.setColor( Color.green );

        for (i =0; i<9;i++)
            g.fillRect(x0+30*i,y0,i+1,i+1);

        g.setColor( Color.yellow );;
        for (i =0; i<9;i++)
            g.fillOval(x0+30*i,y0+60, i+1,i+1);
      }
   }
 class  thickp2
 {  public static void main(String[] args)
        { VP vp1= new VP( 360,200);
        };
 }
```

If you run this program, you will get the following output.

Output

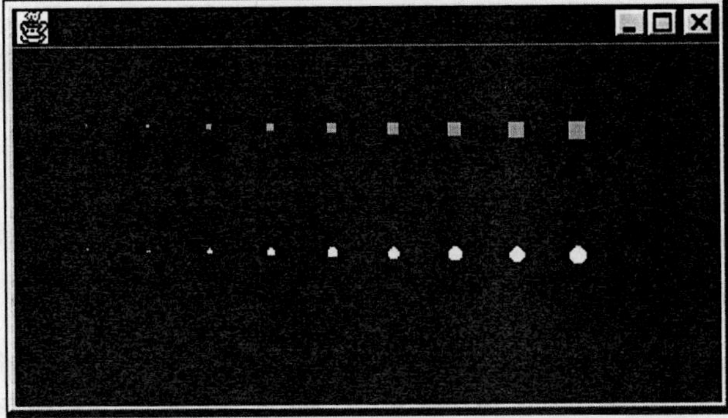

Does this output remind you of options in `brush` tool of any painting software?

Table 13.1 summarizes the constructors for class `Color`.

Table 13.1 Summary of Constructors Class `Color`

`Color``(ColorSpace cspace, float[] components, float alpha)`	Creates a colour in the specified ColorSpace with the colour components specified in the float array and the specified alpha.
`Color``(float r, float g, float b)`	Creates an opaque sRGB colour with the specified red, green, and blue values in the range (0.0–1.0).
`Color``(float r, float g, float b, float a)`	Creates an sRGB colour with the specified red, green, blue, and alpha values in the range (0.0–1.0).
`Color``(int rgb)`	Creates an opaque sRGB colour with the specified combined RGB value consisting of the red component in bits 16–23, the green component in bits 8–15, and the blue component in bits 0–7.
`Color``(int rgba, boolean hasalpha)`	Creates an sRGB colour with the specified combined RGBA value consisting of the alpha component in bits 24–31, the red component in bits 16–23, the green component in bits 8–15, and the blue component in bits 0–7.
`Color``(int r, int g, int b)`	Creates an opaque sRGB colour with the specified red, green, and blue values in the range (0–255).
`Color``(int r, int g, int b, int a)`	Creates an sRGB colour with the specified red, green, blue, and alpha values in the range (0–255).

Table 13.2 summarizes the methods for class `Color`.

Please note that first column states return type. Second column specified method as well as its description.

Table 13.2 Summary of Methods Class `Color`

`Color`	**`brighter()`**	Creates a new colour that is a brighter version of this color.
`PaintContext`	**`createContext (ColorModel cm, Rectangle r, Rectangle2D r2d, AffineTransform xform, RenderingHints hints)`**	Creates and returns a PaintContext used to generate a solid colour pattern.
`Color`	**`darker()`**	Creates a new colour, that is a darker version of this colour.
`static Color`	**`decode(String nm)`**	Converts a string into an integer and returns the specified opaque colour.
`boolean`	**`equals(Object obj)`**	Determines whether another object is equal to this colour.
`int`	**`getAlpha()`**	Returns the alpha component in the range 0–255.
`int`	**`getBlue()`**	Returns the blue component in the range 0–255 in the default sRGB space.
`static Color`	**`getColor(String nm)`**	Finds a colour in the system properties.
`static Color`	**`getColor(String nm, Color v)`**	Finds a colour in the system properties.
`static Color`	**`getColor(String nm, int v)`**	Finds a colour in the system properties.
`float[]`	**`getColorComponents (ColorSpace cspace, float[] compArray)`**	Returns a float array containing only the colour components of the colour in the ColorSpace specified by the cspace parameter.
`float[]`	**`getColorComponents (float[] compArray)`**	Returns a float array containing only the colour components of the colour in the ColorSpace of the colour.
`ColorSpace`	**`getColorSpace()`**	Returns the ColorSpace of this colour.

(Continued)

Table 13.2 (*Continued*)

float[]	**getComponents (ColorSpace cspace, float[] compArray)**	Returns a float array containing the colour and alpha components of the colour, in the ColorSpace specified by the cspace parameter.
float[]	**getComponents (float[] compArray)**	Returns a float array containing the colour and alpha components of the colour, in the ColorSpace of the colour.
int	**getGreen()**	Returns the green component in the range 0–255 in the default sRGB space.
static Color	**getHSBColor(float h, float s, float b)**	Creates a colour object based on the specified values for the HSB colour model.
int	**getRed()**	Returns the red component in the range 0–255 in the default sRGB space.
int	**getRGB()**	Returns the RGB value representing the colour in the default Srgb ColorModel.
float[]	**getRGBColorComponents (float[] compArray)**	Returns a float array containing only the colour components of the colour, in the default sRGB colour space.
float[]	**getRGBComponents (float[] compArray)**	Returns a float array containing the colour and alpha components of the colour, as represented in the default sRGB colour space.
int	**getTransparency()**	Returns the transparency mode for this colour.
int	**hashCode()**	Computes the hash code for this colour.
static int	**HSBtoRGB(float hue, float saturation, float brightness)**	Converts the components of a colour, as specified by the HSB model, to an equivalent set of values for the default RGB model.
static float[]	**RGBtoHSB(int r, int g, int b, float[] hsbvals)**	Converts the components of a colour, as specified by the default RGB model, into an equivalent set of values for hue, saturation, and brightness that are the three components of the HSB model.
String	**toString()**	Returns a string representation of this colour.

Table 13.3 summarizes the methods for class Graphics.

Table 13.3 Summary of Methods Class Graphics

abstract void	**clearRect(int x, int y, int width, int height)**	Clears the specified rectangle by filling it with the background colour of the current drawing surface.
abstract void	**clipRect(int x, int y, int width, int height)**	Intersects the current clip with the specified rectangle.
abstract void	**copyArea(int x, int y, int width, int height, int dx, int dy)**	Copies an area of the component by a distance specified by d*x* and d*y*.
abstract Graphics	**create()**	Creates a new graphics object that is a copy of this graphics object.
Graphics	**create(int x, int y, int width, int height)**	Creates a new graphics object based on this graphics object, but with a new translation and clip area.
abstract void	**dispose()**	Disposes of this graphics context and releases any system resources that it is using.
void	**draw3DRect(int x, int y, int width, int height, boolean raised)**	Draws a three-dimensional highlighted outline of the specified rectangle.
abstract void	**drawArc(int x, int y, int width, int height, int startAngle, int arcAngle)**	Draws the outline of a circular or elliptical arc covering the specified rectangle.
void	**drawBytes(byte[] data, int offset, int length, int x, int y)**	Draws the text given by the specified byte array, using this graphics context's current font and colour.
void	**drawChars(char[] data, int offset, int length, int x, int y)**	Draws the text given by the specified character array, using this graphics context's current font and colour.
abstract boolean	**drawImage(Image img, int x, int y, Color bgcolor, ImageObserver observer)**	Draws as much of the specified image as is currently available.

(*Continued*)

Table 13.3 (*Continued*)

abstract boolean	**drawImage(Image img, int x, int y, ImageObserver observer)**	Draws as much of the specified image as is currently available.
abstract boolean	**drawImage(Image img, int x, int y, int width, int height, Color bgcolor, ImageObserver observer)**	Draws as much of the specified image as has already been scaled to fit inside the specified rectangle.
abstract boolean	**drawImage(Image img, int x, int y, int width, int height, ImageObserver observer)**	Draws as much of the specified image as has already been scaled to fit inside the specified rectangle.
abstract boolean	**drawImage(Image img, int dx1, int dy1, int dx2, int dy2, int sx1, int sy1, int sx2, int sy2, Color bgcolor, ImageObserver observer)**	Draws as much of the specified area of the specified image as is currently available, scaling it on the fly to fit inside the specified area of the destination drawable surface.
abstract boolean	**drawImage(Image img, int dx1, int dy1, int dx2, int dy2, int sx1, int sy1, int sx2, int sy2, ImageObserver observer)**	Draws as much of the specified area of the specified image as is currently available, scaling it on the fly to fit inside the specified area of the destination drawable surface.
abstract void	**drawLine(int x1, int y1, int x2, int y2)**	Draws a line, using the current colour, between the points (X1, Y1) and (X2, Y2) in this graphics context's coordinate system.
abstract void	**drawOval(int x, int y, int width, int height)**	Draws the outline of an oval.
abstract void	**drawPolygon(int[] xPoints, int[] yPoints, int nPoints)**	Draws a closed polygon defined by arrays of X and Y coordinates.
void	**drawPolygon (Polygon p)**	Draws the outline of a polygon defined by the specified polygon object.

(*Continued*)

Table 13.3 *(Continued)*

abstract void	**drawPolyline(int[] xPoints, int[] yPoints, int nPoints)**	Draws a sequence of connected lines defined by arrays of X and Y coordinates.
void	**drawRect(int x, int y, int width, int height)**	Draws the outline of the specified rectangle.
abstract void	**drawRoundRect(int x, int y, int width, int height, int arcWidth, int arcHeight)**	Draws an outlined round-cornered rectangle using this graphics context's current colour.
abstract void	**drawString(AttributedCharacterIterator iterator, int x, int y)**	Draws the text given by the specified iterator, using this graphics context's current colour.
abstract void	**drawString(String str, int x, int y)**	Draws the text given by the specified string, using this graphics context's current font and colour.
void	**fill3DRect(int x, int y, int width, int height, boolean raised)**	Paints a three-dimentional highlighted rectangle filled with the current colour.
abstract void	**fillArc(int x, int y, int width, int height, int startAngle, int arcAngle)**	Fills a circular or elliptical arc covering the specified rectangle.
abstract void	**fillOval(int x, int y, int width, int height)**	Fills an oval bounded by the specified rectangle with the current colour.
abstract void	**fillPolygon(int[] xPoints, int[] yPoints, int nPoints)**	Fills a closed polygon defined by arrays of *x* and y coordinates.
void	**fillPolygon(Polygon p)**	Fills the polygon defined by the specified polygon object with the graphics context's current colour.
abstract void	**fillRect(int x, int y, int width, int height)**	Fills the specified rectangle.
abstract void	**fillRoundRect(int x, int y, int width, int height, int arcWidth, int arcHeight)**	Fills the specified round-cornered rectangle with the current colour.

(Continued)

Table 13.3 *(Continued)*

void	**finalize()**	Disposes of this graphics context once it is no longer referenced.
abstract Shape	**getClip()**	Gets the current clipping area.
abstract Rectangle	**getClipBounds()**	Returns the bounding rectangle of the current clipping area.
Rectangle	**getClipBounds (Rectangler)**	Returns the bounding rectangle of the current clipping area.
Rectangle	**getClipRect()**	Deprecated. As of Java Development Kit (JDK) version 1.1, replaced by getClipBounds().
abstract Color	**getColor()**	Gets this graphics context's current colour.
abstract Font	**getFont()**	Gets the current font.
FontMetrics	**getFontMetrics()**	Gets the font metrics of the current font.
abstract FontMetrics	**getFontMetrics (Font f)**	Gets the font metrics for the specified font.
boolean	**hitClip(int x, int y, int width, int height)**	Returns true if the specified rectangular area intersects the bounding rectangle of the current clipping area.
abstract void	**setClip(int x, int y, int width, int height)**	Sets the current clip to the rectangle specified by the given coordinates.
abstract void	**setClip(Shape clip)**	Sets the current clipping area to an arbitrary clip shape.
abstract void	**setColor(Color c)**	Sets this graphics context's current colour to the specified colour.
abstract void	**setFont(Font font)**	Sets this graphics context's font to the specified font.
abstract void	**setPaintMode()**	Sets the paint mode of this graphics context to overwrite the destination with this graphics context's current colour.
abstract void	**setXORMode(Color c1)**	Sets the paint mode of this graphics context to alternate between this graphics context's current colour and the new specified colour.
String	**toString()**	Returns a string object representing this graphics object's value.

(Continued)

Table 13.3 (*Continued*)

`abstract void`	**`translate(int x, int y)`**	Translates the origin of the graphics context to the point (*x*, *y*) in the current coordinate system.

Keywords

alpha value, animation, circle, `color`, `copyArea()`, `drawLine()`, `drawOval()`, `drawRect`, `fillOval()`, `Frame`, line, pixel, Point, rectangle, `setBackground()`, `setColor()`, `setSize()`, `setTitle()`, `setXORMode()`, transparence.

C++ Corner

There is no equivalent of `putpixel()` in Java. Use of `drawLine()` has to be made to draw a point. There is no method to draw a circle. We have to use `drawOval` method for this task.

Review Questions

1. What are the ways to draw a point on the screen?
2. How to draw a circle on the screen?
3. Which are the three primary colours?
4. What is the use of method `setXORMode()`?

Exercises

1. Assume a company has five divisions. Assuming turn over of each division is known, draw a pie chart.
2. Given sales figures for twelve months, draw a bar graph.
3. A sine wave is generated by a rotating phasor. Assuming the value of omega, show the generation of one cycle of sine wave.
4. Draw a circle of unit radius and an enclosing rectangle. Generate 10,000 random number pairs representing a point (*x* and *y* coordinates). If a point is within a circle, draw it in one colour. If it is outside, draw in another colour. At the end, count the number of points in the circle. From this, calculate the value of "pi".

5. Write a program to draw the following figure on the screen:

Hint: All the circles are of equal radius.

6. Write a program to draw a woven design as shown in Figure 13.4.

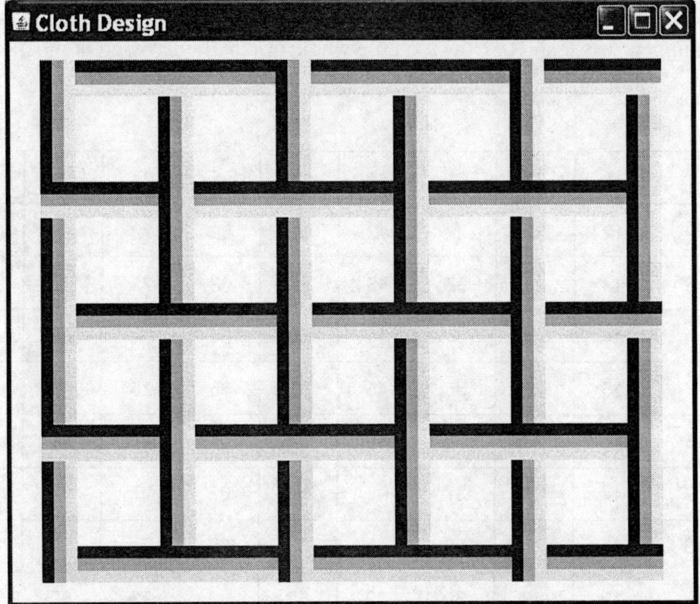

Figure 13.4 Problem Cloth Design

CHAPTER 14

COLLECTION OF ACADEMIC PROGRAMS

14.1 Prime Numbers

Prime numbers are very important in mathematics as well as in computer science. There are many algorithms for finding prime numbers. Let us write programs based on two common algorithms.

14.1.1 Sieve of Eratosthenes

Sieve of Eratosthenes algorithm is taught in high school mathematics. This is a simple algorithm. It is not necessarily the most efficient. The idea behind it is very simple. Cross out (remove) all numbers which are multiples of any prime numbers. Naturally, all those numbers which remain intact are prime numbers.

The working procedure can be explained as follows.

First, draw a 10 by 10 grid and write numbers 1 to 100 in it (Figure 14.1). Next draw a square around 1, as it is not a prime number. Next number is 2. Select it as a prime number. Mark a circle around it. Cross out all multiples of 2, that is numbers 4, 6, up to 100. Find the next uncrossed number. It is 3. Mark it as a prime number by circling it. Cross out all its multiples. Find next uncrossed number it is 5. Repeat the earlier procedure until you exhaust all prime numbers less than 10. Now scan the whole grid. All uncrossed numbers are prime numbers.

1	11	21	31	41	51	61	71	81	91
2	12	22	32	42	52	62	72	82	92
3	13	23	33	43	53	63	73	83	93
4	14	24	34	44	54	64	74	84	94
5	15	25	35	45	55	65	75	85	95
6	16	26	36	46	56	66	76	86	96
7	17	27	37	47	57	67	77	87	97
8	18	28	38	48	58	68	78	88	98
9	19	29	39	49	59	69	79	89	99
10	20	30	40	50	60	70	80	90	100

Figure 14.1 Sieve of Eratosthenes

Problem: Write a program to find prime numbers by sieve of Eratosthenes.

Solution: Let us simplify the algorithm little bit. It will simplify coding. Actually, we have to cross out multiples of prime numbers only (for efficiency), but there is no harm in crossing out multiples of non-primes as well. It means we cross out multiples of 2 to 10.

We will set an array *a* of 100 Booleans and set all elements to false. It will signify that initially every number is uncrossed. When we have to cross any number say *k*, we will set *a*[*k*] to true. It will signify that *k*th number is crossed. This will help us to get all uncrossed numbers in the end.

See Program 14.1.

PROGRAM 14.1 Sieve of Eratosthenes

```
//      prime1.java
// Finding prime numbers by
// Sieve Erato-Sthenes (SOE) method
class prime1
{ public static void main(String arg[])
    { boolean a[];
      a=new boolean[101];
      int i,j,k,count;

      for(i=2;i<=100;++i)
        {  a[i]=false;
        }

      for(i=2;i<=10;++i)
        { k=2;
          while((i*k) <=100)
            { a[i*k]=true;
              k++;
            }
        }
      count = 0 ; // for printing
      for(i=2;i<=100;i++)
        { if(a[i]==false )
            { System.out.printf("%4d",i);
              if ( ++count%10 == 0)
              System.out.println();
            }
        }
    }
}
```

If you run the program, you will get the following output.

Output

```
  2   3   5   7  11  13  17  19  23  29
 31  37  41  43  47  53  59  61  67  71
 73  79  83  89  97
```

Implementing the algorithm exactly (crossing out multiples of prime numbers only) is left to the readers as an exercise.

14.1.2 Prime numbers: A more efficient method

In the sieve method, many numbers are crossed again and again. Hence, it will be a good idea to find prime numbers by an alternative algorithm.

A simple solution will be to take all numbers one by one and test if they are prime numbers. A simple test is to try dividing by all numbers less than that number. This method can be improved by trying to divide by prime numbers only.

Problem: Write a program to find all prime numbers between 2 and 1,000.

Solution: Here we will have to maintain an array of prime numbers. As and when a new prime is found, it will be added to it. Naturally, we will have to keep a track of how many numbers are currently in the array. See Program 14.2.

PROGRAM 14.2 Prime Numbers

```
//      prime2.java
// finding prime numbers from
// 2 to 1000 by more efficient method

class prime2
{ static int prime[];
  static int i,j,k;
  static int n;
  static boolean cont;

  public static void main(String arg[])
    { prime=new int[2001];
      prime[0]=1;prime[1]=2;
      prime[2]=3;prime[3]=5;
      prime[4]=7;
      n=4;

      for(i=8;i<=1000;++i)
       { cont=true;
         k=1;
         do
           { if((i % prime[k]) ==0)
                 cont=false;
              else
                k++;
           } while((cont!=false) && (k < n));
             if (cont==true)
               { n=n+1;
                 prime[n]=i;
               }
       }
      for(i=0;i<=n;++i)
           { System.out.printf("%5d",prime[i]);
             if ( (i+1)%8 == 0 )
                System.out.println();
           }
    }
}
```

If you run the program, you will get the following output.

Output

```
  1     2     3     5     7    11    13    17
 19    23    29    31    37    41    43    47
 53    59    61    67    71    73    79    83
 89    97   101   103   107   109   113   127
131   137   139   149   151   157   163   167
173   179   181   191   193   197   199   211
223   227   229   233   239   241   251   257
263   269   271   277   281   283   293   307
311   313   317   331   337   347   349   353
359   367   373   379   383   389   397   401
409   419   421   431   433   439   443   449
457   461   463   467   479   487   491   499
503   509   521   523   541   547   557   563
569   571   577   587   593   599   601   607
613   617   619   631   641   643   647   653
659   661   673   677   683   691   701   709
719   727   733   739   743   751   757   761
769   773   787   797   809   811   821   823
827   829   839   853   857   859   863   877
881   883   887   907   911   919   929   937
941   947   953   967   971   977   983   991
997
```

You will notice that all the lines are displayed properly. This is because of method `printf()`.

14.2 Date, Time, and Calendar

For professional programs we need to handle dates and time. Java has provided various classes for programmers to use these quantities directly. These classes are placed in the package `java.util`. Let us start our study with class `Date`.

14.2.1 Class `Date`

Java provided class `Date` to handle an instance of time in a program. It has two constructors

```
Date()
Date(long n)
```

The first constructor constructs the date object and initializes all the fields (date, month, hour, etc.) with the values of those quantities at the time of construction.

The second constructor defines the fields of the date object from parameter n. Here, n represents the delay in milliseconds since the standard base time known as "the epoch", namely 1 January 1970, 00:00:00 GMT.

To help converting it into string for printing, a class `SimpleDateFormat` is also provided.

Let us see them in action in a program.

Problem: Write a program to introduce class `Date` and `SimpleDateFormat`.

Solution: See Program 14.3.

PROGRAM 14.3 Class `Date`

```
//    date6.java
import java.util.* ;
import java.text.* ;
class date6
{ public static void main(String arg[])
    { Date dt1 = new Date();
      String st = new String();
      SimpleDateFormat sdf = new SimpleDateFormat() ;
      System.out.println("<---date6.java starts--->");
      System.out.println(dt1);
      System.out.println(sdf.format(dt1) );
    }
}
```

If you run the program, you will get the following output.

Output

```
<---date6.java starts--->
Fri Nov 09 17:38:35 IST 2007
11/9/07 5:38 PM
```

Please note that output indicates that the program was run on ninth of November.

14.2.2 Method `getTime()` from class `Date`

We have started studying class `Date`. It contains many methods one of which is `getTime()`. This method returns the number of milliseconds since 1 January 1970, 00:00:00 GMT represented by this date object. This time can be used imaginatively in many applications. Our programs need a `delay()` function for getting understandable outputs. We can use this method to produce the required delay.

Problem: Write a program to develop a method for time delay.

Solution: Let us develop a time delay method `delay1(long n)` where *n* specifies the delay in milliseconds. The algorithm will be very simple. Initially, we will create a date object and call `getTime()` method. This gives a time in seconds from a specific date. This is stored as initial reading. Now in a loop, fresh readings are taken until the difference between the fresh reading and old reading equals the required time delay.

See Program 14.4.

PROGRAM 14.4 Time Delay Using Class `java.util.Date`

```
//    time1.java
import java.util.Date ;
class time1
{ public static void main(String arg[])
    { System.out.println("--->time1.java starts<---");
      System.out.println(" waiting for 5 seconds");
      delay1(5000);
      System.out.println( "time over" );
    }
```

```
  public static void delay1(long n)
    { Date d1 = new Date() ;
      long t1,t2;
      int i,j,k,m=0;
      t1= d1.getTime();
      t1 = t1 + n;
      t2= d1.getTime();
      while ( t2 < t1 )
        { d1 = new Date() ;
          t2 = d1.getTime();
        }
    }
}
```

If you run the program, you will get the following output.

Output

```
--->time1.java starts<---
waiting for 5 seconds
time over
```

Please note that initially only first two lines appear in output. After a delay of 5 seconds, the last line, that is "time over" appears.

You may ask yourself the following questions.

- Is the program efficient?
- How much system resources it uses?

Can you use information in Program 14.4 to measure execution time of any given method?

Principle used in this method can be used to measure the time delay between two events (just like a stop watch). We will develop and use a class `BPtimer` for this purpose at later stage.

14.2.3 Class `GregorianCalendar`

After introduction of class `Date`, Java developers felt for a better handling of its functions. Hence, most of its methods were deprecated.

For working with calendar, Java has provided a new class `Calendar`. However, it is an abstract class. You cannot instantiate it. A class derived from it known as `GregorianCalendar` is available for use. Let us study with a simple program.

Problem: Write a program to introduce class `GregorianCalendar`.

Solution: See Program 14.5.

PROGRAM 14.5 Introduction to `GregorianCalendar`

```
//   calendar1.java
import java.util.* ;
class calendar1
{  public static void main(String arg[])
   { GregorianCalendar cnd = new GregorianCalendar();
```

```
        String st = new String();
        System.out.println("--->calendar1.java starts<---");
        System.out.println(cnd);
    }
}
```

If you run the program, you will get the following output.

Output

```
--->calendar1.java starts<---
java.util.GregorianCalendar[time=1133782848080,
areFieldsSet=true,areAllFieldsSet=true,lenient=true,
zone=java.util.SimpleTimeZone[id=Asia/Calcutta,offset=19800000,
dstSavings=3600000,useDaylight=false,startYear=0,startMode=0,
startMonth=0,startDay=0,startDayOfWeek=0,
startTime=0,endMode=0,endMonth=0,endDay=0,endDayOfWeek=0,
endTime=0],firstDayOfWeek=1,minimalDaysInFirstWeek=1,
ERA=1,YEAR=2005,MONTH=11,WEEK_OF_YEAR=50,WEEK_OF_MONTH=2,
DAY_OF_MONTH=5,DAY_OF_YEAR=339,DAY_OF_WEEK=2,
DAY_OF_WEEK_IN_MONTH=1,AM_PM=1,HOUR=5,HOUR_OF_DAY=17,MINUTE=10,
SECOND=48,MILLISECOND=80,ZONE_OFFSET=19800000,DST_OFFSET=0]
```

Please note that this program was run on the afternoon of 5 December 2005. The output on the screen was continuous. We have added a few line breaks only to increase readability. Please note the line marked in bold. When we subject any object to printing its default string representation gets printed. Hence, the output is not easily understandable. However, language provides many useful methods to display its contents. One method is `get()`. It returns the string representation of its parameter. For example,

```
get(Calendar.YEAR)
```

returns the string representing the year.

Let us see this in action in Program 14.6.

Problem: Write a simple program to print fields of `GregorianCalendar`.

Solution: See Program 14.6.

PROGRAM 14.6 GregorianCalendar II

```
//          calendar2.java
import java.util.* ;
class calendar2
{ public static void main(String arg[])
    { GregorianCalendar date1 = new GregorianCalendar(2004,12,9);
        String st = new String();
        System.out.println("--->calendar2.java starts<---");
        System.out.println(" YEAR: " + date1.get(Calendar.YEAR));
        System.out.println("MONTH: " + date1.get(Calendar.MONTH));
        System.out.println(" DATE: " + date1.get(Calendar.DATE));
    }
}
```

If you run the program, you will get the following output.

Output

```
--->calendar2.java starts<---
YEAR:   2005
MONTH:    0
DATE:   9
```

What went wrong? Why 2005? The answer is month value is put as 12. First month number is zero. Hence last month number is 11 not 12. Hence, there was a roll over to next year.

14.2.4 Incrementing a date

Many applications like fixed deposits of banks will need to calculate a new date by adding certain period to a specified date. For this purpose class `Date` supports a method `add()`, which has the format

```
add( int field int amount)
```

It will add `amount` of specified time to the field. It implies that we can add number of months only to months and so on.

Problem: Write a program to add a specified period say 1 year to a given date.

Solution: To make the program a little interesting, let us take the initial date as 29th February of a leap year 2004 (see Program 14.7).

PROGRAM 14.7 Incrementing Date

```
//          calendar3.java
//     convertion from class Date
import java.util.* ;
import java.text.* ;

class calendar3
{ public static void main(String arg[])
   { GregorianCalendar cal1 = new GregorianCalendar(2004,1,29);
     Date date1 = new Date();
     date1 = cal1.getTime(); // date set from caledar
     SimpleDateFormat sdf = new SimpleDateFormat();

     System.out.println("--->calender3.java starts<---");

     date1 = cal1.getTime(); // date set from caledar
     System.out.println("old value of date1 : " + sdf.format(date1) );
     System.out.println("Now add 1 year ");
     cal1.add(Calendar.YEAR,1) ;
     date1 = cal1.getTime(); // date set again from caledar
     System.out.println("new value for date1 : " + sdf.format(date1));
   }
}
```

If you run the program, you will get the following output.

Output

```
--->calender3.java starts<---
old value of date1 : 2/29/04 12:00 AM
Now add 1 year
new value for date1 : 2/28/05 12:00 AM
```

We decided to test this facility rigorously. Hence, we gave the data from a leap year. The date was 29th February. We got the answer correctly as 28th February of the next year. If someone develops this algorithm without applying his mind, the output may have been a non-existent date like 29th February 2005.

You will agree that this is a great help from the Java language.

14.3 Matrix

Most of the time, we have to study two-dimensional matrices. Hence, we will write a few programs using it. As we will develop and use classes, they can be easily reused in similar programs.

14.3.1 Matrix addition

Let us develop a program for matrix addition.

Problem: Write a program to add two given matrices.

Solution: The task of adding matrices is straightforward. The algorithm is simple. An element of resultant matrix is the sum of the corresponding elements.

```
C[i][j] = A[i][j] * B[i][j]
```

Since, typically, we solve three-by-three matrices, let us develop a class named `mat3x3` to represent a matrix (see Program 14.8).

PROGRAM 14.8 Matrix Addition

```
//      matrix1.java
//    matrix addition
class mat3x3
  { int[][] ele = new int[3][3];
    mat3x3( int[] A )
      { int i,j,k=0;
        for(i=0;i<=2;i++)
          for(j=0;j<=2;j++)
                ele[i][j]=A[k++];
      }
  mat3x3()   //  creates matrix without assigning values
        {
        };
  }
class matrix1
{
  public static void main(String arg[])
    { int X[] = { 1,2,3, 4,5,6, 7,8,9 } ;
```

```
        int Y[] = { 1,2,3, 14,15,16, 27,28,29 };

        mat3x3 mat1 = new mat3x3(X) ;
        mat3x3 mat2 = new mat3x3(Y) ;
        mat3x3 mat3 = new mat3x3();

        int i,j;
        System.out.println("--->matrix1.java<---");
//       calculating
          for(i=0;i<=2;i++)
            for(j=0;j<=2;j++)
              mat3.ele[i][j] = mat1.ele[i][j] + mat2.ele[i][j];

        System.out.println("mat1");
        for(i=0;i<=2;++i)
          { for(j=0;j<=2;++j)
                System.out.print("\t" + mat1.ele[i][j]);
            System.out.println();
          }

        System.out.println("mat2");
        for(i=0;i<=2;++i)
          { for(j=0;j<=2;++j)
                System.out.print("\t" + mat2.ele[i][j]);
            System.out.println();
          }

        System.out.println("mat3");
        for(i=0;i<=2;++i)
          { for(j=0;j<=2;++j)
                System.out.print("\t" + mat3.ele[i][j]);
            System.out.println();
          }
    }
}
```

If you run the program, you will get the following output.

Output

```
--->matrix1.java<---
mat1
        1       2       3
        4       5       6
        7       8       9
mat2
        1       2       3
        14      15      16
        27      28      29
mat3
        2       4       6
        18      20      22
        34      36      38
```

14.3.2 Matrix multiplication

Matrix multiplication is a very common matrix operation. Let us write a program for it.

Problem: Write a program to multiply two given matrices.

Solution: When we want to multiply two matrices, the number of rows of the first matrix should be same as columns of the second matrix. The element of the resultant matrix is the sum of product of elements taken from corresponding row of the first matrix and column of the second matrix.

```
C[i][j] = ∑ A[i][k] * B[k][j]
```

Let us continue with class `mat3x3` here (see Program 14.9).

PROGRAM 14.9 Matrix Multiplication

```
//       matrix2.java
//     matrix multiplication
class mat3x3
   { int[][] ele = new int[3][3];
     mat3x3( int[] A )
       { int i,j,k=0;
         for(i=0;i<=2;i++)
           for(j=0;j<=2;j++)
                  ele[i][j]=A[k++];
       }
     mat3x3()
       {
       };
   }
class matrix2
{
   public static void main(String arg[])
      {  int X[] = { 1,0,0, 0,1,0, 0,0,1 } ;
         int Y[] = { 1,2,3, 14,15,16, 27,28,29 };

         mat3x3 mat1 = new mat3x3(X) ;
         mat3x3 mat2 = new mat3x3(Y) ;
         mat3x3 mat3 = new mat3x3();

         int i,j,k,sum;
         System.out.println("--->mat2.java<---");
//        calculating
          for(i=0;i<=2;i++)
              for(j=0;j<=2;j++)
               {  sum=0;
                  for(k=0;k<=2;k++)
                  sum+=mat1.ele[i][k] * mat2.ele[k][j];
                  mat3.ele[i][j]=sum;
               }

         System.out.println("mat1");
         for(i=0;i<=2;++i)
           {   for(j=0;j<=2;++j)
```

```
                System.out.print("\t" + mat1.ele[i][j]);
            System.out.println();
      }
      System.out.println("mat2");
      for(i=0;i<=2;++i)
        {  for(j=0;j<=2;++j)
                System.out.print("\t" + mat2.ele[i][j]);
            System.out.println();
        }
      System.out.println("mat3");
      for(i=0;i<=2;++i)
        {   for(j=0;j<=2;++j)
                System.out.print("\t" + mat3.ele[i][j]);
             System.out.println();
        }
   }
}
```

If you run the program, you will get the following output.

Output

```
--->mat2.java<---
mat1
        1       0       0
        0       1       0
        0       0       1
mat2
        1       2       3
        14      15      16
        27      28      29
mat3
        1       2       3
        14      15      16
        27      28      29
```

14.4 Handling Complex Numbers

Java has no in-built support for complex numbers. However, we can develop a class ourselves and give the desired functionality to it. Let us try with a program.

Problem: Write a program to define and print a complex number.

Solution: See Program 14.10.

PROGRAM 14.10 Introduction to Complex Numbers

```
//    comp1.java
class Complex
  { double x, y ;
```

```
    void show()
      { System.out.print(" Complex number: " );
        System.out.println(x +" +j "+ y);
      };
    Complex(double x1, double y1)
      { x=x1;
        y=y1;
      };
   } ;

class comp1
{   public static void main(String arg[])
     { Complex a, b, c ;
       System.out.println("<---comp1.java--->");
       a= new Complex(3,4);
       a.show();
     }
}
```

If you run the program, you will get the following output.

Output

```
<---comp1.java--->
Complex number: 3.0 +j 4.0
```

Problem: Write a program to add and multiply complex numbers.

Solution: See Program 14.11.

PROGRAM 14.11 Adding and Multiplying Complex Numbers

```
//   comp2.java
class Complex
  { double x, y ;
    void show()
      { System.out.print(" Complex number: " );
        System.out.println(x +"  +j "+ y);
      };
    Complex(double x1, double y1)
      {  x=x1;
         y=y1;
      };
    Complex add( Complex num )
      { Complex z = new Complex(0,0);
        z.x = (this.x) + (num.x);
        z.y = (this.y) + (num.y);
        return(z);
      }

     public static Complex mult( Complex a , Complex b)
       { Complex z = new Complex(0,0);
         z.x = ((a.x)*(b.x)) - ((a.y)*(b.y));
```

```
            z.y = ((a.x)*(b.y)) + ((a.y)*(b.x));
            return(z);
        }
    } ;

class comp2
{  public static void main(String arg[])
    { Complex a, b, c ;
      c = new Complex(0,0);
      System.out.println("<---comp2.java starts--->");
      a= new Complex(3,4);
      b= new Complex(5,6);
      System.out.println("Adding complex numbers");
      c= a.add(b);
      c.show();
      System.out.println("Multiplying complex numbers");
//    c= a.mult(a,b);        // this also works!
      c = Complex.mult(a,b);
      c.show();
    }
}
```

If you run the program, you will get the following output.

Output

```
<---comp2.java starts--->
Adding complex numbers
Complex number: 8.0 +j 10.0
Multiplying complex numbers
Complex number: -9.0 +j 38.0
```

Please note the line marked in bold. It is not present in the program. However, this works well and will give the same result as the next statement. A static method can be invoked with the help of a class name or any object of that class.

14.5 Astrology and Numerology

14.5.1 Astrology

Popularity of astrology is increasing day by day. Let us develop simple applications based on astrology. In this section, we will make use of **interface** for storing and using names of planets and signs in North Indian style. As not all the readers may be familiar with these names, we present Tables 14.1 and 14.2 giving equivalent English names.

Table 14.1 lists the Indian and English names of the planets.

Table 14.1 English and Indian Names of Planets

Number	English name	Indian name
1	Sun	Ravi
2	Moon	Chandra

(*Continued*)

Table 14.1 (*Continued*)

3	Mercury	Budh
4	Venus	Shukra
5	Mars	Manga
6	Jupiter	Guru
7	Saturn	Shani
8	Herschel	Harshel
9	Neptune	Neptune
10	Pluto	Pluto
11	Dragon's head	Rahu
12	Dragon's tail	Ketu

Table 14.2 lists English and Indian names of twelve signs.

Table 14.2 **English and Indian Names of Signs**

Number	English name	Indian name
1	Aries	Mesha
2	Taurus	Vrishabha
3	Gemini	Mithun
4	Cancer	Kark
5	Leo	Sinha
6	Virgo	Kanya
7	Libra	Tula
8	Scorpio	Vrischik
9	Sagittarius	Dhanu
10	Capricorn	Makar
11	Aquarius	Kumbha
12	Pisces	Meena

In the simplest form, horoscope (called *Patrika* or *Kundali* in Indian languages) contains information regarding position of all the planets and the ascendant. By position, we mean the position of these planets on the zodiac, at the time of birth. For a simple horoscope, only sign in which these planets are located is sufficient.

Problem: Write a program to enter the data for all planets in a *Patrika* (horoscope).

Solution: See Program 14.12.

PROGRAM 14.12 **Data Entry for Horoscope**

```
//   astro1.java
import java.io.* ;
class Console1
  {  static BufferedReader Jin ;
```

```
    Console1()
    { Jin = new BufferedReader
                (new InputStreamReader (System.in) );
    }
   public static int getint() throws IOException
      { String st1 ;
        st1= Jin.readLine();
        Integer temp = new Integer (st1.trim());
        return temp.intValue();
      } ;
   } ;
interface horo
   { final String[] Pname =
          { "ravi", "chandra", "mangal", "budh" ,
            "guru" , "shukra", "shani", "rahu" ,
            "ketu", "harshal", "neptune", "pluto"
          } ;
     final String[] Rname =
          { "mesha", "vrishabha", "mithun", "kark",
            "sinha", "kanya", "tula", "vrischik",
            "dhanu", "makar", "kumbha", "meena"
          };
   }
class Patrika implements horo
{ int [] Planets = new int[12] ;
  Patrika()
    { int i , k=0;

    } ;
  public void readData()
  { int i, k=0;
    Console1 input = new Console1();
    System.out.println("Enter data 0..11 " ) ;
    for ( i=0 ;i<12 ; i++)
      { k=0;
        System.out.print( Pname[i] +": " );
          try {
                  k = Console1.getint() ;
                  if ( ! valid (k) ) k = 0;
                }
          catch (IOException e)
                { } ;
        Planets[i] = k ;
      }
  }
  public void showData()
  { int i, k=0;
    System.out.println("displaying data");
    for ( i=0 ;i<12 ; i++)
      { System.out.print(  Pname[i] +" in" +
```

```
                              Rname[Planets[i]] +"\t\t");
        if ( i%2 !=0 ) System.out.println();
          //  artificial for fine printing
      }
    }
    boolean valid(int k)
    { boolean flag = true; // valid
      if ( k < 0 ) flag = false;
      if ( k > 11) flag = false;
      return flag;
    }
  }

class astro1 implements horo
{ public static void main (String argv[])
    { int i ; // , k = -1;
      int[] store = new int[12] ;
      System.out.println("---astro1.java---");
      Patrika ashok =new Patrika();
      ashok.readData();
      ashok.showData();
    }
}
```

If you run the program, you will get the following output.

Output

```
---astro1.java---
Enter data 0..11
ravi: 0
chandra: 1
mangal: 9
budh: 5
guru: 3
shukra: 11
shani: 6
rahu: 1
ketu: 7
harshal: 2
neptune: 3
pluto: 33
displaying data
ravi in mesha               chandra in vrishabha
mangal in makar                    budh in kanya
guru in kark                shukra in meena
shani in tula               rahu in vrishabha
ketu in vrischik                   harshal in mithun
neptune in kark                  pluto in mesha
```

Note the line marked in bold. While entering data for Pluto, number 33 was typed. Valid *rashi* numbers are 0 to 11 only. Hence, the entry is checked by `valid()` and corrected (of course arbitrarily) to mesha.

You will see another useful program in a later chapter.

14.5.2 Numerology

Numerology is the science of numbers. Every number from one to nine represents some characteristics. Every person is supposed to have a number which describes his nature and other traits. This number is decided by the name of a person. Every alphabet in assigned a number. The following table illustrates the numbers assigned to different alphabet.

A, I, J, Q, Y	1
B, K, R	2
C, G, L, S	3
D, M, T	4
E, H, N, X	5
U, V, W	6
O, Z	7
F, P	8

Please note that number 9 is not assigned to any character.

To find a lucky number, we have to add numbers associated to every character of a given name. If addition results in number greater than 9, we have to add all the digits to get the number. For example, if the addition results in say 15, then 1 + 5, that is 6, is the lucky number.

Problem: Write a program to read a name and find the lucky number.

Solution: See Program 14.13.

PROGRAM 14.13 Numerology

```
//              num1.java
import java.io.*;
class num1
{ public static void main(String args[])
    {
       String st1="";
       System.out.println("What is your name?");
       try
        { st1 = readString();
        }
        catch (IOException e){ };
        System.out.println("Your name is : " + st1);
        System.out.println("Your Number is " + val(st1) );
    }
  public static String readString()
            throws IOException // note1
    { BufferedReader jin =new BufferedReader(new
            InputStreamReader(System.in) ) ;
```

```
        String st1;
        st1 = jin.readLine();
        return st1 ;
    }
  public static int val(String st1 )
  { int sum = 0,sum1,sum2;
    int N,i,x=0;
    char ch ;
    N = st1.length() ;
    for( i=0;i<N;i++)
      {  ch = st1.charAt(i) ;
         ch = Character.toLowerCase(ch);
         switch ( ch )
           { case 'a': x =1;break;
             case 'b': x =2;break;
             case 'c': x =3;break;
             case 'd': x =4;break;
             case 'e': x =5;break;
             case 'f': x =8;break;
             case 'g': x =3;break;
             case 'h': x =5;break;
             case 'i': x =1;break;
             case 'j': x =1;break;
             case 'k': x =2;break;
             case 'l': x =3;break;
             case 'm': x =4;break;
             case 'n': x =5;break;
             case 'o': x =7;break;
             case 'p': x =8;break;
             case 'q': x =1;break;
             case 'r': x =2;break;
             case 's': x =3;break;
             case 't': x =4;break;
             case 'u': x =6;break;
             case 'v': x =6;break;
             case 'w': x =6;break;
             case 'x': x =5;break;
             case 'y': x =1;break;
             case 'z': x =7;break;
             case ' ': x =0;break;

           }
         sum = sum + x ;
         sum1 = sum /10 ;
         sum2 = sum % 10 ;
         sum = sum2 ;
         if ( sum1 == 1 ) sum++; // add one

      }
     return sum ;
  }
}
```

A sample output is shown hereafter.

Output

```
What is your name?
mahesh
Your name is : mahesh
Your Number is 5
```

Note: In this program we are developing and using the method `readString()`. This method invokes reading from console. Under unexpected circumstances, it will throw an exception. We have to tell the compiler that this method may throw an exception. Hence, the clause `throws IOException`. We will be discussing "Exceptions" in detail in Chapter 19.

14.6 Playing Cards

Playing cards are popular among all age groups. Figure 14.2 displays some of the cards. If we want to simulate card games in a computer, we will have to handle playing cards in a program. Earlier to object-oriented programming, programs written were assigning numeric values to cards. Processing was a bit cumbersome then. Java is object oriented. Therefore, cards can be handled in a natural way in a program.

In the following programs, we will develop classes for a card and a deck.

14.6.1 Shuffling of cards I

Before any game starts, we shuffle the deck of cards. If we watch the action, we will notice that the middle portion of the deck is removed and put on top. Instead of this, we can use a simple algorithm. We will exchange two cards (picked randomly). We will repeat exchanging cards for reasonably large number. This can be done in a program very easily. Let us see this in action in Program 14.14.

Problem: Write a program to shuffle a deck of cards.

Solution: Initially we will create a deck which is in order (sorted). While shuffling the deck we will exchange cards 1,000 times. See Program 14.14.

Figure 14.2 Playing Cards

PROGRAM 14.14 Deck of Cards I

```
//        cards4.java
import java.util.Random ;
import java.lang.String ;
class Card
  { private int n ;
    private int suit;
    private int val;
    Card( int i)  // constructor
      { if ( (i<0) && (i>=52) )
        { System.out.println("Invalid card");
          System.exit(1);
          i=0;
        }
        n= i;
        suit = n / 13 ;
        val = n % 13 ;
      };
    public String show()
        { String s0;
          String[] s1 = {  "Spade", "Heart", "Diamond", "Club"};
          String[] s2 = {   "A","K","Q","J","T","9",
                            "8","7","6","5","4","3","2"};

          return s1[suit] +" " + s2[val] ;
      };
  };

class Deck
     { static final int FiftyTwo =52;
       Card[] crd;
       Deck()
       { crd =new Card[FiftyTwo];
         for( int i=0;i<FiftyTwo;i++)
               crd[i] = new Card(i);
       }
       public void shuffle()
         { int N = 1000;
           int i , x , y ;
           Card temp;
           Random random = new Random();
           for( i=0;i<N;i++)
             { x = random.nextInt(FiftyTwo) ;
               y = random.nextInt(FiftyTwo) ;
               temp = crd[x];
               crd[x] = crd[y];
               crd[y] = temp;
           }
       };
     }
class cards4
```

```
{
  public static void main(String args[])
    {
      Deck myDeck = new Deck();

      System.out.println("<---cards4.java--->");
      System.out.println("First three cards");
      System.out.println("before shuffling");
      System.out.println(myDeck.crd[0].show() + "-" +
                              myDeck.crd[1].show()+ "-" +
                              myDeck.crd[2].show());
      //shuffle
      myDeck.shuffle();
      System.out.println("after shuffling");
      System.out.println(myDeck.crd[0].show() + "-" +
                              myDeck.crd[1].show() + "-" +
                              myDeck.crd[2].show() );
    }
}
```

If you run the program, you will get the following output.

Output

```
<---cards4.java--->
First three cards
before shuffling
Spade A-Spade K-Spade Q
after shuffling
Club T-Spade 5-Diamond 7
```

In the earlier program, we have used random numbers to pick two cards. Well when we have a random number generator with us, why not generate the deck itself with its help? The only hitch is that there is no guarantee that the same card will not be generated again. If we take care of this, then there will be no problem.

14.6.2 Generate a fresh deck of cards

Problem: Write a program to arrange a fresh deck of cards using random number generator.

Solution: First, we will generate the deck. When we use a random number, it is possible that it will suggest a card already in the deck. Hence, we will use a separate array of Booleans to store information regarding the availability of the suggested card. If the suggested card is not available, we will discard that suggestion and try again. After generating the deck, we will test it for duplicate entries (see Program 14.15).

PROGRAM 14.15 Deck of Cards II

```
//   cards3.java
import java.util.Random ;
import java.lang.String ;
interface BPcards
{  final int FiftyTwo =52;
} ;
```

```
class Card implements BPcards
  { private int n ;
    private int suit;
    private int val;
    Card( int i) // constructor
      { if ( (i<0) && (i>=FiftyTwo ) )
          { System.out.println("Invalid card ");
            System.exit(1);
            i=0;
          }
        n = i;
        suit = n / 13 ;
        val = n % 13 ;
      };
    public String show()
      { String s0;
        String[] s1 = { "Spade", "Heart", "Diamond", "Club"};
        String[] s2 = { "A","K","Q","J","T","9",
                        "8","7","6","5","4","3","2"};
        return s1[suit] +" " + s2[val] ;
      };
    public int value()
       { return n; }
  };
class Deck implements BPcards
    { //static
      Card[] crd;
      Deck()
      { crd =new Card[FiftyTwo];
      }
      public boolean checkDuplicate()
        { boolean answer =true;
          int i,j;
          here:for( i=0;i<FiftyTwo-1;i++)
            { for( j=i+1;j<FiftyTwo;j++)
              if ( crd[i].value() == crd[j].value() )
                { //System.out.println("error");
                  answer = false;
                  break here;
                }
            }
           return answer;
        }
    }
class cards3 implements BPcards
{
  public static void main(String args[])
    { int k,i;
      Deck myDeck = new Deck();
      boolean[] flag = new boolean[52];
      System.out.println("<---cards3.java--->");
      int attempt=0; int ind =0 ;
```

```
      for(i=0;i<FiftyTwo;i++)
            flag[i] =true ;
      Random random = new Random();
// Now generating a shuffled deck of cards
     System.out.println("attempt numbers when next card is selected");
     while (ind< FiftyTwo)
     { k = random.nextInt(FiftyTwo);
       if ( flag[k] )
             { flag[k]=false;
             myDeck.crd[ind] = new Card(k);
//             System.out.println("ind ="+ind+" attempt ="+attempt);
             System.out.print( attempt +", ");
             ind++;
             }
         attempt++;
      };
    System.out.println("\n.....Printing deck");
    for(i=0;i<FiftyTwo;i++)
        {   System.out.print(myDeck.crd[i].show() +" ," );
            if ( (i+1) % 4 == 0 )
System.out.println();
          }
 // forcing duplicate
 //      myDeck.crd[51] = myDeck.crd[10] ;
 // checking duplicate
      System.out.println(".....Checking for Duplicates");
    if ( myDeck.checkDuplicate() )
        System.out.println("No duplicates" ) ;
      else System.out.println("Duplicates found Error !!!!!!");
  }
 }
```

If you run the program, you will get the following output.

Output

```
<---cards3.java--->
attempt numbers when next card is selected
0, 1, 2, 3, 4, 5, 6, 7, 8, 9, 10, 12, 13, 15, 16, 17, 18, 19,
20, 21, 24, 26, 31, 33, 34, 35, 39, 43, 46, 52, 55, 56, 58, 60,
70, 71, 76, 78, 80, 82, 83, 86, 88, 92, 104, 116, 118, 120, 140,
179, 255, 308,
.....Printing deck
Heart 7 , Heart T , Club 9 , Club 5 ,
Heart 6 , Diamond Q , Heart 5 , Heart 9 ,
Club 8 , Spade 2 , Diamond T , Diamond 5 ,
Diamond 8 , Club 3 , Heart 4 , Spade A ,
Heart Q , Spade 3 , Heart 2 , Heart 3 ,
Spade J , Spade 6 , Diamond 2 , Heart J ,
Club K , Club A , Club 6 , Spade 5 ,
Diamond J , Club 2 , Spade Q , Heart K ,
Club J , Spade T , Spade 7 , Club T ,
```

```
Diamond 9 , Club 7 , Spade 4 , Spade 9 ,
Diamond 7 , Diamond 6 , Club 4 , Diamond 3 ,
Diamond 4 , Spade 8 , Club Q , Diamond K ,
Heart 8 , Spade K , Diamond A , Heart A ,
.....Checking for Duplicates
No duplicates
```

You may want to test whether checking duplicates is really working or not. Bring the commented statement

```
// myDeck.crd[51] = myDeck.crd[10] ;
```

back in the program. This forces a duplicate in the deck. If our code is correct, it should point it out.

You may wonder why we are displaying the attempt numbers. When we select cards with this algorithm, after most of the cards are selected we have to waste a lot of attempts. This is clear from the output.

Can we have a faster algorithm such that there is a guarantee that a suggested card is always available?

If you feel shuffling is cumbersome, then there is a gift to you from Java developers. There is a method `shuffle()` available in collections. See a program in Chapter 23 on "Collection Framework".

14.7 Searching and Sorting

Searching is the eternal activity in life. Hence, it is no surprise that it is the most important activity in computer programming. We have studied two programs on searching in Chapter 7 on "Arrays". There are only two main algorithms for searching. When data is not in order, we use linear search algorithm. For efficient searching, we use binary search algorithm. However, for this algorithm, data is required to be in order (sorted). Therefore, sorting also becomes a prime activity. Computer scientists and mathematicians have developed and analysed many algorithms. In this section, we will develop a few programs implementing some of these sorting algorithms.

The most logical or natural algorithm is selection sort. Let us start our study with this sort.

14.7.1 Selection sort

Selection sort algorithm is very natural. If we are sorting without a computer, we are likely to use the same technique. We will pick up the smallest number first and place it in first position. Then we will continue to pick the smallest number from the remaining numbers and put next.

Problem: Write a program to sort an array using selection sort algorithm.

Solution: See Program 14.6.

PROGRAM 14.16 Selection Sort

```
//    select1.java
//    selection sort
import java.util.Random ;
class select1
{ static int findsmall( int[] a , int si , int fi)
      {  int i,temp,ind;
```

```
      temp = a[si];
      ind = si;
        for(i=si+1;i<=fi;i++)
          { if (temp > a[i] )
          { temp =a[i];
            ind = i ;
          }
          }
        return ind ;
      }
  public static void main(String args[])
      { int[] a ;
        int temp0, z ;
        Random random = new Random();
        a=new int[10];
        for(int i=0;i<10;i++)
          { a[i]= random.nextInt(100);
            System.out.print( a[i] +" " );
          }
        System.out.println();
        System.out.println(" sorting starts");
        for(int i=0;i<10;i++)
          {  z= findsmall(a, i , 10-1);
             System.out.println("index is " + z);
             temp0= a[i];
             a[i] = a[z];
             a[z] = temp0;
          }
        for(int i=0;i<10;i++)
          {  System.out.print( a[i]+" " );
          }
      } // main
}
```

If you run the program, you will get the following output.

Output

```
44   47   63   60   79   22   88   46   20   93
sorting starts
index is 8
index is 5
index is 8
index is 7
index is 5
index is 7
index is 8
index is 7
index is 8
index is 9
20   22   44   46   47   60   63   79   88   93
```

14.7.2 Quick sort

As the name suggests, quick sort is the fastest of the available algorithms. This is also sometimes called partition sort. All sorting algorithms basically have passes. However, efforts of one pass have no effect on the next pass. In this particular algorithm, partitioning work done in one pass reduces the efforts in the next pass. It makes this algorithm the fastest.

Problem: Write a program to sort an array using quick sort algorithm.

Solution: See Program 14.17.

PROGRAM 14.17 Quick Sort

```
//              quick2.java
import java.util.Random ;
class quick2
{ static int a[] ;
  static int N =10 ;
  public static void main(String args[])
    { int avg=0 ;
      int i ;
      Random random = new Random();
      a=new int[N];
      System.out.println("The data for sorting is as follows:");
      for( i=0;i<N;i++)
         { a[i]= random.nextInt();
           a[i]= Math.abs(a[i]) % 100 ;
           System.out.print(a[i] + " " );
         }
      System.out.println(""); // go to new line
      System.out.println("Sorting starts");
      quick_sort(0,N-1) ;
      System.out.println("\nThe final output is");
      print_line();
    }
  static void quick_sort(int l, int r) // array a implied
  { int i,j,k,x,w,ind;
    i=l;j=r;
    k=(i+j)/2;
    x=a[k];
    do
      { while (a[i] < x) i++;
        while (x < a[j] ) j =j-1;
        if (i<=j )
          {  w=a[i];a[i]=a[j];a[j]=w;
                i++;j--;
             print_line();
          }
      }while (i<= j);
    if (l<j) quick_sort(l,j);
    if (i<r) quick_sort(i,r);
  }
```

```
  static void print_line()
    { int i;
      for( i=0;i<N;i++)
        System.out.print (a[i] +" " );
      System.out.println("");// go to new line
    }
}    // class quick2 ends here
```

If you run the program, you will get the following output.

Output

```
The data for sorting is as follows:
10      7      11     73     67     47     92     27     15     96
Sorting starts
10      7      11     15     67     47     92     27     73     96
10      7      11     15     27     47     92     67     73     96
10      7      11     15     27     47     92     67     73     96
7      10      11     15     27     47     92     67     73     96
7      10      11     15     27     47     92     67     73     96
7      10      11     15     27     47     67     92     73     96
7      10      11     15     27     47     67     73     92     96
7      10      11     15     27     47     67     73     92     96
The final output is
7      10      11     15     27     47     67     73     92     96
```

There is a saying "Rome was not built in a day". Similarly, large programs are not written in one go. They are developed step by step. The principle of stepwise refinement is used. Same can be said about algorithm development. They are improved in steps. Bubble sort is a very common and well-known algorithm. Let us use it as an example of algorithmic development

14.7.3 Bubble sort

Let us explain the working principle of bubble sort. Let us say that we are arranging the numbers in ascending order. The basic idea is to compare two consecutive numbers, say $a[j]$ and $a[j + 1]$. If $a[j]$ is less than $a[j + 1]$, it is fine. Otherwise, we swap both the numbers. This is continued from $a[0]$ to a[last − 1]. This action constitutes one pass. In general, we have $(N - 1)$ passes to sort the array completely.

In one pass, the heaviest element goes to the bottom, and the lightest element moves up by one position.

Assume we have an array as shown here:

23 18 67 5 42 1 38

After one pass, it will be as follows:

18 23 5 42 1 38 67

Notice that the heaviest element 67 has reached the bottom.

Let us see the complete program.

Problem: Write a program to sort an array using bubble sort algorithm.

Solution: See Program 14.18.

PROGRAM 14.18 Bubble Sort 1

```
//    bubble1.java
class bubble1
{  public static void main(String args[])
    { int i,j,N,temp;
      int[] a = {23,18,67,5,42,1,38};
      N=7 ;  //  size of the array
      System.out.println("<---bubble1.java--->");
      System.out.println("data before sorting");
      for( i=0;i<N;i++)
        System.out.print(a[i] + " ");
      System.out.println();
//    Now sorting sorting starts
      for(i=0;i< N-1;i++)
          { for (j=0;j<N-1;j++)
            { if ( a[j] > a[j+1] )
                          { temp = a[j];
                            a[j] = a[j+1];
                            a[j+1]= temp;
                          }
            }
          }
    System.out.println("data after sorting");
    for (i=0;i<N;i++)
       System.out.print(a[i]+" ");
    System.out.println();
  }
}
```

If you run the program, you will get the following output.

Output

```
<---bubble1.java--->
data before sorting
23 18 67 5 42 1 38
data after sorting
1 5 18 23 38 42 67
```

This program is fine, but the data is directly given in the program. It will be a nice thing to generate data. One solution is to use a random number generator. Let us create data with a random number generator.

Problem: Rewrite a program using random number generator for input data.

Solution: See Program 14.19.

PROGRAM 14.19 Bubble Sort 2

```
//        bubble3.java
//     adds random number generator for data
import java.util.Random ;
class bubble3
```

```
{ public static void main(String args[])
   {  int i,j,N,temp;
      N=7 ; // size of the array
      int[] a = new int[N];
      System.out.println("<---bubble3.java--->");
//   generating data
      Random random = new Random();
        for( i=0;i<N;i++)
            a[i]= random.nextInt(100);
      System.out.println("data before sorting");
      for( i=0;i<N;i++)
        System.out.print(a[i] +" ");
      System.out.println();
//    Now sorting sorting starts
      for(i=0;i< N-1;i++)
            { for (j=0;j<N-1;j++)
              { if ( a[j] > a[j+1] )
                   { temp = a[j];
                     a[j] = a[j+1];
                     a[j+1]= temp;
              }
          }
        }
      System.out.println("data after sorting");
      for (i=0;i<N;i++)
        System.out.print(a[i]+" ");
      System.out.println();
   }
}
```

If you run the program, you will get the following output.

Output

```
<---bubble3.java--->
data before sorting
97    43    11    58    94    55    54
data after sorting
11    43    54    55    58    94    97
```

If we study the bubble sort algorithm, we will notice that small-value (lighter) elements move up slower, and heavy elements move down faster. Actually, in any one pass the largest element takes its final place at the bottom. In other words, after three passes, largest three elements are already in the last three positions. (This is not true for the smallest value elements.) Therefore, when we start the fourth pass, we need not go until the end of an array. We can consider that an array has only $N - 3$ elements instead of N. This will speed up the operation.

The second change is regarding the variable N. Actually we are using it as a constant. Hence, we should declare it as a constant. It saves us of any serious errors (if we inadvertently modify it). Also as a constant, it should be available to any other method in the code. Hence, we have to move it outside the method main.

Problem: Rewrite a program with improved algorithm.

Solution: See Program 14.20.

PROGRAM 14.20 Bubble Sort 3

```
//        bubble4.java
//       improved algorithm

import java.util.Random ;
class bubble4
{ final static int N = 7 ; // size of the array
  public static void main(String args[])
    { int i,j,temp;
      int[] a = new int[N];
      System.out.println("<---bubble4.java--->");
//    generating data
      Random random = new Random();
      for( i=0;i<N;i++)
          a[i]= random.nextInt(100);

      System.out.println("data before sorting");
      for( i=0;i<N;i++)
        System.out.print(a[i] + " ");
      System.out.println();

//        Now sorting starts
      for(i=0;i< N-1;i++)
        { for (j=0;j<N-i-1;j++)
          { if ( a[j] > a[j+1] )
                        { temp = a[j];
                          a[j] = a[j+1];
                          a[j+1]= temp;
                    }
          }
        }
    System.out.println("data after sorting");
    for (i=0;i<N;i++)
       System.out.print(a[i]+" ");
    System.out.println();
  }
}
```

If you run the program, you will get the following output.

Output

```
<---bubble4.java--->
data before sorting
93  85  19  78  13  47  22
data after sorting
13  19  22  47  78  85  93
```

So far, development is on track. But we see that random number generates different data every time. So we have to check the output thoroughly. It would be nice if we get the same data every time. Does it sound paradoxical to make random data consistent? No. We want to get the same data every time. But the generated (data) sequence is random. This is possible if we use random number generator with a seed. When we create a random number generator with same seed every time, we get identical sequence every time. If you check the sequence, you will notice that it is not following any specific rule; it is a random sequence.

Another point is that we have embedded the bubble sort algorithm inside the method main. It is not a good design. If we want to reuse the code, the sorting must be done by a method. A reasonably general method can be easily copied from one program to another. Let us implement these changes in the code.

Problem: Rewrite the program to use method `bubble_sort1`.

Solution: See Program 14.21.

PROGRAM 14.21 Bubble Sort 4

```
//      bubble6.java
//    uses method bubble_sort1
//    uses Random with seed
import java.util.Random ;
class bubble6
{ final static int N = 7 ; // size of the array
  static void bubble_sort1(int [] X, int l, int r)
    { int i,j,temp ;
      for ( i = l ; i < r-1 ; i++ )
       { for ( j = l ; j < r ; j++ )
             if ( X[j] > X[j+1] )
                    {  temp = X[j] ;
                       X[j] = X[j+1] ;
                       X[j+1] = temp ;
                    }
       }
     }  // method bubble_sort1 ends here

  public static void main(String args[])
    { int i;
      int[] a = new int[N];
      System.out.println("<---bubble6.java--->");
//    generating data
      Random random = new Random(1000);
      for( i=0;i<N;i++)
           a[i]= random.nextInt(100);
      System.out.println("data before sorting");
      for( i=0;i<N;i++)
        System.out.print(a[i] + " ");
      System.out.println();

//    Now calling method bubble_sort
      bubble_sort1(a,0,N-1);
      System.out.println("data after sorting");
      for (i=0;i<N;i++)
        System.out.print(a[i]+" ");
      System.out.println();
    }
}
```

If you run the program, you will get the following output.

Output

```
<---bubble6.java--->
data before sorting
87   35   76   24   92   49   41
data after sorting
24   35   41   49   76   87   92
```

You may wonder why parameter list contains *l* and *r*. Actually, *l* symbolizes left and *r* stands for right. Most of the computer teachers draw an array horizontally on the blackboard. Hence, if we want to focus only on the part of an array and not the whole array, then names of the limits naturally become *l* and *r*.

Why write a method which sorts a part of an array? First, by initializing $l = 0$ and $r = N - 1$, we can sort the whole array. The second method can be easily modified if we want to improve or change the algorithm.

The bubble sort is a simple algorithm, but it is not a fast one. If the array size is huge, it takes a long time to finish. It is possible to speed up an algorithm. Assume that the data is somewhat ordered. Consider a case that at the start, the last three elements are already in place. In the first pass, we can make note of that. The second pass can now be restricted to 0 to $N - 3 - 1$ elements. This method is known as bubble sort with flag. In the program, we set a flag to indicate up to which limit we should sort (as elements further than that are already sorted).

Now you will appreciate why we used *l* and *r* in Program 14.21.

Problem: Rewrite a program to implement bubble sort with flag.

Solution: See Program 14.22.

PROGRAM 14.22 Bubble Sort 5

```
//     bubble7.java
//     uses method bubble_sort with flag
import java.util.Random ;
class bubble7
{ final static int N = 20 ; // size of the array
  static void bubble_sort2(int [] X, int left, int right)
    { int j,temp ;
      int l,r,flag;
      l =left ; // copying parameter values
      r = right ; // in variables l and r
//      for ( i = l ; i < r-1 ; i++ )
      while ( l < r )
       {  flag = l;
          for ( j = l ; j < r ; j++ )
            if ( X[j] > X[j+1] )
                  {  temp = X[j] ;
                     X[j] = X[j+1] ;
                     X[j+1] = temp ;
                     flag = j;
                  }
          r= flag; // right limit is set as per flag
       }
    }  // method bubble_sort2 ends here

  public static void main(String args[])
```

```
   { int i;
     int[] a = new int[N];
     System.out.println("<---bubble7.java--->");
//   generating data
     Random random = new Random(1000);
     for( i=0;i<N;i++)
          a[i]= random.nextInt(100);
     System.out.println("data before sorting");
     for( i=0;i<N;i++)
        System.out.print(a[i] +" ");
     System.out.println();
//   Now calling method bubble_sort
     bubble_sort2(a,0,N-1);
     System.out.println("data after sorting");
     for (i=0;i<N;i++)
        System.out.print(a[i]+" ");
     System.out.println();
    }
}
```

If you run the program, you will get the following output.

Output

```
<---bubble7.java--->
data before sorting
87 35 76 24 92 49 41 45 64 50 79 59 72 83 36 75 46 2 23 41
data after sorting
2 23 24 35 36 41 41 45 46 49 50 59 64 72 75 76 79 83 87 92
```

You must have noticed that we have changed *N* to 20. This is because while sorting only seven elements, there may not be any occasion to really test the algorithm. You may change it to 200 if you want to see if any the process is speeding up. Also, you should try different seeds to get different data.

Consider a case where data is almost sorted, except the heaviest element in the top. With the present algorithm, it will come to the bottom in the first pass. The second pass will set the flag to the top (left), indicating that no more passes are required. It means sorting is over very fast indeed.

Now consider a case when the smallest element is in the bottom. It moves up only one place per pass. We do not get any improvement.

Now the last change: The heavy element moves down in one pass because we scan from left to right. If we scan from right to left, the light element will move to top in one pass. If we combine both techniques, we will get the best benefit of using flag. Since the data is scanned once from left to right and then from right to left, the algorithm is also known as shaker sort.

Problem: Rewrite a program using shaker sort algorithm.

Solution: See Program 14.23.

PROGRAM 14.23 Bubble Sort 6

```
//      bubble8.java
//      uses shaker sort algorithm
```

```
import java.util.Random ;
class bubble8
{ final static int N = 20 ; // size of the array
  static void bubble_sort3(int [] X, int left, int right)
     {  int j,temp ;
        int l,r,flag;
        l =left ; // copying parameter values
        r = right ; // in variables l and r
//        for ( i = l ; i < r-1 ; i++ )
        while ( l < r )
         {  flag = l;
            for ( j = l ; j < r ; j++ ) // forward direction
              if ( X[j] > X[j+1] )
                    { temp = X[j] ;
                      X[j] = X[j+1] ;
                      X[j+1] = temp ;
                      flag = j;
                    }
            r = flag; // right limit is set as per flag

            flag=r; // check
            for ( j = r ; j > l ; j-- ) // reverse direction
              if ( X[j-1] > X[j] )
                    {  temp = X[j] ;
                       X[j] = X[j-1] ;
                       X[j-1] = temp ;
                       flag=j-1;
                    }
            l=flag;
         }
      } // method bubble_sort3 ends here
  public static void main(String args[])
    { int i;
      int[] a = new int[N];
      System.out.println("<---bubble8.java--->");
//   generating data
      Random random = new Random(1000);
      for( i=0;i<N;i++)
          a[i]= random.nextInt(100);
      System.out.println("data before sorting");
      for( i=0;i<N;i++)
        System.out.print(a[i] +" ");
      System.out.println();

//    Now calling method bubble_sort
      bubble_sort3(a,0,N-1);
      System.out.println("data after sorting");
      for (i=0;i<N;i++)
         System.out.print(a[i]+" ");
      System.out.println();
  }
}
```

If you run the program, you will get the following output.

Output

```
<---bubble8.java--->
data before sorting
87 35 76 24 92 49 41 45 64 50 79 59 72 83 36 75 46 2 23 41
data after sorting
2 23 24 35 36 41 41 45 46 49 50 59 64 72 75 76 79 83 87 92x
```

I hope you have enjoyed this episode with bubble sort.

Table 14.3 summarizes various methods from class `Random`.

Table 14.3 **Class `Random`: Method Summary**

`protected int`	**`next`**`(int bits)`	Generates the next pseudorandom number.
`boolean`	**`nextBoolean`**`()`	Returns the next pseudorandom, uniformly distributed `boolean` value from the sequence of this random number generator.
`void`	**`nextBytes`** `(byte[] bytes)`	Generates random bytes and places them into a user-supplied byte array.
`double`	**`nextDouble`**`()`	Returns the next pseudorandom, uniformly distributed `double` value between `0.0` and `1.0` from the sequence of this random number generator.
`float`	**`nextFloat`**`()`	Returns the next pseudorandom, uniformly distributed `float` value between `0.0` and `1.0` from the sequence of this random number generator.
`double`	**`nextGaussian`**`()`	Returns the next pseudorandom, Gaussian ("normally") distributed `double` value with mean `0.0` and standard deviation `1.0` from the sequence of this random number generator.
`int`	**`nextInt`**`()`	Returns the next pseudorandom, uniformly distributed `int` value from the sequence of this random number generator.
`int`	**`nextInt`**`(int n)`	Returns a pseudorandom, uniformly distributed `int` value between zero (inclusive) and the specified value (exclusive), drawn from the sequence of this random number generator.

(Continued)

Table 14.3 *(Continued)*

long	**nextLong**()	Returns the next pseudorandom, uniformly distributed long value from the sequence of this random number generator.
void	**setSeed**(long seed)	Sets the seed of this random number generator using a single long seed.

Table 14.4 summarizes various methods from class Date

Table 14.4 Method Summary: Class Date

boolean	**after**(Date when)	Tests if this date is after the specified date.
boolean	**before**(Date when)	Tests if this date is before the specified date.
Object	**clone**()	Returns a copy of this object.
int	**compareTo**(Date anotherDate)	Compares two dates for ordering.
boolean	**equals**(Object obj)	Compares two dates for equality.
long	**getTime**()	Returns the time in milliseconds since 1 January 1970, 00:00:00 GMT represented by this date object.
int	**hashCode**()	Returns a hash code value for this object.
void	**setTime**(long time)	Sets this date object to represent a point in time, that is time in milliseconds after 1 January 1970, 00:00:00 GMT.
String	**toString**()	Converts this date object into a string.

Table 14.5 summarizes the fields of class Calendar. Though this class is abstract, class GregorianCalendar extends this class. Therefore, fields and methods of class Calendar are important.

Table 14.5 Summary of Fields from Class Calendar

static int	**AM**	Value of the AM_PM field indicating the period of the day from midnight to just before noon.
static int	**AM_PM**	Field number for get and set indicating whether the HOUR is before or afternoon.

(Continued)

Table 14.5 *(Continued)*

static int	**APRIL**	Value of the MONTH field indicating the fourth month of the year.
protected boolean	**areFieldsSet**	True if fields[] are in sync with the currently set time.
static int	**AUGUST**	Value of the MONTH field indicating the eighth month of the year.
static int	**DATE**	Field number for get and set indicating the day of the month.
static int	**DAY_OF_MONTH**	Field number for get and set indicating the day of the month.
static int	**DAY_OF_WEEK**	Field number for get and set indicating the day of the week.
static int	**DAY_OF_WEEK_IN_MONTH**	Field number for get and set indicating the ordinal number of the day of the week within the current month.
static int	**DAY_OF_YEAR**	Field number for get and set indicating the day number within the current year.
static int	**DECEMBER**	Value of the MONTH field indicating the twelfth month of the year.
static int	**DST_OFFSET**	Field number for get and set indicating the daylight savings offset in milliseconds.
static int	**ERA**	Field number for get and set indicating the era, for example AD or BC in the Julian calendar.
static int	**FEBRUARY**	Value of the MONTH field indicating the second month of the year.
static int	**FIELD_COUNT**	The number of distinct fields recognized by get and set.
protected int[]	**fields**	The field values for the currently set time for this calendar.
static int	**FRIDAY**	Value of the DAY_OF_WEEK field indicating Friday.
static int	**HOUR**	Field number for get and set indicating the hour of the morning or afternoon.
static int	**HOUR_OF_DAY**	Field number for get and set indicating the hour of the day.

(Continued)

Table 14.5 (*Continued*)

protected boolean[]	**isSet**	The flags which tell if a specified time field for the calendar is set.
protected boolean	**isTimeSet**	If true, then the value of time is valid.
static int	**JANUARY**	Value of the MONTH field indicating the first month of the year.
static int	**JULY**	Value of the MONTH field indicating the seventh month of the year.
static int	**JUNE**	Value of the MONTH field indicating the sixth month of the year.
static int	**MARCH**	Value of the MONTH field indicating the third month of the year.
static int	**MAY**	Value of the MONTH field indicating the fifth month of the year.
static int	**MILLISECOND**	Field number for get and set indicating the millisecond within the second.
static int	**MINUTE**	Field number for get and set indicating the minute within the hour.
static int	**MONDAY**	Value of the DAY_OF_WEEK field indicating Monday.
static int	**MONTH**	Field number for get and set indicating the month.
static int	**NOVEMBER**	Value of the MONTH field indicating the eleventh month of the year.
static int	**OCTOBER**	Value of the MONTH field indicating the tenth month of the year.
static int	**PM**	Value of the AM_PM field indicating the period of the day from noon to just before midnight.
static int	**SATURDAY**	Value of the DAY_OF_WEEK field indicating Saturday.
static int	**SECOND**	Field number for get and set indicating the second within the minute.
static int	**SEPTEMBER**	Value of the MONTH field indicating the ninth month of the year.

(*Continued*)

Table 14.5 *(Continued)*

static int	**SUNDAY**	Value of the DAY_OF_WEEK field indicating Sunday.
static int	**THURSDAY**	Value of the DAY_OF_WEEK field indicating Thursday.
protected long	**time**	The currently set time for this calendar, expressed in milliseconds after 1 January 1970, 00:00:00 GMT.
static int	**TUESDAY**	Value of the DAY_OF_WEEK field indicating Tuesday.
static int	**UNDECIMBER**	Value of the MONTH field indicating the thirteenth month of the year.
static int	**WEDNESDAY**	Value of the DAY_OF_WEEK field indicating Wednesday.
static int	**WEEK_OF_MONTH**	Field number for get and set indicating the week number within the current month.
static int	**WEEK_OF_YEAR**	Field number for get and set indicating the week number within the current year.
Static int	**YEAR**	Field number for get and set indicating the year.
Static int	**ZONE_OFFSET**	Field number for get and set indicating the raw offset from GMT in milliseconds.

Table 14.6 summarizes methods of class Calendar.

Table 14.6 Summary of Methods from Class Calendar

abstract void	**add**(int field, int amount)	Adds or subtracts the specified amount of time to the given calendar field, based on the calendar's rules.
boolean	**after**(Object when)	Returns whether this Calendar represents a time after the time represented by the specified Object.
boolean	**before**(Object when)	Returns whether this Calendar represents a time before the time represented by the specified Object.

(Continued)

Table 14.6 (*Continued*)

void	**clear**()	Sets all the calendar field values and the time value (millisecond offset from the Epoch) of this Calendar undefined.
void	**clear**(int field)	Sets the given calendar field value and the time value (millisecond offset from the Epoch) of this Calendar undefined.
Object	**clone()**	Creates and returns a copy of this object.
int	**compareTo**(Calendar anotherCalendar)	Compares the time values (millisecond offsets from the Epoch) represented by two Calendar objects.
protected void	**complete**()	Fills in any unset fields in the calendar fields.
protected abstract void	**computeFields**()	Converts the current millisecond time value time into calendar field values in fields[].
protected abstract void	**computeTime**()	Converts the current calendar field values in fields[] into the millisecond time value time.
boolean	**equals**(Object obj)	Compares this Calendar to the specified Object.
int	**get**(int field)	Returns the value of the given calendar field.
int	**getActualMaximum** (int field)	Returns the maximum value that the specified calendar field could have, given the time value of this Calendar.
int	**getActualMinimum** (int field)	Returns the minimum value that the specified calendar field could have, given the time value of this Calendar.
Static Locale[]	**getAvailableLocales**()	Returns an array of all locales for which the getInstance methods of this class can return localized instances.
int	**getFirstDayOfWeek**()	Gets what the first day of the week is; for example SUNDAY in the United States, MONDAY in France.
abstract int	**getGreatestMinimum** (int field)	Returns the highest minimum value for the given calendar field of this Calendar instance.

(*Continued*)

Table 14.6 (*Continued*)

Static Calendar	**getInstance**()	Gets a calendar using the default time zone and locale.
Static Calendar	**getInstance**(Locale aLocale)	Gets a calendar using the default time zone and specified locale.
Static Calendar	**getInstance** (TimeZone zone)	Gets a calendar using the specified time zone and default locale.
Static Calendar	**getInstance**(TimeZone zone, Locale aLocale)	Gets a calendar with the specified time zone and locale.
abstract int	**getLeastMaximum** (int field)	Returns the lowest maximum value for the given calendar field of this `Calendar` instance.
abstract int	**getMaximum**(int field)	Returns the maximum value for the given calendar field of this `Calendar` instance.
int	**getMinimalDays InFirstWeek**()	Gets what the minimal days required in the first week of the year are; for example if the first week is defined as one that contains the first day of the first month of a year, this method returns 1.
abstract int	**getMinimum**(int field)	Returns the minimum value for the given calendar field of this `Calendar` instance.
Date	**getTime**()	Returns a `Date` object representing The time value of this `Calendar` (millisecond offset from the Epoch").
long	**getTimeInMillis**()	Returns the time value of this calendar in milliseconds.
TimeZone	**getTimeZone**()	Gets the time zone.
int	**hashCode**()	Returns a hash code for this calendar.
protected int	**internalGet**(int field)	Returns the value of the given calendar field.
boolean	**isLenient**()	Tells whether date/time interpretation is to be lenient.
boolean	**isSet**(int field)	Determines if the given calendar field has a value set, including cases that the value has been set by internal fields calculations triggered by a `get` method call.

(*Continued*)

Table 14.6 (*Continued*)

abstract void	**roll**(int field, boolean up)	Adds or subtracts (up/down) a single unit of time on the given time field without changing larger fields.
void	**roll**(int field, int amount)	Adds the specified (signed) amount to the specified calendar field without changing larger fields.
void	**set**(int field, int value)	Sets the given calendar field to the given value.
void	**set**(int year, int month, int date)	Sets the values for the calendar fields YEAR, MONTH, and DAY_OF_MONTH.
void	**set**(int year, int month, int date, int hourOfDay, int minute)	Sets the values for the calendar fields YEAR, MONTH, DAY_OF_MONTH, HOUR_OF_DAY, and MINUTE.
void	**set**(int year, int month, int date, int hourOfDay, int minute, int second)	Sets the values for the fields YEAR, MONTH, DAY_OF_MONTH, HOUR, MINUTE, and SECOND.
void	setFirstDayOfWeek (int value)	Sets what the first day of the week is; for example SUNDAY in the United States, MONDAY in France.
void	**setLenient**(boolean lenient)	Specifies whether or not date/time interpretation is to be lenient.
void	**setMinimalDays InFirst Week**(int value)	Sets what the minimal days required in the first week of the year are; for example if the first week is defined as one that contains the first day of the first month of a year, call this method with value 1.
void	**setTime**(Date date)	Sets this calendar's time with the given Date.
void	**setTimeInMillis** (long millis)	Sets this calendar's current time from the given long value.
void	**setTimeZone** (TimeZone value)	Sets the time zone with the given time zone value.
String	**toString**()	Return a string representation of this calendar.

Table 14.7 summarizes methods of class GregorianCalendar.

Table 14.7 Summary of Methods from Class `GregorianCalendar`

void	**add**(int field, int amount)	Adds the specified (signed) amount of time to the given calendar field, based on the calendar's rules.
Object	**clone**()	Creates and returns a copy of this object.
protected void	**computeFields**()	Converts the time value (millisecond offset from the Epoch) into calendar field values.
protected void	**computeTime**()	Converts calendar field values into the time value (millisecond offset from the Epoch).
boolean	**equals**(Object obj)	Compares this `GregorianCalendar` to the specified `Object`.
int	**getActualMaximum** (int field)	Returns the maximum value that this calendar field could have, taking into consideration the given time value and the current values of the `getFirstDayOfWeek`, `getMinimalDaysInFirstWeek`, `getGregorianChange` and `getTimeZone` methods.
int	**getActualMinimum** (int field)	Returns the minimum value that this calendar field could have, taking into consideration the given time value and the current values of the `getFirstDayOfWeek`, `getMinimalDaysInFirstWeek`, `getGregorianChange` and `getTimeZone` methods.
int	**getGreatestMinimum** (int field)	Returns the highest minimum value for the given calendar field of this `GregorianCalendar` instance.
Date	**getGregorianChange**()	Gets the `GregorianCalendar` change date.
int	**getLeastMaximum** (int field)	Returns the lowest maximum value for the given calendar field of this `GregorianCalendar` instance.
int	**getMaximum**(int field)	Returns the maximum value for the given calendar field of this `GregorianCalendar` instance.

(Continued)

Table 14.7 *(Continued)*

`int`	**`getMinimum`**`(int field)`	Returns the minimum value for the given calendar field of this `GregorianCalendar` instance.
`TimeZone`	**`getTimeZone`**`()`	Gets the time zone.
`int`	**`hashCode`**`()`	Generates the hash code for this `GregorianCalendar` object.
`boolean`	**`isLeapYear`**`(int year)`	Determines if the given year is a leap year.
`void`	**`roll`**`(int field, boolean up)`	Adds or subtracts (up/down) a single unit of time on the given time field without changing larger fields.
`void`	**`roll`**`(int field, int amount)`	Adds a signed amount to the specified calendar field without changing larger fields.
`void`	**`setGregorianChange`**`(Date date)`	Sets the `GregorianCalendar` change date.
`void`	**`setTimeZone`**`(TimeZone zone)`	Sets the time zone with the given time zone value.

Exercises

1. Write a method Boolean `checkDate(int yy, int mm, int dd)` which checks whether the date specified is a valid date or not.
   i. *Note 1*: 04, 12, 9 in the previous program was not a valid date as months are numbered 0 to 11.
   ii. *Note 2*: Similarly, 29, 1, 2005 is invalid as 2005 is a non-leap year. Hence, February would not have date 29. All these factors are to be considered in the program. You should not use any in-built classes of Java.
2. Solve the same problem using class `GregorianCalendar.`
3. Write a program for bank to add 180 days to a given date.
4. Write a program to find whether a given matrix is symmetrical.
5. Write a program to find whether a given matrix is a diagonal matrix.
6. Write a program to find the determinant of a given matrix.
7. Develop the program to find the solution of simultaneous equations by Gauss–Seidel iterative method.
8. Write a program to solve simultaneous equations using Gauss method of triangularization.
9. Write a program based on Gauss–Jordan method to solve a set of linear equations.
10. Write a program to find the inverse of a given matrix.
11. Write a program to find the best possible straight line passing through the given points.

12. Write a program to find an area of a circle with unit radius, using Monte Carlo method. (Hint: generate 10,000 random points and decide how many of them are within a circle.)
13. Write a program to print a histogram of a given data.
14. Assume you are a taxpayer with 30% income tax. You are planning to borrow "home loan" from HDFC at a rate of 8.5% Assume that interest paid to HDFC is completely free from income tax. (It is to be subtracted from your income.) Compute the effective rate of interest you bear on your loan.
15. Write a program to read a file containing savings bank transactions and calculate the interest. Interest is given on a minimum balance between 10th of a month and the end of month. (As we have not discussed files as yet, you may either enter data interactively or embed it in the program.)

MISCELLANEOUS TOPICS

15.1 Packages

15.1.1 Defining and using packages

When one has too many files, one needs to organize them in folders (directories). Similarly, when one has too many classes (developed by him) to use, some organization or grouping is needed. Java offers it in the form of `package`. We know that Java gives us many useful classes to use directly in our programs. These classes are also grouped into packages. The few common packages are `applet, awt, color, event, io, lang, math` and `swing`. The complete list of JDK application programming interface (API) packages is presented in the appendix.

A package can be defined as "a collection of related classes and interfaces that provides access protection and 'namespace management'". There are many advantages of this organization. It makes classes easier to find and use. It helps in avoiding naming conflicts. It helps in controlling the access. We are permitted to develop new packages and put our own classes and interfaces in it. Putting classes in a package should not be arbitrary. We should bundle related classes into a single package. Let us study the rules of the game.

Defining a package

Consider a case where you want to write a program `test2.java`. We want to use a user-defined method for time delay in it. Since time delay is a general method, we would like to keep it separately in a package so that other programs can also use it.

The solution is to define a class named `delay` with a method named `millisec()` for time delay in milliseconds in it. This class must belong to some specific package say `mypkg2`. We can import this package in our program `test2.java`. Let us first create class `delay`.

Program: Write a program to demonstrate creation of class in a specific package.

Solution: We will create a class `delay`. It will have a method `millisec()`. This method will provide delay in milliseconds. First, we will write this file. As it has a class `delay`, name must be `delay.java`. We will make this class as a part of package `mypkg2` (see Program 15.1).

PROGRAM 15.1 Class delay in Package mypkg2

```
//   delay.java
package mypkg2;
public class delay
  {  public static void milisec(int n)
```

```
    {   long i,j,k;
        for(k=0;k<n;k++)
        {   j=100000;
            for(i=1;i<30000;i++)
                    j=j-i;
        }
    }
}
```

Now we will compile this file to create a file `delay.class`. Please note that the statement `package mypkg2;`

This is the first non-comment statement in the file. Also, the class is specifically declared as public. Now we will make a folder `mypkg2` in the current directory. We will move file `delay.class` in this directory.

Using a package

To use this class in a program, we need an import statement. An import statement starts with a keyword import, followed by the fully qualified class `name` (i.e. `packagename.classname`). In general, if we want to import all the classes from the package, we can use wildcard notation (i.e. `packagename.*`).

Now we will write the program to test it.

Problem: Write a program to demonstrate use of a package.

Solution: See Program 15.2.

PROGRAM 15.2 Use of Package I

```
//   test2.java
import mypkg2.delay ;
class test2
  {
   static void main(String args[])
    {   System.out.println("---test2.java---");
        System.out.println("start");
           delay.milisec(5000);
        System.out.println("stop");
    };
  }
```

If you run the program, you will get the following output

Output

```
---test2.java---
start
stop
```

Please note that word stop appears after a delay of 5 seconds (= 5,000 milliseconds). Please note that when we ran this program, the current directory contained folder `mypkg2` and this folder contained the file `delay.class`. If any one of the above is not true, you will get following error message:

Error

```
---test2.java---
start
Exception in thread "main" java.lang.NoClassDefFoundError: mypkg2/delay
at test2.main(test2.java:8)
```

Note: The program starts executing. Hence, you see the word start. The error says class definition not found. It does not specify details. It is possible that program could not find folder `mypkg2.` (Actually, we changed the folder name temporarily.) Alternately, the folder was very much in place, but the class was not present in the folder.

The success of this program depends on the fact that the system variable `classpath` contains the current directory in our computer. If it does not, then the program will fail to run. See Box 15.1 for more details.

BOX 15.1 CLASSPATH

A Java program uses many classes, which are scattered in the computer. Just as disk operating system (DOS) uses the PATH command to locate a file, Java uses the CLASSPATH environment variable. It tells where to look for classes needed by the program. This variable is set by the command as shown below:

```
set classpath = .; E:\java;E:\java\myPackage
```

Different paths are separated by semicolon. The dot indicates current directory. In Windows, you can issue this command from command prompt.

You can put this command in `autoexec.bat` file. Alternately, user can set classpath through windows control panel.

Both the above methods set the path permanently. Some experts are of the opinion that classpath should be set using the -classpath runtime option every time you compile a program or run an interpreter.

When a running program requires any class, it searches it in folders specified in the classpath. The folders are searched in the order they are present in the classpath. As soon as the class is found, it is used. It is possible that a class `file` with the same name may be present in some directory specified later. The program does not worry about such possibility. It ignores any such classes.

We have now created a package and put a class in it in an informal manner. Now let us look at the whole process little systematically. Here are few short questions and answers.

Short Questions and Answers

Q. How does one create a package say `abcd`?

A. Step 1: Write suitable classes and interfaces with appropriate syntax and compile them. This will create `.class` files.

Step 2: Create a folder named `abcd` and move these `.class` files to this folder.

Q. Can we add another class to this package at a later stage?

A. Yes, by all means. Simply write the code in a `.java` file. It goes without saying that first statement must be `package abcd`. Compile it and move the class `file` to this folder.

Q. If two classes from different packages have same name, how do we resolve the conflict?

A. We can resolve the conflict by fully qualifying the class name as `package_name.class_name`. If we talk of earlier program, `mypkg2.delay` will identify it from any other classes named `delay` present somewhere else.

Q. Do packages contain only classes and interfaces?

A. No, it can contain sub-packages also.

So far, we have studied effects of access specifier in single file programs. Now we have studied concept of a package. Now it is time to study phenomenon of access specification in any (read complex or advanced) Java program.

Table 15.1 illustrates the access mechanism as provided in Java.

Table 15.1 Access Specification in any Java Program

	Access specification			
Method in	**Private**	**No modifier (default)**	**Protected**	**Public**
Same class	Yes	Yes	Yes	Yes
Same package sub-class	No	Yes	Yes	Yes
Same Package non sub-class	No	Yes	Yes	Yes
Different package sub-class	No	No	Yes	Yes
Different package non sub-class	No	No	No	Yes

Now to understand this table better, you can split the table in two parts.

Consider that we are discussing a case of a single package. Class B wants to access member of class A, where both the classes belong to same package. Following rules will apply in this case:

Rule 1: If a method of class B wants to access member of its own class, it can do so irrespective of access specifier of the member (variables or methods).

Rule 2: If a method of class B wants to access member of class A, it can do so if access specifier is any thing other than private.

Consider that we are discussing a case with different packages. Class B from package, say, `pkg2` wants to access member of class A, belonging to package, say, `pkg1`. Following rules will apply in this case:

- If specifier is public, the member is accessible.
- If specifier is protected, member is accessible only if class B extends class A, not otherwise.
- If specifier is default or private, then member is not accessible.

Let us write a program and study the effect of protected access when calling from methods of other packages.

Let us take the example discussed in program `multi4.java` in earlier chapter. We will make subtle changes in it. We will name this file as `C.java`. We will make classes as part of package `pkgABC`. The file is as follows:

File c.java

```
//    C.java
package pkgABC ;
class A
    {  protected String name;
       A(String st1)
         {  name = st1; }
       public void show()
         {  System.out.println("name");
         }
    }
class B extends A
    {
       protected long telephone ;
       B(String st1,long tn)
         {   super(st1);
            telephone = tn ;
         }
       public void show()
         {  System.out.println(super.name + " "z + telephone);
         }
    }
public class C extends B
    { public String city ;
       public C(String st1, long n, String st3 )
         {  super(st1, n);
            city = st3 ;
         }
      public void show()
       {  System.out.println(name + " " + telephone+ " " + city);
       }
    }
```

Please note the important changes. The first non-comment statement is

```
package pkgABC ;
```

The class C is declared public. Its constructor is declared public.

Now we will use class C in program multi5.

Problem: Write a program to study the access specifier protected with respect to use by classes in the different package.

Solution: Let us use the same program with only one change. In method main of class multi5 will use a protected variable telephone from class B. Initially, we will keep it commented (note 1). Please note that classes A, B, and C are part of package pkgABC, while our program multi5 is in different (an unnamed) package (see Program 15.3).

PROGRAM 15.3 Protected in Different Package

```
//   multi5
import pkgABC.* ;
  class multi5
  {   public static void main (String argv[])
    {
      System.out.println("<---multi5.java--->");
      System.out.println("");
      C me = new C("prof",24567890,"Mumbai");
      me.show();
      //    System.out.println( me.telephone); // note 1
    };
  }
```

If you compile and run the program, it will give following output.

Output

```
<---multi5.java--->
prof 24567890 Mumbai
```

Now let us remove the comment from line marked note 1. It will bring following line in the program:

```
System.out.println( me.telephone);
```

Now if we will compile the program, we will get following error message:

```
Compilation error multi5.java
Compiling javac multi5.java
multi5.java:10: telephone has protected access in pkgABC.B
    System.out.println( me.telephone);
                          ^
1 error
```

It proves the point that protected acts as private for classes outside the package.

Please note that folder `pkgABC` is kept in the (current) folder which contains file `multi5.class`.

15.1.2 Static import

From Java 5, we can add keyword static in importing classes. If we import the class with static keyword, we are allowed to use methods or fields from this class, without using the associated class name. This facility is called static import.

Earlier when we wanted to use method `pow()` from class `Math`, we have to always call it `Math.pow();` Now with static import, we can simply say `pow()`. See Program 15.4.

Problem: Write a program to demonstrate concept of "static import". Find the amount returned from a fixed deposit after a period of 100 years.

Solution: We will assume rate of interest as 10%. The deposit amount is assumed as Rs. 1,000 (see Program 15.4).

PROGRAM 15.4 Static Import

```
import static java.lang.Math.*;
import static java.lang.String.*;
public class pow4
{
  public static void main(String args[])
    { double deposit= 1000.00 ;
      double R = 10.0 ;// Rate of interest
      double r = R /100.0 ;
      double amount=0;
      System.out.println("<---pow4.java--->");
      System.out.println("R = " + valueOf(R));//note 1
      amount = deposit * pow( (1.0+r) , 100);//note2
      System.out.println("The amount is : " + (long)amount);
    }
}
```

If you run the program, you will get the following output.

Output

```
<---pow4.java--->
R = 10.0
The amount is : 13780612
```

Note 1: `valueOf(R)` is a method of class `String`.
Note 2: `pow()` is a method of class `Math`.

Because these classes have been imported with keyword `static`, we can compile this program. If you try to compile by removing word static, there will be compilation error.

15.2 Command Line Arguments

So far we have always used following line in our programs:

```
public static void main(String args[])
```

Now let us study what this `String args[]` means. In DOS, you run an application by typing application (`.exe` file) name on command prompt. DOS also allows you to put few arguments to this command. These arguments are known as command line arguments. Modern operating systems, like Windows and Linux, also support this feature. Java allows you get these arguments as strings in your application. `args[0]` stands for first argument, `args[1]` stands for second argument, and so on. The total numbers of arguments supplied are known from `args.length`. These arguments are treated as strings. Let us see a simple program.

Problem: Write a program to demonstrate use of command line arguments.

Solution: See Program 15.5.

PROGRAM 15.5 Command Line Arguments I

```
//    cla1.java
//    command line arguments
```

```
class cla1
{   public static void main(String args[])
        { int i,num;
          num = args.length ;
          System.out.println("Program cla1.java starts ");
          System.out.println("Number of arguments are " + num );
          for(i=0;i<num;i++)
              System.out.println(i+ " ) " + args[i] );
        }
}
```

If you run the program from command line as

```
D:\>java cla1 good morning
```

you will get the following output.

Output

```
Program cla1.java starts
Number of arguments are 2
0 ) good
1 ) morning
```

The above program was simple. It only illustrated the principle. Actually, arguments can be useful parameters. Let us see another example.

Problem: Write a program to demonstrate use of command line arguments.

Solution: Let us say we want to write a program to add two integers. Normally we give data interactively. Here we can give data as command line arguments (see Program 15.6).

PROGRAM 15.6 Command Line Arguments II

```
//    add.java
//    command line arguments
class add
{   public static void main(String args[])
        {   int i,j,k,num;
          num = args.length ;
          System.out.println("Program add.java starts ");
          i = Integer.parseInt(args[0]);
          j = Integer.parseInt(args[1]);
          k = i + j ;
          System.out.println("adding" );
          System.out.println( i + " and " + j );
          System.out.println("you get " + k );
        }
}
```

If you run the program from command line as

```
D:\> java add 2 3
```

you will get the following output.

Output

```
Program add.java starts
adding
2 and 3
you get 5
```

Please note the lines marked in bold. Command line arguments are accepted as strings. Hence to convert them into integers, we have to use method `parseInt()`.

15.3 Inner and Outer Classes

Now it is a time to look at inner classes. You will ask me what about outer classes? The class which contains the inner class is termed as outer class. Hence, no separate study of outer classes is required. Let us first start with a preparatory program.

Problem: Write a program to define class `time100` to represent time and use (instantiate) this class.

Solution: See Program 15.7.

PROGRAM 15.7 Preparatory Program

```
//    time555.java
class time555
{   public static void main (String argv[])
    {   int total ;
        time100 t1= new time100() ;
        t1.hour = 10 ;
        t1.minute =10 ;
        t1.second = 10;
        total =t1.hour * 60 *60 + t1.minute*60 + t1.second ;
       System.out.println("<---time555.java--->");
       System.out.println("Total seconds " + total);
    };
}
class time100
    {   int hour;
        int minute;
        int second ;
    };
```

If you run the program, you will get the following output.

Output

```
<---time555.java--->
Total seconds 36610
```

This is very simple. What if you have to put class `time100` inside class `time555`? No problem. See Program 15.8.

Problem: Rewrite Program 15.7 with class `time100` placed inside the main class.

Solution: Let us rename the programs main class as `time556` and place class `time100` inside it (see Program 15.8).

PROGRAM 15.8 Trial Program

```
//   time556.java
class time556
{
   class time100
    {  int hour;
         int minute;
         int second ;
      };
public static void main (String argv[])
     {  int total ;
        time100 t1= new time100() ;
        t1.hour = 10 ;
        t1.minute =10 ;
        t1.second = 10;
        total =t1.hour * 60 *60 + t1.minute*60 + t1.second ;
        System.out.println("<---time556.java--->");
        System.out.println("Total seconds " + total);
     };
  }
```

If you run the program, you will get the following compilation error.

Output

```
Compiling javac time556.java
time556.java:12: non-static variable this cannot be referenced from a static
context
time100 t1= new time100() ;
            ^
1 error
press any key to continue
```

The error message is quite confusing. Older versions used to give highly verbose error message. Well it can be avoided if we just add word static to it.

Let us test with a program.

Problem: Rewrite Program 15.8 by making class `time100` static.

Solution: To avoid conflict with previous program, let us rename program main class as `time557`. We will put this program in separate directory named `time557` (see Program 15.9).

PROGRAM 15.9 Nested class

```
//   time557.java
class time557
  {
    static class time100
      { int hour;
        int minute;
        int second ;
      };
public static void main (String argv[])
      {   int total ;
          time100 t1= new time100() ;
          t1.hour = 10 ;
          t1.minute =10 ;
          t1.second = 10;
          total =t1.hour * 60 *60 + t1.minute*60 + t1.second ;
          System.out.println("<---time557.java--->");
          System.out.println("Total seconds " + total);
      };
  }
```

If you run the program, you will get the following output.

Output

```
<---time557.java--->
Total seconds 36610
```

Well everything is going smooth. If you see the directory of this application (we have started every program/application in separate directory), you will see one file named `time557$time100.class`. The class `time100` was inside class `time557`. Hence, the compiled version of this class is named as stated.

Some experts do not consider this type of class as inner class at all. It is sometimes referred as "nested class".

With so much attention now, let us come to a real inner class. We will use same example but will not make class `time100` static.

Problem: Write a program to demonstrate concept of inner class.

Solution: For proper demonstration, we will have a separate program class named `inner1`. We will define class `time558`. It will have inner class `time100` (see Program 15.10).

PROGRAM 15.10 Inner class I

```
//   inner1.java
public class inner1
  { public static void main (String argv[])
      {  int total=0 ;
        time558 t1= new time558() ;
        System.out.println("<---inner1.java--->");
        System.out.println("Total seconds " + t1.myTime);
      };
  }
```

```
class time558
  { String myTime ;
    class time100
      { int hour = 10;
        int minute=10;
        int second =10 ;
        public int convert()
         { return hour *3600 + minute*60 + second ; }
      };
    time558()
      { time100 abc = new time100();
         myTime = String.valueOf (abc.convert()) ;
      }
}
```

If you run the program, you will get the following output.

Output

```
<---inner1.java--->
Total seconds 36610
```

This program works fine. Let us have a look at the code carefully. We may now call class `time558` as outer class. Class `time100` becomes inner class. In the constructor of outer class, an object (named abc) of inner class is defined and used.

Topic of inner class is highly complex. We have just provided an introduction. Inner class is extensively used in advanced programming.

15.4 BigInteger

In many applications, we may need integers which are huge and having values larger than type long. Hence, Java has supplied a class `BigInteger`. The object of this class can store an arbitrary precision integer. The class also provides methods which can be used to operate on this large integer. We can use it in many different applications. It is also useful in finding large prime numbers.

Let us write a program and study this class.

Problem: Write a program to introduce class `BigInteger`.

Solution: In order to verify that this class handles integers larger than long, let us multiply the value `MAX_LONG` by 100 and verify (see Program 15.11).

PROGRAM 15.11 BigInteger

```
import java.math.*;
public class bigint1
{
      public static void main(String args[])
      {   BigInteger bg1 =new BigInteger("9223372036854775807");
          BigInteger bg2 =new BigInteger("100");
          System.out.println("<---bigint1--->");
          System.out.println(" bg1 is " + bg1);
```

```
        bg1=bg1.multiply(bg2);
        System.out.println("new value " + bg1);
    }
}
```

If you run the program, you will get the following output.

Output

```
<---bigint1--->
bg1 is     9223372036854775807
new value 922337203685477580700
```

Please note that we have chosen the maximum value of long as the value of bg1.

The program could multiply it by 100. This proves that class `BigInteger` can handle really big integers.

15.5 Enumeration

Enumeration adds elegance to the code. Earlier we have seen use of interface to get enumeration constant. That was only an ad hoc solution. Hence, Java has added class `Enum` in version 1.5. This is to give functionality of enumerated data types somewhat similar to one provided in language C++. However, please note that since Java is a very strict language as far as types are concerned, we cannot use facilities as freely as in C++. Nevertheless, it is a good addition.

At the heart of enumeration there is a class called `Enum`. This is the common base class of all Java language enumeration types.

Table 15.2 illustrates methods from this class.

Table 15.2 Method Summary: Class Enum

protected Object	`clone()`	Throws `CloneNotSupportedException`.
int	`compareTo(E o)`	Compares this enum with the specified object for order.
boolean	`equals(Object other)`	Returns true if the specified object is equal to this enum constant.
Class<E>	`getDeclaringClass()`	Returns the Class `object` corresponding to this enum constant's enum type.
int	`hashCode()`	Returns a hash code for this enum constant.
String	`name()`	Returns the name of this enum constant, exactly as declared in its enum declaration.
int	`ordinal()`	Returns the ordinal of this enumeration constant (its position in its enum declaration, where the initial constant is assigned an ordinal of zero).
String	`toString()`	Returns the name of this enum constant, as contained in the declaration.

(Continued)

Table 15.2 (*Continued*)

static <T extends Enum,<T>>T	valueOf(Class,<T>. enumType, String name)	Returns the enum constant of the specified enum type with the specified name.

When we want to have enumeration in our program, we will use keyword enum.

A typical declaration goes as follows:

```
enum Suits { spade, heart, diamond, club };
```

Here we are declaring enumerated type named Suits. We are defining four elements of this type as spade, heart, diamond, and club. After this declaration, we can define a variable of class `Suits`. It can take any of the above four values. We can perform various operations (as shown in Table 15.2) on it.

Let us study it with the help of a simple program.

Problem: Write a program to study class Enum.

Solution: See Program 15.12.

PROGRAM 15.12 Enumeration

```
//    enum2.java
enum Suits
  {   spade, heart, diamond, club };
class enum2
 {
  public static void main(String args[])
     {   System.out.println("<---enum2.java--->");
         Suits m =Suits.spade;
         Suits n = Suits.diamond;
         System.out.println(" 1.  " + m);
         System.out.println(" 2.  " + m.toString());
         System.out.println(" 3.  " + m.name());
         System.out.println(" 4.  " + m.ordinal() ) ;
         System.out.print(" 5. n as compare to m is ");
         if (n.compareTo(m) <0 )
         System.out.println("less");
                else if(n.compareTo(m)>0)
         System.out.println("more");
                else
         System.out.println("equal");
     }
 }
```

If you run the program, you will get the following output.

Output

```
<---enum2.java--->
1. spade
2. spade
```

```
3. spade
4. 0
5. n as compare to m is more
```

Note:

1. First line shows that we can print the value by using method `println()`.
2. The method `toString()` prints similarly in this case. If we want to have a shorter or longer name for the type we have to overload the `toString()` method.
3. The method name returns a string exactly as declared.
4. Since spade is the first name in declaration, its ordinal value is zero.
5. Demonstrates `compareTo()`.

15.6 Labelled `break` and Labelled `Continue`

15.6.1 Labelled `break`

Earlier we have seen `break` statement. It helps to jump out of the innermost loop. Sometimes a need may arise that on some condition we would like to jump out not of the innermost loop but out side a deeply nested loop.

Java being a structured language does not support `goto`. It supports labelled `break` instead.

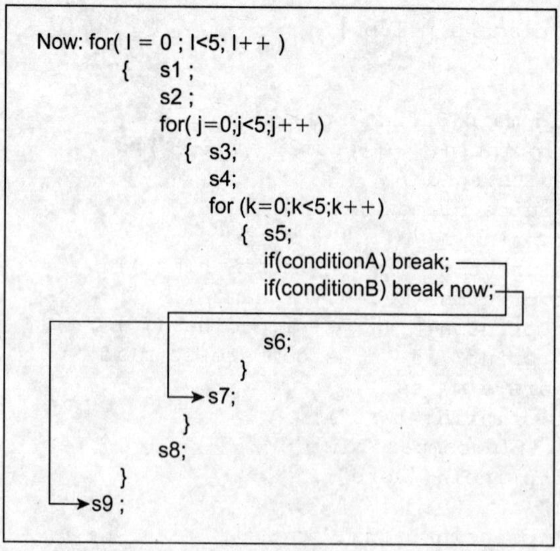

```
Now: for( I = 0 ; I<5; I++ )
        {   s1 ;
            s2 ;
            for( j=0;j<5;j++ )
              {  s3;
                 s4;
                 for (k=0;k<5;k++)
                   {  s5;
                      if(conditionA) break;
                      if(conditionB) break now;
                      s6;
                   }
                 s7;
              }
            s8;
        }
     s9 ;
```

Figure 15.1 Labelled **Break**

To use this facility, we must assign a label say `Now` (or any other name) to a loop at any level. A statement

```
break Now;
```

will move the control out of this labelled loop. Figure 15.1 can explain the action better.

It must be understood that such a labelled `break` statement must be inside that loop. In Figure 15.1 label is attached to outermost loop. However, label can be attached to any inner loop too.

Problem: Write a program to illustrate labelled break statement.

Solution: Let us take an example of gambling. A man takes some initial amount to Las Vegas. Assume he puts Rs. 10 every time. Most of the times, he wins nothing or a minor amount. Once in a blue moon, he may collect more than Rs. 10,000. In that case, he decides to stop gambling immediately (see Program 15.13).

PROGRAM 15.13 Demo of Break

```
/  break4.java
class break4
 {  public static void main ( String args[ ] )
     {  int amount = 120 ;
        int i,j,k;
        System.out.println("<---break4.java--->" ) ;
        Now: for (j= 0; j<3; j++)
              {   for(i=0;i<4;i++)
                   {  amount = amount - 10;
                      k = gamble();
                       amount = amount + k ;
                       if (  k >10000)
                         {  System.out.println("Won  " + k +
                                "\n Time to break " );
                            break Now;
                         }
                   }
              }
        System.out.println("Out side the Labeled loop" );
        System.out.println("Amount left =" +amount);
     }
   public static int gamble()
     {  return 12000;
     }
 }
```

If you run the program, you will get the following output.

Output

```
<---break4.java--->
Won 12000
Time to break
Out side the Labeled loop
Amount left =12110
```

In the above example, method `gamble` should contain sophisticated random number generator. This is left to the readers as an exercise.

15.6.2 Labelled `continue`

Just like labelled `break`, Java provided labelled `continue` statement. The only difference is that when executed, control goes back to beginning of labelled loop. It means it skips over any unfinished code below it.

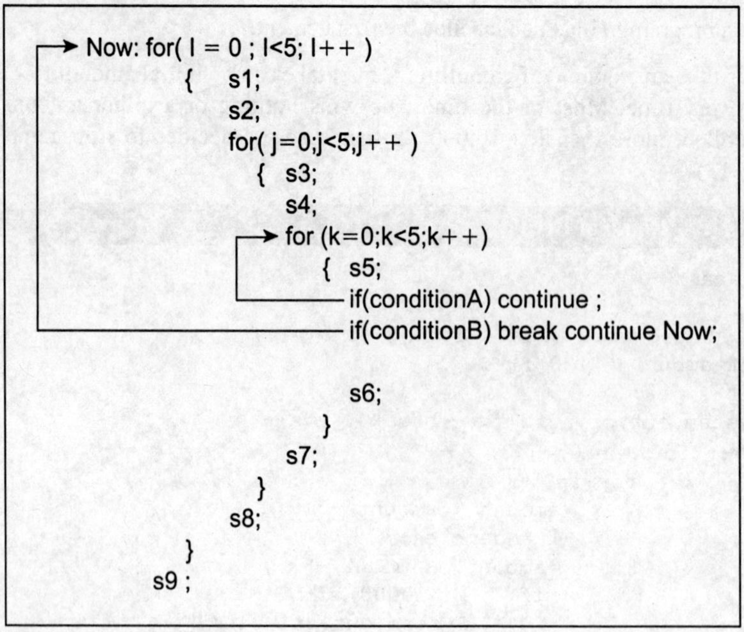

```
Now: for( I = 0 ; I<5; I++ )
     {  s1;
        s2;
        for( j=0;j<5;j++ )
           { s3;
             s4;
             for (k=0;k<5;k++)
                { s5;
                  if(conditionA) continue ;
                  if(conditionB) break continue Now;

                  s6;
                }
             s7;
           }
        s8;
     }
  s9 ;
```

Figure 15.2 Labelled Continue

Figure 15.2 can explain the action better.

As specified, earlier such a `break` statement must be inside the labelled loop. It cannot be outside the labelled loop. Otherwise there will be a compiler error.

Problem: Write a program to illustrate the use of `continue` statement with a label.

Solution: In this program, we will set a simple for loop. Inside the loop, we will test marks obtained by the students. If a student gets less than 40 marks, last line in the loop is not printed (see Program 15.14).

PROGRAM 15.14 Labelled continue

```
//    continue2.java
class continue2
{   public static void main ( String args[ ] )
     {   int marks[] ={ 55 , 35, 88 , 10 } ;
         System.out.println("--->continue2.java<---") ;
         int i,j;
Label1 : for(j=0;j<2;j++)
          {System.out.println("j= " + j);
           for(i=0;i<4;i++)
             { System.out.println("i= " + i + " Marks =" + marks[i]);
               if (marks[i] <40) continue Label1;
               System.out.println("---last line in loop " + i );
             }
          }
     }
}
```

If you run the program, you will get the following output.

Output

```
--->continue2.java<---
j= 0
i= 0 Marks =55
---last line in loop 0
i= 1 Marks =35
j= 1
i= 0 Marks =55
---last line in loop 0
i= 1 Marks =35
```

15.7 Operators Revisited

15.7.1 Conditional operator (? :)

The function of this operator is somewhat similar to `if-then` statement. There is a condition and a selection is based on the evaluation of condition. The only difference is this is an operator and hence returns values. It does not execute different statements. Its syntax is as follows:

```
( condition ) ? A : B
```

The condition is a Boolean expression. If it evaluates to true, value A is returned, otherwise value B is returned. Please note that A and B can be constants or expressions. The brackets shown around the condition are for readability. They are not compulsory. They may or may not be present.

Problem: Write a program to demonstrate use of conditional operator. Given two array indices, get the value of the array element with higher index.

Solution: See Program 15.15.

PROGRAM 15.15 Conditional Operator

```
//    cond1.java
//    conditional operator
class cond1
{ public static void main(String args[])
   {  int A = 55, B = 65, max,min ;
      System.out.println("<---cond1--->");
      max = A > B ? A :B;
      min =  (A<B)? A:B;
      System.out.println("maximum is "+ max);
      System.out.println("minimum is "+ min);
   }
}
```

If you run the program, you will get the following output.

Output

```
<---cond1--->
maximum is 65
minimum is 55
```

In our opinion, this is not a great facility. It may have been retained in Java for compatibility with C++ code. However, as this returns a value, certain cryptic uses can be found out for this construct. For example, this construct can appear as an array index (see Program 15.16). Here we will show that as conditional operator is an operator, it can have an exclusive usage which will not be possible with `if`, which is a statement. We will use it as an index of an array.

Using conditional expression as an array index

Problem: Write a program to demonstrate use of conditional operator as an array index.

Solution: In this example, we will put the conditional expression as an index of array (see Program 15.16).

PROGRAM 15.16 Conditional Operator Cond2.Java

```
//    cond2.java
//    conditional operator
class cond2
{   public static void main(String args[])
    {   int[] box = { 22, 33, 44, 51, 93 };
          int i=3, j = 2, result ;
          System.out.println("<---cond2--->");
          result= box[ (i > j ) ? i : j] ;
          System.out.println("result is "+ result);
    }
}
```

If you run the program, you will get the following output.

Output

```
<---cond2--->
result is 51
```

15.7.2 Operator `instanceof`

This is a binary operator. It returns a value of type Boolean. If `operand1`, which is an object, is instance of `operand2`, which is a class, the result is true. Else, result is false. At the beginning, one will wonder what the use of such an operator is. When we write a program, it is we who decide variables (objects) names and its types (class). Well this is a general picture. In specific cases, we are allowed to move super-class references to (point to) sub-class object. This creates a possibility that reference of a particular type may or may not be referencing to object of its own class. Therefore, operator instanceof will be helpful to us. Let us write a simple program and get familiar with it.

Problem: Write a program to demonstrate operator `instanceof`.

Solution: We will define a super class and a sub-class. Then we will make reference of super-class point to object of sub-class and check the result (see Program 15.17).

PROGRAM 15.17 Operator instanceof

```
//   inst1.java
class time0
      { public int numsec ; // (int n) ;
       } ;
class clock extends time0
        {  String st1;
         } ;
class inst1
 {  public static void main (String argv[])
    {
     System.out.println("<---inst1.java--->");
     clock clk1 = new clock();
     time0 t1 = new time0();
     time0 t2 ;

     System.out.println("1. t1 instanceof time0 " + ( t1 instanceof time0) );
     System.out.println("2. t1 instanceof clock " + (t1 instanceof clock) ) ;
     t2 = t1 ;
     t1= clk1;

     System.out.println("3. t1 instanceof clock " + (t1 instanceof clock) ) ;

     System.out.println("4. clk1 instanceof clock "
             + (clk1 instanceof clock) ) ;
     System.out.println("5. clk1 instanceof time0 "
             + (clk1 instanceof time0) ) ;
    };
 }
```

If you run the program, you will get the following output.

Output

```
<---inst1.java--->
1. t1 instanceof time0 true
2. t1 instanceof clock false
3. t1 instanceof clock true
4. clk1 instanceof clock true
5. clk1 instanceof time0 true
```

You will appreciate this program better after you read Chapter 16 "Inheritance Revisited".

15.7.3 Operator >>>

Earlier we have studied operator >> It is used for shifting bits right. Shifting right philosophically means dividing by 2. The operator takes care of the sign bit. Digit-wise it means that whatever is earlier leftmost bit, is added as new leftmost bit.

Java has additional operator >>> It works similar to operator >> and shifts the bits in the number to right. It adds zero as leftmost bit. Therefore, its action on positive numbers is identical to operator >>. However, for negative numbers, it gives different result.

Problem: Write a program to demonstrate operator >>>.

Solution: See Program 15.18.

PROGRAM 15.18 Operator >>>

```
//   shift3.java
public class shift3
 {
    public static void main(String[] args)
    { int i = 32;
      int j= -32 ;
      int k1,k2,l1,l2;
      System.out.println("<---shift3--->");
      System.out.println("i is " + i ); //Integer.toBinaryString(i));
      System.out.println("j is " + j ); //Integer.toBinaryString(j));
      k1= i>>>2;
       // System.out.println(k1);
       k2= i>>2;
       System.out.println(" using >>> using >>");
       System.out.printf(" i : %10d%10d\n",k1,k2);
       l1=j>>>2;
       //System.out.println(l1);
       l2=j>>2;
       System.out.printf(" j : %10d%10d\n",l1,l2);
    }
 }
```

If you run the program, you will get the following output.

Output

```
<---shift3--->
i is 32
j is -32
    using  >>> using >>
i :          8        8
j : 1073741816       -8
```

At this stage, you may wonder why there is no matching operator <<<. Try to find the answer yourself.

15.8 Interface `Cloneable`

Package `java.lang` has defined an interface `Cloneable`. It is interesting to note that there is no method defined in it. When a class implements this interface, it indicates to the compiler that it is legal for this object to use method clone from class `Object`.

15.8.1 Method `clone()`

The class `Object` has a method `clone()`. It has the following format:

```
protected Object clone()
                         throws CloneNotSupportedException
```

Method `clone` makes a field-for-field copy of the instances of invoking object.

If a class (actually method of it) calls method clone when it does not implements `Cloneable`, an exception `CloneNotSupportedException` is thrown.

Since the method is protected, we use it by overriding with a public method.

If a class contains only primitive fields or references to immutable objects (read strings), it is safe to use method `clone` directly. In all other cases (say trees) use of this method requires additional work.

Let us see a simple program using the aforementioned concepts.

PROGRAM 15.19 Cloning an Object

```
//   clone1.java
class time5 implements Cloneable
 {int myTime;
  time5(int n)
  { myTime = n;
  }
  public time5 clone()
  { try
   { return (time5) super.clone();
   }
   catch(CloneNotSupportedException e)
   { System.out.println("Clone Not Supported");
   }
   return this; // note 1
  }
}
public class clone1
{
public static void main (String argv[])
   { int total=0 ;
     time5 t1= new time5(3) ;
     time5 t2= t1.clone();
     System.out.println("<---clone1.java--->");
     System.out.println("Total seconds " + t1.myTime);
     System.out.println("Total seconds " + t2.myTime);
   };
}
```

If you run this program, you will get the following output.

Output

```
<---clone1.java--->
Total seconds 3
Total seconds 3
```

You may wonder about the fuss regarding simple fields. Consider a case of a binary tree. If you say, you are cloning the root node, there is no meaning to copy only that node. It is the starting point of whole big tree. A bit-by-bit copy may point to previous tree. There may be dangerous side effects. Hence cloning using this interface should be restricted to only simple objects.

15.9 Generics

Many times, we come across a situation when we have developed a method say sorting for one type of object. If we want to sort any other type of objects, we have to rewrite or tune this method. Such exercise is also open to errors. The question arises why we cannot write a routine once and use it without modification for different kind of data? This facility is available in C++ under templates. Java introduced "generics" for this purpose. This facility was first introduced in version 5. A good programming practice requires that we should catch as many errors at the compiling. When the program is complete, there should not be any errors as far as possible. It is claimed that generics help us in this direction. This is the advantage of generics. Now we can have generic classes or generic methods in Java.

15.9.1 Generic types

For using generic facility in programming, we can study classes and methods using this facility. However, term generic types is used in literature in place of generic classes. We will assume both the things as identical. We will not worry about nomenclature but study the principle.

Let us imagine a simple class named `Box`. It contains two numbers of same types. Types can be `Integers` or `Double` or even `Long`. We do not want to define separate classes for individual types. This is now possible with generics that we can start our class definition as

```
class Box (T)
```

Here, `T` stands for a type variable. At a later stage, it will stand for either `Integer` or `Double` or any other class. Please note that `T` cannot represent primitive data types. Let us see the class definition.

```
class Box<T>
  { T x,y ;
    boolean k;
    Box ( T a, T b )
      { x=a;
        y=b;
        k = x.equals(y);
  }
}
```

A close scrutiny will tell us that this class contains two objects and a Boolean variable which stores the information regarding whether both the objects are equal. We can declare an object with `T` representing type `Integer` as follows:

```
Box integerBox = new Box<Integer>(a,b);
```

Note that word Integer within angled brackets tell the compiler that we are using type `Integer` in place of `T`.

Let us study it with a simple program.

Problem: Write a program to study a generic class.

Solution: We will use the example of the class `Box` discussed earlier (see Program 15.20).

PROGRAM 15.20 Generic Class

```
//     gen2.java
class Box<T>
   { T x,y ;
     boolean k;
     Box ( T a, T b )
      { x=a;
        y=b;
        k = x.equals(y);
      }
   }
class gen2
  {
    public static void main(String[] args)
    { Integer a ,b ;
     a = new Integer(4);
     b = new Integer(4);
     Box integerBox = new Box<Integer>(a,b);
     System.out.println("<---gen2.java--->");
     System.out.println(integerBox.k);
    }
  }
```

If you run the program, you will get the following output.

Output

```
<---gen2.java--->
true
```

The result is as expected.

15.9.2 Generic methods

Just like classes, we can have generic methods too. Actually, in Program 15.20 we have used a generic constructor. We know that constructor is nothing but a method. We can have independent methods which use generic principle.

Let us say we want to develop a method to add an element to a vector. As vectors can be of different types, we will have a method `add` which is generic. For example,

```
static <T> void add(T a, Vector<T> v)
```

If the vector stores elements of some particular class, we can add the element of that class in it with this method. The <T> after keyword `static` in the declaration tells the compiler that this is a generic method using generic type `T`.

Problem: Write a program to study generic methods.

Solution: See Program 15.21.

PROGRAM 15.21 Generic Method

```
//      gen3b.java
import java.util.* ;
class gen3b
{
   static <T> void add(T a, Vector<T> v)
   { v.add(a) ;
   }
public static void main(String args[])
       { int i ;
        Vector<Integer> vec1 = new Vector<Integer>(10);
        add(3,vec1);
        System.out.println("<---gen3b--->");
        System.out.println(vec1.size());
       }
}
```

If you run the program, you will get the following output.

Output

```
<---gen3b--->
1
```

As methods have no existence outside the class (like C++), a typical general purpose generic method will be independent of the class in which it is present. It means such methods will have to be declared as `static`.

Generics is a tough topic. If you do not follow the rules of the game, you do not get the full benefit of it. Consider a case that you develop a program say `gen1.java` by violating the rules, you may get following compilation error:

Error

```
gen1.java uses unchecked or unsafe operations.
Recompile with -Xlint:unchecked for details.
```

If you recompile with–Xlint parameter

```
prompt>javac -Xlint gen1.java
```

you will get only a warning and not an error.

Warning

```
gen1.java:26: warning: [unchecked] unchecked call to XXXX.
1 warning
```

After the warning, you are allowed to run the program. We can run our program but we are not getting the full benefit of generic programming.

Generics is an advanced topic. At this stage, we do not want to go in details of it. You will find extensive use of generics in Chapter 23 "Collection Framework".

15.10 Guidelines for Forming Identifiers

Java is case-sensitive language. It is a deliberate design. Languages C/C++ are case-sensitive too. Hence, C programming habits can be continued in Java. Using upper-case and lower-case letters in an identifier can increase readability. Java Language Specifications recommend certain conventions. If we do not follow them in our programs, our programs will still compile. However, if we use them, our programs will be more readable. Also readers who themselves follow these conventions will be comfortable in reading our code. The recommendations are as follows:

- The general rule is that all characters should be in lower case.
- If an identifier is multi-word, then the first character of every word except the first word should be in upper case. For example, `lastAction`, `cleanBold`, and `outOfFashion`.
- First character of variable, method, or package should be in lower case.
- First character of class name or interface name should be in upper case.
- Class names should be nouns and method name should be verbs.
- Constants declared with final should be all in upper case

Table 15.3 illustrates the above guidelines.

Table 15.3 Forming Identifiers

Kind of identifier	Examples	
class	`TestOut`	`MyWindow`
interface	`Money`	`HindiNames`
method	`show()`	`byeBye()`
variable	`myMarks`	`runsScored`
package	`mypkg2`	`myUtils`
constant	`RED`	`HUNDRED`

For further details, please see "Java Language Specifications" from Web site of Sun Microsystems.

15.11 Parameter Passing Re-visited

In Chapter 6 on functions, we have seen method `swap` has to take curious path. This is because Java claims not to have pointers and does contain pointers internally. The language C became popular on the advocacy of strength of pointers and it became its nemesis.

Java claims that it does not support pointer and therefore it is simple and secure. This is partially true. Java does not support user-defined pointers and pointer manipulation or arithmetic. It does use pointers internally. The type reference is nothing but a pointer.

In old days of DOS, main memory was limited. When more memory was available (rather processors with more addressing capacity became available), there was a tricky situation. The computer has 640 KB of memory but only 64 KB was addressable by simple means. This created an artificial divide in the main memory. 64 KB was allocated to program's data and remaining memory was called heap. Programs started using pointers and command `new` to use this heap memory. This was called dynamic memory allocation.

In modern computers and with very high amount of memory available, this divide still continued.

In earlier languages, like PASCAL, there were two types of parameters: value parameters and variable parameters. This continued in C/C++ with different nomenclature and syntax. Value parameters became parameter passed by value and variable parameters became parameter passed by reference.

The parameters which a method can modify were variable parameters. They were passed with pointer (or address).

The parameters whose values are not supposed to change were passed as copies. This could ensure that after the method is over, any changes occurring during method execution are not reflected back. To achieve this, such parameter values were pushed on stack. It was not economically possible in those days to pass arrays or large data structures on stack. (The available RAM memory was limited.) Therefore, such parameters were passed by reference even when programmer has used them as pass by value.

In Java, this old policy was got converted into a rule. In Java, philosophically there is only one method of parameter passing. That is "pass by value".

Let us see the implications of this strategy. In Java, we cannot swap (by writing a method) two integers. Actually, we cannot swap any primitive data types. We are forced to write that famous three-line code.

We can swap or modify non-primitive data types, like arrays, strings, and objects. However, we have to understand that the reference is still passes by value. We must manipulate actual fields. If we pass object `MyStudent raja` as a parameter, we should modify fields like `raja.name` or `raja.marks`. We cannot simply use `raja`. It will not work.

15.12 Dynamic Data Structures

For many years, "Data Structures" was taught as the next subject after basic programming course. Dynamic data structures were a part of the said subject. Writing programs using such structures was considered as "Advanced programming". Many excellent textbooks are available for this subject. We advise our readers to get details from these textbooks.

The name dynamic suggests that the size of the data structure is not fixed. It changes as per our (programmers) wish. We have studied arrays. It is static data structure. Once we declare an array, its size cannot be changed.

In this section, we will show that in Java you can handle dynamic data structures easily. We will discuss two popular structures, that is linked list and tree.

15.12.1 Linked list

Linked list is the simplest of all data structures. Here the nodes which are the basic data elements are linked to each other. The linked list starts from the main pointer. From early texts, this is termed as root. Figure 15.3 displays a typical linked list.

It is convenient to add a node at the root. Hence, the algorithm for creating a linked list is as follows:

- Generate first node. It should point to "Null" (no where). Let the root point to this node.
- Generate next node and add it at the root.

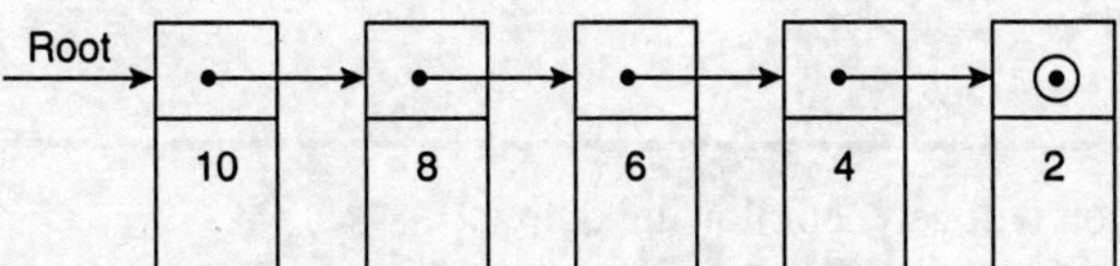

Figure 15.3 Linked List

- This node should point to where root was pointing earlier.
- Repeat above step until data is exhausted.

Problem: Write a program to create and scan a linked list.

Solution: We will assume our node consists of an object of type (class) Book. At present, it will contain a book number and pointer to next elements. For simplicity, we will accept data about book numbers from an array. The first task is to create a linked list. The second one is to scan and print all the book numbers (see Program 15.22).

PROGRAM 15.22 Linked List I

```
//         linked1.java
//    linked list first program
//  only a start
class Book
   { int key; // isbn number
    Book next;
    Book(int n) // constructor
       { key = n ;
         next = null ;
       }
   };
class linked1
  { static void main(String args[])
       { Book root ;
        Book temp ;
        int i;
        int A[] = { 2, 4, 6, 8, 10 } ;
          System.out.println("<---linked1.java--->");

          temp =new Book(A[0]);
          root = temp;
          for( i=1;i<5;i++)
           { temp =new Book(A[i]);
            temp.next = root;
            root = temp;
           }
         // now scanning the list
         temp = root ;
         while(temp != null)
            { System.out.println(temp.key);
```

```
                temp = temp.next;
            }
        }
    }
```

If you run the program, you will get the following output.

Output

```
<---linked1.java--->
10
8
6
4
2
```

In the above programs, the last number entered is at the root. So when we get the numbers back they appear in reverse. In this program, we entered the new node at the root because it is very simple. If we are ready to write few more lines, it is possible that the new node is entered at the tail. In that case, the elements in the linked list will be in the order of their arrival.

15.12.2 Binary search tree

Another useful data structure is tree. A special case of the general tree is binary tree. In a binary tree, each node can have at most two child nodes. A recursive definition of binary tree can be stated as follows:

"Binary tree is either null or a node with a possible left and right sub-tree. A subtree is a tree".

If we organize the elements of the binary tree in a disciplined manner, it is possible to search the data quickly. Therefore, it is named as binary search tree (BST) (Figure 15.4). Every data value in left sub-tree is less than that of the node. Every data value in right sub-tree is greater than that of the node.
If we collect all the elements of a binary search tree, they are in sorted order. Hence, it is useful in sorting too. Let us try sorting using BST.

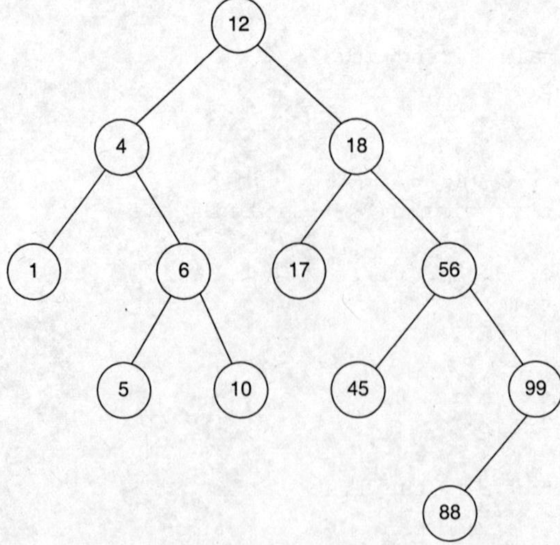

Figure 15.4 Binary Search Tree

Problem: Write a program to sort given data using BST.

Solution: The first step will be to create a BST from a given data and then collect all elements (see Program 15.23).

PROGRAM 15.23 Binary Search Tree

```
//      tree1.java
//     tree program
//
class Node

    { int key;    // isbn number
      Node left, right;
      Node(int n) // constructor
         { key = n ;
           left = null ;
           right = null ;
         }
    };
class tree1
{static void main(String args[])
   {Node root ;
    Node temp ;
    int i;
    int A[] = { 12, 4, 6, 18, 10,56,1,45,99,88,5,17 } ;
    System.out.println("<---tree1.java--->");
    root = new Node(A[0]); // First nodeof the tree
    // building tree
    for( i=1;i<A.length;i++)
          { build(root,A[i]) ;
          }
    // now scanning the tree
    visitAll(root);
}
 static void build( Node root, int num )
 { if (root == null)
      { System.out.println("error!");
        System.exit(1);
      }
     else
       if(root.key > num)
           { if ( root.left == null )
                          root.left = new Node(num);
                else build(root.left, num);
           }
     else
           {if( root.right == null )
                          root.right = new Node(num);
                else      build(root.right,num);
           }
       }
```

```
static void visitAll( Node root )
{ if(root != null)
      {visitAll(root.left);
       System.out.println(root.key);
       visitAll(root.right);
    }
}
}
```

If you run the program, you will get the following output.

Output

```
<---tree1.java--->
1
4
5
6
10
12
17
18
45
56
88
99
```

In the above program, we have to develop algorithms on our own. Java has recently added a facility what is known as "collection framework". The above programs can easily be written with the help of classes and methods of it. The collection framework is described in detail at the Chapter 23.

15.13 Package `Java.util`

Package `util` supports many useful interfaces and classes. Name util is a short for utility. Utilities improve the productivity of a programmer. In programming, "nothing is impossible". Even a novice programmer can write a complex code. However, it takes long time. Hence, any programming environment provides utilities. We have already used facilities like class `Random` and class `Scanner` earlier. In this section, we will study few more utilities.

15.13.1 Arrays

Package `Java.util` provides this interesting class named `Arrays`. There are no constructors direct or indirect for this class. You will ask me what the use of such a class is. Well this class contains many useful methods to work with arrays.

The most important methods being `sort()` and `binary-search()`. These methods can be applied to arrays of `byte, char, double,` float, `int, long, object`, or `short`.

If the specified array reference is null, then methods in this class all throw a `NullPointerException`. This class is a member of the "Java Collections Framework".

Let us study method sort from this class.

Problem: Write a program to demonstrate method `sort()` from class `Arrays`.

Solution: See Program 15.24.

PROGRAM 15.24 Sorting with Arrays

```
//     sort1.java
//     uses Arrays
import java.util.*;
class sort1
{  public static void main(String args[])
   {  int i,j,n,x,k;
      int[] a = {23,18,67,5,42,1,38};
     System.out.println("<---sort1--->");
     // Now sorting
     Arrays.sort(a);
     // Now printing
     System.out.println("Sorted output");
     for (i=0;i< a.length;i++)
     System.out.println( a[i]);
   }
}
```

If you run the program, you will get the following output.

Output

```
<---sort1--->
Sorted output
1
5
18
23
38
42
67
```

15.13.2 Class `BitSet`

Consider a situation of a very large factory with more than 10,000 workers. One can think of storing the attendance in an array of Boolean. We know that the information is only true or false. But the system designates 1 byte (8 bits) for it. If we can store a single binary digit, it can very well represent attendance. But there is no data type called bit. Also addressing every bit as a variable will be inefficient. With this background in mind, we can appreciate the class `BitSet`.

Java offers us a class named `BitSet`. As the name suggest, it is a set of bits. Strictly speaking, it is a vector of Boolean bits. As we know, vectors can grow in size when needed. We can address every bit with the help of an index. Initially all the bits are set to `false`.

It has rich set of methods. These are described in the table at the end of the chapter. There are two constructors. One creates the bit set of default size. The other constructor creates the bit set of specified size.

Problem: Write a program to demonstrate class `BitSet`.

Solution: In this program, we will define a variable `absent` of type bit set. For simplicity, we will keep the data of absent employees in array A. We will set the bits corresponding to absent employees. Next, we will scan the bit set for bits with value 1 (see Program 15.25).

PROGRAM 15.25 BitSet1

```
import java.util.* ;
public class bitset1
{  public static void main(String args[])
     {  final int max =2000;
        int [] A = { 23 , 34, 305,340, 701};

        BitSet absent = new BitSet(max);
        System.out.println("<---bitset1--->");
        for(int i =0; i<A.length;i++)
             absent.set(A[i]);
        // now list out
        for(int i =0; i<max; i++)
           { if (absent.get(i))
                System.out.println(i);
           }
     }
}
```

If you run the program, you will get the following output.

Output

```
<---bitset1--->
23
34
305
340
701
```

Let us study one more program on bit set based on data compression.

Data compression

Data compression interests computer scientists from ages. Earlier it was storage problem which was asking for the data compression. Now internet bandwidth problems give boost to study of data compression. There are many algorithms for compressing the data. Here we are studying class `BitSet`. We are interested in finding out how we can use it for data compression. In Java, type integer is 32 bits. Consider a small number like 5. It will have only 3 useful bits. All other leading bits will be zero. We can hope to find some algorithm to use this fact. In implementing that algorithm, we will be required to transfer the relevant bits to a `BitSet` object. Also, we will be required to extract the given number of bits, construct, and integer from it. We will focus on these activities in the following program.

Problem: Write a program to demonstrate use of class `BitSet` in data compression.

Solution: In this program, we will develop two complimentary methods.

1. Method `add()` will add useful bits of an integer value to bit set.
2. Method `extract()` will extract those bits and convert it into an integer value.

PROGRAM 15.26 Methods for Data Compression

```
//   bitset2.java
import java.util.* ;
public class bitset2
{
  public static int add(BitSet bs, int n, int loc )
  { int count =0;
    int k;
     while (n>0)
     {  k= n % 2;// last bit
        System.out.println(count + "\t"+k);
        if (k==1) bs.set(loc);
        loc++;
        n=n/2;
        count++;
     }
     return count;
  }
  public static int extract(BitSet bs, int loc,int digits)
  {
  int result =0;
  for(int i= loc; i<loc+digits;i++)
      { result = result*2;
        if ( bs.get(i) )
        result =result+1;
      }
  return result ;
  }
 public static void main(String args[])
   { final int max =200;
     int Z = 17;
     int i=0,k=0;
     int temp=0;

     BitSet absent = new BitSet(max);
     System.out.println("<---bitset2--->");
     add ( absent, Z,5);
     add ( absent, Z+1,1001);
     System.out.println("part II");

     // now list out
     for(i =0; i<absent.length(); i++)
        { if (absent.get(i))
```

```
                System.out.println(i);
            }
        System.out.println("part II");
        System.out.println(extract(absent,5,5) );

        System.out.println("length ="+absent.length());
        System.out.println(" size ="+absent.size());
    }
}
```

If you run the program, you will get the following output.

Output

```
<---bitset2--->
0  1
1  0
2  0
3  0
4  1
0  0
1  1
2  0
3  0
4  1
part II
5
9
1002
1005
part II
17
length =1006
size =1024
```

Program 15.26 forms the backbone of a package for integer data compression. You have to define the rules for general strategy effecting data compression. The above methods will be highly useful in implementing that strategy.

15.14 Class Runtime

In the package `java.lang`, a very useful class named `Runtime` is defined. When any Java application starts running, a single instance of class `Runtime` is generated by the system. This allows application to interface with the environment in which it is running. Please note that we cannot create an instance of this class on our own. The method `getRuntime` helps us to obtain this object. This class has many useful methods. The following table illustrates some of them.

`exec()`	This method has the following format: `Process exec(String command)` This method executes the specified string command in a separate process. We are able to initiate any executable file or a batch file with the help of this command.
`exit()`	This method has the following format: `void exit(int status)` This method terminates the currently running Java virtual machine (JVM) by initiating its shutdown sequence. You will see this method in action in many of the programs in present text.
`freeMemory()`	This method has the following format: `long freeMemory()` This method returns the amount of free memory in the JVM when our program is running.
`gc()`	This method has the following format: `void gc()` This method runs the garbage collector. Memory will be reclaimed by the JVM. We can conveniently and conventionally too invoke this method as `System.gc();`
`getRuntime()`	This method has the following format: `static Runtime getRuntime()` This method returns the runtime object associated with the current Java application.
`load()`	This method has the following format: `void load(String filename)` This method loads the specified filename as a dynamic library (dll).
`totalMemory()`	This method has the following format: `long totalMemory()` This method returns the total amount of memory in the JVM.

Let us study two useful methods with the help of a program

15.14.1 Methods `freeMemory()` and `totalMemory()`

Problem: Write a program to find total and free memory in our computer.

Solution: The methods `freeMemory()` and `totalMemory()` from class `Runtime` are useful for this task (see Program 15.27).

PROGRAM 15.27 Memory I

```
//     memory1.java
class memory1
{
  public static void main(String arg[])
   {
      System.out.println("<---memory1.java--->");
      Runtime sys = Runtime.getRuntime();
      System.out.println("Total Memory " + sys.totalMemory() );
      System.out.println(" Free Memory " + sys.freeMemory() );
      System.out.println();
      byte b1[] = new byte[1000] ;

      System.out.println(
         "After allocating 1000 bytes " + sys.freeMemory() );
      short s1[] = new short[1000] ;
      System.out.println(
         "After allocating 1000 short " + sys.freeMemory() );
      int i1[] = new int[1000] ;
      System.out.println(
         "After allocating 1000 int " + sys.freeMemory() );
      long l1[] = new long[1000] ;
      System.out.println(
         "After allocating 1000 long " + sys.freeMemory() );
   }
}
```

If you run the program, you will get the following output.

Output

```
 <---memory1.java--->
Total Memory 1048576
Free Memory 675040

After allocating 1000 bytes 674000
After allocating 1000 short 671968
After allocating 1000 int   667936
After allocating 1000 long  659904
```

Please note that odd looking figure or total memory is actually 1 MB (1,024 × 1,024 Kb). We know that memory needed by data type byte, short, int, and long is one, two, four, and eight bytes, respectively. This can be checked with the above results.

15.15 Class `System`: Time Delay Routine

Java offers a static method named `currentTimeMillis()` in its class `System`.

This method returns a long telling, number of milliseconds passed from midnight of 1 January 1970. This time stored at the beginning and end of any activity leads to the time taken by that activity. This principle can be used to get time delay. Here the activity is simply "do nothing".

Problem: Write a program to define time delay method `delay9(long n)`. This method should provide delay of *n* milliseconds.

Solution: See Program 15.28.

PROGRAM 15.28 Time Delay

```
//   time2.java
class time2
{ public static void main(String arg[])
   { System.out.println("--->time2.java starts<---");
     System.out.println(" waiting for 5 seconds");
     delay9(5000);
     System.out.println(" time over" );
   }
public static void delay9(long n)
   { long t1,t2;
     t1 = System.currentTimeMillis();
     t1 = t1 + n;
     t2= System.currentTimeMillis();
     while ( t2 < t1 ) t2= System.currentTimeMillis();
   }
}
```

If you run the program, you will get the following output.

Output

```
--->time2.java starts<---
waiting for 5 seconds
time over
```

Stopwatch: Here we have created a time day. Many times, we are interested in measuring time required by some process. The situation is just opposite to one encountered above. The method `currentTimeMillis()` can also be used to create a class which can be used as a stopwatch. In this class, we need methods `start()` and `stop()`. We have developed the class `BPtimer` for this task. In this class, method `stop()` also displays the time. Both the methods are static. You can see them in action in Chapter 17 on "Files".

15.16 Assertion

When we write programs, there are many assumptions. The code is written with these assumptions. It is quite possible that at certain times they may not be valid. The program either will fail or will give disastrous result.

To avoid this, we will have to test these assumptions every now and then. To do it in elegant manner, Java has offered assertion. Those who have studied C++ will know that it is available in that language too. In Java, we can use assert statement in two forms. Let us start with the first one.
It will take the following form:

```
assert condition;
```

We compile programs with assertion normally. However, for running the programs, we have to use flag `ea` or `enableassertions`. If assertion error occurs during program run, you will get following message:

```
Exception in thread "main" java.lang.AssertionError.
```

If you do not use the flag, such exception will not be raised.
The second form has following syntax:

```
assert condition : expression ;
```

In this case, an exception will be constructed with the expression. Typically, expression will be a string. We have to design this string in such a way that when it is displayed, we get proper insight about the error.

Problem: Write a program to demonstrate assertions.

Solution: In this program, we will set the assertion such that denominator is not zero (see Program 15.29).

PROGRAM 15.29 Assertion

```
//    assrt.java
//    command line arguments
class assrt
{  public static void main(String args[])
        {  int x=5,y=0, num;
           assert y!=0;
           num = x/y ;
           System.out.println("<---assrt.java--->");
           System.out.println( y );
        }
}
```

When you run the program from command prompt as

```
Prompt>java -ea assrt
```

you will see the following output.

Output

```
Exception in thread "main" java.lang.AssertionError
    at assrt.main(assrt.java:6)
Please note that as assertion is enabled and the condition fails, we get
Exception of type assertion. Note that as the program fails, actual division
by zero does not occur.
```

When you run the program from command prompt as

Prompt>java assrt

you will see the following output.

Output

```
Exception in thread "main" java.lang.ArithmeticException: / by zero
at assrt.main(assrt.java:7)
```

Please note that we have not enabled the assertion. Hence, division by zero occurs in the program. Hence, exception of this specific type is raised.

Problem: Write a program to demonstrate second form of assert statement.

Solution: Basically we will use the same code as previous program (see Program 15.30).

PROGRAM 15.30 Assertion with Expression

```
//    assrt1.java
//    command line arguments
class assrt1
{ public static void main(String args[])
      { int x=5,y=0, num;
        assert y!=0 : "dividing by zero";
        num = x/y ;
        System.out.println("<---assrt1.java--->");
        System.out.println( y );
      }
}
```

When you run the program from command prompt as

Prompt>java -ea assrt1

you will get the following output.

Output

```
Exception in thread "main" java.lang.AssertionError: dividing by zero at as-
srt1.main(assrt1.java:6)
```

When you run the program from command prompt as

Prompt>java assrt1

you will get the following output.

Output

```
Exception in thread "main" java.lang.ArithmeticException: / by zero at
assrt1.main(assrt1.java:7)
```

Prima facie, the facility of assertion appears to be unimportant. Also, the same action can be obtained from other constructs. In the opinion of experts, this is not true. This is a very good facility. All of us stop at developing the program. We do not attach importance to debugging and testing. In this particular phase of programming, assertion is a very good tool in the hands of a disciplined programmer.

15.17 Description of Advanced Java Program

In this chapter, we have introduced user-defined packages. Though we will be studying many more chapters, the development is complete as far as structure of a Java program is concerned. Now we are capable of writing advanced Java programs. Let us now describe the features of advanced Java programs.

Advanced Java programs:

1. Program lines no restriction
2. Program may be in more than one file
3. User-defined classes or interfaces allowed
4. User-defined packages allowed
5. Generic classes and methods allowed
6. Inner classes allowed

Special suggestions:

1. Use conventions prescribed for identifiers
2. Main program class in separate folder with same name
3. All packages must be sub-folders of main folder.
4. Use static variables and methods if needed

Comments:

1. Large programs are normally written in a group. They must satisfy principles taught in "Software Engineering". At the simplistic level, we must use convention for identifiers. It increases readability as well as uniformity.
2. Since we may be using many user-defined packages, we must keep main program in a folder with same name.
3. When all packages are sub-folders of this package, chances of errors or clashing of names get reduced.
4. As we have come up to a level in programming, we should not be afraid of using static variables and methods. We mean this in the sense of global.

15.18 The Untold Story: Java Criticized

In early days of programming, every program used to start with a keyword program. Languages FORTRAN and Pascal are the main examples. From the days of language C, this keyword disappeared. However, in those days, there was no Internet so there was no HTML and no classes or scripts. Every code written was basically a program or an application as it is called today.

Programs were moderate in size and libraries were always provided by the compilers. Hence, programs could be fitted in a single file. So when we compile a file it was undoubtedly a program file. Things have changed. But the concept of a file and the program containing in it has not changed.

Though Java officially ignores or underplays this fact, it has to live with it. Hence, it makes such rules which defy logic. So far, we have not come across the following rule:

"A file should contain only one public class".

If access modifier public is so simple and non-restrictive, why such a rule? If there are 100 default classes or even protected classes in a file are allowed why not more than one public class?

The reason is that there is tacit understanding that this is not really a class but a program in C/C++ jargon. That is why it has a method `main()`. Imagine two classes both public with method `main` in each. Then computer (means Java runtime environment, JRE) cannot decide where to start.

If such a public class is a class then program runs without instantiating it. Also, in GUI programs, instantiating a class within its own `main` method is making programs look complicated. It smells recursion. And people claim Java is simple.

We do not mean to suggest that Java is not simple. It only has certain rules and conventions which are not so simple. If we ignore them, Java is definitely a simple language.

In our opinion in next version, developers of Java should introduce two key words: program (or application) and applet; then every apparent complexity will be removed.

Table 15.4 summarizes various methods from class `Runtime`.

Table 15.4 Method Summary: Class `Runtime`

`Void`	`addShutdownHook (Thread hook)`	Registers a new virtual-machine shutdown hook.
`Int`	**`availableProcessors`**`()`	Returns the number of processors available to the JVM.
`Process`	**`exec`**`(String command)`	Executes the specified string command in a separate process.
`Process`	**`exec`**`(String[] cmdarray)`	Executes the specified command and arguments in a separate process.
`Process`	**`exec`**`(String[] cmdarray, String[] envp)`	Executes the specified command and arguments in a separate process with the specified environment.
`Process`	**`exec`**`(String[] cmdarray, String[] envp, File dir)`	Executes the specified command and arguments in a separate process with the specified environment and working directory.
`Process`	**`exec`**`(String command, String[] envp)`	Executes the specified string command in a separate process with the specified environment.
`Process`	**`exec`**`(String command, String[] envp, File dir)`	Executes the specified string command in a separate process with the specified environment and working directory.
`Void`	**`exit`**`(int status)`	Terminates the currently running JVM by initiating its shutdown sequence.

(Continued)

Table 15.4 (*Continued*)

Long	**freeMemory**()	Returns the amount of free memory in the JVM.
void	**gc**()	Runs the garbage collector.
InputStream	**getLocalizedInputSt ream**(InputStream in)	**Deprecated**. As of JDK 1.1, the preferred way to translate a byte stream in the local encoding into a character stream in Unicode is via the InputStreamReader and BufferedReader classes.
OutputStream	**getLocalizedOutputStr eam**(OutputStream out)	**Deprecated**. As of JDK 1.1, the preferred way to translate a Unicode character stream into a byte stream in the local encoding is via the OutputStreamWriter, BufferedWriter, and PrintWriter classes.
Static Runtime	**getRuntime**()	Returns the runtime object associated with the current Java application.
void	**halt**(int status)	Forcibly terminates the currently running JVM.
void	**load**(String filename)	Loads the specified filename as a dynamic library.
void	**loadLibrary** (String libname)	Loads the dynamic library with the specified library name.
long	**maxMemory**()	Returns the maximum amount of memory that the JVM will attempt to use.
boolean	**removeShutdownHook** (Thread hook)	De-registers a previously registered virtual-machine shutdown hook.
void	**runFinalization**()	Runs the finalization methods of any objects pending finalization.
static void	**runFinalizersOnExit** (Boolean value)	**Deprecated.** This method is inherently unsafe. It may results in finalizers being called on live objects while other threads are concurrently manipulating those objects, resulting in erratic behaviour or deadlock.
long	**totalMemory**()	Returns the total amount of memory in the JVM.
void	**traceInstructions** (Boolean on)	Enables/disables tracing of instructions.
void	**traceMethodCalls** (Boolean on)	Enables/disables tracing of method calls.

Table 15.5 summarizes various methods from class Arrays.

Table 15.5 Method Summary: Class Arrays Simplified

static **<T> List<T>**	asList(T... a)	Returns a fixed-size list backed by the specified array.
static int	binarySearch(byte[] a, byte key)	Searches the specified array of bytes for the specified value using the binary search algorithm.
static int	binarySearch	Identical methods available for types byte, char, double, float, int, long, object or short.
static boolean	deepEquals(Object[] a1, Object[] a2)	Returns true if the two specified arrays are deeply equal to one another.
static int	deepHashCode (Object[] a)	Returns a hash code based on the "deep contents" of the specified array.
Static String	deepToString (Object[] a)	Returns a string representation of the "deep contents" of the specified array.
static boolean	equals(array a, array b)	Returns true if the two specified arrays of same type are equal to one another. Arrays can be Boolean, byte, char, double, float, int, long, object or short.
static void	fill(boolean[] a, boolean val)	Assigns the specified Boolean value to each element of the specified array of Booleans.
Static void	fill(boolean[] a, int fromIndex, int toIndex, boolean val)	Assigns the specified Boolean value to each element of the specified range of the specified array of Booleans.
static void	fill	Methods shown above for type Boolean. identical fill methods available for types byte, char, double, float, int, long, object, or short.
Static int	hashCode(array a)	Returns a hash code based on the contents of the specified array. Array can be Boolean, byte, char, double, float, int, long, object, or short.
Static void	sort(array a)	Sorts the specified array into ascending numerical order. Array can be Boolean, byte, char, double, float, int, long, object, or short.
Static void	sort(array a, int fromIndex, int toIndex)	Sorts the specified range of the specified array into ascending numerical order. Array can be Boolean, byte, char, double, float, int, long, object, or short.

(Continued)

Table 15.4 *(Continued)*

Static **<T> void**	sort(T[] a, Comparator,<? super T.> c)	Sorts the specified array of objects according to the order induced by the specified comparator.
static **<T> void**	sort(T[] a, int fromIndex, int toIndex, Comparator<? super T> c)	Sorts the specified range of the specified array of objects according to the order induced by the specified comparator.

Table 15.6 summarizes various constructors for class `BitSet`.

Table 15.6 Constructor Summary: Class `BitSet`

BitSet()	Creates a new bit set.
BitSet(int nbits)	Creates a bit set whose initial size is large enough to explicitly represent bits with indices in the range 0 through `nbits-1`.

Table 15.7 summarizes various methods from class `BitSet`.

Table 15.7 Method Summary: Class `BitSet`

void	**and**(BitSet set)	Performs a logical **AND** of this target bit set with the argument bit set.
void	**andNot**(BitSet set)	Clears all of the bits in this `BitSet` whose corresponding bit is set in the specified `BitSet`.
int	**cardinality**()	Returns the number of bits set to `true` in this `BitSet`.
void	**clear**()	Sets all of the bits in this `BitSet` to `false`.
void	**clear**(int bitIndex)	Sets the bit specified by the index to `false`.
void	**clear**(int fromIndex, int toIndex)	Sets the bits from the specified `fromIndex` (inclusive) to the specified `toIndex` (exclusive) to `false`.
Object	**clone**()	Cloning this `BitSet` produces a new `BitSet` that is equal to it.
boolean	**equals**(Object obj)	Compares this object against the specified object.
void	**flip**(int bitIndex)	Sets the bit at the specified index to the complement of its current value.

(Continued)

Table 15.4 ***(Continued)***

void	**flip**(int fromIndex int toIndex)	Sets each bit from the specified `fromIndex` (inclusive) to the specified `toIndex` (exclusive) to the complement of its current value.
boolean	**get**(int bitIndex)	Returns the value of the bit with the specified index.
BitSet	**get**(int fromIndex, int toIndex)	Returns a new `BitSet` composed of bits from this `BitSet` from `fromIndex` (inclusive) to `toIndex` (exclusive).
int	**hashCode**()	Returns a hash code value for this bit set.
boolean	**intersects** (BitSet set)	Returns true if the specified `BitSet` has any bits set to `true` that are also set to `true` in this `BitSet`.
boolean	**isEmpty**()	Returns true if this `BitSet` contains no bits that are set to `true`.
int	**length**()	Returns the "logical size" of this `BitSet`: the index of the highest set bit in the `BitSet` plus one.
int	**nextClearBit** (int fromIndex)	Returns the index of the first bit that is set to `false` that occurs on or after the specified starting index.
int	**nextSetBit**(int fromIndex)	Returns the index of the first bit that is set to `true` that occurs on or after the specified starting index.
void	**or**(BitSet set)	Performs a logical **OR** of this bit set with the bit set argument.
void	**set**(int bitIndex)	Sets the bit at the specified index to `true`.
void	**set**(int bitIndex, boolean value)	Sets the bit at the specified index to the specified value.
void	**set**(int fromIndex, int toIndex)	Sets the bits from the specified `fromIndex` (inclusive) to the specified `toIndex` (exclusive) to `true`.
void	**set**(int fromIndex, int toIndex, boolean value)	Sets the bits from the specified `fromIndex` (inclusive) to the specified `toIndex` (exclusive) to the specified value.
int	**size**()	Returns the number of bits of space actually in use by this `BitSet` to represent bit values.
String	**toString**()	Returns a string representation of this bit set.
void	**xor**(BitSet set)	Performs a logical **XOR** of this bit set with the bit set argument.

Keywords

>>> operator, Arrays, BigInteger, Binary Search tree, BitSet, CLASSPATH, clone(), Cloneable, CloneNotSupportedException, command line arguments, currentTimeMillis(), dynamic data structures, Enum, Enumeration, freeMemory(), generic class, generic methods, generic types, generics, getRuntime(), import, inner classes, instanceof, Java Collections Framework, labelled break, labelled continue, linked list, namespace management, nested class, NullPointerException, outer classes, package, static import, totalmemory()

RuleBook

labelled break labelled continue	Labelled break and labelled continue statements must be inside the loop so labelled.
command line arguments	All command line arguments are passed as a string to method main.
package statement	If any program contains package statement it has to be the first statement.
Inner	Objects declared within the inner scope will NOT be visible outside it
Cloneable Comparable, and Runnable	Interfaces defined by java.lang are Cloneable Comparable, and Runnable.
Garbage collection	When all references to an object are gone, the memory used by the object is automatically reclaimed.
native	The native keyword indicates that the method is implemented in another language like C/C++.
Cloneable	A Cloneable interface defines no members.
import statement	Import statement must come before all other statements except package statement.

C++ Corner

Packages in Java are like precompiled header files in C++. Just as precompiled files are ready to use (with out compilation), contents of a package is also ready to use.

In C++ precompiled headers, you can also see constants and functions. In Java, constants and functions (methods) do not have any existence outside a class. Hence, all required constants have to be embedded in either a class or an interface. All required methods are required to be put inside some suitable class.

Review Questions

1. What are the advantages of using packages?
2. Explain the two different methods of specifying the classpath.

3. What is the data type of command line arguments as received by the application?
4. What is the advantage of labelled break (or continue)?
5. In which situation, conditional operator scores over if-else statement?
6. Is parameter passing in Java too restrictive?
7. What are the advantages of inner class?
8. What do you understand by the term "name space management"?
9. Distinguish between packages and interfaces with examples.
10. Write short note on instance of operator.
11. Write short note on Utility classes.
12. Write short note on garbage collection in Java.
13. Why <<< operator is not defined in Java?

Exercises

1. Develop any three utility methods and keep the corresponding classes in a package named `myutil`.
2. Write a program to create a linked list in such a way that node at the root is the one which arrived first. (Hint: Add arriving elements at the tail.)
3. Develop a method which retrieves the data from a BST in descending order.

CHAPTER 16

INHERITANCE REVISITED

We have studied the basic concepts in inheritance in Chapter 12. Now, let us study a few advanced concepts.

Java is a highly object-oriented language. It is most suitable for studying object orientation. Java has class `Object` as the base (super) class for every other class. Hence, it is a good idea to study this class before we study advanced concepts in inheritance.

16.1 Class `Object`

In Java, a public class `Object` is at the root of the class hierarchy. Every class in Java whether defined by us or supplied by various packages has this class as a superclass. The methods of this class are implemented by all classes including arrays.

Table 16.1 illustrates various methods from this class.

Table 16.1 Method Summary: Class Object

protected Object	`clone()`	Creates and returns a copy of this object.
boolean	`equals(Object obj)`	Indicates whether some other object is "equal to" this one.
protected void	`finalize()`	Called by the garbage collector on an object when garbage collection determines that there are no more references to the object.
Class<? extends Object>	`getClass()`	Returns the runtime class of an object.
int	`hashCode()`	Returns a hash code value for the object.
void	`notify()`	Wakes up a single thread that is waiting on this object's monitor.
void	`notifyAll()`	Wakes up all threads that are waiting on this object's monitor.
String	`toString()`	Returns a string representation of the object.

(*Continued*)

Table 16.1 *(Continued)*

void	`wait()`	Causes current thread to wait until another thread invokes the `notify()` method or the `notifyAll()` method for this object.
void	`wait(long timeout)`	Causes current thread to wait until either another thread invokes the `notify()` method or the `notifyAll()` method for this object, or a specified amount of time has elapsed.
void	`wait(long timeout, int nanos)`	Causes current thread to wait until another thread invokes the `notify()` method or the `notifyAll()` method for this object, or some other thread interrupts the current thread, or a certain amount of real time has elapsed.

When we started studying Java, we did not start with this class. Hence, while studying, we had many unanswered questions. We wondered why Java behaves like this. Many of these questions will now be answered.

Let us first study the method `toString()`. This method returns a string representation of the object. When we define a class say `Point`, we may not redefine this method. But when we write a code like

```
System.out.println( p1)
```

something is printed on the screen. This is because when method `println()` prints an object, it actually prints the string returned by the `toString()` of the point. As point is a sub-class of class `Object`, `println` invokes this method.

Similarly, when we say `s1.equals(s2)`, it returns correct Boolean result when s1 and s2 are `Strings`. This is because class `String` has overridden `equals()` method. If we try

```
p1.equals(p2)
```

the code will compile and may give wrong result. If we want accurate result, our class point must override the `equals()` method.

Let us study this with simple programs.

Problem: Write a program to demonstrate that when not defined, the class uses its super-class objects methods `equals()` and `toString()`.

Solution: See Program 16.1.

PROGRAM 16.1 Methods from Class `Object`

```
//     point1.java
class point1
{
  public static void main(String args[])
    {   point p1,p2 ;
        System.out.println("<---point1.java--->");
        p1 = new point(3.0,2.0);
        p2 = new point(3.0,2.0);
```

```
        System.out.println(p1);
        System.out.println( p1.equals(p2) );
    }
}
class point
   {  private double x,y ;
      point(double a, double b)
          { x=a;y=b;}
   };
```

If you run this program, you will get the following output.

Output

```
<---point1.java--->
point@82ba41
false
```

Problem: Rewrite Program 16.1 with class point defining overriding methods `toString()` and `equals()`.

Solution: See Program 16.2.

PROGRAM 16.2 Overriding Methods of Class `Object`

```
//     point2.java
class point2
{
  public static void main(String args[])
    { point p1,p2 ;
      System.out.println("<---point2.java--->");
      p1 = new point(3.0,2.0);
      p2 = new point(3.0,2.0);
      System.out.println("p1 = " + p1);
      System.out.println("p2 = " + p2);
      System.out.println( "They are equal : "
                                 + p1.equals(p2) );
    }
}
class point
   {  private double x,y ;
      point(double a, double b)
          { x=a;y=b;}
      public String toString()
       { return ( "point["+ String.valueOf(x) + " , " +
                  String.valueOf(y)+" ]" ) ;
       }
      public boolean equals( point p2)
       { if( ( this.x == p2.x) && (this.y ==p2.y) )
                          return true;
               else       return false ;
       }
   };
```

If you run this program, you will get the following output.

Output

```
<---point2.java--->
p1 = point[3.0 , 2.0 ]
p2 = point[3.0 , 2.0 ]
They are equal : true
```

In the above program, we have overridden the method `equals()`. Remove this method from the above program and compile and run the program. You will get results that points are not equal. The points p1 and p2 are different objects. The method of class `Object` does not check for equality of the contents. This task is left to us the programmers!

The methods `wait()`, `notify()`, and `notifyAll()` work with threads. We will be discussing threads in Chapter 18. The method `hashCode()` returns a hashcode which is an integer. This code is very useful in searching and sorting. You will see classes like `HashTable` and `HashSet` that are discussed in Chapter 23.

16.2 Multiple Inheritance

In C++ a class can have two different classes as its super-classes. Such a scheme of inheritance is termed as *multiple inheritance*. Java does not allow this type of inheritance.

This has been shown symbolically in Figure 16.1.

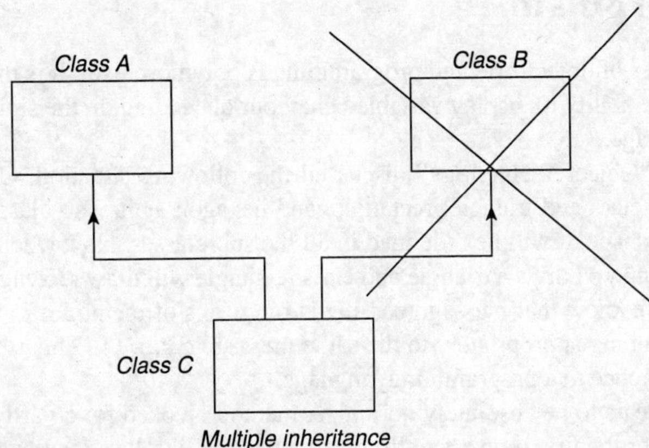

Figure 16.1 Multiple Inheritance not Allowed

However, Java allows a class to extend one class and implement one (or more) interface. This is shown in Figure 16.2.

In the opinion of many experts, this qualifies for calling multiple inheritance. We feel that this should not be called as multiple inheritance. When a class extends another class, it has access to all the fields and has a free use of the already developed methods. When you implement an interface, you only get what is to be developed. No cooked food!

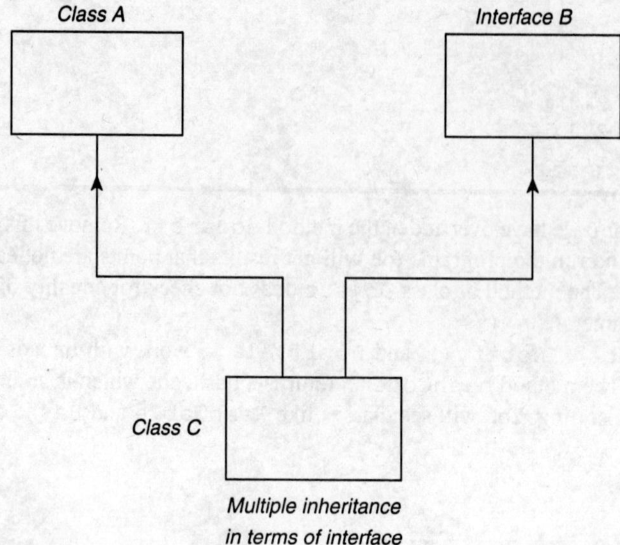

Figure 16.2 Multiple Inheritance in Terms of Inheritance

In our opinion, we hardly need the facility of multiple inheritance. Its absence cannot be considered as a disadvantage.

16.3 Polymorphism

One of the useful features of object-oriented programming is polymorphism. It is the ability of the objects to take different forms. The ability to display variable behaviour depending on the situation is a great facility in any programming language.

All early texts on "Object Technology" discussed the following situation. Consider a case when we define shape as a super-class and triangle, rectangle, and hexagon as its sub-classes. If we have a method `draw()` in super-class shape, it will be redefined in all the sub-classes. Now when we invoke draw on sub-class, the triangle program will draw a triangle and class rectangle will draw rectangle, that is different action for the same method. We know that message passing is by means of method `call` in Java. So we see that every sub-class is responding appropriately to the same message `draw()`. This is precisely the meaning of *polymorphism* with reference to a programming language.

At first sight, it appears to be absolutely normal. A method invoked for a particular class has to execute its own class method. For the first time a strictly typed language like Java is allowing a little freedom to its users. It will allow us to assign a sub-class reference value to a variable (reference) of super-class. As in the above example, a variable reference of type shape can refer to variable of type triangle. And when you invoke draw, it does not draw a shape but a triangle.

Before continuing with polymorphism, let us study the intricacies of assigning subclass reference to super-class variable.

We have said that Java allows super-class reference to point to sub-class object. However, its converse is not true. Java does not allow sub-class reference to point to super-class object. These rules are shown pictorially in Figure 16.3.

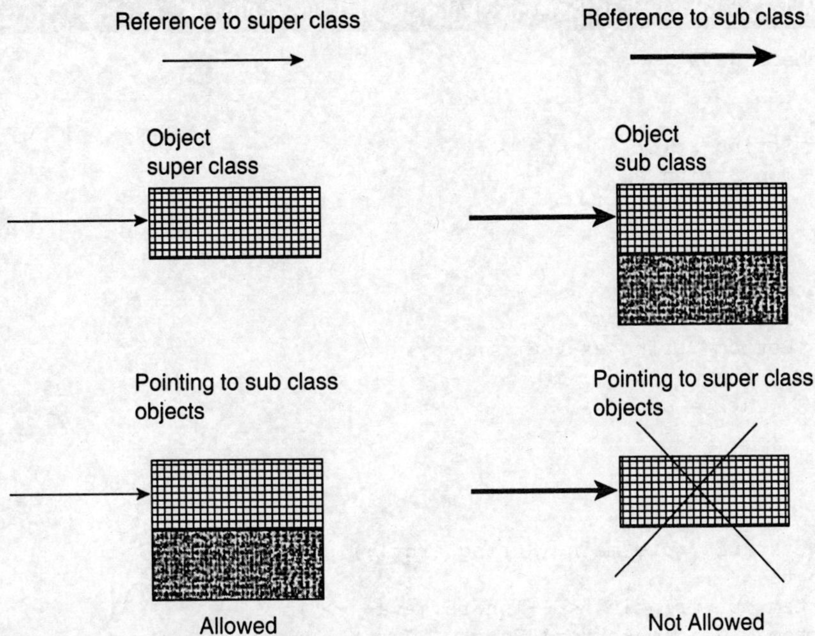

Figure 16.3 **Super- and Sub-class References**

16.3.1 A super-class variable can reference a sub-class object

We are familiar with both super-class and sub-class. We can define reference variables for both the classes. We have seen assignment operation working with reference variables as well. So far, we have assigned one reference variable to another reference variable of the same class.

Now consider the following declarations:

```
Top king1, king2;
Bottom joker1, joker2;
```

where class `Bottom` extends class `Top`

Here assignment

```
king1 = king2 ;
```

is fine; What about the following assignment?

```
king1 = joker1 ;
```

Java is a strict language. Will it allow a variable of super-class to be assigned a value of sub-class reference? Surprisingly, the answer is yes. If this happens, such variables points to sub-class object. However, there are certain restrictions. Such variable can reference only that data and code which relate to super-class only.

Problem: Write a program to demonstrate that super-class reference can be assigned the value of sub-class reference.

Solution: See Program 16.3.

PROGRAM 16.3 Super-class Reference Points to Sub-class Object I

```
//      inher5.java

class Top
      {   String st1 ;
          Top(String sx)
           { st1 = sx ; }
      } ;

class Bottom extends Top
      {   String st2;
          Bottom(String sx , String sy)
           { super(sx);
             st2 = sy ;
           }
      }

class inher5
{   public static void main (String argv[])
    { Top t1 ;
      System.out.println("<---inher5.java--->");
      Bottom b1 = new Bottom("Hero", "Joker") ;
      System.out.println("-st1 is -->"+ b1.st1) ;
      System.out.println("-st2 is -->"+ b1.st2) ;
      t1 = b1 ;
      System.out.println("-st1 is -->"+ t1.st1) ;
      System.out.println("-st2 is -->"+ t1.st2) ;// Note 1
    };
}
```

If you compile the program, you get an error.

Compilation Error

```
inher5.java:26: cannot find symbol
symbol: variable st2
location: class Top
System.out.println("-st2 is -->"+ t1.st2) ;// Note 1
                                         ^
1 error
press any key to continue
```

If you remove the line marked `note1` (and rename the program as `inher5A`), you will get the following output.

Output

```
<---inher5a.java--->
-st1 is -->Hero
-st2 is -->Joker
-st1 is -->Hero
```

It may be noted that reference to class `TOP t1` is assigned a value b1, which is a reference to class `BOTTOM`. After this, we are allowed to refer to those variables which are defined in super-class. We are not allowed to refer to those variables which are defined in sub-class.

Figure 16.4 clearly illustrates this principle.

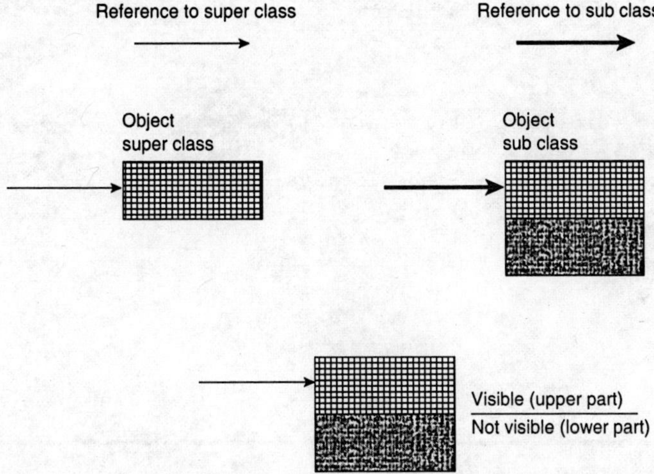

Figure 16.4 Super-class Reference Points to Sub-class

This is fine for field variables, but what about methods? Fundamentally, only those methods which are defined in super-class are usable. This is fine, but many times subclasses have overridden methods from super-class. This means that with a given method name, there are two codes: one written in super-class definition and another in sub-class definition. Which code will be executed? The answer is the code from sub-class is executed.

Let us verify this fact with the following program.

Problem: Write a program to demonstrate that when a super-class reference is assigned a value of sub-class variable, it refers to methods of sub-class.

Solution: See Program 16.4.

PROGRAM 16.4 Super-class Reference Points to Sub-class Object II

```
//      inher15.java
class TOP
  {  String st1 ;
     void init1(String sx )
     { st1 = sx ; } ;
       public void show()
        { System.out.println("method show(): from TOP "
                 + st1) ;
        };
     } ;
```

```
class BOTTOM extends TOP
  { String st2;
    void init2 (String sy)
      {st2 = sy ; }
      public void show()
        {System.out.println("method show(): from BOTTOM "
                          + st2) ;
      }
  }
class inher15
 { public static void main (String argv[])
     { TOP t1 ;
       System.out.println("<---inher15.java-->");
       BOTTOM b1 = new BOTTOM() ;
       b1.init2("Joker");
       b1.init1("Hero");
       b1.show();
       t1 = b1 ;
       t1.show();
     };
 }
```

If we run this program, we will get the following output.

Output

```
<---inher15.java-->
method show(): from BOTTOM Joker
method show(): from BOTTOM Joker
```

Note the line marked in bold. It assigns value b1 to t1. Now t1 refers to the sub-class object. When we invoke the method `show()`, it executes the method `show` of sub-class.

For C++ Programmers

In Java, there is no keyword `virtual`. If you study the aforementioned program, you will notice that similar output will occur in C++ program if and only if the `show()` function in super-class (base class in C++ jargon) is declared virtual.

With this much preparation, we are in a position to understand and appreciate polymorphism.

16.3.2 Polymorphism in action

Decades ago, when we used to say library, we could only think of books. Let us take a case of modern library. It will contain not only books but also audiotapes and video CDs. We may say that libraries now store reference material.

Problem: Write a program to demonstrate polymorphism.

Solution: Here we will have one super-class with method `show()`. Two subclasses will override this method. When we invoke it with a super-class variable, which is pointing to a sub-class, method from that sub-class will be executed (see Program 16.5).

PROGRAM 16.5 Polymorphism in Action I

```
//     lib1.java
class refmat
 {String st1 ; // short for reference material
  refmat( String sx )
    { st1 = sx ;
    } ;
  public void show()
    { System.out.println("method show(): from refmat "
                                  + st1) ;
    };
 } ;
class book extends refmat
 {int numpage ;
  book( String sy , int num )
    { super (sy);
      numpage = num;
    }
  public void show()
    { System.out.println("method show(): from book " );
      System.out.println("pages = " + numpage) ;
    }
 } ;

class cassette extends refmat
    {int time ;
      cassette( String sy , int t )
        { super (sy);
          time = t;
        }
    public void show()
      {System.out.println("method show(): from cassette " );
      System.out.println("time in minutes = " + time) ;
      }
    } ;

class lib1
{   public static void main (String argv[])
    { book b1 = new book( "myJAVA", 300);
      System.out.println("---lib1.java---");
      refmat r1 = b1;
      r1.show();
      cassette ac1 = new cassette("sound of Music" ,60);
      r1= ac1;
      r1.show();
    }
  };
```

If we run this program, we will get the following output.

Output

```
---lib1.java---
method show(): from book
pages = 300
method show(): from cassette
time in minutes = 60
```

16.4 Dynamic Method Dispatch

We have just seen that a variable of super-class can refer to a sub-class object.

There may be two or three sub-classes. They may be having method from super-class which is overridden. Now when the compiler sees a method `call` (see last line in Program 16.5), it may or be able to decide which method to call. Hence, the decision to invoke a method is postponed to runtime. At runtime when such a method `call` is to be executed, the compiler selects an appropriate method. This behaviour is termed as "dynamic method dispatch".

Since this behaviour is also seen in C++, it will be a good thing to look at similar situations and terms.

When the compiler decides which method to execute, it is termed as static binding. It is termed as compile time polymorphism.

When compiler does not decides which method to execute and leaves the decision to runtime environment (JVM in case of Java), it is termed as dynamic binding or late binding. It is also termed as runtime polymorphism. In other words, dynamic dispatch means run time polymorphism.

There is a subtle difference between Java and C++. In C++, if the super-class method is declared as virtual, then only the method from sub-class is executed. In Java, there is no keyword `virtual`. When super-class reference invokes an overridden method, it invokes only the sub-class method.

16.5 Collection of Programs

16.5.1 Sub-class reference cannot be assigned a super-class value

Problem: Write a program to demonstrate that sub-class reference cannot be assigned super-class value.

Solution: See Program 16.6.

PROGRAM 16.6 Sub-class Reference Assigned to Super-class I

```
//      inher5c.java
class TOP
        {  String st1 ;
           void init1(String sx )
             { st1 = sx ; }
        } ;
class BOTTOM extends TOP
          {  String st2;
             void init2 (String sy)
             { st2 = sy ; }
          }
class inher5c
```

```
{   public static void main (String argv[])
    { TOP t1 = new TOP(); ;
      System.out.println("---inher5c.java---");
      BOTTOM b1 = new BOTTOM() ;
      b1.init2("Jokar");
      b1.init1("Hero");
      b1= t1; // = b1 ;
    };
}
```

If we run the program, we will get the following compilation error.

Output

```
Compiling D:\java\bin\javac inher5c.java
inher5c.java:19: Incompatible type for =. Explicit cast needed to convert TOP
to BOTTOM.
b1= t1; // = b1 ;
   ^
1 error
```

Hold your breath. If you are feeling that typecasting will solve the problem, you are wrong. The program will get compiled, But when you run it, you will get runtime error. See the following program.

Problem: Write a program to illustrate that attempt of typecasting super-class object into sub-class fails at runtime.

Solution: See Program 16.7.

PROGRAM 16.7 Sub-class Reference Assigned to Super-class II

```
//     inher5d.java
class TOP
       { String st1 ;
         void init1(String sx )
          { st1 = sx ; }
       } ;
class BOTTOM extends TOP
        {  String st2;
           void init2 (String sy)
             { st2 = sy ; }
        }
class inher5d
{   public static void main (String argv[])
    { TOP t1 = new TOP(); ;
      System.out.println("---inher5d.java---");
      BOTTOM b1 = new BOTTOM() ;
      b1.init2("Jokar");
      b1.init1("Hero");
      b1= (BOTTOM) t1; // = b1 ;
    };
}
```

If we run the above program, we will get the following exception (error).

Output

```
---inher5d.java---
Exception in thread main
java.lang.ClassCastException
void inher5d.main(java.lang.String[])
```

This is natural. In general, the sub-class object is larger (contains more data) than the super-class object. If super-class object, which has less data, has to transform into sub-class object, it must get additional data. Since this is impossible, language does not permit it.

16.5.2 Arrays of dissimilar elements

In arrays, all the elements (or objects) are required to be of the same type (or class). Arrays are the most powerful data structure. It effortlessly jumps to any element with the help of the index (in other words random access). Some people felt that it would be great if arrays can be made of dissimilar elements. Certain category of problems will be easy to solve (write code).

In Java though we cannot easily have arrays of totally dissimilar elements, we can have arrays of objects belonging to different sub-classes of a particular super-class. This is possible because Java allows us to use super-class reference to point to a sub-class object.

Let us study this with the help of a program.

Problem: Write a program to demonstrate an array of dissimilar elements.

Solution: Let us consider books and cassettes as library material. We will have super-class `Libmat` extended by sub-classes `Book` and `Cassette`. Now we create a single array, add elements to it, and then get them back (see Program 16.8).

PROGRAM 16.8 Array of Dissimilar Objects

```
//      array1.java
import java.io.*;
class LibMat  // short for Library material
  {String title ;
   LibMat( String sx )
     { title = sx ;
     } ;
   public void show()
     {  System.out.println("method show(): from LibMat "
                          + title) ;
     };
  } ;

class Book extends LibMat
  {int numpage ;
   Book( String sy , int num )
     { super (sy);
       numpage = num;
```

```
    }
  public void show()
    { System.out.println(" Title : " + title );
      System.out.println(" pages = " + numpage) ;
    }
 } ;
class Cassette extends LibMat
  { int time ;
    Cassette( String sy , int t )
      { super (sy);
        time = t;
      }
    public void show()
     { System.out.println(" Cassette ->" + title);
       System.out.println(" time in minutes = "
                                  + time) ;
     }
  } ;
class array1
{public static void main (String argv[])
            throws IOException
  {int i ;
   String st1;
   LibMat box[] = new LibMat[3] ;
   BufferedReader Jin = new BufferedReader
                (new InputStreamReader (System.in) );

   System.out.println("---array1.java---");
   box[0] = new Book( "JAVA FAQ", 300);
   box[1] = new Cassette("sound of Music" ,60);
   box[2] = new Book( "JAVA Tips and Trics", 200);
//       Note box is of class LibMat still we are allowed
//       to create an object of subclass with it!

   for(i=0;i<3;i++)
      { System.out.println("Material Index "+i);
        box[i].show() ;
      }
  }
};
```

If you run the program, you will get the following output.

Output

```
---array1.java---
Material Index 0
Title : JAVA FAQ
pages = 300
Material Index 1
Cassette ->sound of Music
```

```
time in minutes = 60
Material Index 2
Title : JAVA Tips and Trics
pages = 200
```

At this stage, you may have noticed an important thing. `box` is of class `LibMat`. Still we are allowed to create an object of sub-class with it. A constructor constructs an object and returns a reference. This is assigned to a super-class variable. Hence, this is permissible!

RuleBook

super-class variable	Super-class reference variable can be assigned a sub-class reference value
sub-class variable	Sub-class reference variable cannot be assigned a super-class reference value
multiple inheritance	Java does not allow for multiple inheritances, where a class has more than one super-class.
object class	By default, classes inherit from the `Object` class, which is a super-class of all classes in the Java class hierarchy.

C++ Corner

In Java, there is no keyword `virtual`. Consider a case that there is a method in sub-class with same name as the one in super-class. When a super-class reference refers to sub-class object, it always invokes methods in sub-class. This means what a C++ programmer achieves by declaring a function `virtual`, a Java program achieves it automatically.

Review Questions

1. What is polymorphism?
2. Explain the advantages of super-class reference being assigned a sub-class value.
3. Explain the terms compile time polymorphism and runtime polymorphism.
4. Explain dynamic method dispatch with the help of an example.

CHAPTER 17

FILES

The ability of the computer to store alphanumeric data, graphic images, and so on in files, and its ability to retrieve the contents has revolutionized applications in almost all aspects of life. Therefore, life without files is unimaginable.

Even the programs which we write are stored in files. We write our programs in `.java` file. It is a text file. We compile our program and create `.class` file. It is a bytecode file. A file is nothing but a sequential collection of bytes stored with a name.

In Windows OS, file names have optional extension. It helps in identifying the nature of contents of the file. A `.class` extension tells us that this is a bytecode file. A `.wav` extension tells us that the file contains sound.

In this chapter, we will explain how to perform reading and writing operations on files on a disk.

17.1 Why Files?

When we work on a computer, data and programs are stored in RAM, which is a volatile memory device. When we switch off the power, the data as well as the program present in it vanishes. When we restart the computer, we may wish to run the same program again. But it is not present in the memory. Therefore, we require a non-volatile memory. It stores our programs (and data too) even when the power is switched off. In computers, floppies, hard disks, and CDs form the secondary memory. The data and programs are stored in it in the form of a file. Thus, the study of files becomes very important.

17.2 File Classification

Let us start our study of file classification with a few questions and answers.

Short Questions and Answers

Q. What are the two basic types of files?

A. Files can be classified as either text files or binary files.

Q. How does the internal construction of binary and text files differ?

A. Text files are those which contain normal ASCII text characters (printable). These files are line oriented. An end of line can be represented by new-line character. In DOS, a new line is signified by two characters, LF and FF (ASCII values 10 and 13). The number of characters in a line is not fixed.

Binary files are files of bytes. There is no concept of line. Binary file is a plain sequential collection of (data) bytes.

Q. What are the advantages of text file?

A. They are many:

1. Text is the most primary method of expressing ourselves. Kids learn "ABC" even before joining a school.
2. Text file can be created with simple tools like Notepad or sophisticated word processors like Microsoft Word.
3. It can easily be read or printed.
4. It can be used to store input as well as output data.

Q. What are the advantages of binary files?

A. There are two main advantages:

Their size is smaller than corresponding text files.

The speed at which programs can read data from them is very high (as compared to text files).

Q. What is the disadvantage of binary files?

A. They cannot be easily read or written by ordinary tools. They need special programs for it.

Q. How can we sub-classify binary files?

A. Binary files can be sub-classified as (1) binary data files and (2) binary program files.

Q. How can we sub-classify data files?

A. Data files can be classified as either input file or output file. An input file can only be read and output files can only be written. This description is only simplistic. But it helps our understanding of files. (It is possible to open a file for both input and output. More of it shall be discussed at a later stage.)

Q. How can we classify data files on the basis of how they are accessed?

A. Data files can be classified as either sequential access files or direct access files. In a sequential access file, components are accessed one after the other (sequentially) whereas in direct access files, any component can be accessed directly (without accessing its previous components). Hence, these files are also called as random access files.

So far, files have been classified as follows:

- text files versus binary files
- input files versus output files
- data files versus program files
- sequential access file versus direct access file

We do not want to complicate the issue by trying permutation and combination of these classes though it is understood that a particular file can simultaneously belong to multiple classes (types). A file can be binary sequential data file. A text file can be an input file or an output file. The only thing to note is that text files cannot be random access files.

17.3 Class `File`

To handle files, Java offers us a very useful class named `File`. This class has many constructors and methods. Let us study it in an informal way.

We can construct an object of this class by simply calling a constructor as shown as follows.

```
File f1 = new File( "abc.txt");
```

The computer creates an object of class `File` with name `abc.txt`. Here we have not specified any directory. Hence, our default working directory is assumed. The computer associates this symbolic name f1 with an actual file name (as understood by the OS) `abc.txt`. The file with this name may or may not exist in the current directory. Please note that this constructor has created an object of type file and not an actual file.

To test whether such a file exists or not, Java provides Boolean method `exists()`. Let us study this with the help of a program.

Problem: Write a program to test whether a given file exists in the current directory.

Solution: See Program 17.1.

PROGRAM 17.1 Test for File Existence

```
//              file1.java
import java.io.* ;
class file1
  { public static void main(String[] args) throws Exception
     { File f1 = new File("abc.txt");
       System.out.println("<---file1.java starts--->");
       if( f1.exists() ) System.out.println("File exists");
            else System.out.println(" File does not exists");
     };
  }
```

If you run this program, you will get the following output.

Output

```
<---file1.java starts--->
File does not exists
```

We know that files can be used for either input or output. When we create data files and want to use them for reading, we do not want the program to accidentally delete or modify it. The simplest way is to make it read-only. (This is possible in every OS.) Once a file is made "read-only", a program cannot write to it.

Java allows us to test whether files are read-only or not. It supports two methods `canRead()` and `canWrite()` for this purpose.

Problem: Write a program to test whether a file exists in the current directory. Also, test if you can read from or write to that file.

Solution: If a file is read-only, we cannot write to it. However, Java has provided two separate methods. So we will use both of them (see Program 17.2).

PROGRAM 17.2 Test for Read–Write

```
//              file2.java
import java.io.* ;
class file2
  { public static void main(String[] args) throws Exception
     { File f1 = new File("abc.txt");
       System.out.println("<---file2.java starts--->");
       if( f1.exists() ) System.out.println("File exists");
            else System.out.println(" File does not exists");
```

```
        if( f1.canRead() ) System.out.println("can read ");
            else System.out.println(" cannot read");
        if( f1.canWrite() ) System.out.println("can write ");
            else System.out.println("cannot write");
    };
}
```

If you run this program, you will get the following output.

Output

```
<---file2.java starts--->
File exists
can read
cannot write
```

Before running Program 17.2, a file with this name was created in the current directory. We deliberately made it read-only (by setting property in Windows OS). Hence, we get this particular output.

While working with methods in this class, many times we have to deal with the name of the path where the file is placed. We can use absolute pathname or abstract pathname. Absolute pathname specifies the path starting from the drive letter. Abstract pathname indicates the relative path, that is relative to current working directory.

Table 17.1 illustrates all the important methods supported by class `File`.

Table 17.1 Summary of Methods: Class `File`

boolean	**canRead()**	Tests whether the application can read the file denoted by this abstract pathname.
boolean	**canWrite()**	Tests whether the application can modify the file denoted by this abstract pathname.
int	**compareTo(File pathname)**	Compares two abstract pathnames lexicographically
int	**compareTo(Object o)**	Compares this abstract pathname to another object.
boolean	**createNewFile()**	Atomically creates a new, empty file named by this abstract pathname, if and only if a file with this name does not exist.
static File	**createTempFile(String prefix, String suffix)**	Creates an empty file in the default temporary-file directory, using the given prefix and suffix to generate its name.
static File	**createTempFile(String prefix, String suffix, File directory)**	Creates a new empty file in the specified directory, using the given prefix and suffix strings to generate its name.
boolean	**delete()**	Deletes the file or directory denoted by this abstract pathname.

(Continued)

Table 17.1 *(Continued)*

void	**deleteOnExit()**	Requests that the file or directory denoted by this abstract pathname be deleted when the virtual machine terminates.
boolean	**equals(Object obj)**	Tests this abstract pathname for equality with the given object.
boolean	**exists()**	Tests whether the file denoted by this abstract pathname exists.
File	**getAbsoluteFile()**	Returns the absolute form of this abstract pathname.
String	**getAbsolutePath()**	Returns the absolute pathname string of this abstract pathname.
File	**getCanonicalFile()**	Returns the canonical form of this abstract pathname
String	**getCanonicalPath()**	Returns the canonical pathname string of this abstract pathname.
String	**getName()**	Returns the name of the file or directory denoted by this abstract pathname.
String	**getParent()**	Returns the pathname string of the parent of this abstract pathname, or null if this pathname does not name a parent directory.
File	**getParentFile()**	Returns the abstract pathname of the parent of this abstract pathname, or null if this pathname does not name a parent directory.
String	**getPath()**	Converts this abstract pathname into a pathname string.
int	**hashCode()**	Computes a hash code for this abstract pathname.
boolean	**isAbsolute()**	Tests whether this abstract pathname is absolute.
boolean	**isDirectory()**	Tests whether the file denoted by this abstract pathname is a directory.
boolean	**isFile()**	Tests whether the file denoted by this abstract pathname is a normal file.
boolean	**isHidden()**	Tests whether the file named by this abstract pathname is a hidden file.
long	**lastModified()**	Returns the time that the file denoted by this abstract pathname was last modified.
long	**length()**	Returns the length of the file denoted by this abstract pathname.

(Continued)

Table 17.1 *(Continued)*

String[]	**list()**	Returns an array of strings naming the files and directories in the directory denoted by this abstract pathname.
String[]	**list(FilenameFilter filter)**	Returns an array of strings naming the files and directories in the directory denoted by this abstract pathname that satisfy the specified filter.
File[]	**listFiles()**	Returns an array of abstract pathnames denoting the files in the directory denoted by this abstract pathname.
File[]	**listFiles(FileFilter filter)**	Returns an array of abstract pathnames denoting the files and directories in the directory denoted by this abstract pathname that satisfy the specified filter.
File[]	**listFiles(FilenameFilter filter)**	Returns an array of abstract pathnames denoting the files and directories in the directory denoted by this abstract pathname that satisfy the specified filter.
static File[]	**listRoots()**	List the available file system roots.
boolean	**mkdir()**	Creates the directory named by this abstract pathname.
boolean	**mkdirs()**	Creates the directory named by this abstract pathname, including any necessary but non-existent parent directories.
boolean	**renameTo(File dest)**	Renames the file denoted by this abstract pathname.
boolean	**setLastModified(long time)**	Sets the last-modified time of the file or directory named by this abstract pathname.
boolean	**setReadOnly()**	Marks the file or directory named by this abstract pathname so that only read operations are allowed.
String	**toString()**	Returns the pathname string of this abstract pathname.
URL	**toURL()**	Converts this abstract pathname into a file: URL.

Many other facilities can be seen in Section 17.11 (Program 17.13). Now, after studying class `File`, we want to use files for reading and writing. To begin with, let us start our study with text files.

17.4 Text Files

Let us first study how to create a text file and write to it. For this purpose, we need class `FileWriter`. Let us try a simple program.

Problem: Write a program to create a text file. Write in this file `Name` of a person and his weight in kilograms.

Solution: See Program 17.3.

PROGRAM 17.3 Introduction to Text File

```
//            fo3.java
import java.io.* ;
class fo3
  {   public static void main(String[] args) throws Exception
        {   String s1 = "Anthony Gonsalves";
            String s2 = new String("56.3") ;
            System.out.println("<---fo3.java--->");

            FileWriter f2 = new FileWriter("fo3.dat");

            f2.write("my name = " + s1 + "\n");
            f2.write("My Weight = " + s2);
            f2.close();
            System.out.println("file fo3.dat created");
        }
  } ;
```

If you run this program, you will get the following output.

Output

```
<---fo3.java--->
file fo3.dat created
```

If you try to inspect the created text file, it will appear as follows:

Text File **fo3b.dat**

```
my name = Anthony Gonsalves
My Weight = 56.3
```

Please note that method `close()` belongs to class `FileWriter`. It closes this writer and flushes any pending data. In effect, it closes the file too.

Now it is the time to read a file. Text files can be read one character at a time, but it is advantageous to read the entire line at a time. Java supports a very useful class `String`. It is suitable for reading one line of text at a stretch. We can get (extract) all the characters from a string easily.

Problem: Write a program to open and read a text file line by line.

Solution: See Program 17.4.

PROGRAM 17.4 Reading a Text File

```
//             fi2.java
import java.io.* ;
class fi2
{  public static void main(String[] args) throws Exception
    {  String s1 ;
    //    String s2 ;
       boolean flag ;
       System.out.println("<---fi2.java--->");
       FileReader f1 = new FileReader("fi2.dat");
       BufferedReader fin = new BufferedReader(f1);

       while ( fin.ready() )
            {  s1 = fin.readLine();
               System.out.println(s1);
            }
       fin.close();
    }
}
```

If you run this program, you will get the following output.

Output

```
<---fi2.java--->
Hello!
This is a text file.
You are reading line by line.
Thank You for reading me.
```

Note the function `fin.ready()`.

17.5 Formatted File Input

Text files can be used to store the data in a formatted manner. Consider a case of a text file which stores the colours. A colour has a name and values of RGB colour components. A typical file is shown as follows:

Input Text File— **`col_values.text`**

```
0123456789012345678901234567890123456789 <-column numbers
gray          7f        7f        7f
black         00        00        00
white         ff        ff        ff
yellow        ff        ff        00
```

It is possible to read such a file and extract data from it.

For reading files, we use class `FileReader`. It is capable of reading files. However, for efficiency purpose, it is necessary to use a class `BufferedReader` along with the `FileReader` class. Consider the following program.

Problem: Write a program to read an input file named `col_values.txt` and get colour names and RGB values.

Solution: When we inspect the input file, we note that

- 15 columns are reserved for colour name (string).
- There are three colour values in 10 columns each.
- Colour values are in hexadecimal notation.

Now we read one line at a time in a string. Get name and values of colours in sub-strings. As sub-strings may have leading and trailing blanks, we trim them. Lastly, hexadecimal colour values are converted into integer by method `parseInt()` (see Program 17.5).

PROGRAM 17.5 Reading a Formatted File

```
//    format3.java
//    Simple table
//    formatted input.
import java.io.* ;
class format3
{ public static void main(String[] args) throws IOException
      {  int i,j,k ;
         char box[] = new char[51];
         FileReader f1 = new FileReader("col_values.txt");
         BufferedReader Jin = new BufferedReader(f1) ;
         System.out.println("<---format3.java--->");

         for(i=1; i<=4; i++) // knowing 4 lines in file
            {  String sb0, sb1,sb2,sb3,sb4,stemp ;
               int red, green, blue=0 ;
               sb0 = Jin.readLine();
               k= sb0.length();
               stemp = sb0.substring(0,15);
               sb1= stemp.trim();
               stemp = sb0.substring(15,25);
               sb2 = stemp.trim();
               red = Integer.parseInt(sb2,16);
               stemp = sb0.substring(25,35);
               sb3 = stemp.trim();
               green = Integer.parseInt(sb3,16);
               stemp = sb0.substring(35,37);
               sb4 = stemp.trim();
               blue = Integer.parseInt(sb4,16);
               System.out.println(sb1+ "\t" + red + "\t" +green +"\t"+blue);
            }
      }
 } ;
```

If you run this program, you will see the following output.

Output

```
<---format3.java starts--->
gray    127     127     127
black   0       0       0
white   255     255     255
yellow  255     255     0
```

You may wonder what the use of this program is. Well, it shows you how to read and accept colour data. With little modification, you can build an array of colour information and use it in graphics programs.

17.6 Reading File with Format-Free Data

Old programming languages like Fortran and COBOL accepted only formatted data. In a formatted data, elements appear in fixed columns. Many times data may not be properly formatted. Programming languages like Pascal boasted of reading format-free data. This facility continued in languages like C and C++.

When data elements are separated by any number of separating characters like blanks and tabs, such data is called format-free data. To read such data, Java provides a class `StringTokenizer.` It extracts tokens from a string. It implies that it automatically skips all separating characters. Once we have a string which contains a known type of data like integer or double, extracting data from it becomes very simple.

Problem: A data file contains the data of a SUDOKU puzzle. Every line contains a row number, a column number, and the value. These numbers (integers) are separated by any number of blanks and/or tabs. In other words, they are present in format-free manner. Write a program to read this data in an array.

Solution: We will read data line by line in a string. Subject this string to `StringTokenizer.`

As data may have maximum 81 rows, array will have 81 rows and three columns (see Program 17.6).

PROGRAM 17.6 Using `StringTokenizer`

```
//      token1.java
import java.io.* ;
import java.util.* ;
class token1
{ public static void main(String[] args) throws IOException
     {  int a[][] = new int[81][3] ;
        String line = null;
        String str1,str2,str3 ;
        int i,j,N;
        i=0;

        try {
                FileReader f1 = new FileReader("token1.txt");
                BufferedReader br = new BufferedReader( f1);
                while ((line = br.readLine()) != null)
                 {      System.out.println("line read is: " + line);
                        j=0;
                        StringTokenizer st = new StringTokenizer(line);
                        while (st.hasMoreTokens())
                          {  str1 = st.nextToken() ;
```

```
                        a[i][j] = Integer.parseInt(str1);
                        j++;
                    }
            i++;
        }
        br.close();
    }
    catch(Exception e)
      {   System.out.println("Some Error"); }
    N=i-1;
    System.out.println("Now printing array a");
    for(i=0;i<=N;i++)
      {   for(j=0;j<3;j++)
              System.out.print(a[i][j]+"\t");
              System.out.println();
      }
   }
}
```

If you run the program, you will get the following output.

Output

```
line read is: 1       2  3
line read is: 3  4     5
line read is: 5  6     7
Now printing array a
1       2       3
3       4       5
5       6       7
```

17.7 Binary Files

As mentioned earlier, there are certain advantages of binary files. Let us try to create and use binary files. These files are used to store data. Hence, the simplest example will be of storing a few integers. Study the following program.

As we are writing binary data in a file, we have to use class `FileOutputStream` embedded in class `DataOutputStream`.

Problem: Write a program to create a binary data file `binfile1.dat`. The file should contain first 10 odd integers.

Solution: See Program 17.7.

PROGRAM 17.7 Creating Binary File

```
//      binfile1.java
import java.io.* ;
class binfile1
  {  public static void main(String[] args) throws Exception
```

```
        {  int i;
           System.out.println("<---binfile1--->");
           FileOutputStream fx = new
                FileOutputStream("binfile1.dat");
           DataOutputStream f2 = new DataOutputStream(fx);
           for(i = 1;i<20;i=i+2)
             { f2.writeInt(i);
             }
           f2.close();
           System.out.println("file created successfully");
        }
};
```

This program creates the file `binfile1.dat`. As stated earlier, you cannot see this file in word processor and will need a program to see the contents of that file. One may ask what is the use of such binary files. Practically, every large data file is stored as binary file. Large databases are also binary files. But DBMS software comes with built-in programs to view them. Let us write a simple program to read a binary file.

When we want to read a binary file, we have to use class `FileInputStream` embedded in class `DataInputStream`.

Problem: Write a program to read a binary data file `binfile1.dat` and display its contents. It is known that the file contains 10 integers.

Solution: See Program 17.8.

PROGRAM 17.8 Reading a Binary File

```
//       binfile2.java
import java.io.* ;
class binfile2
{ public static void main(String[] args) throws Exception
      {  int i,k;
         System.out.println("<---binfile2--->");
         FileInputStream fy = new
              FileInputStream("binfile1.dat");
         DataInputStream f1 = new DataInputStream(fy);
           for(i = 0;i<10;i++)
              {  k=f1.readInt();
                 System.out.println(k + " ");
              }
           f1.close();
      }
};
```

If you run this program, you will get the following output.

Output

```
<---binfile2--->
1
3
5
```

```
7
9
11
13
15
17
19
```

This console output displays the contents of binary file `binfile1.dat` generated by Program 17.7.

17.8 Files for Objects

In the previous section, we first created and then read a binary file consisting of integers. We can do that for any other primary data type like float, long, and double. A file can contain different data types as well. In early days of computer programming, binary files were used to contain records (see Box 17.1). In terms of object-oriented language, an object represents a record. Hence, a binary file can be used to store objects. (Of course, all belong to the same class.) (See Box 17.2.)

BOX 17.1 Record

Record is a very popular term of old programming languages. A record means collection of variables in a bundle. In C/C++, it is called `struct`. Actually, an object is improvised version of `struct`. Type class can also represent `struct`. In C++, both `class` and `struct` are available. Java developers decided to drop the type `struct`.

BOX 17.2 Why all Elements of Binary File should be Identical

Theoretically, it is possible that a binary file can contain variables of different primitive types. But when you read such a file, you must know the exact sequence of the data in that file. This is practically a very difficult task. We will need another file to keep this information, and the speed with which we read will also decrease. Also, we will not be able to jump to the *n*th record directly. This prevents any arbitrary combination of primitive data types in a file. Hence, a binary file will have all integers or all bytes or all doubles. Though we said primitive data types, the point is valid for objects too.

Let us write a program which creates a file for objects and reads it back.

Problem: Write a program to create a (binary data) file of objects. The file should contain five objects of class complex number. Next, open that file for reading and fill the array of complex numbers from the file.

Solution: To write binary data, we have to use class `FileOutputStream` embedded in class `DataOutputStream`. When we want to read that file, we have to use class `FileInputStream` embedded in class `DataInputStream` (see Program 17.9).

PROGRAM 17.9 File for Objects

```
//      objfile2.java
import java.io.* ;

class Complex
    { double x, y ;
```

```
        void show()
           {   System.out.print(" Complex number: " );
               System.out.println(x +" +j "+ y);
           };
       Complex(double x1, double y1)
           {   x=x1;
               y=y1;
           };
       } ;

class objfile2
{ public static void main(String arg[]) throws Exception
       {   int i;
           Complex n1, n2, n3, n4, n5 ;
           System.out.println("--->objfile2.java starts<---");
           double x, y ;

FileOutputStream fx = new
           FileOutputStream("objfile2.dat");
           DataOutputStream f1 = new DataOutputStream(fx);

           n1 = new Complex(3.1, 5.1);
           n2 = new Complex(5.1, 7.2);
           n3 = new Complex(7.1, 9.3);
           n4 = new Complex(9.1, 11.4);
           n5 = new Complex(11.1,13.5);

           System.out.println("Writing data to file");
           f1.writeDouble(n1.x);
           f1.writeDouble(n1.y);
           f1.writeDouble(n2.x);
           f1.writeDouble(n2.y);
           f1.writeDouble(n3.x);
           f1.writeDouble(n3.y);
           f1.writeDouble(n4.x);
           f1.writeDouble(n4.y);
           f1.writeDouble(n5.x);
           f1.writeDouble(n5.y);
           f1.close();
//         Now the same file will be open for input

           FileInputStream fy = new
           FileInputStream("objfile2.dat");
           DataInputStream f2 = new DataInputStream(fy);
           Complex A[] = new Complex[5];

//         reading from file into an array
           System.out.println("Reading data from file");

           for (i=0 ; i< 5; i++)
               {   x = f2.readDouble();
                   y = f2.readDouble();
                   A[i] = new Complex(x, y);
```

```
            }
        System.out.println("Displaying data from array");
        for (i=0 ; i< 5; i++)
            A[i].show();
    }
}
```

If you run this program, you will get the following output.

Output

```
--->objfile2.java starts<---
Writing data to file
Reading data from file
Displaying data from array
Complex number: 3.1 +j 5.1
Complex number: 5.1 +j 7.2
Complex number: 7.1 +j 9.3
Complex number: 9.1 +j 11.4
Complex number: 11.1 +j 13.5
```

Important: So for we have not discussed any limitations on objects that can be stored in a binary file. The object must contain only basic data types. It should not contain strings. Strings have no fixed length. Hence, different objects will have different lengths. It will be difficult to handle them. In other words, the object we want to handle must get converted into a fixed number of bytes. This was not the case with text files. Text files can have every line of different length.

17.9 Random Access File

As mentioned earlier, a file can be opened for either reading or writing. This is a simplistic model of files. Nevertheless, it helps us in understanding and using the files easily. In early days of computing, files were strictly sequential. Data was to be read and processed from these files, and the output was kept in another file. For example, the basic pay of an employee was to be read as the data file, and salary statements (or salary slips) were written to output file.

Nowadays the scenario has changed. Databases have become common. Transaction processing has become "online". It calls for a file to be read and written simultaneously. In such a case, there is no meaning to sequential accessing of a file. Access has to be "random", and such files are called random access files. Random means we should be able to reach to a particular position directly. Therefore, such files are also known as direct access files. Such access puts a restriction on the file. All the elements of the file should be of same type. The type can be either elementary type or an object in general.

Figure 17.1 shows a schematic random access file. To allow us to work with such files, Java provides a class `RandomAccessFile`.

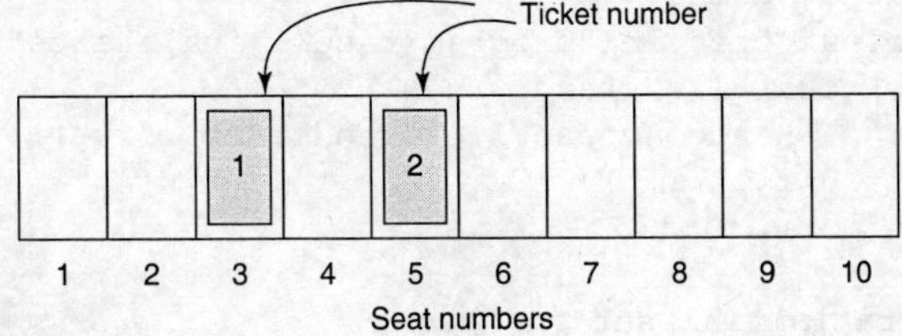

Figure 17.1 Random Access File

This class implements interfaces `DataInput` and `DataOutput`. These interfaces define basic input/output methods.

There are two constructors for this class.

```
RandomAccessFile(File fileObject , String access) throws
FileNotFoundException
```

and

```
RandomAccessFile( String filename, String access) throws
FileNotFoundException
```

Access string can be either "r" or "rw" signifying read or read–write operation.

Let us study this class with a program.

Problem: Write a seat reservation program using random access file. Consider a hill station with a tourist helicopter. Assume that it has 10 seats numbered 1 to 10. Assume the following situation:

- A tourist comes to a booking counter.
- He demands a particular seat (number).
- Computer checks if seat is available.
- If so, it issues a ticket with the requested seat number.
- If the seat is already booked, tourist must request another seat.

Solution: To begin with, all seats are free. Hence, all are marked with value 0. Please note that the ticket numbers start from 1. Hence, writing ticket number 0 is same as no ticket is issued for this seat.

When a seat number is requested, using seek instruction, we try to find the data (ticket number). If the ticket number is zero, we write the current ticket number to this seat.

At the end of the day, we want to have a summary. It may be noted that random access file can be accessed sequentially as well.

Hence, we go to the first record and keep on reading the seat numbers.

See Program 17.10.

PROGRAM 17.10 Random Access File

```
//          rand1.java
import java.io.* ;

class rand1
  {  public static void main(String[] args) throws Exception
          {  int i,k,num,Tnum;
             int request = 0 ;
             int data[] = { 3, 5, 6, 5, 3, 4 , 9, 7, 2, 1 } ;
             int ticket_number = 1 ;
             System.out.println("program rand1.java starts");
             RandomAccessFile frand = new
                       RandomAccessFile("rand1.dat","rw");
             for(i = 0;i<11;i++)
                {  frand.writeInt(0);
                }
             // data initialisation over
```

```
            // live transation starts 6 in number
            while (request < 6)
                {   k = data[request++];
                    System.out.println("Requested seat number : "+ k);
                    frand.seek(4 * k );
                    num = frand.readInt();
                    if( num == 0 ) // seat availble
                        {   frand.seek(4 * k ); //very important
                            frand.writeInt(ticket_number); // to file
                            System.out.print("Seat reserved ");
                            System.out.print(" ticket number "
                                                + ticket_number);
                            System.out.println(" seat number " + k );
                            ticket_number++;
                        }
                    else
                            System.out.println(" sorry this seat is booked");
                }
        // printing summary
        System.out.println(" printing summary " );
        System.out.println("seat ticket");
        frand.seek(4 * 0 );
        for(i=0;i<10;i++)
                {   Tnum = frand.readInt();
                    System.out.println(i + "\t" + Tnum);
                }
        frand.close();
    }
}
```

If you run this program, you will get the following output.

Output

```
Requested seat number : 3
Seat reserved ticket number 1 seat number 3
Requested seat number : 5
Seat reserved ticket number 2 seat number 5
Requested seat number : 6
Seat reserved ticket number 3 seat number 6
Requested seat number : 5
 sorry this seat is booked
Requested seat number : 3
 sorry this seat is booked
Requested seat number : 4
Seat reserved ticket number 4 seat number 4
 printing summary
seat ticket
0       0
1       0
2       0
3       1
```

```
4    4
5    2
6    3
7    0
8    0
9    0
```

17.10 Object Serialization

While the text was in development, one of my friends pointed out that the title "file for objects" is incorrect. It should be "file of objects". I politely pointed out that the use of word "for" was deliberate. What we have created was not the file of objects. He asked, "Is it because no strings?" (He was right in a way. Strings are also objects but they require unequal memory. The present model requires that every object must need the same number of bytes.) I replied, "No. The main reason is in that in this model we could not allow even reference!"

As mentioned earlier, there are two dynamic data structures, namely, linked list and binary tree. In these structures, it is possible for an object to refer to one or many objects. Those objects can refer to still more objects.

Hence, if we claim to store one object, we may have to store 100 objects with complex interlinking. This appears to be a very difficult task. But Java makes it amazingly simple. Java allows serialization of the object. It also allows us to simply call one particular write method. However, this topic is beyond the scope of this chapter.

17.11 End of Chapter Programs

17.11.1 Large binary file

It is a known fact that data stored in binary form is read very quickly. However, it is not possible to test the premise when we deal with small size files. In practice, files are of very large size in applications like databases. Hence, it will be a good idea to measure the time needed to read a large binary file.

Problem: Write a program to demonstrate reading of large binary files.

Solution: Let us first create a binary file storing 10,000,000 integers. Then we will read them back. For measuring time, we will use methods from class `BPtimer` (see Program 17.11).

PROGRAM 17.11 Large Binary File

```
//        binfile12.java
//    Creating LARGE Binary file

import java.io.* ;
class binfile12
  {  public static void main(String[] args) throws Exception
        {  int i,k=0;
           System.out.println("<---binfile12.java starts--->");

           FileOutputStream fx = new
```

```
                FileOutputStream("binfile1.dat");
            BufferedOutputStream bos = new
            BufferedOutputStream(fx);
            DataOutputStream f2 = new DataOutputStream(bos);//(fx);
            for (i=1;i<=10000000;i++)

        // while( f2.ready() )
                {  f2.writeInt(i);
                }
            f2.close();
            System.out.println("file created successfully");
            FileInputStream fy = new
            FileInputStream("binfile1.dat");
            BufferedInputStream bis = new BufferedInputStream(fy);
            DataInputStream f1 = new DataInputStream(bis);//(fy);
            System.out.println("reading starts");
               BPtimer.start();
            for (i=1;i<=10000000;i++)
                     k=f1.readInt();
            System.out.println("file read successfully");
            System.out.println(k + " ");
            f1.close();
            BPtimer.stop();
        }
   } ;
class BPtimer
  {   private static long t0;
      private static long t1;

      public static void start()
          {   t0 = System.currentTimeMillis();
          }

      public static void stop()
          {   t1 = System.currentTimeMillis() - t0 ;
              System.out.println("time measured = " + t1
                 + "\n milliSeconds");
          }
}
```

If you run this program, you will get the following output.

Output

```
<---binfile12.java starts--->
file created successfully
reading starts
file read successfully
10000000
time measured = 1063
 milliseconds
```

17.11.2 Large text file

We have just seen a large binary file. For comparison purpose, we are required to work with a large text file which will take much more time to read and write. Computer scientists have developed the concept of buffering (hardware) to reduce this time. Java offers us the classes `BufferedReader` and `BufferedWriter` for this purpose. Let us study it with help of a program.

Problem: Write a program to show that one can read faster with the help of `BufferedReader`.

Solution: To appreciate the speed, we must have a very large file. Here we will create a large text file and keep natural numbers from 1 to 10,000,000 in it (one number in one line). Then we will read this file. We will use methods from class `BPtimer` to measure the time (see Program 17.12).

PROGRAM 17.12 Large Text File

```
// big size text files
//       fo4.java
import java.io.* ;
public class fo4
  {   public static void main(String[] args) throws Exception
          {  String s1 ;
             int i =10 ;
             int k =0;
             System.out.println("<---fo4.java--->");
             System.out.println("Creating Data file");
             FileWriter f2 = new FileWriter("fo4.dat");
             BufferedWriter bw = new BufferedWriter (f2) ;
                for (i=1;i<=10000000;i++)
                   bw.write(i+ "\n" );
             bw.close();
             System.out.println("file fo4.dat created");

             FileReader f1 = new FileReader("fo4.dat");
             BufferedReader fin = new BufferedReader(f1);
             System.out.println("file reading starts");
             BPtimer.start();
                while ( fin.ready() )
                {   s1 = fin.readLine();
                    k=Integer.parseInt(s1);

                }
          //        System.out.println(k); // for debugging
             fin.close();
             BPtimer.stop();
             System.out.println("program over");
          }
      } ;
class BPtimer
  {   private static long t0;
      private static long t1;
      public static void start()
```

```
        {   t0 = System.currentTimeMillis();
        }
    public static void stop()
        {   t1 = System.currentTimeMillis() - t0 ;
            System.out.println("time measured = " + t1
                                   + "\n in milli seconds");
        }
}
```

If we run this program, we will get the following output.

Output

```
<---fo4.java--->
Creating Data file
file fo4.dat created
file reading starts
time measured = 5797
  in milli seconds
program over
```

You may modify the program in such a way that `BufferedReader` is not used. Find the time to read in that case.

The contents of this text file were same as binary file of the previous program. Compare the time recorded in both the programs.

17.11.3 List of files

Problem: Write a program to find and list all the files in a given directory.

Solution: Java supports a very interesting method named `list()`. It gets all the names of all the files in the directory and put it in an array of string. See Program 17.13.

PROGRAM 17.13 Listing Files from a Directory

```
//      file3.java
import java.io.* ;
class file3
  {   public static void main(String[] args) throws Exception
          {   int i, k ;
              String dname = new String("c:/jprog/ch17/file3");
              File d1 = new File( dname);
              String[] filelist ;
              System.out.println("<---file3.java starts--->");
              if( d1.isDirectory() )
                    System.out.println("Yes it is a directory");
                  else
                      {   System.out.println(
                                  " File named is not a directory");
                          System.exit(0);
                      }
```

```
            filelist = d1.list();
            k = filelist.length;
            System.out.println("no of entries are " + k);
            for(i=0;i<k;i++)
               System.out.println(i+") " + filelist[i] );
        }
}
```

If you run this program, you will get the following output.

Output

```
<---file3.java starts--->
Yes it is a directory
no of entries are 2
0) file3.class
1) file3.java
```

As expected, the program lists all the files in the specified directory. Unfortunately, this method also lists folders (directories) as files when they exist. It is left to the readers to improve the program such that the output contains only files and not the folders (directories).

17.11.4 Reading matrices from binary files

Problem: Write a program to read a matrix from a binary data file.

Solution: Earlier we solved a problem on 3 × 3 matrix addition. We will use the same program but will add a new constructor which will accept the file name as a parameter (see Program 17.14).

PROGRAM 17.14 Reading an Array from Binary File

```
//       matrix3.java
//    reading from binary file
//       matrix addition
import java.io.* ;
class mat3x3
    {  int[][] ele = new int[3][3];
       mat3x3( int[] A )
          {  int i,j,k=0;
             for(i=0;i<=2;i++)
                for(j=0;j<=2;j++)
                   ele[i][j]=A[k++];
          }
       mat3x3()       // creates matrix without assigning values
       {
       };
       mat3x3(String fname) throws Exception
             // creates matrix from file
       {  int i,j,k;
          FileInputStream fy = new
                 FileInputStream(fname);
```

```
                DataInputStream f1 = new
                DataInputStream(fy);
          System.out.println("constructor invoked");

          for(i=0;i<=2;i++)
             for(j=0;j<=2;j++)
                 {   k=f1.readInt();
                     System.out.print(k + " "); // for debugging only
                     ele[i][j] = k ;
                 }
             System.out.println();
          fy.close();
        };
    }
class matrix3
{
  public static void main(String arg[]) throws Exception
    {   mat3x3 mat1 = new mat3x3("mat1.dat") ;
        mat3x3 mat2 = new mat3x3("mat2.dat") ;
        mat3x3 mat3 = new mat3x3();

        int i,j;
        System.out.println("--->matrix3.java<---");
//      calculating
        for(i=0;i<=2;i++)
           for(j=0;j<=2;j++)
              mat3.ele[i][j] = mat1.ele[i][j] + mat2.ele[i][j];

        System.out.println("mat1");
        for(i=0;i<=2;++i)
           {  for(j=0;j<=2;++j)
                    System.out.print("\t" + mat1.ele[i][j]);
              System.out.println();
           }

        System.out.println("mat2");
        for(i=0;i<=2;++i)
           {  for(j=0;j<=2;++j)
                    System.out.print("\t" + mat2.ele[i][j]);
              System.out.println();
           }

        System.out.println("mat3");
        for(i=0;i<=2;++i)
           {  for(j=0;j<=2;++j)
                 System.out.print("\t" + mat3.ele[i][j]);
              System.out.println();
           }
    }
}
```

If you run this program, you will get the following output.

Output

```
constructor invoked
1   2   3   4   5   6   7   8   9
constructor invoked
1   2   3   14   15   16   27   28   29
--->matrix3.java<---
mat1
      1              2              3
      4              5              6
      7              8              9
mat2
      1              2              3
      14             15             16
      27             28             29
mat3
      2              4              6
      18             20             22
      34             36             38
```

Note that line

"constructor invoked"

tells us that the constructor with file name as parameter is invoked.

17.11.5 Listing all the files including those in the sub-folders

File structure in most of the OSs is tree structure. We can see only one folder at a time. We cannot see or list all the files easily. Hence, an application which can list all the files in a given directory is highly desirable. Let us try our knowledge of files to do this task.

Problem: Write a program to find (using recursion) all the files in a given directory and all of its sub-directories.

Solution: Writing a solution without recursion will be difficult. Recursion makes the program simple and short. In essence, we should develop a recursive method which gets all the files. Let us name such method as `getThemAll` (see Program 17.15).

PROGRAM 17.15 Listing all Files

```
//    ftree3.java
//    uses recursion to list all files.
//
import java.io.* ;
class ftree3
  {   static File[] filelist ;
      static FileWriter f2;
      static int fileCount =0;
      static void getThemAll(File d1) throws IOException
          {   int i,k,dind;
```

```
            System.out.println("Yes it is a directory-> "+ d1);
            filelist = d1.listFiles();
            k = filelist.length;
            System.out.println("no of entries are " + k);
            File dirArray[] = new File[k] ;
            dind =0 ; // index for darray
            for(i=0;i<k;i++)
                { if(filelist[i].isDirectory() )
                      { dirArray[dind++] = filelist[i] ;
                      }
                  else
                      { System.out.println(fileCount
                                 + ") " + filelist[i] +" "+"file");
                        f2.write(fileCount + ") " + filelist[i] +"\n");
                        fileCount++;
                      }
                }
            for(i=0;i<dind;i++)
                { System.out.println( i + ") " + dirArray[i] );
                  getThemAll ( dirArray[i] );
                }
    }
    public static void main(String[] args) throws Exception
        {  int i, k ;
           String dname = new String("C://Jprog");
           File d1 = new File( dname);
           f2 = new FileWriter("ftree3.out");
           System.out.println("<---ftree3.java starts--->");
           if( d1.isDirectory() == false)
              { System.out.println(" File named is not adirectory");
                return ;
              }
           getThemAll( d1);
           f2.close();
        }
}
```

If you run this program, you will get the output on screen as well as stored in the file. When I ran this program, there were more than 12,000 lines in the output. Only the first few lines are presented in the following output.

Output

```
0) C:\Jprog\JXP7.bat
1) C:\Jprog\JXP6n.bat
2) C:\Jprog\cmdJdk6.bat
3) C:\Jprog\BPJA6new.bat
4) C:\Jprog\BPJA6N.EXE
5) C:\Jprog\xxBPJA6NEW.EXE
6) C:\Jprog\Latest Java_prog_list.txt
7) C:\Jprog\BPJA6N.PIF
8) C:\Jprog\bubgral.class
9) C:\Jprog\ch3\bit1\bit1.class
```

```
10) C:\Jprog\ch3\bit1\bit1.java
11) C:\Jprog\ch3\area1\area1.class
12) C:\Jprog\ch3\area1\area1.ctxt
13) C:\Jprog\ch3\area1\area1.java
14) C:\Jprog\ch3\area1\bluej.pkg
15) C:\Jprog\ch3\area1\bluej.pkh
16) C:\Jprog\ch3\char1\char1.java
17) C:\Jprog\ch3\char1\char1.class
18) C:\Jprog\ch3\char1\char1.out
19) C:\Jprog\ch3\char3\char3.java
20) C:\Jprog\ch3\char3\char3.class
21) C:\Jprog\ch3\char3\char3n.class
22) C:\Jprog\ch3\char3\char3n.out
23) C:\Jprog\ch3\char3\char3n.java
24) C:\Jprog\ch3\const1\const1.java
25) C:\Jprog\ch3\const1\const1.class
26) C:\Jprog\ch3\final1a\final1a.err
27) C:\Jprog\ch3\final1a\final1a.java
28) C:\Jprog\ch3\final1\final1.java
29) C:\Jprog\ch3\final1\final1.class
30) C:\Jprog\ch3\line1\line1.java
31) C:\Jprog\ch3\line1\line1.class
32) C:\Jprog\ch3\line1\line1.out
33) C:\Jprog\ch3\logical1\logical1.java
34) C:\Jprog\ch3\logical1\logical1.class
35) C:\Jprog\ch3\modulo1\modulo1.java
36) C:\Jprog\ch3\modulo1\modulo1.class
37) C:\Jprog\ch3\relop1\relop1.java
38) C:\Jprog\ch3\shift1\shift1.java
39) C:\Jprog\ch3\shift1\shift1.class
40) C:\Jprog\ch3\trunc1\trunc1.java
41) C:\Jprog\ch3\trunc1\trunc1.class
42) C:\Jprog\ch3\unicode1\unicode1.class
43) C:\Jprog\ch3\unicode1\unicode1.java
44) C:\Jprog\ch3\first\abc1.doc
45) C:\Jprog\ch3\first\first.class
46) C:\Jprog\ch3\first\first.java
47) C:\Jprog\ch3\first\first.out
48) C:\Jprog\ch3\unicode2\unicode2.out
49) C:\Jprog\ch3\unicode2\unicode2.java
50) C:\Jprog\ch3\unicode2\unicode2.class
```

If you study the output, you will find that this program first lists all the files from a given directory namely `C:\Jprog`. Then it prints files in the sub-directories also.

Keywords

absolute pathname, abstract pathname, binary files, `BufferedReader`, `BufferedWriter`, `canRead()`, `canWrite()`, class `File`, `DataInputStream`, `DataOutputStream`, `delete()`, `deleteOnExit()`, direct access file, `exists()`, `FileInputStream`, `FileNotFoundException`, `FileOutputStream`,

Format-free data, formatted data, `getAbsoluteFile()`, `getAbsolutePath()`, `getParent()`, `getParentFile()`, input file, `isAbsolute()`, `lastModified()`, `list()`, `listFiles()`, `mkdir()`, object serialization, output file, random access files, record, sequential access file, text files.

Review Questions

1. What are the various ways of classifying files?
2. What are the advantages of binary file?
3. What are the advantages of text files?
4. What are the advantages of random access files?
5. What is object serialization?
6. What is the use of class `StringTokenizer`?
7. What is the difference between abstract pathname and absolute pathname?

Exercises

1. Write a program to read your name, roll number, address, and marks obtained in physics, chemistry, and mathematics from keyboard and place it in file.
2. Write a program to read the biodata of 20 applicants and write them to a file.
3. Write a program to display a specified text file on console. Assume that the file is specified as command line argument. (Hint: show only 20 lines at a time.)
4. Assume that a data file is a text file. Write a program that will read integer *n*, and display the *n*th line on the screen.
5. Write a program to encrypt and decrypt files.
6. Write a program to generate directory of colleges in Mumbai city. The entries must be the name of the college, telephone number, and the degree offered. Allow interactive data entry and retrieval.
7. Write a program that finds and print the total number of characters and total number of words in a text file. The program should ask the user to enter the name of file.
8. Write a program to display the mobile number of your classmates when you enter his roll number. Assume that the roll numbers are starting from 601. Assume that the data is stored in a random access file.
9. Repeat the aforementioned program for whole institute. Assume that there are about 1,500 students. Roll numbers start from 1 and end at 3,999. (Naturally, all the roll numbers are not assigned.)
10. Write a Java program for counting the number of characters, words, and lines in a file.
11. Write a program to create a data file containing the following information.

Sr_no	Merit_no	Name	Total_marks
1	03	Madura	92
2	02	Vrunda	97
3	01	Sarika	98

The information should be entered using console.

MULTI-THREADED PROGRAMMING

So far, we have written many programs. All of them can be termed as single threaded. For last many years, programming languages were producing single-threaded programs. Only recently, multi-threading support has appeared in programming languages. Java is providing an elegant, easy-to-use multi-threading environment to programmers.

Let us first understand what a thread is.

18.1 What are Threads?

When we start running a program, execution begins with method main. Executing of a method means executing statement after statement in sequence. Please note that loops like for and while are considered as a single (may be complex) statement. As CPUs started becoming faster and faster and OS started supporting multi-tasking, it becomes apparent that we should be able to run more than one method at a time. This brings in the concept of thread. One method (or group of some statements) is put in one envelope and sent for execution. At the same time, another code is sent for execution. The program controls them through some invisible monitoring mechanism. We imagine that these envelopes are tied to the programs by a thread.

Let us not bother how a single processor can execute two codes simultaneously. We will discuss it later.

18.2 Why Use Threads?

One of the main motives behind the introduction of threads is to maximize the use of resources. In simple terms, we want to run our programs faster. Consider a case in which we want to run a simple program of searching an array. It involves two tasks: reading data from file and specifying interactively the number N which we want to search.

Consider a pseudo code:

```
Read data from file;
Get N from console;
```

It is possible to run these actions in an overlapped manner, thereby saving time.

Let us take another example. Consider a case in which we want to compare bubble sort and quick sort. The methods for the same are available to us. We want both the methods to execute simultaneously. With our present programming knowledge, we can execute these methods one after the other. We cannot run them simultaneously.

This action is possible only when we do it with two threads. This excellent demonstration is available in *The Java Tutorial*. Readers are advised to see it to appreciate the power of threads. With so much motivation to study threads, let us start with creating and running threads.

18.3 Creating and Running a Thread

There are two ways to create a new thread of execution. One way is to declare a class to be a sub-class of `Thread`. This sub-class should override the run method of class `Thread`. The other way to create a thread is to declare a class that implements the `Runnable` interface. That class then implements the run method.

Let us start with the first method of creating thread. It will require the following steps.

Define a sub-class which extends class `Thread`.

The code we want to execute has to be placed in a method `run()` of this sub-class.

Next, create an object of this sub-class and execute the run method.

For example, a sub-class `FirstThread` could be written as follows:

```
class FirstThread extends Thread
   { // declarations
     // constructor if required
      public void run ()
         {
            // The code we want to run comes here.
         }
   }
```

Next, the following code can be used to create the thread and set it running.

```
FirstThread th1 = new FirstThread();
th1.start();
```

As the concept of thread is quite complex, let us write a small program which runs only one thread. This will help us in getting familiar with a thread.

Problem: Write a program to demonstrate running of a single thread.

Solution: Since we have to run some useful code in a thread, let us take a simple example of sorting. We will sort a small array of integers in the thread (see Program 18.1).

PROGRAM 18.1 A Single Thread

```
//     thr1.java
class FirstThread extends Thread
      {    int A[] = {35,7,23,1,14} ;

   public static void sort(int [] A)
            {  int i,j,temp;

               System.out.println("Initial data");
               for(i=0; i<5;i++)
                     System.out.print(A[i]+"\t");
               System.out.println();
               // now sorting
               for(i=0; i<5-1;i++)
                  for(j=0; j<5-1;j++)
```

```
                if( A[j]> A[j+1] )
                    { temp = A[j];
                      A[j] = A[j+1];
                      A[j+1] = temp;
                    }

            System.out.println("data after sorting");
            for(i=0; i<5;i++)
                System.out.print(A[i]+"\t");
        }

    public void run()
    {  sort(A);
    }
  }
class thr1
  { public static void main( String args[] )
      { System.out.println("<---thr1.java--->");
        FirstThread th1 = new FirstThread();
        th1.start();
      }
  };
```

If we run the program, we will get the following output.

Output

```
<---thr1.java--->
Initial data
35    7     23    1     14
data after sorting
1     7     14    23    35
```

You will ask me why is the running of a single thread shown in a chapter of multi-threading? Well, running many threads at a time is no different from running a single thread. And of course, if you cannot run even one thread, you cannot run many.

18.4 Creating Multiple Threads

After studying how a single thread comes into action, we are in a position to study what is called multi-threading, that is many threads in action (simultaneously). We have to start various threads one after the other by calling their start method.

Here, every thread is expected to run a specific code. By the word code, we mean a group of Java statements. We know that most of the time we have a single processor in a computer. Naturally, not all the threads are going to run simultaneously. The Java runtime machine switches execution of threads at short intervals. It gives us the illusion that all the threads are running simultaneously. Analogy can be drawn to a multi-tasking OS like Windows running various tasks simultaneously.

As every good thing has to come to an end, so does the thread. It is born, passes through different phases, and then comes to an end. This brings us to the life cycle of a thread.

18.5 Life Cycle of a Thread

A thread in its lifetime goes through various states. Let us study the life cycle of a thread in brief.

When we create a thread naturally, it is in "new" state. The most noticeable state is when the thread is running. We call it the "running" state. If there is any visible action (on screen), we can easily notice it. But as the time comes to run another thread, the current thread must go to another state.

In the next state, the thread is not running, but is ready to run when given a chance. This state is therefore called "runnable" state. (We may also call it "ready" state.)

Sometimes a thread requires some input data. It cannot proceed unless it is made available by the OS. Such a state is called a "blocked" state.

When a thread comes to the end of its code, naturally its life gets over. Hence, it enters a "dead" state.

Any thread starts with the new state and ends up in a dead state. During its life cycle, it moves from state to state. Figure 18.1 shows the state transition diagram of a thread's life cycle.

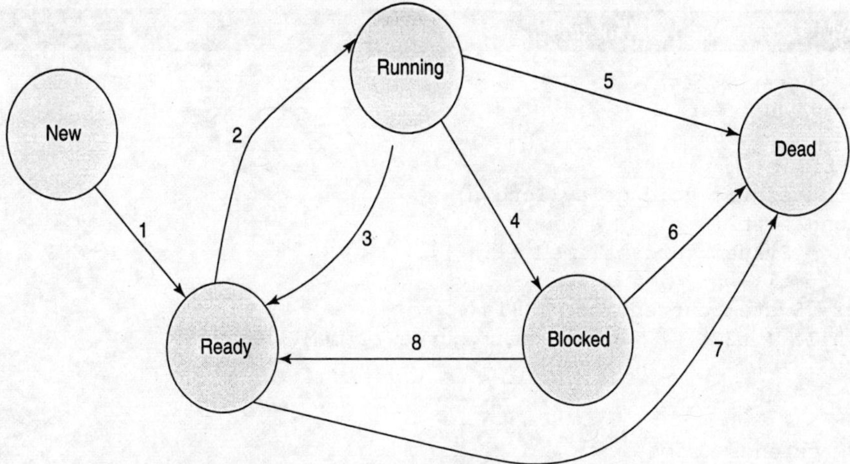

Figure 18.1 Life Cycle of a Thread

We will describe these state transitions in the following table.

Path No	Description
1	When we create a thread, it is normally in a position to run. Hence, it acquires ready state.
2	In a program, there may be many threads in the ready state. The JRE decides which one to start running. It selects a thread and starts executing it. Therefore, such a thread will move to the running state.
3	When the allocated (CPU) time of a thread is over, a running thread has to make way for another thread. Hence, JRE puts it back in the ready state.
4	Sometimes, a running thread may ask for disk input or may wait for some other event to occur. If such a thread keeps running, it will waste CPU time. Hence, JRE puts it in a state which can be described as the blocked state.
5	At a particular time, a running thread will come to its codes last statement (return). It implies that it is coming to its end. Naturally, it enters a state named "dead".

(Continued)

6 & 7	Earlier it was possible to stop a thread by sending a stop command. In such a case, a thread which either is blocked or is in waiting state enters the dead state. Now since the method stop is deprecated, these paths are no more valid.
8	A thread in blocked state is actually waiting for something to happen. When that thing happens (say data available from disk), then the thread is capable of running again. Hence, it is put back in the ready state.

After studying the life cycle of a thread, now let us write a program with three threads. To make it interesting, let us use graphics.

Problem: Write a program which contains three threads.

Solution: See Program 18.2.

PROGRAM 18.2 Demo of Threads

```
//      thgraph2.java
import java.awt.* ;

class BPtimer
  { public static void delay(long n)
    { long t1,t2;
      t1 = System.currentTimeMillis();
      t1 = t1 + n;
      t2= System.currentTimeMillis();
      while ( t2 < t1 ) t2= System.currentTimeMillis();
    }
  }

class VP extends Frame
   { Graphics g1;
     VP (int xdim, int ydim) //constructor
        { setSize(xdim,ydim);
        setBackground(Color.white );
        setVisible(true);
        g1=getGraphics();
        g1.setColor(Color.blue);
   }

class A extends Thread
{ public void run()
   { for (int i = 0; i< 30;i++)
        { BPtimer.delay(150);
        g1.drawLine(100,100,100+i*10,100);
        }
        g1.drawString(" Exit from A",120,100-30);
   }
}

class B extends Thread
   { public void run()
     { for (int j = 0; j< 30;j++)
```

```
        { BPtimer.delay(150);
          g1.drawLine(100,200,100+j*10,200);
        }
          g1.drawString(" Exit from B",120,200-30);
      }
    }

class C extends Thread
    { public void run()
      { for (int k = 0; k< 30 ;k++)
        { BPtimer.delay(110);
          g1.drawLine(100,300,100+k*10,300);
        }
        g1.drawString(" Exit from C",120,300-30);
      }
    }

public void show_me()
    { new A().start();
      new B().start();
      new C().start();
    }
}

class thgraph2
    { public static void main( String args[] )
      { VP vp1= new VP( 500,400);
        vp1.show_me();
        // System.exit(0);
      }
}
```

If you run this program, you will see all the three lines growing. The last line grows fastest. Thread C exits first. When all threads complete their execution, the following screen appears.

Output

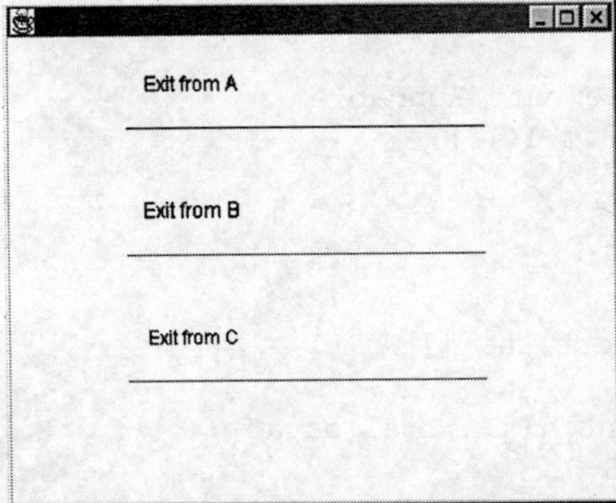

Note the last line marked in bold. It is removed by commenting out. If it is included, we do not see any output. Please note that it is not the last line but one line above that starts the running of the threads. They start running. At that time, if we close the program (actually Java runtime machine), everything gets closed.

18.6 Implementing Runnable Interface

As stated earlier, Java provides an alternate way to create a thread. We can declare a class that implements the Runnable interface. In this class, we have to implement the run method. To start a thread, first we have to pass the instance of this class as an argument.

```
Class SecondThread implements Runnable
{       // declarations
        // constructor if required
        public void run()
         {
            // The code we want to run comes here.
         }
}
```

Now the following code can be used to create a thread and set it running.

```
SecondThread th2 = new SecondThread();
Thread some_name = new Thread(th2).start();
```

Please note the above carefully. th2 is the object of type SecondThread. We create a new Thread some_name with this object as a parameter. We call this method as the start for running this thread. This method invokes the run method of object th2. The above example can be reduced to the following code.

```
SecondThread th2 = new SecondThread();
new Thread(th2).start();
```

Let us study it with an example.

Problem: Write a program to demonstrate the use of interface Runnable.

Solution: Let us rewrite the earlier program (thr1.java) where we sort a small array of integers in the thread (see Program 18.3).

PROGRAM 18.3 Interface Runnable

```
//      thr2.java
//      Demonstrates interface Runnable

class secondThread implements Runnable
   {  int A[] = {35,7,23,1,14} ;
      public void run()
       {  sort(A);
       }

   public static void sort(int [] A)
      {  int i,j,temp;
         System.out.println("Initial data");
         for(i=0; i<5;i++)
              System.out.print(A[i]+"\t");
         System.out.println();
         //  now sorting
```

```
            for(i=0; i<5-1;i++)
                for(j=0; j<5-1;j++)
                  if( A[j]> A[j+1] )
                    {  temp = A[j];
                       A[j] = A[j+1];
                       A[j+1] = temp;
                    }
            System.out.println("data after sorting");
            for(i=0; i<5;i++)
                System.out.print(A[i]+"\t");
        }
    }
class thr2
  {   public static void main( String args[] )
       {  System.out.println("<---thr2.java--->");
          System.out.println("Demonstrates interface Runnable");
          secondThread th2 = new secondThread();
          new Thread(th2).start();
       }
  };
```

If you run the program, you will see the following output.

Output

```
<---thr2.java--->
Demonstrates interface Runnable
Initial data
35    7     23     1      14
data after sorting
1     7     14     23     35
```

18.7 Thread Priority and Thread Scheduling Policy

It is possible to set a priority value to a thread. Java provides three predefined constants for this purpose, as shown in Table 18.1.

Table 18.1 Thread Priority Constants

Constant	Meaning
MAX_PRIORITY	The maximum priority that a thread can have.
MIN_PRIORITY	The minimum priority that a thread can have.
NORM_PRIORITY	The default priority that is assigned to a thread.

Please note that Java depends on thread scheduling policy of the OS, which is discussed further in the text for Windows XP . It uses the "preemptive thread scheduling" policy. When a higher priority thread becomes ready for execution, currently running lesser priority thread is stopped. A lower priority thread cannot preempt higher priority running thread. It has to wait until the running thread either completes or goes to blocking state for some reason.

If there are many threads with same priority, they are given an opportunity to run in round robin fashion. Let us study a simple program to study this concept.

Problem: Write a program to demonstrate thread priority.

Solution: See Program 18.4.

PROGRAM 18.4 Thread Priority

```
//      thread2.java
//      thread priority

class BPtimer
   { public static void delay(long n)
      { long t1,t2;
        t1 = System.currentTimeMillis();
        t1 = t1 + n;
        t2= System.currentTimeMillis();
        while ( t2 < t1 ) t2= System.currentTimeMillis();
      }
   }

class A extends Thread
   { public void run()
       {  for (int i = 1; i< 5;i++)
           { BPtimer.delay(500);
             System.out.println("== from thread A = " + i );
           }
         System.out.println(" Exit from A");
       }
   }

class B extends Thread
   { public void run()
       {  for (int j = 1; j< 5;j++)
           { BPtimer.delay(500);
             System.out.println("------ from thread B =" + j );
           }
         System.out.println(" Exit from B");
      }
   }
class C extends Thread
   { public void run()
        {  for (int k = 1; k< 5;k++)
            { BPtimer.delay(500);
              System.out.println("********* from thread C = " + k );
            }
          System.out.println(" Exit from C");
       }
   }
```

```
class thread2
    { public static void main( String args[] )
      { System.out.println("<---thread2.java--->");
        A th1= new A();
          th1.setPriority(Thread.MIN_PRIORITY);
          th1.start();
        B th2 = new B();
          th2.setPriority(Thread.NORM_PRIORITY);
          th2.start();
        C th3 = new C();
          th3.setPriority(Thread.MAX_PRIORITY);
          th3.start();
      }
    }
```

If you run the program, you will see the following output.

Output

```
<---thread2.java--->
********* from thread C = 1
********* from thread C = 2
********* from thread C = 3
********* from thread C = 4
   Exit from C
------ from thread B =1
------ from thread B =2
------ from thread B =3
------ from thread B =4
   Exit from B
== from thread A = 1
== from thread A = 2
== from thread A = 3
== from thread A = 4
   Exit from A
```

Let us modify our previous graphics program.

Problem: Write a program to demonstrate thread priority using graphics.

Solution: See Program 18.5.

PROGRAM 18.5 Threads Demo II

```
//     th3.java
import java.awt.* ;
import javax.swing.* ;

class BPtimer
  { public static void delay(long n)
      { long t1,t2;
        t1 = System.currentTimeMillis();
```

```
         t1 = t1 + n;
         t2= System.currentTimeMillis();
         while ( t2 < t1 ) t2= System.currentTimeMillis();
      }
    }

class VP extends JFrame
    {  Graphics g1;
       VP (int xdim, int ydim) //constructor
          {  setSize(xdim,ydim);
             setBackground(Color.white);
             setVisible(true);
             g1=getGraphics();
             g1.setColor(Color.blue);
          }

    class A extends Thread
    {  public void run()
       {  for (int i = 0; i< 30;i++)
          {  BPtimer.delay(150);
             g1.drawLine(100,100,100+i*10,100);
          }
             g1.drawString(" Exit from A",120,100-30);
       }
    }

    class B extends Thread
      {  public void run()
         {  for (int j = 0; j< 30;j++)
            {  BPtimer.delay(250);
               g1.drawLine(100,200,100+j*10,200);
            }
               g1.drawString(" Exit from B",120,200-30);
         }
      }

    class C extends Thread
      {  public void run()
         {  for (int k = 0; k< 30 ;k++)
          {  BPtimer.delay(100);
             g1.drawLine(100,300,100+k*10,300);
          }
          g1.drawString(" Exit from C",120,300-30);
         }
      }

public void show_me()
  {  A th1 = new A();
       th1.setPriority(Thread.NORM_PRIORITY);
       th1.start();
       System.out.println(th1.toString());
       B th2 = new B();
```

```
        th2.setPriority(Thread.MAX_PRIORITY);
        th2.start();
        System.out.println(th2.toString());

        C th3 = new C();
        th3.setPriority(Thread.NORM_PRIORITY);
        th3.start();
        System.out.println(th3.toString());
    }
  }
public class th3
{  public static void main( String args[] )
   {  VP vp1= new VP( 500,400);
      vp1.setDefaultCloseOperation(JFrame.EXIT_ON_CLOSE);
      //  vp1.setVisible(true);
      BPtimer.delay(150); // note 1
      vp1.show_me();
      //System.exit(0);
   }
 }
```

If you run the program, at the end you will see the following output.

Output

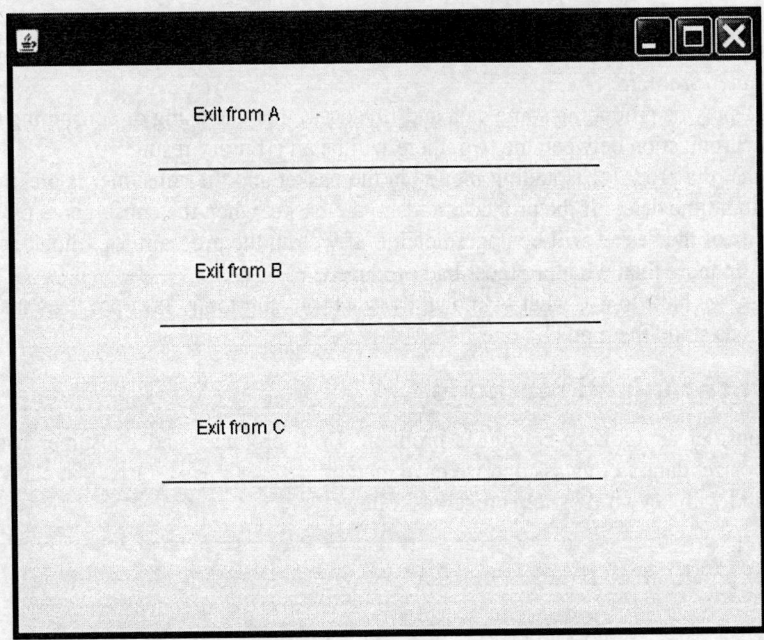

We have to watch this application while running. As Thread B is set to maximum priority, it runs and runs. It finishes before others could put even first step. Afterwards, both threads A and C start moving. As the priority of both C and A is the same, both run together.

There are many points to note in Program 18.5. Basically, code is repeated from `thgraph2.java`. However, delay in thread B is more that delay in A and delay in C. Still it starts as well as finishes even before others two could be visible. Delay in C is less than that of A. Hence, it runs faster than thread A. Lastly, we have added one more statement.

```
BPtimer.delay(150); // note 1
```

You may wonder why a delay is called at this place. Strictly speaking, this is not necessary. When we run the program without it, at times thread B started running even before the frame could become properly visible. When the frame becomes visible, whatever has been drawn before vanishes. This delay helps in getting proper output. Alternatively, we may add

```
vp1.setVisible(true);
```

to achieve the same result.

There are two types of threads in the system. The first one is called "Daemon thread". The second type is normal or non-Daemon thread. In a program, many threads run. Eventually they die. Whenever all normal threads finish (terminate), the program comes to an end. The program does not wait for Daemon thread to terminate. Can we declare a thread as Daemon thread? Find the answer for yourself.

18.8 Synchronization

When we write multi-threaded programs, we may not imagine that there may be complications in the programs. Those of you who have studied the subject of "Operating System" are aware that there are problems like deadlocks. Without going into details, we may say that if two threads are using common data, there is a possibility of erroneous behaviour in the program. Let us take an example of standard producer–consumer problem.

A `thread1` may be producing some data and `thread2` may be using or consuming that data. If there is no proper synchronization between the two, there will be an arbitrary result.

Let us say that the producer is adding money in the basket and the consumer is picking it up. Both are acting with random time delay. If the producer adds to the basket when the consumer is picking it up, after a while the contents of the basket will be unpredictable. If we run the program for 1 hour, at the end the consumer may pick up more than what producer had produced.

To avoid this, we have to use what is known as synchronizing tools. Java provides many tools for synchronization. Let us study them one by one.

18.8.1 Synchronized methods

Let us again consider a producer–consumer problem. Both producer and consumer use object of class `basket` to put or get data. Let us assume we have method `put_or_get(){...}` in class `basket`. Let us define this method with keyword **synchronised** as follows:

```
class basket
      {  synchronised put_or_get()
               {
               //  method body .
               }
      }
```

Now assume that both consumer and producer processes are running from different threads. If both of them want to use `put_or_get()` method simultaneously, the system will not allow them to do so. One of the threads has to wait until other thread finishes. This will solve any concurrency-related problem.

18.8.2 Synchronized statements

Synchronized statements offer another way to create synchronized code. A word synchronized placed before a block makes the block synchronized. Synchronized statements must specify the object that provides the intrinsic lock. Consider the following example. Here instead of a method, a statement (block) is `synchronized`.

```
public void someName( )
    {  synchronized (this) {
         //  statements
         }
```

In the previous paragraph, we talked of intrinsic lock. In Java, the whole process of Synchronization is based on the concept of intrinsic lock or monitor lock. We may simply call it as "monitor".

Every object has an intrinsic lock associated with it. For proper working every thread must acquire this lock (monitor) before using object fields. The thread should release the monitor when it has finished its work. During this time, we can say that this thread owns the monitor and no other thread can acquire the same lock.

18.8.3 Methods `wait()`, `notify()`, and `notifyAll()`

We can use inter-thread communication for proper coordination among the threads. A thread may sleep until it is notified by the other thread. The "`Object` class" provides methods `wait`, `notify`, and `notifyAll` for this purpose.

Method `wait()` makes the thread to wait for getting the monitor. Since it is possible that this thread may be interrupted, it has to be used with `try-catch` block.

Method `notify()` wakes up a single thread that is waiting on this object's monitor. Method `notifyAll()` wakes up all threads that are waiting on this object's monitor.

It is important to note that all these methods must be called only when they own the monitor of that object. Otherwise, they throw `IllegalMonitorStateException`.

A thread becomes the owner of the object's monitor by executing a synchronized instance method of that object. Alternately, it can do so by executing a synchronized statement which specifies that object.

18.8.4 Method `join()`

Java offers method `join()` in class Thread. It is quite useful in co-coordinating Threads. This method makes the current thread to wait until other specified thread terminates. Let us see this in action in the following program.

Problem: Write a program to demonstrate the use of method `join()`.

Solution: Let us continue our example of drawing horizontal lines. Thread "A" draws the line undisturbed. In thread "B" we will draw only first 15 units. Then we will call join on thread "A". This will suspend thread B until thread "A" ends. After that thread, "B" resumes and draws the remaining line.

PROGRAM 18.6 Demo of Method Join()

```
//      th5.java
import java.awt.* ;
import javax.swing.*;

class VP extends JFrame
   {  Graphics g1;
      VP (int xdim, int ydim) //constructor
        {  setSize(xdim,ydim);
           setBackground(Color.white);
           setVisible(true);
           g1=getGraphics();
           g1.setColor(Color.blue);
        }

class A extends Thread
   {  public void run()
      {  for (int i = 0; i< 30;i++)
         {  try
               {  sleep(250);}
           catch(Exception e){ };
           g1.drawLine(100,100,100+i*10,100);
         }
           g1.drawString(" Exit from A",120,100-30);
      }
   }
   static A th1;
   static B th2;
class B extends Thread
   {  public void run()
       {
       for (int j = 0; j< 15;j++)
        {  try
             {  sleep(200);}
           catch(Exception e){ };
          g1.drawLine(100,200,100+j*10,200);
        }
          g1.drawString(" waiting for A to finish",120,200-20);

          try
            {  th1.join() ;}
          catch(Exception e){ };
          g1.drawString(" Resuming operation",120,200+20);

          for (int j = 16; j< 30;j++)
            {  try
                 {  sleep(250);}
               catch(Exception e){ };
               g1.drawLine(100,200,100+j*10,200);
            }
```

```
            g1.drawString(" Exit from B",120,200+40);
            }
         }
    //   static B th2;
public void show_me()
   {  th1 = new A();
      th1.setPriority(Thread.NORM_PRIORITY);
      th1.start();
      th2 = new B();
      th2.setPriority(Thread.NORM_PRIORITY);
      th2.start();
   }
}
class th5
   {  public static void main( String args[] )
      {  VP vp1= new VP( 500,400);
         vp1.setTitle("Demo Of join() " );
         vp1.setDefaultCloseOperation(JFrame.EXIT_ON_CLOSE);
         vp1.setVisible(true);
         vp1.show_me();
      }
}
```

When we run Program 18.6, we first see both threads A and B start drawing corresponding lines. Midway we see that thread B halts with the message "waiting for A to finish". Thread A continues and finishes operation. Now thread B resumes with message "Resuming operation". It continues until it completes its drawing task. It exits with the message "Exit from B". The following figure shows the screenshot at the end of the program.

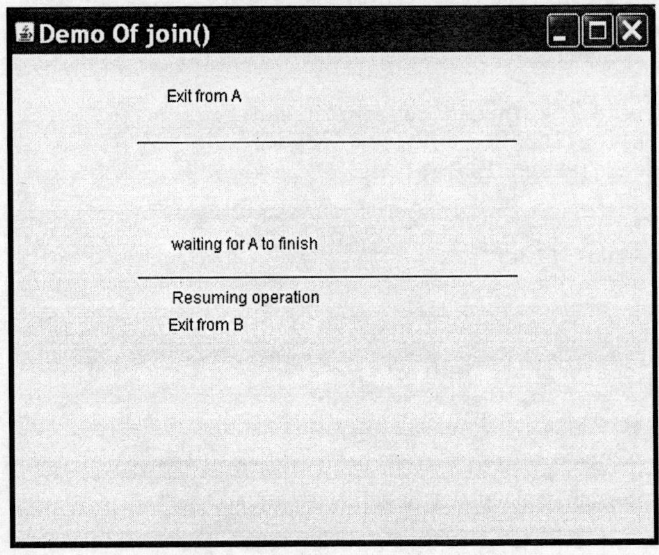

Remember the famous tale of hare and tortoise? You may imagine thread A as tortoise. Thread B represents the hare which sleeps in between. It wakes up only when the tortoise wins the race.

Consider a case of reading an array from a file and sorting it. There is no way of sorting an array unless it is fully read. If the two actions of reading and sorting are in different threads, sorting can begin only when reading is complete, if we use the method `join()`.

18.9 Timer and TimerTask

The package `Java.util` provides two important classes namely `Timer` and `TimerTask`. These are normally used in conjunction. Java offers the facility of running a thread in background. This thread schedules tasks for future execution. It can run thread once or repeatedly at regular intervals.

It goes without saying that tasks so scheduled should finish quickly. Also note that that there is no absolute guarantee that the task will be scheduled at specified time.

Let us study these classes with the help of an example.

Problem: Write a program to demonstrate `Timer` and `TimerTask` classes.

Solution: In this example, we will create a `Timer` object say `timea`. We want the program to run for say 5 seconds. We will put the main thread to sleep for 5,000 milliseconds. During this time, `TimerTask` will execute every 1000 milliseconds. In the timer `Task`, we will print word `hello` (see Program 18.7).

PROGRAM 18.7 TimerTask

```
//   timer1.java
import java.util.*;

public class timer1
   {  public static void main(String args[])
       {  System.out.println("<---timer1.java--->");
          Timer timea = new Timer(true);
          timea.scheduleAtFixedRate( new MyTask(), 0, 1000);
          try
           {  Thread t = Thread.currentThread();
              t.sleep(5000);
           }  catch  (Exception e){};
     }
   }
class MyTask extends TimerTask
    {
      public void run()
        {
          System.out.println("Hello");
        }
    }
```

If you run the above program, you will get the following output.

Output

```
  <---timer1.java--->
Hello
```

```
Hello
Hello
Hello
Hello
Hello
```

Please note that the word hello is printed six times. One expects it to print only five times. Change the sleep time by few milliseconds, less than 5,000 milliseconds, and you will get the word printed only five times.

You will ask me, why force main thread to sleep? The answer is that otherwise the program comes to an end immediately. The action we want to watch is guaranteed by the timer. We have to ensure that the program runs for a finite time.

Table 18.2 summarizes the constructors from class Timer.

Table 18.2 Constructor Summary: Class Timer

`Timer()`	Creates a new timer.
`Timer(boolean isDaemon)`	Creates a new timer whose associated thread may be specified to run as a daemon.
`Timer(String name)`	Creates a new timer whose associated thread has the specified name.
`Timer(String name, boolean isDaemon)`	Creates a new timer whose associated thread has the specified name, and may be specified to run as a daemon.

Table 18.3 summarizes the methods from class Timer.

Table 18.3 Method Summary: Class Timer

`void cancel()`	Terminates this timer, discarding any currently scheduled tasks.
`int purge()`	Removes all cancelled tasks from this timer's task queue.
`void schedule(TimerTask task, Date time)`	Schedules the specified task for execution at the specified time.
`void schedule(TimerTask task, Date firstTime, long period)`	Schedules the specified task for repeated fixed-delay execution, beginning at the specified time.
`void schedule(TimerTask task, long delay)`	Schedules the specified task for execution after the specified delay.

(Continued)

Table 18.3 (*Continued*)

`void schedule(TimerTask task, long delay, long period)`	Schedules the specified task for repeated fixed-delay execution, beginning after the specified delay.
`void scheduleAtFixed-Rate (TimerTask task, Date firstTime, long period)`	Schedules the specified task for repeated fixed-rate execution, beginning at the specified time.
`void scheduleAtFixed-Rate (TimerTask task, long delay, long period)`	Schedules the specified task for repeated fixed-rate execution, beginning after the specified delay.

Table 18.4 summarizes the methods from class TimerTask.

Table 18.4 **Methods Summary: Class TimerTask**

`boolean cancel()`	Cancels this timer task.
`abstract void run()`	The action to be performed by this timer task.
`long scheduledExecutionTime()`	Returns the scheduled execution time of the most recent actual execution of this task.

Table 18.5 summarizes the constructors from class Thread.

Table 18.5 **Constructor Summary: Class Thread**

`Thread()`	Allocates a new Thread object.
`Thread(Runnable target)`	Allocates a new Thread object.
`Thread(Runnable target, String name)`	Allocates a new Thread object.
`Thread(String name)`	Allocates a new Thread object.
`Thread(ThreadGroup group, Runnable target)`	Allocates a new Thread object.
`Thread(ThreadGroup group, Runnable target, String name)`	Allocates a new Thread object so that it has target as its run object, has the specified name as its name, and belongs to the thread group referred to by group.

(*Continued*)

Table 18.5 *(Continued)*

`Thread(ThreadGroup group, Runnable target, String name, long stackSize)`	Allocates a new Thread object so that it has target as its run object, has the specified name as its name, belongs to the thread group referred to by group, and has the specified stack size.
`Thread(ThreadGroup group, String name)`	Allocates a new Thread object.

Table 18.6 summarizes the methods from class Thread.

Table 18.6 **Methods Summary: Class Thread**

`static int activeCount()`	Returns the current number of active threads in this thread's thread group.
`void checkAccess()`	Determines if the currently running thread has permission to modify this thread.
`int countStackFrames()`	Deprecated. The definition of this call depends on `suspend()`, which is deprecated. Further, the results of this call were never well defined.
`static Thread currentThread()`	Returns a reference to the currently executing thread object.
`void destroy()`	Destroys this thread, without any clean-up.
`static void dumpStack()`	Prints a stack trace of the current thread.
`static int enumerate (Thread[] tarray)`	Copies into the specified array every active thread in this thread's thread group and its sub-groups.
`ClassLoader getContextClassLoader()`	Returns the context ClassLoader for this Thread.
`String getName()`	Returns this thread's name.
`int getPriority()`	Returns this thread's priority.
`ThreadGroup getThreadGroup()`	Returns the thread group to which this thread belongs.
`void interrupt()`	Interrupts this thread.
`static boolean interrupted()`	Tests whether the current thread has been interrupted.
`boolean isAlive()`	Tests if this thread is alive.

(Continued)

Table 18.6 (*Continued*)

`boolean isDaemon()`	Tests if this thread is a Daemon thread.
`boolean isInterrupted()`	Tests whether this thread has been interrupted.
`void join()`	Waits for this thread to die.
`void join(long millis)`	Waits at most millis milliseconds for this thread to die.
`void join(long millis, int nanos)`	Waits at most millis milliseconds plus nanos nanoseconds for this thread to die.
`void resume()`	Deprecated. This method exists solely for use with `suspend()`, which has been deprecated because it is deadlock-prone.
`void run()`	If this thread was constructed using a separate Runnable run object, then that Runnable object's run method is called; otherwise, this method does nothing and returns.
`void setContextClassLoader (ClassLoadercl)`	Sets the context ClassLoader for this Thread.
`void setDaemon (boolean on)`	Marks this thread as either a Daemon thread or a user thread.
`void setName(String name)`	Changes the name of this thread to be equal to the argument name.
`void setPriority(int newPriority)`	Changes the priority of this thread.
`static void sleep(long millis)`	Causes the currently executing thread to sleep (temporarily cease execution) for the specified number of milliseconds.
`static void sleep(long millis, int nanos)`	Causes the currently executing thread to sleep (cease execution) for the specified number of milliseconds plus the specified number of nanoseconds.
`void start()`	Causes this thread to begin execution; the JVM calls the run method of this thread.
`void stop()`	Deprecated. This method is inherently unsafe. Stopping a thread with Thread.stop causes it to unlock all of the monitors that it has locked (as a natural consequence of the unchecked ThreadDeath exception propagating up the stack).
`void stop(Throwable obj)`	Deprecated. This method is inherently unsafe. See `stop()` (with no arguments) for details. An additional danger of this method is that it may be used to generate exceptions that

(*Continued*)

Table 18.6 *(Continued)*

	the target thread is unprepared to handle (including checked exceptions that the thread could not possibly throw, were it not for this method).
`void suspend()`	Deprecated. This method has been deprecated, as it is inherently deadlock-prone. If the target thread holds a lock on the monitor protecting a critical system resource when it is suspended, no thread can access this resource until the target thread is resumed. If the thread that would resume the target thread attempts to lock this monitor prior to calling resume, deadlock results. Such deadlocks typically manifest themselves as "frozen" processes.
`String toString()`	Returns a string representation of this thread, including the thread's name, priority, and thread group.
`static void yield()`	Causes the currently executing thread object to temporarily pause and allow other threads to execute.

Keywords

blocked state, Daemon thread, dead state, `getName()`, `getPriority()`, `interrupt()`, `isAlive()`, `isDaemon()`, `join()`, `MAX_PRIORITY`, `MIN_PRIORITY`, `NORM_PRIORITY`, preemptive thread scheduling, ready state, run, `Runnable`, running state, `start()`, `sleep()`, synchronized, thread, thread life cycle, thread priority, `Timer`, `TimerTask`, `yield()`

RuleBook

`NORM_PRIORITY`	`NORM_PRIORITY` is the default priority of a newly created thread.
Thread priority	Threads may yield to threads of lower priority.
Thread simultaneous access	It is possible for two threads to access the same variable or the same method of the same object at the same time. However, the net result will be unpredictable.
Thread class	By using a thread class, multi-threaded program can be created.
Synchronized	Every object that has synchronized methods has a monitor.
Monitor	The `sleep()` method tells the calling thread to give up monitor until some other thread enters the same monitor.
Preemptive switching	A thread priority is used to decide when to move from one running thread to the next. This is called preemptive switching.
`sleep()`	The `sleep()` method is used to temporarily stop the execution of the thread.
`join()`	The `join()` method suspends the current thread until that thread object dies.
`start()`	After the `start()` method is called, the thread is in a Runnable state.

Review Questions

1. What is a thread?
2. What is the advantage of having threads?
3. Which are the two different ways to create a thread?
4. Describe various states of a thread.
5. Draw the diagram for the life cycle of a thread and label the paths with appropriate methods for thread execution.
6. Can we assign priority to a thread? If yes, how?
7. What is the default priority?
8. Explain inter-thread communication.
9. Write a short note on Daemon threads.
10. Write a short note on multi-threading.
11. Write a short note on thread synchronization.

Exercises

1. Write a program of threads in Java showing inter-leaving of actions from two threads: t1 and t2 synchronizing on a shared object.

   Let t1 print message `ping-->` and t2 print message `<--pong`. Take as command line arguments the following inputs to the program:

   Sleep Interval for thread t1

   Sleep Interval for thread t2

   Messages per cycle

   No. of cycles
2. Write a small Java program to illustrate the use of `Runnable` interface.

EXCEPTION HANDLING

CHAPTER 19

An unusual situation may occur sometimes while running the programs. There might be errors and some of them may be fatal. Take a simple case of divide by zero. Older languages give some error message and halt the execution of the program. If the errors are fatal, one cannot do anything about it but if they are non-fatal, the language should allow us to do some damage control exercise. Java provides elegant way of exception handling precisely for this purpose.

19.1 Why Use Exception Handling

One of the most important reasons for handling exception is that when a program terminates abruptly many undesirable things happen. Certain resources, like open files and the World Wide Web (WWW) connection, remain blocked. The operating system (OS) does not get them back. If your program has done any important work or calculations, the efforts are lost. When exception occurs, the program stops running. We cannot do anything about it afterwards. But if we handle exceptions properly, we can do some damage control exercise. We can give the allocated resources back to the OS and save some results. In lighter vain, we can send SOS to our friends.

Let us start our study with a simple example.

Problem: Write a program to show divide by zero exception.

Solution: See Program 19.1.

PROGRAM 19.1 Divide by zero exception

```
//    ex2.java
class ex2
{ public static void main (String args [] )
    { int num = 20;
      int den = 0 ;
      int result;
      result = num / den ;
      System.out.println("--->ex2.java starts<---");
      System.out.println("result is " + result );
    }
}
```

If you run this program, you will get the following output.

Output

```
Exception in thread main
java.lang.ArithmeticException: / by zero
        void ex2.main(java.lang.String[])
```

The program aborts if there is exception. This is `ArithmeticException`. The great thing about it is that Java is highly object oriented and converts exceptions into objects. Java also provides some nice ways to handle these exceptions (objects). Let us study it in detail.

19.2 Types of Exceptions

There are two types of exceptions. The first one represents error. These are hard situations and lead to abrupt termination of the program. Also, these are unrecoverable exceptions. A table describing various types of error is given in Section 19.8. Exceptions of second type are not so hard. They can be handled properly. Here program is not required to terminate immediately. Of course, we are required to code using rules of the game.

Package `java.lang` defines a class `Throwable`. This class has two sub-classes namely `Error` and `Exception`. Errors or exception occurring in the programs are objects of these classes.
Figure 19.1 Illustrates hierarchy of exception classes.

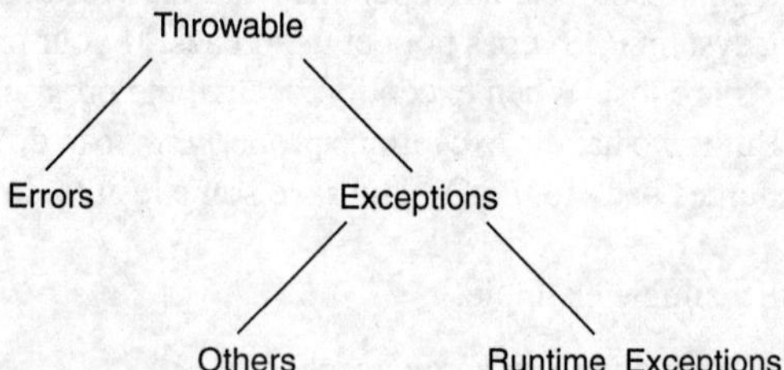

Figure 19.1 Hierarchy of Exceptions

19.3 Checked and Unchecked Exceptions

Exceptions can be divided in two groups, runtime exceptions and non-runtime exception. Runtime exceptions occur within the Java runtime system. The examples are the following:

- arithmetic exceptions, such as dividing by zero,
- pointer exceptions, such as trying to access an object's members through a null reference, and
- indexing exceptions, such as trying to access an array element with an index that is too large or too small.

Java has defined a class `RuntimeException` which acts as super-class for all individual runtime error classes. When we write methods, we need not catch or specify these exceptions. Hence, they can be termed as "unchecked exceptions". The name is somewhat misleading as the JVM does check for these exceptions.

The other exceptions are those occurring in our code. Consider a case of exceptions that occur during input/output. The compiler ensures that we either catch or specify them. That is why they are called "checked exceptions". It is possible that we may forget putting "`try` block" around critical code, which is likely to produce say IOException. The compiler will refuse to compile the code. It will give the following error message.

unreported exception java.io.IOException; must be caught or declared to be thrown

If we add words **throws Exception** to any method, it will compile without giving any error message.

19.4 Exception Handling Constructs

Java offers an elegant solution to exception handling. It provides two constructs, try and catch. A try construct consists of keyword `try` followed by block. (Block is a group of statements enclosed in curly brackets.) We will term this block as try block.

The code which is likely to produce exception is kept in this block. This is followed by catch construct. It consists of keyword `catch` followed exception parameter (in round brackets) followed by a block. We will term this block as catch block. When executing code from try block raises an exception, the control is handed over to catch block. After this block ends, the control goes to next sentence in the program. Please note that the control does not go to try block again (see Program 19.2).

Problem: Write a program to illustrate try–catch action.

Solution: See Program 19.2.

PROGRAM 19.2 Try–Catch demo

```
//      ex21.java

class ex21
{  public static void main (String args [] )
      {  int num = 20;
         int den = 0 ;
         int result=0;
         System.out.println("--->ex21.java starts<---");
         try {
                  result =   num / den ;
                  System.out.println("Just for test");
            }
         catch(Exception e)
            {  System.out.println("Exception is caught");
            }
         System.out.println("result is " + result );
      }
}
```

If you run this program, you will get the following output.

Output

```
--->ex21.java starts<---
Exception is caught
result is 0
```

All the aforementioned points can be verified from the output. Note the absence of string

```
Just for test
```

in the output.

These actions are shown pictorially in Figure 19.2.

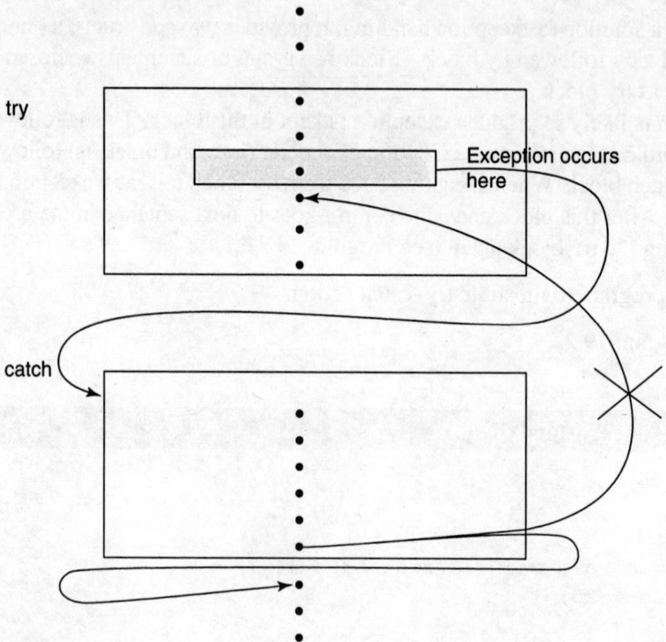

Figure 19.2 try–catch mechanism

Let us see a small program.

Problem: Write a program to demonstrate NullPointerException.

Solution: See Program 19.3.

PROGRAM 19.3 NullPointerException

```
//      ex31.java
class ex31
{  public static void main (String args [] )
   {  int j =0;
      String str ="welcome" ;
      System.out.println("<---ex31.java--->");
      try {
            str = null;
            j = str.length();
```

```
            System.out.println(j);
          }
        catch( NullPointerException e)
          {  System.out.println("Exception is caught");
             System.out.println(e.toString());
          }
        System.out.println("last line of the program" );
    }
}
```

If you run this program, you will get the following output.

Output

```
<---ex31.java--->
Exception is caught
java.lang.NullPointerException
last line of the program
```

One more program in Section 19.8 illustrates the NumberFormatException.

Warning!

Remember the proverb "a stitch in time saves nine". Some programmers may bypass the mechanism of checked exception. The compiler will not issue a warning. But such shortcuts may prove disastrous in the long range. When you write a method which has many statements throwing different exceptions, the code fails to compile. You get the following message.

"unreported exception java.io.IOException; must be caught or declared to be thrown".

There is a tendency to add `throws Exception`. The program compiles without any objection. But the program may fail when exception is thrown and we will have no chance to recover. In a professional application, this will not be acceptable.

19.5 Keyword finally

As an extension to try and catch, Java offers another facility in terms of keyword `finally`. If we place a block labelled as `finally`, just after the catch block, it will always be executed. Let us see its action in a program.

Problem: Write a program to illustrate keyword `finally`.

Solution: See Program 19.4.

PROGRAM 19.4 Keyword finally

```
 //     ex23.java
class ex23
{  public static void main (String args [] )
```

```
    {  int num = 20;
       int den = 0 ;
       int result=0;
       System.out.println("--->ex23.java starts<---");
       try {
               result =   num / den ;
               System.out.println("Just for test");
           }
       catch(Exception e)
           {  System.out.println("Exception is caught");
           }
       finally
          {   System.out.println(
                  "All resources may be released here");
          }
       System.out.println("result is " + result );
    }
}
```

If you run this program, you will get the following output.

Output

```
--->ex23.java starts<---
Exception is caught
All resources may be released here
result is 0
```

Note that the catch block is executed followed by finally block. Afterwards, the control goes to next statement after `finally`. Hence, the line "result is 0" appears in the output.

In the aforementioned program, if we change the denominator to 20, there will be no exception. As stated earlier, `finally` block will still be executed. You can see the program `ex23a.java` in Section 19.8.. You will notice that `finally` block is executed when catch block is not.

19.6 `Throw` Statement

So far we have only seen exception objects being generated because of some peculiarity in our code. Java allows us to define our own exceptions. It is called user-defined exception. For this, we must define a sub-class of `Exception`. The `throw` statement is used to throw the object of type exception.

Let us take a simple program from banking. One wants to withdraw money from an account. Naturally, for the operation to succeed, balance has to be greater than withdrawal. If someone tries to withdraw more than the balance there should be exception. Let us name it as insufficient balance.

See the following program.

Problem: Write a program to show that a new exception class can be defined.

Solution: Let us take a simple program from banking. We will define a class `IBException` (IB = Insufficient Balance). See Program 19.5.

PROGRAM 19.5 Insufficient Balance Exception

```
//      ex5a.java
class  IBException extends Exception
  {  public  String toString()
        { return ( "Transaction denied\n"
                 +"Insufficient balance");
        }
  } ;
class ex5a
{ public static void main (String args [] ) throws IBException
    { int balance = 20;
      int withdraw = 30 ;
      int result;
      System.out.println("<---ex5a.java starts--->");
      try
        { result = balance - withdraw ;
          if ( result <  0 ) throw new IBException() ;
          balance = result;
          System.out.println("balance is " + balance );
        }
      catch (IBException e)
        { System.out.println(e.toString());
        }
    }
}
```

If you compile this program, you will get the following output.

Output

```
 <---ex5a.java starts--->
Transaction denied
Insufficient balance
```

Well the action on exception was very simple in this case. In real-life situation, action that is more appropriate will be required. If it is an ATM rather than a bank, *an alarm in watchman's cabin may be sounded.*

19.7 Multiple Catch Blocks

Java allows multiple catch blocks after a try bloc. Any given code is likely to raise different possible exceptions. The action in response cannot be easily unified. For clarity of code, we should use different catch blocks for each exception.

When an exception occurs, the system tries to match with the type of exception one by one. When it finds a suitably matching catch block, system executes this block. Any further catch blocks are ignored.

Let us study this by a suitable example.

Problem: Write a program to demonstrate multiple catch blocks.

Solution: See Program 19.6.

PROGRAM 19.6 Multiple Catch Blocks I

```
//      ex43.java
class ex43
{ public static void main (String args [] )
   { int A[] ={0,1,2};
     int j,k = 0 ;
     String str ="welcome" ;
     System.out.println("<---ex43.java--->");
     try {
          str = null;    // note 1
          j = str.length();
          System.out.println("string length : "+ j) ;
          k=5 ;
          A[k]=0;
          System.out.println(A[k]);
          }
     catch( NullPointerException e)
          { System.out.println("Exception is caught");
            System.out.println(e.toString());
          }
     catch(ArrayIndexOutOfBoundsException e)
            {  System.out.println("Exception is caught");
               System.out.println(e.toString());
            }
   }
}
```

If you run this program, you will get the following output.

Output

```
<---ex43.java--->
Exception is caught
java.lang.NullPointerException
```

If you comment out line marked note 1, you will get the following output.

Output

```
 <---ex43.java--->
string length : 7
Exception is caught
java.lang.ArrayIndexOutOfBoundsException: 5
```

When we write multiple catch blocks, the exception classes should be independent. If not, they should be properly structured. Let us study the following program before discussing the same.

Problem: Write a program to demonstrate unstructured multiple catch blocks.

Solution: See Program 19.7.

PROGRAM 19.7 Multiple Catch Blocks II

```
//      ex42.java
class ex42
{  public static void main (String args [] )
   {  int A[] ={0,1,2};
      int k = 0 ;
      System.out.println("<---ex42.java--->");
      try {   k=5 ;
              A[k]=0;
              System.out.println(A[k]);
          }
      catch(Exception e)
          {
          }
      catch(ArrayIndexOutOfBoundsException e)
          {  System.out.println("Exception is caught");
             System.out.println(e.toString());
          }
      System.out.println("last line of the program" );
   }
}
```

If you run this program, you will get the following compilation error.

Output

```
Compiling javac ex42.java
ex42.java:14: exception java.lang.ArrayIndexOutOfBoundsException has already
bee
n caught
        catch(ArrayIndexOutOfBoundsException e)
        ^
1 error
press any key to continue
```

Please note the following points:

ArrayIndexOutOfBoundsException is a derivative (sub-subclass) of class Exception. We have stated a rule that exceptions are matched sequentially. Though Exception matches ArrayIndexOutOfBoundsException, such an exception clause will never get executed because exception is caught by earlier catch block. Hence, Java flags it as compilation error.

It is possible for Java developers to ignore such a case, but in certain circumstances, it can mar the real and correct action. This will reduce the quality of a program and also introduce bugs. Hence, this strictness on the part of Java should be appreciated.

After catch block, control flows out to the statement after `try` block. We have not coded any action here. You will appreciate the example if you consider an ATM in place of a bank counter.

19.8 Collection of End of Chapter Programs

19.8.1 Clause finally

Problem: Write a program to show that clause `finally` is executed even when there is no exception.

Solution: See Program 19.8.

PROGRAM 19.8 Clause finally

```
//      ex23a.java
class ex23a
{  public static void main (String args [] )
     {  int num = 20;
        int den = 20 ;
        int result=0;
        System.out.println("--->ex23a.java starts<---");
        try {
               result =   num / den ;
               System.out.println("Just for test");
            }
        catch(Exception e)
           {  System.out.println("Exception is caught");
           }
        finally
          {   System.out.println(
                 "All resources may be released here");
          }
        System.out.println("result is " + result );
     }
}
```

If you run this program, you will get the following output.

Output

```
--->ex23a.java starts<---
Just for test
All resources may be released here
result is 1
```

19.8.2 Number format exception

Earlier, in chapter on Wrapper classes, we studied a method `parseByte(String str)` which returns the byte equivalent of number contained in the string specified by str. It assumes radix 10. This throws NumberFormatException. The reason is that not every string can conforms to a number.

Problem: Write a program to demonstrate NumberFormatException.

Solution: See Program 19.9.

PROGRAM 19.9 NumberFormatException I

```
//        ex35.java
class ex35
{  public static void main (String args [] )
     {  byte num ;
        System.out.println("<---ex35.java--->");
        num = Byte.parseByte("XY");
        System.out.println("num is " + num );
     }
}
```

If you run this program, you will get the following error output.

Output

```
<---ex35.java--->
Exception in thread "main" java.lang.NumberFormatException:
For input string: "XY"
        at java.lang.NumberFormatException.forInputString(Unknown Source)
        at java.lang.Integer.parseInt(Unknown Source)
        at java.lang.Byte.parseByte(Unknown Source)
        at java.lang.Byte.parseByte(Unknown Source)
        at ex35.main(ex35.java:6)
```

Please note that string `XY` does not represent a number in radix 10. Therefore, there is an exception. Had the string been `23`, you would have got the following output.

```
<---ex35a.java--->
num is 23
```

In the aforementioned program, we have not caught the exception. It is known that `parseByte()` is likely to throw the exception. Hence, a better idea is to use a `catch` statement which writes a suitable comment like

```
"parameter is not a valid byte value."
```

on the screen.

Java has large numbers of exceptions. They are organized in deep hierarchy. It is not possible to list all of them here. We have selected few common exceptions for ready reference. Readers are advised to refer to API specifications for complete details.

Table 19.1 lists the important sub-classes of class `Exception`.

Table 19.1 Selected Sub-Classes of Class `Exception`

Exception sub-classes	Description
`AWTException`	Signals AWT exception
`ClassNotFoundException`	Occurs when an application fails to find the class to load
`DataFormatException`	Thrown when data format error occurs

(Continued)

Table 19.1 (*Continued*)

`FontFormatException`	Thrown by create font method
`InterruptedException`	Occurs when thread is interrupted
`IOException`	Input/output exception
`NoSuchFieldException`	Occurs when a class does not have a specified field
`NoSuchMethodException`	Occurs when a class does not have a specified method
`PrinterException`	Indicates exceptional conditions in print system
`RuntimeException`	This is a super-class of the exceptions that gets thrown during normal JVM Operation
`UnsupportedAudioFileException`	Occurs when audio file does not conform to specified format

Table 19.2 describes the various kinds of checked and unchecked exceptions supported in Java. Please note that we have selected only few common exceptions.

Table 19.2 Summary of Checked and Unchecked Exceptions

Exception	Description
Part I The following exceptions are derived from class `RuntimeException`. Therefore, they are **unchecked exceptions.**	
`ArithmeticException`	Thrown when an exceptional arithmetic condition has occurred
`ArrayIndexOutOfBoundsException`	Thrown to indicate that an array has been accessed with an illegal index
`ArrayStoreException`	Thrown to indicate that an attempt has been made to store the wrong type of object into an array of objects
`ClassNotFoundException`	Thrown when an application tries to load in a class through its string name using `The forName` method in class `Class`
`IllegalArgumentException`	Thrown to indicate that a method has been passed an illegal or inappropriate argument
`IllegalMonitorStateException`	Thrown to indicate that a thread has attempted to wait on an object's monitor or to notify other threads waiting on an object's monitor, without owning the specified monitor

(*Continued*)

Table 19.2 (*Continued*)

`IllegalStateException`	Signals that a method has been invoked at an illegal or inappropriate time
`IllegalThreadStateException`	Thrown to indicate that a thread is not in an appropriate state for the requested operation
`IndexOutOfBoundsException`	Thrown to indicate that an index of some sort (such as to an array, to a string, or to a vector) is out of range
`NegativeArraySizeException`	Thrown if an application tries to create an array with negative size
`NullPointerException`	Thrown when an application attempts to use null in a case where an object is required
`NumberFormatException`	Thrown to indicate that the application has attempted to convert a string to one of the numeric types, but that the string does not have an appropriate format
`RuntimeException`	`RuntimeException` is the super-class of those exceptions that can be thrown during the normal operation of the JVM
`SecurityException`	Thrown by the security manager to indicate a security violation
`StringIndexOutOfBoundsException`	Thrown by the `charAt` method in class String and by other string methods to indicate that an index is either negative or greater than or equal to the size of the string
`UnsupportedOperationException`	Thrown to indicate that the requested operation is not supported

Part II

The following exceptions are not the sub-classes of class `RuntimeException`. Therefore, they are **checked exceptions**.

`ClassCastException`	Thrown to indicate that the code has attempted to cast an object to a sub-class, of which it is not an instance.
`InstantiationException`	Thrown when an application tries to create an instance of a class using the `newInstance` method in class `Class`, but the specified class object cannot be instantiated because it is an interface or is an abstract class.

(*Continued*)

Table 19.2 *(Continued)*

`InterruptedException`	Thrown when a thread is waiting, sleeping, or otherwise paused for a long time and another thread interrupts it using the `interrupt` method in class `Thread`.
`NoSuchFieldException`	Signals that the class does not have a field of a specified name
`NoSuchMethodException`	Thrown when a particular method cannot be found
`CloneNotSupportedException`	Thrown to indicate that the `clone` method in class `Object` has been called to clone an object, but that the object's class does not implement the `Cloneable` interface
`IllegalAccessException`	Thrown when an application tries to load in a class, but the currently executing method does not have an access to the definition of the specified class because the class is not public and in another package
`EOFException`	Thrown when an end of file or end of stream has been reached unexpectedly during input
	Thrown when attempt to open the specified file fails

Table 19.3 describes the various kinds of errors supported in Java.

Table 19.3 **Summary of Errors**

`AbstractMethodError`	Thrown when an application tries to call an abstract method
`ClassCircularityError`	Thrown when circularity has been detected while initializing a class
`ClassFormatError`	Thrown when the JVM attempts to read a class `file` and determines that the file is malformed or otherwise cannot be interpreted as a class `file`
`Error`	An error is a sub-class of `Throwable` that indicates serious problems which a reasonable application should not try to catch
`ExceptionInInitializerError`	Signals that an unexpected exception has occurred in a static initializer

(Continued)

Table 19.3 (*Continued*)

`IllegalAccessError`	Thrown if an application attempts to access or modify a field, or to call a method that it does not have an access to
`IncompatibleClassChangeError`	Thrown when an incompatible class change has occurred to some class definition
`InstantiationError`	Thrown when an application tries to use the Java new construct to instantiate an abstract class or an interface
`InternalError`	Thrown to indicate that some unexpected internal error has occurred in the JVM
`LinkageError`	Sub-classes of `LinkageError` indicate that a class has some dependency on another class; however, the latter class has its incompatibly changed after the compilation of the former class
`NoClassDefFoundError`	Thrown if the JVM or a classloader tries to load in the definition of a class (as part of a normal method call or as a part of creating a new instance using the new expression) and no definition of the class is found
`NoSuchFieldError`	Thrown if an application tries to access or modify a specified field of an object, and the object no longer has that field
`NoSuchMethodError`	Thrown if an application tries to call a specified method of a class (either static or instance), and that class no longer has a definition of that method
`OutOfMemoryError`	Thrown when the JVM cannot allocate an object because it is out of memory, and no more memory could be made available by the garbage collector
`StackOverflowError`	Thrown when a stack overflow occurs because an application recurses too deeply
`ThreadDeath`	An instance of ThreadDeath is thrown in the victim thread when the `stop` method with zero arguments in class `Thread` is called
`UnknownError`	Thrown when an unknown but serious exception has occurred in the JVM
`UnsatisfiedLinkError`	Thrown if the JVM cannot find an appropriate native-language definition of a method declared native

(*Continued*)

Table 19.3 (*Continued*)

`UnsupportedClassVersionError`	Thrown when the JVM attempts to read a class `file` and determines that the major and minor version numbers in the file are not supported
`VerifyError`	Thrown when the "verifier" detects that a class `file`, though well formed, contains some sort of internal inconsistency or security problem
`VirtualMachineError`	Thrown to indicate that the JVM is broken or has run out of resources necessary for it to continue operating

Keywords

`ArithmeticException`, `ArrayIndexOutOfBoundsException`, `catch` block, checked exceptions, class `Throwable`, divide by zero exception, `Exception`, finally, `NullPointerException`, `NumberFormatException`, `throw` statement, `throws`, `try` block, unchecked exceptions, user-defined exception

RuleBook

`try`	A `try` block must be followed by a `catch` block. `Catch` block need not be present if `finally` block is present
`finally`	When a `finally` block is present it is always executed irrespective of occurrence of exception
`finally`	A `finally` block is optional
`Exception class`	The root class of all the exception classes is the `Exception` class
`Instantiationexception`	Instantiation exception means an attempt to create an abstract class or interface
Stack overflow `Runtime` exception	Stack overflow is an example of `Runtime` exception
`Exception`	An exception is an abnormal condition that disrupts normal program flow
`throw`	A throw statement causes an exception to be thrown
`throws`	A special clause called throws is used in method "definition" to indicate that a method may possibly throw an exception
checked Exceptions	Only runtime exceptions are checked exceptions, all others are unchecked exceptions.

C++ Corner

It may be noted that `finally` keyword (and the facility thereof) is not present in C++.

Review Questions

1. What do you understand by the term checked exception?
2. What do you understand by the term unchecked exception?
3. Does the control go back to try block, after catch block is executed?
4. What is the advantage of clause `finally`?
5. What is the difference between keywords `throw` and `throws`.
6. List ten different exceptions defined in Java.
7. List any five errors defined in Java.
8. What is the difference between a runtime error and a compile time error? Explain using a suitable example.
9. Write short note on exception handling in Java.
10. Distinguish between error and exception.
11. What are the advantages of exception handling?
12. Explain multiple catch clauses in exception handling.

Exercises

1. Write a program to demonstrate `IndexOutOfBoundsException`.
2. Write a program to demonstrate `NullPointerException`.
3. Write a program to demonstrate `StringIndexOutOfBoundsException`.
4. State whether the following program will compile. If yes, describe the output. If no, give reasons.

```
***********************************************************

//      ex37.java
class ex37
{  public static void main (String args [] )
     {  byte num = 20;
        System.out.println("<---ex37.java starts--->");

        try {
               num = Byte.parseByte("128");
            }
        catch(Exception e) {
                System.out.println("Exception is caught" );
                System.out.println(e);
        };
        System.out.println("num is " + num );
     }
}

***********************************************************
```

5. State whether the following program will compile. If yes, describe the output. If no, give reasons.

```
*************************************************

//   ex52.java
class ex52
{
  public static void main (String args [ ] )
   {
     try
      {
         double x = 0.0;
         throw (new Exception ("Thrown") ) ;
         //return ;  Note 1
      }
     catch (Exception e)
      {
         System.out.println("Exception caught");
         return ;
      }
     finally
         { System.out.println("***finally***"); }
   }
}

*************************************************
```

6. State whether the following program will compile. If yes, describe the output. If no, give reasons.

```
*********************************************************

//      ex3a.java
class  E extends Exception
  { } ;
class ex3a
{  public static void main (String args [] )
     {  int balance = 20;
        int withdraw = 10 ;
        int result;
        System.out.println("--->ex3a.java starts<---");
        result = balance - withdraw ;
        if ( result <  0 ) throw new E() ;
        balance = result;
        System.out.println("balance is " + balance );
     }
}

**********************************************************
```

JAVA APPLETS

Right when computers were invented, programs started running on them. There were stand-alone programs. Then Internet came into existence. In a short time frame, it became popular. The world got transformed into a global village. However, initially, people could see only static text while browsing the Internet. There was no action and no dynamism. There was necessity of the small programs running while browsing. To fulfil this need, Java applets were introduced.

20.1 Applet Basics

Applets are nothing but special tiny programs (applications). They are not supposed to execute independently. They are for embedding inside a web page. As we surf the Internet with help of browsers, the browser will display the web pages. If the page contains an applet, it starts running (inside a browser). These days every browser supports applets. Alternately, we can view them with Java Applet Viewer (tool).

Let us develop the standard Hello World applet.

Problem: Write a Hello World applet.

Solution: See Program 20.1.

PROGRAM 20.1 Applet Hello World

```
//        first.java
import java.applet.*;
import java.awt.*;
public class first extends Applet
   {
      public void paint(Graphics g)
         {
            g.drawString("Hello World" , 30,30);
         }
   }
```

The first step is to write a code. We have written this code in a file named `first.java`. Next we have to compile the code. It will produce a class file named `first.class`. The next step is to write a Hyper Text Markup Language (HTML) file as shown hereafter. We have named the file as `first.html`. However, there is no restriction on the name of this HTML file. It could have been anything else. Only important thing is that parameter code should specify the name of the class which represents the applet, that is `first` in this example.

first.html

```
<applet
code = "first" width =300 height =200 >
</applet>
```

This HTML file is very small. It contains only three pieces of information namely

`code = first`: meaning that the applet class file is `first.class`,

`width = 300`: meaning that width of the applet is 300 pixels, and

`height = 200`: meaning that height of the applet is 200 pixels.

This information is placed in applet tag (<applet> </applet>).

Now we are ready to run our first ever applet. There are two ways to see the applet in action:

Using tool appletviewer provided by Java development kit (JDK).

Using any of the popular browsers.

If you run the applet using applet viewer, you will get following output.

Output

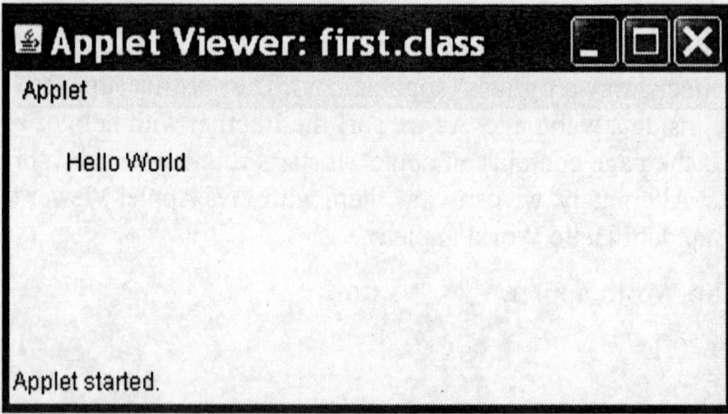

BOX 20.1 Appletviewer

When we develop applets, we would like to test them immediately. Hence, Java has provided this tool. When we use this tool, we do not need any browser. Most of the integrated development environments (IDE) will allow us to use this tool directly (without leaving the environment we are using for development).

From command prompt, running an appletviewer is simple. Issue appletviewer command with HTML file as parameter. For example,

```
d:\some_folder> appletviewer first.html
```

Please note that file `first.html` must be in the current folder. The paths have to be properly set for command operation. In case of any doubt, use full path name for appletviewer like

```
d:\some_folder> d\:jd6\bin\ appletviewer first.html
```

Also note that parameter to appletviewer command is not necessarily an HTML file. It can be any text file. Only requirement is that it should contain applet tag. The tool reads the tag and decides to run the specified applet.

If you like so, you can verify that height and width are as specified in HTML file. If you observe this HTML file through a browser, you will get following output

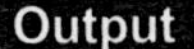

The browser details are not shown in the figure.

20.2 The Applet Class

Earlier we said that applet is a tiny program. Hence, if we see the syntax, it will have some rules common with the applications. First note that just like any application, the file name of `*.java` file matches with the basic class name. In the earlier applet, file is `first.java`. It contains class `First`. Note that it **"extends Applet".**

An applet may override some of the following methods from class `Applet`:

- `init()`
- `start()`
- `stop()`
- `destroy()`

Details of these will be discussed later.

The difference with the application can be noted as absence of method `main()`. The applet class is inherited from component. Hence, to draw the applet on the screen, we override the paint method. The `drawstring` method from graphics class is the only executable statement in the whole applet.

Figure 20.1 shows the hierarchy of class `Applet`.

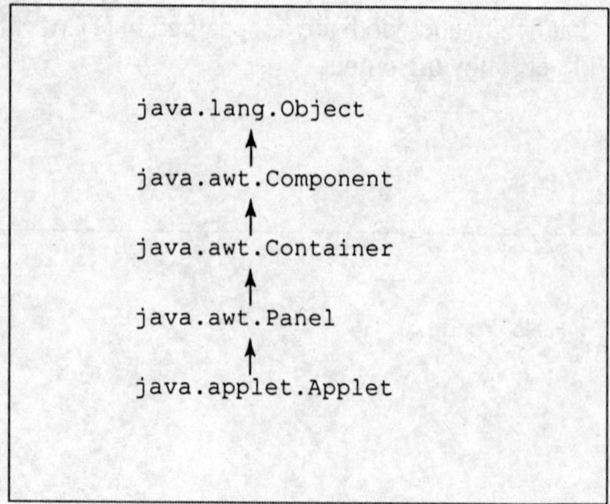

Figure 20.1 **Hierarchy of Class Applet**

20.3 Applet Architecture

From the earlier hierarchy, it is clear that applet is a container for AWT (advanced windows toolkit) objects. At this stage, we have not studied AWT package. We are going to study it in detail later. However, it can be mentioned here that applets will use event-driven model of computing. They will use graphical user interface (GUI).

Let us now specify how an applet can be constructed. Let us say we want to create an applet say `myApplet`.

- We must prepare (write) a class `myApplet`. This should extend (class) `Applet`.
- This must be kept in a file `myApplet.java`.
- There must be a method `paint()` which does the actual job of showing the applet on the screen.
- We may put data elements and methods in an applet.
- Please note that there is no method `main()` in an applet.
- Initialization of variables and other preliminary tasks are to be put in method `init()`.

Short Questions and Answers

Q. What is the difference between "applet" and `Applet`?

A. "applet" is a package while `Applet` is a class in this package.

20.4 Applet Life Cycle

The aforementioned applet was too primitive. It has no data of its own. There was no action. We have not overloaded few important methods in the aforementioned applet. At this stage, let us study the life cycle of the applet. The most important method in class `Applet` is method `init()`. This method is automatically called when the applet is initialized in the beginning. The method `stop()` is executed when the page displaying object is removed from the screen. The method `start()` is executed every time the display of the applet brought back on the screen (it is possible to minimize the page displaying the applet. When the page is again restored, the `start` method is invoked again.)

The method `destroy()` is called just before the web page is closed permanently. Right from the loading of applet till its exit from the browser, an applet passes through various states.

Let us write a program to study applet life cycle.

Figure 20.2 shows the state transition diagram for the applet.

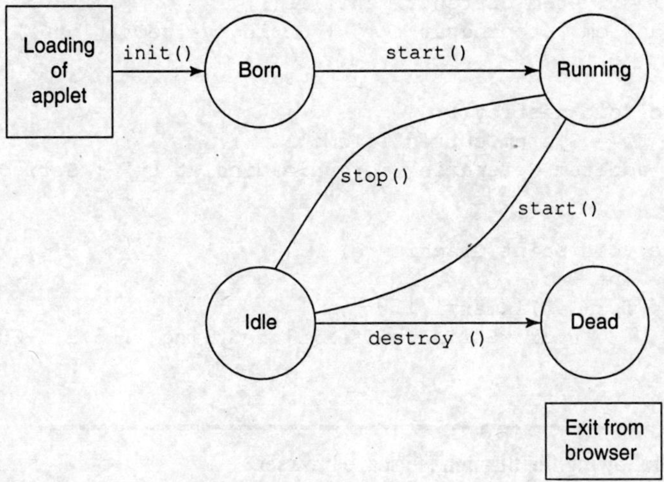

Figure 20.2 State Transition Diagram of Applet Life Cycle

Problem: Write an applet to study applet life cycle.

Solution: See Program 20.2.

PROGRAM 20.2 Demo of Applet Life Cycle

```
//       simple2.java
import java.applet.*;
import java.awt.*;
public class simple2 extends Applet
  {  final int max = 10;
     StringBuffer[] buffer= new StringBuffer[max];
     int i,count =0;
     long t0,t1;
     void addItem(String newWord )
        {    if ( count < max)
             { buffer[count].append(newWord);
               count ++;
             }
        }

     public void init()
        {  for(i=0;i<max;i++)
                 buffer[i] = new StringBuffer("");
           t0 = System.currentTimeMillis();
           addItem( " Executing init() at t = 0 " );
        }
     public void start()
     {  // addItem(" Executing start ");
        t1 = System.currentTimeMillis();
        addItem( " Executing start at t = " + String.valueOf(t1-t0) );
```

```
    }

    public void stop()
      { t1 = System.currentTimeMillis();
        addItem("stoping at t =" + String.valueOf(t1-t0));
      }

    public void destroy()
      {   t1 = System.currentTimeMillis();
          addItem("preparing for unloading.at t=" + String.valueOf(t1-t0));
      }

    public void paint(Graphics g)
        {  int i ;
           for(i=0;i<max;i++)
               g.drawString(buffer[i].toString(), 5, 15+20*i);
        }
   }
```

If we open the following file through Netscape browser,

```
simple2.html
<applet code = "simple2" width =500 height =300 >
</applet>
```

we will get sample output as follows:

Output

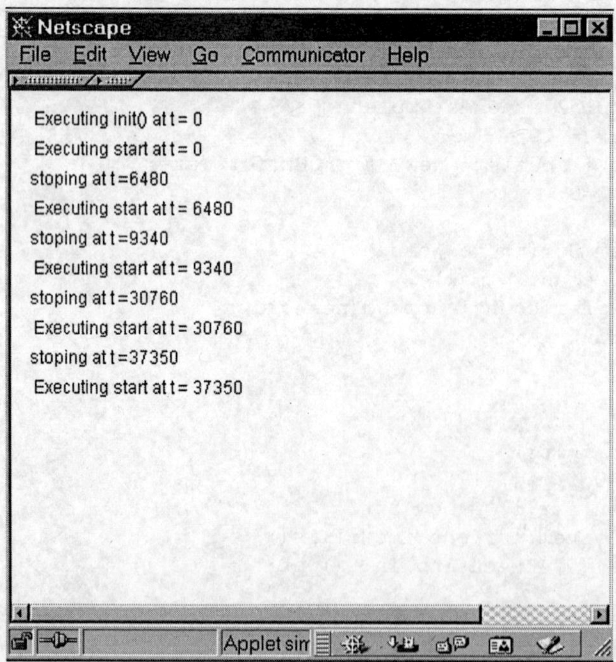

Note that executing `init()` has appeared only once. That is, at the beginning of the applet. Whenever we resize the applet, we get stop and start messages. If we minimize and restore, no action takes place. It indicates that when a web page displaying applet moves on the desktop, first `stop` method is executed. When it settles on a new position on the desktop, it is started again. Simply minimizing does not call for `stop()` method.

Important: The earlier discussion is for older versions of Java. If we compile with JDK 5, we will get slightly different answer. The method `init` will not execute only once. It will be expected every time before start is executed. It also means that there is no great distinction between init and start.

When the applet starts executing for the very first time, method `paint` is called after method `start()`. At a later stage when applet moves (repositioned) on the screen, method `paint()` is called once again. It goes without saying that this also implies the case when we restore an applet from minimized position.

20.5 Comparison of Applet and Application

At this stage, one would like to know the difference between applet and application. Table 20.1 summarizes various points.

Table 20.1 Comparison of Applet and Application

Applications	Applets
Applications are executed by Java compatible virtual machine.	Applets gets automatically loaded and executed by the browser.
Applications may or may not use GUI.	Applets must use GUI supplied by AWT.
Applications need method `main()`. Execution starts with it.	Applets do not need method `main()`. Execution of the applet starts with method `init()`.
Applications can read or write to local disk.	Applets cannot write to local disk.

Please note the last point. Applications must be capable of writing to disk. Otherwise, its usefulness will be practically zero. On the contrary allowing applets to write to local disk is a potential threat to our machine. Applets are embedded in HTML files, which come from millions of unknown sources. They may contain malicious code like viruses, or unintended erroneous code. In either case, our data is at the risk. Hence, Java is right in its design, not allowing access to our (local) disk.

20.6 Setting Font and Changing Style, Size, Type, Foreground and Background Colour

Modern computers (operating systems) support various fonts. We can see the text in various fonts. Any selected font will have different styles, like plain, bold, and italic. Also, fonts can be seen in any colour. Applets allow us to specify and use fonts efficiently and in friendly manner. We have to use method `setFont` from graphics class. Table 20.2 shows few fonts in different sizes and styles.

Table 20.2 Sample Fonts Size and Style

Font name	Font size	Font style	Sample
Arial	16	Plain	I love Java
Arial	20	Bold	**I love Java**
Arial	24	Italic	*I love Java*
Courier	24	Plain	`I love Java`
Verdana	24	Plain	I love Java

Problem: Write an applet to study various fonts.

Solution: We will write a string `I love Java` in various fonts with different sizes and styles (see Program 20.3).

PROGRAM 20.3 Fonts Demo

```
//      font1.java
import java.awt.* ;
import java.applet.* ;
public class  font1 extends Applet
   {  public void paint (Graphics g)
      {  String st1 = new String("I love Java");
         g.setColor(Color.red);
         Font f1 = new Font("Arial"   , Font.PLAIN , 16);
         g.setFont(f1);
         g.drawString(st1,50,50 );
         Font f2 = new Font("Arial"   , Font.BOLD , 20);
         g.setFont(f2);
         g.drawString(st1,50,100 );
         Font f3 = new Font("Arial"   , Font.ITALIC , 24);
         g.setFont(f3);
         g.drawString(st1,50,150 );
         Font f4 = new Font("courier"  , Font.PLAIN , 24);
         g.setFont(f4);
         g.drawString(st1,50,200 );
         Font f5 = new Font("Verdana", Font.PLAIN , 24);
         g.setFont(f5);
         g.drawString(st1,50,250 );
      }
}
```

If you see the applet in Appletviewer or with the help of an HTML file, you will get following output.

Output

I love Java

I love Java

I love Java

I love Java

I love Java

If your system has fancy fonts, you can replace present fonts in Program 20.3 and recompile the program file. Also note that if the system does not have a specific font, it uses some similar font to display the text.

20.7 Using Graphics Methods in Applets

We have studied various methods to draw various shapes like circle, rectangle, line, round-cornered rectangle, and ellipse in Chapter 13 on "Graphics". All these methods can also be used creatively in applets too. Let us study a simple program.

Problem: Write an applet with graphical constructs like line, rectangle, oval, and arc.

Solution: See Program 20.4.

PROGRAM 20.4 Graphics in Applet I

```
//      appgra5.java
//     drawing
import java.awt.* ;
import java.applet.* ;
public class  appgra5 extends Applet
{  public void paint (Graphics g)
      {  g.drawLine(20,20,300,20);
         g.setColor(Color.red);
         g.drawRect(50,30,50,50);
         g.setColor(Color.pink);
         g.draw3DRect(200,30,50,50,true);
         g.setColor(Color.black);
         g.drawOval(60,150,60,40);
         g.setColor(Color.blue);
         g.drawArc(140,150,60,40,0,300);
         g.setColor(Color.green);
         g.fillArc(220,150,60,40,0,300);

      }
}
```

If we open the following file through any browser

Applet `appgra5.html`

```
<applet code="appgra5" width="320"
height="300"></applet>
```

we will get sample output as follows:

Output

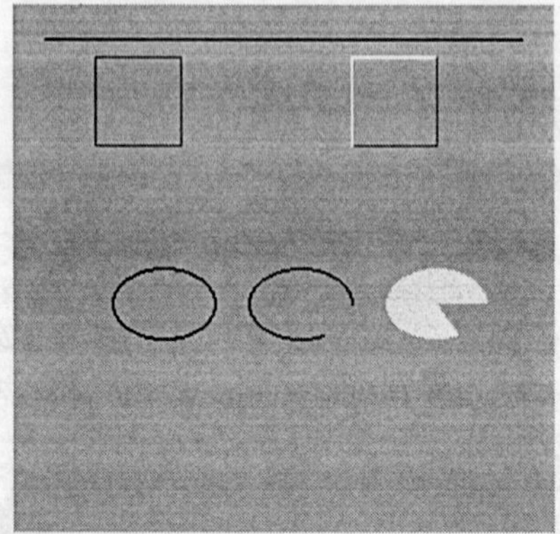

Let us study drawing circles with the help of a simple program. In Chapter 13, we have noted that there is no direct method for drawing circle. We have to use method `drawOval` for this purpose.

Problem: Write an applet to study drawing circles.

Solution: Drawing one circle is simple. However, we can create beautiful figures using circles. Here we will draw 36 circles to create an artistic pattern (see Program 20.5).

PROGRAM 20.5 Circles

```
//     circle1.java
import java.awt.* ;
import java.applet.* ;
class  circle1 extends Applet
   {
     public void init()
      {  setBackground(Color.white);
      }

   public  void delay(long  n)
     { long t1,t2;
       t1 = System.currentTimeMillis();
       t1 = t1 + n;
       t2 = System.currentTimeMillis();
       while ( t2 < t1 )   t2= System.currentTimeMillis();
     }

    public void paint (Graphics g)
      {int k ;
```

```
        int x0=100, y0=100, r1=50;
        int x1 , y1 ;
        double mult = 3.1416 /180.0 ;
        g.setColor( Color.blue  );
        for(k=0; k< 36; k++)
          {  delay(100);
             x1 = (int) Math.ceil( x0 + r1* Math.cos(10.0*mult*k) ) ;
             y1 = (int) Math.floor( y0 + r1* Math.sin(10.0*mult*k) ) ;
             g.drawOval(x1,y1,2*r1,2*r1);
          }
     }
}
```

If we open the following file through any browser

circle1.html

```
<applet code = "circle1" width =500 height =400 >
</applet>
```

We will get following output.

Output

20.8 Colours and Applets

Class `Applet` extents AWT class component. This gives an ability to use colours. Let us study with a simple program, how applet can display any desired colour.

Problem: Write an applet to study various shades of colours.

Solution: We have studied colours in Java earlier in Chapter 13. Let us develop an applet to display various colour shades. Any colour consists of red, green, and blue components, that is three parameters. Unfortunately, our monitor screens and pages of the book are plane, that is two-dimensional. Therefore, it is not possible to show all possible colours on it.

Hence, in this applet we will set one of the three colours say blue to constant value and vary the values of two other colours, that is red and green. This will allow us to display different shades on the monitor screen. We will set colour red on *x*-axis and green on *y*-axis. Let us have a matrix of five by five squares and fill them with various shades (see Program 20.6).

PROGRAM 20.6 colors1.java

```
//      colors1.java
import java.awt.* ;
import java.applet.* ;
public class  colors1 extends Applet
 { public static void delay()
    { double a,b;
      long i,j=300000;
      for(i=0;i<100000;i++)
        { j--;
          a = 2.33 /3.11 ;
        }
    };
  public void paint (Graphics g)
    { int k, line, red, green=0, blue=0 ;
      int x0, y0, x1, y1;
      int xdim =60,ydim = 60 ;
      for(line=0; line<5; line++)
       for(k=0; k<5; k++)
        { g.setColor( new Color(128,128,128) );
          delay();
          x0 = 20 + k * (xdim+20);
          y0= 20+line*(ydim+10);
          g.drawRect(x0, y0, xdim, ydim);
          g.setColor( new Color(k*xdim, line*xdim, blue) );
          g.fillRect(x0, y0, xdim, ydim);
        }
    }
}
```

If we open the following file through any browser

colors1.html

```
<applet code="colors1.class" width=500 height=500
</applet>
```

We will get the following output.

Output

In Program 20.6, red and green colour values are changed using for loop. They are shown here in tabular form.

0,0	0,60	0,120	0,180	0,240
60,0	60,60	60,120	60,180	60,240
120,0	120,60	120,120	120,180	120,240
180,0	180,60	180,120	180,180	180,240
240,0	240,60	240,120	240,180	240,240

Please note that top left colour appears black. It is natural as here all colour components are zero. Bottom right colour appears yellow. When we mix equal red and green, we get shades of yellow depending on the colour value.

20.9 Images in Applet

So far, we have seen text and graphical drawings in an applet. Applets are also able to show images. Java provides an abstract class `Image` in package AWT. To display an image in the applet following points should be noted:

1. The image must be available in the system.
2. The image can be of only certain types like `gif` or `JPG`, but not `bmp`.
3. Method `getImage()` should be used to get image from the system into the applet.
4. The parameter `getDocumentBase()` specifies the URL (i.e. location of the image).
5. The next parameter is the name of the image file.
6. The method `drawImage()` draws the image in the applet.
7. The parameters of this method are
   - image to be drawn,
   - *x* and *y* coordinates of top left corner where the image is to be displayed, and
   - the reference to the component (this).

Problem: Write an application to write an applet with image.

Solution: See Program 20.7.

PROGRAM 20.7 Displaying Image

```
//      image1.java
import java.awt.* ;
import java.applet.* ;

public class image1 extends Applet
   {  Image img;
      String st;
      public void init()
       { setBackground(Color.blue);
```

```
        st = getParameter("imgx");
        img = getImage(getDocumentBase(),st);
      }
    public void paint(Graphics g)
      {  g.drawImage(img,10,10,this);
      } ;
  }
```

If we open the following file through any browser

File image1.html

```
<applet code = "image1" width =420 height =320 >
<param name ="imgx" value ="butterfly.gif">
</applet>
```

we can use the following HTML file `image1.html` shown earlier to view the applet. You will get the following output.

Output

Please note that in this example, image parameter is given name `imgx`. If you like, you could use any other name like `myImage`. Its value is specified as `butterfly.gif`. This is the name of the file on the disk. Also, note the blue colour border. We have not drawn any border ourselves. We have set background colour as blue. Actually, when applet starts the first the rectangular area with specified by width and height parameters is painted by the background colour. Then any further action takes place. You may modify width and height parameters and study yourself.

One possible reason for not supporting `bmp` format is that these files are very large in size. In early days, bandwidth was small. Internet would take very long time to load. Hence, Java allows only those types which store images in a small space (number of bytes).

20.10 Sound in Applets

Applets support sound too. Images and sound together make applets a complete multimedia experience.

We can play audio clips in applet in two different ways. Let us see one of the methods first. In the class `Applet`, there is method `play()`. It accepts two parameters, an URL and a string. In simple terms, it looks for an audio file named by the string in directory suggested by the URL. Then it plays that file once.

Problem: Write an applet to play sound (`*.wav`) files.

Solution: To make a program little interesting we will make eight wav files named sa, re, ga etc. which stores basic notes in it. The ratio of next note to previous note is fixed. The last note (saa) frequency is exactly two times the frequency of first note (sa). This leads to formulae 7th root of 2 for the ratio.

As far as creating sound files, you can record the notes from any musical instrument. Alternately, software like "Audacity" can be used to create notes directly.

We will play them one by one using a `for` loop (see Program 20.8).

PROGRAM 20.8 Sound I

```
//     sound3.java
import java.awt.* ;
import java.applet.* ;
public class  sound3 extends Applet
{  String note[] =
   { "sa.wav", "re.wav", "ga.wav", "ma.wav",
     "pa.wav", "dha.wav", "ni.wav", "saa.wav"};

   public static void delay(int t)
        { long i,j,k=300000;
          for(j=0;j<t;j++)
          for(i=0;i<1000000;i++)
           k--;
        };

    public void paint (Graphics g)
       {  int k ;
         for (k=0; k<8;k++)
           { //g.setColor(Color.blue);
             //g.fillRect(20,20,100,100);
             g.drawString(note[k],20,20+20*k);
             play(getCodeBase(), note[k] );
             delay(280);
           } ;
        }
}
```

We will use the following HTML file.

File sound3.html

```
<applet code="sound3" width="400" height="300"></applet>
```

If you run the applet, you will start hearing notes. Before note is played, file name will appear on the screen. The following is the screen snap shot at the end of the applet.

Output

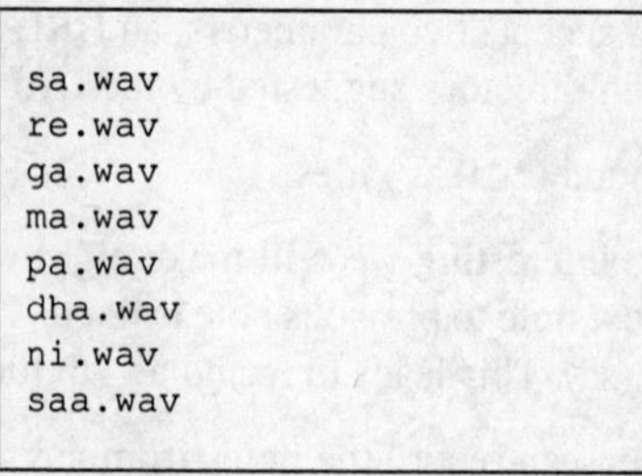

This program has its drawbacks too. The delay must be properly estimated. Large delay will mean lot of pause between notes. Small delay will results in second note starting before first note ends. In that case, two notes play simultaneously.

English music uses what is known as Equally Tempered scale. Here octaves remain as before but 11 notes are introduced between them, the intervals being made equal and each 12√2, that is 1.0595. The London International Conference of May 1939 agreed that the international standard for concert pitch should be based on 440 for the treble A, that is 264 for middle C'. With this, the frequency table becomes as shown in Table 20.3.

Table 20.3 **Equally Tempered Scale**

Note	Frequency
C'	261.6
C#	277.2
D	293.7
D#	311.1
E	329.6
F	349.2
F#	370
G	392
G#	415.3
A	440
A#	466.2
B	493.9
C''	523.3

Can you modify Program 20.8 using these notes?

A better alternative to work with sound is to use `AudioClip` interface. It helps us playing a sound clip.

Problem: Write an applet to use alternative method for playing sound.

Solution: We will declare an `AudioClip` say my`Clip` and initialize with the method

```
getAudioClip(getCodeBase(), st1);
```

In this program, instead of separate files, we will use another file named `saregal.wav`. This file contains all the eight tones. (You are free to use any available sound file instead.) We will define a string depending upon whether the file is found or not. Then first we will display the string and next keep on repeatedly playing (looping) the sound clip (see Program 20.9).

PROGRAM 20.9 Sound II

```
//     sound4.java
import java.applet.*;
import java.awt.*;
public class sound4 extends Applet
{   String s1 = "Found", s2 = "NOT Found", s3;
    String st1  = "saregal.wav";
   AudioClip myClip;
    public void init()
     {   myClip =    getAudioClip(getCodeBase(), st1 );
         if (myClip == null) s3 =s2;
         else s3 = s1;
     }
    public void paint(Graphics g)
      {  g.drawString(s3,20,20);
      }
     public void start()
       {   myClip.loop();
       }
};
```

The following file is used to run the applet.

sound4.html

```
<applet code="sound4" width="300" height="200"></applet>
```

When you run the applet, you will get the following screen. You also get repeated play of the clip.

Output

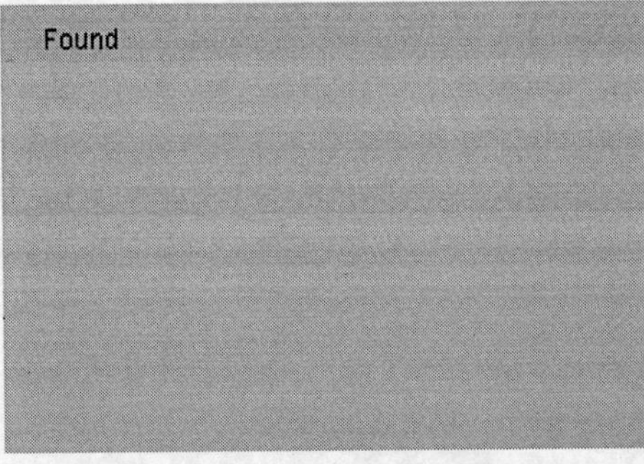

You will ask me what advantage you get by the second method (using `AudioClip`). First you will note that we are getting automatic looping. Though we have not shown in this example, it is possible to play the clip only once. It is also possible to stop the clip while running.

However, to display all these aspects we will need buttons or some other GUI components.

20.11 Applet Tag Attributes

Table 20.4 indicates the various attributes of applet tag. They help in positioning the applet on the web page.

Table 20.4 Applet Tag Attributes

Attribute	Description
CODE	We have to set this attribute as name of the class file which contains applet.
CODEBASE	We have to specify the URL of the directory where applet is present. If applet is in same directory as HTML file this attribute need not be specified.
WIDTH	For reserving horizontal space (width) on the HTML page.
HEIGHT	For reserving vertical space (height) on the HTML page.
NAME	To help other applets on the page to communicate we may specify a name.
ALIGN	To align the applet on the page we can specify one of the following values: TOP, BOTTOM, LEFT, RIGHT, MIDDLE, ABSMIDDLE, ABSBOTTOM, TEXTTOP, and BASELINE.
HSPACE	Used to specify horizontal space in pixels. Valid only if attribute align is set to left or right.
VSPACE	Used to specify vertical space in pixels. Valid only if attribute align is set top or bottom.
ALT	The specified text is displayed when the browser displaying the page is a NON-Java browser.

20.12 JAR Files

Java provides us an excellent utility called JAR. Actually, JAR stands for Java ARchive. It is a platform-independent file format. It allows us to bundle many files together. There is another aspect to it. If required we can use compression too.

You will ask me what the use of this facility in applets is. When an applet needs few images, sound, and other files, these files have to flow in the Internet. If there is only one file instead of many, moving becomes simple. If the file is compressed it takes less time. In either way, there is benefit of using JAR files.

The general form of JAR command is

```
cmd prompt>jar options jar_filename list_of_files
```

Table 20.5 displays various options for the JAR command.

Table 20.5 JAR Command Options

-c	create new archive
-t	list table of contents for archive
-x	extract named (or all) files from archive
-u	update existing archive
-v	generate verbose output on standard output
-f	specify archive file name
-m	include manifest information from specified manifest file
-0	store only; use no ZIP compression
-M	Do not create a manifest file for the entries
-C	change to the specified directory and include the following file

Consider a case of previous applet sound4. The applet uses one more file `saregal.wav`. Now we can club the `sound4.class` and `saregal.wav` in one bundle. Let us try to use our knowledge of JAR to this applet.

To be on safer side, let us first create a new directory named `jar1`. Now we will copy both `sound4.class` and `saregal`.wav to this directory. Let us assume that we are in this directory called jar1. From this directory we issue following command:

```
command prompt > jar cf asound.jar sound4.class saregal.wav
```

It will create a JAR file named `asound.jar`. This JAR file contains both files `sound4.class` and `saregal.wav`. For this demonstration, we will create a new HTML file called `asound.html`. In this file we have to set archive attribute to `asound.jar`. It will tell the browser that this JAR file supplies the necessary files. The HTML file will be as follows:

File `asound.html`

```
<applet code="sound4.class" archive="asound.jar"
width="150"
height="150"></applet>
```

If we browse this HTML file, we will get same output as we have got in earlier case with file `sound4.html`. Please note that when browser runs file `asound.html` it needs the file `asound.jar`. When this file is available in current directory, browser does not need any other files separately, not even `sound4.class`. Reason is simple. All the needed files are contained in a JAR.

20.13 Introduction to HTML

So far we have used HTML files without discussing them. This is the right time to study HTML files. HTML stands for Hyper Text Markup Language. We mark the text with the help of tags. This decides how the text is displayed in the browser.

Table 20.6 HTML Tags

<HTML>	This tag specifies that the contents are in HTML format.
<HEAD>	This tag specifies main heading on the page.
<TITLE>	Text marked with this tag is displayed in the title bar of the browser.
<BODY>	Signifies the body of the text. Applet tag is inside this tag
<H1 tag>	Declares that text should be displayed in Header1 format. There can be up to six header formats.
<CENTER>	Puts the text in the centre of the page.
<APPLET>	The applets (discussed in this chapter) are to be put in this tag.
<PARAM>	User defined parameters. Optional.
<B>	Displays the text in bold
 	Signifies line break
<P>	Specifies a paragraph. Paragraph always starts on a new line. No end tag is necessary for this tag.
<IMG>	Specifies image.
<HR>	Marks a horizontal line.
<FONT>	Used to specify a font.
<! ...>	This is a comment. It is ignored by the browser.

Let us prepare a small text file. Then add few tags to it and convert it into an html file.

HTML file demo1.html

```
<TITLE> *** HTML Demo ***</TITLE>
<body>
<h1> H1:Text is displayed in Header1 format. </h1>
<h2> H2: There can be up to six header formats.</h2>
HTML :This tag specifies that the contents are in HTML format.<br>
TITLE:Text marked with this tag is displayed in the title bar of the
browser.<br>
BODY :Signifies the body of the text. Applet tag is inside this tag
<center>This text in the center of the page.</center>
APPLET :The applets (discussed in this chapter) are to be put in this
tag.<br>
PARAM : user defined parameters. Optional.<br>
<b>B : Displays the text in Bold </b><br>
<p>
```

```
BR: Signifies Line-break<br> P : Specifies a paragraph.
Paragraph always start on a new line.<br>
No end tag is necessary for this tag. IMG : Specifies Image.<br>
HR : Marks a horizontal line.<br>
<HR>
<font face="Courier New">
FONT : Courier new is used to specify a font</font><br>
<! This is a comment. It is ignored by the Browser.>
</body>
```

If you watch the file through the browser you will get the following display.

Output

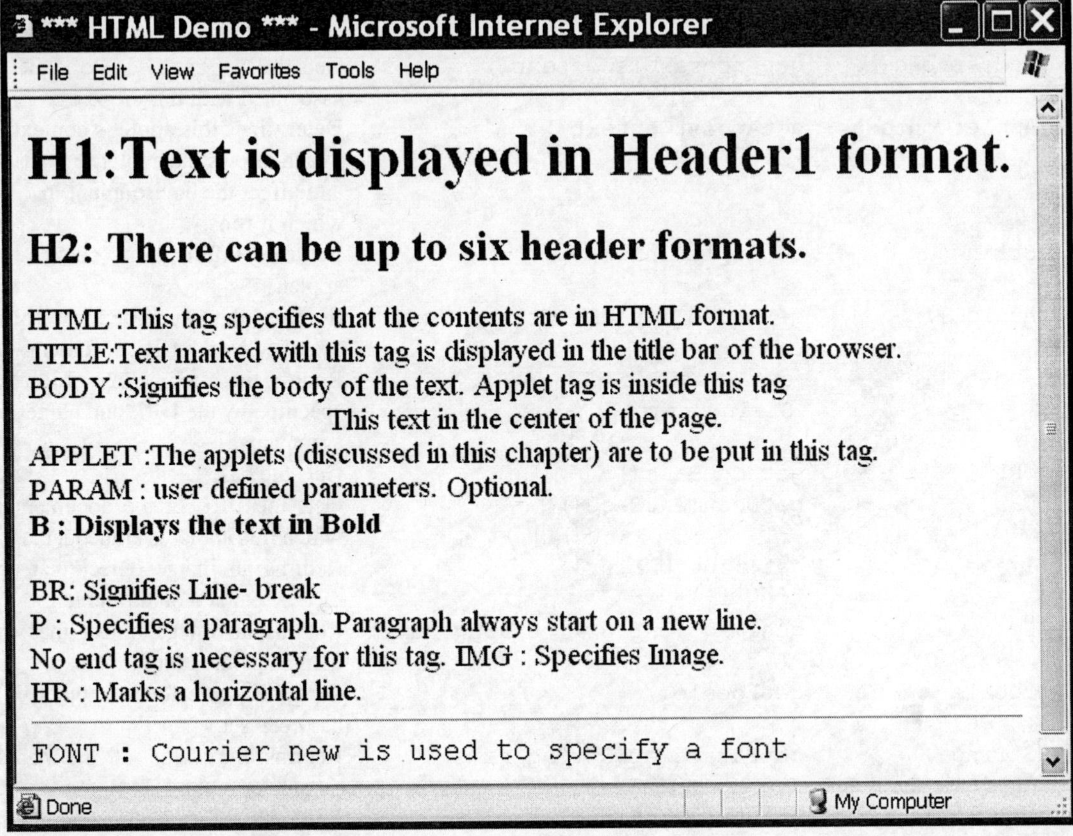

In the output you may note following points:

1. Please note *** HTML Demo *** in the title bar.
2. Header1 is very big.
3. Header2 is big.
4. Display text in Bold.

5. Paragraph on new line.
6. Horizontal line running throughout the page.
7. font "Courier New" in the last line.
8. The comment is ignored by the browser.

Table 20.7 displays useful methods from class `Applet`.

Table 20.7 Method Summary: Class `Applet`

`void`	`destroy()`	Called by the browser or applet viewer to inform this applet that it is being reclaimed and that it should destroy any resources that it has allocated.
`AccessibleContext`	`getAccessibleContext()`	Gets the `AccessibleContext` associated with this `Applet`.
`AppletContext`	`getAppletContext()`	Determines this applet's context, which allows the applet to query and affect the environment in which it runs.
`String`	`getAppletInfo()`	Returns information about this applet.
`AudioClip`	`getAudioClip(URL url)`	Returns the `AudioClip` object specified by the URL argument.
`AudioClip`	`getAudioClip(URL url, String name)`	Returns the `AudioClip` object specified by the URL and name arguments.
`URL`	`getCodeBase()`	Gets the base URL.
`URL`	`getDocumentBase()`	Gets the URL of the document in which this applet is embedded.
`Image`	`getImage(URL url)`	Returns an image object that can then be painted on the screen.
`Image`	`getImage(URL url, String name)`	Returns an image object that can then be painted on the screen.
`Locale`	`getLocale()`	Gets the locale for the applet, if it has been set.
`String`	`getParameter(String name)`	Returns the value of the named parameter in the HTML tag.
`String[][]`	`getParameterInfo()`	Returns information about the parameters that are understood by this applet.
`void`	`init()`	Called by the browser or applet viewer to inform this applet that it has been loaded into the system.

(Continued)

Table 20.7 *(Continued)*

boolean	`isActive()`	Determines if this applet is active.
static AudioClip	`newAudioClip(URL url)`	Get an audio clip from the given URL.
void	`play(URL url)`	Plays the audio clip at the specified absolute URL.
void	`play(URL url, String name)`	Plays the audio clip given the URL and a specifier, that is relative to it.
void	`resize(Dimension d)`	Requests that this applet be resized.
void	`resize(int width, int height)`	Requests that this applet be resized.
void	`setStub(AppletStub stub)`	Sets this applet's stub.
void	`showStatus(String msg)`	Requests that the argument string be displayed in the "status window".
void	`start()`	Called by the browser or applet viewer to inform this applet that it should start its execution.
void	`stop()`	Called by the browser or applet viewer to inform this applet that it should stop its execution.

Keywords

ALIGN, ALT, applet, APPLET, applet life cycle, applet tag, Applet Viewer, `AudioClip` interface, BODY, Bold, BR, CENTRE, CODE, CODEBASE, Color, `destroy()`, `drawImage()`, FONT, fonts, `getAudioClip`, `getDocumentBase()`, HEIGHT, HR, HSPACE, HTML, image, IMG, `init()`, italic, JAR, NAME, P, PARAM, Plain, `play()`, sound, `start()`, `stop()`, TITLE, URL, VSPACE, WIDTH

RuleBook

class `Applet`	The `Applet` class must be the super class of any applet, that is to be embedded in a web page or viewed by the Java Applet Viewer.
applet writing to disk	Java does not allow applets to write to local disk.
applet `main()`	Applets do not need a `main()` method.
applet `i/o`	User I/O is NOT accomplished with Java's stream I/O classes
applet `i/o`	User I/O is accomplished with AWT or swing objects
Java-compatible browser	Applets should be run under a Java-compatible browser.
Initialization	Initialization can happen only ones in the applets lifetime. However, currently this rule has changed.

web page	To change Web Page background colours you use the BG COLOR attribute in the <BODY> tag.
APPLET tag	The APPLET tag is used to start an applet from both an HTML document and from an applet viewer.

C++ Corner

The concept of applets has been introduced for the first time in Java. Hence, there is no equivalence of it C++.

Review Questions

1. What is an applet?
2. What are the two different ways to see applets in action?
3. Explain the steps needed in developing and testing applets.
4. Describe the applet life cycle.
5. Describe the use of PARAM tag.
6. Distinguish between Java applets and Java applications.
7. Write a short note on applet architecture.

Exercises

1. Write an applet which draws a human face with few ovals and arcs.
2. Write an applet which displays a given string in blinking manner.
3. Write a program to roll (horizontally) a given string.
4. Write an applet with background consisting of randomly coloured pixels.

EVENT HANDLING AND AWT

Older computing models revolved about the console input and output. In modern days we (most of the time) use GUI and various components like buttons, scroll bars, and textboxes. Programming model has also changed to event-driven programming. It has made events very important. In this chapter, we will be studying events and event handling.

Events are strongly associated with components. It will not be prudent to study event handling without studying the components. For this purpose, we have to get familiar to components. This requires that we study a very useful package called Advanced Window Toolkit known by the acronym "AWT".

As of today, Java recommends using swing package for GUI. The majority of components are redefined (with prefix J) in swing. We will be discussing those components in detail in a chapter on swing. To avoid duplication, we have kept the discussion on AWT very brief. It may also be noted that only few classes like color are present only in AWT.

21.1 Abstract Window Toolkit

Java offers to its users a package called Abstract Window Toolkit.

This package contains all of the classes for creating user interfaces and for supporting graphics and images. A user-interface object such as a button or a scrollbar is called a component in AWT terminology. The `Component` class is the root of all AWT components.

Direct-known sub-classes are listed as follows:

```
Box.Filler,    Button,         Canvas,        Checkbox,
Choice,        Container,      Label,         List,
Scrollbar,     TextComponent
```

To hold these components, we need a container. For this purpose, a class known as container is defined in Java AWT package. The container allows us to position the components it contains.

The sub-class of container known as panel is very useful. We can imagine a panel as a sort of screen component. It may be noted that it is a super-class of class `Applet`. Method `add()` is defined to add components to a panel.

Another sub-class of container is `Window`. An object of this is a top-level window with no borders and menu bar. The default layout for a window is BorderLayout. A window must have a frame, dialog, or another window defined as its owner when it is constructed. This is the reason why we normally do not use this class directly and use a class known as `Frame`.

We have studied a class called `Frame` earlier in Chapter 13 on "Graphics". We will use this class `Frame` to hold the components. Frame is the main class of our program when we want to use GUI for our programs. Figure 21.1 describes the hierarchy of the components.

Class `Canvas` is a sub-class of class `Component`. It is useful for drawing. It is a rectangular area. For better results, we are advised to sub-class it and then use. It goes without saying that we override its `paint` method.

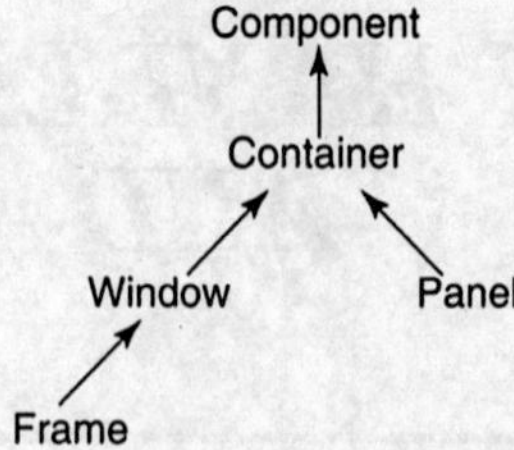

Figure 21.1 Class Hierarchy

With this much introduction, we are in a position to enter a new world. So far, our programming was console based. Now we are entering GUI-based programming. There are two main changes to be noticed.

1. The display is no more monochrome text screen. It is colourful and capable of showing images as well as text in various fonts.
2. The programming model changes to event-driven programming. The events decide the flow of the program.

Let us start our study with a simple component `Button`.

21.1.1 Using Button

Button is an important GUI component. It is supposed to trigger some specific action. When we click the button, it appears to have been pressed. Let us study it with a program.

Problem: Write a program to study `Button`.

Solution: See Program 21.1.

PROGRAM 21.1 Study of button

```
//      button1.java

import java.awt.* ;
import java.awt.event.* ;
class button1 extends Frame implements ActionListener
   {  Button bt1 ;
      public button1()
          {  super("***button1***") ;
             setSize(400,300);
             bt1 = new Button ("Quit");
             add(bt1);
             bt1.addActionListener(this);
             setLayout(new GridLayout() ) ;
             setVisible(true);
          }
      public void actionPerformed(ActionEvent ev)
          {  String st = ev.getActionCommand();
         if    ( st.equals("Quit") )
                {  System.exit(0);
                }
          }
```

```
    public static void main( String args[])
        {   button1 bt1 = new button1();
        }
}
```

If you run this program, you will see the following window.

Output

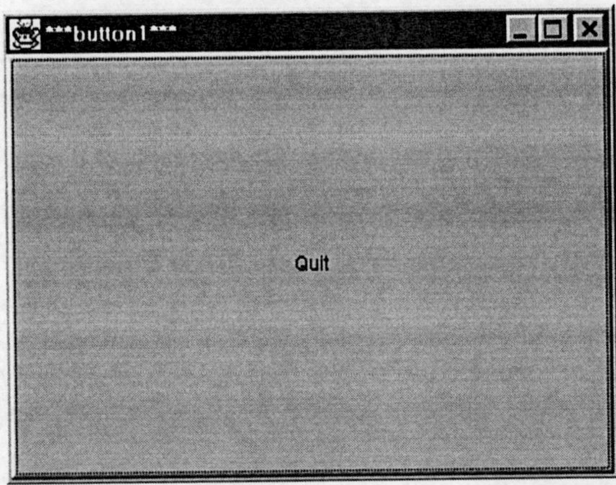

If you click on the button, the program will get closed. The reason is when we click the button, action `event` takes place. It is recognized as the quit command. The action set for this command is `System.exit(0);`. It closes the application.

21.1.2 Using TextField

The component for writing single line text is `TextField`. We can write a text at the time of initialization through constructor. At a later stage, we can use `setText()` method.

Text fields can be used for both input and output. We can type in text in the text field. Alternately, we can display some text in it. For typing in the `TextField`, we must first click it with a mouse. It brings this component in focus and a cursor appears in it. Now, we can type in our text.

Problem: Write a program to study `TextField`.

Solution: In this program, we will use one `TextField` as input and the other for output (see Program 21.2).

PROGRAM 21.2 TextField

```
//      textfil.java
//    implements textfield

import java.awt.* ;
import java.awt.event.* ;
//import java.awt.Toolkit ;
//import javax.swing.* ;

class textfil extends Frame implements ActionListener
```

```
{ TextField tx1,tx2;
  Button bt1 ;
  public textfil()
      {   super(" text field demo") ;
          setSize(400,300);
          tx1 = new TextField(20) ;
          add(tx1);
          tx1.setText("");
          tx2 = new TextField(25) ;
          add(tx2);
          bt1 = new Button ("copy"); // note 1
          add(bt1);
          bt1.addActionListener(this);
          setLayout(new GridLayout() ) ; // note 2
          setVisible(true);
      }
  public void actionPerformed(ActionEvent ev)
  {   String st = ev.getActionCommand();
        if ( st.equals("copy") ) // note 3
          {   tx2.setText(tx1.getText());
          }
  }
  public static void main( String args[])
  {       textfil t1 = new textfil();
  }
}
```

When we run the program, we have to type something in the leftmost `TextField`. If we type "Hello World" and then press copy button, "Hello World" will be copied in the second `TextField`. We will get the following output. We have used grid layout in this program. We will discuss Layouts in detail in Chapter 22 on "Swing".

Output

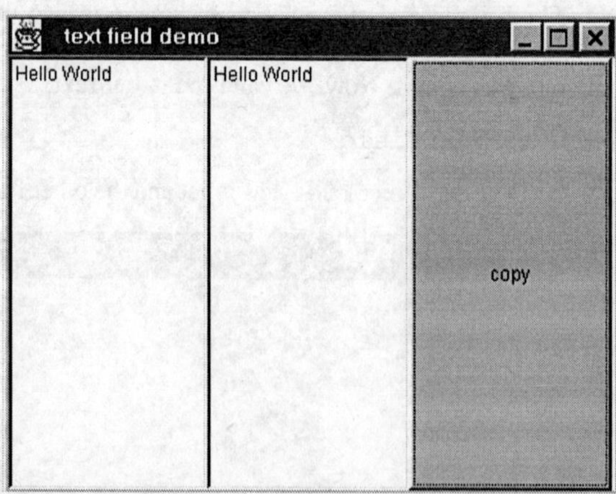

Please note the line marked note1. This creates a button with name "copy". Mark the line note3. This checks whether the action command is `copy`.

21.1.3 Using checkbox

The component checkbox comes handy when user has to select zero or more choices. When we click a checkbox, it is marked. A small check symbol appears in the box. If we click once again, it becomes unmarked. Let us try a small program.

Problem: Write a program to study checkbox.

Solution: In this program, we will define a checkbox. To put up a simple application, we will test this checkbox in a loop. We will terminate the application the moment checkbox is found marked (see Program 21.3).

PROGRAM 21.3 Checkbox

```
//      cb1
//      program stops after box is checked.
import java.awt.*;
class myFrame extends Frame
  {   Checkbox b1 ;
      public myFrame()
          {   super("***check box demo***") ;
              setSize(400,300);
              b1 = new Checkbox("abc");
              add(b1);
              setVisible(true);
          }
  }
class cb1
  {   public static void main( String args[])
          {   boolean flag = false;
              myFrame fm = new myFrame();
              while (flag == false) // this loop waits
                  {   flag = fm.b1.getState();
                  }
              if (flag == true) System.exit(0);
          } ;
  };
```

If you run this program, you will see the following window.

Output

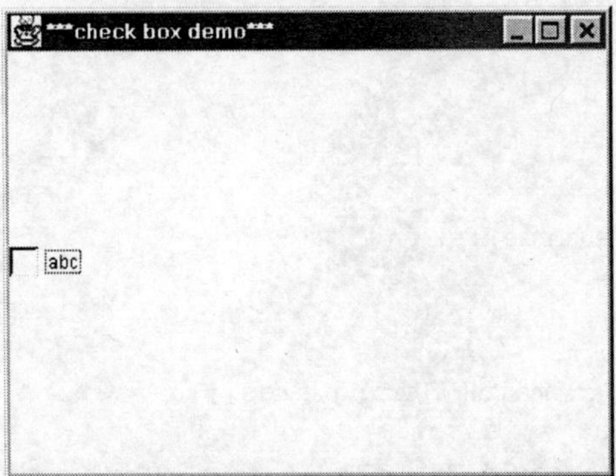

If you check the box (i.e. click it with mouse) named `abc`, the program will end. In this program, we are using a continuous loop to check the flag. The flag is set when the box is checked. In effect, this ends the program.

21.1.4 Using radio button

Radio buttons are groups of buttons. By convention, we can select only one button at a time. The concept of radio buttons is similar to checkboxes except one difference. By convention, there are no limits as to how many items can be selected at a time in case of checkboxes.

It is interesting to note that there is no component named as radio button. The general name checkbox is used for it. Java defines a class named `CheckboxGroup`. Checkboxes added in the group are nothing but radio buttons. Also note that the shape of a radio button is circular while that of a checkbox is square.

Problem: Write a program to study radio buttons.

Solution: In this program, we will loop till button C is selected. A method `getState()` tells us whether a radio button is selected or not (see Program 21.4).

PROGRAM 21.4 Radio Button

```
//      rb1
//      program stops after
//      box c is checked.

import java.awt.*;

class myFrame extends Frame
{
      CheckboxGroup g1 ;
      Checkbox a,b,c;
      static String AString = "A";
      static String BString = "B";
      static String CString = "C";

      public myFrame()
         {    super("***radio button demo***") ;
              setSize(400,300);
              setLayout( new GridLayout (3,1) ) ;
              g1 = new CheckboxGroup();
              a  = new Checkbox(AString, g1, true);
              b  = new Checkbox(BString, g1, false);
              c  = new Checkbox(CString, g1, false);

              add(a);
              add(b);
              add(c);
              setVisible(true);
         }
}
class rb1
  {   public static void main( String args[])
         {   boolean flag = false;
              myFrame fm = new myFrame();
```

```
            while (flag == false) // this loop waits
                {   flag = fm.c.getState();
                }
            if (flag == true) System.exit(0);
        } ;
    };
```

If you run this program, you will see the following window.

Output

When we select button "C", the program terminates.

21.1.5 Using canvas

As the name suggests, it is a component to draw things on. Earlier, we have drawn on the frame itself. Canvas is the most appropriate component to draw things on. To use it, we have to define a class which extends class `Canvas`. We should define method `paint` for this class. Whenever we want to refresh this canvas, we have to call the method `paint()`.

Problem: Write a program to study class `canvas`.

Solution: In this program, we will use a canvas to draw a filled rectangle. We will define a button such that every click will increase the size of the rectangle by five pixels (see Program 21.5).

PROGRAM 21.5 Canvas

```
//    canvas1.java

import java.awt.* ;
import java.awt.event.* ;

class myCanvas extends Canvas
  {   static int x1 =30, y1= 30,x2 =50,y2=50;

      public void paint(Graphics g)
```

```
        {   g.setColor(Color.green );
            g.fillRect(x1,y1,x2,y2);
        }
      public void inc()
      {   x2=x2+5; y2 =y2+5;
          paint( getGraphics());
      };
   }
class canvas1 extends Frame implements ActionListener
   {  myCanvas c1 ;
      Button b1;
      public canvas1()
        {   super(" ***canvas1*** ") ;
            setSize(400,300);
            c1 = new myCanvas();
            add(c1);
            b1 =new Button("button");
            add(b1);
            b1.addActionListener(this);
            setLayout(new GridLayout() ) ;
            setVisible(true);
      }
   public void actionPerformed(ActionEvent ev)
      {   String st = ev.getActionCommand();
          if ( st.equals("button") )
            { c1.inc();
            }
      }
   public static void main( String args[])
     { canvas1 c = new canvas1();
     }
}
```

If you run this program and click the button four to five times, you will see the following output.

Output

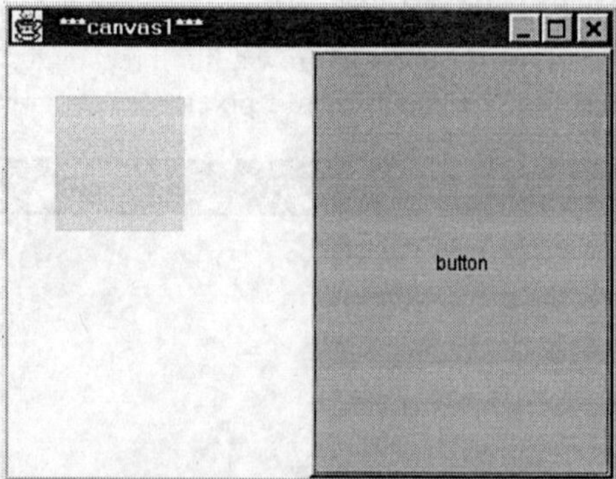

The most interesting point is that when you click the button, the size of the square increases by five pixels.

21.2 Event Handling

Events can be separated in two groups: higher-level events and lower-level events. The events generated by AWT components can be considered as higher-level events. Events generated by hardware devices like keyboard and mouse can be called lower-level events. Let us start our study with AWT component events.

Whenever we click a checkbox or click a button or type a key in a text field, an event occurs. This generates an object of a particular class. The system (or simply the application) transmits this object to those objects which have registered to receive this object.

Once this event object is received, the `actionPerformed` method is executed. A properly coded method takes appropriate action.

Let us have a close look at our program `button1.java`. Only relevant lines are reproduced for ready reference.

```
//     button1.java
import java.awt.event.* ;
class button1 extends Frame implements ActionListener
bt1.addActionListener(this);
public void actionPerformed(ActionEvent ev)
String st = ev.getActionCommand();
if ( st.equals("Quit") ){ System.exit(0)};
```

The statement

```
class button1 extends Frame implements ActionListener
```

tells the program that class `button1` wants to listen to events.

```
bt1 = new Button ("Quit");
bt1.addActionListener(this);
```

This statement creates an object of type button. It is labelled as `Quit`.

Whenever a button bt1 is clicked, an event object is generated. This object carries the string `Quit` with it. As the event occurs, it is notified to the class `button1`. Its method `actionPerformed` is executed. The first step of this method is to identify the event. This is done by the following statement:

```
st = ev.getActionCommand();
```

When it is executed and event is clicking of button bt1, st gets the value `Quit`.

Once we identify the event, an appropriate action can be easily taken. In this case, it is quitting the program.

Short Questions and Answers

Q. When is an event generated?

A. An event is generated on clicking an AWT component. When we press a key on the keyboard or click a mouse, an event is generated.

Q. What is an event object?

A. Java being a highly object-oriented language creates an object of an appropriate class, whenever an event occurs.

Q. To whom is this object delivered?

A. All the classes that have registered to listen to this event get this event.

Q. What happens then?

A. The classes registering for events have a defined method `actionPerformed` which gets executed.

21.2.1 Delegation event model

Applications based on GUI are a bit different from ordinary console applications. A typical GUI application will have many different AWT components. Different events occur in an application. It is possible that every event reaches every component. But it will be a sheer waste of time and energy. Hence, a mechanism exists such that certain events reach only certain components. To achieve this, components tell the application which events they should be notified. These components will take cognizance of these events in their method `actionPerformed`. Components will not be delivered events in which they are not interested. The application will delegate events only as per the previously declared policy. This is known as the delegation event model. It may be noted that one event can be delegated to more than one component. See Box 21.1 for more details about event class in Java 1.0.

BOX 21.1 Events in Java 1.0

Event is a platform-independent class that encapsulates events from the platform's GUI in the Java 1.0 event model. In Java 1.1 and later versions, the class `Event` is maintained only for backwards compatibility. In the text, we have used more powerful classes provided in later versions.

21.2.2 Event classes and event listener interfaces

Package `java.awt.event` provides interfaces and classes for dealing with different types of events fired by AWT components. The `java.awt.AWTEvent` class describes the AWT event model in detail. Events are fired by event sources. An event listener registers with an event source to receive notifications about the events of a particular type. This package defines events and event listeners, as well as event listener adapters, which are convenience classes to make the process of writing event listeners easier.

The following is a list of classes from Package `java.awt.event`.

```
ActionEvent,                  AdjustmentEvent,
AWTEventListenerProxy,        ComponentAdapter,
ComponentEvent,               ContainerAdapter,
ContainerEvent,               FocusAdapter,
FocusEvent,                   HierarchyBoundsAdapter,
HierarchyEvent,               InputEvent,
InputMethodEvent,             InvocationEvent,
ItemEvent,                    KeyAdapter,
KeyEvent,                     MouseAdapter,
MouseEvent,                   MouseMotionAdapter,
MouseWheelEvent,              PaintEvent,
TextEvent,                    WindowAdapter,
WindowEvent,
```

Interfaces defined in Package `java.awt.event` are given at the end of the chapter.

So far we have discussed the events generated by the components. Input devices like the keyboard and mouse also generate events. These events are termed as low-level events. Let us have a close look at events generated by these devices.

21.2.3 KeyEvent

To work with keyboard, Java offers a class known as KeyEvent. Many text components generate this event when we press a key.

Those who have a little hardware knowledge will know that when we actually type a key, three different actions occur. First, the key is pressed; it remains in that stage for sometime and is then released.

To take cognizance of this event, keyListener interface has to be used. This interface has three methods:

```
keyTyped()
keyPressed()
keyReleased()
```

These methods are invoked when the corresponding action takes place. It goes without saying that a programmer has to define these methods as they are declared in an interface.

Problem: Write a program to study keyboard events.

Solution: In this program, we will use KeyListener interface. It requires us to define methods keyTyped, keyPressed, and keyReleased. The actions of these three methods will be displayed in separate lines. Whenever we press and release a key, we will get corresponding key code and print in a specific line. When our actions will invoke a keyTyped method, we will put the corresponding character in the line.

PROGRAM 21.6 Key Demo I

```
//   key1.java
import java.awt.* ;
import java.awt.event.* ;

class myFrame extends Frame implements KeyListener
  {  public static String str1 = "", str2 ="", str3="" ;
     public static Graphics myG ;
     public myFrame()
        {  super("***key1***") ;
           setSize(500,350);
           setVisible(true);
           myG = getGraphics() ;
        }
     public void keyTyped(KeyEvent ke)
        {  char ch; // int n ;
           ch = ke.getKeyChar();
           str1 = str1 + ch ;
           myG.drawString(str1,50,100);
        }
     public void keyPressed(KeyEvent ke)
        {  int n;
           n = ke.getKeyCode() ;
           str2 = str2 + n +" ";
           myG.drawString(str2,50,200);
        }
  public void keyReleased(KeyEvent ke)
     {  int n;
        n = ke.getKeyCode() ;
```

```
        str3 = str3 + n + " ";
        myG.drawString(str3,50,300);
    }
  public void paint(Graphics myG)
    {   addKeyListener(this);
        Font f1 = new Font("Arial" , Font.BOLD , 20);
        myG.setFont(f1);
        myG.drawString("Key Typed ",50,50 );
        myG.drawString("key pressed",50,150 );
        myG.drawString("key released",50,250 );
        Font f2 = new Font("Arial" , Font.BOLD , 16);
        myG.setFont(f2);
    }
  }
class key1
  {  public static void main( String args[])
    {   myFrame k1 = new myFrame();
    }
  };
```

When the program started running, we pressed the following keys in the following order.

a, Caps Lock, b, keypad 9, Num Lock, keypad 9, Tab, Escape, w,9.

The following output is received on screen

Output

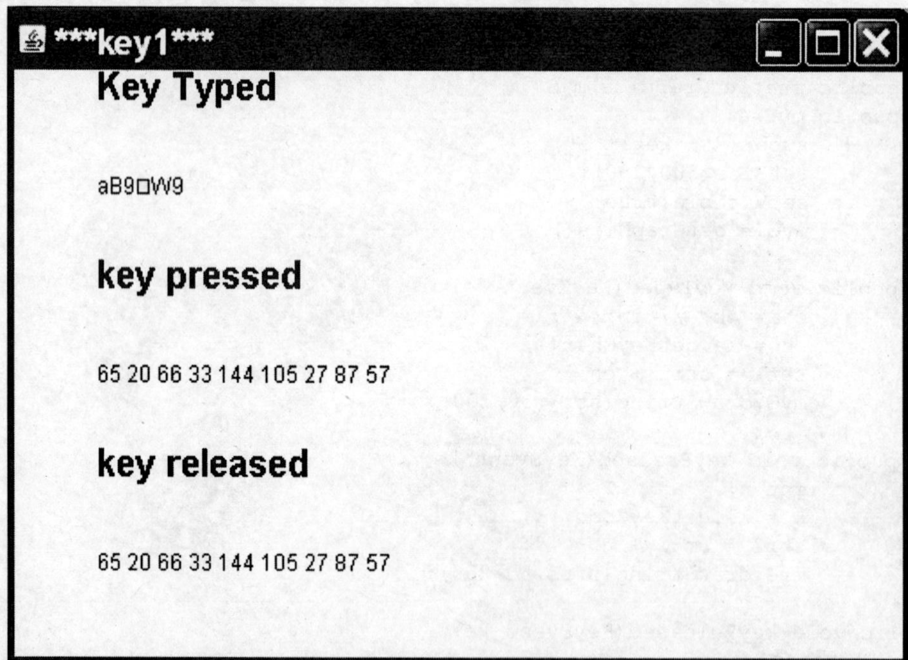

Please note that

- Key pressed and released lines show nine integer key codes.
- `KeyTyped` line shows only six characters.
- Caps Lock, PgUp (= keypad 9), and Num Lock did not produced any character (`keyTyped`).
- Character generated by Escape is shown as square box.
- Character generated by Tab is not shown in any list.

On running this program in older versions of Java, `keyTyped` was shown by a square box. The value of the key pressed was 9.

After an application, let us write an applet responding to keys.

Problem: Write an applet to study keyboard events.

Solution: In this applet, we will sense a key. If a key is r, g, or b, the background colour of the applet will be changed as red, green, and blue. If we type any other key, we will set the background colour as grey. See the following applet.

PROGRAM 21.7 Key Demo II

```
//   key2.java
import java.awt.event.*;
import java.awt.*;
import java.applet.*;
class key2 extends Applet implements KeyListener
{ static Color col1 = Color.yellow;
      public void init()
         {   addKeyListener(this);
             // requestFocus();
         }
      public void paint(Graphics g)
         {   setBackground(col1);
             g.drawString("applet demo of keyTyped",100,100);
             g.drawString("R-red G-green B-blue default-gray",100,150);
         };

      public void keyPressed(KeyEvent ke)
         {   int n;
             n = ke.getKeyCode() ;
         }
      public void keyReleased(KeyEvent ke)
         {   char ch; int n ;
             n = ke.getKeyCode() ;
         }
      public void keyTyped(KeyEvent ke)
         {   char ch; int n ;
             ch = ke.getKeyChar();
             switch (ch) {
                case 'r': col1 =Color.red; break;
                case 'g': col1 =Color.green; break;
```

```
                case 'b': col1 =Color.blue; break;
                default :col1=Color.gray;
                }
               repaint();
        }
}
```

If you run the aforementioned applet, you will get the following screen with yellow background. If you press keys r, g, or b, colour changes to red, green, or blue, respectively. Pressing any other key makes background grey. If you press key "g", you will get the following screen output.

Output

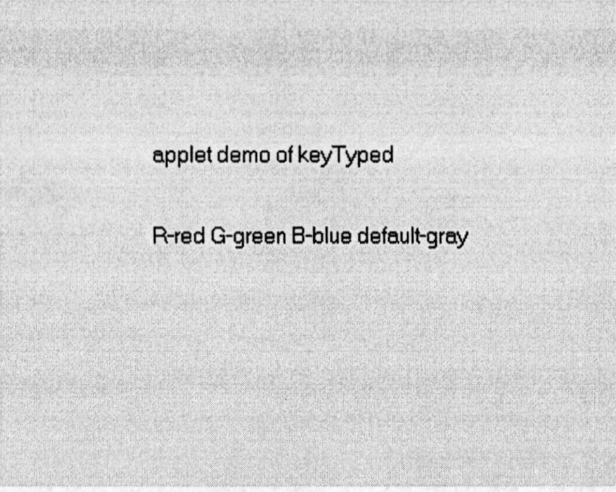

Please note that `keyPressed` or `keyReleased` methods are not doing any useful work. We are forced to define them as they are declared in `keyListener` interface.

21.2.4 Mouse events

Mouse is another important input device. When we move the mouse or click a mouse button, a mouse event is generated. Mouse events are grouped in two categories: mouse events and mouse motion events.

Mouse Events: If we want to work with mouse events like press, release, click, enter, and exit on a component, we have to implement `MouseListener` interface. It means that we have to define methods declared in this interface. When a mouse event occurs, the relevant method in the listener object is invoked, and the `MouseEvent` is passed to it.

Mouse Motion Events: If we want to work with movement of mouse (moved or dragged) on a component, we have to implement `MouseMotionListener` interface. It means that we have to define methods declared in that interface. When a mouse movement occurs, the relevant method in the listener object is invoked, and the `MouseEvent` is passed to it.

Tables 21.1 and 21.2 describe all the methods from both the interfaces.

Table 21.1 Methods Summary: Interface MouseListener

Event	Method
Mouse is clicked on a component	mouseClicked(MouseEvent e)
Mouse enters a component	mouseEntered(MouseEvent e)
Mouse exits a component	mouseExited(MouseEvent e)
Mouse button is pressed on a component	mousePressed(MouseEvent e)
Mouse button is released on a component	mouseReleased(MouseEvent e)

Table 21.2 Methods Summary: Interface MouseMotionListener

Event	Method
Mouse button is pressed on a component and then dragged	mouseDragged(MouseEvent e)
Mouse button is moved on a component (with no button down)	mouseMoved(MouseEvent e)

Please note that events are generated with respect to a component in Java, for example `Frame`.

Problem: Write a program to study methods from `MouseListener` interface.

Solution: In this program, we will demonstrate `MousePressed` method. Every time a mouse is clicked on the component that is `Frame` in this example, the colour of the frame will change (see Program 21.8).

PROGRAM 21.8 Interface MouseListener

```
//   mouse1.java
import java.awt.* ;
import java.awt.event.* ;
import java.awt.Color ;

class myFrame extends Frame implements MouseListener
   {  public static Graphics myG ;
      static int ind=0;
      static int max = 10;
      static Font f1 = new Font("Arial" , Font.BOLD , 20);
      Color fc,bc; // forground and background
      Color[] col = { Color.white , Color.blue , Color.cyan ,
                      Color.gray , Color.green , Color.magenta,
                      Color.orange , Color.pink , Color.red ,
                      Color.yellow } ;
      String[] name = {  "white" , "blue" , "cyan" ,
                         "gray" , "green" , "magenta",
                         "orange" , "pink" , "red" ,
                         "yellow",/*"bye bye"*/ } ;
      public myFrame()
```

```
        {   super("***mouse1***") ;
            setSize(400,300);
            setVisible(true);

            fc = Color.black;
            bc= Color.white;
        }
    public void paint(Graphics g)
        {   this.setBackground(bc);
            g.setColor(fc);
            g.setFont(f1);
            g.drawString(name[ind],50,100);
        }
    public void init()
        {   addMouseListener(this);
            requestFocus();
        }
    public void mousePressed(MouseEvent e)
        {   ind++;
            if ( ind < max)
                    {   bc=col[ind];
                        this.repaint();
                    }
                else System.exit(0);
        }
    public void mouseReleased(MouseEvent e) { }
    public void mouseEntered(MouseEvent e) { }
    public void mouseExited(MouseEvent e) { }
    public void mouseClicked(MouseEvent e) { }
  }
class mouse1
  {   public static void main( String args[])
      {   myFrame k1 = new myFrame();
          k1.init();
      }
  };
```

The screen at the start will be seen as follows. The background colour will change every time we click the mouse. The name of the colour will also be displayed.

Output

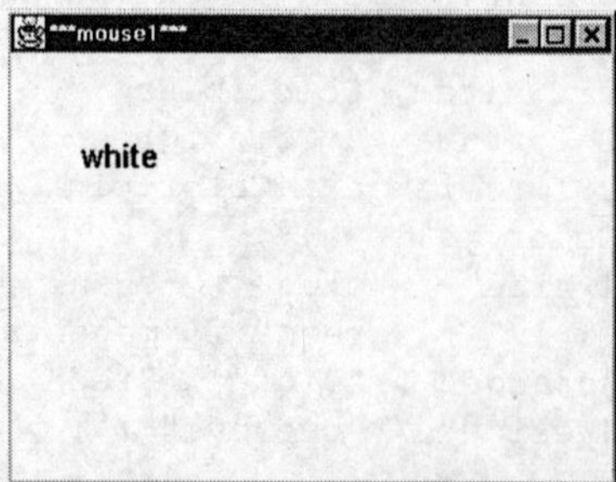

We have not actively implemented other methods like `mouse entered`. You can add a small code and test the concept yourself.

You can see the `MouseMotionListener` interface demo in a program on free-hand drawing in Chapter 26 on "Collection of Programs".

21.2.5 Adapter classes

If we inspect Program 21.8, we will see lot of empty methods. The class `myFrame` implements `MouseListener` interface. We are required to define all the methods of this interface. In our program, we wanted to use only one method `mousePressed(MouseEvent e)`. Still we have to define all other methods. To handle such situation, Java offers Adapter classes. An adapter class is essentially a hollow (in a way a dummy) class. It implements all methods of a given interface without any action. Instead of implementing an interface, we should extend the respective adapter class. In that case, we have to define only one or two required methods. No other method needs to be defined. Let us rewrite the aforementioned program using `MouseAdapter` class.

Problem: Write a program to class `MouseAdapter`.

Solution: As we are demonstrating the use of `MouseAdapter` class instead of `MouseListener` interface, we will use previous program and modify it suitably. See Program 21.9.

PROGRAM 21.9 Adapter Class

```
//   adapt1.java

import java.awt.* ;
import java.awt.event.* ;
import java.awt.Color ;

class myFrame extends Frame
  {  public static Graphics myG ;
     static int ind=0;
     static int max = 10;
     static Font f1 = new Font("Arial" , Font.BOLD , 20);
     Color fc,bc; // forground and background
     Color[] col = { Color.white , Color.blue , Color.cyan ,
                        Color.gray , Color.green , Color.magenta,
                        Color.orange , Color.pink , Color.red ,
                        Color.yellow } ;
     String[] name = { "white" , "blue" , "cyan" ,
                        "gray" , "green" , "magenta",
                        "orange" , "pink" , "red" ,
                        "yellow",/*"bye bye"*/ } ;

     public myFrame()
         {  super("***adapt1***") ;
            setSize(400,300);
            setVisible(true);

            fc = Color.black;
            bc= Color.white;
         }
     public void paint(Graphics g)
         {  this.setBackground(bc);
```

```
            g.setColor(fc);
            g.setFont(f1);
            g.drawString(name[ind],50,100);
        }

    public void init()
        {   addMouseListener(new demo());
            requestFocus();
        }
void action()
{ repaint();
}
class demo extends MouseAdapter
  {  public void mousePressed(MouseEvent e)
     {   ind++;
            if ( ind < max)
                {   bc=col[ind];
                    action();
                }
             else System.exit(0);
     }
   }
  }
  public class adapt1
    { public static void main( String args[])
        {   myFrame k1 = new myFrame();
            k1.init();
        }
    };
```

If you run this program, you will get absolutely the same output as that of the Program 21.8.

For smooth running, we have to make minor changes. First, we define a new class. We have deliberately named it as "demo". It extends `MouseAdapter` class and contains mouse pressed method. In the original program it contained the code `this.repaint()`. Here this stands for `myframe`. This part is handled by a new method `action()`.

The following table lists various adapter classes.

Adapter classes	ListenerInterface
MouseAdapter	MouseListener
MouseMotionAdapter	MouseMotionListener
KeyAdapter	KeyListener
WindowAdapter	WindowListener
ComponentAdapter	ComponentListener
Container Adapter	Container Listener
Focus Adapter	FocusListener

21.2.6 Virtual key code constants

Table 21.3 illustrates the virtual key codes supported by Java.

Table 21.3 Virtual Key Code Constants

Number keys	
VK_0 to VK_9	These are the same as ASCII "0" through "9" (0 × 30 – 0 × 39)
Character keys	
VK_A through VK_Z	These are the same as ASCII "A" through "Z" (0 × 41 – 0 × 5A)
Numbers from numpad	
VK_NUMPAD0 to VK_NUMPAD9	Keys from numpad
Function keys	
VK_F1 to VK_F19	Constant for function keys, F1 to F19
Key pad arrow key	
VK_KP_DOWN	Keypad arrow down function key
VK_KP_LEFT	Keypad arrow left function key
VK_KP_RIGHT	Keypad arrow right function key
VK_KP_UP	Keypad arrow up function key
Other keys	
VK_ALT	
VK_AMPERSAND	
VK_ASTERISK	
VK_AT	Constant for the "@" key
VK_BACK_QUOTE	
VK_BACK_SLASH	
VK_BACK_SPACE	
VK_BRACELEFT	
VK_BRACERIGHT	
VK_CAPS_LOCK	

(Continued)

Table 21.3 (*Continued*)

VK_CIRCUMFLEX	Constant for the "^" key
VK_CLEAR	
VK_CLOSE_BRACKET	
VK_COLON	Constant for the ":" key
VK_COMMA	
VK_CONTROL	
VK_COPY	
VK_CUT	
VK_DECIMAL	
VK_DELETE	
VK_DIVIDE	
VK_DOLLAR	Constant for the "$" key
VK_DOWN	
VK_END	
VK_ENTER	
VK_EQUALS	
VK_ESCAPE	
VK_EXCLAMATION_MARK.	Constant for the "!" key
VK_GREATER	
VK_HOME	
VK_INSERT	
VK_INVERTED_EXCLAMATION_MARK	Constant for the inverted exclamation mark key
VK_LEFT	
VK_LEFT_PARENTHESIS.	Constant for the "(" key
VK_LESS	
VK_MINUS.	Constant for the "-" key
VK_NUM_LOCK	
VK_NUMBER_SIGN.	Constant for the "#" key
VK_OPEN_BRACKET	

(*Continued*)

Table 21.3 (*Continued*)

VK_PAGE_DOWN	
VK_PAGE_UP	
VK_PASTE	
VK_PAUSE	
VK_PERIOD	
VK_PRINTSCREEN	
VK_QUOTE	
VK_QUOTEDBL	
VK_RIGHT	
VK_RIGHT_PARENTHESIS	Constant for the ")" key
VK_SCROLL_LOCK	
VK_SEMICOLON	
VK_SHIFT	
VK_SLASH	
VK_SPACE	
VK_STOP	
VK_SUBTRACT	
VK_TAB	
VK_UNDERSCORE	Constant for the "_" key.
VK_UP	

Table 21.4 illustrates the various interfaces from the Package java.awt.event.

Table 21.4 Interface Summary: Package java.awt.event

ActionListener	The listener interface for receiving action events
AdjustmentListener	The listener interface for receiving adjustment events
AWTEventListener	The listener interface for receiving notification of events dispatched to objects that are instances of Component or MenuComponent or their sub-classes
ComponentListener	The listener interface for receiving component events

(*Continued*)

Table 21.4 (*Continued*)

`ContainerListener`	The listener interface for receiving container events
`FocusListener`	The listener interface for receiving keyboard-focus events on a component
`HierarchyBoundsListener`	The listener interface for receiving ancestor-moved and resized events
`HierarchyListener`	The listener interface for receiving hierarchy-changed events
`InputMethodListener`	The listener interface for receiving input method events
`ItemListener`	The listener interface for receiving item events
`KeyListener`	The listener interface for receiving keyboard events (keystrokes)
`MouseListener`	The listener interface for receiving "interesting" mouse events (press, release, click, enter, and exit) on a component
`MouseMotionListener`	The listener interface for receiving mouse motion events on a component
`MouseWheelListener`	The listener interface for receiving mouse wheel events on a component
`TextListener`	The listener interface for receiving text events
`WindowFocusListener`	The listener interface for receiving WindowEvents, including `WINDOW_GAINED_FOCUS` and `WINDOW_LOST_FOCUS` events
`WindowListener`	The listener interface for receiving window events
`WindowStateListener`	The listener interface for receiving window-state events

Table 21.5 illustrates various classes from Package `java.awt.event`.

Table 21.5 Class Summary: Package `java.awt.event`

`ActionEvent`	A semantic event which indicates that a component-defined action has occurred
`AdjustmentEvent`	The adjustment event emitted by adjustable objects
`AWTEventListenerProxy`	A class which extends the `EventListenerProxy`, specifically for adding an `AWTEventListener` for a specific event mask

(*Continued*)

Table 21.5 ***(Continued)***

`ComponentAdapter`	An abstract adapter class for receiving component events
`ComponentEvent`	A low-level event which indicates that a component has moved, changed size, or changed visibility (also, the root class for the other component-level events)
`ContainerAdapter`	An abstract adapter class for receiving container events
`ContainerEvent`	A low-level event which indicates that the contents of a container have changed because a component was added or removed
`FocusAdapter`	An abstract adapter class for receiving keyboard focus events
`FocusEvent`	A low-level event which indicates that a component has gained or lost the input focus
`HierarchyBoundsAdapter`	An abstract adapter class for receiving ancestor moved and resized events
`HierarchyEvent`	An event which indicates a change to the component hierarchy to which a component belongs
`InputEvent`	The root event class for all component-level input events
`InputMethodEvent`	Input method events contain information about text that is being composed using an input method
`InvocationEvent`	An event which executes the `run()` method on a `Runnable` when dispatched by the AWT event dispatcher thread
`ItemEvent`	A semantic event which indicates that an item was selected or deselected
`KeyAdapter`	An abstract adapter class for receiving keyboard events
`KeyEvent`	An event which indicates that a keystroke occurred in a component
`MouseAdapter`	An abstract adapter class for receiving mouse events
`MouseEvent`	An event which indicates that a mouse action occurred in a component
`MouseMotionAdapter`	An abstract adapter class for receiving mouse motion events
`MouseWheelEvent`	An event which indicates that the mouse wheel was rotated in a component
`PaintEvent`	The component-level paint event
`TextEvent`	A semantic event which indicates that the text of an object has changed

(Continued)

Table 21.5 (*Continued*)

`WindowAdapter`	An abstract adapter class for receiving window events
`WindowEvent`	A low-level event that indicates that a window has changed its status

Keywords

Abstract Window Toolkit, `ActionListener`, `actionPerformed`, AWT, button, canvas, Canvas, checkbox, Container, Delegation Event Model, `event`, `Frame`, `getActionCommand()`, `KeyEvent`, `keyPressed()`, `keyReleased()`, `keyTyped()`, low-level events, mouse event, `MouseListener`, `MouseMotionListener`, `MousePressed`, Panel, radio button, `System.exit()`, `TextField`, Virtual key code, Window

RuleBook

Key events	Key events are generated when a user presses or releases a key on the keyboard
multiple listeners	A component can have multiple listeners for events of different type
graphics	Graphic class is defined in `java.awt` package.
container event	Container event class is generated when a component is added to or removed from a container.
add	The add method for attaching GUI components is a `Container` class method and not of class `Component`.

Review Questions

1. Describe the event-handling model in Java.
2. Describe various methods from `KeyListener` interface. What are the mouse event-handling interfaces and their corresponding methods? Explain in brief.
3. Describe various methods from `MouseListener` interface.
4. Describe various methods from `MouseMotionListener` interface.
5. What is delegation event model in Java? Explain in brief.
6. Describe various interfaces and classes from package AWT.

Exercises

1. Write a program to print the corresponding virtual key code when a key is typed.
2. Write an applet which responds to mouse events.
3. Write an AWT application with checkbox such that all cable TV channels will be displayed from the selected category.
4. Write an AWT application with radio button such that first file lines are displayed from a selected file.
5. An old kid's game (named Briano) consisted of two lists: one of the names of states and the other that of the capital cities. Along the names, there were electric contacts. If you connect a wire between the correct names, a small bulb glows. Simulate this game using two sets of radio buttons. A bulb should be replaced by a `TextField` showing the string "you are right" in bold.

INTRODUCTION TO SWING

Earlier we have studied components from AWT package. These components depend on the methods and facilities of similar components from the base platform. That is the reason they are termed as "heavyweight components". This design has certain advantages. As expected, there are disadvantages too. Now Java provides a set of components termed as "lightweight" components. They are also called all-Java components. These components are coded in Java language. They do not depend on platform facilities. These components are defined in a package `Javax.swing`. These components practically work the same way on all platforms. The package swing is fairly big and will be a subject of a full text. In this chapter, we will introduce few basic components so that we can write simple applications with GUI.

22.1 JFrame

The most fundamental and important component of this package is `JFrame`. Actually, this component extends class `Frame` of package "awt". We have studied this class earlier. All what we have studied is true for `JFrame`.

Let us start our study with a simple program.

Problem: Write a program to demonstrate use of `JFrame`.

Solution: See Program 22.1.

PROGRAM 22.1 JFrame Demo

```
//       jframe1.java
import javax.swing.*;
import java.awt.Color;
class jframe1
{  public static void main(String[] args)
    {    JFrame f1= new JFrame("java5");
         f1.setDefaultCloseOperation(JFrame.EXIT_ON_CLOSE);
         f1.setSize(300,200);
         f1.setVisible(true);
    }
}
```

Output

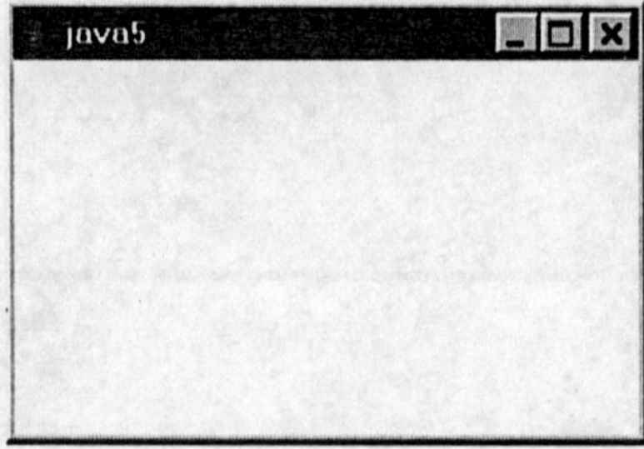

Note the title `java5`. This program does not compile in earlier versions. Also notice the statement

```
f1.setDefaultCloseOperation (JFrame.EXIT_ON_CLOSE);
```

As the method name suggests, the application closes when we click the X button. Before this method was added, we have to use following code for this purpose:

```
f1.addWindowListener(new WindowAdapter()
    {   public void windowClosing(WindowEvent e)
            { System.exit(0); }
    });
```

22.2 JOptionPane for (Output) Message

Just like console programming, first and foremost task in visual programming will be input/output. The simplest form of input/output is handled by `JOptionPane` in swing package. `JOptionPane` can be used with both input and output. Let us first study a simple program for its use for output. The useful method is `showMessageDialog()`.

Problem: Write a program to demonstrate use of `JOptionPane` for displaying an output message.

Solution: See Program 22.2.

PROGRAM 22.2 JOptionPane for Output

```
//   jop11.java
import java.awt.* ;
import java.awt.event.* ;
import javax.swing.* ;

class jop11 // extends JFrame implements ActionListener
 {
   public static void main( String args[])
      {   JFrame frame = new JFrame("JOption Pane Demo");
          frame.addWindowListener(new WindowAdapter()
             {   public void windowClosing(WindowEvent e)
                    {    System.exit(0); }
             });
          frame.setBounds(150,150,350,350);
```

```
        frame.setResizable(false); // works
        frame.getContentPane().setLayout( new BorderLayout() );
        frame.setVisible(true);
        JOptionPane.showMessageDialog(null,"In the Center");//works
        JOptionPane.showMessageDialog(frame,"In the frame");
    }
}
```

If you run this program, you will first get the following output.

Output

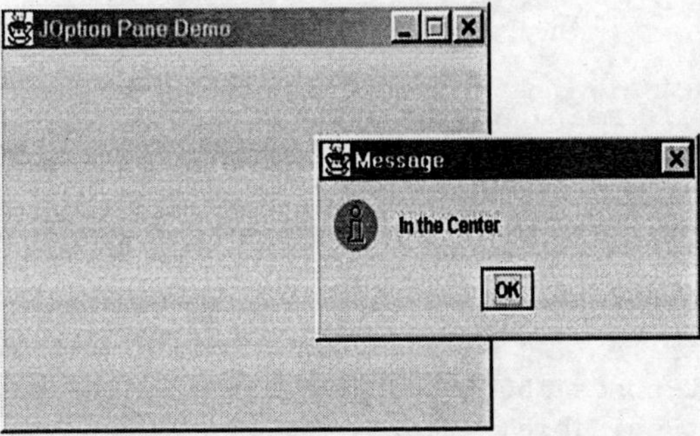

If you click the OK button then this message will close and new message will appear, as shown in following output.

Output

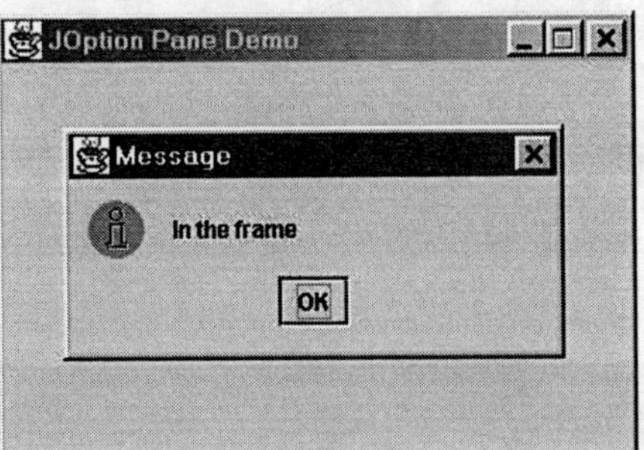

Note that the new message has appeared inside the main frame. If we click OK button this message will vanish leaving the frame on the screen. We can click exit button to end the program.

Also note that in this program, we have used setBounds() to locate the main frame at an absolute location on the computer screen. Now let us study the input dialog box.

22.3 Input Dialog `JOptionPane`

In the aforementioned example, we have used method `showMessageDialog()` for output. Now, for using with input we have another method named

`showInputDialog()`.

Let us study it with a program.

Problem: Write a program to demonstrate use of `JOptionPane` for inputting the data.

Solution: See Program 22.3.

PROGRAM 22.3 `JOptionPane` for Input

```
//     jop22.java
import java.awt.* ;
import java.awt.event.* ;
import javax.swing.* ;
class jop22
  {
      public static void main( String args[])
        {    JFrame frame = new JFrame("JOption Pane Demo");
             frame.addWindowListener(new WindowAdapter()
                {    public void windowClosing(WindowEvent e)
                     {    System.exit(0); }
                });
             String str1;
             frame.setBounds(150,150,350,350);
             frame.setResizable(false); // works
             frame.getContentPane().setLayout( new BorderLayout() );
             frame.setVisible(true);
             str1= JOptionPane.showInputDialog(frame,"How old are You ?");
             JOptionPane.showMessageDialog(frame,"Your age is "+ str1);
             System.exit(0);
        }
  }
```

If you run this program, you will get the following output.

Output

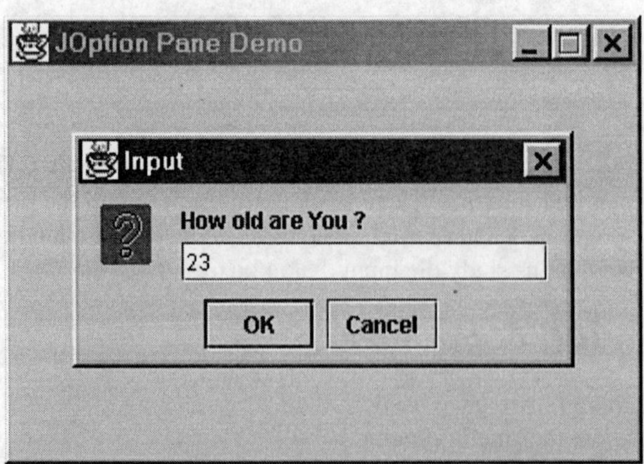

Type your age, say 23, and press "OK" button. Then you will get the following output.

Output

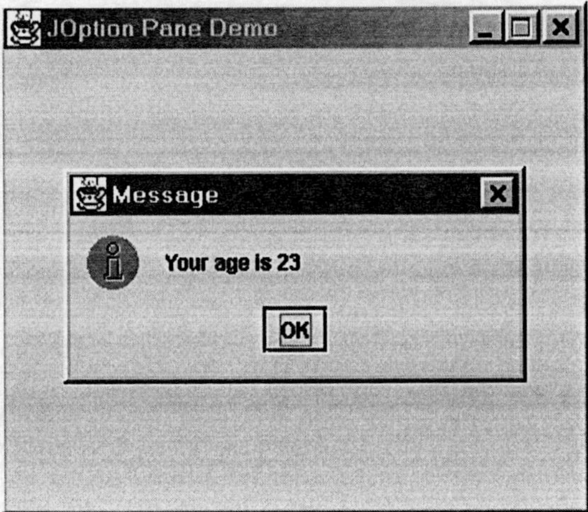

Please note that when you press "OK" button, program terminates. This is because we have included `exit()` method just after the last `showMessageDialog()` method.

In India, minimum age for voting is 18. Can you modify the program so that a proper message "Well eligible for voting" or "Sorry too young to vote" appears in the message window?

The class `JOptionPane` has many constructors. Also, methods `showInputDialog` and `showMessageDialog` are overloaded. Hence, one can have lots of variations in input/output. Interested readers are requested to see the "API" specification.

22.4 Class `JButton`

In Chapter 21 on AWT, we have studied class `Button`. `JButton` is an improved version. In GUI-based event-driven programming, buttons are used to start a particular action. Let us study it with a simple program.

Problem: Write a program to introduce class `JButton`.

Solution: In this program, we will introduce two buttons. Out of them, one button will be associated with closing the present program (see Program 22.4).

PROGRAM 22.4 Class `JButton`

```
//      jbut3.java

import java.awt.* ;
import java.awt.event.* ;
import javax.swing.* ;

class jbut3 extends JFrame implements ActionListener
  {  JButton b1,b2 ;
```

```
    public jbut3() // constructor
      { b1 = new JButton("Do nothing");
        b1.addActionListener(this);
        b1.setActionCommand("Do nothing");

        b2 = new JButton("Close");
        b2.addActionListener(this);
        b2.setActionCommand("Close");

        this.getContentPane().setLayout( new FlowLayout(FlowLayout.CENTER) );
        this.getContentPane().add(b1);
        this.getContentPane().add(b2);
      };

  public static void main( String args[])
      { jbut3 thisprog = new jbut3();
        thisprog.addWindowListener(new WindowAdapter()
        {   public void windowClosing(WindowEvent e)
              {    System.exit(0); }
        });

        thisprog.setBounds(150,150,400,400);
        thisprog.setResizable(false); // works
        thisprog.pack();
        thisprog.setVisible(true);
      }
  public void actionPerformed(ActionEvent e)
    {
      if (e.getActionCommand().equals("Close") )
            {    System.exit(0); }
      if (e.getActionCommand().equals("Do nothing") )
          { // Do nothing
          }
    }
  }
```

If you run the program, you will get the following output.

Output

There are following points to note:

1. We have given command

   `thisprog.setBounds(150,150,400,400);`

   The output faithfully appeared at 150 × 150 pixels away from the top left corner of the monitor, but the size is not 400 × 400 pixels. This is because of `pack()` instruction. It has packed the frame to bare minimum size.

2. If you write close in place of Close in "action performed" command, program does not work properly. The reason being Java is case sensitive.
3. Note "do nothing". This is deliberate. If you want to take any other action, you have to simply add the code in place of comment // do Nothing. You can use this program as a template for any two button program.

22.5 Class `JLabel`

The name label itself indicates what the use of this component is. It displays useful information (typically for neighbouring components). Information can be a text string or an image or both. Class `JLabel` supports various constructors for this purpose. Please note that `JLabel` is a passive component. No action will start if we click it with the mouse.

Problem: Write a program to illustrate use of class `JLabel`.

Solution: In this program, we will show three labels. The first one will be a pure text. The second one will be an image. The third one will be with both text and image (see Program 22.5).

PROGRAM 22.5 Demo of `JLabel`

```
//      label2.java
import java.awt.*;
import java.awt.event.*;
import javax.swing.*;
import javax.swing.border.Border;

public class label2 extends JFrame
{    label2(String s1)
       { super(s1);
       }
      public static void main(String s[])
       {    label2 thisprog = new label2("JLabel demo");
            thisprog.addWindowListener(new WindowAdapter() {
                 public void windowClosing(WindowEvent e) {System.exit(0);}
            });
            thisprog.setSize(240,260);
            thisprog.getContentPane().add(new form());
            thisprog.setVisible(true);
       }
}
class form extends JPanel {

    JLabel lab1,lab2,lab3;
    public form()
    {
       lab1 = new JLabel(" This is simple text label ");
       lab2 = new JLabel( new ImageIcon("bell1.jpg") ) ;
       lab3 = new JLabel(" CAR ",
       new ImageIcon("car1.jpg"),JLabel.CENTER ) ;
```

```
        setLayout(new BoxLayout(this,BoxLayout.Y_AXIS) ) ;
        Border line = BorderFactory.createLineBorder(Color.blue);

        add(lab1);
        add(lab2);
        add(lab3);

      lab1.setBorder(line);
      lab2.setBorder(line);
      lab3.setBorder(line);
   }
}
```

If you run the program, you will get the following output.

Output

In the output, there is a text label on the top. An image label is in the middle. The label at the bottom has both text and image.

There are following two new things in this program:

- A line border
- A box layout

Borders and the layout managers are discussed at the end of this chapter.

22.6 JCheckBox

Many interactive GUI programs allow us to select some options. This is typically done with the help of checkboxes. Hence, checkboxes are useful components in GUI programming. We see checkboxes in application forms (say for college admission). It is a convenient tool to input standardized information. Therefore, GUI-based applications support checkboxes. Swing package has provided class `JCheckBox` for this purpose.

Problem: Write a program to introduce `JCheckBox`.

Solution: We have studied colours in Chapter 13 on graphics. Let us use them in this program. Let us denote three checkboxes for basic colours red, green, and blue. The background colour of the frame will be selected on the basis of the combination of these three basic colours (see Program 22.6).

PROGRAM 22.6 Check Box

```
import java.awt.*;
import java.awt.event.*;
import javax.swing.*;
public class cb1 extends JPanel
{

     JCheckBox red;
     JCheckBox green;
     JCheckBox blue;
     boolean r = false, g = false, b =false;

     public cb1()
     {    // Create the check boxes
          red = new JCheckBox("RED");
          red.setMnemonic(KeyEvent.VK_R);
          red.setSelected(false);

          green = new JCheckBox("GREEN");
          green.setMnemonic(KeyEvent.VK_G);
          green.setSelected(false);

          blue = new JCheckBox("BLUE");
          blue.setMnemonic(KeyEvent.VK_B);
          blue.setSelected(false);

          // Register a listener for the check boxes.
          CheckBoxListener myListener = new CheckBoxListener();
          red.addItemListener(myListener);
          green.addItemListener(myListener);
          blue.addItemListener(myListener);
          this.setBackground(Color.black);

          // Put the check boxes in a column in a panel
          JPanel checkPanel = new JPanel();
          checkPanel.setLayout(new GridLayout(0, 1));
          checkPanel.add(red);
          checkPanel.add(green);
          checkPanel.add(blue);

          setLayout(new BorderLayout());
          add(checkPanel, BorderLayout.WEST);
```

```
        //  add(pictureLabel, BorderLayout.CENTER);
        setBorder(BorderFactory.createEmptyBorder (20,20,20,20));
    }

    /** Listens to the check boxes. */
class CheckBoxListener implements ItemListener
{   public void itemStateChanged(ItemEvent e) {
        int index = 0;
        char c = '-';
        Object source = e.getItemSelectable();

        if (source == red) r = !r;
        if (source == green) g = !g;
        if (source == blue) b = !b;

        if (r && !g && !b)    setBackground(Color.red);
        if (!r && g && !b)    setBackground(Color.green);
        if (!r && !g && b)    setBackground(Color.blue);

        if (r && g && !b)    setBackground(Color.yellow);
        if (r && !g && b)    setBackground(Color.magenta);
        if (!r && g && b)    setBackground(Color.cyan);

        if (r && g && b)    setBackground(Color.white);
        if (!r && !g && !b)    setBackground(Color.black); }
}
  public static void main(String s[])
  { JFrame frame = new JFrame("check box demo");
    frame.addWindowListener(new WindowAdapter() {
        public void windowClosing(WindowEvent e) {
            System.exit(0);
        }
      });
        frame.setContentPane(new cb1());
        frame.pack();
        frame.setVisible(true);
  }
}
```

If you run the program, you will get the following output.

Output

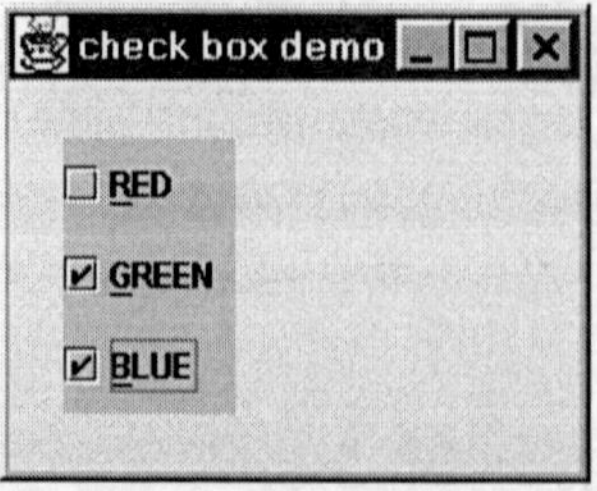

Please note that as we have checked two primary colours, green and blue, we get background colour as cyan. If we select all three, background will be "white". If no box is selected background will be black.

22.7 Introduction to `JRadioButtons`

Checkboxes allow us to select any number of choices (parameters). Sometimes, application demands that we have to select only one of the available choices. For this purpose, we have to use Radio Buttons.

In discussion on AWT package, we have seen that there was no separate class for `RadioButtons`. We have to use only "checkbox". Luckily in package `swing`, Java has provided a separate class named `JRadioButton`. To hold these buttons, we have a class `ButtonGroup`

Problem: Write a program to introduce `RadioButtons`.

Solution: In kindergarten, kids are taught "A for apple". The characters are associated with the objects. If we want to write a program to simulate this, we can have radio buttons. On clicking these buttons, corresponding image can be shown (see Program 22.7).

PROGRAM 22.7 RadioButton Demo

```
//      rb4.java
import java.awt.*;
import java.awt.event.*;
import javax.swing.*;

public class rb4 extends JFrame implements ActionListener{  rb4()
    {    super("Radio Button Demo");
    }
    public static void main(String s[])
    {  rb4 thisprog = new rb4();

          thisprog.addWindowListener(new WindowAdapter()
            {  public void windowClosing(WindowEvent e)
                   {  System.exit(0); }
            });

       thisprog.setBounds(50,50,500,500);
       thisprog.setResizable(true); // works

       thisprog.getContentPane().add(new form(), BorderLayout.CENTER);
       thisprog.setVisible(true);
    }
    public void actionPerformed(ActionEvent e)
      {
      }
}

class form extends JPanel {
```

```
    static String A = "Apple";
    static String B = "Ball";
    static String C = "Cat";

    JLabel picture;

    public form() {
    //  Create the radio buttons.
    JRadioButton AButton = new JRadioButton(A);
    AButton.setMnemonic(KeyEvent.VK_A);
    AButton.setActionCommand(A);
    AButton.setSelected(true);

    JRadioButton BButton = new JRadioButton(B);
    BButton.setMnemonic(KeyEvent.VK_B);
    BButton.setActionCommand(B);

    JRadioButton CButton = new JRadioButton (C);
    CButton.setMnemonic(KeyEvent.VK_C);
    CButton.setActionCommand(C);

    //  Group the radio buttons.
    ButtonGroup group = new ButtonGroup();
    group.add(AButton);
    group.add(BButton);
    group.add(CButton);

    //  Register a listener for the radio buttons.
    RadioListener myListener = new RadioListener();
    AButton.addActionListener(myListener);
    BButton.addActionListener(myListener);
    CButton.addActionListener(myListener);

    //  Set up the picture label
    picture = new JLabel(new ImageIcon("images/apple.jpg"));

    //  Put the radio buttons in a column in a panel
    JPanel radioPanel = new JPanel();
    radioPanel.setLayout(new GridLayout(0, 1));
    radioPanel.add(AButton);
    radioPanel.add(BButton);
    radioPanel.add(CButton);

    setLayout(new BorderLayout());
    add(radioPanel, BorderLayout.WEST);
    add(picture, BorderLayout.CENTER);

setBorder(BorderFactory.createEmptyBorder(20,20,20,20));
    }

    /** Listens to the radio buttons. */
    class RadioListener implements ActionListener {
```

```
        public void actionPerformed(ActionEvent e) {
          picture.setIcon(new ImageIcon("images/" + e.getActionCommand()
                                                       + ".jpg"));

        }
      }
  };
```

When we start running this program, we will get following output. If we click radio button named Ball or Cat, the corresponding figure will appear in place of apple.

Output

22.8 Introduction to Class Canvas

As the name suggests, it is a component to draw things on. Earlier, we have drawn on the frame itself. That was fine because we were just learning. We wanted to get things done without studying too many additional things. Now we are studying in detail. The frame is a top layer container for holding various components, like buttons, checkboxes, and others. So we have to look for a new component for drawing. Canvas is the most appropriate place to draw things. We can place canvas on the frame along with the other components.

Here we will study two programs. In these programs, we will also use `TextField` for getting input.

Problem: Write a program to study class `Canvas`.

Solution: In this program, we will use canvas to draw an oval. The parameter *k* will be accepted from `TextField`. The width of the oval will be set to 20 times of *k*, while height will be fixed at 100. To add additional functionality, we will print a string describing the value of *k* (see Program 22.8).

PROGRAM 22.8 Canvas I

```
//    canvas1a.java

import java.awt.* ;
import java.awt.event.* ;
import javax.swing.* ;

class da extends Canvas    // da drawing area
   { public int k ;
      static String str[] = {"zero","one","two","three"}; da()
        { k=0;
          setBounds(20,20,150,150);
          this.setBackground(new Color(220,220,255)) ;
        }
  public void paint(Graphics g)
     { g.drawOval(20,20,k*20,100);
       if(k==0) g.drawString(str[0],10,10);
       if(k==1) g.drawString(str[1],10,10);
       if(k==2) g.drawString(str[2],10,10);
       if(k==3) g.drawString(str[3],10,10);
     }
   }

class canvas1a extends JFrame implements ActionListener
{   JTextField tf1;
    da can ;
    static int n = 100;
    canvas1a() // constructor
     { super("canvas1a");
       tf1 = new JTextField(20);
       tf1.setText("");
       tf1.setBackground(new Color(255,220,200) ) ;
       tf1.addActionListener(this);
       tf1.setActionCommand("txt");
       tf1.setBounds(20,180,150,50);
       tf1.setBorder( BorderFactory.createLineBorder(Color.green) );
       tf1.setVisible(true);
       can = new da();

       this.getContentPane().setLayout(null);
       this.getContentPane().setBackground(Color.white);
       this.getContentPane().add(tf1);
       this.getContentPane().add(can);
```

```
    };
  public static void main( String args[])
        {  canvas1a thisprog = new canvas1a();
           thisprog.addWindowListener(new WindowAdapter()
             {  public void windowClosing(WindowEvent e)
                  {  System.exit(0); }
             });

        thisprog.setBounds(50,50,190,280);
 //      thisprog.setResizable(true); // works
        thisprog.setVisible(true);
        thisprog.repaint();
        }
  public void actionPerformed(ActionEvent e)
   {  String st9;
      if (e.getActionCommand().equals("quit") )
            {  System.exit(0);
            };
      if (e.getActionCommand().equals("txt") )
            {  st9 = tf1.getText();
               st9 = st9.trim();
               n = Integer.parseInt(st9);
               can.k = n ;
               can.repaint();
            }
   }
}
```

If you run this program, you will get the following output.

Output

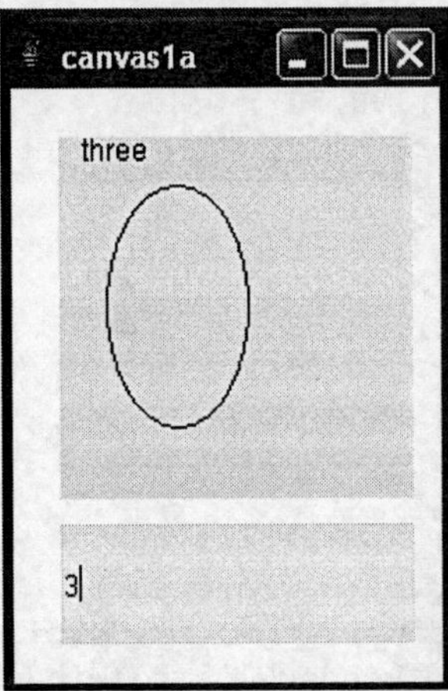

Problem: Rewrite Program 22.8 such that a circle is drawn instead of oval. When we give new input, new output should not erase the old output.

Solution: As we are planning to have many circles, we will dispense with writing the value of the parameter on screen (see Program 22.9).

PROGRAM 22.9 Canvas II

```
//      canvas3.java

import java.awt.* ;
import java.awt.event.* ;
import javax.swing.* ;

class da extends Canvas // da drawing area
{ public int k ;
  da()
  { k = 0;
    setBounds(20,20,150,150);
    this.setBackground(new Color(220,220,255) ) ; //light blue
  }
  public void draw()
    { Graphics gx = getGraphics();
      gx.drawOval(20,20,k*20,k*20);
    };
}

class canvas3 extends JFrame implements ActionListener
  { JTextField tf1;
    da can ;
    static int n = 100;
    canvas3() // constructor
      { super("canvas3");
        tf1 = new JTextField(20);
        tf1.setText("");
        tf1.setBackground(new Color(255,255,220)) ;//light yellow
        tf1.addActionListener(this);
        tf1.setActionCommand("txt");
        tf1.setBounds(20,180,150,50);
        tf1.setBorder( BorderFactory.createLineBorder(Color.green) );
        tf1.setVisible(true);
        can = new da();
        this.getContentPane().setLayout(null);
        this.getContentPane().setBackground(Color.white);
        this.getContentPane().add(tf1);
        this.getContentPane().add(can);
      };

  public static void main( String args[])
        { canvas3 thisprog = new canvas3();
          thisprog.addWindowListener(new WindowAdapter()
            { public void windowClosing(WindowEvent e)
                  { System.exit(0); }
            });

        thisprog.setBounds(50,50,190,280);
        thisprog.setVisible(true);
        thisprog.repaint();
```

```
        }
  public void actionPerformed(ActionEvent e)
    {  String st9;
       if (e.getActionCommand().equals("quit") )
             {  System.exit(0);
             };
       if (e.getActionCommand().equals("txt") )
             {  st9 = tf1.getText();
                st9 = st9.trim();
                n=Integer.parseInt(st9);
                can.k = n ;
                can.draw();
             }
       }
  }
```

If you run this program, you will get the following output.

Output

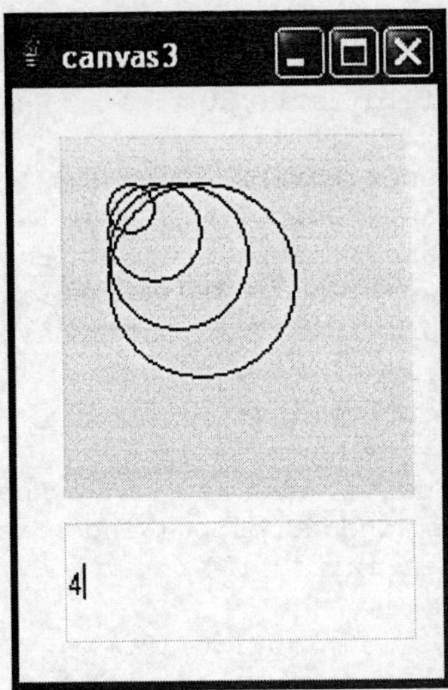

The output was observed when input data was 1, 2, 3, and 4.

22.9 Class `JTextField`

In Program 22.9, we had used `TextField` for the input. Let us study it in detail, what it offers to us. As the name suggests, this component is for working with text. By working, we mean both input and output. We can edit the `TextField` and then accept the text as a string. Alternately, we can use to display a text (string) in it.

This component is basically meant for one line of text. There are many constructors available. They essentially allow us to (optionally) define width as well as any text appearing initially. Let us try our first program.

22.9.1 Simple demo

Problem: Write a program to introduce class `JTextField`.

Solution: Class `JTextField` gives us an editable textbox. However, in this program, we will not do any editing inside the box. We will define two strings such that second one appears to be first string shifted right. On clicking a button, we will display these strings alternately in the `TextField`. This will create an illusion that we are shifting the text at the mouse click. (see Program 22.10)

PROGRAM 22.10 Class JTextField

```
//    textb4.java
import java.awt.* ;
import java.awt.event.* ;
import javax.swing.* ;
class textb4 extends JFrame implements ActionListener
  {  JTextField tf1;
     String st1 = new String(" ***Welcome***");
     String st2 = new String("***Welcome*** ");
     JButton b2 ;
     public textb4() // constructor
        {  tf1 = new JTextField( st1 ,30);
           b2 = new JButton("shift");
           b2.addActionListener(this);
           b2.setActionCommand("shift");
           this.getContentPane().setLayout( new BorderLayout() );
           this.getContentPane().add(tf1, BorderLayout.NORTH);
           this.getContentPane().add(b2, BorderLayout.SOUTH);
  };
  public static void main( String args[])
        {  textb4 thisprog = new textb4();
           thisprog.addWindowListener(new WindowAdapter()
              {  public void windowClosing(WindowEvent e)
                    {  System.exit(0); }
              });
           thisprog.setBounds(150,150,150,150);
           thisprog.setResizable(true); // works
           thisprog.pack();
           thisprog.setVisible(true);
        }
  public void actionPerformed(ActionEvent e)
     {
     if (e.getActionCommand().equals("shift") )
           { if ( tf1.getText().compareTo(st1) == 0 )
                 tf1.setText(st2);
              else tf1.setText(st1);
           }
     }
  }
```

If you run the program, you will get the following output.

By clicking the button shift, we will see the output string shifting back and forth.

Let us try one more program.

22.9.2 Finding a square of a number

Problem: Write a program to find a square of a given number.

Solution: The strategy is very simple. Get the input as a text, convert to number, and then square it (see Program 22.11).

PROGRAM 22.11 Finding Square of a Given Number

```
//    textb5.java
//   squaring numbers
import java.awt.* ;
import java.awt.event.* ;
import javax.swing.* ;

class textb5 extends JFrame implements ActionListener
  {  JTextField tf1;
//  String st1 = new String(" ***Welcome***");
//  String st2 = new String("***Welcome*** ");
    JButton b2 ;
    public textb5() // constructor
       {  tf1 = new JTextField( 30);
          tf1.addActionListener(this);
          tf1.setActionCommand("txt");
          b2 = new JButton("quit");
          b2.addActionListener(this);
          b2.setActionCommand("quit");
          this.getContentPane().setLayout( new BorderLayout() );
          this.getContentPane().add(tf1, BorderLayout.NORTH);
          this.getContentPane().add(b2, BorderLayout.SOUTH);
       };
  public static void main( String args[])
         {  textb5 thisprog = new textb5();
            thisprog.addWindowListener(new WindowAdapter()
               {  public void windowClosing(WindowEvent e)
                    {  System.exit(0); }
               });
            thisprog.setBounds(150,150,150,150);
            thisprog.setResizable(true); // works
            thisprog.pack();
            thisprog.setVisible(true);
         }
```

```
   public void actionPerformed(ActionEvent e)
     { String st9;
     int n;
       if (e.getActionCommand().equals("quit") )
             { System.exit(0);
             };
       if (e.getActionCommand().equals("txt") )
           { st9 = tf1.getText();
             st9 = st9.trim();
             n = Integer.parseInt(st9);
             tf1.setText(String.valueOf(n*n) ) ;
           }
     }
   }
```

If you run this program and type value 12 (even with leading and trailing blanks), then you will get the following output.

Output **textb5.out**

This was just a sample program. You can modify it for any mathematical or trigonometric function. If you add one more `TextField`, you can display both input as well as output simultaneously.

22.10 JTextArea

Since we know that `TextField` can handle only one line of text, we need another more powerful text component. Java provides us with `JTextArea`. This can handle multiple lines of texts. This class offers many constructors. We can specify the height and width in terms of columns and rows. We can also select the initial text to be displayed.

Problem: Write a program to demonstrate `JTextArea`.

Solution: In this program, we have a `JTextArea` and a button. We will define three strings. Initially we will keep text as null (blank). Initially the display will be blank. On every click of a button, we will add one string to the display (text area).

See Program 22.12.

PROGRAM 22.12 JTextArea Demo

```
//    jtrea.java
//
import java.awt.* ;
import java.awt.event.* ;
```

```
import javax.swing.* ;

class jtarea extends JFrame implements ActionListener
  {  JTextArea ta;
     int count = 0;
     String str0 = new String("1    ***Welcome***");
     String str1 = new String("\n\n2    to");
     String str2 = new String("\n\n3    JTextArea Demo \n\n *************");
     JButton b2 ;
     jtarea() // constructor
       {  super("JTextarea Demo");
          ta = new JTextArea("",10,40);
          b2 = new JButton("next");
          b2.addActionListener(this);
          b2.setActionCommand("next");
          b2.setVisible(true);
          this.getContentPane().setLayout( new BorderLayout() );
          this.getContentPane().add(ta, BorderLayout.NORTH);
          this.getContentPane().add(b2, BorderLayout.SOUTH);
           b2.setVisible(true);
  };

  public static void main( String args[])
       {  jtarea thisprog = new jtarea();
          thisprog.addWindowListener(new WindowAdapter()
           {  public void windowClosing(WindowEvent e)
                   {  System.exit(0); }
           });

       thisprog.setBounds(50,50,250,350);
       thisprog.setResizable(true); // works
       thisprog.pack();
       thisprog.setVisible(true);
       }
  public void actionPerformed(ActionEvent e)
    {  String st9 = "";

       if (e.getActionCommand().equals("next") )
         {  switch ( count++ )
              {  case 0 : st9 = str0;break;
                 case 1 : st9 = str1; break;
                 case 2 : st9 = str2;
              }
               ta.append(st9);
               //ta.setText(st9 ) ;
         }
    }
  }
```

If you run this program, you will first get following output with blank text area. When you start clicking button next, every time one string (starting with 1) will appear on screen. Any further clicking will have no effect on the text area.

Output

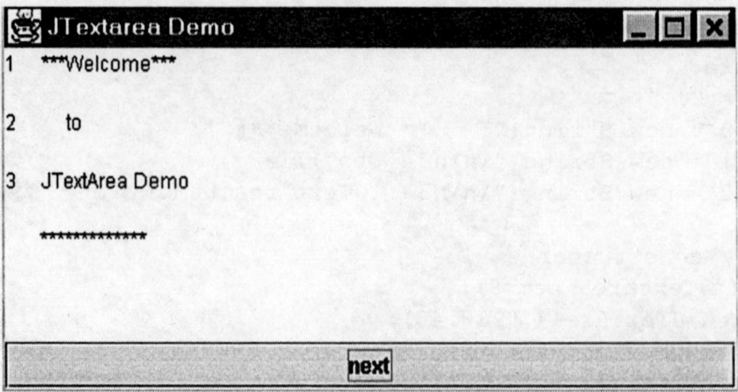

Please note that we do not have any positional control on the display. When we are adding say third line, we are actually appending the display string. In C++, we have methods like `outtextxy()`, which print the string at a given position on the string. This is not possible here. Of course in programming, nothing is impossible. You can write few lines of intelligent code with additional `TextField` for input and achieve the same. Any takers for this project?

22.11 JMenu

Once upon a time, an interviewer asked the candidate about the difference between software and a program. The reply was small application is a program and collection of applications is a software. Whether the answer is right or wrong is left to you. But if you want many programs in one program, what you need is menus. Let us study it with a program.

Problem: Write a program to study `Menu` facility.

Solution: The solution revolves around class `JMenu` (see Program 22.13).

PROGRAM 22.13 Menus

```
//      menu1.java

import java.awt.*;
import java.awt.event.*;
import javax.swing.*;

public class menu1 extends JFrame implements ActionListener
{
  JMenuBar mb = new JMenuBar();
  JMenu menuA, menuB;
  static JLabel lab;
  menu1()
    { super("Menu1");
      setJMenuBar(mb) ;
      menuA = new JMenu("one");
      menuB = new JMenu("two");
      mb.add(menuA);
```

```
    mb.add(menuB);
    JMenuItem item1;
    item1 = new JMenuItem("show");
    item1.addActionListener(this);
    JMenuItem item2;
    item2 = new JMenuItem("hide");
    item2.addActionListener(this);
    menuA.add(item1);
    menuB.add(item2);
    lab = new JLabel(" SHOW or HIDE");
  }

  public static void main(String s[])
  { menu1 thisprog = new menu1();

       thisprog.addWindowListener(new WindowAdapter()
         { public void windowClosing(WindowEvent e)
              {  System.exit(0); }
         });

    thisprog.setBounds(50,50,200,200);

    thisprog.add(lab);
    lab.setLocation(50,50);
    lab.setVisible(true);
    thisprog.setVisible(true);

  }
 public void actionPerformed(ActionEvent e)
  {  String name;
    name = e.getActionCommand();
    if ( name.equals("hide") )
      { lab.setVisible(false);repaint(); };

    if ( name.equals("show") )
      { lab.setVisible(true);repaint(); };
  }
}
```

When you run the program, you will get the following output.

Output

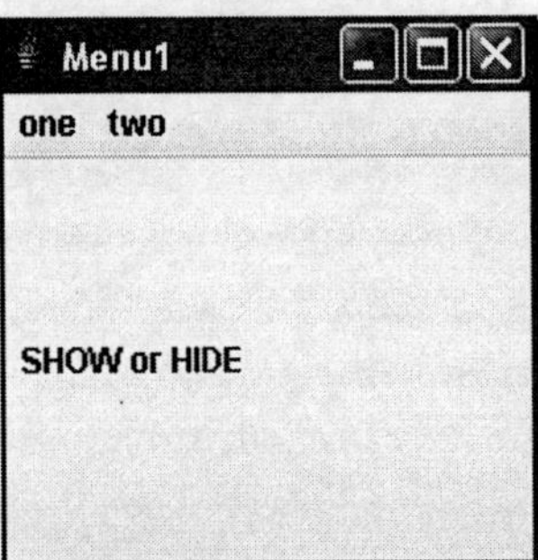

When you take mouse over one of the main menu items like "one" or "two", you see sub-menus show and hide, respectively. If you click hide, the message disappears and if you click show, message appears.

22.12 JFileChooser

In many applications, we have to choose a particular file from our computer. For this, we should be able to navigate through a directory structure and reach the desired file. Java provides us with a component `JFileChooser` for this purpose. Let us study it in a program.

Problem: Write a program to demonstrate "File Chooser Dialog".

Solution: We will use a button and a textbox in this program. The button will open the file chooser dialog. The text area will display the suitable comment at the end (see Program 22.14).

PROGRAM 22.14 Choosing a File

```
import java.io.*;
import java.awt.*;
import java.awt.event.*;
import javax.swing.*;
import javax.swing.filechooser.*;

public class fchoose extends JFrame
  { JTextArea log = new JTextArea(10,30);
    public fchoose()
      { super("fchoose");

          log.setEditable(false);

          //Create a file chooser
          final JFileChooser fc = new JFileChooser();

          //Create the open button
          JButton openButton = new JButton("Open a File...");
          openButton.addActionListener(new ActionListener() {
            public void actionPerformed(ActionEvent e) {
              int returnVal = fc.showOpenDialog(fchoose.this);

          if (returnVal == JFileChooser.APPROVE_OPTION) {
              File file = fc.getSelectedFile();
              //this is where a real application would open the file.
              log.append("Opening: " + file.getName() );
           } else {
              log.append("Open command cancelled by user." );
         }
      }
  });
          openButton.setBounds(50,30,140,30);
          log.setBounds(20,70,200,200);

          openButton.setVisible(true);
```

```
            log.setVisible(true);
            setLayout(null);

            add(openButton);
            add(log);
    }
      public static void main(String[] args) {
        JFrame frame = new fchoose();
        frame.addWindowListener(new WindowAdapter() {
            public void windowClosing(WindowEvent e) {
               System.exit(0);
            }
        });
        frame.setBounds(20,20,240,310);
        frame.setVisible(true);
      }
    }
```

When you run this program, the output frame with a button marked "open a file" appears. If you click that button then following file chooser dialog box appears. Actually, we have reached four layer down in directory structure.

Output

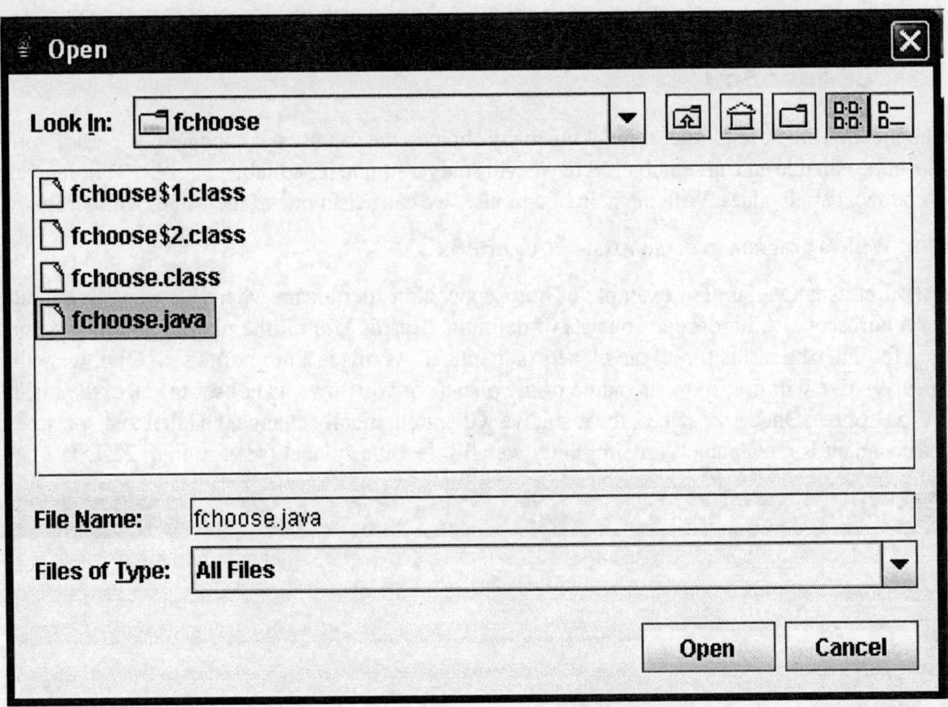

Suppose we chose the file `fchoose.java`, it gets highlighted. Now pressing the button "Open" selects this file and closes the dialog box. Now you will see the original frame with a message in the text box.

Output

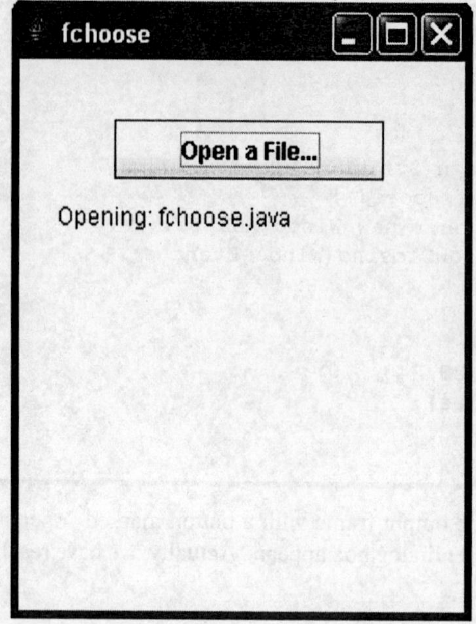

We have shown only basic functionality in this program. You can study additional features yourself.

22.13 JComboBox

If in an application we have to select one of the many choices, we can use a component `JComboBox`. It comes in two flavours, editable and un-editable. Here we will study a simple un-editable `JComboBox`. It gives a button and a dropdown list of values. With the help of a mouse, we can select one of the values from dropdown list.

Problem: Write a program to demonstrate `JComboBox`.

Solution: Let us take a familiar example of horoscope. Consider a case where we want an interactive data input for a horoscope. A horoscope consists of defining "Rashis" for all the planets and the ascendant. The procedure for entering rashis for all the planets is identical. As this is a program using GUI, we will not set a loop ourselves. We will first show the name of the planet for which we want user to select the rashi (we will use `JLabel` for it.). Once user selects the rashi, we will automatically change the label to display next planet. Though ascendant is not a planet, for simplicity we will treat it as planet (see Program 22.15).

PROGRAM 22.15 JComboBox

```
//     combo1.java
import java.awt.*;
import java.awt.event.*;
import javax.swing.*;

class combo1 extends JPanel
  { JLabel lab1 ;
    JTextArea ta ;
    int count = 0 ;
```

```
    public combo1() {
    final String[] Rname =
       {  "mesha",        "vrishabha","mithun",     "kark",
          "sinha",        "kanya",    "tula",       "vrischik",
          "dhanu",        "makar",    "kumbha",     "meena"
       };
    final String[] Pname =
       {  "Ascendent",  "ravi",      "chandra",   "mangal",   "budh",
          "guru",       "shukra",    "shani",     "rahu",
          "ketu",       "harshal",   "neptune",   "pluto"
       } ;
// Create the combo1 box
final JComboBox rashiList = new JComboBox(Rname);
rashiList.setSelectedIndex(7);
rashiList.addActionListener(new ActionListener() {

public void actionPerformed(ActionEvent e) {
     JComboBox cb = (JComboBox)e.getSource();
     String rashiName = (String)cb.getSelectedItem();
     ta.append( Pname[count] + " in " + rashiName +"\n");

     count++;
     if ( count > 12)
     { lab1.setText(" PROGRAM OVER");
       rashiList.setVisible(false);
     }
    else
       lab1.setText(" what is rashi of " + Pname[count]+" ? " );
     }
    });
    // Layout the demo
    setLayout(new BoxLayout(this,BoxLayout.Y_AXIS));
    lab1 = new JLabel(" what is rashi of " + Pname[count]+" ? " );
    ta = new JTextArea("",10,40);
    add(ta);
    add(lab1);
    add(rashiList);

 setBorder(BorderFactory.createEmptyBorder(20,20,20,20));
    }

    public static void main(String s[])
    {
    JFrame frame1 = new JFrame("Demo of JComboBox");
    frame1.addWindowListener(new WindowAdapter() {
      public void windowClosing(WindowEvent e) {System.exit(0);}
 });
      frame1.setContentPane(new combo1());
      frame1.setSize(300,400);;
      frame1.setVisible(true);
     }
 }
```

A sample partial output is as follows.

Output

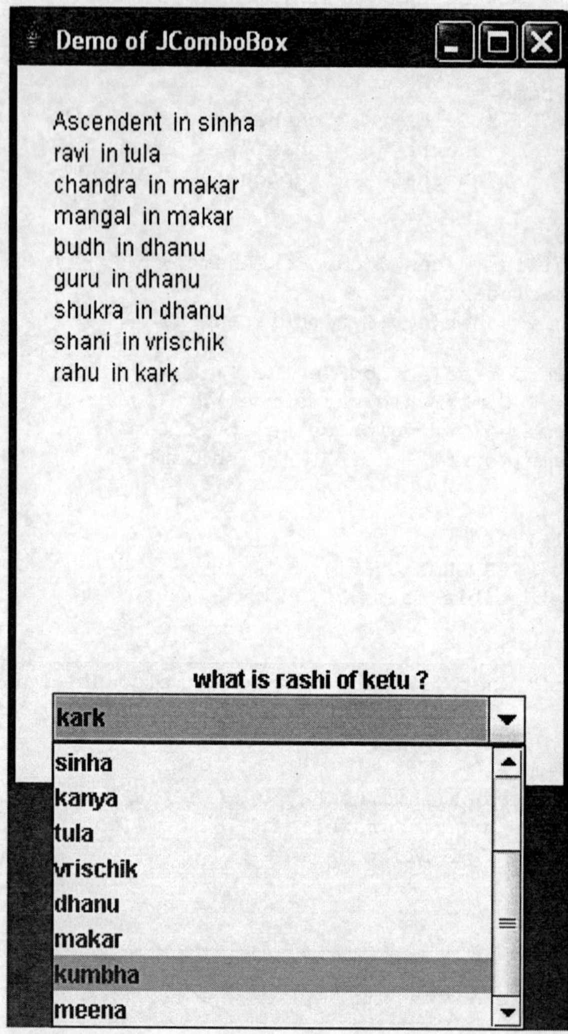

So far, we have seen many programs using swing components. We have placed (laid out) the components on the frame in different manner. Now is the time to introduce this facility formally. Let us study the layout manger.

22.14 Layout Manager

A typical swing application will contain many components. There are two ways to lay (place) these components in a container. We can place components at fixed specified locations. Alternately, we can use layout managers.

Package AWT support many classes, which provide layout managers for general use. These classes are as follows:

- `BorderLayout`
- `CardLayout`
- `FlowLayout`
- `GridBagLayout`
- `GridLayout`

A swing application can use any of the above mangers. In addition, there are some more managers defined in swing. Some of them are as follows:

- `BoxLayout`
- `SpringLayout`

In this chapter, we have already used some of them without any discussion. Let us take a close look at few of them.

22.14.1 BorderLayout

`BorderLayout` divides the content pane in five areas. One is at top, one at bottom, and three in the middle. These positions are identified by constants NORTH, SOUTH, EAST, CENTER, and WEST.

Let us study it with a program.

Problem: Write a program to demonstrate `BorderLayout`.

Solution: In this program, we will set five buttons. As this is only showing locations, we will not assign any action with these buttons (see Program 22.16).

PROGRAM 22.16 `BorderLayout`

```
//      layout1.java

import java.awt.* ;
import java.awt.event.* ;
import javax.swing.* ;

class layout1 extends JFrame implements ActionListener
  {  JButton b1,b2,b3,b4,b5 ;
     public layout1() // constructor
       { b1 = new JButton("One,top");
         b2 = new JButton("Two,left");
         b3 = new JButton("Three,middle");
         b4 = new JButton("Four,east");
         b5 = new JButton("Five,bottom");

         this.getContentPane().setLayout( new BorderLayout() );
         this.getContentPane().add(b1,BorderLayout.NORTH);
         this.getContentPane().add(b2,BorderLayout.WEST);
         this.getContentPane().add(b3,BorderLayout.CENTER);
         this.getContentPane().add(b4,BorderLayout.EAST);
         this.getContentPane().add(b5,BorderLayout.SOUTH);
```

```
    };

public static void main( String args[])
      { layout1 thisprog = new layout1();
        thisprog.addWindowListener(new WindowAdapter()
          { public void windowClosing(WindowEvent e)
               { System.exit(0); }
          });
      thisprog.setBounds(0,0,300,300);

//      thisprog.pack();
      thisprog.setVisible(true);
      }
  public void actionPerformed(ActionEvent e)
    {
    }
  }
```

When you run the program, you will get the following output.

Output

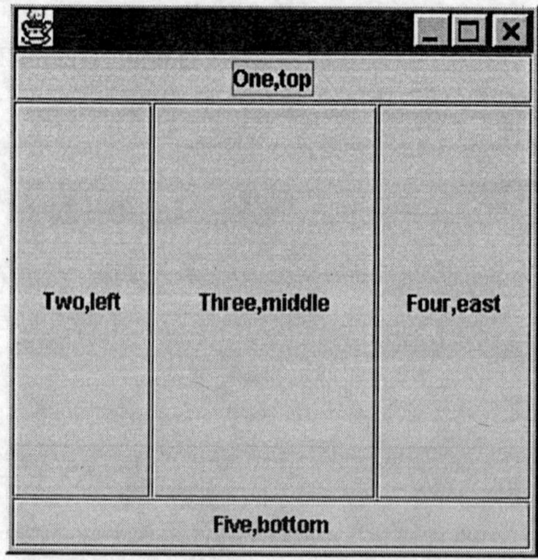

Please note the following points:

1. Top and bottom areas are of low height. Most of the height of the pane is filled by the three central areas.
2. The middle area is in general the largest area.
3. If we do not define any size for the buttons, these buttons occupy the whole area.
4. When we resize the window, the shapes of buttons start changing.
5. In this program, we have used buttons. However, layout manger is a general tool. We can use it for any component. Actually, there can be different components in different area.

The earlier constants like NORTH and SOUTH can be replaced by new set of constants as given hereafter.

New name	Old name
PAGE_START	NORTH
PAGE_END	SOUTH
LINE_START	WEST
LINE_END	EAST
CENTER	CENTER

Please note that the new names are available in JDK 5 onwards. Let us study one more program with these constants.

Problem: Write a program to demonstrate use of `BorderLayout`.

Solution: See Program 22.17.

PROGRAM 22.17 `BorderLayout` Demo

```
//      layout2.java
//
import java.awt.* ;
import java.awt.event.* ;
import javax.swing.* ;

class layout2 extends JFrame implements ActionListener
  { JButton b1,b2,b3,b4,b5 ;
    public layout2() // constructor
      { b1 = new JButton("One,PAGE_START");
        b2 = new JButton("Two,LINE_START");
        b3 = new JButton("Three,CENTER");
        b4 = new JButton("Four,LINE_END");
        b5 = new JButton("Five,PAGE_END");

        this.getContentPane().setLayout( new BorderLayout() );

this.getContentPane().add(b1,BorderLayout.PAGE_START);
this.getContentPane().add(b2,BorderLayout.LINE_START);
this.getContentPane().add(b3,BorderLayout.CENTER);
this.getContentPane().add(b4,BorderLayout.LINE_END);
this.getContentPane().add(b5,BorderLayout.PAGE_END);
      };

  public static void main( String args[])
      { layout2 thisprog = new layout2();
        thisprog.addWindowListener(new WindowAdapter()
        { public void windowClosing(WindowEvent e)
```

```
                { System.exit(0); }
        });
        thisprog.setBounds(0,0,400,300);
        thisprog.setVisible(true);
    }
public void actionPerformed(ActionEvent e)
    {
    }
  }
```

If you run this program, you will get the following output.

Output

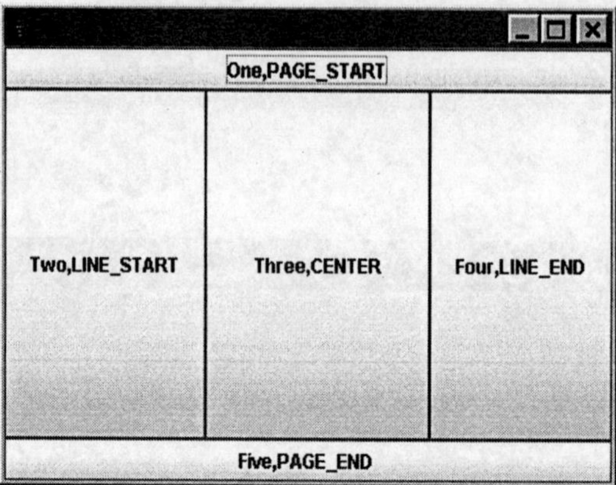

22.14.2 BoxLayout

In this style, components can be laid in a specified axis. By axis, we basically mean vertical or horizontal. Strictly speaking, there are two more axis named line axis and page axis. Let us study a simple program using this layout.

Problem: Write a program to demonstrate BoxLayout.

Solution: In this program, we will again use five buttons.

PROGRAM 22.18 BoxLayout

```
//    layout3.java
import java.awt.* ;
import java.awt.event.* ;
import javax.swing.* ;

class myPanel extends JPanel
  { JButton b1, b2, b3, b4, b5 ;
```

```
   myPanel()
   {
     b1 = new JButton("One");
     b2 = new JButton("Two");
     b3 = new JButton("Three");
     b4 = new JButton("Four");
     b5 = new JButton("Five");

     setLayout ( new BoxLayout(this,BoxLayout.Y_AXIS) );
     add(b1);
     add(b2);
     add(b3);
     add(b4);
     add(b5);
   }
 };

class layout3 extends JFrame implements ActionListener
 { static myPanel thisone = new myPanel();

    public static void main( String args[])
      { layout3 thisprog = new layout3();
        thisprog.addWindowListener(new WindowAdapter()
          { public void windowClosing(WindowEvent e)
                  { System.exit(0); }
          });
    thisprog.setBounds(0,0,150,250);
    thisprog.add(thisone );
    thisprog.setVisible(true);
      }
  public void actionPerformed(ActionEvent e)
    {
    }
  }
```

When you run the program, you will get the following output.

Output

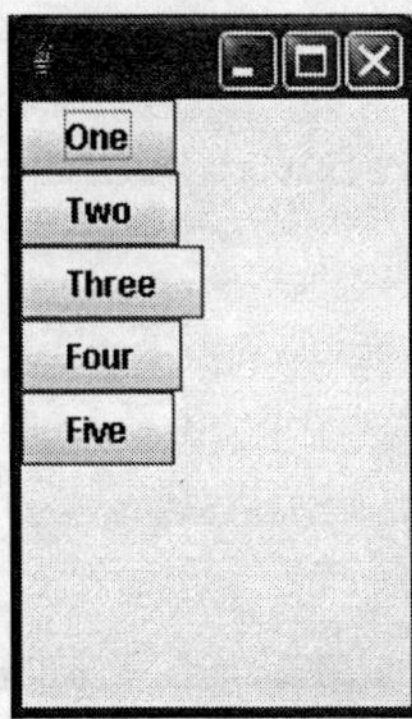

As we have selected "Y Axis" the buttons are placed one below the other.

22.14.3 GridLayout

In this layout, we can divide the container in rectangular grid. It will define equal-sized rectangular areas. Grid can have more than one rows and columns. Let us study a simple program.

Problem: Write a program to demonstrate `GridLayout`.

Solution: In this program, we will again use five buttons.

PROGRAM 22.19 GridLayout

```
//    layout4.java
//     GridLayout

import java.awt.*;
import java.awt.event.*;
import javax.swing.*;

public class layout4 extends JPanel
    { static JPanel myPanel;
      static JButton b1 = new JButton("One");
      static JButton b2 = new JButton("Two");
      static JButton b3 = new JButton("Three");
      static JButton b4 = new JButton("Four");
      static JButton b5 = new JButton("Five");

       public static void main(String s[]) {
         JFrame frame = new JFrame("gridLayout demo");
         frame.addWindowListener(new WindowAdapter() {
           public void windowClosing(WindowEvent e) {
             System.exit(0);
         }
       });
       frame.setSize(300,300);
       myPanel = new JPanel();
       frame.add(myPanel);
       myPanel.setLayout(new GridLayout(3, 1));

       myPanel.add(b1);
       myPanel.add(b2);
       myPanel.add(b3);
       myPanel.add(b4);
       myPanel.add(b5);

       frame.setVisible(true);
    }
}
```

When you run the program, you will get the following output.

Output

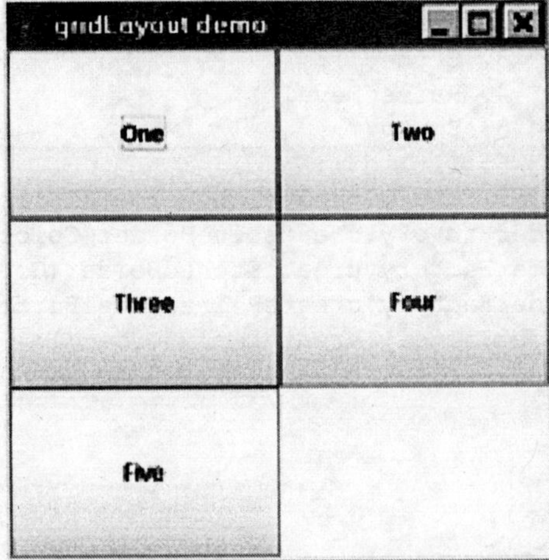

22.15 Using Borders

In some of the previous programs, we have seen the components having borders. In Java, we can have border for any `JComponent` like `JButton`. It means that we cannot have borders for AWT components like `Button`. The reason is method `setBorder()` is defined in `JComponent` class from package `javax.swing`

Borders are useful in improving the appearance of the `JComponent` on the screen. Borders not only support lines but also allow us to provide titles and empty space around the component.

Problem: Write a program to demonstrate various borders.

Solution: In this program, we will again use five labels and have following type of borders around them.

```
LineBorder
EtchedBorder
RaisedBevelBorder
EmptyBorder
TitledBorder
```

PROGRAM 22.20 Borders

```
//      borl.java
import java.awt.*;
import java.awt.event.*;
import javax.swing.*;
import javax.swing.border.Border;
import javax.swing.border.TitledBorder;
```

```
class myform extends JPanel
{ JLabel lab1,lab2,lab3,lab4,lab5,lab6;
  public myform()
  { lab1 = new JLabel(" 1. Line");
    lab2 = new JLabel(" 2. Line thickness");
    lab3 = new JLabel(" 3. Etched");
    lab4 = new JLabel(" 4. RaisedBevel");
    lab5 = new JLabel(" 5. Empty");
    lab6 = new JLabel(" 6. Titled");
    Border line1 = BorderFactory.createLineBorder(Color.red);
    Border line2 = BorderFactory.createLineBorder(Color.green, 5);
    Border line3 = BorderFactory.createEtchedBorder(Color.blue,Color.yellow);
    Border line4 = BorderFactory.createRaisedBevelBorder();
    Border line5 = BorderFactory.createEmptyBorder();
    Border line6 = BorderFactory.createTitledBorder("Bhave Patekar");
    lab1.setBorder(line1);
    lab2.setBorder(line2);
    lab3.setBorder(line3);
    lab4.setBorder(line4);
    lab5.setBorder(line5);
    lab6.setBorder(line6);
    setLayout(null);
    lab1.setBounds (20,30,150,50);
    lab2.setBounds (20,100,150,50);
    lab3.setBounds (20,170,150,50);
    lab4.setBounds (20,270,150,50);
    lab5.setBounds (20,310,150,50);
    lab6.setBounds (20,380,150,50);

    add(lab1);
    add(lab2) ;
    add(lab3) ;
    add(lab4);
    add(lab5) ;
    add(lab6) ;
  }
}
public class bor1
  { public static void main(String[] args)
     { JFrame frame = new JFrame();
       frame.addWindowListener(new WindowAdapter() {
        public void windowClosing(WindowEvent e)
            { System.exit(0); }
                               });
       frame.getContentPane().add(new myform()); // , BorderLayout.EAST);
       frame.setSize(170+50,430+50);
       frame.setVisible(true);
     }
  };
```

When you run the program, you will get the following output.

Output

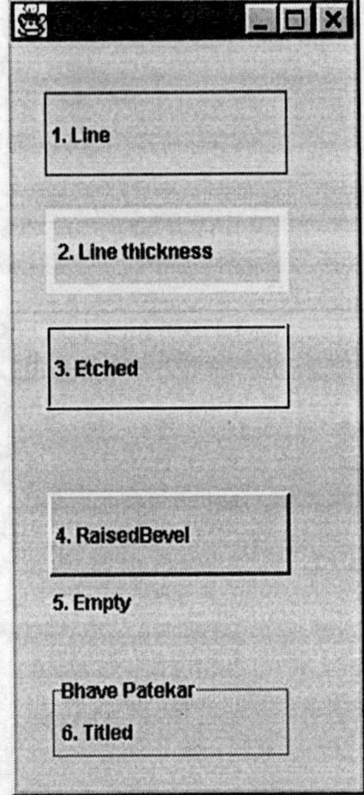

22.16 Java Foundation Classes

Java foundation classes known as JFC exhibit very rich features for developing GUI-based applications. Now we can write Java programs with better interactivity and graphical support. The features are as follows:

- Swing GUI components
- Pluggable look-and-feel support
- Accessibility API
- Java 2D API
- Drag-and-drop support
- Internationalization

Java has large number of APIs spread over different packages. Its discussion is out of the scope of the present text. As swing components are part of JFC, they can make use of its features. Because of this, swing architecture provides a number of advantages in the following areas:

- Wide variety of components
- Pluggable look and feel
- MVC architecture
- Keystroke handling
- Action objects
- Nested containers
- Generic undo capabilities
- Virtual desktops
- Compound borders
- Customized dialogs
- Standard dialog classes
- Structured table and tree components
- Powerful text manipulation
- Accessibility support

Discussion of these features is beyond the scope of present text. You may study these and utilize them on your own.

Table 22.1 describes various methods from the class `BorderFactory`.

Table 22.1 Creating a Border with `BorderFactory`

Method	Purpose
`Border createLineBorder (Color)` `Border createLineBorder (Color, int)`	Create a line border. The first argument is a `java.awt.Color` object that specifies the colour of the line. The optional second argument specifies the width in pixels of the line.

`Border createEtchedBorder()`
`Border createEtchedBorder (Color, Color)`
`Border createEtchedBorder(int)`
`Border createEtchedBorder (int, Color, Color)`
	Create an etched border. The optional Color arguments specify the highlight and shadow colours to be used. In release 1.3, methods with int arguments were added that allow the border methods to be specified as either `EtchedBorder.RAISED` or `EtchedBorder.LOWERED`. The methods without the int arguments create a lowered etched border.

`Border createLoweredBevelBorder()`	Create a border that gives the illusion of the component being lower than the surrounding area.
`Border createRaisedBevelBorder()`	Create a border that gives the illusion of the component being higher than the surrounding area.
`Border createBevelBorder (int, Color, Color)` `Border createBevelBorder (int, Color, Color, Color, Color)`	Create a raised or lowered beveled border, specifyibg the colours to use. The integer argument can be either `BevelBorder.RAISED` or `BevelBorder.LOWERED`. With the three-argument constructor, you specify the highlight and shadow colours. With the five-argument constructor, you specify the outer highlight, inner highlight, outer shadow, and inner shadow colours, in that order.
`Border createEmptyBorder()` `Border createEmptyBorder(int, int, int, int)`	Create an invisible border. If you specify no arguments, then the border takes no space, which is useful when creating a titled border with no visible boundary. The optional arguments specify the number of pixels that the border occupies at the top, left, bottom, and right (in that order) of whatever component uses it. This method is useful for putting empty space around your components.
`MatteBorder createMatteBorder (int, int, int, int, Color)` `MatteBorder createMatteBorder(int, int, int, int, Icon)`	Create a matte border. The integer arguments specify the number of pixels that the border occupies at the top, left, bottom, and right (in that order) of whatever component uses it. The colour argument specifies the colour with which the border should fill its area. The icon argument specifies the icon with which the border should tile its area.

(Continued)

Table 22.1 ***(Continued)***

`Titled Border createTitled Border (String)`
`TitledBorder createTitled Border(Border)`
`TitledBorder createTitled Border (Border, String)`
`TitledBorder createTitled Border (Border, String, int, int)`
`TitledBorder createTitled Border(Border, String, int, int, Font)`
`Titled Border createTitled Border(Border, String, int, int, Font, Color)`
	Create a titled border. The string argument specifies the title to be displayed. The optional font and colour arguments specify the font and colour to be used for the title's text. The border argument specifies the border that should be displayed along with the title. If no border is specified, then a look-and-feel-specific default border is used.
	By default, the title straddles the top of its companion border and is left-justified. The optional integer arguments specify the title's position and justi fication, in that order. `TitledBorder` defines these possible positions: ABOVE_TOP, TOP (the default), BELOW_TOP, ABOVE_BOTTOM, BOTTOM, and BELOW_BOTTOM. You can specify the justification as LEADING (the default), CENTER, or TRAILING. In locales with Western alphabets LEADING is equivalent to LEFT and TRAILING is equivalent to RIGHT.

`CompoundBorder createCompoundBorder (Border, Border)`	Combine two borders into one. The first argument specifies the outer border; the second, the inner border.

Table 22.2 summarizes the classes available in package `Javax.swing`.

Table 22.2 **Class Summary: `Javax.swing`**

`AbstractAction`	This class provides default implementations for the JFC `Action` interface.
`AbstractButton`	Defines common behaviours for buttons and menu items.
`AbstractCellEditor`	
`AbstractListModel`	The abstract definition for the data model provides a list with its contents.
`ActionMap`	`ActionMap` provides mappings from objects (called keys or action names) to actions.
`BorderFactory`	Factory class for vending standard border objects.
`Box`	A lightweight container that uses a `BoxLayout` object as its layout manager.
`Box.Filler`	An implementation of a lightweight component that participates in layout but has no view.

(Continued)

Table 22.2 *(Continued)*

BoxLayout	A layout manager that allows multiple components to be laid out either vertically or horizontally.
ButtonGroup	This class is used to create a multiple exclusion scope for a set of buttons.
CellRendererPane	This class is inserted in between cell renderers and the components that use them.
ComponentInputMap	A ComponentInputMap is an InputMap associated with a particular JComponent.
DebugGraphics	Graphics sub-class supporting graphics debugging.
DefaultBoundedRangeModel	A generic implementation of BoundedRangeModel.
DefaultButtonModel	The default implementation of a button component's data model.
DefaultCellEditor	The default editor for table and tree cells.
DefaultComboBoxModel	The default model for combo boxes.
DefaultDesktopManager	This is an implementaion of the DesktopManager.
DefaultFocusManager	Default swing focus manager implementation.
DefaultListCellRenderer	Renders an item in a list.
DefaultListCellRenderer.UIResource	A sub-class of DefaultListCellRenderer that implements UIResource.
DefaultListModel	This class implements the java.util.Vector API and notifies the ListDataListeners when changes occur.
DefaultListSelectionModel	Default data model for list selections.
DefaultSingleSelectionModel	A generic implementation of SingleSelectionModel.
FocusManager	Swing Focus Manager
GrayFilter	An image filter that "disables" an image by turning it into a greyscale image, and brightening the pixels in the image.
ImageIcon	An implementation of the icon interface that paints icons from images.
InputMap	InputMap provides a binding between an input event (currently only KeyStrokes are used) and an object.

(Continued)

Table 22.2 ***(Continued)***

`InputVerifier`	The purpose of this class is to help clients support smooth focus navigation through GUIs with text fields.
`JApplet`	An extended version of `java.applet.Applet` that adds support for the JFC/swing component architecture.
`JButton`	An implementation of a "push" button.
`JCheckBox`	An implementation of a check box—an item that can be selected or deselected, and which displays its state to the user.
`JCheckBoxMenuItem`	A menu item that can be selected or deselected.
`JColorChooser`	`JColorChooser` provides a pane of controls designed to allow a user to manipulate and select a colour.
`JComboBox`	A component that combines a button or text field and a drop-down list.
`JComponent`	The base class for all swing components except top-level containers.
`JDesktopPane`	A container used to create a multiple-document interface or a virtual desktop.
`JDialog`	The main class for creating a dialog window.
`JEditorPane`	A text component to edit various kinds of content.
`JFileChooser`	`JFileChooser` provides a simple mechanism for the user to choose a file.
`JFrame`	An extended version of `java.awt.Frame` that adds support for the JFC/swing component architecture.
`JInternalFrame`	A lightweight object that provides many of the features of a native frame, including dragging, closing, becoming an icon, resizing, title display, and support for a menu bar.
`JInternalFrame.JDesktopIcon`	This component represents an iconified version of a `JInternalFrame`.
`JLabel`	A display area for a short text string or an image, or both.
`JLayeredPane`	`JLayeredPane` adds depth to a JFC/swing container, allowing components to overlap each other when needed.
`JList`	A component that allows the user to select one or more objects from a list.

(*Continued*)

Table 22.2 *(Continued)*

`JMenu`	An implementation of a menu—a pop-up window containing `JMenuItems` that is displayed when the user selects an item on the `JMenuBar`.
`JMenuBar`	An implementation of a menu bar.
`JMenuItem`	An implementation of an item in a menu.
`JOptionPane`	`JOptionPane` makes it easy to pop up a standard dialog box that prompts users for a value or informs them of something.
`JPanel`	`JPanel` is a generic lightweight container.
`JPasswordField`	`JPasswordField` is a lightweight component that allows the editing of a single line of text where the view indicates something was typed, but does not show the original characters.
`JPopupMenu`	An implementation of a popup menu—a small window that pops up and displays a series of choices.
`JPopupMenu.Separator`	A popup menu-specific separator.
`JProgressBar`	A component that displays an integer value within a bounded interval.
`JRadioButton`	An implementation of a radio button—an item that can be selected or deselected, and which displays its state to the user.
`JRadioButtonMenuItem`	An implementation of a radio button menu item.
`JRootPane`	A lightweight container used behind the scenes by `JFrame`, `JDialog`, `JWindow`, `JApplet`, and `JInternalFrame`.
`JScrollBar`	An implementation of a scrollbar.
`JScrollPane`	Provides a scrollable view of a component.
`JSeparator`	An implementation of a menu separator—a divider between menu items that breaks them up into logical groupings.
`JSlider`	A component that lets the user graphically select a value by sliding a knob within a bounded interval.
`JSplitPane`	`JSplitPane` is used to divide two (and only two) Components.

(Continued)

Table 22.2 *(Continued)*

JTabbedPane	A component that lets the user switch between a group of components by clicking on a tab with a given title and/or icon.
JTable	JTable is a user-interface component that presents data in a two-dimensional table format.
JTextArea	A TextArea is a multi-line area that displays plain text.
JTextField	JTextField is a lightweight component that allows the editing of a single line of text.
JTextPane	A text component that can be marked up with attributes that are represented graphically.
JToggleButton	An implementation of a two-state button.
JToggleButton.ToggleButtonModel	The ToggleButton model
JToolBar	JToolBar provides a component that is useful for displaying commonly used Actions or controls.
JToolBar.Separator	A toolbar-specific separator.
JToolTip	Used to display a "Tip" for a Component.
JTree	A control that displays a set of hierarchical data as an outline.
JTree.DynamicUtilTreeNode	DynamicUtilTreeNode can wrap vectors/hashtables/arrays/strings and create the appropriate children tree nodes as necessary.
JTree.EmptySelectionModel	EmptySelectionModel is a TreeSelectionModel that does not allow anything to be selected.
JViewport	The "viewport" or "porthole" through which you see the underlying information.
JWindow	A JWindow is a container that can be displayed anywhere on the user's desktop.
KeyStroke	A KeyStroke instance represents a key being typed on the keyboard—it contains both a char code for the key and a modifier (alt, shift, ctrl, meta, or a combination).
LookAndFeel	Completely characterizes a look and feel from the point of view of the pluggable look and feel components.
MenuSelectionManager	A MenuSelectionManager owns the selection in menu hierarchy.

(Continued)

Table 22.2 *(Continued)*

`OverlayLayout`	A layout manager to arrange components over the top of each other.
`ProgressMonitor`	A class to monitor the progress of some operation.
`ProgressMonitorInputStream`	Monitors the progress of reading from some `InputStream`.
`RepaintManager`	This class manages repaint requests, allowing the number of repaints to be minimized, for example by collapsing multiple requests into a single repaint for members of a component tree.
`ScrollPaneLayout`	The layout manager used by `JScrollPane`.
`ScrollPaneLayout.UIResource`	The UI resource version of `ScrollPaneLayout`.
`SizeRequirements`	For the convenience of layout managers, calculates information about the size and position of components.
`SizeSequence`	A `SizeSequence` object efficiently maintains an ordered list of sizes and corresponding positions.
`SwingUtilities`	A collection of utility methods for swing.
`Timer`	Causes an action to occur at a predefined rate.
`ToolTipManager`	Manages all the `ToolTips` in the system.
`UIDefaults`	A table of defaults for swing components.
`UIDefaults.LazyInputMap`	`LazyInputMap` will create an `InputMap` in its `createValue` method.
`UIDefaults.ProxyLazyValue`	This class provides an implementation of `LazyValue` which can be used to delay loading of the Class for the instance to be created.
`UIManager`	This class keeps track of the current look and feel and its defaults.
`UIManager.LookAndFeelInfo`	Provide a little information about an installed `LookAndFeel` for the sake of configuring a menu or for initial application set up.
`ViewportLayout`	The default layout manager for `JViewport`.

Keywords

`BorderLayout`, `BoxLayout`, `ButtonGroup`, Canvas, CENTER, `createBevelBorder()`, `createCompoundBorder()`, `createEmptyBorder()`, `createEtchedBorder()`, createLineBorder(), createLoweredBevelBorder(), createMatteBorder(), createRaisedBevelBorder(), createTitledBorder(), EAST, EmptyBorder, EtchedBorder, GridLayout, JButton, Jcheckbox, JComboBox, JFileChooser, JFrame, JFrame.EXIT_ON_CLOSE, JLabel, JMenu, JOptionPane, JRadioButton, JTextArea, JTextField, lightweight components, LineBorder, NORTH, pack(), RaisedBevelBorder, setBounds(), setDefaultCloseOperation, showInputDialog(), showMessageDialog(), SOUTH, TitledBorder, WEST

RuleBook

Jpanel	Jpanel is a Container.
Javax.swing	Javax.swing is the high level swing package, primarily consists of components, adapters, default component models and interfaces for all the delegates and models.
RadioButtons	RadioButtons are implemented in swing through the JRadioButtons class.

Review Questions

1. Write short note on FlowLayoutManager.
2. Write short note on Layout Manager.
3. What is the difference between AWT and swing?
4. Write a short note on JFC.

Exercises

1. A small game consisting of 15 squares is very popular. A small toy consists of in a fixed enclosure 15 plastic pieces numbered 1 to 15. They are in a 4 × 4 grid with one empty slot. This slot helps to move a piece adjoining to it. Initially the pieces are in random order. Aim of the game is to bring all pieces in order.
2. Write a program named displayFile.java. It should have two menus. The first one will help selecting a text file. The second one will display it.
3. Write a java applet program using swing methods and classes to find the factorial of a number, which is accepted from keyboard. Use the recursive method for factorial. Also, write the HTML code for displaying the applet.
4. Write a Java Applet using swing methods and classes to find maximum out of *n* given numbers.
5. Write a program using swing and awt to design a digital clock.
6. Design a simple text editor capable of editing new as well as existing files.

COLLECTION FRAMEWORK

When we start studying a programming language, we work with simple primitive data types. Then we study objects and arrays. When we start programming for real-life problems, two things happen: the size of data we handle increases and the processing also gets involved.

At this stage the program development time increases. The execution time of the program also becomes significant.

Therefore, at this stage when we want to handle huge data, we must have appropriate tools with us. Java comes with the answer—a "collection framework".

By collection, we mean an object which groups multiple elements in a single group. The elements in general are data objects. Examples are library books, student records, and so on. The equivalent of Collections in C++ is known as Standard Template Library (STL) which offers container classes and algorithms.

A framework means a skeleton, an arrangement, or an organization. Hence, collection framework provides us a nice organization to handle large amount of data. It consists of interfaces, implementations, and algorithms.

The basic entity in this collection framework is the interface. The Java collection framework provides the following interfaces.

- `Collection`
- `Set`
- `SortedSet`
- `List`
- `Queue`
- `Map`
- `SortedMap`

Their hierarchical relationship is displayed in Figure 23.1.

A close look will reveal that there are two distinct groups. The `Map` and `SortedMap` belong to a separate group. A typical element of this group is a "pair of object", while in the other group, an element is nothing but a single object.

There are many benefits of the Java collection framework. However, at this level we can appreciate only two of them.

Using collections reduces programming effort. It provides us with ready-made implementations of data structures and algorithms. In any medium-size program, one will have to devote about 70% time to these things. If we have mastered the collection framework, writing related code will settle to writing only a few lines. It means there will be substantial reduction in programming efforts.

It also increases program speed and quality. As these data structures and algorithms are implemented by experts, the chance is that programs using them will execute faster than those developed by an average programmer. Also by using collection framework, we save substantial time for program development. This time can be utilized to tune and improve the performance of the program.

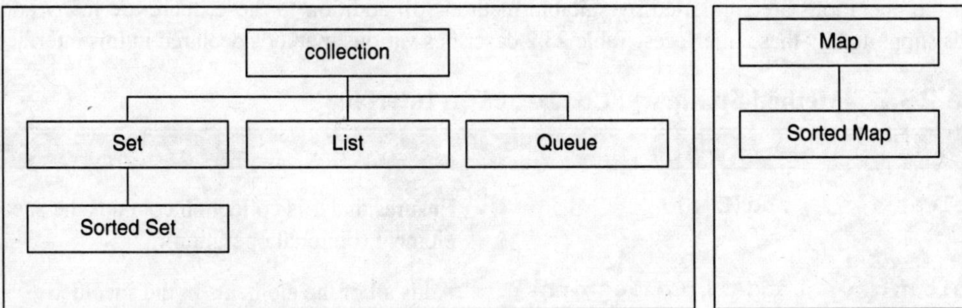

Figure 23.1 Hierarchical Relationship of `Collection` Interfaces

It is possible to implement these interfaces using different data structures like resizable array, `LinkedList`, `Hashtable`, among others. It gives these implementations different performance parameters. It is possible to have a given interface to have different implementations. Table 23.1 illustrates general-purpose implementations of various `Collection` interfaces.

Table 23.1 Collection Framework: General-Purpose Implementations

Interfaces	Implementations				
	Hashtable	Resizable array	Tree	LinkedList	Hashtable + LinkedList
Set	HashSet		TreeSet		LinkedHashSet
List		ArrayList		LinkedList	
Queue					
Map	HashMap		TreeMap		LinkedHashMap

These interfaces and the classes which implement them are available in the package `java.util.` With this much background, let us start our detailed study with `Collection` interface.

23.1 `Collection` Interface

The `Collection` interface provides the basic functionality for the collection. As the name collection suggests collecting objects, we can imagine on our own what methods (for operations) this interface should support.

The basic operations we expect are as follows:

- Add an element to the collection.
- Remove the element from the collection.
- Find the number of elements in the collection.
- Move from element to element for which we need an iterator.

All the operations are supported by suitable methods. In addition to these, there are many additional methods supported by these interfaces. Table 23.2 describes various methods declared in this interface.

Table 23.2 Method Summary: Collection Interface

boolean	add(E o)	Ensures that this collection contains the specified element (optional operation).
boolean	addAll(Collection<? extends E> c)	Adds all of the elements in the specified collection to this collection (optional operation).
void	clear()	Removes all of the elements from this collection (optional operation).
boolean	contains(Object o)	Returns true if this collection contains the specified element.
boolean	containsAll (Collection<?> c)	Returns true if this collection contains all of the elements in the specified collection.
boolean	equals(Object o)	Compares the specified object with this collection for equality.
int	hashCode()	Returns the hash code value for this collection.
boolean	isEmpty()	Returns true if this collection contains no elements.
Iterator<E>	iterator()	Returns an iterator over the elements in this collection.
boolean	remove(Object o)	Removes a single instance of the specified element from this collection, if it is present (optional operation).
boolean	removeAll(Collection <?> c)	Removes all elements of this collection that are also contained in the specified collection (optional operation).
boolean	retainAll(Collection <?> c)	Retains only the elements in this collection that are contained in the specified collection (optional operation).
int	size()	Returns the number of elements in this collection.
Object[]	toArray()	Returns an array containing all of the elements in this collection.
<T> T[]	toArray(T[] a)	Returns an array containing all of the elements in this collection; the runtime type of the returned array is that of the specified array.

23.2 List Interface

The first interface based on Collection interface that we are going to study is List interface. Here the collection is an ordered collection. We may call it a sequence. It may be noted that duplicates are allowed in this collection.

This interface provides operations for the following tasks:

- *Positional access*: We can manipulate elements based on position in the list (similar to the index of an array).
- *Search*: We can search for a specified object in the list and get its position
- *Iteration*: We can iterate over the list.
- *Range view*: We can perform arbitrary range operations on the list.

You may want to compare the List interface with class Vector. The class Vector is a concrete implementation while list is only an interface. However, both have similar functionality. It is reported that List interface is better than Vector as it has removed some of its minor deficiencies. The class Vector has been retrofitted to implement List.

Table 23.3 describes the various methods from Interface List.

Table 23.3 Method Summary: Interface List

Boolean	add(E o)	Appends the specified element to the end of this list (optional operation).
void	add(int index, E element)	Inserts the specified element at the specified position in this list (optional operation).
boolean	addAll(Collection <? extends E> c)	Appends all of the elements in the specified collection to the end of this list, in the order that they are returned by the integrator of the specified collection (optional operation).
boolean	addAll(int index, Collection <? extends E> c)	Inserts all the elements in the specified collection into this list at the specified position (optional operation).
void	clear()	Removes all the elements from this list (optional operation).
boolean	contains(Object o)	Returns true if this list contains the specified element.
boolean	containsAll (Collection<?> c)	Returns true if this list contains all the elements of the specified collection.

(*Continued*)

Table 23.3 *(Continued)*

boolean	equals(Object o)	Compares the specified object with this list for equality.
E	get(int index)	Returns the element at the specified position in this list.
int	hashCode()	Returns the hash code value for this list.
int	indexOf(Object o)	Returns the index in this list of the first occurrence of the specified element, or −1 if this list does not contain this element.
boolean	isEmpty()	Returns true if this list contains no elements.
Iterator<E>	iterator()	Returns an iterator over the elements in this list in proper sequence.
int	lastIndexOf(Object o)	Returns the index in this list of the last occurrence of the specified element, or −1 if this list does not contain this element.
ListIterator<E>	listIterator()	Returns a list iterator of the elements in this list (in proper sequence).
ListIterator<E>	listIterator(int index)	Returns a list iterator of the elements in this list (in proper sequence), starting at the specified position in this list.
E	remove(int index)	Removes the element at the specified position in this list (optional operation).
boolean	remove(Object o)	Removes the first occurrence in this list of the specified element (optional operation).
boolean	removeAll (Collection<?> c)	Removes from this list all the elements that are contained in the specified collection (optional operation).

(Continued)

Table 23.3 (*Continued*)

`boolean`	`retainAll(Collection <?> c)`	Retains only the elements in this list that are contained in the specified collection (optional operation).
`E`	`set(int index, E element)`	Replaces the element at the specified position in this list with the specified element (optional operation).
`int`	`size()`	Returns the number of elements in this list.
`List<E>`	`subList(int fromIndex, int toIndex)`	Returns a view of the portion of this list between the specified fromIndex, inclusive, and toIndex, exclusive.
`Object[]`	`toArray()`	Returns an array containing all of the elements in this list in proper sequence.
`<T> T[]`	`toArray(T[] a)`	Returns an array containing all of the elements in this list in proper sequence; the runtime type of the returned array is that of the specified array.

Java offers two general-purpose `List` implementations: `ArrayList` and `LinkedList`. Most of the times, programmers will be using `ArrayList`. We can access any element with the help of the index. The time for accessing any element is the same. This behaviour is known as "constant-time" performance. Also, the access is very fast. `ArrayList` is similar to legacy class `Vector`.

In the early days of computer science, detailed study had proved that frequent insertion and deletion taxed (burden) the computer. Hence, a data structure called `LinkedList` was invented. It is good for frequent insertions and/or deletions. Hence, Java supports another concrete implementation of `List` interface known as `LinkedList`.

Now, let us start our study of concrete implantations of `List` interface with `ArrayList`.

23.3 ArrayList

The class `ArrayList` offers all the benefits of an array with complete functionality of the `List` interface. Let us write a program to study it.

Problem: Write a program to demonstrate the working of an `ArrayList` class.

Solution: We will first create a new class `myStudent`. We will also develop a method `getData` to create data of 10 students and put it in array "A". The main program will pick data from array "A".

Now we will create an `ArrayList` with this data from array "A". First, we will print the collection `ArrayList` with default option. Then we will write this data as one element on one line. (see Program 23.1).

PROGRAM 23.1 ArrayList

```
//       alist1.java
import java.util.*;
public class alist1
{ static public myStudent[] A = new myStudent[10];
  static myStudent myStd ;
  static Integer myKey ;
public static void main(String args[] ) throws Exception
  { int i ;
    ArrayList< myStudent>
       tabl = new ArrayList< myStudent>();
    System.out.println("<---alist1--->");
    getData(A);
/* for debugging only
       for (i=0;i<10;i++)
       System.out.println(A[i]);
*/
// Putting all elemnets in the ArrayList
   for (i=0;i<10;i++)
      tabl.add(A[i]) ;
// listing all elements
   System.out.println( tabl );
    System.out.println();
// line by line
   for (i=0;i<tabl.size();i++)
        System.out.println( tabl.get(i) ) ;
}
static void getData(myStudent[] X)
  { X[0]= new myStudent(101, "Vikas");
  X[1]= new myStudent(111, "Nilesh");
  X[2]= new myStudent(151, "Mandar");
  X[3]= new myStudent(301, "Anil");
  X[4]= new myStudent(422,"Dilip");
  X[5]= new myStudent(501, "Jyotsna");
  X[6]= new myStudent(524, "Payal");
  X[7]= new myStudent(635, "Gurprasad");
  X[8]= new myStudent(701, "porus");
  X[9]= new myStudent(801, "Glenn");
  }
}
class myStudent
  { public Integer BPnumber ;
    public String name;
    myStudent( int n, String s )
      { BPnumber = new Integer(n);
        name = s;
      }
public String toString()
   { return ( BPnumber + "--" + name);
   }
}
```

If you run the program, you will get the following output.

Output **alist1.out**

```
<---alist1--->
[101--Vikas, 111--Nilesh, 151--Mandar, 301--Anil, 422--Dilip, 501--Jyotsna,
524--Payal, 635--Gurprasad, 701--porus, 801--Glenn]
101--Vikas
111--Nilesh
151--Mandar
301--Anil
422--Dilip
501--Jyotsna
524--Payal
635--Gurprasad
701--porus
801-Glenn
```

Notice the use of square brackets in default printout.

It is possible to construct an `ArrayList` in three different ways. Table 23.4 illustrates these constructors.

Table 23.4 Constructor Summary: `ArrayList`

`ArrayList()`	Constructs an empty list with an initial capacity of 10.
`ArrayList(Collection<? extends E> c)`	Constructs a list containing the elements of the specified collection, in the order they are returned by the collection's iterator.
`ArrayList(int initialCapacity)`	Constructs an empty list with the specified initial capacity.

Table 23.5 illustrates various methods from the class `ArrayList`.

Table 23.5 Method Summary: `ArrayList`

`boolean`	`add(E o)`	Appends the specified element to the end of this list.
`void`	`add(int index, E element)`	Inserts the specified element at the specified position in this list.
`boolean`	`addAll(Collection<? extends E> c)`	Appends all of the elements in the specified collection to the end of this list, in the order that they are returned by the specified collection's iterator.

(Continued)

Table 23.5 (*Continued*)

`boolean`	`addAll(int index, Collection<? extends E> c)`	Inserts all of the elements in the specified collection into this list, starting at the specified position.
`void`	`clear()`	Removes all of the elements from this list.
`Object`	`clone()`	Returns a shallow copy of this `ArrayList` instance.
`boolean`	`contains(Object elem)`	Returns true if this list contains the specified element.
`void`	`ensureCapacity(int minCapacity)`	Increases the capacity of this `ArrayList` instance, if necessary, to ensure that it can hold at least the number of elements specified by the minimum capacity argument.
`E`	`get(int index)`	Returns the element at the specified position in this list.
`int`	`indexOf(Object elem)`	Searches for the first occurrence of the given argument, testing for equality using the `equals` method.
`boolean`	`isEmpty()`	Tests if this list has no elements.
`int`	`lastIndexOf(Object elem)`	Returns the index of the last occurrence of the specified object in this list.
`E`	`remove(int index)`	Removes the element at the specified position in this list.
`boolean`	`remove(Object o)`	Removes a single instance of the specified element from this list, if it is present (optional operation).
`protected void`	`removeRange(int fromIndex, int toIndex)`	Removes from this `List` all of the elements whose index is between from Index, inclusive and toIndex, exclusive.
`E`	`set(int index, E element)`	Replaces the element at the specified position in this list with the specified element.
`int`	`size()`	Returns the number of elements in this list.
`Object[]`	`toArray()`	Returns an array containing all of the elements in this list in the correct order.

(*Continued*)

Table 23.5 (*Continued*)

`<T> T[]`	`toArray(T[] a)`	Returns an array containing all of the elements in this list in the correct order; the runtime type of the returned array is that of the specified array.
`void`	`trimToSize()`	Trims the capacity of this `ArrayList` instance to be of the current size of the list.

23.4 LinkedList

Another concrete implementation of interface `List` is `LinkedList`. Those who have studied the subject of "Data Structure" know that this technique of organizing list offers very easy and quick insertion and deletions. If in our application the list is constantly being modified with insertions and deletions, then this is our best bet. We have already developed a linked list ourselves in a program in an earlier chapter. Let us write a small program to become familiar with this ready-made implementation.

Note: In this chapter, we will frequently talk of speed and performance. Today's computers are very fast. If we compare implementations with moderate data of one or two thousand objects, all implementations will look equally fast. Only when the data is large and applications start needing say more than 30 seconds to run, then only we can test various hypothesis regarding performance. You can generate large data with the help of random number generator and then compare different implementations.

Problem: Write a program to demonstrate `Collection` Class `LinkedList`.

Solution: In this program, we will again use an array A to store data of class `myStudent`. Then we will create a linked `List` and also print it. Next, we will remove the first element and add it at the end. We will print the list to check the list.

PROGRAM 23.2 LinkedList

```
//      linked1.java
import java.util.*;
public class linked1
{ static public myStudent[] A = new myStudent[10];
  static myStudent myStd ;
  static Integer myKey ;
public static void main(String args[] ) throws Exception
  { int i ;
    myStudent temp;
    LinkedList< myStudent>
        tab1 = new LinkedList< myStudent>();
    System.out.println("<---linked1.java--->");
    getData(A);
 // Putting all elements in the LinkedList
    for (i=0;i<10;i++)
       tab1.add(A[i]) ;
 // listing all elements line by line
    for (i=0;i<tab1.size();i++)
          System.out.println( tab1.get(i) ) ;
```

```
    temp = tab1.remove() ;
    tab1.addLast(temp);
 // listing again after change
    System.out.println("\nafter change");
    for (i=0;i<tab1.size();i++)
          System.out.println( tab1.get(i) ) ;
 }
 static void getData(myStudent[] X)
   { X[0]= new myStudent(101, "Vikas");
     X[1]= new myStudent(111, "Nilesh");
     X[2]= new myStudent(151,"Mandar");
     X[3]= new myStudent(301, "Anil");
     X[4]= new myStudent(422, "Dilip");
     X[5]= new myStudent(501, "Jyotsna");
     X[6]= new myStudent(524, "Payal");
     X[7]= new myStudent(635, "Gurprasad");
     X[8]= new myStudent(701, "porus");
     X[9]= new myStudent(801, "Glenn");
   }
 }
 class myStudent
   { public Integer BPnumber ;
     public String name;
     myStudent( int n, String s )
       { BPnumber = new Integer(n);
         name = s;
   }
   public String toString()
     { return ( BPnumber + "--" + name);
   }
 }
```

If you run the program, you will get the following output:

Output

```
<---linked1.java--->
101--Vikas
111--Nilesh
151--Mandar
301--Anil
422--Dilip
501--Jyotsna
524--Payal
635--Gurprasad
701--porus
801--Glenn

after change
111--Nilesh
151--Mandar
301--Anil
```

```
422--Dilip
501--Jyotsna
524--Payal
635--Gurprasad
701--porus
801--Glenn
101-Vikas
```

Please note that record `101--Vikas` moved from the first position to the last one.

Java provides two constructors for this class. They are as shown in Table 23.6.

Table 23.6 Constructor Summary: `LinkedList`

`LinkedList()`	Constructs an empty list.
`LinkedList(Collection<? extends E> c)`	Constructs a list containing the elements of the specified collection, in the order they are returned by the collection's iterator.

Table 23.7 lists all the methods offered by class `LinkedList`.

Table 23.7 Method Summary: `LinkedList`

`boolean`	`add(E o)`	Appends the specified element to the end of this list.
`void`	`add(int index, E element)`	Inserts the specified element at the specified position in this list.
`boolean`	`addAll(Collection<? extends E> c)`	Appends all of the elements in the specified collection to the end of this list, in the order that they are returned by the specified collection's iterator.
`boolean`	`addAll(int index, Collection<? extends E> c)`	Inserts all of the elements in the specified collection into this list, starting at the specified position.
`void`	`addFirst(E o)`	Inserts the given element at the beginning of this list.
`void`	`addLast(E o)`	Appends the given element to the end of this list.
`void`	`clear()`	Removes all of the elements from this list.
`Object`	`clone()`	Returns a shallow copy of this `LinkedList`.

(*Continued*)

Table 23.7 *(Continued)*

`boolean`	`contains(Object o)`	Returns true if this list contains the specified element.
`E`	`element()`	Retrieves, but does not remove, the head (first element) of this list.
`E`	`get(int index)`	Returns the element at the specified position in this list.
`E`	`GetFirst()`	Returns the first element in this list.
`E`	`GetLast()`	Returns the last element in this list.
`int`	`indexOf(Object o)`	Returns the index in this list of the first occurrence of the specified element, or −1 if the `List` does not contain this element.
`int`	`lastIndexOf(Object o)`	Returns the index in this list of the last occurrence of the specified element, or −1 if the list does not contain this element.
`ListIterator <E>`	`listIterator(int index)`	Returns a list iterator of the elements in this list (in proper sequence), starting at the specified position in the list.
`boolean`	`offer(E o)`	Adds the specified element as the tail (last element) of this list.
`E`	`peek()`	Retrieves, but does not remove, the head (first element) of this list.
`E`	`poll()`	Retrieves and removes the head (first element) of this list.
`E`	`remove()`	Retrieves and removes the head (first element) of this list.
`E`	`remove(int index)`	Removes the element at the specified position in this list.
`boolean`	`remove(Object o)`	Removes the first occurrence of the specified element in this list.
`E`	`removeFirst()`	Removes and returns the first element from this list.
`E`	`removeLast()`	Removes and returns the last element from this list.
`E`	`set(int index, E element)`	Replaces the element at the specified position in this list with the specified element.

(Continued)

Table 23.7 (*Continued*)

int	size()	Returns the number of elements in this list.
Object[]	toArray()	Returns an array containing all of the elements in this list in the correct order.
<T> T[]	toArray(T[] a)	Returns an array containing all of the elements in this list in the correct order; the runtime type of the returned array is that of the specified array.

23.5 Interface Set

We have studied Sets in Mathematics. This idea is put in practice by a collection named `Set`. We know that a set cannot contain duplicates. The `Set` interface contains methods which are inherited from `Collection`. It also enforces the condition that there are no duplicates. To achieve this, we must define methods `equals` and `hashCode` properly.

Table 23.8 illustrates various methods from interface `Set`.

Table 23.8 Method Summary: Interface Set

Boolean	add(E o)	Adds the specified element to this set if it is not already present (optional operation).
Boolean	addAll(Collection<? extends E> c)	Adds all of the elements in the specified collection to this set if they are not already present (optional operation).
void	clear()	Removes all of the elements from this set (optional operation).
Boolean	contains(Object o)	Returns true if this set contains the specified element.
Boolean	containsAll(Collection<?> c)	Returns true if this set contains all of the elements of the specified collection.
Boolean	equals(Object o)	Compares the specified object with this set for equality.
int	hashCode()	Returns the hash code value for this set.
Boolean	isEmpty()	Returns true if this set contains no elements.

(*Continued*)

Table 23.8 (*Continued*)

Iterator <E>	iterator()	Returns an iterator over the elements in this set.
Boolean	remove(Object o)	Removes the specified element from this set if it is present (optional operation).
boolean	removeAll(Collection<?> c)	Removes from this set all of its elements that are contained in the specified collection (optional operation).
boolean	retainAll(Collection<?> c)	Retains only the elements in this set that are contained in the specified collection (optional operation).
int	size()	Returns the number of elements in this set (its cardinality).
Object[]	toArray()	Returns an array containing all of the elements in this set.
<T> T[]	toArray(T[] a)	Returns an array containing all of the elements in this set; the runtime type of the returned array is that of the specified array.

In Java, there are three implementations of interface Set. They are HashSet, TreeSet, and LinkedHashSet. Out of these, we will be studying the first two in detail. The HashSet is used for speed while TreeSet offers the facility of ordering.

At this stage, we have to introduce the concept of an iterator.

23.5.1 Iterator

So far, we have studied two collections. We did not find any difficulty navigating them. ArrayList behaves as an Array. We could use index comfortably. LinkedList is more complex. It still supported the method get(i) to return the ith element. What about structures that are more complex? There may not be anything like the index. We need something to move from one element of object to another: enter interface Iterator. It helps to move from one object to another effortlessly. This defines three methods.

The method **hasNext()** returns the Boolean value true if the iteration has more elements. The method **next()** returns the next element in the iteration. The method **remove()** removes the element from the collection, returned by the iterator.

With this much introduction, we are in a position to study any complex collection. Let us start with the TreeSet.

23.6 TreeSet

The class TreeSet is a concrete implementation of the Set interface. Hence, it cannot tolerate duplicates. If we try to find an element which is already in the TreeSet, such an attempt will fail. This is the reason for using the return type Boolean for this method `add()`. When we retrieve the elements of this collection, we find them in (normally) ascending order.

Problem: Write a program to demonstrate Collection class `TreeSet`.

Solution: Let us continue with our data class `myStudent`. But in this example, we will face some trouble. Hence, we will use the same class but with enhancement (see Program 23.3).

PROGRAM 23.3 `TreeSet`

```
//     tset2.java
import java.util.*;
public class tset2
{ static public myStudent[] A = new myStudent[10];
  static myStudent myStd,myStd1 ;
  static myStudent temp;
public static void main(String args[] ) throws Exception
  { int i ;
    TreeSet < myStudent>
      tab1 = new TreeSet<myStudent >();
    System.out.println("<---tset2--->");
    getData(A);
// Putting all elements in the TreeMap
    for (i=0;i<10;i++)
    tab1.add(A[i]) ;
// listing all elements
    System.out.println("Listing Elements");
    Iterator it = tab1.iterator();
    while( it.hasNext() )
      { temp =(myStudent )it.next() ;
        System.out.println( temp);
      }
    System.out.println("No of Elements are " + tab1.size());
// Creating and adding duplicate element
    myStd = new myStudent(701, "porus");//A[2];
    if( tab1.add(myStd) )System.out.println("New element added");
      else System.out.println("Operation failed");

}

// please note index 2 and 8 are deliberately switched
  static void getData(myStudent[] X)
   { X[0]= new myStudent(101, "Vikas");
     X[1]= new myStudent(111, "Nilesh");
     X[8]= new myStudent(151, "Mandar");
     X[3]= new myStudent(301, "Anil");
     X[4]= new myStudent(422, "Dilip");
     X[5]= new myStudent(501, "Jyotsna");
     X[6]= new myStudent(524, "Payal");
     X[7]= new myStudent(635, "Gurprasad");
     X[2]= new myStudent(701, "porus");
     X[9]= new myStudent(801, "Glenn");
   }
```

```
}
final class myStudent implements Comparable <myStudent>
  {
    public int BPnumber ;
    public String name;
    myStudent( int n, String s )
     { BPnumber = n;
       name = s;
     }
    public String toString()
      { return ( BPnumber + "--" + name);
      }
    public int compareTo(myStudent m)
      { if (this.BPnumber >m.BPnumber ) return +1 ;
        else if (this.BPnumber == m.BPnumber ) return 0 ;
           else return -1;
      }
    public boolean equals( Object o)
      { if (!(o instanceof myStudent))
           return false;
        myStudent m = (myStudent) o ;
        if ( ( this.BPnumber == m.BPnumber)
            && (this.name == m.name) ) return true;
            else return false;
      }
    public int hashCode() {
        return 31*BPnumber + name.hashCode();
    }
  }
```

If you run the program, you will get the following output:

Output

```
<---tset2--->
Listing Elements
101--Vikas
111--Nilesh
151--Mandar
301--Anil
422--Dilip
501--Jyotsna
524--Payal
635--Gurprasad
701--porus
801--Glenn
No of Elements are 10
Operation failed
```

Please note that in the input elements x[2] and x[8] are interchanged. This means input data is unsorted.

In the output, the students are in ascending order (of their `BPnumber`). When we try to add a duplicate entry (701, "porus") the operation fails.

We have said that `TreeSet` keeps elements in an ordered form. We have defined class `myStudent`. The compiler has no special knowledge of it. Hence, we have to tell how to compare objects of this class. Here we have added three methods, `compareTo()`, `equals()`, and `hashCode()`, to our class definition.

Table 23.9 illustrates the constructors from class `TreeSet`.

Table 23.9 Constructor Summary: Class `TreeSet`

`TreeSet()`	Constructs a new, empty set sorted according to the natural order of the elements.
`TreeSet(Collection<? extends E> c)`	Constructs a new set containing the elements in the specified collection, sorted according to the natural order of the elements.
`TreeSet(Comparator<? super E> c)`	Constructs a new, empty set sorted according to the specified comparator.
`TreeSet(SortedSet<E> s)`	Constructs a new set containing the same elements as the specified sorted set, sorted according to the same ordering.

Table 23.10 illustrates the methods from the class `TreeSet`.

Table 23.10 Method Summary: Class `TreeSet`

`boolean`	`add(E o)`	Adds the specified element to this set if it is not already present.
`boolean`	`addAll(Collection<? extends E> c)`	Adds all of the elements in the specified collection to this set.
`void`	`clear()`	Removes all of the elements from this set.
`Object`	`clone()`	Returns a shallow copy of this `TreeSet` instance.
`Comparator<? super E>`	`comparator()`	Returns the comparator used to order this sorted set, or null if this tree set uses the natural ordering of its elements.
`boolean`	`contains(Object o)`	Returns true if this set contains the specified element.
`E`	`first()`	Returns the first (lowest) element currently in this sorted set.
`SortedSet<E>`	`headSet(E toElement)`	Returns a view of the portion of this set whose elements are strictly less than toElement.

(Continued)

Table 23.10 (*Continued*)

boolean	isEmpty()	Returns true if this set contains no elements.
Iterator<E>	iterator()	Returns an iterator over the elements in this set.
E	last()	Returns the last (highest) element currently in this sorted set.
boolean	remove(Object o)	Removes the specified element from this set if it is present.
int	size()	Returns the number of elements in this set (its cardinality).
SortedSet<E>	subSet(E fromElement, E toElement)	Returns a view of the portion of this set whose elements range from fromElement, inclusive, to toElement, exclusive.
SortedSet<E>	tailSet(E fromElement)	Returns a view of the portion of this set whose elements are greater than or equal to fromElement.

23.7 HashSet

When we want a set with very fast retrieval, we use the implementation `HashSet`. As the name suggest, it uses Hashing for storing and retrieval.

Problem: Write a program to demonstrate `Collection` class `HashSet`.

Solution: Let us continue with the data from class `myStudent`. Here we will add the data in the `HashSet`. Since there is no ordering, we will get the data out with the help of the iterator. Then we will create a new object and test the method `contains()` (see Program 23.4).

PROGRAM 23.4 HashSet

```
//     hset1.java
import java.util.*;
public class hset1
{ static public myStudent[] A = new myStudent[10];
  static myStudent myStd ;
  static Integer myKey ;
public static void main(String args[] ) throws Exception
  { int i ;
    HashSet< myStudent>
      tab1 = new HashSet< myStudent>();
    System.out.println("<---hset1--->");
    getData(A);
```

```
// Putting all elements in the HashSet
   for (i=0;i<10;i++)
    tab1.add(A[i]) ;
// listing all elements
   Iterator it = tab1.iterator();
   while( it.hasNext() )
     { myStd = (myStudent ) it.next() ;
       System.out.println( myStd) ;
     }
   myStd = new myStudent(151, "Mandar");
//   myStd = A[2];                // note2
   System.out.println(myStd.hashCode());
   System.out.println(A[2].hashCode());
   if ( tab1.contains( myStd ) )
        System.out.println( "Student found") ;
     else System.out.println( "Not found") ;
   }
static void getData(myStudent[] X)
  { X[0]= new myStudent(101, "Vikas");
    X[1]= new myStudent(111, "Nilesh");
    X[2]= new myStudent(151, "Mandar");
    X[3]= new myStudent(301, "Anil");
    X[4]= new myStudent(422, "Dilip");
    X[5]= new myStudent(501, "Jyotsna");
    X[6]= new myStudent(524, "Payal");
    X[7]= new myStudent(635, "Gurprasad");
    X[8]= new myStudent(701, "porus");
    X[9]= new myStudent(801, "Glenn");
  }
}
class myStudent
{
    public Integer BPnumber ;
    public String name;
    myStudent( int n, String s )
     { BPnumber = new Integer(n);
       name = s;
     }
    public String toString()
     { return ( BPnumber + "--" + name);
     }
}
```

If you run the program, you will get the following output:

Output

```
<---hset1--->
101--Vikas
524--Payal
151--Mandar
111--Nilesh
```

```
801--Glenn
701--porus
501--Jyotsna
635--Gurprasad
422--Dilip
301--Anil
27553328
19972507
Not found
```

Prima facie, you will be surprised by the result. Mr. Mandar is very much in the set, still it is said to be not found. The hash codes for the object in the `HashSet` (A[2]) and that of `myStd` which we check are different. Please note the line commented out as note 2. Replace the previous statement by this statement and check the result.

To your surprise, you will get the answer "Student found". Please note that this is a set. We have put A[2] object in it. So it is found. Its copy is not found.

Now you will appreciate why we have put additional methods in Program 23.4. Try the definition of class `myStudent` from previous class in this program and see the result.

Table 23.11 illustrates constructors from class `HashSet`.

Table 23.11 Constructor Summary: `HashSet`

`HashSet()`	Constructs a new, empty set; the backing `HashMap` instance has default initial capacity (16) and load factor (0.75).
`HashSet(Collection<? extends E> c)`	Constructs a new set containing the elements in the specified collection.
`HashSet(int initialCapacity)`	Constructs a new, empty set; the backing `HashMap` instance has the specified initial capacity and default load factor, which is 0.75.
`HashSet(int initialCapacity, float loadFactor)`	Constructs a new, empty set; the backing `HashMap` instance has the specified initial capacity and the specified load factor.

Table 23.12 illustrates the methods from class `HashSet`.

Table 23.12 Method Summary: `HashSet`

`boolean`	`add(E o)`	Adds the specified element to this set if it is not already present.
`void`	`clear()`	Removes all of the elements from this set.

(Continued)

Table 23.12 ***(Continued)***

`Object`	`clone()`	Returns a shallow copy of this `HashSet` instance; the elements themselves are not cloned.
`boolean`	`contains(Object o)`	Returns true if this set contains the specified element.
`*boolean`	`isEmpty()`	Returns true if this set contains no elements.
`Iterator<E>`	`iterator()`	Returns an iterator over the elements in this set.
`boolean`	`remove(Object o)`	Removes the specified element from this set if it is present.
`int`	`size()`	Returns the number of elements in this set (its cardinality).

23.8 Interface Map

The `Collection` interfaces seen so far has only one parameter. Now we are going to study a new interface called `Map`. It has two parameters known as key and value. This interface takes the place of abstract class `Dictionary`. We know that a typical entry (object) in any dictionary contains a pair a word and its meaning. The word is small and is the most basic (equivalent to key or pointer). Its meaning may be given in a paragraph. A large object! A dictionary meaning of the word "program" is "descriptive notice of series of events". Here, the word "program" is a key and its meaning is the "object". This has been depicted in Figure 23.2.

We can understand `Map` as a collection of objects of type keys such that each key points uniquely to an object known as values. There is unbreakable bond between a key and its corresponding value.

In simple applications, we use an array of objects. The array index, an integer, acts as if it is a pointer to the object. If we use primitive type objects, like integer, as the key, there are many advantages. But we loose generality. Many keys in real-life applications will be strings. Since strings are objects in Java, defining keys as objects provides tremendous generality to the interface `Map`. We can use strings for keys. But what about the use of primitive data types? Java provides us with wrapper classes, which can effectively represent primary data types.

Table 23.13 describes the methods from interface `Map`.

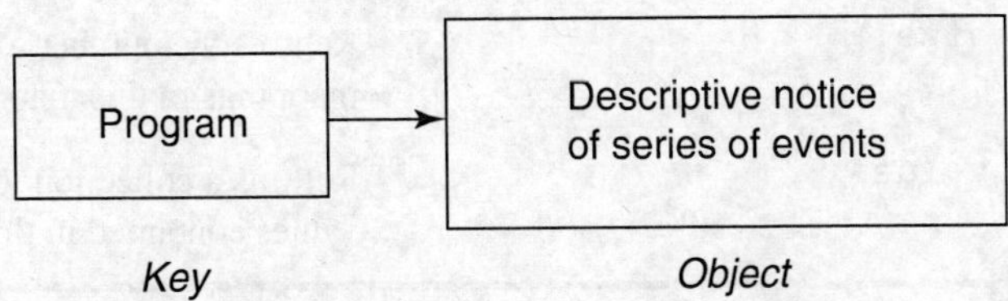

Figure 23.2 **Element of `Map` Interface**

Table 23.13 Method Summary: Interface Map

void	clear()	Removes all mappings from this map (optional operation).
boolean	containsKey(Object key)	Returns true if this map contains a mapping for the specified key.
boolean	containsValue(Object value)	Returns true if this map maps one or more keys to the specified value.
Set<Map.Entry<K,V>>	entrySet()	Returns a set view of the mappings contained in this map.
boolean	equals(Object o)	Compares the specified object with this map for equality.
V	get(Object key)	Returns the value to which this map maps the specified key.
int	hashCode()	Returns the hash code value for this map.
boolean	isEmpty()	Returns true if this map contains no key-value mappings.
Set<K>	keySet()	Returns a set view of the keys contained in this map.
V	put(K key, V value)	Associates the specified value with the specified key in this map (optional operation).
void	putAll(Map<? extends K,? extends V> t)	Copies all of the mappings from the specified map to this map (optional operation).
V	remove(Object key)	Removes the mapping for this key from this map if it is present (optional operation).
int	size()	Returns the number of key-value mappings in this map.
Collection<V>	values()	Returns a collection view of the values contained in this map.

23.9 HashMap

The `Map` interface is implemented by concrete classes like `HashMap` and `TreeMap`. Let us first study `HashMap`.

Table 23.14 describes constructors for class `HashMap`.

Table 23.14 Constructor Summary: `HashMap`

`HashMap()`	Constructs an empty `HashMap` with the default initial capacity (16) and the default load factor (0.75).
`HashMap(int initialCapacity)`	Constructs an empty `HashMap` with the specified initial capacity and the default load factor (0.75).
`HashMap(int initialCapacity, float loadFactor)`	Constructs an empty `HashMap` with the specified initial capacity and load factor.
`HashMap(Map<? extends K,? extends V> m)`	Constructs a new `HashMap` with the same mappings as the specified `Map`.

Table 23.15 describes various methods from the class `HashMap`.

Table 23.15 Method Summary: `HashMap`

`void`	`clear()`	Removes all mappings from this map.
`Object`	`clone()`	Returns a shallow copy of this `HashMap` instance; the keys and values themselves are not cloned.
`boolean`	`containsKey (Object key)`	Returns true if this map contains a mapping for the specified key.
`boolean`	`containsValue (Object value)`	Returns true if this map maps one or more keys to the specified value.
`Set<Map.Entry<K,V>>`	`EntrySet()`	Returns a collection view of the mappings contained in this map.
`V`	`get(Object key)`	Returns the value to which the specified key is mapped in this identity `HashMap`, or null if the map contains no mapping for this key.
`boolean`	`isEmpty()`	Returns true if this map contains no key-value mappings.
`Set<K>`	`keySet()`	Returns a set view of the keys contained in this map.

(Continued)

Table 23.15 ***(Continued)***

V	put(K key, V value)	Associates the specified value with the specified key in this map.
void	putAll(Map <? extends K,? extends V> m)	Copies all of the mappings from the specified map to this map These mappings will replace any mappings that this map had for any of the keys currently in the specified map.
V	remove (Object key)	Removes the mapping for this key from this map if present.
int	size()	Returns the number of key-value mappings in this map.
Collection <V>	values()	Returns a collection view of the values contained in this map.

In earlier versions of Java, a concrete class known as `Hashtable` was supported. Now this class has been made compliant to `Map` interface. This class is more or less identical to `HashMap`. Since we are studying the `Hashtable` class in detail, we will not develop any program for `HashMap` interface at this stage. We will demonstrate it at the end of the chapter.

23.10 TreeMap

This class uses `Tree`. Hence, the class is suitable for getting the output in a sorted manner. This organization assures ($n \log n$) performance. Let us study it with a program.

Problem: Write a program to demonstrate `TreeMap`.

Solution: We know that when we add elements to a `TreeMap`, it maintains the order. To verify this fact, we need data which is unsorted. As we want to continue with our standard data, we will simply exchange any two elements say at index 2 and 8. It makes the data unsorted (see Program 23.5).

PROGRAM 23.5 TreeMap

```
//      tmap1.java
import java.util.*;
public class tmap1
{ static public myStudent[] A = new myStudent[10];
  static myStudent myStd ;
  static Integer myKey ;
public static void main(String args[] ) throws Exception
  { int i ;
    TreeMap<Integer, myStudent>
      tab1 = new TreeMap<Integer, myStudent>();
    System.out.println("<---tmap1--->");
    getData(A);
```

```
//  Putting all elements in the TreeMap
   for (i=0;i<10;i++)
      tab1.put(A[i].BPnumber,A[i]) ;
// listing all elements
   Set s1 =tab1.entrySet();
   Iterator it = s1.iterator();
   while( it.hasNext() )
    {
    Map.Entry kvpair = (Map.Entry )it.next() ;
    myStd = (myStudent ) kvpair.getValue() ;
    System.out.println( mySTd) ;
   }
}
// please note index 2 and 8 are deliberately switched
   static void getData(myStudent[] X)
   { X[0]= new myStudent(101, "Vikas");
     X[1]= new myStudent(111, "Nilesh");
     X[8]= new myStudent(151, "Mandar");
     X[3]= new myStudent(301, "Anil");
     X[4]= new myStudent(422, "Dilip");
     X[5]= new myStudent(501, "Jyotsna");
     X[6]= new myStudent(524, "Payal");
     X[7]= new myStudent(635, "Gurprasad");
     X[2]= new myStudent(701, "porus");
     X[9]= new myStudent(801, "Glenn");
   }
}
class myStudent
   {
    public Integer BPnumber ;
    public String name;
    myStudent( int n, String s )
       { BPnumber = new Integer(n);
         name = s;
       }
         public String toString()
       { return ( BPnumber + "--" + name);
       }
}
```

If you run the program, you will get the following output:

Output

```
<---tmap1--->
101--Vikas
111--Nilesh
151--Mandar
301--Anil
422--Dilip
501--Jyotsna
524--Payal
```

```
635--Gurprasad
701--porus
801--Glenn
```

Please note that in the input (data) index 2 and 8 were changed. The input was thus unsorted. While we iterate over the `TreeMap`, we get an output which is in order.

Table 23.16 describes various constructors for class `TreeMap`.

Table 23.16 Constructor Summary: `TreeMap`

`TreeMap()`	Constructs a new, empty map sorted according to the natural order of the keys.
`TreeMap(Comparator<? super K> c)`	Constructs a new, empty map sorted according to the given comparator.
`TreeMap(Map<? extends K,? extends V> m)`	Constructs a new map containing the same mappings as the given map, sorted according to the natural order of the keys.
`TreeMap(SortedMap<K,? extends V> m)`	Constructs a new map containing the same mappings as the given `SortedMap`, sorted according to the same ordering.

Table 23.17 describes various methods from class `TreeMap`.

Table 23.17 Method Summary: `TreeMap`

`void`	`Clear()`	Removes all mappings from this `TreeMap`.
`Object`	`Clone()`	Returns a shallow copy of this `TreeMap` instance.
`Comparator<? super K>`	`comparator()`	Returns the comparator used to order this map, or null if this map uses the natural order of its keys.
`boolean`	`containsKey (Object key)`	Returns true if this map contains a mapping for the specified key.
`boolean`	`containsValue (Object value)`	Returns true if this map maps one or more keys to the specified value.
`Set<Map. Entry<K,V>>`	`EntrySet()`	Returns a set view of the mappings contained in this map.
`K`	`FirstKey()`	Returns the first (lowest) key currently in this sorted map.

(*Continued*)

Table 23.17 *(Continued)*

V	get(Object key)	Returns the value to which this map maps the specified key.
SortedMap <K,V>	headMap(K toKey)	Returns a view of the portion of this map whose keys are strictly less than toKey.
Set<K>	keySet()	Returns a Set view of the keys contained in this map.
K	lastKey()	Returns the last (highest) key currently in this sorted map.
V	put(K key, V value)	Associates the specified value with the specified key in this map.
void	putAll(Map<? extends K,? extends V> map)	Copies all of the mappings from the specified map to this map.
V	remove(Object key)	Removes the mapping for this key from this TreeMap if present.
int	size()	Returns the number of key-value mappings in this map.
SortedMap <K,V>	subMap(K fromKey, K toKey)	Returns a view of the portion of this map whose keys range from fromKey, inclusive, to toKey, exclusive.
SortedMap <K,V>	tailMap (K fromKey)	Returns a view of the portion of this map whose keys are greater than or equal to fromKey.
Collection <V>	values()	Returns a collection view of the values contained in this map.

23.11 Hashtable

This class was available as a custom class even before the collection framework came into existence. However, at present it is retrofitted with the Collection framework. When our data is suitable for using the Map technique, we have a choice between TreeMap and Hashtable. We know that Hashing gives very fast response for insertion/deletion operations. It is even better than (n log n). However, this technique does not order the data. Hence, when fast operations are desirable and we are not interested in any specific (ascending or descending) ordering, we prefer Hashtable. Let us study it with a program.

Problem: Write a program to demonstrate Hashtable.

Solution: In this program, we will use our standard data. First, we will add all elements and then list them. Then we create a new object and search it in the collection (see Program 23.6).

PROGRAM 23.6 Hashtable

```
//      hash2.java

import java.util.*;

public class hash2
{ static public myStudent[] A = new myStudent[10];
  static myStudent myStd ;
  static Integer myKey ;

public static void main(String args[] ) throws Exception
  { int i ;
    Hashtable<Integer, myStudent>
        tabl = new Hashtable<Integer, myStudent>();
    System.out.println("<---hash2.java--->");
    getData(A);
//      Putting all elemnets in the hashtable
        for (i=0;i<10;i++)
          tabl.put(A[i].BPnumber,A[i]) ;
// listing all elements
      System.out.println(" listing all elements ");
      Enumeration <myStudent> allvalues = tabl.elements();
      while( allvalues.hasMoreElements() )
        { myStd = allvalues.nextElement() ;
          System.out.println( myStd) ;
        }
// listing all keys using for each statement
      System.out.println(" listing only keys ");
      for( Integer N :tabl.keySet() )
            System.out.println(N) ;
    myStd = new myStudent(151, "Mandar");
//    myStd = A[2];
   System.out.println("\n Hash codes for A[2] and myStd");
   System.out.println(myStd.hashCode());
   System.out.println(A[2].hashCode());
   if ( tabl.contains( myStd ) )
           System.out.println( "Student found") ;
     else   System.out.println( "Not found") ;
}
static void getData(myStudent[] X)
  { X[0]= new myStudent(101, "Vikas");
    X[1]= new myStudent(111, "Nilesh");
    X[2]= new myStudent(151, "Mandar");
    X[3]= new myStudent(301, "Anil");
    X[4]= new myStudent(422, "Dilip");
    X[5]= new myStudent(501, "Jyotsna");
    X[6]= new myStudent(524, "Payal");
    X[7]= new myStudent(635, "Gurprasad");
    X[8]= new myStudent(701, "porus");
    X[9]= new myStudent(801, "Glenn");
  }
```

```
}
class myStudent
  { public Integer BPnumber ;
    public String name;
    myStudent( int n, String s )
      { BPnumber = new Integer(n);
        name = s;
      }
public String toString()
    { return ( BPnumber + "--" + name);
    }
}
```

If you run the program, you will get the following output:

Output

```
<---hash2.java--->
  listing all elements
801--Glenn
111--Nilesh
501--Jyotsna
524--Payal
635--Gurprasad
151--Mandar
701--porus
101--Vikas
422--Dilip
301--Anil
  listing only keys
801
111
501
524
635
151
701
101
422
301
  Hash codes for A[2] and myStd
8567361
9584176
Not found
```

Please note that the new object `myStd` is initialized with the data which is basically same as A[2]. Still their hash codes are different. Hence, when we search for this object, it is not found. Replace the statement

```
myStd = new myStudent(151, "Mandar");
```

with the following statement

```
myStd = A[2];
```

You will be surprised to know that now you get both hash codes as identical and the object is found.

Table 23.18 describes various constructors for the class Hashtable.

Table 23.18 Constructor Summary: Hashtable

Hashtable()	Constructs a new, empty Hashtable with a default initial capacity (11) and load factor, which is 0.75.
Hashtable(int initialCapacity)	Constructs a new, empty Hashtable with the specified initial capacity and default load factor, which is 0.75.
Hashtable(int initialCapacity, float loadFactor)	Constructs a new, empty Hashtable with the specified initial capacity and the specified load factor.
Hashtable(Map<? extends K,? extends V> t)	Constructs a new Hashtable with the same mappings as the given Map.

Table 23.19 describes various methods from the class Hashtable.

Table 23.19 Method Summary: HashTable

void	clear()	Clears this Hashtable so that it contains no keys.
Object	clone()	Creates a shallow copy of this Hashtable.
boolean	contains(Object value)	Tests if some key maps into the specified value in this Hashtable.
boolean	containsKey (Object key)	Tests if the specified object is a key in this Hashtable.
boolean	containsValue (Object value)	Returns true if this Hashtable maps one or more keys to this value.
Enumeration <V>	elements()	Returns an enumeration of the values in this Hashtable.
Set<Map. Entry<K,V>>	EntrySet()	Returns a Set view of the entries contained in this Hashtable.
boolean	equals (Object o)	Compares the specified Object with this Map for equality, as per the definition in the Map interface.

(Continued)

Table 23.19 (*Continued*)

V	get(Object key)	Returns the value to which the specified key is mapped in this Hashtable.
int	hashCode()	Returns the hash code value for this Map as per the definition in the Map interface.
boolean	isEmpty()	Tests if this Hashtable maps no keys to values.
Enumeration <K>	keys()	Returns an enumeration of the keys in this Hashtable.
Set<K>	keySet()	Returns a Set view of the keys contained in this Hashtable.
V	put(K key, V value)	Maps the specified key to the specified value in this Hashtable.
void	putAll(Map<? extends K,? extends V> t)	Copies all of the mappings from the specified Map to this Hashtable. These mappings will replace any mappings that this Hashtable had for any of the keys currently in the specified Map.
protected void	rehash()	Increases the capacity and internally reorganizes this Hashtable, in order to accommodate and access its entries more efficiently.
V	remove(Object key)	Removes the key (and its corresponding value) from this Hashtable.
int	size()	Returns the number of keys in this Hashtable.
String	toString()	Returns a string representation of this Hashtable object in the form of a set of entries, enclosed in braces and separated by the ASCII characters ", " (comma and space).
Collection <V>	values()	Returns a Collection view of the values contained in this Hashtable.

23.12 Algorithms

After coming up with the collection framework, Java developers have also supported a lot of algorithms in the collection framework, thus helping the programmers. These are polymorphic algorithms. Please note that methods with same name operate on collection of any type, and still produce correct result. That is why the term polymorphic is used. With these in-built methods, programming has nearly become a child's play now.

Please note that we started with study of *Collection interface*. Java has also defined a class with the same name `Collection`. This class holds all the algorithms.

Most of the algorithms apply to the class `List`. Some of them are listed below.

`sort`	Sorts a `List` using a merge sort algorithm, which provides a fast, stable sort. (A stable sort is one that does not reorder equal elements.)
`shuffle`	Randomly permutes the elements in a `List`.
`reverse`	Reverses the order of the elements in a `List`.
`rotate`	Rotates all the elements in a `List` by a specified distance.
`swap`	Swaps the elements at specified positions in a `List`.
`replaceAll`	Replaces all occurrences of one specified value with another.
`fill`	Overwrites every element in a `List` with the specified value.
`copy`	Copies the source `List` into the destination `List`.
`binarySearch`	Searches for an element in an ordered `List` using the binary search algorithm.
`indexOfSubList`	Returns the index of the first sub-list of one `List` that is equal to another.
`lastIndexOfSubList`	Returns the index of the last sub-list of one `List` that is equal to another.

Table 23.20 describes the various methods from class `Collections`. Many of them are actually implementations of algorithms.

Table 23.20 Method Summary: Class `Collections`

static <T> boolean	addAll(Collection<? super T> c, T... a)	Adds all of the specified elements to the specified collection.
static <T> int	binarySearch(List<? extends Comparable<? super T>> list, T key)	Searches the specified list for the specified object using the binary search algorithm.
static <T> int	binarySearch(List<? extends T> list, T key, Comparator<? super T> c)	Searches the specified list for the specified object using the binary search algorithm.

(Continued)

Table 23.20 ***(Continued)***

static <E> Collection<E>	checkedCollection (Collection<E> c, Class<E> type)	Returns a dynamically type-safe view of the specified collection.
static <E> List<E>	checkedList(List<E> list, Class<E> type)	Returns a dynamically type-safe view of the specified list.
static <K,V> Map<K,V>	checkedMap(Map<K,V> m, Class<K> keyType, Class<V> valueType)	Returns a dynamically type-safe view of the specified map.
static <E> Set<E>	checkedSet(Set<E> s, Class<E> type)	Returns a dynamically type-safe view of the specified set.
static <K,V> SortedMap <K,V>	checkedSortedMap (SortedMap<K,V> m, Class<K> keyType, Class<V> valueType)	Returns a dynamically type-safe view of the specified sorted map.
static <E> SortedSet<E>	checkedSortedSet (SortedSet<E> s, Class<E> type)	Returns a dynamically type-safe view of the specified sorted set.
static <T> void	copy(List<? super T> dest, List<? extends T> src)	Copies all of the elements from one list and add to another.
static boolean	disjoint(Collection<?> c1, Collection<?> c2)	Returns true if the two specified collections have no elements in common.
static <T> List<T>	emptyList()	Returns the empty list (immutable).
static <K,V> Map<K,V>	emptyMap()	Returns the empty map (immutable).
static <T> Set<T>	emptySet()	Returns the empty set (immutable).
static <T> Enumeration<T>	enumeration(Collection <T> c)	Returns an enumeration over the specified collection.
static <T> void	fill(List<? super T> list, T obj)	Replaces all of the elements of the specified list with the specified element.
static int	frequency(Collection <?> c, Object o)	Returns the number of elements in the specified collection equal to the specified object.

(Continued)

Table 23.20 (*Continued*)

static int	indexOfSubList(List <?> source, List<?> target)	Returns the starting position of the first occurrence of the specified target list within the specified source list, or −1 if there is no such occurrence.
static int	lastIndexOfSubList (List<?> source, List<?> target)	Returns the starting position of the last occurrence of the specified target list within the specified source list, or −1 if there is no such occurrence.
static <T> ArrayList<T>	list(Enumeration <T> e)	Returns an `ArrayList` containing the elements returned by the specified enumeration in the order they are returned by the enumeration.
static <T extends Object & Comparable <? super T>> T	max(Collection<? extends T> coll)	Returns the maximum element of the given collection, according to the natural ordering of its elements.
static <T> T	max(Collection<? extends T> coll, Comparator<? super T> comp)	Returns the maximum element of the given collection, according to the order induced by the specified comparator.
static <T extends Object & Comparable <? super T>> T	min(Collection<? extends T> coll)	Returns the minimum element of the given collection, according to the natural ordering of its elements.
static <T> T	min(Collection<? extends T> coll, Comparator<? super T> comp)	Returns the minimum element of the given collection, according to the order induced by the specified comparator.
static <T> List<T>	nCopies(int n, T o)	Returns an immutable list consisting of n copies of the specified object.
static <T> boolean	replaceAll(List<T> list, T oldVal, T newVal)	Replaces all occurrences of one specified value in a list with another.
static void	reverse(List<?> list)	Reverses the order of the elements in the specified list.

(*Continued*)

Table 23.20 *(Continued)*

static <T> Comparator<T>	reverseOrder()	Returns a comparator that imposes the reverse of the natural ordering on a collection of objects that implement the Comparable interface.
static <T> Comparator<T>	reverseOrder (Comparator<T> cmp)	Returns a comparator that imposes the reverse ordering of the specified comparator.
static void	rotate(List<?> list, int distance)	Rotates the elements in the specified list by the specified distance.
static void	shuffle(List<?> list)	Randomly permutes the specified list using a default source of randomness.
static void	shuffle(List<?> list, Random rnd)	Randomly permutes the specified list using the specified source of randomness.
static <T> Set<T>	singleton(T o)	Returns an immutable set containing only the specified object.
static <T> List<T>	singletonList (T o)	Returns an immutable list containing only the specified object.
static <K,V> Map<K,V>	singletonMap(K key, V value)	Returns an immutable map, mapping only the specified key to the specified value.
static <T extends Comparable <? super T>> void	sort(List<T> list)	Sorts the specified list into ascending order, according to the natural ordering of its elements.
static <T> void	sort(List<T> list, Comparator<? super T> c)	Sorts the specified list according to the order induced by the specified comparator.
static void	swap(List<?> list, int i, int j)	Swaps the elements at the specified positions in the specified list.
static <T> Collection<T>	synchronized Collection(Collection <T> c)	Returns a synchronized (thread-safe) collection backed by the specified collection.
static <T> List<T>	synchronizedList (List<T> list)	Returns a synchronized (thread-safe) list backed by the specified list.

(Continued)

Table 23.20 (*Continued*)

`static <K,V> Map<K,V>`	`synchronizedMap (Map<K,V> m)`	Returns a synchronized (thread-safe) map backed by the specified map.
`static <T> Set<T>`	`synchronizedSet (Set<T> s)`	Returns a synchronized (thread-safe) set backed by the specified set.
`static <K,V> SortedMap<K,V>`	`synchronizedSortedMap (SortedMap<K,V> m)`	Returns a synchronized (thread-safe) sorted map backed by the specified sorted map.
`static <T> SortedSet<T>`	`synchronizedSortedSet (SortedSet<T> s)`	Returns a synchronized (thread-safe) sorted set backed by the specified sorted set.
`static <T> Collection <T>`	`unmodifiableCollection (Collection<? extends T> c)`	Returns an unmodifiable view of the specified collection.
`static <T> List<T>`	`unmodifiableList (List<? extends T> list)`	Returns an unmodifiable view of the specified list.
`static <K,V> Map<K,V>`	`unmodifiableMap (Map<? extends K,? extends V> M)`	Returns an unmodifiable view of the specified map.
`static <T> Set<T>`	`unmodifiableSet (Set<? extends T> s)`	Returns an unmodifiable view of the specified set.
`static <K,V> SortedMap<K,V>`	`unmodifiableSortedMap (SortedMap<K,? extends V> m)`	Returns an unmodifiable view of the specified sorted map.
`static <T> SortedSet<T>`	`unmodifiableSortedSet (SortedSet<T> s)`	Returns an unmodifiable view of the specified sorted set.

Now it is the time to use these in programs. Let us start with sorting of data.

23.12.1 Sorting

Java offers ready-made method `sort()`. It comes in two flavours. We can sort using natural order of elements. Alternately, we may specify the order ourselves. It goes without saying that computer understands the natural order for wrapper classes and strings. However, computer cannot understand what the natural order for any given object is. Hence, the objects we want to sort must define `Comparable` interface. Unfortunately, we may be asked to write applications for a given class which does not implement this interface. In that case, we have to define a method compare for the objects of this class. Let us study this with a program.

Problem: Write a program to sort a data consisting of objects of class `myStudent`.

Solution: In the class `myStudent`, we have a field called `name` which is a string. To sort the data, let us choose this string. One of the parameters of sort is `Comparator`. In this program, we will define the `Comparator` in the parameter list itself (see Program 23.7).

PROGRAM 23.7 Sorting with Strings

```
//      sort1.java
import java.util.*;
public class sort1
{ static public myStudent[] A = new myStudent[10];
  static myStudent myStd ;
  static Integer myKey ;
public static void main(String args[] ) throws Exception
  { int i ;
    ArrayList< myStudent>
        tab1 = new ArrayList< myStudent>();
    System.out.println("<---sort1--->");
    getData(A);
// Putting all elemnets in the ArrayList
    for (i=0;i<10;i++)
        tab1.add(A[i]) ;
// Now sorting
   Collections.sort(tab1,new Comparator<myStudent>()
        { public int compare(myStudent A, myStudent B)
             { return A.name.compareTo(B.name );
             }
    });
// listing all elements after sort
    for (i=0;i<tab1.size();i++)
        System.out.println( tab1.get(i) ) ;
  }
 static void getData(myStudent[] X)
  { X[0]= new myStudent(101, "Vikas");
    X[1]= new myStudent(111, "Nilesh");
    X[2]= new myStudent(151, "Mandar");
    X[3]= new myStudent(301, "Anil");
    X[4]= new myStudent(422, "Dilip");
    X[5]= new myStudent(501, {"Jyotsna");
    X[6]= new myStudent(524, "Payal");
    X[7]= new myStudent(635, "Gurprasad");
    X[8]= new myStudent(701, "porus");
    X[9]= new myStudent(801, "Glenn");
   }
}
class myStudent
 {
   public Integer BPnumber ;
   public String name;
   myStudent( int n, String s )
     { BPnumber = new Integer(n);
```

```
        name = s;
     }
     public String toString()
    { return ( BPnumber + "--" + name);
     }
}
```

If you run the program, you will get the following output:

Output

```
<---sort1--->
301--Anil
422--Dilip
801--Glenn
635--Gurprasad
501--Jyotsna
151--Mandar
111--Nilesh
524--Payal
101--Vikas
701-porus
```

Let us study another algorithm.

23.12.2 Algorithm shuffle

So far, we have talked about sorting, that is moving from unordered collection to ordered collection. What about its reverse? You may wonder whether at any time we need to move from an ordered collection to a disordered collection. Well, we may if want to play cards. There will be no fun if we are dealt with the same cards in every game. Java supplies us with a general algorithm named shuffle. We can use it for applications for playing cards.

Problem: Write a program to shuffle a deck of cards.

Solution: In this program, we will use an `ArrayList` to hold the 52 cards. At the beginning, we will generate the list with all cards in order. (as that is most simple.) Then we will call the method `shuffle()` (see Program 23.8).

PROGRAM 23.8 Algorithm shuffle

```
//      sort2.java
import java.util.* ;
import java.lang.String ;
class Card
  { private int n ;
    private int suit;
    private int val;
    Card( int i) // constructor
       { if ( (i<0) && (i>=52) )
          { System.out.println("Invalid card ");
            System.exit(1);
```

```
                i=0;
              }
          n= i;
          suit = n / 13 ;
          val = n % 13 ;
    };
public String show()
    {     String s0;
          String[] s1 = { "Spade", "Heart", "Diamond", "Club"};
          String[] s2 = { "A","K","Q","J","T","9",
                          "8","7","6","5","4","3","2"};
          return s1[suit] + " " + s2[val] ;
      };
 };
 class sort2
 { static Card crd ;
   public static void main(String args[])
     { final int FiftyTwo =52;
       ArrayList <Card> myDeck = new ArrayList< Card>() ;
       System.out.println("<---sort2.java--->");
       for( int i=0;i<FiftyTwo;i++)
         { crd = new Card(i);
           myDeck.add(crd);
         }
 // before Shuffling
       System.out.println("\nBefore shuffling");
       System.out.println(myDeck.get(0).show());
       System.out.println(myDeck.get(1).show());
       System.out.println(myDeck.get(2).show());
       Collections.shuffle(myDeck, new Random());
 // After Shuffling
       System.out.println("\nafter shuffling");
       System.out.println(myDeck.get(0).show());
       System.out.println(myDeck.get(1).show());
       System.out.println(myDeck.get(2).show());
   }
 }
```

If you run the program, you will get the following output:

Output

```
<---sort2.java--->
Before shuffling
Spade A
Spade K
Spade Q
after shuffling
Club J
Club A
Heart K
```

You will agree that the collection framework, in general, and algorithms, in particular, have made our jobs much easier.

23.12.3 Binary search

For fast searching, we can use binary search algorithm. Only the pre-condition is that the data has to be sorted. With collection framework, sorting can be very simple. So will be the searching with binary search algorithm. Let us write a small program to study it.

Java is a case-sensitive language. If you type "Audioclip" in place of "AudioClip", you will get compilation error. It is quite annoying when we know that there is such a class (Interface). If some system can tell whether such a class possibly exists, it will be great help. Let us try an elementary program for this. We will also use this program as a demonstration of algorithm search.

Problem: Write a program to demonstrate algorithm `binarySearch` from collection framework.

Solution: Let us collect all known Java classes and interfaces in a file named `allclass.txt.` We will put one name on one line so that reading this file becomes simple. We will use `ArrayList`, as it offers us the facility to sort as well as search the objects. Here the object is a string. We will read an input string, convert it into lower case, and then put it in the collection.

Success of binary search depends on the data being sorted. Hence, we will first sort the Collection. It then becomes a simple task. First, get the string to search, and then pass its lower-case version to the method `Collections.binarySearch()` (see Program 23.9).

PROGRAM 23.9 Algorithm binarySearch

```
//      alist3.java
import java.io.* ;
import java.util.*;
public class alist3
{
public static void main(String args[] ) throws Exception
  { int i,k ;
    String s1 ,toSearch;
    ArrayList< String>
      tab1 = new ArrayList< String >();
    System.out.println("<---alist3--->");
    FileReader f1 = new FileReader("allclass.txt");
    BufferedReader fin = new BufferedReader(f1);
    Scanner sc = new Scanner(System.in);
    i=0;
    while ( fin.ready() )
      { s1 = fin.readLine();
// System.out.println(i + " " +s1); for debugging
   i++;
   tab1.add(s1.toLowerCase());
   }
   fin.close();
   System.out.println( i + " Stings added");
   Collections.sort(tab1);
```

```
    toSearch = "AudioClip";
    k =
  Collections.binarySearch(tab1,toSearch.toLowerCase() );
    if (k<0) System.out.println("Not found");
       else System.out.println( "found at location" + k);
    }
  }
```

If you run the program, you will get following output.

Output

```
<---alist3--->
3279 Stings added
found at location227
```

The first few lines of file `allclass.txt` are shown below.

File **`allclass.txt`**

```
AbstractAction
AbstractBorder
AbstractButton
AbstractCellEditor
AbstractCollection
AbstractColorChooserPanel
AbstractDocument
AbstractDocument.AttributeContext
AbstractDocument.Content
AbstractDocument.ElementEdit
AbstractExecutorService
AbstractInterruptibleChannel
AbstractLayoutCache
AbstractLayoutCache.NodeDimensions
AbstractList
AbstractListModel
AbstractMap
AbstractMethodError
AbstractPreferences
AbstractQueue
AbstractQueuedSynchronizer
AbstractSelectableChannel
AbstractSelectionKey
AbstractSelector
AbstractSequentialList
AbstractSet
AbstractSpinnerModel
AbstractTableModel
AbstractUndoableEdit
AbstractWriter
```

23.13 HashMap

So far, we have not demonstrated the use of HashMap. Its power can be enjoyed in the backdrop of Program 23.9.

The aforementioned program was very nice but only elementary. It is not sufficient to know whether any class exists or not. If it exists, we must know how to spell it (Which characters are in upper case?). This calls for two strings: One a correct class name, and other all of its lower-case versions. These two strings are associated with each other. This is an excellent situation for a map. The second string will be the key and the first string (actual class name) will be the value.

Problem: Write a program to demonstrate class HashMap from collection framework.

Solution: Let us continue with Program 23.9. It does not help us to know whether the sting exists. If it exists, we must print both the actual class name and the string which we were searching. (See Program 23.10)

PROGRAM 23.10 HashMap

```
//      hmap1.java
import java.io.* ;
import java.util.*;
public class hmap1
{
public static void main(String args[] ) throws Exception
  { int i ;
    String s1,s2,toSearch;
    HashMap< String,String>
        tab1 = new HashMap< String,String >();
    System.out.println("<---hmap1--->");
    FileReader f1 = new FileReader("allclass.txt");
    BufferedReader fin = new BufferedReader(f1);
    Scanner sc = new Scanner(System.in);
    i=0;
    while ( fin.ready() )
      { s1 = fin.readLine();
        // System.out.println(i + " " +s1); for debugging
        i++;
        tab1.put(s1.toLowerCase(),s1);
      }
    fin.close();
    System.out.println( i + " Strings added");
    toSearch = "Audioclip";
    s2 = tab1.get( toSearch.toLowerCase() ) ;
    if ( s2 == null) System.out.println("Not found");
       else
          { System.out.println( " searching " + toSearch );
            System.out.println( " found " + s2 );
          }
  }
}
```

If we run the program, we will get following output.

Output

```
<---hmap1--->
3279 Strings added
searching Audioclip
found AudioClip
```

You will agree that such a program (module) will be very useful in any Java IDE.

23.14 Enhanced For Loop

You may feel that there is a sudden change in the topic. Well the discussion on collections has ended. We have discussed the enhanced for loop in Chapter 7. However, our intelligent readers must have found that the introduction as trivial. Well, the real power of enhanced for loop can be appreciated with the backdrop of `HashSet`.

When we add objects in `HashSet`, they go into a space depending on the hash code. There in no explicit indexing. `Collection` framework offers the facility of an iterator to get all the elements. We can even delete an object with the help of an iterator.

If we are interested in only visiting all the elements (no deletions), we can use the for loop. The generalized syntax of such a loop is

```
for ( type variable : collection ) { } ;
```

Let us take the example similar to one we had used for `HashSet`. The use of iterator will now be replaced by an enhanced for loop.

Problem: Write a program to demonstrate the use of enhanced for loop with the class `HashSet`.

Solution: See Program 23.11.

PROGRAM 23.11 Enhanced For Loop

```
//      forhset.java
import java.util.*;
public class forhset
{ static public myStudent[] A = new myStudent[10];
  static myStudent myStd ;
  static Integer myKey ;
public static void main(String args[] ) throws Exception
   { int i ;
     HashSet< myStudent>
       tabl = new HashSet< myStudent>();
     System.out.println("<---forhset--->");
     getData(A);
 // Putting all elements in the HashSet
    for (i=0;i<10;i++)
      tabl.add(A[i]) ;
 // listing all elements
    for ( myStudent x : tabl )
        { System.out.println( x );
        }
    }
```

```
static void getData(myStudent[] X)
   { X[0]= new myStudent(101, "Vikas");
     X[1]= new myStudent(111, "Nilesh");
     X[2]= new myStudent(151, "Mandar");
     X[3]= new myStudent(301, "Anil");
     X[4]= new myStudent(422, "Dilip");
     X[5]= new myStudent(501, "Jyotsna");
     X[6]= new myStudent(524, "Payal");
     X[7]= new myStudent(635, "Gurprasad");
     X[8]= new myStudent(701, "porus");
     X[9]= new myStudent(801, "Glenn");
   }
}
```

If we run the program, we will get following output.

Output

```
<---forhset--->
301--Anil
635--Gurprasad
524--Payal
501--Jyotsna
101--Vikas
111--Nilesh
701--porus
151--Mandar
422--Dilip
801-Glenn
```

Please note that the order is not the one in which the objects arrived. But this is natural in a `HashSet`.

Keywords

binary search algorithm, algorithm shuffle, `ArrayList`, class `Collections`, collection framework, `Collection` interface, `HashMap`, `HashSet`, `Hashtable`, `Interface`, `Map`, `Set`, `Interface`, `List`, Linked List, `LinkedList`, `shuffle()`, `sort()`, `TreeMap`, `TreeSet`

RuleBook

Collection framework	Components of "collection framework" are available in the package `java.util`
`Set`	`Set` is a collection interface used to maintain unique elements.

Review Questions

1. Which two interfaces are at the top of the hierarchies in the Java collection framework?
2. Which interfaces does not allow duplicate objects?

3. Is `Collection` an interface or a class?
4. In order to sort objects in a `List`, which interface and method has to be implemented by these objects?

Exercises

1. A file consists of records of students. Write a program and to read the records and create a new file which does not contain duplicates.
2. Create a large data file (more than 100,000 objects) using random number generator. Write a code to compare the performance of binary search algorithm with searching using Hashing.
3. Write a program to generate and shuffle a deck of playing cards.
4. Write a method (on your own) to reverse the elements of a given `List`. Compare the performance of your method with method reverse from Java collection framework.
5. Write a program to demonstrate the following methods from class `ArrayList`: `indexOf()`, `lastIndexOf()`, and `remove()`. For simplicity, use wrapper class integer as data.
6. Create an `ArrayList` of 100,000 integers. Covert it into `HashSet`. Create 50 integers using random numbers. Compare the time required to search them in the above two data structures.

MULTIMEDIA EXPERIENCE

Early computers were monsters. Scientists worked with them only through monochrome terminals. Things have changed slowly and silently for many years. Now computers are not restricted to black and white text. Computers have now multimedia ability. They can handle fonts, images (graphics), and sound too. Modern applications are now expected to give users a complete multimedia experience.

Let us start our study with images.

24.1 Images

In this section, we will see simple programs with images. Let us start with the simple introduction.

24.1.1 Introducing image

These days we have lot of images stored in our computer. Images are stored in different formats (using specific extensions). The images we are discussing here are two-dimensional images. Such an image consists of rows and columns of points called "Pixels". These days, images are coloured images as compared to monochrome images many years before. In RGB colour model, values of red, green, and blue are stored for every pixel.

In Java, we can display an image on the screen by simple `drawImage()` method. Let us study the method with the help of a simple program.

Problem: Write a program to display an image available in a file.

Solution: See Program 24.1.

PROGRAM 24.1 Introducing Image

```
//       image2.java
import java.awt.* ;
import javax.swing.*;

class image2 extends JFrame
  {   Image img;
      image2(Color col) //constructor
          {   setSize(500,400);
              setTitle("***image2***");
              setBackground(col);
              setDefaultCloseOperation(EXIT_ON_CLOSE);
              setVisible(true);
          }
      public void paint(Graphics g)
```

```
    {   g.clearRect(0,0,500,400);
        Image img = getToolkit().getImage("butterfly.gif");
        g.drawImage(img,50,50,this);
    }

  public static void main(String[] args)
    {   image2 thisprog = new image2(Color.pink);
    }
}
```

If you run the program, you will get the following output.

Output

Please note the following statement:

```
Image img = getToolkit().getImage("butterfly.gif");
```

The method `getImage()` gets the image for us. This method is defined in class `Toolkit`. To get the instance of the toolkit we use method `getToolkit()`.

24.1.2 Converting image to an array

This task is assigned to a class named `PixelGrabber`. As the name suggests, it grabs the pixels, meaning it converts the image into an array. The task is simple and straightforward. However, it needs intermediate steps. If we miss them or their order, we may not be successful.

To store an image in an array we must have array of sufficient size. Hence, we must first know height and width of the image. Methods

```
img.getWidth(null);
img.getHeight(null);
```

return the necessary information.

But there is a catch. These functions return value 1 when the image is not fully loaded. Hence, we have to wait for loading of the image completely.

To know that whether an image is completely loaded we have to use another class named "MediaTracker". A method called `waitForID()` helps us in this task.

We have seen how to convert a given image to an array. We can also convert an array into an image. The class `MemoryImageSource` is an implementation of the `ImageProducer` interface. It uses an array for creating an image. Method `createImage` is present in class "`java.awt.Component`". It creates an image from the specified image producer. By using both these entities, we can construct an image.

Let us see all these concepts in action in a simple program.

Problem: Write a program to demonstrate class `PixelGrabber`.

Solution: Let us first take an image from a disk. Then grab it in an array. To show that we are painting the image from the array let us deliberately print only half the image (see Program 24.2).

PROGRAM 24.2 Class `PixelGrabber`

```
//      image5.java
// shows half the image

import java.awt.* ;
import java.applet.* ;
import java.awt.image.* ;
public class image5 extends Applet
{ String st;
  Image oldImg, newImage;
  int w , h ;
  MemoryImageSource mis ;
  public void init()
     {  st = getParameter("img");
        oldImg = getImage(getDocumentBase(),st);
        setBackground(Color.pink);
        try
           {  MediaTracker mt = new MediaTracker (this) ;
              mt.addImage(oldImg,0);
              mt.waitForID(0);
           }
        catch (InterruptedException e){};

        w = oldImg.getWidth(null);
        h = oldImg.getHeight(null);
        int info[] = new int[w*h] ;
        PixelGrabber p = new
                PixelGrabber(oldImg,0,0,w,h/2,info,0,w);
        // Note parameter values
```

```
        try{   p.grabPixels();
            }
        catch (InterruptedException e){};
        mis = new MemoryImageSource(w,h,info,0,w) ;
        newImage = createImage( mis );
    }
  public void paint(Graphics g)
        {  g.clearRect(0,0,500,400);
           g.drawImage(newImage,0,0,this);
        } ;
}
```

Following box shows file "image5.htm" which runs class image5.

file **image5.htm**

```
<applet code = "image5" width = 400 height = 300
hspace = "20" vspace = "20" >
<param name = img value = butterfly.gif>
</applet>
```

If you run the file in a browser, you will get the following output.

Output

In Program 24.2, we have used variable "oldImage" to get image from the disk. Note that name of the file does not appear in the program. It is specified in the html file.

Note the parameters of the constructor "PixelGrabber". Here (h/2) is responsible for selecting only top half of the image.

24.1.3 Processing image

Once we grab the image in an array, we can apply all of our Java programming knowledge to processing this image. Let us take a standard task of converting a colour image to grey scale image.

Problem: Write a program to convert the image to grey scale image.

Solution: See Program 24.3.

PROGRAM 24.3 Grey Scale

```
//     image6.java

import java.awt.* ;
import java.applet.* ;
import java.awt.image.* ;

public class image6 extends Applet
{ String st;
Image oldImg, newImage;
int w , h ;
int r,g,b,temp,avg;
int bmask,gmask,rmask,tmask;
MemoryImageSource mis ;
public void init()
   {  st = getParameter("img");
      oldImg = getImage(getDocumentBase(),st);
      setBackground(Color.pink);
      try
         {  MediaTracker mt = new MediaTracker (this) ;
            mt.addImage(oldImg,0);
            mt.waitForID(0);
         }
      catch (InterruptedException e){};

      w = oldImg.getWidth(null);
      h = oldImg.getHeight(null);
      int info[] = new int[w*h] ;
      PixelGrabber p = new
                PixelGrabber(oldImg,0,0,w,h,info,0,w);
      try{  p.grabPixels();
         }
      catch (InterruptedException e){};

      bmask =255;
      gmask =255<<8 ;
      rmask = 255<<16 ;
      for(int i=0;i<w*h;i++)
         {  temp = info[i];
            b = temp&255 ;
            g = (temp>>8) &255;
            r = (temp>>16) &255;
```

```
            avg= (int)(r*0.33+g*0.56 +b*0.11) ;
            if(avg>255) avg = 255;
            if(avg<0) avg=0;
            r=g=b= avg ;

            info[i]= 255<<24 | r<<16 | g<<8 | b;
        }
        mis = new MemoryImageSource(w,h,info,0,w) ;
        newImage = createImage( mis );
    }
  public void paint(Graphics g)
      {   g.clearRect(0,0,500,400);
          g.drawImage(newImage,0,0,this);
      } ;
}
```

We will use the following html file to observe the result.

HTML file

```
<applet code = "image6" width = 120 height = 120 hspace = "20"
vspace = "20" >
<param name = img value = c3.jpg>
</applet>
```

We have created an input file with six colours, namely red, yellow, green, cyan, blue, and magenta. You can see them properly only on a colour monitor.

Input **Image File**

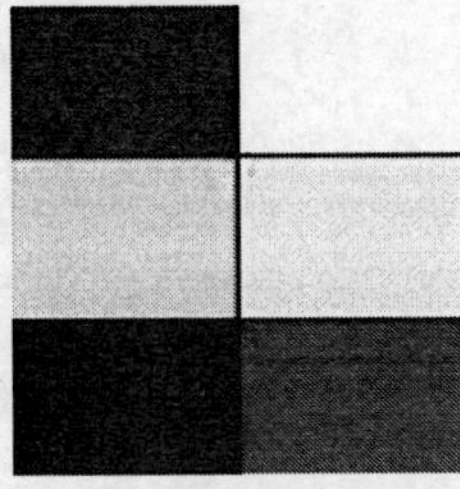

When we open the html file in any browser we will get the following output.

Output

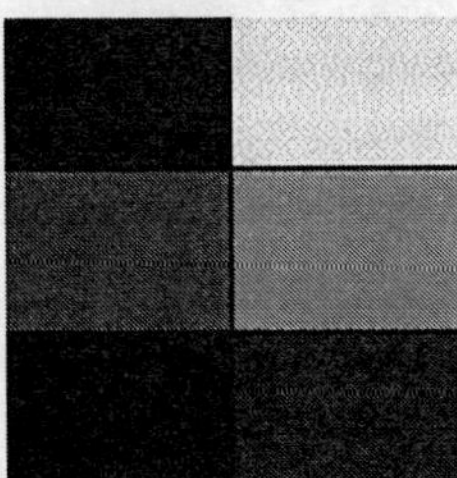

If you see both figures as identical, it proves that our program is successful.

24.1.4 Study of transparency

Java allows you to have transparent images. You can have a transparency level of 0 to 255. To understand its effect, let us create a special image of a glass plate. A glass plate can be easily imagined as a transparent image/object (see Figure 24.1).

In Figure 24.1, there are 10 strips. Their colour and transparency values (or alpha value) are specified as follows.

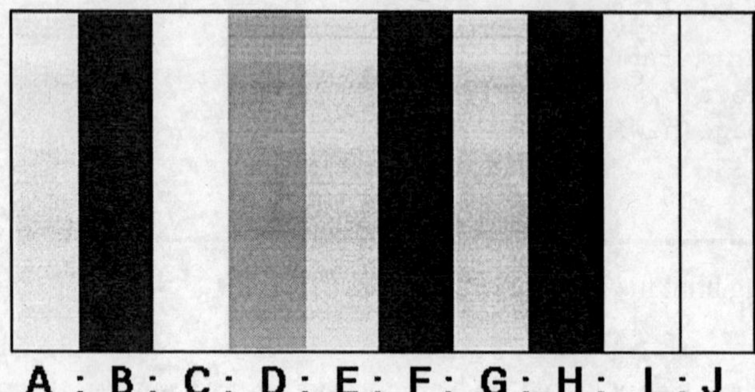

Figure 24.1 Transparent Glass

Plate	Colour	Alpha value
A	red	40
B	red	200
C	green	40
D	green	200
E	blue	40
F	blue	200
G	black	40
H	black	200
I	white	40
J	white	200

Problem: Write a program to study transparency.

Solution: In this program, we will create an image of the plate as shown hereafter. Then we will draw few concentric circles in different colours. Then we will place this glass image on upper half of those circles. To understand imaging better, we will again place this image on lower half of circles, but with XOR mode (see Program 24.4).

PROGRAM 24.4 Study of Transparency

```
//      image35.java
//      application
import java.awt.* ;
import java.applet.* ;
import java.awt.image.* ;
//      study of transparency 40 200

class VIEWPORT extends Frame
  {  static Image img;
     static MemoryImageSource mis;
     VIEWPORT (Color col) //constructor
        {   setSize(450,450);
            setBackground(col);
            setVisible(true);
            int w = 400;
            int h = 200 ;
            int info[] = new int[w*h] ;
            int transp = 0 ;
            int i,j ,k=100;
            for(i=0; i<40; i++)                  // first block 0 transp red
            for(j=0; j<h;j++)
               {  transp = 40 ;
                  info[j*w+i] = (transp << 24) | 255<<16;
               }
            for(i=40; i<80; i++)                 // second block 255 transp red
            for(j=0; j<h;j++)
               {  transp = 200 ;
                  info[j*w+i] = (transp << 24) | 255<< 16;
               }
            for(i=80; i<120; i++)                // third block 0 transp green
            for(j=0; j<h;j++)
               {  transp = 40 ;
                  info[j*w+i] = (transp << 24) | 255<<8 ;
               }
            for(i=120; i<160; i++)               // fourth block 255 transp green
            for(j=0; j<h;j++)
               {  transp = 200 ;
                  info[j*w+i] = (transp << 24) | 255<<8 ;
               }
            for(i=160; i<200; i++)               // fifth block 0 transp blue
            for(j=0; j<h;j++)
               {  transp = 40 ;
                  info[j*w+i] = (transp << 24) | 255;
               }
            for(i=200; i<240; i++)               // sixth block 255 transp blue
            for(j=0; j<h;j++)
               {  transp = 200 ;
                  info[j*w+i] = (transp << 24) | 255;
               }
```

```
        for(i=240; i<280; i++)              // seventh block 0 transp black
        for(j=0; j<h;j++)
            {   transp = 40 ;
                info[j*w+i] = (transp << 24) | 0;
            }
        for(i=280; i<320; i++)              // eight block 255 transp black
        for(j=0; j<h;j++)
            {   transp = 200 ;
                info[j*w+i] = (transp << 24) | 0;
            }

        for(i=320; i<360; i++)              // nine block 0 transp white
        for(j=0; j<h;j++)
            {   transp = 40 ;
                info[j*w+i] = (transp << 24) | 255<<16 | 255<<8 | 255 ;
            }

        for(i=360; i<400; i++)              // ten block 255 transp white
        for(j=0; j<h;j++)
            {   transp = 200 ;
                info[j*w+i] = (transp << 24) | 255<<16 | 255<<8 | 255 ;
            }

        mis = new MemoryImageSource(w,h,info,0,w) ;
        img = getToolkit().createImage(mis );
    }

    public void paint(Graphics g)
    {   int i,j,k=330;
        for( i=0;i<10;i++)
            {   if( i%4 == 0 ) g.setColor(Color.red);
                if( i%4 == 1 ) g.setColor(Color.green);
                if( i%4 == 2 ) g.setColor(Color.blue);
                if( i%4 == 3 ) g.setColor(Color.black);

                for(j=0;j<10;j++)
                    g.drawOval( 10+20*i+j, 10+20*i+j,
                                400-40*i-2*j,400-40*i-2*j);
            }

        g.drawImage(img, 0, 0, this);
        g.setXORMode(Color.white);
        g.drawImage(img, 0, 200 , this);
    } ;
}
public class image35 extends Applet
  {  public static void main(String[] args)
        {   VIEWPORT win1= new VIEWPORT(Color.white);
        }
}
```

If you run the program, you will get the following output.

Output

Sometimes printed images do not show colours properly. Your computer monitor is the best place to view this output.

24.1.5 Subtitles

When we see regional films on television, we need subtitles. In early days of television, subtitles use to obscure the image behind it. Actually, we can have subtitles which are transparent. Then we have a glimpse of the image in the background. Let us try this with a simple program.

Problem: Write a program to demonstrate superimposing of a text on an image in a transparent manner.

Solution: In Java, a pixel is stored using 24 bits. Most significant 8 bits decide the level of transparency. If we want to make an image transparent, then we have to set the most significant 8 bits. If we logically `AND` a pixel with 16,777,215 then the most significant bytes (MSBs) are set to zero without modifying the red, green, and blue values. Now if we logically `OR` it with (127<<24) the MSBs are set to 127. As transparency values are in the range of 0 to 255, a value of 127 makes it moderately transparent.

In the following program, we will use an image of a butterfly as background image. We will create an image which shows a text say "BHAVE PATEKAR". We will use it as `tryImage`. We will convert it into `newImage` which will be transparent. Now we will draw the new image on the old image (see Program 24.5).

PROGRAM 24.5 Subtitles

```
//      image8.java
//

import java.awt.* ;
import java.applet.* ;
import java.awt.image.* ;
import java.util.* ;
import javax.swing.* ;

public class image8 extends JFrame
{ String st;

   Image firstImage, newImage, tryImage;
   int temp,w,h;
   int[] info ;
   MemoryImageSource mis ;
   image8()
      {  super("image8");
         setSize(500,430);
         int i,j;
         int trans= 255;
         // setBackground(Color.yellow);
         firstImage =getToolkit().getImage("butterfly.gif");

         tryImage =getToolkit().getImage("bp1.gif");
            try
            {  MediaTracker mt = new MediaTracker (this) ;
               mt.addImage(tryImage,0);
               mt.waitForID(0);
            }
         catch (InterruptedException e){};
         w = tryImage.getWidth(null);
         h = tryImage.getHeight(null);
         info = new int[w*h] ;
         PixelGrabber p = new PixelGrabber(tryImage,0,0,w,h,info,0,w);
      // Note parameter values
      try{   p.grabPixels();
         }
      catch (InterruptedException e){};

      for(i=0;i<info.length;i++)
            info[i]= ( 127<<24)|(info[i]& 16777215);
      mis = new MemoryImageSource(w,h,info,0,w) ;
      newImage = createImage( mis );
```

```
    }
  public void paint(Graphics g)
      {   g.setColor(Color.yellow);
          g.fillRect(0,0, 500,430);
          g.drawImage(firstImage,50,80,this);
          // g.drawImage(tryImage,5,80,this);
          g.drawImage(newImage,50,80,this);
      } ;

  public static void main(String args[])
  {   image8 myprog = new image8();
      myprog.setDefaultCloseOperation(JFrame.EXIT_ON_CLOSE);
      myprog.setVisible(true);
      myprog.repaint();
  }
}
```

When you run the program, you will get the following output.

Output

The following figure displays file bp1.jif.

Image **bp1.jif**

BHAVE
PATEKAR

24.2 Sound

We have seen two programs using sound in Chapter 20 on "Applets". In that chapter, we had developed only applets. It is possible to have sound in applications too. Only thing to note is that AudioClip and related methods are from class Applet. We have to use this class in the application. Let us study it with a program.

24.2.1 Sound in applications

PROGRAM 24.6 Sound in Application

```
//          sound8.java
import java.applet.*;
import java.awt.*;
import javax.swing.*;
import java.net.URL;
import java.net.MalformedURLException;

public class sound8 extends JFrame //
{ sound8()
     {  super("sound8");
     }
  public static void main(String args[])
     {  sound8 myprog =new sound8();
        myprog.setDefaultCloseOperation(JFrame.EXIT_ON_CLOSE);
        myprog.setSize(300,300);
        myprog.setVisible(true);
        ABC x = new ABC();
        myprog.add(x);
        x.setVisible(true);
        x.init();
        JOptionPane.showMessageDialog(myprog,"Start sound?");
        x.start() ;
     }
};

class ABC extends JApplet
{ String s1 = "Found", s2 = "NOT Found", s3;
  String st1 = "saregal.wav";
```

```
    AudioClip myClip;
    static URL thisone ;
    public void init()
    {
        try
        {   thisone = new URL("file:" + System.getProperty("user.dir")+ "/");
        myClip = Applet.newAudioClip(new URL(thisone, st1) ) ;
        } catch (MalformedURLException e) { }
        }
        public void start()
            {   myClip.loop();
            }
}
```

If you run the program, you will get the following screen.

Output

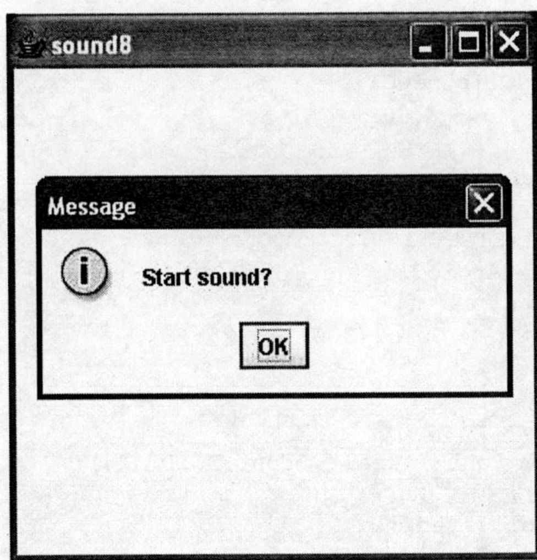

When you click the "OK" button, you start hearing the "saregama… ". Actually, initially program was developed without `JOptionPane`. As soon as the program start executing, you start hearing sound even before the Frame window appears on the screen. The simplest way to delay the execution of statement "`x.start()`" was to use the `JOptionPane`. You can try using a button, at the cost of at least four extra lines.

24.2.2 A musical keyboard

Just as it is said that "no life without wife", similarly the singing is unattractive without accomplishment. There comes the musical keyboard. Casio and many other keyboards are around for many years. Since we have studied that Java can handle sound, let us try to develop a small program, which will simulate a keyboard.

Problem: Write an applet to play basic notes.

Solution: We will use notes from Indian music. There are basic eight notes named sa, re, ga, ma, pa, dha, ni, and saa. There are normally three octaves of these notes. We will use only one octave.

We have to record one ".wav" file for each note using harmonium or digital keyboard. Alternately, there are softwares like "Audacity" which can generate tones in a jiffy. (For this program, we have first created raw sound files with the help of a Java program later these raw files were converted to .wav files).

Once sound files are in place, a simple switch statement can play each note. For simplicity, we have assigned numeric keys 1 to 8 for sa to saa in the order (see Program 24.7).

PROGRAM 24.7 Musical Keyboard

```
 //      sound7.java
import java.awt.* ;
import java.awt.event.*;
import java.applet.* ;

public class sound7 extends Applet implements KeyListener
{ static String note[] = { "sa.wav", "re.wav", "ga.wav", "ma.wav",
                    "pa.wav", "dha.wav", "ni.wav", "saa.wav"};

  static final int EIGHT = 8;
  static AudioClip ac[] = new AudioClip[EIGHT] ;
  static AudioClip oldClip,newClip;

  public void init()
     {  addKeyListener(this);
        requestFocus();
        for(int i=0;i<EIGHT;i++)
           ac[i] = getAudioClip(getCodeBase(), note[i] );
        oldClip=ac[0];
        setBackground(new Color(230,230,255) );
     } ;

  public void paint(Graphics g)
     {  Font f1 = new Font("Arial", Font.BOLD, 24);
        g.setFont(f1);
        g.setColor(Color.red);
        g.drawString(" Welcome to",100,80);
        g.drawString("Musical Keyboard",100,120);
        g.drawString(" Use keys " , 100,200);
        g.drawString("1,2,3,4,5,6,7,8",100, 230);
     } ;

  public void keyPressed(KeyEvent ke)
     {  int n;
        n = ke.getKeyCode() ;
     }
  public void keyReleased(KeyEvent ke)
     {  char ch; int n ;
        n = ke.getKeyCode() ;
     }

  public void keyTyped(KeyEvent ke)
     {  char ch; int ind;
```

```
            ch = ke.getKeyChar();
            switch (ch) {
                case '1': ind = 0 ;  ; break;
                case '2': ind = 1 ;  ; break;
                case '3': ind = 2 ;  ; break;
                case '4': ind = 3 ;  ; break;
                case '5': ind = 4 ;  ; break;
                case '6': ind = 5 ;  ; break;
                case '7': ind = 6 ;  ; break;
                case '8': ind = 7 ;  ; break;
                default : ind = -1;  ; break ;
                }
            if ( (ind < EIGHT) && (ind >=0) )
                  {  newClip = ac[ind];
                     newClip.play();
                     if (oldClip != newClip) oldClip.stop();
                         oldClip=newClip;
                  } ;

            }
    }
```

The html file to run this applet is as shown hereafter.

file **sound7.html**

```
<applet code = "sound7" width = "400" height = "300"></applet>
```

When you run the html file in the browser, you will see the following screen.

Output

Welcome to
Musical Keyboard

Use keys
1,2,3,4,5,6,7,8

In Program 24.7, we have created notes of frequencies as suggested in Indian musical instruments. In western countries, a scale known as "Equally Tempered Scale" is used.

24.3 Complete Multimedia Experience

So far, we have written programs using only images or sound. It is possible to combine these with text and graphical user interface (GUI). This will give us a rich experience.

Problem: Write a program to display text and play selected nursery rhyme.

Solution: In Program 24.8 we will use three nursery rhymes namely "Jack and Jill", "Twinkle Twinkle", and "Baa Baa Black Sheep". We will record these rhymes in separate audio files. Also, we will prepare three separate text files, which contain the text. At the start of the program, we will use a radio button to select the rhyme. When we click the "Show & Play" button, the text of the rhyme will be displayed in the text box as well as corresponding audio clip will also start playing (see Program 24.8).

PROGRAM 24.8 Nursery Rhymes

```
//              multi1.java

import java.applet.* ;
import java.awt.*;
import java.awt.event.* ;
import java.io.* ;
import java.util.*;

import java.net.URL;
import java.net.MalformedURLException;
import javax.swing.* ;

public class multi1 extends JFrame implements ActionListener
{
  JTextArea ta;
  JButton b2;
  static String s1,s2,s3 ,select;
  MyPanel radio ;

  static String poem[] = {"jack.wav","twinkle.wav","baabaa.wav"};
  static final int THREE = 3;
  static AudioClip ac[] = new AudioClip[THREE] ;
  static AudioClip oldClip,newClip;
  static URL thisone ;

  multi1()
     {  super(" multi media demo 1");
        setLayout(null);

        ta = new JTextArea("",10,10);
        ta.setFont(new Font("Arial",Font.BOLD,16) ); // PLAIN
        add(ta);
        ta.setBounds(50,50,250,170);

        b2 = new JButton("Show & Play");
        b2.addActionListener(this);
        b2.setActionCommand("show");
        add(b2);
        b2.setBounds(50,270,200,30);
        b2.setVisible(true);
        radio = new MyPanel();
```

```
        add(radio);
        radio.setBounds(50,330,150,150);
        radio.setVisible(true);
    }

  public static void main(String[] args) throws Exception
    {   String temp;
        StringBuffer sb1= new StringBuffer(100);
        int k=0;
        boolean flag ;

        try
         { thisone = new URL("file:" +
System.getProperty("user.dir") + "/");

              for(int i=0;i<THREE;i++)
                 ac[i] = Applet.newAudioClip(new URL(thisone, poem[i]) );
           }  catch (MalformedURLException e) { }

        s1 = new String ( getFile("a.txt") ) ;
        s2 = new String ( getFile("b.txt") ) ;
        s3 = new String ( getFile("c.txt") ) ;
        select = s1;
        newClip=ac[0];

        multi1 thisprog = new multi1();
           thisprog.addWindowListener(new WindowAdapter()
              {   public void windowClosing(WindowEvent e)
                    {   System.exit(0); }
              });

        thisprog.setBounds(0,0,400,450);
        thisprog.setResizable(true); // works

        thisprog.setVisible(true);

    }

  public void actionPerformed(ActionEvent e)
    {
        if (e.getActionCommand().equals("show") )
           {   ta.setText(select ) ;
               newClip.play();
           }
    }

  static String getFile(String fname) throws Exception
  {
      String temp;
      StringBuffer sb1= new StringBuffer(100);
      FileReader f1 = new FileReader(fname);
      BufferedReader fin = new BufferedReader(f1);
```

```
        while ( fin.ready() )
            {   temp = fin.readLine();
                sb1.append(temp+'\n');
            }
        fin.close();
        return sb1.toString();

    }

class MyPanel extends JPanel
    {
        String A = "1. Jack and Jill";
        String B = "2. Twinkle twinkle";
        String C = "3. Baa, baa, black sheep";

        JLabel picture;

        public MyPanel()
            {
                // Create the radio buttons.
                JRadioButton AButton = new JRadioButton(A);
                AButton.setActionCommand(A);
                AButton.setSelected(true);
                JRadioButton BButton = new JRadioButton(B);
                BButton.setActionCommand(B);

                JRadioButton CButton = new JRadioButton(C);
                CButton.setActionCommand(C);

                // Register a listener for the radio buttons.
                RadioListener myListener = new RadioListener();
                AButton.addActionListener(myListener);
                BButton.addActionListener(myListener);
                CButton.addActionListener(myListener);

                ButtonGroup group = new ButtonGroup();
                group.add(AButton);
                group.add(BButton);
                group.add(CButton);

                // Put the radio buttons in a column in a panel
                JPanel radioPanel = new JPanel();
                radioPanel.setLayout(new GridLayout(0, 1));
                radioPanel.add(AButton);
                radioPanel.add(BButton);
                radioPanel.add(CButton);

                setLayout(new BorderLayout());
                add(radioPanel, BorderLayout.NORTH);
            }

        // Listens to the radio buttons.
```

```
    class RadioListener implements ActionListener
    {
        public void actionPerformed(ActionEvent e)
            {
                if ( e.getActionCommand()== A )
                  {  select = s1; newClip=ac[0];
                  }
                if ( e.getActionCommand()== B )
                  {  select = s2; newClip= ac[1];
                  }
                if ( e.getActionCommand()== C )
                  {  select = s3; newClip= ac[2];
                  }
            }
    }
  }//MyPanel
} // muti1
```

If you run the program and click the "Show & Play" button a sample output will look as follows. Simultaneously you will hear the rhyme.

Output

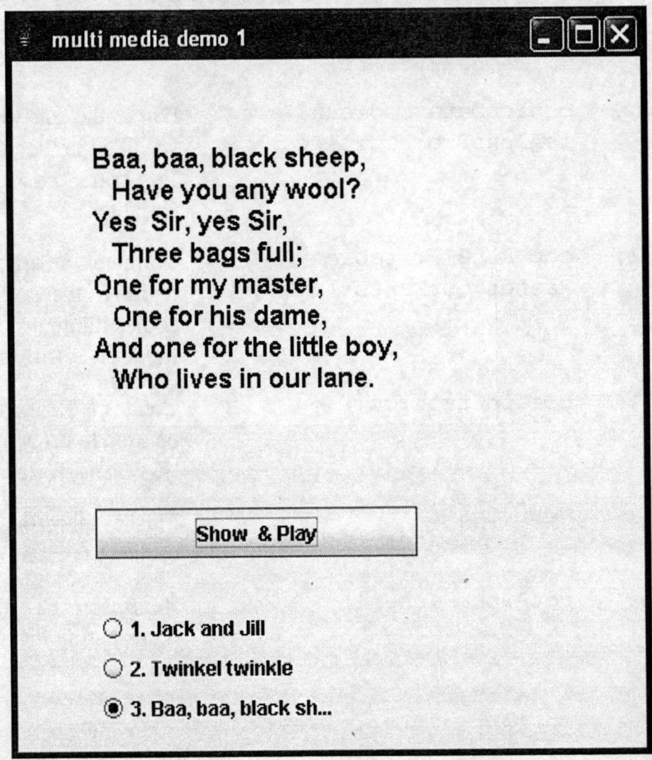

Well, we hope you have enjoyed this chapter.

Table 24.1 describes various constructors from class `BufferedImage`.

Table 24.1 Constructor Summary: Class `BufferedImage`

`BufferedImage(ColorModel cm, WritableRaster raster, boolean isRasterPremultiplied, Hashtable<?,?> properties)`	Constructs a new `BufferedImage` with a specified `ColorModel` and `Raster`.
`BufferedImage(int width, int height, int imageType)`	Constructs a `BufferedImage` of one of the predefined image types.
`BufferedImage(int width, int height, int imageType, IndexColorModel cm)`	Constructs a `BufferedImage` of one of the predefined image types: `TYPE_BYTE_BINARY` or `TYPE_BYTE_INDEXED`.

Table 24.2 describes various methods from class `BufferedImage`.

Table 24.2 Method Summary: Class `BufferedImage`

`void`	`addTileObserver (TileObserver to)`	Adds a tile observer.
`void`	`coerceData(boolean isAlphaPremultiplied)`	Forces the data to match the state specified in the `isAlphaPremultiplied` variable.
`WritableRaster`	`copyData(Writable Raster outRaster)`	Computes an arbitrary rectangular region of the `BufferedImage` and copies it into a specified `WritableRaster`.
`Graphics2D`	`createGraphics()`	Creates a `Graphics2D`, which can be used to draw into this `BufferedImage`.
`void`	`flush()`	Flushes all resources being used to cache optimization information.
`WritableRaster`	`getAlphaRaster()`	Returns a `WritableRaster` representing the alpha channel for `BufferedImage` objects with `ColorModel` objects that support a separate spatial alpha channel such as `ComponentColorModel` and `DirectColorModel`.

(Continued)

Table 24.2 ***(Continued)***

ImageCapabilities	getCapabilities(GraphicsConfiguration gc)	This overrides Image.getCapabilities(gc) to get the capabilities of its surfaceManager.
ColorModel	getColorModel()	Returns the ColorModel.
Raster	getData()	Returns the image as one large tile.
Raster	getData(Rectangle rect)	Computes and returns an arbitrary region of the BufferedImage.
Graphics	getGraphics()	This method returns a Graphics2D, but is here for backwards compatibility.
int	getHeight()	Returns the height of the BufferedImage.
int	getHeight(ImageObserver observer)	Returns the height of the BufferedImage.
int	getMinTileX()	Returns the minimum tile index in the *x* direction.
int	getMinTileY()	Returns the minimum tile index in the *y* direction.
int	getMinX()	Returns the minimum *x* coordinate of this BufferedImage.
int	getMinY()	Returns the minimum y coordinate of this BufferedImage.
int	getNumXTiles()	Returns the number of tiles in the *x* direction.
int	getNumYTiles()	Returns the number of tiles in the *y* direction.
Object	getProperty(String name)	Returns a property of the image by name.
Object	getProperty(String name, ImageObserver observer)	Returns a property of the image by name.
String[]	getPropertyNames()	Returns an array of names recognized by getProperty(String) or null, if no property names are recognized.

(Continued)

Table 24.2 (*Continued*)

`WritableRaster`	`getRaster()`	Returns the `WritableRaster`.
`int`	`getRGB(int x, int y)`	Returns an integer pixel in the default RGB colour model (`TYPE_INT_ARGB`) and default sRGB colour space.
`int[]`	`getRGB(int startX, int startY, int w, int h, int[] rgbArray, int offset, int scansize)`	Returns an array of integer pixels in the default RGB colour model (`TYPE_INT_ARGB`) and default sRGB colour space, from a portion of the image data.
`SampleModel`	`getSampleModel()`	Returns the `SampleModel` associated with this `BufferedImage`.
`ImageProducer`	`getSource()`	Returns the object that produces the pixels for the image.
`Vector<RenderedImage>`	`getSources()`	Returns a vector of `RenderedImage` objects that are the immediate sources, not the sources of these immediate sources, of image data for this `BufferedImage`.
`BufferedImage`	`getSubimage(int x, int y, int w, int h)`	Returns a sub-image defined by a specified rectangular region.
`Raster`	`getTile(int tileX, int tileY)`	Returns tile `(tileX, tileY)`.
`int`	`getTileGridXOffset()`	Returns the x offset of the tile grid relative to the origin, For example, the *x* coordinate of the location of tile (0, 0).
`int`	`getTileGridYOffset()`	Returns the *y* offset of the tile grid relative to the origin, For example, the *y* coordinate of the location of tile (0, 0).
`int`	`getTileHeight()`	Returns the tile height in pixels.
`int`	`getTileWidth()`	Returns the tile width in pixels.
`int`	`getTransparency()`	Returns the transparency.

(*Continued*)

Table 24.2 *(Continued)*

int	getType()	Returns the image type.
int	getWidth()	Returns the width of the BufferedImage.
int	getWidth(ImageObserver observer)	Returns the width of the BufferedImage.
WritableRaster	getWritableTile(int tileX, int tileY)	Checks out a tile for writing.
Point[]	getWritableTileIndices()	Returns an array of point objects indicating which tiles are checked out for writing.
boolean	hasTileWriters()	Returns whether or not any tile is checked out for writing.
boolean	isAlphaPremultiplied()	Returns whether or not the alpha has been premultiplied.
boolean	isTileWritable(int tileX, int tileY)	Returns whether or not a tile is currently checked out for writing.
void	releaseWritableTile(int tileX, int tileY)	Relinquishes permission to write to a tile.
void	removeTileObserver(TileObserver to)	Removes a tile observer.
void	setData(Raster r)	Sets a rectangular region of the image to the contents of the specified Raster r, which is assumed to be in the same coordinate space as the BufferedImage.
void	setRGB(int x, int y, int rgb)	Sets a pixel in this BufferedImage to the specified RGB value.
void	setRGB(int startX, int startY, int w, int h, int[] rgbArray, int offset, int scansize)	Sets an array of integer pixels in the default RGB colour model (TYPE_INT_ARGB) and default sRGB colour space, into a portion of the image data.
String	toString()	Returns a string representation of this BufferedImage object and its values.

Keywords

alpha value, AudioClip, class Toolkit, createImage(), getImage(), getToolkit(), image, ImageProducer, MediaTracker, MemoryImageSource, PixelGrabber, transparency, waitForID()

Review Questions

1. Find for yourselves the various audio formats supported by Java.

Exercises

1. Modify the musical instrument program to add additional notes ("mand" and "teevra").
2. Convert the musical instrument program to three octaves.
3. Rewrite the program `sound7.java` using Equally Tempered Scale (English notes).
4. Write a program which simulates a simple tape recorder. The program should be able to load the existing file. It should be able to play, stop, and loop this file.
5. Write a program (with pre-recorded voice scripts) to accept a train number and platform number and make an announcement. (Sometimes on a busy railway station, trains do not arrive on a specific platform.)

MOVING FROM C++ TO JAVA

Many programmers learn C++ before learning Java. Unwittingly, one starts comparing the two languages. Since both the languages are object oriented and Java has kept the basic syntax of C++, learning Java can be much faster (if not simpler) for C++ programmers.

This section is divided in three parts. In the first part, we will compare keywords in the two languages and the effect thereof. In the second part, we will examine all the differences in the two languages in detail. In the third part, we will show how small- and medium-sized C++ programs can be converted into Java programs.

25.1 Part I: Comparing Keywords

25.1.1 Keywords

Let us start on a positive note. If you know C++, you know the heart of Java. The following is the list of keywords which are common to both C++ and Java. They are used in more or less the same manner.

```
abstract    break      case        catch
char        class      continue    default
do          double     else        float
for         if         int         long
new         private    protected   public
return      short      static      switch
this        throw      try         void
volatile    while
```

Now, let us see the keywords which are different in the two languages. The following are the keywords of C++ which are absent in Java.

```
asm         auto       delete      enum        extern
friend      inline     operator    register    signed
sizeof      struct     template    typedef     union
unsigned    virtual
```

In Java, keywords `const` and `goto` are reserved for future use.

Java is developed as a machine-independent, safe, and secure language. Naturally, it debars any attempts which are machine dependent as well as potentially unsafe. Most of the keywords of C++ which are removed by Java fall in this category. Let us see the impact of their removal in brief. (See Table 25.1)

Table 25.1 Keywords of C++ not Supported by Java

Keyword	Implications of absence
`asm`	No support for assembly language. We cannot embed assembly code in the source
`auto`	As it is a default behaviour, its absence has no implications
`delete`	No freeing of memory per force. This task is assigned to in-built mechanism called garbage collection
`enum`	Cannot associate names to numbers. (This facility adds elegance to a code. The new version of Java has introduced some functionality recently. It has introduced class `Enum`.)
`extern`	No external variables in a file
`friend`	A non-class method cannot access private data of the class
`inline`	No high-speed execution of certain functions
`operator`	No operator overloading
`register`	Cannot force a variable to be located in a high-speed register
`signed`	No implications, as all numeric data are signed in Java
`sizeof`	Cannot find size of variables and objects directly
`struct`	No implication as a class can represent a `struct`
`template`	Generic programming not available. (However, from version 5 generic programming is supported by Java.)
`typedef`	Cannot specify complex data type
`union`	Memory sharing by different types of variables is not possible
`unsigned`	A chance to handle twice the larger number is lost
`virtual`	Cannot force child class to redefine a function
`const`	Cannot declare a `const` directly (However, keyword `final` gives a somewhat similar result)

After looking at what is not supported, let us see the keywords which are newly added in Java. The following are the keywords of Java which are not part of C++.

```
boolean      byte       extends      final          finally
implements   import     instanceof   interface      native
package      strictfp   super        synchronised   throws
transient
```

Its implications in brief are described in Table 25.2.

Table 25.2 Keywords of Java which are not Present in C++

Keyword	Implications of addition
`boolean`	Natural handling of conditions and other Boolean quantities
`byte`	Natural handling of most primitive data type. Also reduces the memory requirement if data needs only a byte
`extends`	Just emphasizes inheritance. Replaces ":" from C++
`final`	Makes a variable non-modifiable. Another way to declare constants
	Prevents a method being overridden
	Makes a class non-inheritable
`finally`	Adds power to `try-catch` mechanism
`implements`	Support for interface
`import`	Allows us to use packages. Somewhat equivalent to `#include`
`instanceof`	Allows verifying whether an object belongs to a particular class
`interface`	New way of looking at objects. No equivalence in C++
`native`	Allows using methods developed in languages other than Java
`package`	Allows user to keep reusable code together. In some way similar to pre-compiled header files
`strictfp`	Forces strictness while performing floating-point calculations
`super`	Helps in reaching base class variables
`synchronised`	Helps prevent threads from invoking methods concurrently
`throws`	Used in exceptions
`transient`	Marks the field which is not used in serialization

25.2 Part II: Differences as a Programming Language

Now let us turn our attention to the differences in the two languages from the perspective of programming language. Let us discuss them in step by step.

Identifiers: Character $ is not allowed as a part or start of a variable name in C++. It is allowed in Java. As Java uses Unicode, many non-English letters are available as characters for forming identifiers.

Data types: In Java, all integer types are stored as `signed` quantities. There is no `unsigned` tag in Java. This is not a great disadvantage. Modern computers have memory in Megabytes. Saving of few bytes has no significance today. Many years before, when personal computers were introduced, they had only 640 kilobytes of memory (RAM). Unsigned integers were relevant those days as the maximum value stored by them was twice as that of the signed variable.

There is no direct equivalent of `enum` in Java. However, its effect can be obtained by defining an interface. In our opinion, `enum` adds elegance to a code. It may be noted that from version 5 (JDK 5) that Java supports `enum` in some peculiar object-oriented way. In our opinion, it is not very user-friendly. However, use of interface is simpler in place of `enum`.

Java does not support **pointers** as a data type. Those switching from C/C++ find some difficulty. However, computer scientists have discussed advantages and disadvantages of pointers at length. Inadvertent use of pointers many times produce errors which are difficult to debug. The decision of the developers of Java not to allow user-defined pointers is a very good decision in our opinion. It must be stated that generic advantages of pointers are not lost in Java. Java internally uses pointers as object references. We can have dynamic data structures in Java without any difficulty.

At present, Java does not support keyword `const`. If we want C++ like action of `const` on a variable, we have to make use of keyword `final`.

Operators and expressions: Java has added an operator ">>>". While shifting bits to right, it treats the number as unsigned.

Relational expressions return Boolean value in Java. In C++, such expressions return integer. In C/C++ **true** and **false** are represented by 1 and 0, respectively. However, change by Java adds more elegance and safety from inadvertent errors.

In Java modulo operator `(%)` can accept floating-point operands. This is a useful operator with integer operands. However, so far we have not found a great use of this operator with floating-point operands.

In Java, you can assign a character variable to integer but not vice versa, whereas in C++ you are allowed to do so. Actually, in C++ the size of `char` and `int` is same. Also, language tacitly tries to consider both data types as identical. In Java, the type `int` is four bytes. Hence, direct assignment to `char` (which is two bytes) is not possible.

Java does not allow floating-point values to be assigned to integer-type variables directly (without typecasting).

The operators ">>" and "<<" are no longer used in input/output. We have to use methods from various classes available from `io` package.

Initialization of variables: C++ does not flag compilation error, when un-initialized variables are used. This is sure to create unexpected errors. Java refuses to compile such a code. In this case, Java is a better language than C++.

Statements: `j+k;`, which is a valid expression statement in C++, is invalid in Java. Actually, such a statement cannot have any action. Hence, Java is right in disallowing it.

`break` and `continue` statements in C++ cannot have labels. Java supports labelled `break` and `continue`. This allows a structured way of leaving a loop.

Loops: Both the languages allow declaring a control variable inside the `for loop`. In Java, such a variable is visible only within the scope of the `for loop`. But in C/C++, it is visible even outside the scope of the `for loop`.

Functions: In C/C++ (old style), if a method does not have any parameter, we can write `void` as the parameter list. This is not allowed in Java.

In Java, every function is a method belonging to some class. There is no concept like general or global (not belonging to a class) functions as in C/C++.

In Java, basic parameter passing is only by value. C++ allows parameter passing both by value and by reference. Primitive data types are strictly passed by value. It implies that you cannot write method `swap(int x, int y)`.

Aggregate data types are to be passed by reference. The programmer does not have any choice over it. Hence, swapping of objects is possible but you have to write the code properly.

In C++, you can add keyword `const` to parameters. This facility is absent in Java. Thus, parameter passing is far less flexible in Java than in C/C++. In C++, it is the programmer who decides how to pass any parameter.

Local variables of methods could be **static** in C++. They retain their values after invocation of the method. This concept is not supported in Java. Keyword `static` cannot be applied to local variables.

In C++, function `main` returns `int`. In Java, it returns `void`. In C++, for `main()` parameters are optional, while for Java parameter (`String[] args`) is mandatory.

Arrays: In Java, if an array index value is out of range, runtime error occurs. This is a very good feature. It does not produce unintended errors. This feature is not supported in C/C++.

In Java arrays are created (memory allocated) **only** using operator `new`. In C/C++, the operator `new` may or may not be used.

Strings: Strings in Java are not null terminated as in C++. Strings are objects of class String. This class is very rich in methods. In C++, strings are not immutable while in Java they are.

To provide mutable strings, Java offers a separate class called `StringBuffer`. C++ does not need such a separate class.

Strings cannot be lexicographically compared using operators like ">" or "<=" in Java. This is possible in C++.

Constructors: The concepts of default constructor in C++ and Java are a bit different. When you define a class without any constructor, the System supplies a default constructor. In Java, it initializes the members to zero values whereas in C++ members are not initialized to zero values.

In case we have defined one or more constructors and one of them is without parameters, that constructor becomes the default constructor.

In C++, when you declare an object without any constructor, default constructor gets called. In Java, there is no way an object comes in to existence without call to `new`. It naturally needs explicit call to some constructor, one without parameters (default) or otherwise.

In Java, when you write a sub-class constructor, call to `super` is optional, when a super-class constructor without parameter exists. Only in this context, Java has any significance to the term "default constructor".

Access specifier: In Java, access specifier applies only to what it precedes. In C++, access specifier is followed by ":". The access specifier applies to all variables that follow.

Inheritance: Java does not support multiple inheritance. In this case, C++ can be considered as more powerful than Java. However, there is very limited use of this facility. It also brings in its own complications. (See *Programming in* C++ by Bhave Patekar.)

Polymorphism: In Java, there is no keyword `virtual`. Consider a case where there is a method in sub-class with the same name as one in super-class. When a super-class reference refers to sub-class object, it always invokes methods in sub-class. It means what a C++ programmer achieves by declaring a function `virtual`, a Java program achieves it automatically.

Interface: There is no direct equivalent of interface in C++. Hence, C++ cannot give a uniform look and feel to its objects in a simple and straightforward manner. In this regard, Java scores over C++.

Graphics: There is no equivalent of method `putpixel` in Java. Use of `drawLine` has to be made to draw a point.

Packages: Packages are like header files in C++. Just as header files are ready to use, contents of a package is also ready to use. Both of them contain classes. In C++, header files can contain constants and functions. In Java, constants and functions (methods) do not have any existence outside a class. Hence, all required constants have to be embedded in either a class or an interface. All required methods are required to be put inside some suitable class. Packages can contain only classes and interfaces.

Exception Handling: Java supports keyword `finally`. This provides additional functionality to exception handling. As this keyword is absent in C/C++, this functionality is not available to programmers.

C++ does not require that an exception should be caught.

Applets: The concept of applets has been introduced for the first time in Java. Hence, there is no equivalence of it in C++. In this case, Java is more useful than C++.

25.2.1 Facilities in C++ missing in Java

In this section, we will discuss a few facilities of C++ which are not supported by Java. Those who learn Java as the first language do not find any difficulty in learning and using the language. However, those who know C/C++ before learning Java start comparing facilities of C++ with Java. Not finding many of these may make learners uncomfortable. This section tries to make C++ programmers comfortable while learning Java. We will not only discuss the facilities of C++ which are not supported by Java but also try to show some way out in such circumstances.

1. *No unsigned integers*: Integer types are always signed in Java. We know that signed integer variables can also handle unsigned integer values. Hence, there will not be any difficulty while programming. Simply use the appropriate integer type (`byte`, `short`, `int`, or `long`) in place of an unsigned integer type. (See Program x1.cpp.) It will be worthy to note that if you need to handle very large integers (which you could not do in C++), there is a class `BigInteger` in Java.
2. *No* `typedef`: This facility is grossly under utilized by C/C++ programmers. We find very few situations when it is necessary to use `typedef`. It may be noted that a class can have a member of any user-defined type. Hence, it will be quite easy to create a data structure created using `typedef` by suitably defining one or more classes.
3. *Pre-processor directives*: Though pre-processor is a powerful concept, most C/C++ programmers use only two facilities, that is `#include` and `#define`.

   As far as `#define` is concerned, it only does the textual substitution. If we are using it in place of constants, then we have two choices in Java. We can either use keyword `final` or use an interface to define a constant. (See Program x2.)

   In C++ with `#include` you can put some uncompiled code (text file) in the source file. This facility is not available in Java. You have to actually copy that code in your source file.

   In C++, you can also include pre-compiled code (header files). In Java, you can replace it with `import` statement. Please note that the names of libraries in the two languages can be different. If there is no equivalence in Java, you have to develop a package first and then use `import` statement.
4. *No global variables and functions:* In Java, all variables and function (methods) belong to some class. If we talk of small or medium (single file) programs, the class which is the main program class can contain variables and methods which can work as global. The trick is to declare them as `static` and simply forget that there is nothing like global in Java. (See Program x3 in this regard).

   If you are a serious programmer and writing a very huge program, you have to be a bit careful.
5. *No* `goto`*:* Computer scientists voted out (or vetoed?) `goto` thirty years ago. If you still consider it a necessary statement in programming, something is really wrong with your training.
6. *No automatic-type conversion if loss*: This is really a safety enhancement in Java. No reason to complain.
7. *No structures and* `union`: The concept of class includes type `struct`. A class defined with all public members and no method is 100% substitute for `struct`. (See Program x4.)

As far as union is concerned, Java has no direct solution. Programmers have to think of a suitable alternative. However, this facility is used only remotely in programming. Hence, an average programmer will not feel the loss of facility.

8. *No default arguments*: With say two default arguments, we can call a method in three different ways. This faculty is not present in Java. But we know that Java allows us to overload the methods, that is we can have many methods with same name but different signatures. It means that we will have to define different overloaded methods. If you think that it will be tedious, you are wrong.
9. *Operator overloading*: Java does not support the facility of operator overloading. You know that this facility was added to programming languages later. The programs with objects were written even earlier. So we have to use the old style of writing methods to accomplish the results. (See Program money1.cpp and Program 25.6 in Section 25.3.6)
10. *No destructors*: Java does not support the concept of destructor. When the object goes out of scope, at a suitable time later, the garbage collector does the necessary work of removing the object from memory. If a programmer wants to perform a specific task (like releasing resources), he has to define method `finalize()` in that class. The garbage collector calls this method before removing the object from the memory.
11. *No* `delete` *operator*: This is a natural as the task of deleting objects is assigned to the garbage collector. In C++, one may attempt `new` and `delete` cycles to use the available memory efficiently. In the old days when the memory of the computer was small, it was important to give power of destruction to the programmer. In present times, it is really not necessary. These days, memory is never seen as the bottleneck. Therefore, non-availability is not a disadvantage. On the other hand, inadvertent use of `delete` creates problems. Such problems are automatically avoided in Java.
12. *Operators "<<" and ">>" not overloaded in input/output*: These operators were overloaded to merely add an alternate simple coding to the otherwise use of `scanf/printf` statements. This facility was not available in C. We may say Java in this respect follows C and not C++.

    It may be noted that `printf` statement is added in Java5. It serves the purpose of output. For input, one should use scanner class.
13. *No Pointer arithmetic*: Pointer arithmetic was once considered the greatest tool for a programmer. However, it is not so today. In early days of computers, RAM memory was very less. Programmers had to manage within limited memory. Nowadays, pen drives of the size of a key chain have Megabytes of memory. Hence, any manipulation thereof is simply not required.

    In C/C++, pointers were used to create and manage arrays. Since this concept does not exist in Java, non-availability of pointer arithmetic is in no way a minus point of Java.

    On the other side, it is very hard to detect errors (bugs) entered into programs with the use of pointers. It takes thousands of man-days to remove them. If one starts using Java, these efforts are as good as gained.
14. *Absence of* operator `(->)`: This operator was exclusively designed for use with pointers. As pointers are not supported, there is no place for this operator in Java.
15. *Absence of scope resolution operator*: Since Java class definition includes (textually) the member method definitions, this operator is not required in Java.

    If you see the following method defined in C++, say

```
ThisClass::thatMethod() { }
```

you have to physically move the code of `thatMethod` to `ThisClass` in Java programming.

16. *No multiple inheritance*: Java does not support multiple inheritance. If you have to convert C++ class with multiple inheritance, you have no simple alternative. The whole class has to be redefined. When one of the super-class is `abstract`, we may convert it into an interface and then use it.
17. *Objects as parameter passing only by reference*: You cannot pass objects by value. The only thing you should see is that the method does not modify any of the fields of the parameter. Such fields (variables) should not appear on the left-hand side of the assignment statement.

25.2.2 Facilities in Java not present in C++

As this book is on Java, all the features of Java are discussed in detail in the present text. Therefore, in this section we will discuss very briefly about those features of Java which are absent in C++.

1. *Multi-threading*: Java supports multi-threading. Earlier versions of C/C++ did not support multi-threading. However, modern compilers of C++ have introduced some library functions to support multi-threading.
2. *Package*: Packages are very useful in supplying already developed classes and interfaces. Though this feature is not available in C++, libraries of C++ roughly provide the same functionality.
3. *Interface*: Interface is totally new in Java. There is no equivalence of it in C++. Some authors consider it just as an indirect way of providing multiple inheritance. We do not agree fully with this use. Proper use of interface gives elegant exterior view of objects, which is not possible with any of the available C++ features.
4. *Garbage collection*: Java has provided in-built mechanism of garbage collection, thus reducing the burden on the programmer.
5. *Type String*: Java supports type String and StringBuffer as in-built types. For this reason, its use is much less error prone than a null-terminated string of C/C++.
6. *Documentation comments*: Java supports the facility of documentation comments, which has no equivalence in C/C++.

25.3 C++ to Java Through Programs

In this section, we will see few programs from C++ converted into Java. Let us start with a simple program.

25.3.1 Exercise one

As mentioned earlier, Java does not support unsigned integers. The Java integer can handle far larger values than even unsigned `int` of C++. Let us test this fact with our first conversion program.

Let us consider a simple C++ program using `unsigned int`. We know that in C++, type `int` can handle a maximum positive value of approximately 32 kilobytes. When we use type `int`, we will get an incorrect answer. However, `unsigned int` range extends to approximately 64 kilobytes. Hence, C++ program produces correct answer. If we convert it into Java, the Java program also gives us the correct answer.

Problem: Write a C++ program to demonstrate the use of keyword `unsigned`. Also write an equivalent Java program.

Solution: The following table shows a C++ program and the converted Java program (Program 25.1) side by side.

PROGRAM	x1.cpp	PROGRAM 25.1 Conversion I
Line number	**C++ program**	**Equivalent Java program**
1	// x1.cpp	// x1.java
2	#include<IOSTREAM.H>	
3		class x1
4		{
5	int main()	public static void main(String args[])
6	{ unsigned int k =20000;	{ int k =20000;
7	cout<< k<<endl;	System.out.println(k);
8	k=k*2;	k=k*2;
9	cout<< k<<endl;	System.out.println(k);
10	return 0;	// return 0;
11	}	}
12		}

Both the programs produce identical output. It is shown as follows.

Output

```
20000
40000
```

Note the various points

Line number	Remarks
1	name of program changes from x1.cpp to x1.java
2	#include is absent in Java program.
3	class x1 has no equivalence in C++.
4	
5	main in Java is public static void. It also has parameter "String args[]"
6	
7	println statement replaces cout statement.
8	

9	println statement replaces cout statement.
10	as java main is void it cannot return 0. Statement is commented out.
11	
12	

25.3.2 Exercise two

Here we will show how to handle directive #define in Java.

Let us take the familiar example of pass, fail, and percentage. See the following C++ program.

Problem: Write a simple C++ program to print pass/fail remark and the percentage. For passing, you need minimum 40 marks out of 100. Use #define to define constants MAX and MIN.

Solution: See the following C++ program.

PROGRAM x2.cpp

```
//      x2.cpp
#include<IOSTREAM.H>
#define MAX 100
#define MIN 40
int main()
{ int mark = 75;
     if ( mark >= MIN ) cout<< "1. Passes" <<endl;
        else cout << "1. fails" <<endl;

     cout<< "2. Percentage = "<< 100.0* mark/MAX <<endl;
  return 0;
}
```

We have explained earlier that there are two ways to do this task. In this example, we will demonstrate both the styles in this program.

See the corresponding Java program. (See Program 25.2)

PROGRAM 25.2 Conversion II

```
//      x2.java

class x2 implements exam
{ final static int MIN = 40 ; // Note-1

  public static void main(String args[])
     {
        int mark = 75;
        if ( mark >= MIN )System.out.println("1. Passes" );
              else System.out.println( "1. fails" );
```

```
            System.out.println("2. Percentage = " + 100.0* mark/MAX );
        }
}

interface exam
{ final static int MAX = 100 ; // Note-2
}
```

If we run this program, we will get the following output.

Output

```
1. Passes
2. Percentage = 75.0
```

Let us explain the points involved in comments Note 1 and Note 2.

Note 1: We are using `MIN` as a constant. We have declared it as `static` and `final`.

Note 2: Here we have declared `MAX` as a constant, inside an interface named `exam`. The main class `x2` implements `exam`.

25.3.3 Exercise three

In this section, we will see how to handle global variables and functions in a Java program. First, see the simple C++ program.

Problem: Define a class `Student` with fields for marks and percentage. Define a global variable to represent maximum marks 100. Also define a global method for calculating percentage.

Solution: See the following C++ program.

PROGRAM `x3.cpp`

```
//    x3.cpp
#include<IOSTREAM.H>

int Max = 100; // global variable
float percent( int marks) // global function
   {  return 1.0*marks/Max ;
   } ;
class Student
      {  public:
         int marks ;
         float per ;
         Student(int m)
             {  marks= m;
                  per = percent(marks);
             }
      };

int main()
```

```
{ Student myBest = Student(99);
  cout<< "Percentage = " << myBest.per <<endl;
  return 0;
}
```

Now see the equivalent Java program. (See Program 25.3)

PROGRAM 25.3 Conversion III

```
//    x3.java

class x3
{
     static int Max = 100; // global variable
     static float percent( int marks) // global function
        {  return (float) ( 1.0*marks/Max );
        }

  public static void main(String args[])
        {
           Student myBest = new Student(99);
           System.out.println("Percentage = " + myBest.per);
        }
static class Student
  {       int marks ;
          float per ;
          Student(int m)
     {    marks= m;
          per = percent(marks);
     }
  };
}
```

If you run the program, you will get the sample output as follows.

Output

```
Percentage = 0.99
```

Please note that

1. Global variable `Max` is declared `static`.
2. The global method `percent()` is also declared `static`.
3. Class `Student` is using method `percent` which is global. It is not defined in class `Student`.

25.3.4 Exercise four

In this section, we will see how to handle structures from C++ in a Java program. Let us first see the C++ program using structure.

Problem: Write a C++ program which defines and use structure colour. It should have integer fields red, green, and blue.

Solution: See the following C++ program.

PROGRAM x4.cpp (Uses Structures)

```
//    x4.cpp
#include<IOSTREAM.H>

struct Color { int red,green,blue ;} ;
int main()
{ Color yellow ={256,255,0} ;
  cout<< "red value "<< yellow.red <<endl;
  return 0;
}
```

Let us study the converted Java program. (See Program 25.4)

PROGRAM 25.4 Conversion IV

```
//    x4.Java
class color { int red, green, blue ;}

class x4
{
  public static void main(String args[])
     {
         color yellow = new color();
         yellow.red = 255 ;
         yellow.green = 255 ;
         yellow.blue = 0 ;

         System.out.println("red value "+ yellow.red );
     }
}
```

If you run the program, you will get the following output.

Output

```
red value 255
```

Please note the following points:

1. `struct Color` gets converted into class `color`.
2. There is no constructor for this class.
3. All the members have default access. It is as good as `public`.

25.3.5 Exercise five

In this section, we will try to take a sample program and literally convert it line by line. It will give us a thorough insight in structure of Java program.

Let us take a case of simple factorial program. A code in C++ is given hereafter. We will show how this program can be converted into Java in simple steps.

Problem: Write a C++ program to find the factorial of a given integer.

Solution: See the following program.

C++ Program: Finding Factorial

```
//    factor1.cpp
#include<IOSTREAM.H>
#include<conio.h>
long factor(int n ) ;
int main()
{     int n;
          long fact;
          cout << "program factor1.cpp starts" << endl;
          cout << "give n between 2 to 10 :" ;
          cin >> n;
          if ( (n<1)|| ( n>10) )
                         cout << cout << "error in input" ;
               else
               {    fact =factor(n);
                       cout << "factorial of n " << n
                           << " is " << fact<< endl;
               }
        getch();
        return 0;
}
long factor(int n)
{     int i; long temp =1;
      for (i=2;i<=n;i++)
```

```
24              temp = temp * i ;
25          return temp;
26      }
```

Let us study what changes are needed in the aforementioned program.

Line1	We have to change the file name from `factor1.cpp` to `factor1.java`. Hence, the comment also has to be changed to `factor1.java`.
Line 2	In place of `#include<IOSTREAM.H>` we need `import java.util.* ;` This provides us the input capability.
Line 3	There is no equivalent of `conio.h`. Hence, this line is removed. Consequently, line 18, that is `getch()`, has to be removed.
Line 4	This is function declaration. It is not required in Java. It has to be removed.
Line 5	The syntax of `main` is different. `public static void main(String args[])` takes the place of `int main()`.
Line 19	As `main` is of type `void`, `return 0` at the `main` is to be removed.

With these changes, the program may look like the following:

```
1       //      factor1.java
2       import java.util.* ;
3       //
4       //
5       public static void main(String args[])
6       {  int n;
7               long fact;
8               cout << "program factor1.cpp starts" << endl;
9               cout << "give n between 2 to 10 :" ;
10              cin >> n;
11              if ( (n<1)|| ( n>10) )
12                      cout << cout << "error in input" ;
```

```
            else
                    {    fact =factor(n);
                         cout << "factorial of n " << n
                                     << " is " << fact<< endl;
                    }
    //
    //
    }
    long factor(int n)
    {   int i; long temp =1;
        for (i=2;i<=n;i++)
                 temp = temp * i ;
        return temp;
    }
```

Well, these changes are not sufficient. Let us see what more.

We know that the whole program should be a public class named factor1. Hence, we have to add three lines class factor1, {" and "}. We also know that function factor has to be part of this class. Hence, we have to add the closing curly bracket at the end of program. This will include the function in a class. This function factor has to be declared static.

With these changes, the program may look like the following:

```
//     factor1.java
import java.util.* ;
//
//
public static void main(String args[])
{
{       int n;
          long fact;
          cout << "program factor1.cpp starts" << endl;
          cout << "give n between 2 to 10 :" ;
```

```
                    cin >> n;
                    if ( (n<1)|| ( n>10) )
                              cout << cout << "error in input" ;
                         else
                         { fact =factor(n);
                              cout << "factorial of n " << n
                                   << " is " << fact<< endl;
                         }
          //
          //
     }
     long factor(int n)
     {     int i; long temp =1;
           for (i=2;i<=n;i++)
                temp = temp * i ;
           return temp;
     }
     }
```

Lastly, we know that operator "<<" are not overloaded in Java. Also, there is no `cout`. Hence, we have to replace these output statements with appropriate `System.out.print` statement. Note that different entities printed are separated by plus sign (+) in Java. For input, we have to use the class `Scanner` and method `nextInt()`.

With these changes, the Java program would look like the following: (See Program 25.5)

PROGRAM 25.5 Conversion V

```
// factor1.java
import java.util.* ;
class factor1
{
  public static void main(String args[])
  {   int n;
      long fact;
      System.out.println( "program factor1.java starts");
      System.out.print( "give n between 2 to 10 :" );
      Scanner cin = new Scanner(System.in);
```

```
        n = cin.nextInt();
        if ( (n<1)|| ( n>10) )
                System.out.println("error in input") ;
            else
                {  fact =factor(n);
                   System.out.println("factorial of " + n
                           + " is " + fact );
                }

        return ;
    }
    static long factor(int n)
    {  int i; long temp =1;
      for (i=2;i<=n;i++)
         temp = temp * i ;
      return temp;
    }
}
```

If we run the program, we will get the following output.

Output

```
program factor1.java starts
give n between 2 to 10 :5
factorial of 5 is 120
```

25.3.6 Exercise six

Operator overloading is not supported in Java. The tasks operators perform are to be delegated to methods in Java. In this program, we will define class `Money`. It will have an operator "+" overloaded. This operator will help us to add two amounts (objects of type Money). First, we will see a complete C++ program.

Problem: Write a C++ program to illustrate the overloading of operator "+". For this purpose develop and use class `Money`.

Solution: See the following C++ program.

PROGRAM `money1.cpp`

```
//   money1.cpp

#include<iostream.h>
#include<stdlib.h>
#include<conio.h>

class Money
        {  long rupee, paise ;
           public:
```

```
            void print() ;
            Money() ;
            Money(long p, long q);
            Money operator + ( Money a2 );
        } ;
int main()
{ cout << "program money1.cpp starts" <<endl;
  Money amt1, amt2, amt3 ;
  amt1= Money( 25,15);
  amt2= Money( 22,12);
  amt1.print();
  amt2.print();
  cout << "after adding" << endl ;
  amt3 = amt1 + amt2 ;
  amt3.print();
  getch();
return 0;
}
void Money::print()
{ cout << "Amount is Rs ";
  cout << rupee << "." << paise << "/-"<< endl;
}
Money::Money()
{ rupee = paise=0; //initializing to zero value
}
Money::Money(long p, long q)
{
  if ( (p<0) || (q<0) || (q>99) )
     {  cout<< "initialisation error "<<endl;
          cout << "initialising with ZERO value"<<endl;
          p=q=0 ;
     }
     else
        {  rupee = p;
             paise = q;
        }
}
Money Money::operator+( Money a2 )
{ Money temp;
  temp.rupee = this->rupee + a2.rupee;
  temp.paise = this->paise + a2.paise;
  if (temp.paise >= 100 )
     {  temp.paise -=100;
        temp.rupee += 1;
     }
  return temp;
}
```

Now let us study a Java program. This program will also have class `Money`. Instead of overloaded operator, it will have a method `add()`. It will return the object of type `Money`.

See the complete Java program. (See Program 25.6)

PROGRAM 25.6 Conversion VI

```
//          money1.java

class Money
      {   long rupee, paise ;
          void print()
          {   System.out.println( "Amount is Rs ");
              System.out.println(rupee + "." + paise + "/-") ;
          } ;
        Money()
          {   rupee = paise=0; //initializing to zero value
          } ;
        Money(long p, long q)
          {   if ( (p<0) || (q<0) || (q>99) )
                  {   System.out.println( "initialization error");
                      System.out.println( "initializing with ZERO value");
                      p=q=0 ;
                  }
                  else
                      {   rupee = p;
                          paise = q;
                      }
              } ;
        Money add ( Money a2 )
          {   Money temp= new Money();
              temp.rupee = this.rupee + a2.rupee;
              temp.paise = this.paise + a2.paise;
              if (temp.paise >= 100 )
                  {   temp.paise -=100;
                      temp.rupee += 1;
                  }
              return temp;
          } ;
      } ;
public class money1
{
   public static void main(String argv[])
   {   System.out.println( "program money1.java starts" );
       Money amt1, amt2, amt3 ;
       amt1= new Money( 25,15);
       amt2= new Money( 22,12);
       amt1.print();
       amt2.print();
       System.out.println( "after adding" ) ;
       amt3 = amt1.add( amt2) ;
       amt3.print();
   }
}
```

If we run the program, we will get the following output.

Output

```
program money1.java starts
Amount is Rs
25.15/-
Amount is Rs
22.12/-
after adding
Amount is Rs
47.27/-
```

25.4 Rules for C++ to Java Conversion

1. Replace `unsigned byte,` `unsigned short,` and `unsigned int` by simply `int` in Java. Replace `unsigned long` of C++ by simple `long` in Java.
2. Replace `#define max 100` by either `final int max = 100;` or interface.
3. Replace all `#include` with appropriate `import` statements.
4. In single file program, replace all global variables and functions by static variables and static methods in main program class.
5. Replace structure by class without methods.
6. Replace all C++ strings by `StringBuffer`. If strings in C++ are not being modified in the program, you may use class `String` in Java.

CHAPTER 26

COLLECTION OF PROGRAMS

In this chapter, we will see both applications and applets. We will try to cover problems from different walks of life.

26.1 Projectile

When we see a fielder standing on boundary line, throwing the ball straight into the gloves of the wicket keeper, we think that he is a genius. Well, he may or may not be, but one thing is sure. He has done his college physics seriously. A projectile starting at an angle of 45 degrees travels farthest, before hitting the ground.

Let us develop an applet to show the trajectory of a projectile.

Problem: Write an applet to show the trajectory of a projectile.

Solution: Let us assume the following:

When a projectile starts, it has velocities both in horizontal and vertical direction. Horizontal velocity remains constant with time, whereas the vertical velocity reduces because of gravity. After some time, it becomes negative and the projectile starts coming down. The vertical displacement becomes zero when the projectile touches the ground (see Program 26.1).

PROGRAM 26.1 Projectile

```
//      proj2.java
import java.applet.*;
import java.awt.*;
import java.lang.Math;

public class proj2 extends Applet
{   public void init ()
      { setBackground(Color.white);
        setForeground(Color.red);
      }

    public void paint(Graphics g)
      { char box[] = new char[100];
        int k;
        int X0=20, Y0=200;
        g.setColor(Color.red);
        String st1 = new String("<-------         X axis          ------>");
        Font f1 = new Font("Arial" , Font.PLAIN , 16);
        g.setFont(f1);
        g.drawString(st1,X0+200,Y0+30 );

        g.drawLine(X0,Y0,X0,20); // Y-axis
```

```
        g.drawLine(X0,Y0,540-X0,Y0);//X-axis

        int x=20, y=300;
        int alpha = 45;
        double gravity=9.8,u=70.0;
        float valsin,valcos;
        double t ;
        int totaltime = 10;
        valsin=(float)Math.sin(2*3.14159*alpha/360);
        valcos=(float)Math.cos(2*3.14159*alpha/360);

        g.setColor(Color.blue);
        for(t=0; t<=totaltime; t= t + 0.1)
          { x=X0 + (int)(u * valcos * t );
            y=Y0 - (int)(u * valsin * t -0.5*gravity*t*t);
            g.drawLine(x,y,x,y);
            g.drawLine(x+1,y,x+1,y);
            g.drawLine(x,y+1,x,y+1);
            g.drawLine(x+1,y+1,x+1,y+1);
            delay();
          }
    }

  public static void delay()
    {       double a,b;
            long i,j=350000;
            for(i=0;i<4000000;i++)
                { j--;
                  a = 2.33 /3.11 ;
                }
    }
}
```

To watch the projectile, we need a small HTML file as shown hereafter.

Proj2.html

```
<applet code = "proj2" width =600 height =400 >
</applet>
```

If you use the browser, you will see the projectile moving through the sky. We have taken the snapshot of the flight.

Output

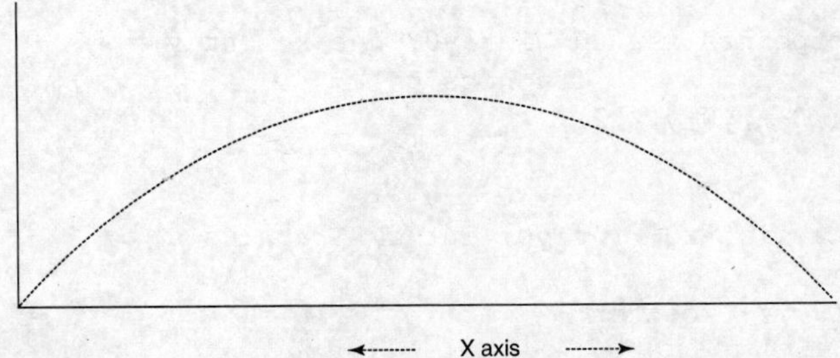

Confession: Though it is enjoyable to watch the applet, the code we have written is not quite ideal. You may show one or two additional projectiles starting at angles little different from the one shown. We have used trial and error method to decide when the projectile hits the ground. Use of `for loop` is a proof of that. You may try `while loop` with suitable condition so that you do not need any trials.

26.2 Wall Clock

All of us glance at the wall clock but we hardly bother to know how it works or what are its components. Let us try to develop an applet which displays a running wall clock.

Problem: Write an applet to display a running wall clock.

Solution: See Program 26.2.

PROGRAM 26.2 Wall Clock

```
// clock2.java
import java.util.*;
import java.awt.*;
import java.applet.*;
import java.text.*;

public class clock2 extends Applet implements Runnable
{
    Thread clock;
    int xcenter=100,ycenter=70;
    int s,m,h;
    int xs,ys,xm,ym,xh,yh,lastxs,lastys,lastxm,lastym,
        lastxh,lastyh;
    Font myclock;
    int degree,i;
    int placex,placey;

    public void init()
    {
        resize(300,300);
        setForeground(Color.red);
        setBackground(Color.black);
        lastxs = lastys = lastxm = lastym
            = lastxh = lastyh = 0;
        myclock=new Font("Arial",Font.BOLD,14);
 }

 public void plotpoints(int x0, int y0, int x, int y,
                             Graphics g )
  {   g.fillRect(x0-x,y0-y,2,2);
  }

public void circle(int x0, int y0, int r, Graphics g)
  {
      int x = x0 ;//+ xcenter;
```

```
        int y = y0 ;//- ycenter;
        g.drawOval(x-2,y-2,4,4);
    }

public void paint(Graphics g)
    {
        SimpleDateFormat formatter;Date currdate;
        currdate=new Date();
        formatter=new
           SimpleDateFormat("HH:mm:ss",Locale.getDefault());
        formatter.applyPattern("ss");
        s=Integer.parseInt(formatter.format(currdate));
        formatter.applyPattern("mm");
        m=Integer.parseInt(formatter.format(currdate));
        formatter.applyPattern("HH");
        h=Integer.parseInt(formatter.format(currdate));
        g.drawRoundRect(40,10,125,115,10,10);

        g.setFont(myclock);
        i=1;

        for(degree=28;degree<=360;degree=degree+30)
        {
        placex=(int) (Math.cos(degree*3.14/180-3.14/2)
          * 45 + xcenter);
        placey=(int) (Math.sin(degree*3.14/180-3.14/2)
        * 45 + ycenter);
        g.drawString(Integer.toString(i),placex,placey);
        i++;
    }

    // following equations calculate the positions of
    // hands in clock.
    xs=(int) (Math.cos(s*3.14/30-3.14/2) *50 +xcenter);
    ys=(int) (Math.sin(s*3.14/30-3.14/2) *50 +ycenter);
    xm=(int) (Math.cos(m*3.14/30-3.14/2) *45 +xcenter);
    ym=(int) (Math.sin(m*3.14/30-3.14/2) *45 +ycenter);
    xh=(int) (Math.cos((h*30+m/2)*3.14/180-3.14/2)
                *30 + xcenter);
    yh=(int) (Math.sin((h*30+m/2)*3.14/180-3.14/2)
                *30 + ycenter);

    // these drawLine functions draw hands.
    g.setColor(getBackground());
    if (xs != lastxs || ys != lastys) {
        g.drawLine(xcenter, ycenter, lastxs, lastys);
        circle(lastxs,lastys,3,g);
    }
    if (xm != lastxm || ym != lastym)
        {  g.drawLine(xcenter, ycenter, lastxm, lastym);
        }
    if (xh != lastxh || yh != lastyh)
        { g.drawLine(xcenter, ycenter, lastxh, lastyh);
```

```
        }
    g.setColor(Color.red);
    g.drawLine(xcenter,ycenter,xs,ys);
    circle(xs,ys,3,g); //circle on second hand
    g.setColor(Color.orange);
    g.drawLine(xcenter,ycenter,xm,ym);
    g.drawLine(xcenter,ycenter,xh,yh);
    lastxs=xs; lastys=ys;
    lastxm=xm; lastym=ym;
    lastxh=xh; lastyh=yh;
  }
  public void start()
  {    clock=new Thread(this);
       clock.start();
  }
  public void update(Graphics g)
  { paint(g);
  }
  public void run()
  {   Thread me=Thread.currentThread();
       while(clock==me)
       {  try {
                Thread.currentThread().sleep(100);
          } catch(InterruptedException e) {}
          repaint();
       }
    }
  }
```

To run the applet, we will write a small HTML file as shown.

clock1.html

```
<applet code = "clock2" width =200 height =150 align=middle vspace=80
hspace=175>
</applet>
```

If you load this HTML page in any browser of your choice, you will get a clock ticking. The following diagram shows a freeze shot of the display.

Output

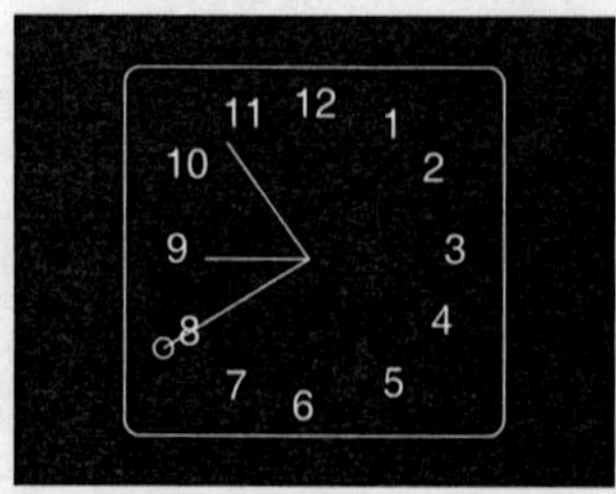

Please note that the clock shows the current time.

26.3 Drawing Ellipses

Problem: Write a program to draw multiple ellipses.

Solution: The method `drawOval` can draw the ellipse in a rectangle with either vertical or horizontal lines. Hence, this method is not suitable for drawing ellipses which are oriented in different directions (angles). Here, we first imagine a point on an ellipse which has zero inclination and then rotate it through desired angle (see Program 26.3).

PROGRAM 26.3 Ellipses

```
 //     ele1.java
import java.awt.* ;
import javax.swing.*;

class  VP extends JFrame
   {  VP (int xdim, int ydim) //constructor
       { setSize(xdim,ydim);
         setBackground(Color.white);
         setVisible(true);
       }
     public void delay(long n)
       { long t1,t2;
         t1 = System.currentTimeMillis();
         t1 = t1 + n;
         t2= System.currentTimeMillis();
         while  ( t2 < t1 ) t2= System.currentTimeMillis();
        }

   public void paint  (Graphics g)
      {  int k ;
         int x0=200, y0=210, r1=100;
         int x1 , y1,x2,y2 ;
         double mult = 3.1416 /180.0 ;
         double abc =0.6 ,mag,ang;
         g.clearRect(0,0,400,400);
         g.setColor( Color.blue );
         for(double z =0;z<180;z=z+30)
         for(k=0; k< 360; k++)
           {  delay(1);
              x1 = (int) Math.ceil( r1* Math.cos(mult*k) ) ;
              y1 = (int) Math.floor( abc*r1* Math.sin(mult*k) ) ;
             mag = Math.hypot(y1,x1);
              ang = Math.atan2(y1,x1)+ Math.toRadians(z);
              x2 = (int) Math.ceil( x0+mag* Math.cos(ang) ) ;
              y2 = (int) Math.floor( y0+mag* Math.sin(ang) ) ;
              g.fillOval(x2,y2,2,2);
           }
      }
 }
public class ele1
```

```
{ public static void main(String[] args)
      { VP vp1= new VP( 400,400);
          vp1.setDefaultCloseOperation(JFrame.EXIT_ON_CLOSE);
      };
}
```

When you run this program, you will see the following output.

Output

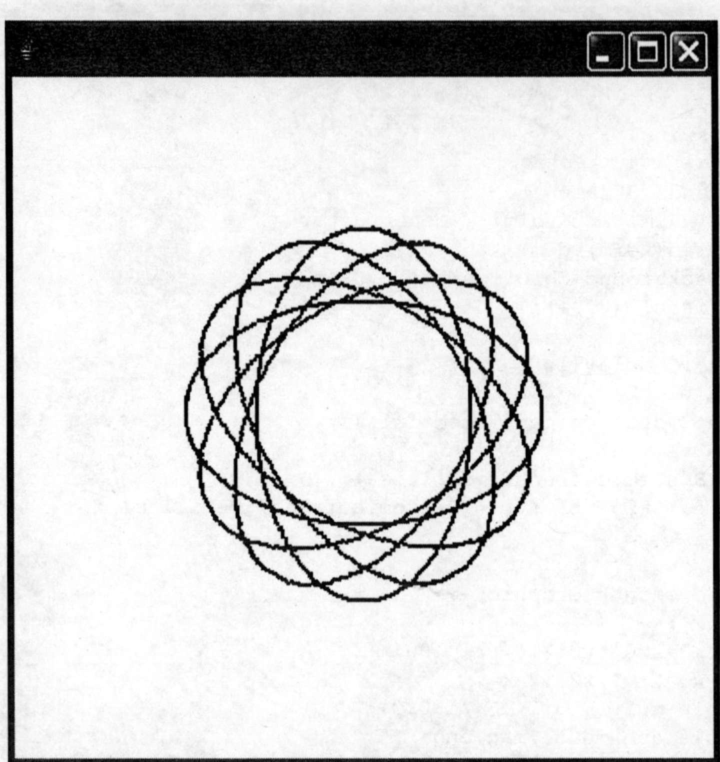

26.4 Area of Circle by Monte Carlo Method

The estimation methods based on statistics are common. Here we will use a method known as Monte Carlo method for finding area of the circle.

Problem: Write a program to find the area of a circle with a unit diameter.

Solution: In this program, we will use Monte Carlo method. We will imagine a square with unit side. Its area will, therefore, be "one" (unit area). We will use random number technique to create a point lying in this area and check mathematically if the point lies in the circle inscribed in the square. In any statistical method, we have to keep the sample size very large. Hence, we will create many such points. The ratio of points lying in the circle to total points will describe/represent the area of circle with unit diameter. See Program 26.4.

PROGRAM 26.4 Area of Circle—Monte Carlo Method

```
import java.awt.* ;
import javax.swing.* ;

import java.util.* ;

class monte2 extends JFrame
{
  monte2 (int xdim, int ydim) //constructor
       { setSize(xdim,ydim);
       { setTitle("Area of circle :Monte carlo Method");
   //      setBackground(Color.white);
       { setVisible(true);
       { setDefaultCloseOperation(JFrame.EXIT_ON_CLOSE);
     }
public static void main(String[] args)
      { monte2 thisprog = new monte2( 400,300);
        thisprog.setVisible(true);
      };

public void delay(long n)
   { long t1,t2;
     t1 = System.currentTimeMillis();
     t1 = t1 + n;
     t2= System.currentTimeMillis();
     while ( t2 < t1 ) t2= System.currentTimeMillis();
   }
int test(int x, int y, int z)
{ int ans = 0;
  Double R = z /2.0;
  Double x1 = x - z/2.0;
  Double y1 = y - z/2.0;
  if ( Math.sqrt( x1*x1 + y1*y1) <= R ) ans =1;
   return ans;
};
public void paint (Graphics g)
  {int x, y;
   Color drawcol;
   long i, count = 0;
   long simu_max =1200*8*2 ;
   float val_pi;
   final int max = 200 ;
   g.setColor(Color.white);
   g.fillRect(0,0,400,300);
   delay(500);
   Random rand = new Random();
   for (i=10;i<simu_max; i++)
    {   x=rand.nextInt(max);
        y=rand.nextInt(max);
        if (test(x, y, max) ==1)
                 {  drawcol = Color.red; //RED
```

```
                    count ++;
                }
                else drawcol = Color.yellow ; //YELLOW
            g.setColor( drawcol ) ;
            g.drawLine(x+50, y+50, x+50 ,y+50);
            if (i %10 == 0) delay(1);

        }
    g.drawString( Double.toString((double)count/simu_max), 50,270);

    }
}
```

When you run this program, you will see the following output.

Output

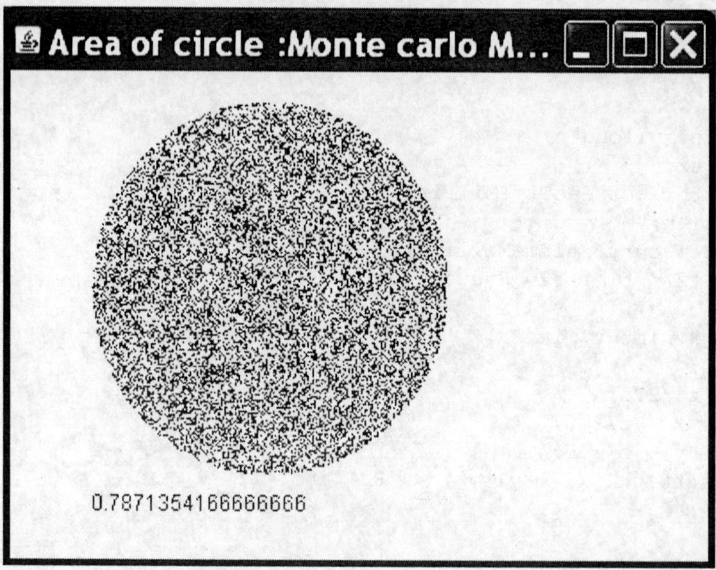

Please note that the value printed at the bottom is the area of circle with unit diameter.

26.5 Display of Binary Tree

Earlier we have worked with a dynamic data structure called binary tree. Teaching and learning such structures is fairly tough task. It will be a nice idea to see (graphically) how a binary tree grows. It will make teaching and learning of this topic somewhat simpler. Let us try this with the help of a program.

Problem: Write a program to display a binary tree on the screen.

Solution: In this program, we will develop a method `show_me` to do the complete task. It will create its own thread. In the `run` method of the thread, we will first build the tree and then visit all nodes. While visiting the nodes, we will plot the nodes on the screen.

Recursion comes very handy for visiting and displaying the nodes. The logic is unbelievably simple. We keep a track of left and right margins as well as the level of the node. The *y* position is proportional to level of the node. The *x* position is the centre of left and right margins (see Program 26.5).

PROGRAM 26.5 Display of Binary Tree

```
//     tree3.java
//   Binary Search Tree
//   graphics version

import javax.swing.*;
import java.awt.Color;
import java.awt.* ;

class BPtimer
 { public static void delay(long n)
    { long t1,t2;
      t1 = System.currentTimeMillis();
      t1 = t1 + n;
      t2= System.currentTimeMillis();
      while ( t2 < t1 ) t2= System.currentTimeMillis();
    }
 }
class Node
 { int key;       // isbn number
   Node left, right;
   Node(int n) // constructor
    { key = n ;
      left = null ;
      right = null ;
    }
 };

class VP extends JFrame
  { static Graphics g1;
    Node root ;
    Node temp ;
    int i;
    int A[] = { 12, 4, 6, 18, 10,56,1,45,99,88,5,17 } ;

    VP (int xdim, int ydim) //constructor
      { setSize(xdim,ydim);
        setDefaultCloseOperation(JFrame.EXIT_ON_CLOSE);
        setBackground(Color.white);
        setVisible(true);
        g1=getGraphics();
        g1.setColor(Color.blue);
      }

class A extends Thread
```

```
  { public void run()
     { root = new Node(A[0]); // First nodeof the tree
       // building tree
       for( i=1;i<A.length;i++)
         { build(root,A[i]) ;
         }
        BPtimer.delay(250);
        // printing tree
         visitAllx(root,1,80,1,g1);
        }
     }

    public void show_me()
     {  A th1 = new A();
        th1.setPriority(Thread.NORM_PRIORITY);
        th1.start();
     }

   static void  build( Node root, int num )
     {if(root == null) { System.out.println("error!");
                          System.exit(1);
                        }
         else
          if(root.key > num)
            {if ( root.left == null ) root.left = new Node(num);
                  else     build(root.left, num);
            }
           else {if(root.right == null) root.right = new Node(num);
                     else build(root.right,num);
     }
 }
 static void visitAllx( Node root, int lm, int rm,
              int h, Graphics g1)
    {int x ;
     if (root != null)
       { x=(lm+rm)/2;
         g1.drawString(String.valueOf(root.key),50+x*3,50+h*40);
         BPtimer.delay(500);
         visitAllx(root.left,lm,x,h+1,g1);
         visitAllx(root.right,x,rm,h+1,g1);
       }
     }
  }
public class tree3
 { public static void main(String args[])
     { VP vp1= new VP( 500,400);
        vp1.setTitle("tree3");
        vp1.setVisible(true);
        vp1.show_me();
     }
 }
```

When you run this program, the tree is constructed node by node. At the end you will see the following output.

Output

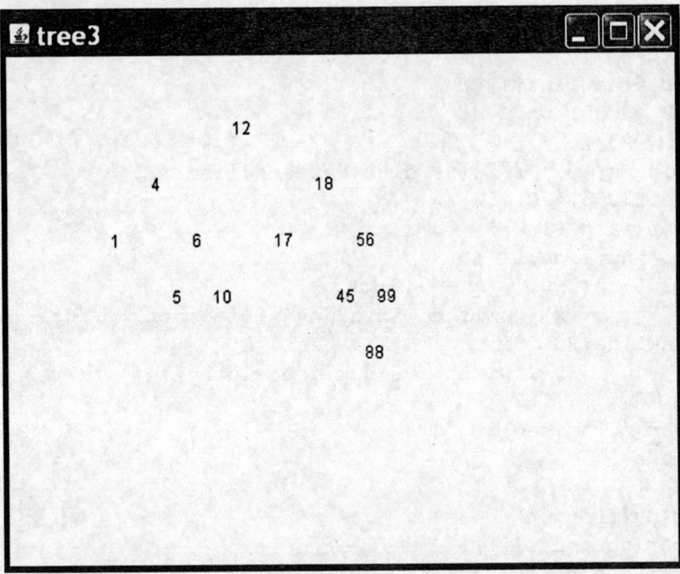

26.6 Drawing with Data from a File

When we draw many diagrams, we have to repeat many patterns like rectangles. If we can create instructions from drawing and put them in a file, it will be very useful. Our program can read it and draw the diagram. If we have to modify something, we have to only make changes in the text file. Let us see this concept in action.

Problem: Write a program to draw rectangles as specified in a file

Solution: See Program 26.6.

PROGRAM 26.6 Drawing Diagrams

```
 //      draw2.java
import java.awt.* ;
import java.io.* ;
import java.util.* ;
import java.awt.event.* ;
import javax.swing.*;

class draw2 extends JFrame
{  static Color faintBlue = new Color(200,200,255);
   static FileReader file1 ;
   static BufferedReader br ;
   static String[] buff;
```

```
   static int buffLength ; // note using buff.length!
/*
   draw2(String str1)
   {super(str1);
   }
*/   public void paint(Graphics g)
    { int i;
      int[] cor = new int[4] ;
      int x0=30,y0=30;
      int width =25 ;
      int numline = 16 ; // also dist between lines 25
      g.clearRect(0,0,450,450);
      g.setColor(faintBlue);
      for(i=0;i<=numline;i++)
        { g.drawLine( x0,    y0+i*width,
                      x0+numline*width,    y0+i*width); //hol line
          g.drawLine(x0+i*width,        y0,
                     x0+i*width, y0+numline*width );    // ver line
        }
      g.setColor(Color.red);
// executing code
      i=0;
      while (i<buffLength)
       {  getcor(cor,buff[i]);
          g.drawRect(cor[0],cor[1],cor[2],cor[3]);
          i++;
       }
   };

public static void main(String[] args) throws IOException
 { String line;
   buff = new String[50] ;
   file1 = new FileReader("draw2.txt");
   br = new BufferedReader( file1);
   buffLength = 0;
   while ((line = br.readLine()) != null)
       { System.out.println("line read is: " + line);
         buff[buffLength++] = new String(line);
       };
//   System.out.println(buffLength);
     draw2 f1= new draw2();
     f1.setDefaultCloseOperation(JFrame.EXIT_ON_CLOSE);
     f1.setTitle("Drawing from file");
     f1.setSize(450,450);
     f1.setBackground(Color.white);
     f1.setVisible(true);
   }

public static void getcor(int[] a, String line)
 { String str1;
   try
```

```
        {
          StringTokenizer st = new StringTokenizer(line);
          int j=0;
          while (st.hasMoreTokens()&& j<4)
              {  str1 = st.nextToken() ;
                 a[j] = Integer.parseInt(str1);
                 j++;
              }

        } catch(Exception e) { System.out.println("Some Error") ;}

      };
    }
/* file draw2.txt
    50 60 40 80
   120 60 40 80
   190 60 40 80
   260 60 40 80
 */
```

If you run this program, you will get the following output.

Output

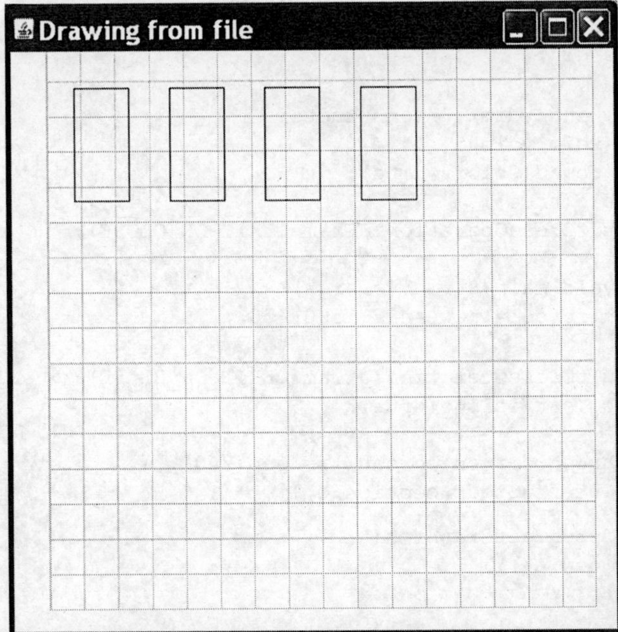

Please note that while reading the data file, program prints data on the console. When we run Java programs with GUI, we can still make use of console. Since the main output is GUI, use of console should be only for debugging information and not for the end-user output. It will be absurd to expect the end-user at both the `Frame` as well as the console.

26.7 Animation

Earlier we had seen a simple animation under Chapter 13 on "Graphics". After studying AWT and `Swing`, we are better equipped to handle animation. Let us try a simple program.

Problem: Write a program to show a rotating red square on the screen.

Solution: We have `fillPoly()` method to plot a filled polygon. When a square is rotating, its vertices will be changing with time. We will have to calculate them first before calling the `fillPoly()`. As in any animation, the following actions are repeated in a loop. First, the previous figure is erased, and then a new figure is drawn. Thereafter we call for a delay (see Program 26.7).

PROGRAM 26.7 Animation

```
import java.awt.* ;
import javax.swing.* ;

import java.util.* ;

class ani2 extends JFrame
{ static double a0   = Math.toRadians(0.0);
  static double a90   = Math.toRadians(90.0);
  static double a180   = Math.toRadians(180.0);
  static double a270   = Math.toRadians(270.0);
  static Graphics g1 ;

  ani2 (int xdim, int ydim) //constructor
       { setSize(xdim,ydim);
         setBackground(Color.white);
         setVisible(true);
         setDefaultCloseOperation(JFrame.EXIT_ON_CLOSE);
       }
  public static void main(String[] args)
        { ani2 thisprog = new ani2( 500,400);

thisprog.setDefaultCloseOperation(JFrame.EXIT_ON_CLOSE);
          thisprog.setVisible(true);
          try
             { Thread.currentThread().sleep(200); }
          catch(InterruptedException e){}

          g1=thisprog.getGraphics();
          A a1 = new A();
          a1.start();
        };

 public void delay(long n)
    {
     try
       {  Thread.currentThread().sleep(100);}
    catch(InterruptedException e){}
```

```
    }
  public static void compute_sq(double theta, int[] x, int[] y ,int len)
  { x[0]=250 +(int) Math.floor( len*Math.sin(theta + a0 ));
    y[0]=250 +(int) Math.floor( len*Math.cos(theta + a0) );

    x[1]=250 +(int) Math.floor( len*Math.sin(theta + a90) );
    y[1]=250 +(int) Math.floor( len*Math.cos(theta + a90) );

    x[2]=250 +(int) Math.floor( len*Math.sin(theta + a180) );
    y[2]=250 +(int) Math.floor( len*Math.cos(theta + a180) );

    x[3]=250 +(int) Math.floor( len*Math.sin(theta + a270) );
    y[3]=250 +(int) Math.floor( len*Math.cos(theta + a270) );

  }
static   class A extends Thread
   { public void run()
       { paint_me( g1) ;
       }
   }
public static void paint_me (Graphics g)
  { int x0=50, y0=50;
    Color drawcol = Color.red ;
    Color bgcol = Color.white ;
    g.setColor(bgcol);
    g.fillRect(0,0,500,500);
    g.setColor(drawcol);
    try
       { Thread.currentThread().sleep(200); }
    catch(InterruptedException e){}

    int i,j,N,temp;
    int [] x = new int[4] ;
    int [] y = new int[4] ;
    N=15 ;    // no of loops

    for (j=0;j<100;j++)
     {
       compute_sq(j*0.01,x,y,100);
       g.fillPolygon(x,y,4);
       try
         { Thread.currentThread().sleep(200); }
       catch(InterruptedException e){}
       g.setColor(bgcol);
       g.fillPolygon(x,y,4);
       g.setColor(drawcol);
     }

   }
 }
```

When you run this program, you see the following output.

Output

26.8 Graphical Display of Bubble Sort

Our teachers emphasized that a figure is worth thousand words. Hence, it is worth trying algorithms like bubble sort be given a graphical display. The famous *Java Tutorials* graphically demonstrates a few sorting techniques, the demo of which is worth studying and enjoying. Let us see whether we can also attempt such a task ourselves.

Problem: Write a program to graphically demonstrate sorting by bubble sort.

Solution: In this program, we will consider a small array of integers as our data for sorting. We will use horizontal lines to represent the data. The length will be the indicator of the data value. The lines corresponding to successive array elements are displayed one below the other (see Program 26.8).

PROGRAM 26.8 Graphic Bubble Sort

```
 //      bubgra2

import java.awt.* ;
import javax.swing.* ;
import java.util.* ;

class  bubgra2 extends JFrame
{
  bubgra2 (int xdim, int ydim) //constructor
        { setSize(xdim,ydim);
          setBackground(Color.white);
          setTitle("Bubble sort");
          setVisible(true);
          setDefaultCloseOperation(JFrame.EXIT_ON_CLOSE);
        }
```

```
public static void main(String[] args)
      { bubgra2 thisprog = new bubgra2( 400,300);
        thisprog.setVisible(true);
      };

public void delay(long n)
   { try
        { Thread.currentThread().sleep(100);}
     catch(InterruptedException e){}
   }

public void paint (Graphics g)
  {int x0=50, y0=50;
   Color drawcol = Color.red ;
   Color bgcol = Color.white ;
   g.clearRect(0,0,400,300);
   g.setColor(drawcol);

 //*****
      int i,j,N,temp;
      int[] a = {50,23,18,67,35,42,15,38,33,15,88,27,77,9,61};
      N=15 ;  // size of the array +1
      for (j=0;j<N;j++)
         g.drawLine(x0,y0+j*10,x0+a[j]*2,y0+j*10);
      delay(1000);
 //   Now sorting starts
      for(i=0;i< N-1;i++)
        { for (j=0;j<N-1;j++)
           { if ( a[j] > a[j+1] )
              { temp = a[j];
                g.setColor(bgcol);
                g.drawLine(x0,y0+j*10,x0+a[j]*2,y0+j*10);
                a[j] = a[j+1];
                g.setColor(drawcol);
                g.drawLine(x0,y0+j*10,x0+a[j]*2,y0+j*10);
                delay(100);
                g.setColor(bgcol);

 g.drawLine(x0,y0+j*10+10,x0+a[j+1]*2,y0+j*10+10);
                a[j+1]= temp;
                g.setColor(drawcol);

 g.drawLine(x0,y0+j*10+10,x0+a[j+1]*2,y0+j*10+10);
                delay(100);
              }
           }
          delay(1000);
         }
       }
 }
```

At the end of sorting, you will get the following output.

Output

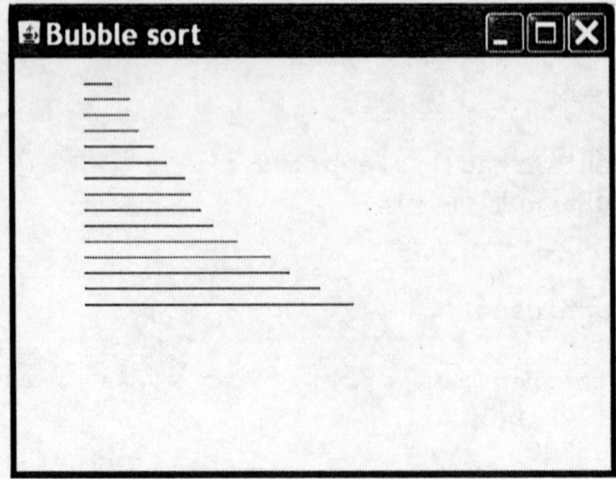

26.9 Astrology: Strength of a Horoscope

It is believed that a person reaches heights in life if his horoscope is strong. It is possible to calculate/specify the strength of a horoscope by a single value. Let us see how far we succeed in the task.

26.9.1 Strength of planets located in different signs

In any horoscope, each planet is placed in any one particular sign. The following table illustrates the **strength of planets located in different signs.**

Signs → Planets ↓	Mesha	Vrishabha	Mithun	Kark	Sinha	Kanya	Tula	Vrischik	Dhanu	Makar	Kumbha	Meena
Ravi	100	15	55	80	90	60	5	80	80	15	15	80
Chandra	60	95	65	85	80	65	35	5	60	40	35	55
Mangal	90	50	20	10	80	20	45	85	80	95	35	80
Budha	40	80	85	30	75	100	80	35	40	60	55	5
Guru	80	20	20	**100**	80	20	20	80	90	10	45	85
Shukra	45	85	80	20	15	10	90	50	35	80	80	95
Shani	**5**	80	60	20	15	60	100	20	45	85	90	50

Planet Guru in sign "Kark" has the highest marks, 100. Planet Shani in sign "Mesha" has only 5 marks. These cells are marked in bold in the aforementioned table.

26.9.2 Strength of planets depending on the position

A planet has different percentage power if located in different position. Position means position from the ascendant. If the planet is in the ascendant, its position is 1. The following table specifies the power of the planet in percentage, depending on the position. This table needs little explanation. The top row represents the power as percentage. Its value ranges from 100% to 11%. The leftmost column represents the planets.

Percentage →	100	91	83	75	67	59	51	43	35	27	19	11
Planets↓												
Ravi	**10**	11	6	3	1	9	5	7	4	2	8	12
Chandra	4	11	3	1	7	9	5	10	2	6	12	8
Mangal	10	11	6	3	9	5	1	4	2	12	8	7
Budha	1	11	10	3	4	5	9	2	6	12	8	7
Guru	9	5	1	11	2	10	4	7	6	12	8	3
Shukra	4	11	5	7	9	2	1	10	3	12	8	6
Shani	11	6	**3**	10	7	9	5	4	2	8	12	1

If the planet Ravi is in the 10th position, then it has 100% power. If the planet Shani is in the 3rd position, then it has 83% power. These entries are marked in bold in the above table.

To avoid interactive computing, we can enter the details of a horoscope in a text file with the following format:

line 1	Name
line 2	Date of birth
line 3	Time of birth
line 4 to 14	Number of the sign in which ascendants and planets Sun, Moon, Mars, Mercury, Jupiter, Venus, Saturn, Herschel, Neptune, and Pluto are present.

Note:

Data in lines 1, 2, and 3 is not processed in this particular program.

Only the ascendant and the first seven planets are used in this program.

File design is done considering the future developments.

The // and contents thereafter are just for information.

A sample data file named `Sunder` is as follows.

```
Sunder A.Rajan      // name
xx:yy:19zz     // date
aa:bb    // time      // data changed to hide identity
9        // Asc
11       // sun
```

```
4      // moon
11      // mars
10      // mercury
11      // Jupiter
12      // venus
6      // Saturn
3      // Harchel
6      //neptune
4      //Pluto
```

The rules or assumptions for evaluating are as follows.

- The planet present in a particular sign has a particular value.
- The planet placed in a particular house (with respect to ascendant) has a particular multiplying factor.
- The final strength of a planet is the product of these two quantities.
- The value is the sum of values of all the seven planets.
- Only seven planets are considered for this evaluation.
- The data needed is location (sign) of all planets and sign of the ascendant.
- In the main evaluation (method A), we take sum of powers of all the seven planets. A power of a planet is computed as position value * percentage/100.
- When a percentage value is low, it reduces the power of a planet significantly. The resulting value may not represent the true planet power. Therefore, an alternate method (say B) is used. Here average of rashi power and position power is found by the formula (rashi power + position power)/2.

With these assumptions, we are in a position to write a program.

Problem: Write a program to evaluate the strength of a given horoscope.

Solution: See Program 26.9.

PROGRAM 26.9 Evaluating Horoscope

```
//      value1.java
import java.io.* ;

interface horo1
    { final int RAVI = 0;
      final int CHANDRA = 0;
      final String[] Pname =
           { " ravi", " chandra", "  mangal", "   budh" ,
             " guru" ," shukra", "   shani", "   rahu",
             " ketu", " harshal", " neptune", "  pluto"
           } ;
     final String[] Rname =
       { "mesha", "vrishabha", "mithun", "kark",
         "sinha", "kanya",     "tula",   "vrischik",
         "dhanu", "makar",     "kumbha", "meena"
       };
final int Rpower[][] =
 {
```

```
  { 100, 15, 55, 80, 90, 60,  5, 80, 80, 15, 15, 80  }, //ravi
  {  60, 95, 65, 85, 80, 65, 35,  5, 60, 40, 35, 55  }, //chandra
  {  90, 50, 20, 10, 80, 20, 45, 85, 80, 95, 35, 80  }, //mangal
  {  40, 80, 85, 30, 75,100, 80, 35, 40, 60, 55,  5  }, //budha
  {  80, 20, 20,100, 80, 20, 20, 80, 90, 10, 45, 85  }, //guru
  {  45, 85, 80, 20, 15, 10, 90, 50, 35, 80, 80, 95  }, //shukra
  {   5, 80, 60, 20, 15, 60,100, 20, 45, 85, 90, 50  }  //shani
 };

final int percent[] =
  { 100, 91, 83, 75, 67, 59, 51, 43, 35, 27, 19, 11}; //percent
final int Lpower[][] =
  {
   { 10, 11,  6,  3,  1,  9,  5,  7,  4,  2,  8, 12  }, //ravi
   {  4, 11,  3,  1,  7,  9,  5, 10,  2,  6, 12,  8  }, //chandra
   { 10, 11,  6,  3,  9,  5,  1,  4,  2, 12,  8,  7  }, //mangal
   {  1, 11, 10,  3,  4,  5,  9,  2,  6, 12,  8,  7  }, //budha
   {  9,  5,  1, 11,  2, 10,  4,  7,  6, 12,  8,  3  }, //guru
   {  4, 11,  5,  7,  9,  2,  1, 10,  3, 12,  8,  6  }, //shukra
   { 11,  6,  3, 10,  7,  9,  5,  4,  2,  8, 12,  1  } // shani
 };
}

class Patrika2 implements horo1
{ String name,date,time;
  int asc ;
  int[] Planets = new int[12] ;
  Patrika2()
     { int i;
       for (i=0;i<12;i++)
         Planets[i]=0;
     } ;
public void showData()
{  int i, k=0;
   System.out.println("name : " + name);
   System.out.println("date : " + date);
   System.out.println("time : " + time);
   System.out.println("Ascendent : " + Rname[asc] );
   for ( i=0 ;i<12 ; i++)
     { System.out.println( Pname[i] +" in " + Rname[Planets[i]] );
     }
}
boolean valid(int k)
{ boolean flag = true; // valid
  if ( k < 0 ) flag = false;
  if ( k > 11) flag = false;
  return flag;
}
public void eval1()
{  int i, j, k, ans, sum1, sum2, sum3 ;
   int box[][] = new int[12][6] ;
   System.out.println("<---evaluation--->");
```

```
// part I
      sum1 = 0;
      for (i=0;i<7;i++)
       {  k = Rpower[i][Planets[i]];
          box[i][0] = k ;
          sum1 = sum1 + k ;
       };
       sum1 = sum1 / 7 ;
       // colomn 0 for rashi power

// part II
      for (i=0;i<7;i++)
         {  k = ( Planets[i] - asc +12) % 12 + 1; // k range 1 to 12
            ans = -1 ;
            for (j=0;j<12;j++)
                if ( k == Lpower[i][j] ) { ans = j; break; } ;
            if ( ans == -1 )
                  { System.out.println("Error 2") ;
                             return;
                  }
                else
                 { box[i][1] = percent[ans] ;}
         } ;
         // column 1 for positional power
// part III
      // column 2 product
       sum2 = 0 ;
       for (i=0;i<7;i++)
         {  box[i][2] = box[i][0] * box[i][1] /100 ;
            sum2 = sum2 + box[i][2];
         }
       sum2 = sum2 / 7 ;

      // column 3 average
       sum3 = 0 ;
       for (i=0;i<7;i++)
         {  box[i][3] = ( box[i][0] + box[i][1] ) / 2 ;
            sum3 = sum3 + box[i][3];
         }
       sum3 = sum3 / 7 ;
       System.out.println("planet Rashi Position   A     B " );
       System.out.println(" name  power power     mult  avg" );
       for (i=0;i<7;i++)
          System.out.println( Pname[i] +" : "
                              + box[i][0] + " "
                              + box[i][1] + " "
                              + box[i][2] + " "
                              + box[i][3]);

          System.out.println("----------------------------------------");
          System.out.println( "  " + sum1 + "  ****  "
```

```
        + sum2 + "      " + sum3 );
  }
public void fetchFromFile() throws IOException
 { int i,j; // ,j,k ;
   String fname,temp;
   String Z[] = new String[13];
   BufferedReader Cin = new BufferedReader
                        (new InputStreamReader(System.in) ) ;
   System.out.println("Give name of the file");
   fname = Cin.readLine();
   File fx = new File(fname);
   if ( ! fx.exists() )
      { System.out.println(" Can not read from named file");
        System.exit(1); //return;
      }
   FileReader f1 = new FileReader(fx);
   BufferedReader Jin = new BufferedReader(f1) ;

   System.out.println("<---reading file starts--->");
   name = Jin.readLine();
   date = Jin.readLine();
   time = Jin.readLine();
   System.out.println("name = " + name);
   System.out.println("date = " + date);
   System.out.println("time = " + time );
   temp = Jin.readLine();
   j=Integer.parseInt(temp.substring(0,3).trim() );
   asc = j-1 ;
   if ( ! valid (asc) ) asc = 0;
   i=0;
   while ( (Jin.ready()) && (i<7) )
   { temp = Jin.readLine();
      j=Integer.parseInt(temp.substring(0,3).trim() );
      j= j-1;
      if ( ! valid (j) ) j = 0;
      Planets[i] = j ;
      i++;
   }
  }
}
class value1
{  public static void main (String argv[])
    { System.out.println("<---value1.java--->");
      Patrika2 p1 = new Patrika2();
      try
        { p1.fetchFromFile(); }
      catch (IOException e ) { } ;
      p1.eval1();
    }
}
```

If you run this program and give the file name as `Sunder`, you will see the following output.

Output

```
<---value1.java--->
Give name of the file
sunder
<---reading file starts--->
name = Sunder A.Rajan // name
date = xx:yy:19zz // date
time = aa:bb // time // data changed to hide identity
<---evaluation--->
planet      Rashi    Position   A       B
name        power    power      mult    avg
   ravi :   15       75         11      45
chandra :   85       11         9       48
 mangal :   35       75         26      55
   budh :   60       43         25      51
   guru :   45       11         4       28
 shukra :   95       100        95      97
  shani :   60       75         45      67
----------------------------------------------
            56       ****       30      55
```

The main evaluation (method A) results in value as 30.

The alternate evaluation (method B) gives value as 55.

In general, value obtained by method B for any horoscope is always higher than the corresponding method A value.

26.10 Freehand Drawing

In school days, we are expected to draw what is known as "freehand drawing". It is really a matter of skill to draw symmetric left and right sides. But with the computer at your disposal, you can do a neat job. We can use the interface `MouseMotionListener` for this task.

Problem: Write a program to draw a "freehand drawing" the mouse.

Solution: We have to draw only one side. The other side will be generated automatically. (see Program 26.10).

PROGRAM 26.10 Freehand Drawing

```
 //   mouse2.java
import java.awt.* ;
import java.awt.event.* ;
import javax.swing.* ;

class myFrame extends JFrame implements MouseMotionListener
{ public static Graphics myG ;
  public static int width =400, height =300;
  myFrame()
```

```
      { super("***mouse2***") ;
        setSize(width,height);
        setResizable(false);
        setBackground(Color.white);
        setVisible(true);
      }
public void init()
 { addMouseMotionListener(this);
   requestFocus();
   myG = getGraphics() ;
   myG.setColor(Color.blue);
 }
public void paint (Graphics myG)
 { myG.clearRect(0,0,width,height);
   myG.setColor(Color.blue);
   myG.drawLine( 200,20,200,300);
 }
public void mouseMoved(MouseEvent e)
     {
     }
public void mouseDragged(MouseEvent e)
  {  int x = e.getX() ;
     int y = e.getY() ;
     myG.drawRect( x,y,1,2);
     myG.drawRect( 400-x,y,1,2);
  }
}
public class mouse2
 {  public static void main( String args[])
    {    myFrame k1 = new myFrame();
         k1.setDefaultCloseOperation(JFrame.EXIT_ON_CLOSE);
         k1.init();
    }
}
```

If you run this program, you create a freehand drawing. A sample drawing is as follows.

Output

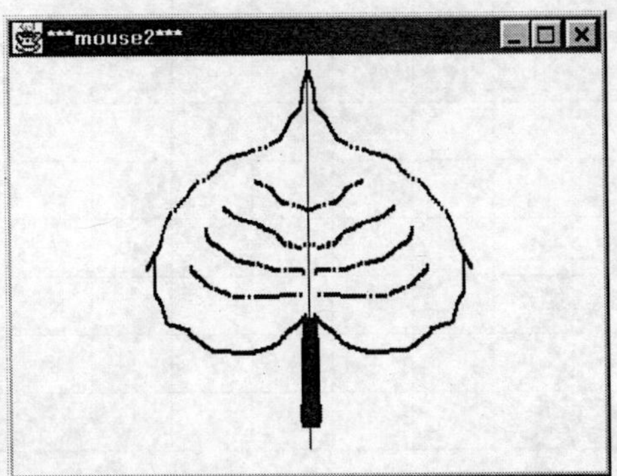

Please note the following statement.

```
myG.drawRect( 400-x,y,1,2);
```

This statement is responsible for drawing on the other side.

26.11 Sudoku I

These days all the newspapers have "Sudoku" puzzles everyday. These are interesting brain-teasers. Let us develop a program to aid the solution of it. The puzzle consists of nine rows of nine cells each. It is further divided into nine 3 × 3 boxes. Initially, 25 to 30 numbers are present in the grid, one number in one cell. All the numbers are between 1 and 9.

Rules of play

Fill the remaining cells with numbers 1 to 9 such that digits 1 to 9 **do not** repeat in the same row, column, or box.

Here is a sample puzzle. (See Figure 26.1)

					2		6	3
				9	6			5
			3					
7		1					2	6
5	4						7	1
6	2					9		4
					1	8		
9			5	8				
4	5		9					7

Figure 26.1 Sudoku Puzzle

When solved correctly, you will get the following answer. (See Figure 26.2)

1	9	4	8	5	2	7	6	3
8	3	7	1	9	6	2	4	5
2	6	5	3	7	4	1	9	8
7	8	1	4	3	9	5	2	6
5	4	9	2	6	8	3	7	1
6	2	3	7	1	5	9	8	4
3	7	2	6	4	1	8	5	9
9	1	6	5	8	7	4	3	2
4	5	8	9	2	3	6	1	7

Figure 26.2 Sudoku Puzzle Solution

Problem: Write a program to solve a given Sudoku puzzle.

Solution: Developing a solution for Sudoku is quite complex. Here is a humble attempt. This program will help you to solve the puzzle.

We know that around 25 to 35 numbers are given (specified) at the start. These numbers predict as to which numbers cannot be present in a particular cell. It is quite possible that some particular cell can have only one number as all the remaining numbers are ruled out. We have to mentally locate such a cell and the corresponding number. It will be a great idea if we can see such a possibility visually. It means that we should be able to see each and every cell and what numbers it can take.

By visual inspection, we will be able to decide the cell and the number. If we put this number in this cell, it will rule out more numbers from some more cells. We can hope that every time we find at least one cell such that there is only one possible number in it. This process will continue till the puzzle is completely solved.

Let us assume that initially there is no given data. Hence, all the 81 cells can have any number. This fact can be displayed by showing all 1 to 9 numbers in each cell.

We say that we start with data entry phase. Now take the first number in the data and put it in its cell. Give effect of this placement. Then take the remaining numbers one by one till the given data is exhausted. Now start solving the puzzle.

By visual inspection, identify the cell which contains only one possible number. Give this data to the program (row number, column number, and value number). The program will enter this data into a puzzle grid and will mark its effect. Now we have to merely repeat this procedure till we mark all the cells.

The program always displays 9×9 grid. Each cell displays (in two rows) all numbers which can occupy this cell. When we enter a number in any cell, it is displayed with two stars before and after (**2**). By chance if we give inconsistent data, program will refuse to accept it and halt.

With this general scheme, we have designed the program as follows. The first phase is called data entry phase. The program prompts you to type data. Give data as say "3 4 5", meaning third row, fourth column, and value 5. Note that at least one blank is necessary between the elements.

Program will accept the data and show **5** in third row fourth column. If for some reason the cell cannot accept this data (error), program will report it and stop. When you finish data entry, just type some single character and press return. Though this is an error, it will be treated as the end of data entry signal.

Now the puzzle-solving phase starts. If the program finds a number for a cell, it will tell you the same. It will request you to press return to accept. Just press return and it will enter that data and go to next one.

With sufficient numbers given as data, you do not have to think yourself. The program will do that for you.

If you wish to solve the puzzle yourself, do not end the data entry phase. After the given data is over, add solution on your own. Data entry phase does not give you ready-made solution. However, it gives you a graphical view to aid your judgement (see Program 26.11).

PROGRAM 26.11 Sudoku I

```
//   sudoku1.java

import java.io.* ;
import java.util.StringTokenizer ;
//   This interface defines Constant TEN = 10
interface STDH
```

```
    { final int TEN = 10;
    };

//     This class defines method getString()
class MyIO
   { public static String getString() throws IOException
     { String st1;
       BufferedReader Jin = new BufferedReader
            (new InputStreamReader (System.in) );
       st1= Jin.readLine();
       return st1;
     }
   } ;

// This Class handles a unit of
// row number,column number and the value

class Unit { int row, col, val; } ;

public class sudoku1 implements STDH
{ static int    a,b,c;
  static String str1 ;
  static boolean flag = true;

  public static boolean readme() throws IOException
  { int k;
    boolean answer = true;
    System.out.println( " type data :" );
    str1 = MyIO.getString();
    StringTokenizer st = new StringTokenizer(str1);
    k=st.countTokens();
    // System.out.println("k="+k);
    if (k!=3) { System.out.println("error in input" );
                answer = false;
              }
        else
            {
              try
                  { a= Integer.parseInt( st.nextToken() );
                    b= Integer.parseInt( st.nextToken() );
                    c= Integer.parseInt( st.nextToken() );
                    // System.out.println(a + "," + b + "," + c);
                    // usefun while debugging
                  }
                  catch (Exception e)
                    { System.out.println(" Exceptin in parse
int ***error in input" );
                  answer = false;
                 }
              } ;
      return answer;
```

```
  };
public static void main(String args[]) throws IOException
    { int k;
      int tdc =0;
      boolean dataEntry = true;
      System.out.println("sudoku1.java starts ");

      T1 box[][] = new T1[TEN][TEN] ;
      Unit z = new Unit();
      int master_count = 0;
      String str1 ;
      char ch ;
      int i,j ;
      for( i=1; i<TEN; i++)
      for( j= 1; j<TEN; j++)
         { box[i][j] = new T1();
         };
      welcome();
      MyIO.getString();

// data entry phase
       display(box);
       while (  dataEntry )
         {
           if ( !readme()) // error in reading
                 { dataEntry =false ;
                   break;//if (!dataEntry) break;
                 }
            master_count++ ;
           if ( effect(a,b,c,box) )
               { display(box);
                 if ( master_count==81 )
                       { flag = false;
                         System.out.print("\n congradulations ") ;
                       };
               }
               else
                 { System.out.print("\n error in data");
                   dataEntry = false;
                   flag = false;
                 } ;
          } ; // while
        System.out.println(" \n\n\n\n\n\n data entry phase over");
        System.out.println("\n\n\n\n press return to continue\n\n");
         MyIO.getString();
         flag = true;
// solving phase
       display(box);
//     flag is initialised at the begining. If there is any error
//     in data entry phase the flag is reseted.
//     Hence solving phase is bypassed.
```

```
      while ( flag )
        { tdc = findSolution(box,z);
          if ( (tdc == 2) )
             { System.out.print("press return to accept - - - ");
               str1 = MyIO.getString();
               a= z.row ; b = z.col ; c = z.val ;
             }
          else
           {
            if (! readme()) // error
               { flag= false ;
                 break;
               }
             }
          //  if (flag )
          //    {
               master_count++ ;
                 if ( effect(a,b,c,box) )
                    { display(box);
                      if ( master_count==81 )
                           { flag = false;
                             System.out.print("\n congradulations ") ;
                           };
                    }
                    else flag = false;
           // } ;
        } ; // while
      System.out.print("program over");
     // return ;
   }; // main
 static void welcome()
 {
   System.out.println("\n\n\n\n              welcome to ");
   System.out.println(         "\n           SUDOKU       ");
   System.out.println("\n\n\n\n              ver 1.0    ");
   System.out.println( "... press return key to start" ) ;
 }
 static void display(T1 box[][])
 {  int i, j,k;
    System.out.println(
    " 1      2      3      4      5      6      7      8      9");
    System.out.println(
    "-------------------------------------------------------------");
    for( i=1; i < TEN; i++)
     {
       for( j= 1; j<TEN; j++)
         { //first line
           if ( box[i][j].free )
              {
                for (k=1;k<6;k++)
                    if ( box[i][j].choise[k] !=0 )
```

```
                    System.out.print( box[i][j].choise[k]) ;
                 else System.out.print(' ');
               System.out.print(" ") ;
               }
             else System.out.print("**" + box[i][j].value + "** " );
         } ;
       System.out.println(" | ");
       //second line
       for( j= 1; j<TEN; j++)
        { //second line
          if ( box[i][j].free )
            { for (k=6;k<TEN;k++)
                if ( box[i][j].choise[k] !=0 )
                    System.out.print( box[i][j].choise[k]) ;
                  else System.out.print(' ');
                System.out.print(" ") ;
            }
           else System.out.print( " ");
         }
        System.out.println(" | " + i );
        if( i%3 == 0)
      System.out.println(
       "----------------------------------------------------------------");

     }
 };

 // this method checks if the choice is acceptable
 // if so it effect i.e accepts it!

 static boolean effect(int row,int col,int val,T1 box[][])
 { int i,j ;
   int R,C;
   boolean returnvalue = true ;
   if  (     (row<1) || (row>9)
         || (col<1) || (col>9)
         || (val<1) || (val>9)
      )
         { System.out.print ( "error1");
           returnvalue = false ;
           return returnvalue ;
           // exit(1);
      };
 if ( box[row][col].free == false )
        { System.out.println( "error2 duplicate entry ") ;
              System.out.println("at " + row +',' + col) ;
              System.out.print("press any key to quit") ;
           //   getch();

           returnvalue = false ;
           return returnvalue ;
```

```
        } ;
 if ( box[row][col].choise[val] != val)
         { System.out.println("error3 choice NOT available ");
              System.out.println("at " + row + ','+ col) ;
              System.out.print( "press any key to quit") ;
           //    getch();
          returnvalue = false ;
          return returnvalue ;

            //   exit(1);
      } ;
 box[row][col].value = val ;
 box[row][col].free = false ;
 for( i=1; i < TEN; i++)
    box[i][col].choise[val] = 0 ;
 for( j=1; j < TEN; j++)
    box[row][j].choise[val] = 0 ;
 R = (row-1) /3*3 +1 ;
 C = (col-1) /3*3 +1 ;
 for( i=0; i < 3 ; i++)
    for( j= 0; j<3 ; j++)
      { box[R+i][C+j].choise[val] =0 ; };

  return returnvalue;
 };

 static int findSolution(T1 box[][] ,Unit z )
 { int result =0;
   int found = 0;
   int flag = 0;
   int i, j, k ;
   int simple_count = 0;
   int cnt[] = new int[TEN] ;
 // simple rule
  for( i=1; i < TEN; i++) // go to all rows
  for( j=1; j < TEN; j++) // and columns ie every cell
   if (box[i][j].free )
    { simple_count = 0;
      for (k=1;k<TEN;k++)
         if ( box[i][j].choise[k] == k ) simple_count++;
      if ( simple_count == 1) // find choice
         { for (k=1;k<TEN;k++)
              if ( box[i][j].choise[k] == k )
               { z.col = j;
                 z.row = i ;
                 z.val = k ;
               }
                 System.out.println( "rule A : suggests ->" +
                                     z.row + " ," + z.col +
                                     " ," + z.val );
                 result = 2;
```

```
                return result;
            }
        }
//  cout << "analysis by rule 3" << endl;
// rule 3A row wise
    for( i=1; i < TEN; i++)         // go to all rows
     { for (k=0;k<TEN;k++)
            cnt [k] = 0;
       for( j=1; j < TEN; j++)     // go to all column of a given row
         { if (box[i][j].free )
            for (k=1;k<TEN;k++)
                 if ( box[i][j].choise[k] == k ) cnt[k]++;
         }
       // inspect cnt for value one!
       k= 1; found = 0;
       while ( ( k < TEN )&& (found ==0) )
         {   if ( cnt[k] == 1 ) found = 1;
                 else k++;
         }
       if ( found ==1 )
         { // now finding the column
            j=1; flag = 0;
                        while ( ( j<TEN ) && ( flag==0 ) )
               if ( (box[i][j].free ) &&
                          (box[i][j].choise[k] == k ) )
                  { flag = 1;
                    z.col = j;
                    z.row = i ;
                    z.val = k ;
                  }   else j++;
                 //
                  System.out.println("rule B : suggests ->" + z.row
                                          + " ," + z.col
                                          + " ," + z.val );
          result = 2;
          return result;
        }
      };
// now by columns
    for( j=1; j < TEN; j++) // go to all colums
      { for (k=0;k<TEN;k++)
              cnt [k] = 0;
        for( i=1; i < TEN; i++) // go to all rows in a given col
          { if (box[i][j].free )
             for (k=1;k<TEN;k++)
                  if ( box[i][j].choise[k] == k ) cnt[k]++;
          }
          // inspect cnt for value one!
          k= 1; found = 0;
          while ( ( k < TEN )&& (found ==0) )
            {   if ( cnt[k] == 1 ) found = 1;
```

```
                    else k++;
            } ;
          if ( found ==1 )
            { // now finding the row
              i=1; flag = 0;
                    while ( ( i<TEN ) && ( flag==0) )
                if ( (box[i][j].free ) &&
                        (box[i][j].choise[k] == k ) )
                  { flag = 1;
                    z.col = j;
                    z.row = i ;
                    z.val = k ;
                  }  else i++;
                     System.out.println("rule C : suggests ->" + z.row
                                          + " ," + z.col
                                          + " ," + z.val);
//             cout << "rule3 -> col"<<i<<",choice "<<k<<endl;
              result = 2;
              return result;
            }
        };
      return result ;
}
}
// class T1 represents a single cell. It has a value
// as well as choices if free
class T1 implements STDH
  {  boolean free ;
     int value ;
     int choise[]= new int[TEN];
     void show()
       {  int i ;
          if ( !free ) System.out.print("**" + value + "**" ) ;
               else
                 {  for( i=1; i < TEN; i++)
                      if ( choise[i] == i )
                           System.out.print( choise[i] ) ;
                 }
          System.out.println( " ; " );
       } ;

      T1()
       { int i ;
         free = true ; // false
         value = -1 ; //invalid value;
         for( i=0; i < TEN; i++) choise [i] = i ;
       }
};
```

If you start running this program and give data as given in the puzzle shown earlier, you will see the following screen.

Output

```
  1      2      3      4      5      6      7      8      9
----------------------------------------------------------------------
**1**           4      4      45   **2**    4    **6**  **3**    |
        789    789     78     7             7                    |  1
  23     3     234     14   **9**  **6**   124     14   **5**    |
  8      78     78     78                   7      8      2      |  2
  2           **5**  **3**    14      4    124     14     2      |
  8    6789                   7      78     7      89     89     |  3
----------------------------------------------------------------------
**7**    3    **1**    4     345    345     35   **2**  **6**    |
         89            8            89                           |  4
**5**  **4**    3      2      23     3      3    **7**  **1**    |
                89     68     6     89                           |  5
**6**  **2**    3      1     135    35    **9**    35   **4**    |
                8      78     7     78              8            |  6
----------------------------------------------------------------------
  23     3      23     24    234   **1**  **8**   345     2      |
         67     67     67     67                   9      9      |  7
**9**    13     23   **5**  **8**    34   1234    134     2      |
         67     67                   7      6                    |  8
**4**  **5**    23   **9**    23     3     123     13   **7**    |
                68            6             6                    |  9
----------------------------------------------------------------------
type data :
```

Now you have two choices to proceed.

If you wish to solve the puzzle on your own, you should continue typing data. The program output is of great help to you. A glance at the console will tell you that in cell (4,7) there is only one choice, that is value 3. You can enter data as 4 7 3. The program will accept it and refresh the screen. Some new cell will start showing single choice.

If you are interested only in getting the solution, you may take active help of the program. For that, you have to end the data entry phase and simply type any character and press return. It will signal an error to data entry section and close that phase. Program will enter the problem-solving phase and show you what data can be entered. You have to simply press return to accept it. In no time, you will come at the end of the puzzle.

Here are some more problems with solution for practice.

puzzle1.rtf

2		8				6		5
	6	4				9	3	
			2		3			
4		1		8		5		9
			1		4			
3		9		7		1		6
			9		8			
	5	2				4	6	
8		7				3		1

sol_puzzle1.rtf

2	3	8	4	1	9	6	7	5
1	6	4	8	5	7	9	3	2
7	9	5	2	6	3	8	1	4
4	7	1	3	8	6	5	2	9
5	2	6	1	9	4	7	8	3
3	8	9	5	7	2	1	4	6
6	1	3	9	4	8	2	5	7
9	5	2	7	3	1	4	6	8
8	4	7	6	2	5	3	9	1

puzzle2.rtf

	4			8			6	
9	2	6			1			
			6					3
	9				3			6
		2		5		1		
6			7				5	
1					5			
			8			9	1	4
	6			9			7	

sol_puzzle2.rtf

3	4	7	2	8	9	5	6	1
9	2	6	5	3	1	7	4	8
5	1	8	6	7	4	2	9	3
7	9	5	4	1	3	8	2	6
4	8	2	9	5	6	1	3	7
6	3	1	7	2	8	4	5	9
1	7	9	3	4	5	6	8	2
2	5	3	8	6	7	9	1	4
8	6	4	1	9	2	3	7	5

puzzle3.rtf

		5	3	8			7	
	8			1	2			6
								9
8	9				1			
	3	7		2		6	5	
			6				9	7
6								
5			2	9			1	
	2			7	8	3		

sol_puzzle3.rtf

9	6	5	3	8	4	1	7	2
7	8	4	9	1	2	5	3	6
3	1	2	5	6	7	4	8	9
8	9	6	7	5	1	2	4	3
4	3	7	8	2	9	6	5	1
2	5	1	6	4	3	8	9	7
6	7	8	1	3	5	9	2	4
5	4	3	2	9	6	7	1	8
1	2	9	4	7	8	3	6	5

puzzle4.rtf

		8	6		2	3		
6			7	5	1			8
2	4						7	5
		3				2		
5	1						3	6
9			1	2	6			3
		5	8		4	9		

sol_puzzle4.rtf

7	9	1	4	8	3	6	5	2
4	5	8	6	9	2	3	1	7
6	3	2	7	5	1	4	9	8
2	4	9	3	6	8	1	7	5
8	6	3	5	1	7	2	4	9
5	1	7	2	4	9	8	3	6
9	7	4	1	2	6	5	8	3
3	2	5	8	7	4	9	6	1
1	8	6	9	3	5	7	2	4

puzzle5.rtf

	5						6	
		2	9		1	3		
		9	6		3	5		
2			4		9			6
	1						5	
7			5		8			1
		8	7		2	4		
		1	3		4	9		
	3						8	

sol_puzzle5.rtf

3	5	4	8	2	7	1	6	9
8	6	2	9	5	1	3	4	7
1	7	9	6	4	3	5	2	8
2	8	5	4	1	9	7	3	6
9	1	3	2	7	6	8	5	4
7	4	6	5	3	8	2	9	1
5	9	8	7	6	2	4	1	3
6	2	1	3	8	4	9	7	5
4	3	7	1	9	5	6	8	2

26.12 Sudoku II

Let us try using GUI for this problem.

Problem: Write a program to solve Sudoku puzzle using swing components.

Solution: This program uses a `JTextArea` to display the output. It uses a `JTextField` to enter data. The same field is also used for flagging error messages.

This is not an ideal design but saves the required components. See Program 26.12.

PROGRAM 26.12 Sudoku II

```
 // su2.java

import java.awt.* ;
import java.awt.event.* ;
import javax.swing.* ;
import java.util.* ;

interface STDH
    {  final int TEN = 10;
    };
class MainData implements STDH // da drawing area
 { public int k ;
   char[] display;

T1 box[][] = new T1[TEN][TEN] ;
MainData()
   { k=0;
     int i,j ;
     display = new char[45*18];
     for(i=0;i<45*18;i++)
        display[i] = ' '; // Character.forDigit(i%10,10);
```

```
    for( i=1; i<TEN; i++)
        for( j= 1; j<TEN; j++)
            { box[i][j] = new T1();
            };
  }
public void draw_Num( int n, int row, int col)
  {
    display[(row-1)*45*2 + (col-1)*5 + 0 ] = ' ';
    display[(row-1)*45*2 + (col-1)*5 + 1 ] = '*';
    display[(row-1)*45*2 + (col-1)*5 + 2 ] =
                                    Character.forDigit(n,10);
    display[(row-1)*45*2 + (col-1)*5 + 3 ] = '*';
    display[(row-1)*45*2 + (col-1)*5 + 4 ] = ' ';
    display[(row-1)*45*2+45 + (col-1)*5 + 0 ] = ' ';
    display[(row-1)*45*2+45 + (col-1)*5 + 1 ] = ' ';
    display[(row-1)*45*2+45 + (col-1)*5 + 2 ] = ' ';
    display[(row-1)*45*2+45 + (col-1)*5 + 3 ] = ' ';
    display[(row-1)*45*2+45 + (col-1)*5 + 4 ] = ' ';
  }

public void draw_String( int n, int row, int col,int k)
{ char ch ='.';
   if (k<6)
    { if ( ( 0< n ) && ( n<TEN ) )
            display[(row-1)*45*2 + (col-1)*5 +k-1 ] =
                                    Character.forDigit(n,10);
          else display[(row-1)*45*2 + (col-1)*5 +k-1] = ch;
    }
    else //secondline
    { if ( ( 0< n ) && ( n<TEN ) )
            display[(row-1)*45*2+45 + (col-1)*5+ k-6 ] =
                                            Character.forDigit(n,10);
          else display[(row-1)*45*2+45 + (col-1)*5 +k-6] = ch;
    }
}

public void paint_me ()
  { int i,j,k;
    final int fc = 4 ;
    int x0,y0;
    for( i=1; i < TEN; i++)
    {for( j= 1; j<TEN; j++)
     {//first line
      if( box[i][j].free == true )
          { for (k=1;k<6;k++)
              if ( box[i][j].choise[k] !=0 )
                   draw_String( box[i][j].choise[k],i,j,k) ;
               else draw_String(-1, i , j ,k);
          }
        else draw_Num( box[i][j].value, i, j );
    }
```

```
  };
  // second line
  for( i=1; i < TEN; i++)
  {for( j= 1; j<TEN; j++)
    {if( box[i][j].free == true )
        {for (k=6;k<TEN;k++)
             if ( box[i][j].choise[k] !=0 )
                  draw_String( box[i][j].choise[k], i,j,k) ;
                else draw_String(-1, i,j,k );
        }
      }
    }
 } //paint_me

String effect(int row,int col,int val)
  {
    int i,j ;
    int R,C;
    String errorMessage ="";
//  boolean returnvalue = true ;
    if (  (row<1) || (row>9)
         || (col<1) || (col>9)
         || (val<1) || (val>9)
       )
          { errorMessage = "error1";
            //returnvalue = false ;
            return errorMessage ; // returnvalue ;
          } ;
   if ( box[row][col].free == false)
         {  errorMessage = "error2 : duplicate entry " ;
            return errorMessage; //returnvalue ;
         } ;
   if ( box[row][col].choise[val] != val)
         { errorMessage= "error3 : choice NOT available ";
           return errorMessage;//returnvalue ;
               //  exit(1);
         } ;
   box[row][col].value = val ;
   box[row][col].free = false;
   for( i=1; i < TEN; i++)
    box[i][col].choise[val] = 0 ;
   for( j=1; j < TEN; j++)
   box[row][j].choise[val] = 0 ;
   R = (row-1) /3*3 +1 ;
   C = (col-1) /3*3 +1 ;
   for( i=0; i < 3 ; i++)
   for( j= 0; j<3 ; j++)
     { box[R+i][C+j].choise[val] -0 ;
     };
   return errorMessage;//returnvalue;
  };
```

```
int findSolution(UNIT z )
{  int result =0;
    int found = 0;
    int flag = 0;
    int i, j, k ;
    int simple_count = 0;
    int cnt[] = new int[TEN] ;
//   simple rule
   for( i=1; i < TEN; i++)   // go to all rows
   for( j=1; j < TEN; j++)   // and columns ie every cell
    if (box[i][j].free == true )
     { simple_count = 0;
       for (k=1;k<TEN;k++)
          if ( box[i][j].choise[k] == k ) simple_count++;
       if ( simple_count == 1) // find choice
          { for (k=1;k<TEN;k++)
               if ( box[i][j].choise[k] == k )
                 { z.col = j;
                   z.row = i ;
                   z.val = k ;
                 }
         // System.out.println( "rule A : suggests ->" +
         // z.row + " ," + z.col + " ," + z.val );
                    result = 2;
                    return result;
          }
   }
// cout << "analysis by rule 3" << endl;
// rule B row wise
  for( i=1; i < TEN; i++)    // go to all rows
   { for (k=0;k<TEN;k++)
          cnt [k] = 0;
     for( j=1; j < TEN; j++) // go to all column of a given row
       { if (box[i][j].free == true )
         for (k=1;k<TEN;k++)
              if ( box[i][j].choise[k] == k ) cnt[k]++;
       }
     // inspect cnt for value one!
     k= 1; found = 0;
     while ( ( k < TEN )&& (found ==0) )
       {   if ( cnt[k] == 1 ) found = 1;
               else k++;
       }
     if ( found ==1 )
         { // now finding the column
           j=1; flag = 0;
                     while ( ( j<TEN ) && ( flag==0 ) )
              if ( (box[i][j].free == true ) &&
                        (box[i][j].choise[k] == k ) )
                 { flag = 1;
                   z.col = j;
```

```
                z.row = i ;
                z.val = k ;
              }   else j++;
          // System.out.println("ruleB : suggests ->" + z.row
          //             + " ," + z.col + " ," + z.val );
          result = 2;
          return result;
        }
    };
// now by columns
  for( j=1; j < TEN; j++)       // go to all colums
    { for (k=0;k<TEN;k++)
          cnt [k] = 0;
      for( i=1; i < TEN; i++)   // go to all rows in a given col
        { if (box[i][j].free == true )
          for (k=1;k<TEN;k++)
              if ( box[i][j].choise[k] == k ) cnt[k]++;
        }
      // inspect cnt for value one!
      k= 1; found = 0;
      while ( ( k < TEN )&& (found ==0) )
        {   if ( cnt[k] == 1 ) found = 1;
                else k++;
        } ;
      if ( found ==1 )
       { // now finding the row
         i=1; flag = 0;
               while ( ( i<TEN ) && ( flag==0) )
           if ( (box[i][j].free == true )
                   && (box[i][j].choise[k] == k ) )
              { flag = 1;
                z.col = j;
                z.row = i ;
                z.val = k ;
              }  else i++;
           // System.out.println("rule3B : suggests ->" + z.row
           //              + " ," + z.col + " ," + z.val);
        //    cout << "rule3 -> col"<<i<<",choice "<<k<<endl;
           result = 2;
           return result;
         }
     };
   return result ;
 }
 } // MainData

 public class su2 extends JFrame implements ActionListener
  { JTextField tf1;
    static Font f = new Font("courier",Font.BOLD,18);
    MainData data ;
    JTextArea jt ;; //= new JTextArea(20,20);
```

```
    static int n=100;
    int master_count = 0 ;
    su2()      // constructor
      { super("SUDOKU II ");
        data = new MainData() ;
        this.getContentPane().setLayout( null );
        tf1 = new JTextField( 20);

        tf1.addActionListener(this);
        tf1.setActionCommand("txt");
        tf1.setBounds(10,490,100,40);
        tf1.setBorder( BorderFactory.createLineBorder(Color.black) );
        this.getContentPane().add(tf1);
        jt = new JTextArea();//45,20);
        jt.setColumns(45);
        jt.setRows(18);
        jt.setLocation(10,10);
        jt.setFont(f);
        jt.setLineWrap(true);
        jt.setText(new String(data.display));
        jt.setBounds(10,10,45*11,550);
        jt.setEditable(false);
        jt.append("hello world");
        this.getContentPane().add(jt);
     //   tf1.setVisible(true);
     //   jt.setVisible(true);
        this.setVisible(true);
    }

public static void main( String args[])
    { su2 thisprog = new su2();
      thisprog.setDefaultCloseOperation(JFrame.EXIT_ON_CLOSE);
      thisprog.setBounds(10,10,520,580);
      thisprog.setResizable(false); //
      thisprog.data.paint_me();
      thisprog.jt.setText( new String(thisprog.data.display) );
    }
public void actionPerformed(ActionEvent e)
 { String stline,s1="",s2="",s3="";
    int a=0,b=0,c=0;
    int T;
    UNIT z= new UNIT();
    if( e.getActionCommand().equals("quit") )
        {  System.exit(0);
        };
    if( e.getActionCommand().equals("txt") )
       {stline= tf1.getText();
        tf1.setText("");
         //   jt.setText(stline);
        StringTokenizer stn = new StringTokenizer(stline);
        if (stn.hasMoreTokens())    s1 = stn.nextToken() ;
```

```
        if (stn.hasMoreTokens())     s2 = stn.nextToken() ;
        if (stn.hasMoreTokens())     s3 = stn.nextToken() ;
        try
          { a=Integer.parseInt(s1);
            b=Integer.parseInt(s2);
            c=Integer.parseInt(s3);
          }
        catch (NumberFormatException nfe) { a=0;b=0;c=0; }
        stline= data.effect(a,b,c) ;
        if( stline.length() == 0) // zero means ok
           {data.paint_me();
            jt.setText(new String(data.display));
            if ( ++master_count==81 )
                 { tf1.setText("Congradulations! you win ");
                 }
               else if ( data.findSolution(z) == 2 )
                         tf1.setText(z.toString() );
            }
            else
              {tf1.setText(stline); // error message
               // jt.setText("MAHESH");    // for debugging
              }
          }
      }
  }
  class T1  implements STDH
      {  boolean free ;
         int value ;
         int choise[]= new int[TEN];
         T1(){ int i ;
               free = true ;
               value = -1 ; //invalid value;
               for( i=0; i < TEN; i++) choise [i] = i ;
              }
       };
  class UNIT
    { int row, col, val;
      public String toString()
        { return String.valueOf(row) + " " +
                 String.valueOf(col) + " " +
                 String.valueOf(val)    ;
        }
    } ;
```

If you start solving the puzzle and type

1 1 1

2 2 2

3 3 3

as data, you will get the following output.

Output

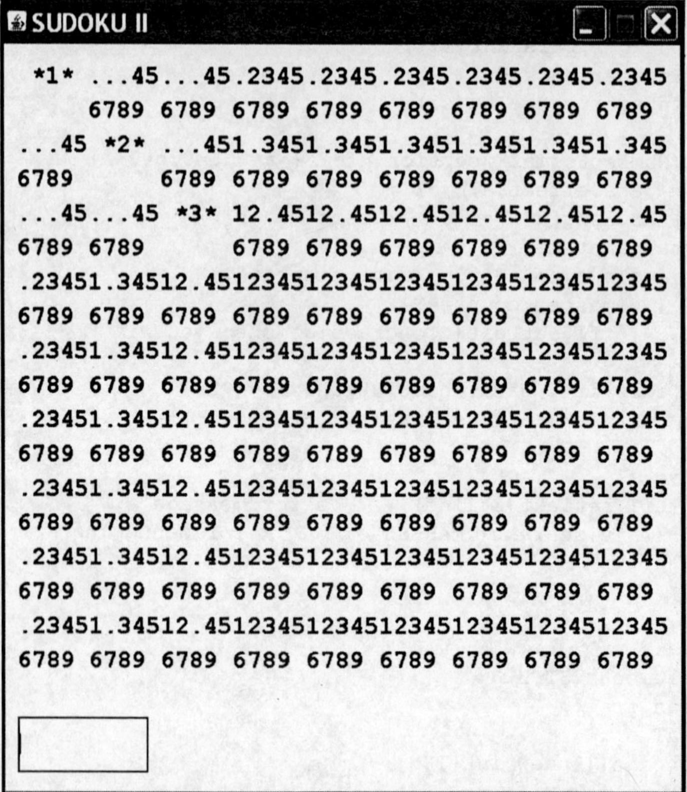

Please note some changes from the console version. There are no separate phases for data entry and solution.

As you go along entering the data and some definite answer is present for some cell, it will appear in the `TextField`. It is upon you to accept or reject it and continue to enter data.

When all the given data is entered and the puzzle has a solution, the program will suggest entries. If you accept them, it will solve the puzzle completely.

You can make this program work similar to the console one by adding a button to signify the end of data entry and slight tuning of the code.

26.13 Moon Revolves Around Earth

Applets and graphics together can be a great tool in computer-aided education. In school physics, there is a topic on stars and planets. Students are taught that Earth is a planet which rotates around the Sun, which is a star. Moon is a sub-planet which revolves around the Earth. It will be interesting to see this in action on a screen. Students will get a better understanding of the topic. Let us write an applet to see this in action.

Problem: Write an applet to show how Moon and Earth revolve around the Sun.

Solution: We will need to make some simplifying assumptions. They are

- Orbits of Earth and Moon are circular.
- Moon, Earth, and Sun are always in a plane.
- Diameter of Sun is 20 pixels.
- Diameter of Earth is 16 pixels.
- Diameter of Moon is 10 pixels.
- Earth is at 100 pixels from Sun.
- Moon is at 30 pixels from Earth.

The other assumptions are that the Earth completes a revolution around the Sun in 365.25 days. The Moon completes one revolution around the Earth in 29.5 days. We will display the positions of each day in a year. We will use delay of 200 milliseconds to symbolize a day and define classes `Planet` and `SubPlanet` (which extends `Planet`). We will assume and display Sun as a circle at the centre. See Program 26.13.

PROGRAM 26.13 The Moon Revolves Around the Earth

```
//     circle1.java
import java.awt.* ;
import java.applet.* ;
class Planet
    { Color myCol =Color.green;
      int rad ;
      int hsize=8;//half size
      double omega ;
      int X0,Y0;
      int x,y;
      public Planet(int xcentre, int ycentre )
       {rad =100 ;
        X0 = xcentre;
        Y0 = ycentre ;
        x=X0;y=Y0;
        omega = 2*Math.PI/365.25;//2 Pi radians in 365.25 days
      };
      void getpos(int t)
       { x = (int) ( X0 + rad * Math.cos ( omega*t ) ) ;
         y = (int) ( Y0 + rad * Math.sin ( omega*t ) ) ;
       } ;
      void show(Graphics g)
       { g.setColor(myCol);
         g.fillOval(x-hsize, y-hsize, 2*hsize, 2*hsize);
       }
      void hide(Graphics g)
       { g.setColor(Color.gray);
         g.fillOval(x-hsize, y-hsize, 2*hsize, 2*hsize);
       };
    } ;
class SubPlanet extends Planet
   { //int rad1 =30;
     int hsize =5; //half size
     Color myCol =Color.blue;
```

```
    void getpos(int t,int a, int b)
      {  x = (int) ( a + rad * Math.cos ( omega*t ) ) ;
         y = (int) ( b + rad * Math.sin ( omega*t ) ) ;
      } ;

    public SubPlanet(int a, int b)
      { super(a,b);
        rad =30;
        omega = 2*Math.PI/29.5; // 2 Pi radians in 29.5 days
      };
    public void show(Graphics g)
      { g.setColor(myCol);
        g.fillOval(x-hsize, y-hsize, 2*hsize, 2*hsize);
      }
    public void hide(Graphics g)
      { g.setColor(Color.gray);
        g.fillOval(x-5, y-5, 10, 10);
      }
   };

public class planet3 extends Applet
 {  final int xcentre = 150, ycentre = 150;
    final int moon_rad = 30 ;
    int moonX =0, moonY = 0 ;
    int moon_temp = 0;
    Planet earth;
    SubPlanet moon;
    public void init()
      {   setBackground(Color.gray);
          earth = new Planet(xcentre, ycentre) ;
          moon = new SubPlanet(xcentre, ycentre) ;
      }

    public void delay(long n)
     { long t1,t2;
       t1 = System.currentTimeMillis();
       t1 = t1 + n;
       t2 = System.currentTimeMillis();
       while ( t2 < t1 ) t2= System.currentTimeMillis();
      }
    public void paint (Graphics g)
      { int j ;
        g.setColor(Color.red ) ;
        g.fillOval(xcentre-10, ycentre-10, 20, 20); // sun
        g.setColor(Color.red ) ;
        g.drawOval(earth.X0-earth.rad, earth.Y0-earth.rad,
      2*earth.rad,2*earth.rad);
//      g.drawString("start",100,100); for debugging only
        for( j= 0 ; j<360; j++)
           {  earth.getpos(j);
              moon.getpos(j,earth.x,earth.y);
              moon.show(g);
```

```
            earth.show(g);
            delay(100);
            earth.hide(g);
            moon.hide(g);
          }
        g.setColor(Color.red ) ;
//      g.drawString("over",100,130); for debugging only
      }
}
```

We will place this applet in a HTML file as follows:

File **planet3.html**

```
<applet code="planet3" width="300"
height="300"></applet>
```

When we see the applet running in the browser, at one moment we will see the following snapshot.

Output

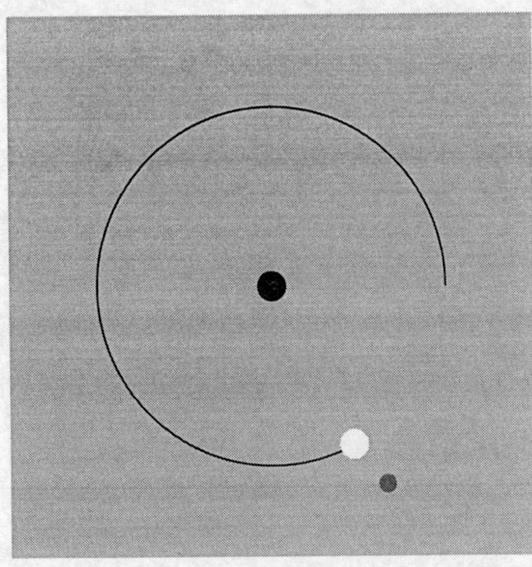

You can very easily modify/develop the applet further to show Full Moon and no Moon days. Is it possible to show when eclipses occur?

26.14 Astronomy: Retrograde Motion

The concept of retrograde motion of a planet is difficult to understand. Here is a simple program which will demonstrate the retrograde behaviour of an outer planet.

Problem: Write a program to demonstrate the retrograde motion of a planet.

Solution: See Program 26.14.

PROGRAM 26.14 Retrograde Demo

```
 //     retro2.java
import java.awt.* ;
import java.applet.* ;
class Planet
    { Color myCol,bgCol;
      int rad ;
      int hsize=8;//half size
      double omega ;
      int X0,Y0;
      int x,y;
      public Planet(int xcentre, int ycentre ,int radius,
                    double orb, Color c1 )
        { rad =radius ;
          X0 = xcentre;
          Y0 = ycentre ;
          myCol=c1;
          bgCol=Color.white;
          x=X0;y=Y0;
          omega = 2*Math.PI/(365*orb);
          // 2 Pi radians in 365.25 days
         };
       void getpos(int t)
         {  x = (int) ( X0 + rad * Math.cos ( omega*t ) ) ;
            y = (int) ( Y0 + rad * Math.sin ( omega*t ) ) ;
         } ;
       void show(Graphics g)
         { g.setColor(myCol);
           g.fillOval(x-hsize, y-hsize, 2*hsize, 2*hsize);
            }
       void hide(Graphics g)
         { g.setColor(bgCol);
           g.fillOval(x-hsize, y-hsize, 2*hsize, 2*hsize);
         };
     } ;

public class retro2 extends Applet
 { final int xcentre = 320, ycentre = 250;
   Planet earth;
   Planet jupitor;
   public void init()
    { setBackground( new Color(250,255,250));
      earth = new Planet(xcentre, ycentre, 20, 1.0, Color.blue) ;
      jupitor= new Planet(xcentre, ycentre,104, 30.0,Color.yellow) ;
    }
   public void delay(long n)
    { long t1,t2;
      t1 = System.currentTimeMillis();
      t1 = t1 + n;
      t2 = System.currentTimeMillis();
```

```
        while ( t2 < t1 )    t2= System.currentTimeMillis();
      }
    public void paint (Graphics g)
     {int j ;
      double angle;
      g.setColor(Color.red ) ;
      g.fillOval(xcentre-10, ycentre-10, 20, 20); // sun
//    g.setColor(Color.red ) ;
      g.drawOval(earth.X0-earth.rad, earth.Y0-earth.rad,
                      2*earth.rad,2*earth.rad);
      drawCircle(earth.X0,earth.Y0,earth.rad,g);
//         g.setColor(Color.yellow ) ;
      drawCircle(earth.X0,earth.Y0,295,g);
      for(int i=-30;i<+30;i=i+3)
         drawLines5 (i,g);
      for( j= 0 ; j<360*2; j+=2)
        { earth.getpos(j);
          earth.show(g);
          jupitor.getpos(j);
          jupitor.show(g);
          g.setXORMode(Color.white);//background
          g.setColor(Color.green);
          g.drawLine(earth.x, earth.y, jupitor.x,
             jupitor.y);
          angle = Math.atan2 ( (jupitor.y - earth.y) ,
                        (jupitor.x - earth.x) );
          g.fillOval(earth.X0+(int)(270*Math.cos(angle)),
              earth.Y0+(int)(270*Math.sin(angle)), 8,8);
          delay(100);
          g.drawLine(earth.x, earth.y, jupitor.x,
            jupitor.y);
          g.fillOval(earth.X0+(int)( 270*Math.cos(angle) ),
              earth.Y0+(int)(270*Math.sin(angle) ), 8,8);
          g.setPaintMode();
          g.setColor(Color.white);
          earth.hide(g);
          jupitor.hide(g);
        }
      g.setColor(Color.red ) ;
//      g.drawString("over",100,130); for debugging only
      }
    public static void drawCircle(int x, int y, int r, Graphics g)
     {    g.drawOval(x-r,y-r,2*r,2*r);
      }
    public void drawLines5( int t, Graphics g)
     {    int x1,y1,x2,y2;
          x1= (int) ( xcentre +
             295 * Math.cos ( Math.toRadians(t)));
          y1= (int) ( ycentre +
             295 * Math.sin ( Math.toRadians(t)));
          x2= (int) ( xcentre +
```

```
        (295+10) * Math.cos ( Math.toRadians(t)));
      y2= (int) ( ycentre +
        (295+10) * Math.sin ( Math.toRadians(t)));
      g.drawLine(x1,y1,x2,y2);
    }
}
```

File **retrol.html**

```
<body>
<applet code="retrol" width="700" height="500"></applet>
</body>
```

The following figure is a snapshot of the output.

Output

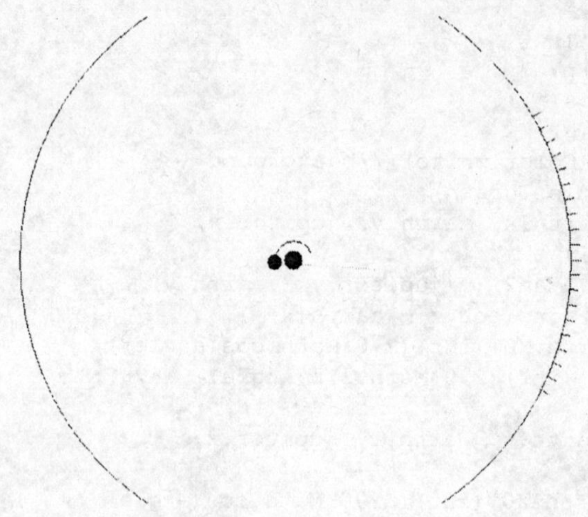

Please note that the Sun is shown in red, Earth in blue, and Jupiter in yellow. Program runs for two rounds of Earth around the Sun, that is two years time. A green straight line is for the proof that the position of Jupiter shown on the zodiac is genuine. The outer red circle represents zodiac. A small green dot indicates visible position of the Jupiter.

APPENDIX A

RULEBOOK

After we study any language, we are not in a position to remember every thing. Therefore, a quick ready reference becomes very useful. In the following table, we have tried to summarize all the important rules, points, and facts about Java programming. If you get some errors and want to get some clue quickly without reading the entire text, the following table will be of great help to you.

Keyword	The rule
`abstract` class	A class containing an abstract method is an abstract class. Such a class must be explicitly declared as abstract.
`abstract` class	An abstract class cannot be instantiated.
`abstract` class extending	If a class extends an abstract class, it must define all the methods of the super class. Otherwise, it has to be declared abstract.
abstract method	A method declared without the body is an abstract method. Such a method has to be declared as Abstract
`add`	The `add` method for attaching GUI components is a `Container` class method and *not* of `Component` class.
Applet writing to disk	Java does not allow applets to write to local disk.
`Applet` class	The `Applet` class must be the super class of any applet that is to be embedded in a Web page or viewed by the Java Applet Viewer.
applet `i/o`	User I/O is *not* accomplished with Java's stream I/O classes.
applet `i/o`	User I/O is accomplished with AWT or swing objects
applet `main()`	Applets do not need a `main()` method.
`APPLET` tag	The `APPLET` tag is used to start an applet from both an HTML document and from an applet viewer.
array index checking	Java checks array index during runtime. If program tries to use index out of bound, a runtime error occurs.
array size	When an array size (dimension) is specified, it cannot be changed later in the program.

(Continued)

arrays methods	Arrays are passed to methods by call-by-reference.
Assignment	You can assign a character variable to integer but not vice versa
Bit-wise operator	Bit-wise operators accept only integral operands (`char, byte, short, int,` and `long`). Float and double are not allowed.
Boolean type	The Boolean type cannot be converted from or to any other data type.
Boolean variable	In Java, Boolean variable *does not* take the value 1 or 0; it takes true or false values only.
`break`	A `break` statement can be used only within loop or switch case statements.
Bytecode	The type of code generated by a Java compiler
Character constant	Character constant (literal) is formed by enclosing a single character in pair of single quotes.
Checked Exceptions	Only runtime exceptions (including its subclasses) are checked exceptions; all others are unchecked exceptions.
`Cloneable, Comparable` and `Runnable`	Interfaces defined by `java.lang` are `Cloneable`, `Comparable`, and `Runnable.`
`Cloneable`	A `Cloneable` interface defines no members.
Collection framework	Components of "Collection framework" are available in the package `java.util`
Comma operator	Java does not support the comma operator (of C++).
command line arguments	All command line arguments are passed as a string to method main.
Comments	Comments increase the readability of the program.
Comments	Comments have no relevance to program (execution) speed.
`const`	In Java `const` is a reserved word, reserved for future use.
constructor	Constructors do not have a return type.
constructor	Name of the constructor is same as that of the class.
constructor	Constructors can be overloaded.
constructor	A class `constructor` may have public or protected keyword before them, nothing else.
constructor	`constructor` is a method is used to initialize the instance variable of a class.
container event	Container event class is generated when a component is added to or removed from a container.

(*Continued*)

cv `for`	The control variable declared in `for` loop is visible only within the scope of the loop. But in C/C++, it is visible even after the loop is exited.
Default constructor	If class definition does not contain a constructor, the compiler provides a default constructor which initializes all data members to null values.
`do-while`	`do-while` loop construct will always be executed at least once.
escape codes	In Java, there are no escape codes defined for vertical tab and the bell character.
`Exception`	An `Exception` is an abnormal condition that disrupts normal program flow.
`Exception` class	The root class of all the exception classes is the `Exception` class.
`expression` statement	Only certain types of expressions are allowed in `expression` statement. They are `assignment, inc/dec`, and method `call`.
Expressions	*Expressions* are combinations of variables, keywords or symbols that evaluate to a value of some type.
final	A final variable cannot change from its initialized value.
`final` class	A class declared final cannot be sub-classed.
`final` method	A method declared as final cannot be overridden.
`finalize()`	Method `finalize()` is called before an unused object is recycled.
finally	When a finally block is present, it is always executed irrespective of occurrence of exception.
finally	A finally block is optional.
`for` loop	The second expression in `for` statement must be a Boolean expression. As a special case, it can be a blank expression which is considered as having value "true".
functions	Every function in Java must be a member of some class. Java uses `term` method for such member functions.
Garbage collection	When all references to an object are gone, the memory used by the object is automatically reclaimed.
`graphics`	`Graphic` class is defined in `java.awt` package.
Implements	A class can use an interface by using the `Implements` clause.
`import`	Java by default imports package `java.lang`. We do not have to import it specifically.

(*Continued*)

`import` statement	Import statement must come before all other statements except package statement.
`in`	The object "in" belongs to class `InputStream`. It is standard input stream.
`in, out, err`	`In, out`, and `err` are predefined stream variables.
Inheritance	Inheritance is a mechanism that enables one class to inherit in general the behavior and attributes of another class. But we cannot say that it inherits **all the** behavior and attributes.
Initialization	Initialization can happen only ones in the applets lifetime. However, currently this rule has changed.
initialization of class variable	JVM automatically initializes every numeric instance of class variable.
inner	Objects declared within the inner scope will *not* be visible outside it
`inputStream`	Abstract class `inputStream` is the super class of all classes used for reading bytes.
Instantiation exception	Instantiation exception means an attempt to create an abstract class or interface.
interface	A class can have more than one interface.
interface	An interface can extend any number of interfaces,
Java-compatible browser	Applets should be run under a Java-compatible browser.
`Javax.swing`	`Javax.swing` is the high-level swing package, and primarily consists of components, adapters, default component models and interfaces for all the delegates and models.
`Join()`	The `join()` method suspends the current thread until *that* thread object dies.
`Jpanel`	`Jpanel` is a Container.
Key events	Key events are generated when a user presses or releases a key on the keyboard.

keywords currently in use	`abstract`	`assert`	`boolean`
	`break`	`byte`	`case`
	`catch`	`char`	`class`
	`continue`	`default`	`do`
	`double`	`else`	`enum`
	`extends`	`final`	`finally`
	`float`	`for`	`if`

(*Continued*)

	`implements`	`import`	`instanceof`
	`int`	`interface`	`long`
	`native`	`new`	`package`
	`private`	`protected`	`public`
	`return`	`short`	`static`
	`strictfp`	`super`	`switch`
	`synchronized`	`this`	`throw`
	`throws`	`transient`	`try`
	`void`	`volatile`	`while`
keywords which are values defined	`false`	`null`	`true`
keywords reserved for future use	`const`	`goto`	

labelled `break` labelled `continue`	Labelled `break` and labelled `continue` statements are allowed in Java.
labeled `break` labeled `continue`	Labelled `break` and labelled `continue` statements must be inside the loop so labelled.
`long`	The number of bytes used by Java primitive long is 8.
`main()`	Java applications begin execution at method `main()`.
`Main()`	`Main()` is a class method, not an object method.
method `interface`	Methods declared in interface must be declared `public` in class definition.
method `interface`	Any normal class (non `Abstract`) must fully define all the methods declared in the interface.
modulo division	Modulo divisor operator can be used with floating point values in Java. This is not allowed in C/C++.
monitor	The `sleep()` method tells the calling thread to give up monitor until some other thread enters the same monitor.
multiple inheritance	Java *does not* allow multiple inheritances, where a class has more than one super class.
multiple inheritances	Java allows multiple inheritances by means of interfaces.
multiple listeners	A component can have multiple listeners for events of different type.
`native`	The `native` keyword indicates that the method is implemented in another language like C/C++.

(*Continued*)

`NORM_PRIORITY`	`NORM_PRIORITY` is the default priority of a newly created thread.
`object` class	By default, classes inherit from the `Object` class, which is a super class of all classes in the Java class hierarchy.
`out`	The object `out`" belongs to class `printStream`. It is standard output stream.
overloading	A method with a given name in a class can have different signatures. Such methods are said to be overloaded.
overloading	A method in a class cannot have two definitions with same signature, even if return types are different.
override	A method is overridden when another method with the same signature is declared in a subclass.
override	A final method cannot be overridden
package statement	If any program contains package statement, it has to be the first statement.
parameter passing	Basic parameter passing in Java is call-by-value. All simple types are passed by call-by-value. However, all aggregate types effectively get passed by call-by-reference
`parseInt`	The method is used to convert `String` to an integer, assuming that the `String` represents an integer.
preemptive switching	A thread priority is used to decide when to move from one running thread to the next. This is called preemptive switching.
program file name	A simple Java application source file must have extension `java`. The name of the file and the name of the public class must be identical (case sensitive)
`RadioButtons`	`RadioButtons` are implemented in swing through the `JRadioButtons` class.
`Reader`	Abstract class `Reader` is the super class of all classes used for reading characters.
Relational expressions	Relational expressions return Boolean value. Note: C++ returns `int`.
`return` statement	If return type of a method is void, `return` statement is optional. For any other return type, it is compulsory.
`Set`	`Set` is a collection interface used to maintain unique elements.
`Sleep()`	The `sleep()` method is used to temporarily stop the execution of the thread.
source file public class	If a source file includes a public class, the class name must match the unextended filename. In other words, there cannot be two public classes in a single source file.

(*Continued*)

Stack overflow `Runtime` exception	Stack overflow is an example of `Runtime` exception.
`Start()`	After the `start()` method is called, the thread is in a `Runnable` state.
`static` for local variables.	Keyword `static` not allowed for local variables of any method.
`static` method	A `static` method cannot make a reference to non-static variables of a class.
`static` method	When a method is made static, it cannot use keywords `this` or `super`.
`static` variable	A `static` variable indicates that there is only one copy of that variable.
String operators	Strings cannot be lexicographically compared using operators like > or <= .
`string` constant	String constant (literal) is formed by enclosing a zero or more characters in pair of double quotes.
String immutable	Strings in Java are immutable, meaning they cannot be changed. The methods which appear to modify a given string actually return a new (separate) string.
`StringBuffer`	When no specific buffer length is requested, `StringBuffer` allocates room for 16 additional characters.
`StringBuffer` mutable	Objects of class `StringBuffer` are very much like strings. However, they are mutable (can be modified).
sub-class variable	Sub-class reference variable *cannot* be assigned a super-class reference value
sub-class constructor	Every constructor of a sub class must have a call to super class constructor as a first statement. Only exception is when super-class has *no* constructor or has a default constructor (one without parameters).
super-class variable	Super-class reference variable can be assigned a sub-class reference value
switch default	Default clause is optional in Java
switch expression	Switch expression can be of basic type `byte, short, int,` or char. It can be also be `Wrapper` class type like `Character, Byte, Short`, or `Integer`. It can be also of any enumerated type.
synchronized	Every object that has synchronized methods has a monitor.
`thread` class	By using a `thread` class, multithreaded program can be created.

(*Continued*)

Thread priority	Threads may yield to threads of lower priority.
Thread simultaneous access	It is possible for two threads to access the same variable or the same method of same object at same time. However, the net result will be unpredictable.
`throw`	A `throw` statement causes an exception to be thrown.
`throws`	A special clause called `throws` is used in method definition to indicate that a method may possibly throw an exception.
`trim()` String	String method `trim()` returns a new String object in which all white-space characters have been removed from the beginning and end of a string.
`try`	A `try` block must be followed by a `catch` block. `Catch` block need not be present if `finally` block is present.
Unicode character	Unicode character can be expressed as `\u` followed by four hexadecimal digits. Note character `u` is in lowercase. There must be exactly four digits no more any less.
Unsigned	Integer types are always signed in Java. There is no unsigned qualifier in Java.
variable initialization	Java flags compilation error if one tries to use ordinary variables without initialization.
variable name	A variable name can contain as well as start with character `$`.
variables interface	Variables in interface must be declared as final.
Vector	Elements of the vector can only be objects. Simple data types like integers are not allowed as elements.
Vector `size()`	The `size()` method determines the number of elements in Vector (not `sizeOf()`).
void	In Java if method does not return any value, then it must be declared as *void.*
Web page	To change Web page background colours, use the `BGCOLOR` attribute in the `<BODY>` tag.
`Writer`	Abstract class `Writer` is the super-class of all classes used for writing characters.

KEYWORDS

Table B.1 illustrates the keywords in Java which are currently in use.

Table B.1 Keywords in Java

abstract	assert	boolean	break	byte
case	catch	char	class	continue
default	do	double	else	enum
extends	final	finally	float	for
if	implements	import	instanceof	int
interface	long	native	new	package
private	protected	public	return	short
static	strictfp	super	switch	synchronized
this	throw	throws	transient	try
void	volatile	while		

Table B.2 illustrates the keywords in Java which are reserved for future use

Table B.2 Keywords in Java reserved for future use

const	goto

Table B.3 illustrates the keywords in Java for which values are defined.

Table B.3 Keywords in Java for which values are defined

false	Null	true

APPENDIX C

OPERATORS

Table C.1 describes various operators in their order of precedence. Operators of same precedence are given same rank.

Table C.1 Operators precedence

Operator	Use	Description or Returns true if	Type	Rank
`[]`	`type []`	Declares an array of unknown length, which contains type elements.	Other	1
`[]`	`type[op1]`	Creates an array with `op1` elements. Must be used with the new operator.	Other	1
`[]`	`op1[op2]`	Accesses the element at `op2` index within the array `op1`. Indices begin at 0 and extend through the length of the array minus one.	Other	1
`.`	`op1.op2`	Is a reference to the `op2` member of `op1`.	Other	1
`()`	`op1(params)`	Declares or calls the method named `op1` with the specified parameters. The list of parameters can be an empty list. The list is comma-separated.	Other	1
`++`	`op++`	Increments `op` by 1; evaluates to the value of `op` before it was incremented	Short Cut	1
`--`	`op–`	Decrements `op` by 1; evaluates to the value of `op` before it was decremented	Short Cut	1
`!`	`! op`	`op` is false	Conditional	2
`~`	`~op2`	bit-wise complement	Logical	2
`+`	`+op`	Promotes `op` to `int` if it is a `byte`, `short`, or `char`	Other Arithmetic	2
`-`	`-op`	Arithmetically negates `op`	Other Arithmetic	2
`++`	`++op`	Increments `op` by 1; evaluates to the value of `op` after it was incremented	Short Cut	2

(*Continued*)

Table C.1 *(Continued)*

<table>
<tr><td>--</td><td>--op</td><td>Decrements op by 1; evaluates to the value of op after it was decremented</td><td>Short Cut</td><td>2</td></tr>
<tr><td>(type)</td><td>(type) op1)</td><td>Casts (converts) op1 to type. An exception will be thrown if the type of op1 is incompatible with type.</td><td>Other</td><td>3</td></tr>
<tr><td>new</td><td>new op1</td><td>Creates a new object or array. op1 is either a call to a constructor, or an array specification.</td><td>Other</td><td>3</td></tr>
<tr><td>*</td><td>op1 * op2</td><td>Multiplies op1 by op2</td><td>Arithmetic</td><td>4</td></tr>
<tr><td>/</td><td>op1/op2</td><td>Divides op1 by op2</td><td>Arithmetic</td><td>4</td></tr>
<tr><td>%</td><td>op1 % op2</td><td>Computes the remainder of dividing op1 by op2</td><td>Arithmetic</td><td>4</td></tr>
<tr><td>+</td><td>op1 + op2</td><td>Adds op1 and op2</td><td>Arithmetic</td><td>5</td></tr>
<tr><td>-</td><td>op1 - op2</td><td>Subtracts op2 from op1</td><td>Arithmetic</td><td>5</td></tr>
<tr><td>>></td><td>op1 >> op2</td><td>shift bits of op1 right by distance op2</td><td>Shift and Logical</td><td>6</td></tr>
<tr><td><<</td><td>op1 << op2</td><td>shift bits of op1 left by distance op2</td><td>Shift and Logical</td><td>6</td></tr>
<tr><td>>>></td><td>op1 >>> op2</td><td>shift bits of op1 right by distance op2 (unsigned)</td><td>Shift and Logical</td><td>6</td></tr>
<tr><td>instanceof</td><td>op1 instanceof op2</td><td>Returns true if op1 is an instance of op2</td><td>Other</td><td>7</td></tr>
<tr><td>></td><td>op1 > op2</td><td>op1 is greater than op2</td><td>Relational</td><td>7</td></tr>
<tr><td>>=</td><td>op1 >= op2</td><td>op1 is greater than or equal to op2</td><td>Relational</td><td>7</td></tr>
<tr><td><</td><td>op1 < op2</td><td>op1 is less than op2</td><td>Relational</td><td>7</td></tr>
<tr><td><=</td><td>op1 <= op2</td><td>op1 is less than or equal to op2</td><td>Relational</td><td>7</td></tr>
<tr><td>==</td><td>op1 == op2</td><td>op1 and op2 are equal</td><td>Relational</td><td>8</td></tr>
<tr><td>!=</td><td>op1 != op2</td><td>op1 and op2 are not equal</td><td>Relational</td><td>8</td></tr>
<tr><td>&</td><td>op1 & op2</td><td>op1 and op2 are both true; always evaluates op1 and op2</td><td>Conditional</td><td>9</td></tr>
<tr><td>&</td><td>op1 & op2</td><td>Bit-wise and</td><td>Logical</td><td>9</td></tr>
<tr><td>^</td><td>op1 ^ op2</td><td>If op1 and op2 are different, that is, if one or the other of the operands is true but not both</td><td>Conditional</td><td>10</td></tr>
<tr><td>^</td><td>op1 ^ op2</td><td>Bit-wise xor</td><td>Logical</td><td>10</td></tr>
<tr><td>|</td><td>op1 | op2</td><td>Either op1 or op2 is true; always evaluates op1 and op2</td><td>Conditional</td><td>11</td></tr>
<tr><td>|</td><td>op1 | op2</td><td>Bit-wise or</td><td>Logical</td><td>11</td></tr>
</table>

(Continued)

Table C.1 (*Continued*)

<table>
<tr><td>&&</td><td>op1 && op2</td><td>op1 and op2 are both true; conditionally evaluates op2</td><td>Conditional</td><td>12</td></tr>
<tr><td>||</td><td>op1 || op2</td><td>Either op1 or op2 is true; conditionally evaluates op2</td><td>Conditional</td><td>13</td></tr>
<tr><td>?:</td><td>op1 ? op2 : op3</td><td>If op1 is true, returns op2. Otherwise, returns op3.</td><td>Other</td><td>14</td></tr>
<tr><td>+=</td><td>op1 += op2</td><td>op1 = op1 + op2</td><td>Assignment</td><td>15</td></tr>
<tr><td>-=</td><td>op1 -= op2</td><td>op1 = op1 - op2</td><td>Assignment</td><td>15</td></tr>
<tr><td>*=</td><td>op1 *= op2</td><td>op1 = op1 * op2</td><td>Assignment</td><td>15</td></tr>
<tr><td>/=</td><td>op1 /= op2</td><td>op1 = op1/op2</td><td>Assignment</td><td>15</td></tr>
<tr><td>%=</td><td>op1 %= op2</td><td>op1 = op1 % op2</td><td>Assignment</td><td>15</td></tr>
<tr><td>&=</td><td>op1 &= op2</td><td>op1 = op1 & op2</td><td>Assignment</td><td>15</td></tr>
<tr><td>|=</td><td>op1 |= op2</td><td>op1 = op1 | op2</td><td>Assignment</td><td>15</td></tr>
<tr><td>^=</td><td>op1 ^= op2</td><td>op1 = op1 ^ op2</td><td>Assignment</td><td>15</td></tr>
<tr><td><<=</td><td>op1 <<= op2</td><td>op1 = op1 << op2</td><td>Assignment</td><td>15</td></tr>
<tr><td>>>=</td><td>op1 >>= op2</td><td>op1 = op1 >> op2</td><td>Assignment</td><td>15</td></tr>
<tr><td>>>>=</td><td>op1 >>>= op2</td><td>op1 = op1 >>> op2</td><td>Assignment</td><td>15</td></tr>
</table>

APPENDIX D

LIST OF IMPORTANT PACKAGES

Java 6 makes available to users a large number of packages. The packages sometimes contain many sub-packages. In this appendix, we list only important packages and sub-packages for ready reference. For complete details, visit the relevant Web site.

Name of package/sub-package	Description
`java.applet`	This package provides the classes necessary to create an applet and the classes an applet uses to communicate with its applet context.
`java.awt`	This package contains all of the classes for creating user interfaces and for painting graphics and images.
`java.beans`	This package contains classes related to developing *beans* – components based on the JavaBeans architecture.
`java.io`	This package provides for system input and output through data streams, serialization and the file system.
`java.lang`	This provides classes that are fundamental to the design of the Java programming language.
`java.math`	This package provides classes for performing arbitrary-precision integer arithmetic (`BigInteger`) and arbitrary-precision decimal arithmetic (`BigDecimal`).
`java.net`	This package provides the classes for implementing networking applications.
`java.nio`	This package defines buffers, which are containers for data, and provides an overview of the other NIO packages.
`java.rmi`	This package supports methods for Remote Method Invocation.
`java.security`	This package provides the classes and interfaces for the security framework.

`java.sql`	This package provides the API for accessing and processing data stored in a data source (usually a relational database) using the Java programming language.
`java.text`	This package provides classes and interfaces for handling text, dates, numbers, and messages in a manner independent of natural languages.
`java.util`	This package contains the collections framework, legacy collection classes, event model, date and time facilities, internationalization, and miscellaneous utility classes (a string tokenizer, a random-number generator, and a bit array).
`javax.crypto`	This package provides the classes and interfaces for cryptographic operations.
`javax.imageio`	This package is the main package of the Java Image I/O API.
`javax.management`	This package provides the core classes for the Java Management Extensions.
`javax.naming`	This package provides the classes and interfaces for accessing naming services.
`javax.net`	This package provides classes for networking applications.
`javax.print`	This package provides the principal classes and interfaces for the Java Print Service API.
`javax.rmi`	Contains user APIs for RMI-IIOP.
`javax.script`	This package consists of interfaces and classes that define Java Scripting Engines and provides a framework for their use in Java applications.
`javax.sql`	This package provides the API for server side data source access and processing from the Java Programs.
`javax.swing`	This package provides a set of "lightweight" (all-Java language) components that work more or less the same way on all platforms.
`javax.tools`	This package provides interfaces for tools which can be invoked from a program, for example, compilers.
`javax.transaction`	This package contains three exceptions thrown by the ORB machinery during unmarshalling.
`javax.xml`	This package defines core XML constants and functionality from the XML specifications.
`java.awt.color`	This package provides classes for colour spaces.

`java.awt.dnd`	This package supports drag-and-drop facility for use in GUI (graphical user interface) applications.
`java.awt.event`	This package provides interfaces and classes for dealing with different types of events fired by AWT components.
`java.awt.font`	This package provides classes and interface relating to fonts.
`java.awt.geom`	This package provides the Java 2D classes for defining and performing operations on objects related to two-dimensional geometry.
`java.awt.im`	Provides classes and interfaces for the input method framework.
`java.awt.image`	This package provides classes for creating and modifying images.
`java.awt.print`	This package provides classes and interfaces for a general printing API.
`java.lang.management`	Provides the management interface for monitoring and management of the Java virtual machine as well as the operating system on which the Java virtual machine is running.
`java.lang.reflect`	Provides classes and interfaces for obtaining reflective information about classes and objects.
`java.util.concurrent`	This package offers utility classes commonly useful in concurrent programming.
`java.util.jar`	This package provides classes for reading and writing the JAR (Java ARchive) file format, which is based on the standard ZIP file format with an optional manifest file.
`java.util.zip`	This package provides classes for reading and writing the standard ZIP and GZIP file formats.
`javax.net.ssl`	This package provides classes for the secure socket package.
`javax.sound.midi`	This package provides interfaces and classes for I/O, sequencing, and synthesis of MIDI (musical instrument digital interface) data.
`javax.sound.sampled`	This package provides interfaces and classes for capture, processing, and playback of sampled audio data.
`javax.swing.border`	This package provides classes and interface for drawing specialized borders around a Swing component.
`javax.swing.event`	This package provides for events fired by Swing components.

`javax.swing.filechooser`	This package contains classes and interfaces used by the `JFileChooser` component.
`javax.swing.plaf`	This package provides one interface and many abstract classes that Swing uses to provide its pluggable look-and-feel capabilities.
`javax.swing.table`	This package provides classes and interfaces for dealing with `javax.swing.JTable`.
`javax.swing.text`	This package provides classes and interfaces that deal with editable and non-editable text components.
`javax.swing.tree`	This package provides classes and interfaces for dealing with `javax.swing.JTree`.

MINI PROJECTS

At the end of the text, we want to present our readers with reasonably advanced exercises. They deserve the status of a mini project. Normally such exercises are open ended. Sometimes students find it difficult to start from a simple definition. Hence, we have illustrated these exercises in detail. For some exercise we have designed levels. One can take up a level as per his level of preparation or time available. We hope our readers will enjoy coding these mini projects.

AE.1 Chess Clock

In competitive chess, a player has a maximum time fixed to make certain moves. If a player fails to make those many moves, he loses. In the first session, players have two and a half hours for 40 moves. In subsequent sessions, time is 1 hour for 16 moves (Please check the rules with chess expert).

Hence, the chess clock should record thinking time for each player and notify if someone fails.

A chess clock consists of two separate clocks: one for each player. It has two press buttons. When the match starts, the clock for player with white pieces starts ticking. When a player with white pieces makes a move, he presses the button on his side. It stops his clock and starts one of his opponent's. When the opponent makes a move, he presses the button on his side. It stops his clock and starts the clock of player with white pieces.

When the clock assigned to any player registers the specified time and number of moves are not completed by that player, he/she loses. A buzzer sounds to indicate that.

Figure AE.1 displays a typical output screen.

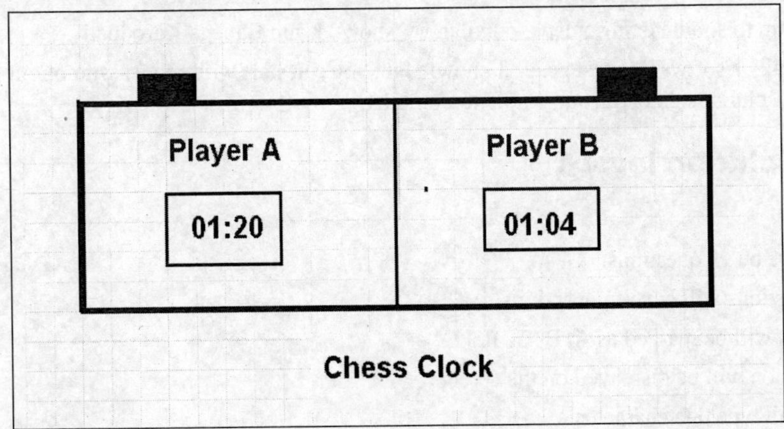

Figure AE.1 Chess Clock

You may assume a time of 2 hours for 40 moves. Assign key "A" to player A and key "L" for player B. While simulating, use actual time of 1 second for 1 minute of game time. You may also show players names as well as true date and time.

Second alternative—Note that a count down timer is equally appropriate substitute for a counting clock. Such a timer will show the amount of time balance (left) instead of time elapsed.

AE.2 Rolling Board

If you visit any bank or any similar establishment, you will notice a rolling display board. It displays various schemes as well as other information. The idea behind this is that it catches customer attention. Let us write a program for it.

Let us make some assumptions:

- 12–15 characters.
- Single row.
- Delay of 1 second.
- Only text characters.
- Message length maximum 45 characters.
- Repeats indefinitely.

A sample output is shown as follows.

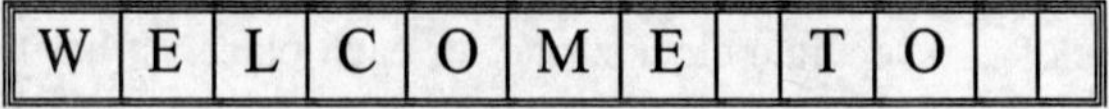

W	E	L	C	O	M	E		T	O		

The repetition rate should be such that the message is easily readable.

Second alternative—After one cycle, colour of the display should change. Typically, three different colours should be used.

AE.3 Kaun Banega Karodpati

Write a program to simulate on screen a popular TV show "Kaun Banega Karodpati".

This is essentially a software to test general knowledge; you can start with some assumptions (specifications). Let us discuss solutions graded from simple to complex.

AE.3.1 Solution level 1

Specifications:

- Let there be 15 questions.
- All questions will have four options
- Options will be marked as A, B, C, and D
- A question will be displayed on the screen.
- User will type one character.
- It will be compared with stored (correct) answer.

- If user wins, he is given 1000 marks/Rupees.
- After answering all questions user will be shown the total score.

Implementation:

This can be written in pseudo-code as

```
for i = 0 to 14 do
  { show i th question
  show options
  get response
  test answer, if correct then score=score + 1000
}
```

AE.3.2 Solution level 2

The above solution will have same questions repeated in every session. Hence, at level 2, when one runs the program second time, he should be presented with different questions altogether. We should have 200 or more questions and use random number technique to select 15 questions.

Instead of a fixed prize of Rs 1000, each question be awarded graded prize as shown in table below. If someone completes 15 questions, he really gets a prize of **rupees one crore**!

Round	Prize (in rupees)
1	1000
2	2000
3	3000
4	4000
5	5000
6	10,000
7	20,000
8	50,000
9	1,00,000
10	3,00,000
11	6,00,000
12	12,00,000
13	25,00,000
14	50,00,000
15	1,00,00,000

AE.3.3 Solution level 3

As the prize increases with every question, the questions at higher level should be tougher and tougher.

We should separate available questions in 15 different groups. Questions in group (n + 1) should be tougher than that of those in group (n).

User may be allowed to use 50/50. In that case, two wrong choices must be removed.

AE.4 Exam Master

These days everything in the world goes "online". Examinations are no exception. As computers can never be as intelligent as human beings, the best way to use the computer in examinations is with multiple choice questions (MCQs). This is essentially a software to conduct online test with MCQs. It goes without saying that questions should be on Java programming language.

We can start with some assumptions (specifications). Let us discuss solutions graded from simple to complex.

AE.4.1 Solution level 1

Specifications:

- There are 15 questions.
- All questions will have four options
- A question will be displayed on the screen.
- Options will be marked as A, B, C, and D
- User will type one character.
- It will be compared with stored (correct) answer.
- If user selects correct answer, he is awarded one marks.
- After answering all questions user will be shown the total score.

Implementation:

A typical implementation can be written in pseudo-code as

```
for i = 0 to  14 do
     { show i th question
         show options
  get response
  test answer, if correct  then  score=score + 1
     }
Show_result ;
```

Important:

The questions and answers should be stored on disk in coded form. The questions should be roughly of same complexity, but from different topics.

AE.4.2 Solution level 2

There should be 100 questions. During the test, questions should be selected in semi-random fashion.

AE.4.1 Solution level 3

There should be only maximum 3 minutes per single question. If no answer comes in that time, the question should be removed. The maximum test time is of only 30 minutes (average per question only 2 minutes). The summary of topics on which there was poor performance should be indicated at the end of the test.

AE.5 Game of Business

This is a very popular game for school going children. It trains them in practices for business. It helps them in handling money. It is available in any local store.
We can start with some assumptions (specifications).

Specifications:

- Number of players: 3–6
- One player acts as Banker
- Each player plays with separate colour pebbles
- Cash Rs 10,00,000
- A board with approximately 40 houses
- Two dices with six faces each

Most of the houses are cities with following properties.

- 1 group colour
- 2 price of the city,
- 3 rent a (complex formula)

Rules

- First, all players are allotted different coloured pebble.
- These pebbles are placed at start (house 0)
- 80% of the available cash is distributed among the players evenly.
- The remaining is with the banker
- Players play turn by turn
- Play ends when all players except one become bankrupt (practically, the game continues forever).

A player's turn

- He throws a dice
- Moves pebble accordingly.
- If he reaches a city not owned by any player, he has an option to purchase it.
- To purchase a city he has to pay the price of city to Banker.
- If he reaches a city owned by another player, he pays rent to that player.

A schematic diagram of a typical board is shown in Figure AE.2.

Figure AE.2 Business

Note: What is stated above a is general description. One must use details as specified in the game sold in the local market.

AE.6 Game: Snake II

These days this game is very popular on mobile handsets. We will develop it for the computer. Using predefined keys, we have to control the movement of a snake. The goal is to earn maximum points.

We can start with some assumptions (specifications).

Specifications:

- Snake original size—5 units
- Display—Main area: 20 units by 10 units
- Buttons for start and quit
- Action keys: up, down, left, right, return, escape
- Food appears randomly, immediately after snake eats previous one.
- Snake gets longer by one unit after eating the food.
- It also gives you one point.
- Snake moves at uniform speed.
- You cannot stop the snake.
- You cannot direct it backwards.
- Points: When snake eats food, you earn one point.
- The Jackpot appears along with every fifth food item.
- Jackpot vanishes after 12 seconds.
- Eating the Jackpot gives you bonus points.

- Points gained are 10* (12–time in seconds)
- Actions are synchronized at interval of 1 second. It means that any key pressed within 1 second of previous will be ignored.
- Aim of the game is to earn maximum points.
- Game ends when either (i) the snake hits its own body or (ii) if you press quit (escape) button.
- Game is played with help of keyboard only. One cannot use the Mouse.

AE.7 Game: Snake and Ladder

This is also a beautiful game to simulate. This is known to any one and every one (see Figure AE.3).

Figure AE.3 Snake and Ladder

AE.7.1 Problem Specification

Simulate the game of snake and ladder with following specifications.

- A board with 100 houses, numbered from 1 to 100.
- Numbering in a particular way.
- House 1 is start, House 100 is the Home.
- Snakes = 11, Ladders = 11, Locations as per standard
- Number of players: 2
- One (or two) dice with 6 faces.
- Two coloured pebbles, one for each player

AE.7.2 Description of the game

- Players play alternately (turn by turn)
- A player throws a dice
- His pebble is moved on the board depending on the dice value
- If at the bottom of the ladder, move it to the top of the ladder
- If at the mouth of the snake, move it to the tail of the snake
- If any player reaches Home (H100), he wins. Play ends.
- If pebble tries to move ahead of Home, it reverses its direction. For example, from H98 two moves take pebble to home, but three moves take it to 99.

You may see the complete solution in C++ in the textbook "Object Oriented Programming with C++" by the same authors.

AE.8 Game of Contract Bridge

This is the most popular card game among intellectuals. It is played with four players. Probably this is the only card game where tournaments are organized even at the international level.

We can start with some assumptions (specifications).

AE.8.1 Cards

- A deck consists of 52 cards.
- Cards are divided in four suits: Spade, Heart, Diamond, and Club
- Suits Club and Spade are black in colour.
- Suits Diamond and Heart are red in colour.
- Every suit consists of 13 cards.

AE.8.2 Shuffling

A deck is shuffled. This action can be simulated with random number generator. You may you use method `shuffle()` from "Collection framework".

AE.8.3 Distribution

A game of bridge is played by four players. These are said to be sitting at positions named North, East, South, and West. It is customary to call the players by these names only. A player termed as dealer distributes the cards. He starts dealing from his left hand side player. If the distributor is west, the cards are dealt in the order North, East, South, and West.

For simplicity assume that dealer is always west.

AE.8.4 Display

A sample display is shown as follows.

```
          NORTH
          S K J 10 2
          H Q J 10
          D 10 8 7
          C K 8 6
WEST              EAST
S 6 3             S 9 7 5 4
H 7 4 2 H A 9 6 7
D Q J 10          D 9 5 4 3
C J 10 9 7 4 C 2

          SOUTH
          S A Q 8
          H K 8 5
          D A K 6
          C A Q 5 3
```

AE.8.5 Solution level 1

Distribute the cards and display all the hands as shown above.

AE.8.6 Solution level 2

In addition, analyze the hands and display its strength. (There are two methods one with points and an older one with tricks.)

AE.8.7 Solution level 3:

Assuming any one bidding system, predict what will be the bidding sequence.

AE.9 Java IDE in Java

This is the most challenging of all the mini projects. It involves the language we are studying in this text. We must have a thorough knowledge of Java to complete this project. We need more knowledge of Java API, which is related to the operating system and GUI.

The goal of this application is to offer facilities for Java programmer to develop Java programs. It goes without saying that the application allows editing, compiling, and running at the click of a button. The user should be able to work with existing programs as well write new ones.

We can start with some assumptions (specifications).

Specifications:

When this program starts, it opens a frame with following menu items.

- File
- Compile
- Run
- Help
- Quit

File menu should have following sub-menus

- New
- Open
- CD

AE.9.1 Solution level 1

The look and feel should be like Borland turbo C++. There should be support for both keyboard as well as mouse.

AE.9.2 Solution level 2

The look and feel should be similar to any popular Java IDE like JCreater or BlueJ.

Hint: For editing purpose, use any available editor like Notepad.

AE.10 Game of Chess

This is a centuries old game still going strong. Even the most powerful computers cannot beat expert players in the game of chess. Actually, simulation of chess game is a topic of mega project. We will try to structure the problem is such a way that it fits the bill of a mini project.

A sample diagram is shown in Figure AE.4.

Figure AE.4 Chessboard

AE.10.1 Solution level 1

It should be a simple two-player version. Here, the onus of playing logic as well as legality of the moves is on the players. The computer only assists in displaying the moves on the board.

General specifications of the game

It consists of a board. It has 64 squares, 8 rows, and 8 columns. Alternate squares are black and white. Each player has an army consisting of 16 pieces as described below:

- King 1
- Queen 1
- Rooks 2
- Bishops 2
- Knights 2
- Pawns 8

Pieces of a type are identical in appearance. All rooks have same shape. However, for player one, the pieces are white, while for player two they are black.
Since black pieces on black squares cannot be seen, the squares are normally made light gray (instead of black) and white.

Rules

Display screen should be in Graph mode. Pieces are shown as images. Number all the squares in the standard chess notation as follows:

- c1, c2...
- b1, b2
- a1, a2....

Action

Now define a cursor. One can move the cursor with cursor keys. Assign a keystroke for pick-up **say** (Pg Up). When this key is pressed, the piece present on the square where the cursor appears is picked up.

Now moving cursor keys moves the piece on the board. Assign a keystroke for putting down say (Pg Dn). Pressing this key should place the piece on the board.

Rules

- Picking from a blank square should not be allowed.
- Putting on an occupied square is allowed.
- The piece present on such a square is considered as killed and taken out of the board.

AE.10.2 Solution level 2

Add mouse support to the simulation. Piece movements by drag and drop.

AE.10.3 Solution level 3

Next improvement relates to legality of move.

When a piece is moved, the move must be legal. If player tries an illegal move, a message should be given and move disallowed.
Some basic simple rules are stated as follows:

Rule 1: movements

Pawn—

- Very first forward move 1 or 2 places
- Consequent move
- Forward only 1 place (if vacant)
- Backward movement NOT allowed
- Diagonal only 1 place (only when capturing an enemy piece)

Bishop—Diagonal no limit

Knight—two and half

Rook—Vertical or horizontal (left or right) no limit

Queen—Like Bishop as well as Rook.

King—any direction one place only

Rule 2: movements

King cannot move to a place where it gets checked!

Rule 3: capturing

A general rule of capturing: A piece can capture only enemy piece.

A possible class definition of **class** piece

```
{   int status; //   0  dead or    1  alive//On or OFF board
    Image img  //   image
    int color   //  0 .. black or   1..white
    int x,y;//  location on board
}
```

Glossary

A

abstract a Java keyword.

abstract class a class defined with keyword abstract. This class cannot be used to create objects. Abstract classes are defined so that other classes can extend them and make them concrete by implementing the abstract methods.

abstract data type a data type. It is not built in the compiler. It is user defined. Normally it is a class. It is defined to implement some idea say a `Queue`. Abstract means user has defined its behaviour (in terms of instance variables and methods).

abstract method a method that has no implementation.

Abstract Window Toolkit (AWT) a collection of Graphical User Interface (GUI) components that were implemented using native-platform versions of the components. These components provide that subset of functionality which is common to all native platforms.

access specifiers keywords public, private, and protected are called access specifiers. They control the access of the entity (class, variable, method, etc.) by other methods in the program.

actual parameter an argument used while calling a method is called actual parameter. It can be a variable, an expression or a constant.

actual parameter list the arguments specified in a particular method call. See also formal parameter list.

adapter class a class that implements all the methods of the interface. Now one can subclass the adapter class and override only those methods in which we are interested.

alpha value a value that indicates the opacity of a pixel.

algorithm the set of the steps or rules required to solve a problem is called algorithm.

API application programming interface. The specification of how a programmer, writing an application, accesses the behaviour and state of classes and objects.

Applet a program written in the Java to run within a web browser compatible with the Java platform.

appletviewer a utility from Java Development Kit which allows to run applets without using a browser.

archive a compressed file designed for space-efficient storage. It contains one or more files.

argument a data item specified in a method call. An argument can be a literal value, a variable, or an expression. An alternate name for parameter.

array a collection of data items, all of the same type, in which each item's position is uniquely designated by an integer (called index).

array of objects we can define an array of objects too. However, as objects are required to have constructors associated with them, generation of array of objects is more specific as compared to arrays of other data types. Once properly constructed, array of objects can be handled exactly like any other array.

ASCII American Standard Code for Information Interchange. A standard assignment of 7-bit numeric codes to characters. See also Unicode.

assignment operator a binary operator represented by "=". Expression on the right-hand side is evaluated and assigned to a variable on the right-hand side. It works with basic data types, as well as strings, arrays, and with reference type too.

assignment expression it assigns the value of the expression on the left-hand side of assignment operator to the variable on the right-hand side.

assignment statement a statement formed with only assignment expression is an assignment statement.

associativity a property of an operator. It decides how to evaluate an expression (from left to right or right to left) having two or more occurrences of the operator.

asynchronous exception an exception caused by an agency outside the program, like keyboard interrupt.

atomic refers to an operation that is never interrupted or left in an incomplete state under any circumstance.

AWT see Abstract Window Toolkit.

base class a super class from which another class inherits its members. All classes have `java.lang.Object` as ultimate base class.

Bean A reusable software component. Beans can be combined to create an application.

binary operator an operator that has two arguments.

binary files files where data is stored in binary form (not in textual form). These files have certain advantages over text files. Program files are binary files.

bit the smallest unit of information in a computer, with a value of either 0 or 1. It stands for binary digit.

bitwise operator an operator that manipulates two values comparing each bit of one value to the corresponding bit of the other value.

bitmap a graphical image usually stored in a file.

block in the Java, any code between matching braces forms a block. Grammar accepts a block in place of a statement.

`boolean` a Java keyword. It refers to an expression or variable that can have only a true or false value. The Java programming language provides the boolean type and the literal values true and false.

boolean expressions logical or relational expressions which result in true or false value, are called boolean expressions.

bounding box for a Raster object, the smallest rectangle that completely encloses all the pixels that are not fully transparent.

braces it means curly brackets. They are used to form a compound statement (block).

brackets it means square brackets. They are used for array subscripts.

`break` a Java keyword. A jump statement. It takes control out of an innermost loop (for, do, while, and switch). Used chiefly in switch statement.

browser see Web browser

bug the unwanted, unintended logical errors in the programs. They prevent programs from giving the desired result.

built-in data types data types intrinsically supported by a language (compiler) like `int`, `float`, etc.

`byte` a sequence of eight bits. The Java supports this type. Memory is normally measured in bytes.

bytecode machine-independent code generated by the Java compiler and executed by the Java interpreter.

C

call invoking user-defined as well as library methods is referred to as calling them.

Call-by-value a technique whereby only values of the parameters are passed to functions (methods in java). This is the basic parameter passing technique used in Java.

call-by-reference a technique whereby addresses (references) of the parameters are passed to functions (methods in java). Fundamentally, this is not supported in Java. However, as objects, strings, and array are defined with reference in Java, when parameters are of these types, effectively this becomes the method of parameter passing.

`case` a Java keyword that defines a group of statements to begin executing if a value specified matches the value defined by a preceding "switch" keyword.

casting explicit conversion from one data type to another.

`catch` a Java keyword used to declare a block of statements to be executed in the event that a Java exception, or run time error, occurs in a preceding "try" block.

Central Processing Unit (CPU) it is the brain of the computer. It interprets and executes the machine language instructions.

`char` a Java keyword used to declare a variable of type character. It supports Unicode characters.

class in the Java, a type that defines the implementation of a particular kind of object. A class definition defines instance and class variables and methods, as well as specifies the interfaces the class implements and the immediate super class of the class. If the super class is not explicitly specified, the super class will implicitly be object.

class method a method that is invoked without reference to a particular object. Class methods affect the class as a whole, not a particular instance of the class. Also called a static method. See also instance method.

`.class` file when a java program is compiled, the byte code file generated has "class" as extension. Such files are called `.class` files.

class variable a data item associated with a particular class as a whole—not with particular instances of the class. Class variables are defined in class definitions. Also called a static field. See also instance variable.

`classpath` a `classpath` is an environmental variable. It tells the Java Virtual Machine (JVM) where to find the class libraries, including user-defined class libraries.

client in the client/server model of communications, the client is a process that remotely accesses resources of a server computer. Server has high computing power and large memory capacity.

closing file It is advisable to close the file opened for input (or output) before the program ends. Otherwise, there is a probability of loss of data.

code A term for any type of program.

code An attribute of the HTML applet tag, which specifies the class to be executed.

`codebase` works together with the code attribute in the <APPLET> tag to give a complete specification of where to find the main applet class file: code specifies the name of the file, and `codebase` specifies the URL of the directory containing the file.

compositing the process of superimposing one image on another to create a single image.

command line arguments arguments passed to an application at the time of execution.

comment the part of the program which is supposed to give more information or explanation to the reader. The compiler does not take any cognizance of it. In Java, comments are enclosed in /* and */. In addition, Java uses // for single-line comments.

comment in a program, explanatory text that is ignored by the compiler. In programs written in Java, comments are delimited using // or /*...*/.

compilation unit The smallest unit of source code that can be compiled. In the current implementation of the Java platform, the compilation unit is a file.

compile time polymorphism if the compiler is able to select the appropriate method for a particular call at the compile time itself, it is called early binding or compile time polymorphism.

compiler a program, which translates source code in higher level language (e.g. C++) into lower level language (machine language).

OR

a program to translate source code into code to be executed by a computer. The Java compiler translates source code written in the Java programming language into bytecode for the JVM.

compiling A process of converting source program into machine program.

compound statement when a series of statements is enclosed in curly brackets, a compound statement is formed. Compound statement is a statement (for grammatical purpose).

concatenate a process of joining of two or more strings.

configurable applet an applet which user can configure by specifying parameters (applet tags) in html document.

`const` a reserved word in Java. However, it is not used by current versions of the Java programming language.

constant a fixed quantity in a program.

constructor a method that creates an object. In Java, constructors are instance methods with the same name as their class. Constructors are invoked using the new keyword.

constructor overloading presence of many definitions of a constructor (in a class definition) is called constructor overloading.

`continue` a Java keyword. A statement which takes control to the end of the loop. In other words, control goes to the starting of the loop.

control structure normally program statements are executed sequentially. Control structure is a statement which manages the flow of execution in pre-defined manner.

critical section a segment of code in which a thread uses resources (such as certain instance variables) that can be used by other threads, but that must not be used by them at the same time.

core class a public class (or interface) that is a standard member of the Java programming language.

core packages the required set of APIs in a Java platform edition which must be supported in any and all compatible implementations.

curly brackets in Java, curly brackets are used as the beginning and the end of a block.

data hiding insulation of the data from direct access by the program is called "data hiding".

deadlock a situation where threads cannot continue execution because they are waiting for resources held by each other.

declaration a statement that establishes an identifier and associates attributes with it, without necessarily reserving its storage (for data) or providing the implementation (for methods). See also definition.

`default` a Java keyword. It is optionally used after all "case" conditions in a "switch" statement. If none of the "case" conditions matches the value of the "switch" variable, the "default" keyword will be executed.

default constructor when classes are defined, we are expected to specify one or more constructors. When we define a class without specifying any constructor, compiler supplies a default constructor. It is used to initialize an object.

deprecation refers to a class, interface, constructor, method or field that is no longer recommended, and may cease to exist in a future version.

derived class a class which inherits properties from (i.e. derived from) another class is called derived class.

dialog box in a GUI, an onscreen message box that conveys or requests information from the user.

direct access file files where we can locate the file component (record/object) directly by specifying the component number are called direct access files. Also known as random access files.

distributed running in more than one address space.

`do` a Java keyword starts a `do while` loop.

`do-while` statement a loop where condition is tested at the end. If condition fails, loop terminates.

`doctags` a special symbol used by the `javadoc` tool to document java packages and methods.

Domain Name Service (DNS) a program that runs on internet and provides automatic translation between domain name and IP address.

dot operator an operator connecting object variable (reference) and data members or method.

`double` a Java keyword used to define a variable of type `double`. A data type for large real numbers.

dynamic binding see runtime polymorphism

early binding see compile time polymorphism.

element components of an array are referred to as elements.

`else` a Java keyword. It is used to execute a block of statements in the case that the test condition with the "if" keyword evaluates to false.

empty statement a statement which contains nothing is an empty statement. As expected, it does nothing. It is only a place holder. However, it creates unimagined bugs like

```
For (i =0;i<max; i++) ;
        sum=sum + a[i] ;
```

Here, an empty statement is repeated maximum number of times instead of the second statement.

encapsulation the localization of knowledge within a module. Since objects encapsulate data and implementation, the user of an object can view the object as a black box that provides services. Instance variables and methods can be added, deleted, or changed, but as long as the services provided by the object remain the same, the code that uses the object can continue to use it without being rewritten. See also instance variable, instance method.

evaluate to compute the value of an expression.

event a system-generated object when something specific (predefined) occurs like mouse click or key pressing.

event-driven programming a new programming paradigm. Here programs normally function in idle loop, waiting for events, such as mouse click, keyboard input etc.

exception An event during program execution that prevents the program from continuing normally; generally, an error. The Java supports exceptions with the try, catch, and throw keywords.

exception handler a block of code that reacts to a specific type of exception. If the exception is for an error that the program can recover from, the program can resume executing after the exception handler has executed.

executable content an application that runs from within an HTML file. See also applet.

execute to perform instructions of a program.

expression a combination of constants, variables, and operators. It has to be evaluated.

`extends` a Java keyword. Class `X` extends class `Y` to add functionality, either by adding fields or methods to class `Y`, or by overriding methods of class `Y`. An interface extends another interface by adding methods. Class `X` is said to be a subclass of class `Y`.

F

`false` a Java keyword. It is literal. It represents a value.

FCS First Customer Ship. The day in which a product is released/shipped to the customer.

field a data member of a class. Unless specified otherwise, a field is not static.

file a sequential collection of data items. It can be stored on and retrieved from a disk (secondary memory).

`final` a Java keyword. You define an entity once and cannot change it or derive from it later. More specifically, a final class cannot be sub classed, a final method cannot be overridden and a final variable cannot change from its initialized value.

`finalize` a method executed (if defined) when the object is destroyed.

`finally` a Java keyword. It executes a block of statements regardless of whether a Java Exception, or runtime error has occurred in a block defined previously by the "try" keyword.

fixed point notation It is a representation for real numbers where position of the decimal point is fixed.

`float` a Java keyword used to define a floating point number variable.

floating point notation a representation for real numbers. It uses scientific notation.

font a complete collection of general and special characters with a consistent and identifiable typeface, weight, posture, and type size.

`for` a Java keyword. It is used to start a `for` statement.

`for` statement a statement using keyword "for". Suitable for repeating code for fixed number of times. Very useful in array processing.

formal parameter arguments used in defining a method are called formal parameters.

formal parameter list the parameters specified in the definition of a particular method. See also actual parameter list.

frame a graphical outline of a window.

FTP the basic Internet file transfer protocol. FTP, which is based on TCP/IP, enables the fetching and storing of files between hosts on the Internet. See also TCP/IP.

G

garbage collection the automatic detection and freeing of memory that is no longer in use. The Java runtime system performs garbage collection. The programmers never explicitly free memory.

GIF Graphics Interchange Format. Storing graphic images in this format requires relatively small size.

`goto` a Java keyword. This is not currently in use. It is reserved for future use.

GUI Graphical User Interface. Refers to the techniques involved in using graphics, along with a keyboard and a mouse, to provide an easy-to-use interface to some program.

H

has-a The containment relationship. It represents has-a relationship.

hexadecimal the numbering system that uses 16 as its base. The marks 0–9 and a–f (or equivalently A–F) represent the digits 0 through 15. In programs written in the Java, hexadecimal numbers must be preceded by 0x.

hierarchy a classification of relationships in which each item, except the top one (known as the root), is a specialized form of the item above it. Each item can have one or more items below it in the hierarchy. In the Java class hierarchy, the root is the `Object` class.

hierarchical inheritance an inheritance scheme (type) where there is one base (super) class and one or more derived (sub) classes. This is the only model supported by Java

HotJava A browser from Javasoft. It is java enabled.

HTML Hyper Text Markup Language. This is a file format, based on SGML, for hypertext documents on the Internet. It is very simple and allows for the embedding of images, sounds, video streams, form fields and simple text formatting. References to other objects are embedded using URLs.

HTTP HyperText Transfer Protocol. The Internet protocol, based on TCP/IP, used to fetch hypertext objects from remote hosts.

hspace An attribute in HTML applet tag. It is used to specify horizontal space.

I

IDE Integrated Development Environment. An environment which allows editing, compiling, and running of programs.

identifier a user-defined name for specific items like variables and methods.

`if` a Java keyword used to form `if` statement.

`if` statement a statement which first evaluates a condition and then decides to execute the following code.

`implements` a Java keyword. When included in the class declaration, it specifies the interfaces that are implemented by this class.

implicit conversions another name for automatic conversion. When expression contains operands of different types, one of the operands is converted automatically to a suitable type.

`import` a Java keyword. It is used at the beginning of a source file that can specify classes or entire packages to be referred to in the code.

index It indicates the position within an array.

information hiding fields declared as private are not available in the program (i.e. outside the class). This means data hiding or information hiding.

inheritance The concept of classes automatically containing the variables and methods defined in their super types. See also super class, subclass.

initialization Assigning values to a variable at the beginning of the program. Assigning initial values to an object at time of declaration is also called initialization.

input the information a program receives from external device such as keyboard.

input stream the source stream that provides data to the program is called the input stream.

instance an object of a particular class. In Java, an instance of a class is created using the new operator.

instance method any method that is invoked with respect to an instance of a class. Also called simply a method. See also class method.

instance variable any item of data that is associated with a particular object. Each instance of a class has its own copy of the instance variables defined in the class. Also called a field. See also class variable.

`instanceof` a Java keyword. Works as if an operator. Returns true when the runtime type of its first operand is assignment compatible with its second operand.

instantiation an object (variable) is considered to be instantiation of a class (type).

`int` a Java keyword. It is used to define a variable of type integer.

`integer` a numerical data type for storing whole numbers.

interactive an adjective given to a program which during its execution interacts with a user (through some I/O device).

`interface` a Java keyword. It is used to define a collection of method definitions and constant values.

Internet an enormous network consisting of literally millions of hosts from many organizations and countries around the world. It is physically put together from many smaller networks and data travels by a common set of protocols.

interpreter a module that alternately decodes and executes every statement in some body of code. The Java interpreter decodes and executes bytecode for the JVM.

IP Internet Protocol. The basic protocol of the Internet. It enables the unreliable delivery of individual packets from one host to another. It makes no guarantees about whether or not the packet will be delivered, how long it will take, or if multiple packets will arrive in the order they were sent. Protocols built on top of this add the notions of connection and reliability. See also TCP/IP.

is-a The inheritance represents is-a relationship.

iterator an iterator points either to an element in the list or to sentinels that conceptually surround the sequence of elements making up the list.

JAR files (.jar) Java ARchive. A file format used for aggregating many files into one.

Java Sun's trademark for a set of technologies for creating and safely running software programs in both stand-alone and networked environments.

Java Database Connectivity (JDBC) an industry standard for database-independent connectivity between the Java platform and a wide range of databases. The JDBC provides a call-level API for SQL-based database access.

Java Development Kit (JDK) a software development environment for writing applets and applications in the Java programming language.

Java Foundation Classes (JFC) an extension that adds GUI class libraries to the Abstract Windowing Toolkit (AWT).

Java platform consists of a language for writing programs ("the Java programming language"); a set of APIs, class libraries, and other programs used in developing, compiling, and error-checking programs; and a virtual machine which loads and executes the class files.

In addition, the Java platform is subject to a set of compatibility requirements to ensure consistent and compatible implementations. Implementations that meet the compatibility requirements may qualify for Sun's targeted compatibility brands.

The Java 2 platform is the current generation of the Java platform.

Java Runtime Environment (JRE) a subset of the JDK for end users and developers who want to redistribute the runtime environment alone. The Java runtime environment consists of the JVM, the Java core classes, and supporting files.

Java virtual machine (JVM) Sun's specification for or implementation of a software "execution engine" that safely and compatibly executes the byte codes in Java class files on a microprocessor (whether in a computer or in another electronic device).

Java HotSpot performance engine—Sun's ultra-high-performance engine for implementing the Java runtime environment which features an adaptive compiler that dynamically optimizes the performance of running applications.

JDBC Java Database Connectivity. An industry standard for database-independent connectivity between the Java platform and a wide range of databases. The JDBC interface provides a call-level API for SQL-based database access.

JPEG Joint Photographic Experts Group. An image file compression standard established by this group. It achieves tremendous compression at the cost of introducing distortions into the image which are almost always imperceptible.

K

keyword the Java sets aside words as keywords; these words are reserved by the language itself and therefore are not available as names for variables or methods.

L

lexical pertaining to how the characters in source code are translated into tokens that the compiler can understand.

linker a module that builds an executable, complete program from component machine code modules. The Java linker creates a runnable program from compiled classes.

linked list it is a dynamic data structure. It consists of nodes. A field in this node points to next node.

list an abstract data type which stores data which can be accessed serially as well as randomly.

literal a collection of characters which represents some constant in the program. For example, 3.0 is a double-precision floating point literal, and "a" is a character literal.

local data data belonging explicitly to a particular method.

local variable a data item known within a block, but inaccessible to code outside the block. For example, any variable defined within a method is a local variable and cannot be used outside the method.

`long` a Java keyword. It is used to define a variable of type long. A data type for storing large integers.

loop a set of statements that are executed repeatedly.

machine language a language consisting of strings of 0's and 1's. The computer hardware is basically capable of executing programs in this language (form).

`main()` name of a method which starts running first, when a JVM runs a program (class).

member a field or method of a class. Unless specified otherwise, a member is not static.

memory it is the space within the computer for holding machine language program as well as the data.

message information sent from one entity (normally an object) to another.

message passing a technique of sending messages. In Java, message passing is in terms of a method call.

method a small independent unit of code. It is called function or subroutine in older languages. Every method in Java must belong to a class. One of the methods must have the name "main".

method a function defined in a class. See also instance method, class method. Unless specified otherwise, a method is not static.

method overloading Java allows different methods of a given class to have the same name. These methods differ in number and/or types of parameters (sometimes called signature of a method).

method overriding when a method is defined in a derived (sub) class and has the same name as that of method in base (super) class, the derived class method overrides the base class method. It means when Method with this name is called, derived class Method is executed.

Mosaic a program that provides a simple GUI that enables easy access to the data stored on the Internet. These data may be simple files or hypertext documents. Mosaic was written by a team at NCSA.

module a part of program which does some specific task. It is practically an independent part.

Multi-level inheritance it is possible that a class is derived from some class which in turn is derived from another class. Such inheritance may be called multi-level inheritance.

multitasking a method by which multiple applications run simultaneously.

multithreaded describes a program that is designed to have parts of its code execute concurrently.

N

`native` a Java keyword. It is used in method declarations to specify that the method is implemented in some other language.

nesting placement of one unit within another is called nesting.

nesting of classes when a class contains objects of another user-defined class, it is called nesting of classes or containership.

`new` a Java keyword. It is used to create an instance of a class. It is an operator.

node an individual element of a tree or linked list.

`null` Java keyword. It is used to specify an undefined value for reference variables.

Oak in early days, this was the name given to language which was later named as Java.

object the principal building blocks of object-oriented programs. Each object is a programming unit consisting of data (instance variables) and functionality (instance methods).

object code (C++) output of the compiler, normally in machine language.

object-oriented analysis method of specifying requirements of the s/w in terms of real-world objects, their behaviour, and their interactions.

object-oriented design to transform the s/w requirements in to specification for objects and derive class hierarchies from which the objects can be created.

object-oriented design a software design method that models the characteristics of abstract or real objects using classes and objects.

object-oriented language a language that has features to support thinking about and implementing solutions in terms of objects is an object-oriented programming language.

object-based programming languages languages that support encapsulation and object identity.

octal the numbering system using 8 as its base, using the numerals 0–7 as its digits. In programs written in the Java, octal numbers must be preceded by 0.

operand the entity required by the operators to form an expression.

operating system a program that manages all operations and resources of the computer.

operator hierarchy if the expression contains more than one operator, then which operator operates first is decided by operator hierarchy (or precedence).

operator precedence when an expression contains different operators, evaluation starts with the operator of the highest precedence. Another name for operator hierarchy.

optional packages the set or sets of APIs in a Java platform edition which are available with and may be supported in a compatible implementation. Over time, optional packages may be required in an edition as the marketplace requires them.

ordinal type a type which contains ordered range of values. It implies that all the values this type can handle are known before using it. For example, `byte` and `char`.

output the programs are written to obtain some result. The result coming from the program is called output.

output stream the destination stream that receives output from the program is called the output stream.

overloaded constructors the constructors for an object having the same name but different number of arguments passed to it are called overloaded constructors.

overloading using one identifier to refer to multiple items in the same scope. In the Java, you can overload methods but not variables or operators. Overloaded methods differ in types of parameters.

overriding Java allows a method in a derived (sub) class to have the same name as that of the base (super) class. But it has a different definition. (It takes some other action.) This principle is called overriding.

`package` a Java keyword. A group of types (classes and interfaces). Packages are declared with the package keyword.

parameter methods normally work in terms of arguments. These are called parameters.

parameterized constructors constructors with parameters are known as parameterized constructors.

pass communication of parameters to and from a method is called passing of parameters.

pass-by-reference a parameter passing technique. Here, address (reference) of the argument is passed. Hence, any changes made inside the method are reflected in the calling method.

pass-by-value a parameter passing technique. Here, only value of the argument is passed. Hence, any changes made inside the method are not reflected in the calling method.

peer in networking, any functional unit in the same layer as another entity.

period operator an operator connecting an object variable and its member (data or method).

pixel the smallest addressable picture element on a display screen or printed page.

pointer a variable that points to another variable. Java does not allow users to define or use pointers. However, internal working of java needs and uses this concept.

polymorphism in general, it is the ability of the objects to take different forms. In particular, when a method is invoked from the reference to super class, it executes the method of subclass, thus showing an appropriate behaviour.

precedence of operators The order in which different operators (present in the expression) are executed.

`private` a Java keyword. It is used in a method or variable declaration. It signifies that the method or variable can only be accessed by other elements of its class.

process a virtual address space containing one or more threads.

program a set of instructions written for the computer to execute.

property characteristics of an object that users can set, such as the colour of a window.

`protected` a Java keyword. It is used in a method or variable declaration.

`public` a Java keyword. It is used in a method or variable declaration. It signifies that the method or variable can be accessed by elements residing in other classes.

R

radio button a component in GUI. Only one button can be selected from a group.

random access in a data structure if we can go to any desired element without passing sequentially over the earlier elements, then this method of access is called random access.

Random Access Memory (RAM) internal memory devices that can be read from or written to in random access manner. This memory is volatile.

random access file another name for direct access file.

raster a line of pixels.

real number a number which may have integral as well as fractional parts. It is represented by either decimal point and or scientific notation. In Java, data types to handle it are `float` and `double`.

record a quantity consisting of one or more components (data variables). This is an old term.

recursion it is a programming technique. Here, a method is allowed to call itself.

reference a data element whose value is an address.

relational expression an expression formed by use of relational operators. Produces Boolean result.

relational operator the operators == != < > <= >= are called relational operators. When operating on operands they produce Boolean results.

`return` a Java keyword used to finish the execution of a method. It can be followed by a value required by the method definition.

return statement it signifies the end of any method. It is compulsory for all methods except those whose return type is void.

reusability it is a property signifying minimal changes in a code before using it in a different program. In Java, a class developed for one program can be used directly without any change in another program.

root in a hierarchy of items, the one item from which all other items are descended. The root item has nothing above it in the hierarchy.

RPC Remote Procedure Call. Executing what looks like a normal procedure call (or method invocation) by sending network packets to some remote host.

runtime system the software environment in which programs compiled for the JVM can run. The runtime system includes all the code necessary to load programs written in the Java programming language, dynamically link native methods, manage memory, handle exceptions, and an implementation of the JVM, which may be a Java interpreter.

Runtime polymorphism if the appropriate method for a particular call is decided at the time of actual execution of the method (running), the process is called "late binding" or "dynamic linking" or "runtime polymorphism".

S

scientific notation a notation for writing numbers. It consists of a mantissa and an exponent.

scope a characteristic of an identifier that determines where the identifier can be used. Most identifiers in the Java programming environment have either class or local scope. Instance and class variables and methods have class scope; they can be used outside the class and its subclasses only by prefixing them with an instance of the class or (for class variables and methods) with the class name. All other variables are declared within methods and have local scope; they can be used only within the enclosing block.

Secure Socket Layer (SSL) a protocol that allows communication between a Web browser and a server to be encrypted for privacy.

sequential access when any particular data (object) can be accessed only after accessing previous data, the method is termed as sequential access. Certain devices like tape drive support only sequential access.

server a computer which gives services to another computer called client.

servlet a server-side program that gives Java technology-enabled servers additional functionality.

set an unordered collection of elements. Elements must be of some ordinal type.

`short` a Java keyword. It is used to define a variable of type short.

shorthand assignment operators general operators like + =, * = etc. are known as shorthand assignment operators.
A + = B; is a shorthand for an assignment statement A = A + B;

single inheritance an inheritance scheme (type) where there is only one base (super) class (not many) for every subclass. In Java, this is the only method of inheritance.

single precision in the Java language specification, describes a floating point number with 32 bits of data. See also double precision.

stand-alone application an application, which can run directly on a computer with the help of java runtime environment. It does not require a browser. In a sense, opposite of applet.

statement it is the simplest form of instruction in a program. Statements are separated by semicolons.

`static` a Java programming language keyword. It is used with variables and methods of a class.

static binding also called early binding. See compile time polymorphism.

static class members they are initialized to zero when they are created. Only one copy of that member is created for the entire class and is shared by all the objects of that class.

static field another name for class variable.

static methods methods declared as static are used to modify only static data members (class variables). Another name for class method.

`strictfp` a Java keyword.

string a data type which stores sequence of characters.

`String` class it is used to instantiate objects that can hold sequences of characters. It is supplied by most of the compilers.

structured type a data type consisting of more than one component of simple data type. There is some structure (ordering) among the components. For example, arrays, structures, files, or strings.

subclass a class that is derived from a particular class, perhaps with one or more classes in between.

subscript an identifier used as an array index.

subtype if type X extends or implements type Y, then X is a subtype of Y. See also super type.

`super` a Java keyword used to access members of a class inherited by the class in which it appears.

superclass a class from which a particular class is derived, perhaps with one or more classes in between.

supertype the super types of a type are all the interfaces and classes that are extended or implemented by that type.

`switch` a Java keyword. It is used to form switch statement.

`switch` statement a statement which helps to select particular action depending on particular case.

symbolic constant a word or literal that represents a value in a program.

`synchronized` a keyword in the Java programming language that, when applied to a method or code block, guarantees that at most one thread at a time executes that code.

syntax error the grammar of programming language is termed as syntax rules. Syntax error is error created by violation of these rules.

T

tag a command (annotation) in HTML.

TCP/IP Transmission Control Protocol based on IP. This is an Internet protocol that provides for the reliable delivery of streams of data from one host to another.

text files files which store characters. They are line oriented and line length is not fixed. All program files are text files.

Thin Client a system that runs a very light operating system with no local system administration and executes applications delivered over the network.

`this` a Java keyword that can be used to represent an instance of the class in which it appears. `this` can be used to access class variables and methods.

thread the basic unit of program execution. A process can have several threads running concurrently, each performing a different job, such as waiting for events or performing a time-consuming job that the program does not need to complete before going on. When a thread has finished its job, the thread is suspended or destroyed.

`throw` a Java keyword that allows the user to throw an exception or any class that implements the "Throwable" interface.

`throws` a Java keyword used in method declarations that specify which exceptions are not handled within the method but rather passed to the next higher level of the program.

`transient` a keyword in the Java programming language that indicates that a field is not part of the serialized form of an object. When an object is serialized, the values of its transient fields are not included in the serial representation, while the values of its non-transient fields are included.

token it is the smallest unit of program (source code). It cannot be divided further.

tree it is a dynamic data structure. It consists of nodes. Here every node points to one or more nodes.

`true` a Java keyword. Actually, it is literal. It represents a value.

`try` a Java keyword that defines a block of statements that may throw a Java language exception. If an exception is thrown, an optional "catch" block can handle specific exceptions thrown within the "try" block. Also, an optional "finally" block will be executed regardless of whether an exception is thrown or not.

`try` block a block prefaced with key word "try". This block can throw exception.

type A class or interface.

type conversions process of conversion of converting value from one data type to another.

type cast casting (converting) a value of one type into another type

U

unary operators those operators which take only one operand.

Unicode a 16-bit character set defined by ISO 10646. See also ASCII. All source code in the Java programming environment is written in Unicode.

UNIX A multiuser operating system.

URL Uniform Resource Locator. A standard for writing a text reference to an arbitrary piece of data in the WWW.

use relationship it gives information such as the various classes a class uses and the way it uses them.

variable Most important component of any programming language. Used for storing data. Every variable has a type, such as `int` or `Object`, and a scope.

virtual machine an abstract specification for a computing device that can be implemented in different ways, in software or hardware. You compile to the instruction set of a virtual machine much like you would compile to the instruction set of a microprocessor. The JVM* consists of a bytecode instruction set, a set of registers, a stack, a garbage-collected heap, and an area for storing methods.

`void` a Java keyword. It is used in method declarations to specify that the method does not return any value. `void` can also be used as a non-functional statement.

`volatile` a Java keyword used in variable declarations that specifies that the variable is modified asynchronously by concurrently running threads.

VRML Virtual Reality Modeling Language.

`vspace` an attribute in HTML applet tag. It is used to specify vertical space.

web browser a web client application that one uses to look at hypertext documents and to follow the links to other documents.

`while` a Java keyword. Forms `while` statement.

`while` statement a loop with condition checking at the beginning.

white-space it is the collective name given to spaces (blanks), horizontal and vertical tabs, newline characters, and comments. White space can serve to indicate where tokens start and end.

widgets a generic term for GUI elements like buttons and checkboxes. Comes from "Window gadgets".

Write Once, Run Any Where (WORA) the philosophy of Java that programs are written only once and run on any platform.

wrapper an object that encapsulates and delegates to another object to alter its interface or behaviour in some way.

WWW World Wide Web. The web of systems and the data in them, that is, the Internet. A huge collection of hypertext pages on the internet.

XML Extensible Markup Language.

Z

zip a file extension. Files of this type hold aggregate of files usually in compressed form.

Bibliography

Bruce Eckel, *Thinking in JAVA*, 3rd edition (Pearson Education, 2003).

C. Thomas Wu, *An Introduction to Object-Oriented Programming with JAVA*, 4th edition (Tata McGraw-Hill, 2006).

Cay S. Horstmann, *Big JAVA*, 2nd edition (John Wiley, 2006).

Cay S. Horstmann and Gary Cornell, *Core JAVA 2*, 7th edition (Pearson Education, 2005).

David Flanagan, *JAVA in Nutshell* (O'reilly Media, 2002).

Doug Lowe, Joel Murach, and Andrea Steelman, *Murach's Beginning Java 2, JDK 5* (SPD, 2005).

E. Balagurusamy, *Programming with JAVA: A Primer*, 3rd edition (Tata McGraw-Hill, 2007).

Harvey Deitel and Paul Deitel, *JAVA How to Program*, 5th edition (Pearson Education, 2003).

Herbert Schildt, *The Complete Reference Java*, 7th edition (Tata McGraw-Hill, 2007).

John Zukowshi, *Mastering Java-2* (New Delhi: Sybex/BPB Publications).

Jonni Kanerva, *The Java FAQ* (Pearson Education, 2004).

Ken Arnold, James Gosling, and David Holmes, *The Java Programming Language*, 3rd edition (Pearson Education, 2005).

Khalid A. Mughal and Rolf W. Rasmussen, *A programmer's Guide to JAVA Certification*, 2nd edition (Pearson Education, 2004).

Rogers Cadenhead, *Teach Yourself Java in 24 Hours* (SAMS Techmedia, 2000).

Index